Medieval and Early Modern
MURDER

Medieval and Early Modern
MURDER
Legal, Literary and Historical Contexts

Edited by
Larissa Tracy

THE BOYDELL PRESS

© Contributors 2018

All Rights Reserved. Except as permitted under current legislation no part of this work may be photocopied, stored in a retrieval system, published, performed in public, adapted, broadcast, transmitted, recorded or reproduced in any form or by any means, without the prior permission of the copyright owner

First published 2018
The Boydell Press, Woodbridge
Paperback edition 2021

ISBN 978 1 78327 311 9 hardback
ISBN 978 1 78327 592 2 paperback

The Boydell Press is an imprint of Boydell & Brewer Ltd
PO Box 9, Woodbridge, Suffolk IP12 3DF, UK
and of Boydell & Brewer Inc.
668 Mt Hope Avenue, Rochester, NY 14620–2731, USA
website: www.boydellandbrewer.com

A CIP catalogue record for this book is available
from the British Library

The publisher has no responsibility for the continued existence or accuracy of URLs for external or third-party internet websites referred to in this book, and does not guarantee that any content on such websites is, or will remain, accurate or appropriate

Contents

List of Illustrations and Tables   vii
Acknowledgements   viii
Contributors   ix
List of Abbreviations   xiv

Introduction: Murder Most Foul   1
Larissa Tracy

I MURDER ON TRIAL: JUSTICE, LAW AND SOCIETY

1 Secret Killing and Murder by Magic in the Law of Adomnán   19
Bridgette Slavin

2 Discursive Murders: The St Brice's Day Massacre, *Beowulf* and *Morðor*   47
Jay Paul Gates

3 Mourning Murderers in Medieval Jewish Law   77
Pinchas Roth

4 Treacherous Murder: Language and Meaning in French Murder Trials   96
Jolanta N. Komornicka

5 'Mordre wol out': Murder and Justice in Chaucer   115
Larissa Tracy

II THE PUBLIC HERMENEUTICS OF MURDER: INTERPRETATION AND CONTEXT

6 Bringing Murder to Light: Death, Publishing and Performance in Icelandic Sagas   139
Ilse Schweitzer VanDonkelaar

7 'I Think This Bacon is Wearing Shoes': Comedy and Murder in the Old French Fabliaux   159
Anne Latowsky

8 'Chevaliers ocirre': Manslaughter, Morality and Meaning in the *Queste del Saint Graal*   179
Lucas Wood

9 Murder, Manslaughter and Reputation: Killing in Malory's *Le Morte Darthur*   206
   Dwayne C. Coleman

10 Poisoning as a Means of State Assassination in Early Modern Venice   227
   Matthew Lubin

11 Defamation, a Murder *More* Foul?: The 'Second Murder' of Louis, Duke of Orleans (d. 1407) Reconsidered   254
   Emily J. Hutchison

12 'A general murther, an universal slaughter': Strategies of Anti-Jesuit Defamation in Reporting Assassination in the Early Modern Period   281
   Andrew McKenzie-McHarg

III MURDER IN THE COMMUNITY: GENDER, YOUTH AND FAMILY

13 Negotiating Murder in the *Historiae* of Gregory of Tours   311
   Jeffrey Doolittle

14 Poisoning, Killing and Murder in the *Edictus Rothari*   333
   Thomas Gobbitt

15 Murder, Foul and Fair, in Shota Rustaveli's *The Man in the Panther Skin*   350
   G. Koolemans Beynen

16 A Multiple Poisoning in the City of Valencia: Sanxo Calbó's Crime (1442)   371
   Carmel Ferragud

17 A Case of Mariticide in Late Medieval France   395
   Patricia Turning

18 Monstrous Un-Making: Maternal Infanticide and Female Agency in Early Modern England   417
   Dianne Berg

19 Imps of Hell: Young People, Murder and the Early English Press   434
   Ben Parsons

   Conclusion   456
   Hannah Skoda

   Select Bibliography   468
   Index   482

Illustrations

FIGURE

10.1 Title Page of Pietro d'Abano, *De Venenis*. Marburg: Johannes Dryander, 1537. Reproduced by kind permission of the Österreichische Nationalbibliothek, Vienna.   237

TABLES

10.1 Documented cases of proposed Venetian state-sponsored assassinations by poison, 1300–1797.   249

14.1 Comparison of fines relating to killing, injury and plotting: poisoning versus 'ordinary' means.   345

The editor, contributors and publishers are grateful to all the institutions and persons listed for permission to reproduce the materials in which they hold copyright. Every effort has been made to trace the copyright holders; apologies are offered for any omission, and the publishers will be pleased to add any necessary acknowledgement in subsequent editions.

Acknowledgements

This project was first inspired by a conversation with Caroline Palmer at the annual International Medieval Congress at Kalamazoo in May 2013. From there, the idea developed into a session at the annual Southeastern Medieval Association Conference in fall 2013 at Appalachian State University: 'On the Edge of Law: Murder in the Middle Ages', sponsored by MEARCSTAPA (Monsters: The Experimental Association for the Research of Cryptozoology Through Scholarly Theory and Practical Application). I owe a considerable debt to Asa Simon Mittman for his editorial guidance and support during the course of this project, and to Jeff Massey for his significant input. I am also grateful to Hannah Skoda for many insightful conversations about medieval violence and murder, and for being willing to write our conclusion. A great deal of work goes into assembling a volume like this, and so my gratitude goes out to Kelly DeVries, David F. Johnson, Dorothy Kim, Wendy Turner and the MEARCSTAPA executive board (Tina Boyer, Massey, Mittman, Stefanie Goyette, Ana Grinberg, Mary Kate Hurley, Mary Leech, Derek Newman-Stille, Melissa Ridley-Elmes, Thea Tomaini and Renée Ward) for their suggestions over the course of this project. I am grateful to Shannon Ambrose, without whose editorial and proof-reading eye this volume would not have been possible. My parents, Nina Zerkich and Robert Tracy, are an unwavering source of support in all my endeavours. I would also like to thank Caroline Palmer for her constant encouragement and the anonymous readers of this volume in its various stages for their prescient suggestions and constructive comments. I am also grateful to Rohais Haughton and her team for their diligence in putting all the pieces together.

This project was supported, in part, by a Visiting Scholarship awarded by the governing body of St John's College, Oxford, for five weeks of resident research at the Bodleian Library, St John's College Library and the British Library, London.

This volume was made possible by a funding grant from Longwood University's Cook-Cole College of Arts and Sciences.

This volume is dedicated to my mom, Nina Zerkich, who likes a good murder mystery as much as I do.

Contributors

Dianne Berg (PhD candidate, English, Tufts University) has a variety of research interests, including literary representations of domestic violence, aggressive female language and behaviour, and constructions of national identity. Her dissertation, '"Strange and Lamentable": True Crime and Domestic Tragedy in Early Modern England', examines how contemporary scandals were appropriated in plays, prose pamphlets and ballads to address anxieties about treason, obedience, gender and the state. Her work has appeared in *Borrowers and Lenders: The Journal of Shakespeare and Appropriation*; *Out of Sequence: The Sonnets Remixed*, ed. D. Gilson (2016) and *Shakespeares from Adaptation to Transformation* (forthcoming).

G. Koolemans 'Bert' Beynen (PhD, Slavic Linguistics, Stanford University) graduated from Leiden University, the Netherlands, and has an MLS from SUNY-Geneseo. He spent a year at Lomonosov Moscow State University on an IREX post-doctoral fellowship and has attended Russian and Georgian language summer schools. He taught Russian language, literature and culture courses at American universities and the University of South Africa, and philosophy courses at a community college. He volunteers as a humanities instructor at Temple University's Osher Lifelong Learning Institute. He publishes on the Georgian writer Shota Rustaveli.

Dwayne C. Coleman (PhD, English, University of Arkansas) is Associate Professor of English at the University of Central Arkansas, where he teaches courses in medieval English literature, English literature surveys and the history and structure of the English language. His research focuses on Thomas Malory and other works of medieval Arthurian literature. His essay 'Talking Heads in Hell: Dante's Use of Severed Heads in *Inferno*' appears in *Heads Will Roll: Decapitation in the Medieval and Early Modern Imagination*, edited by Larissa Tracy and Jeff Massey (2012), and he published '"And here on the othir syde": Thomas Malory's *Amens* as a Textual Marker' in *Medieval Perspectives* 27 (2012).

Jeffrey Doolittle (PhD candidate, History, Fordham University, New York) is a Research Fellow at Fordham University with a great interest in the intellectual cultures of the early Middle Ages. He is completing a dissertation on the monastic medical culture of the early medieval Benedictine abbey of Montecassino under the supervision of Dr Richard Gyug. He has also published a study of the liturgical traditions of Charlemagne as a saint and patron of the city of Girona in *The Charlemagne Legend in Medieval Latin Texts*, ed. William Purkis and Matthew Gabriele (2016).

Carmel Ferragud (PhD, Geography and History, Universitat de València) is Professor of the History of Science in the Universitat de València and a member of Instituto de Historia de la Medicina y de la Ciencia López Piñero (Spain). He has published books and articles about the medical practitioners and the practice of medicine during the Middle Ages, and has edited volumes about medieval documents. He is author of: *Medicina i promoció social a la Baixat Edat Mitjana (Corona d'Aragó, 1350-1410)* (2005); *La cura dels animals: menescals i menescalia a la València medieval* (2009); *Medicina per a un nou regne: el paper de la medicina i els seus practicants en la construcció del regne de València (s. XIII)* (2009); 'The role of doctors in the slave trade during the fourteenth and fifteenth centuries within the kingdom of Valencia (Crown of Aragon)', *Bull Hist Med* 87.2 (2013): 143–69. With Mariluz López Terrada, he edits 'Ciència i medicina a la València foral' (*Afers*, 83; 2015). He is a member of the research group Sciència.cat (Universitat de Barcelona, Spain).

Jay Paul Gates (PhD, English Literature, University of Wisconsin-Madison) is Associate Professor of Anglo-Saxon and Early Medieval Literature at John Jay College in The City University of New York. He co-edited, with Nicole Marafioti, *Capital and Corporal Punishment in Anglo-Saxon England* (2014). He has published on Anglo-Saxon law and literature, the effects of Anglo-Scandinavian cultural contact, and post-Conquest historiographical treatments of the Anglo-Saxon period.

Thomas Gobbitt (PhD, Medieval Studies, University of Leeds) is a postdoctoral researcher at the Institute for Medieval Research of the Austrian Academy of the Sciences, Vienna. His research stands at the intersection of the history of the book and the history of early medieval law, particularly the Anglo-Saxons and the Lombards in the ninth to twelfth centuries. He is currently editing a collected volume for the series Explorations in Medieval Culture. He has published articles on the codicology and manuscript contexts of Anglo-Saxon and Lombard law and law-books, is currently working on a monograph addressing the book cultures of the *Liber Papiensis* and has recently begun a three-year FWF Standalone research project on the production and use of Lombard law-books in the ninth and tenth centuries.

Emily J. Hutchison (PhD, Medieval Studies, University of York) is Associate Professor of History in the Department of Humanities at Mount Royal

University (Calgary, AB). Her dissertation examines the Burgundian propaganda in the first phase of the Burgundo-Armagnac civil war. She has published articles in the *Journal of Medieval History* (2007) and *French Historical Studies* (2012) on early civil war factionalism, and an article in *Speculum* examining the political function of grieving in the outbreak of civil war between 1407 and 1413 (2016). She is currently working on policing mechanisms in late medieval Paris.

Jolanta N. Komornicka (PhD, History, Boston University) is Assistant Professor of History at St Jerome's University, Waterloo, ON. She is the author of several articles on the relationship between crime and society in late medieval Europe, including 'Man as Rabid Beast: Criminals into Animals in Late Medieval France', in *French History*. She teaches on various aspects of high and late medieval society.

Anne Latowsky (PhD, French Studies, University of Washington) is Associate Professor of French at the University of South Florida, Tampa. Her published articles focus on medieval French literature as well as Latin historiography from Late Antiquity to the Middle Ages. She is the author of *Emperor of the World: Charlemagne and the Construction of Imperial Authority, 800–1229* (2013), a project which was supported by a Faculty Research Fellowship from the National Endowment for the Humanities.

Matthew Lubin (PhD, Early Modern European History, University of North Carolina, Chapel Hill) was most recently a Research Associate in the History Department at Duke University. His interests include the intellectual history of Venice and the Venetian Stato da Mar; Christian-Muslim relations during the Middle Ages and Renaissance; the classical tradition both in Italy and in the lands of Islam; and the Greek Orthodox of the eastern Mediterranean, and their diaspora, after 1453. He has co-authored a chapter in *Light and Shadow: Isolation and Interaction in the Shala Valley of Northern Albania*, ed. M.L. Galaty et al. (2013).

Andrew McKenzie-McHarg (PhD, History, University of Erfurt) is a postdoctoral research fellow on the Leverhulme-funded project Conspiracy and Democracy hosted by CRASSH (Centre for Research into the Arts, Social Science and Humanities) at the University of Cambridge. After graduating, he was associated with the Gotha Research Centre of the University of Erfurt. His interests extend from radical streams of thought in late Enlightenment Germany to developments in conceptual history. His book, *The Hidden History of Conspiracy Theory*, which traces the emergence of the concept 'conspiracy theory', is forthcoming.

Ben Parsons (PhD, Literature, University of Sheffield) is Lecturer in Medieval and Early Modern Literature at the University of Leicester. He has published papers on various aspects of medieval and Renaissance culture, including folklore, education, drama, exegesis and notions of adolescence; his work has appeared in journals such as *Medium Aevum, Exemplaria, Viator, Modern Philology*, and *Studies in the Age of Chaucer*. He is the co-author of the critical anthology *Comic Drama in the Low Countries, c. 1450–1560* (2012), and in 2013 was lead researcher on the AHRC-funded project 'Violence in the Late Medieval Classroom'.

Pinchas Roth (PhD, Talmud, Hebrew University of Jerusalem) is Senior Lecturer in the Talmud Department at Bar Ilan University, Ramat Gan, Israel. He has published articles on rabbinic literature and culture in medieval England, France and Provence, including 'Legal Strategy and Legal Culture in Medieval Jewish Courts of Southern France', which appeared in *AJS Review* 38 (2014).

Hannah Skoda (PhD, History, University of Oxford) is Tutorial Fellow in History at St John's College, Oxford. She is the author of *Medieval Violence: Physical Brutality in Northern France 1270–1330* (2013) and co-editor, with Patrick Lantschner and R. L. J. Shaw, of *Contact and Exchange in Later Medieval Europe: Essays in Honour of Malcolm Vale* (2012). Her current research, funded by a Leverhulme prize, focuses on the misbehaviour of fifteenth-century students at the universities of Oxford, Paris and Heidelberg. Drawing on criminological models, her research examines the relationship between the negative stereotypes imposed upon students by a variety of commentators and observers and the ways in which the students negotiated those stereotypes in their actual misbehaviour.

Bridgette Slavin (PhD, Celtic Studies, Sydney University) is currently a Clinical Assistant Professor in the Department of Interdisciplinary Studies at Medaille College in Buffalo, New York. She received her MA in Medieval Studies from Western Michigan University. Her doctoral research focused on the perception of magic and druidry in early Irish texts. In addition to her interest in medieval magic and early Irish law, her other areas of research include kingship, liminality and the experience of women and children in the criminal justice system of Anglo-Norman Ireland.

Patricia Turning (PhD, History, University of California, Davis) is Associate Professor of Medieval and Early Modern History at Albright College. She is the author of *Municipal Officials, Their Public and the Negotiation of Justice in Medieval Languedoc* (2012). Dr Turning has a scholarly focus on crime and punishment at the end of the Middle Ages, and has published works based on jurisdictional disputes from fourteenth-century Southern France. She is currently developing a project which examines felonious women and their experiences in various medieval prisons as a means of assessing how gender affected the development of punitive incarceration.

Larissa Tracy (PhD, Medieval Literature, Trinity College, Dublin) is Professor of Medieval Literature at Longwood University. She is the author of *Torture and Brutality in Medieval Literature* (2012) and *Women of the Gilte Legende* (2003) and has edited several volumes: *Heads Will Roll: Decapitation in the Medieval and Early Modern Imagination*, with Jeff Massey (2012), *Castration and Culture in the Middle Ages* (2013), *Wounds and Wound Repair in Medieval Culture*, with Kelly DeVries (2015) and *Flaying in the Pre-modern World* (2017). She is also the series editor for Explorations in Medieval Culture and the editor of *Eolas: The Journal for the American Society of Irish Medieval Studies*.

Ilse Schweitzer Vandonkelaar (PhD, English, Western Michigan University) is Visiting Assistant Professor of English at Grand Valley State University, Allendale, MI, where she teaches courses in world mythology, critical theory, literature and nature, and Shakespearean drama. She has co-authored articles on pedagogical approaches to environmental literature and digital tools for literary study, though her current research focuses on representations of the environment in Anglo-Saxon texts. She is a series editor for Medieval Institute Publications, Amsterdam University Press and Arc-Humanities Press.

Lucas Wood (PhD, Comparative Literature, University of Pennsylvania) is Assistant Professor of French at Texas Tech University. His research, which explores hermeneutic, generic and ideological tensions within the interlaced literary discourses of chivalry and courtliness through a diverse corpus of mostly twelfth- and thirteenth-century French texts, has generated articles on the literary and spiritual implications of open-ended allegorical interpretation in Arthurian romance, the gender politics of werewolf narratives and tragic love stories, and the vernacular translation of medieval erotology.

Abbreviations

ACCV   Valencia, Arxiu del Reial Col·legi Seminari de Corpus Christi de València
ADN   Lille, Archives départementales du Nord
AL   *The Ancient Laws of Ireland*, ed. and trans. William N. Hancock et al., 6 vols (Dublin: Commissioners for the Publishing of the Ancient Laws and Institutes of Ireland, 1865–1901)
AMT   Archives municipales de Toulouse
AN   Paris, Archives nationales de France
ARV   Valencia, Arxiu del Regne de València
BP   Parma, Biblioteca Palatina
CA   *Cáin Adamnáin*, ed. and trans. Kuno Meyer (Oxford: Clarendon Press, 1905)
CIH   *Corpus Iuris Hibernici*, ed. Daniel A. Binchy, 6 vols (Dublin: Dublin Institute for Advanced Studies, 1978)
eDIL   *Electronic Dictionary of the Irish Language*
EETS o.s.   Early English Text Society, Original Series
JCr   Valencia, Justícia Criminal
MPS   Shot'ha Rust'haveli, *The Man in the Panther's Skin*, trans. Marjorie Wardrop (London: The Royal Asiatic Society of Great Britain and Ireland, 1912; repr. 1966)
PL   *Patrologiae Cursus Completus, Series Latina (Patrologia Latina)*, ed. Jacques Paul Migne, 221 vols (1841–1865)
Preuves   Urban Plancher, *Histoire générale et particulière de Bourgogne et Preuves*, vol. 3 (Dijon, 1748), p. 254, no. 256
RNL   Russian National Library
RSD   Religieux de Saint-Denis, *Chronique du Religieux de Saint-Denys contenant le règne de Charles VI de 1380–1422*, trans. M. Bellaguet, 6 vols (Paris, 1852), 3:730–736

INTRODUCTION

Murder Most Foul*

Larissa Tracy

GHOST: Revenge his foul and most unnatural murder.
HAMLET: Murder?
GHOST: Murder most foul, as in the best it is,
  But this most foul, strange, and unnatural.
                              (*Hamlet* I.v.26–9)[1]

THE GHOST'S WORDS, urging his indecisive son to vengeance, reverberate throughout the corpus of Western literature and popular culture. The 1964 film adaptation of Agatha Christie's *Mrs. McGinty's Dead* (1952) draws its title from these fateful words, luring audiences into a classic whodunnit featuring Miss Jane Marple as the intrepid amateur sleuth, replacing Hercule Poirot in the book. The phrase 'murder most foul' has become an idiomatic, even parodic, catchphrase for referring to cases of homicide.[2] It evokes the dark shadows of Elizabethan drama, the stock murders of pulp fiction and detective novels and the reams of 'true crime' studies about serial killers like Jack the Ripper and H. H. Holmes. However, Shakespeare's iconic phrase captures the insidious nature of this most heinous crime – a crime that has enthralled and horrified societies for centuries. The earliest surviving prohibition of murder occurs in the Sumerian law codes of Ur-Nammu (c. 1900 BCE), the first complete law code in the world, which demands the ultimate penalty: 'If a man commits a murder, that man must be killed.'[3] Murder has always been a feature of human society, recorded not only

---

* My sincerest gratitude goes to Asa Simon Mittman for his comments and suggestions on earlier drafts of the introduction and to Hannah Skoda and Shannon Ambrose for their constant guidance.
[1] William Shakespeare, *Hamlet*, ed. Constance Jordan (New York: Pearson Education, 2004).
[2] E.g.: Mary Papenfuss, 'Murder Most Foul: Medical researchers now believe that homicide, not medical complications, is the leading cause of pregnancy-associated death', *Salon.com* (27 February 2003): http://www.salon.com/2003/02/27/pregnancy_death/ (accessed 31 May 2016).
[3] Joshua J. Mark, 'Ur-Nammu', *Ancient History Encyclopedia*, last modified 16 June 2014, http://www.ancient.eu/Ur-Nammu/ (accessed 26 November 2016).

in the earliest law codes like those of Ur-Nammu, but also present in the archaeological record – 430,000 years ago, an early Neanderthal was beaten around the face with a blunt object and thrown down a cave system in Atapuerca, Spain, where he stayed until 2014 when his remains were discovered among those of twenty-eight other individuals.[4] Biblical tradition claims that the 'first' murder was that of one brother by another with the jawbone of an ass – Cain and Abel – out of envy and spite. Chronicles record numerous murders and assassinations amid accounts of battle and warfare.[5] Murder 'reads the community in which it takes place, calling all relationships into question – mother and infant, husband and wife, lovers, friends, strangers, and mere acquaintances – and posing troubling questions about the moral nature of humankind'.[6]

Modern popular culture makes a killing on murder: crime dramas, true crime, serial killers, detective stories, court-room escapades in novels, films, television series, news and social media. It intrigues and entertains. At any given moment, there are dozens of murder mystery and police dramas on television or in print. Globally, popular authors have devoted long-running series to the mystery of murder that cross periods and geographical boundaries, though British television has capitalised on the genre: *Wallander* (Swedish), *Maigret* (French), *Caïn* (French), *Montalbano* (Italian), *Galileo* (Japan), *Young Sherlock* (China), *Tatort* (German), *Bishaash* (Bangladesh), *C.I.D.* (India), *Cape Town* (South Africa), *The Brokenwood Mysteries* (New Zealand), *Miss Fisher's Murder Mysteries* (Australia), *Murdoch Mysteries* (Canada), *Criminal Minds* (American), *True Detective* (American), *CSI* (American), *Hinterland* (British/Welsh), *Rebus* (British/Scottish), *Midsomer Murders* (British/English), *Foyle's War* (British/English), *Cracker* (British/English), *Touching Evil* (British/English), *Wire in the Blood* (British/English), *Inspector Morse* (British/English), *Inspector Lewis* (British/English) and *Endeavour* (British/English) just to name a few. In these series, detectives – public like Morse and Barnaby, private like Poirot or amateur like Marple – always solve the murder, bringing the murderer to justice. But that is not the reality, and scholars would be hard pressed to find a Poirot in the records of medieval murder, despite modern versions of medieval detectives like Ellis Peters's Cadfael, Umberto Eco's William of Baskerville or Ariana Franklin's Adelia Aguilar.

[4] Erika Engelhaupt, 'World's Oldest Murder Was 430,000 Years in the Making', *National Geographic Phenomena: A Science Salon* (28 May 2015): http://phenomena.nationalgeographic.com/2015/05/28/worlds-oldest-murder-mystery-was-430000-years-in-the-making/ (accessed 31 May 2016).

[5] 'Ancient Roman Murder Victims', *Wikipedia:* https://en.wikipedia.org/wiki/Category:Ancient_Roman_murder_victims (accessed 26 November 2016).

[6] Karen Halttunen, *Murder Most Foul: The Killer and the American Gothic Imagination* (Cambridge, MA: Harvard University Press, 1998), p. 1.

Medieval society, not unlike its modern descendants, was plagued with a series of crimes both petty and capital. In the Middle Ages, according to John Bellamy, an 'overabundance of violent deeds, perhaps also the very harshness of life, seems to have bred a certain callousness which regarded blood-letting as commonplace and even as a form of grim jest'.[7] Late-medieval England was notorious for its high crime rate, including murder, as Edward I lamented in the preamble to the Statute of Winchester (1285) when he 'complained forcefully about the wretched observance of the peace'.[8] But crimes 'involving deliberate cruelty against the victims were relatively few', and to say that medieval people exalted in bloodshed is going too far, for they rarely perpetuated wanton acts of cruelty.[9] Medieval records of murder cases suggest that even instances of justifiable (or simply understandable) killing were not ignored by a society supposedly numbed by hardship. In fact, the literary and legal accounts in this volume reveal that medieval societies were no less horrified by homicide than modern ones. Spectacular crimes, such as regicide, drew public attention because of the grave implications of killings for society. The murder of Edward II in 1327 played a significant role in later propaganda, the supposed method of murder (sodomising with a hot poker) lending currency to rumours of the king's sexual preferences rather than emphasising his political failures.[10] Stories about Richard II's apparent murder by starvation at Pontefract castle in 1400 circulated widely during the reign of his usurper Henry IV.[11] The alleged murder of the princes in the Tower (Edward V and Richard, duke of York) by agents of Richard III achieved mythic proportions, marking the memory of Richard III in popular literature and plays until this day. Often, it is the extraordinary nature of a murder that ensures its popular notoriety or even appeal. But murder is not the simple act of taking a life. *Murder* implies intent, motivation and usually malice.

According to the *Oxford English Dictionary*, a 'murder' is defined as '(an instance of) the unlawful premeditated killing of one human being by another, (a) criminal homicide with malice aforethought; (an instance of) the deliberate killing of a human being in a manner or circumstances tantamount to murder'. The verb 'to murder' means to 'kill (a human being) unlawfully, esp. wickedly or inhumanly; *spec.* kill (a human being) with a premeditated motive, kill with

---

[7] John Bellamy, *Crime and Public Order in England in the Later Middle Ages* (London: Routledge & Kegan Paul, 1973), p. 66.

[8] Ibid., pp. 3–4.

[9] Ibid., pp. 66–67.

[10] Larissa Tracy, *Torture and Brutality in Medieval Literature: Negotiations of National Identity* (Cambridge: D. S. Brewer, 2012), pp. 272–84.

[11] See: Terry Jones, Robert Yeager, Terry Dolan, Alan Fletcher and Juliette Dor, *Who Murdered Chaucer? A Medieval Mystery* (New York: Thomas Dunne, 2003).

malice aforethought'.[12] A killing is only an act of murder if the perpetrator intends to kill, either in that moment, or prior, having planned it in advance. Medieval societies defined murder in much the same way. The word 'murder' in modern English derives from Old English *morþor*, but there are several related forms in other medieval languages: Goth *maurþr*, Old Saxon *morþ*, Old Frisian *morth*, Old Norse *morð*, Middle Dutch *moort*, Old French *mordre* and medieval Latin *murdrum*.[13] Murder is a secret crime, hidden from public view, while manslaughter is publicly claimed and justified. In medieval sources, the term 'homicide' often stands in for the concept of 'manslaughter' or is used interchangeably with 'murder'; but, while all murder is homicide, not all homicide is murder.[14] Thus, each essay here defines murder within its particular context, offering specific and nuanced interpretations of killing in various societies throughout the Middle Ages. Germanic and Norse custom distinguished *morð* 'secret slaughter' from *vig* 'slaying': 'The former involved concealment, or slaying a man by night or when asleep, and was a heinous crime. The latter was not a disgrace, if the killer acknowledged his deed, but he was subject to vengeance or demand for compensation.'[15] French customary laws (custumals) evoked a variety of words to describe taking a life, and each one had a specific meaning that set the context for understanding the crime: *tuer* (infanticide, premeditated murder, battle and manslaughter – by-products of a much larger set of circumstances), *ocir* (murder is the outcome and the meaning, the totality of the event – killing for a purpose or premeditation), *murtrir* (unplanned killing, accidental infanticide, self-defence and manslaughter), *mourir* (*mettre à mort* – a greater degree of intention, used in reference to warfare and vengeance), *traison* (treason, which did not always involve murder, though *murtre* always involved treason) and *homicide* (sudden death, as in a fight or a tournament).[16] As Hannah Skoda writes in reference to French law, killing was defined as murder when 'its context was one of dishonesty, lacking the crucial challenge which would place the act within the framework of vengeance. Legal developments did not simply ban violence,

---

[12] 'murder', n. and v. *The Concise Oxford English Dictionary* (Oxford: Oxford University Press, 2002), pp. 1862–63.

[13] 'murder will out'. Dictionary.com. Online Etymology Dictionary. Douglas Harper, Historian. http://www.dictionary.com/browse/murder--will--out (accessed: 20 May 2016).

[14] See, in this volume: Larissa Tracy, '"Mordre wol out": Murder and Justice in Chaucer', at p. 121.

[15] 'murder will out'. http://www.dictionary.com/browse/murder--will--out (accessed: 20 May 2016).

[16] Hannah Skoda, *Medieval Violence: Physical Brutality in Northern France 1270–1330* (Oxford: Oxford University Press, 2013), pp. 29–31. In this context, 'homicide' is a form of manslaughter.

but tried to direct and mould acceptable forms, as well as suggest how physical gestures should be interpreted.'[17] As medieval laws changed to accommodate the social shifts regarding violence and crime with the help of local communities that were involved in the process of interpreting various forms of violence,[18] murder became more consistently regulated, recorded and adjudicated.

Murder is a facet of most societies. Each has different ways of dealing with it, judging it and punishing it, but the crime itself transcends all geopolitical and chronological boundaries. Other studies have looked at murder in the context of crime in the Middle Ages, as one of a litany of social transgressions or as an offence occurring in a specific time and place.[19] In his comprehensive study on crime in the Middle Ages, Trevor Dean aims to 'recover the history of criminals and victims while also investigating further both the courtroom and the medieval discourse about crime'.[20] This volume follows Dean's lead but with a specific eye on the crime of murder because of its gravity and its profound impact on individual communities and society at large. Murder – the perpetrators, victims, methods and motives – has been the subject of law, literature, chronicles and religion, often crossing genres and disciplines and employing multiple modes of expression and interpretation. It horrifies and edifies; it reveals the worst aspects of humanity, but the study of murder also gives society, and its criminals, a chance for redemption, or at least a chance to build a better society through the deterrence of violent crime. Criminal justice often has limits, while humanity's ability to do harm to its members seems limitless. Murder demands that a community 'come to terms with the crime – confront what has happened and endeavor to explain it, in an effort to restore order to the world'.[21]

As the chapters in this volume demonstrate, definitions of murder, manslaughter and justified or unjustified homicide depend largely on the legal terminology and the laws of the society. Much like modern nations, medieval societies treated

---

[17] Ibid., p. 32.

[18] Ibid., p. 33. For a discussion of secret killing as murder in early Latin law tracts and other early medieval circumstances, see: Warren C. Brown, *Violence in Medieval Europe* (Harlow: Longman, 2011), pp. 50–51 and 81. Brown also addresses instances of murder in later medieval Europe in the broader context of violence.

[19] E.g.: Trevor Dean, *Crime in Medieval Europe 1200–1550* (Harlow: Pearson Education, 2001) which focuses on the broad idea of crime in medieval Europe; Massimo Vallerani, *Medieval Public Justice*, trans. Sarah Rubin Blanshei (Washington, DC: The Catholic University of America Press, 2012), which centres on medieval Italy; and Bellamy, *Crime and Public Order*, which mainly deals with England, as does James Given, *Society and Homicide in Thirteenth-Century England* (Stanford: Stanford University Press, 1977). For murder in the wider context of medieval violence, see: Skoda, *Medieval Violence* and Brown, *Violence in Medieval Europe*.

[20] Dean, *Crime in Medieval Europe*, p. 26.

[21] Halttunen, *Murder Most Foul*, pp. 1–2.

murder and murderers differently based on their social standing, the social standing of the victim, their gender, their mental capacity for understanding their crime, intent, motive and means. As Michel Foucault writes, ever since the Middle Ages 'slowly and painfully built up the great procedure of investigation, to judge was to establish the truth of a crime, it was to determine its author and apply a legal punishment. Knowledge of the offence, knowledge of the offender, knowledge of the law: these three conditions made it possible to ground a judgement in truth.'[22] Almost every medieval society had a system of written laws that adjudicated the nature of various crimes and proscribed appropriate punishments, most of which involved monetary compensation rather than physical punishment.[23] Laws like the Frisian *Lex Frisionum* (c. 802),[24] the Lombard *Edictus Rothari* (643), the Anglo-Saxon laws of Alfred the Great (c. 893),[25] the Icelandic *Grágás* law codes (c. 930 and 1117–18) upon which the laws of the *Jónsbók* (adopted in 1281) are based,[26] the *Coutumes de Beavaisis* of Philippe de

---

[22] Michel Foucault, *Discipline and Punish: The Birth of the Prison*, trans. Alan Sheridan (New York: Vintage Books, 1995), p. 19.

[23] For legal examples in Anglo-Saxon England, see: Jay Paul Gates and Nicole Marafioti, eds., *Capital and Corporal Punishment in Anglo-Saxon England* (Woodbridge: Boydell Press, 2014); discussions of other forms of legal punishments in a variety of medieval societies, see: *Castration and Culture in the Middle Ages*, ed. Larissa Tracy (Cambridge: D. S. Brewer, 2013); *Heads Will Roll: Decapitation in the Medieval and Early Modern Imagination*, ed. Larissa Tracy and Jeff Massey (Leiden: Brill, 2012); and *Flaying in the Pre-modern World: Practice and Representation*, ed. Larissa Tracy (Cambridge: D. S. Brewer, 2017). According to James Given, in thirteenth-century England there was no distinction of punishment for murder or homicide; the legally designated punishment for *any* homicide (except for cases of self-defence or clear accident) was death. However, Given points out that few who were tried for homicide actually faced capital punishment. See: Given, *Society and Homicide*, pp. 91–105, 188–213. In this volume, see: Ilse Schweitzer VanDonkelaar, 'Bringing Murder to Light: Death, Publishing and Performance in Icelandic Sagas', p. 141 at n. 5.

[24] See: Rolf H. Bremmer Jr, 'The Children He Never Had; The Husband She Never Served: Castration and Genital Mutilation in Medieval Frisian Law', in *Castration and Culture*, ed. Tracy, pp. 108–30.

[25] Scott Preston, *King Alfred's Book of Laws* (Jefferson, NC: McFarland, 2012); Lisi Oliver, 'Legal Documentation and the Practice of English Law', *The Cambridge History of Early English Literature*, ed. Clare A. Lees (Cambridge: Cambridge University Press, 2013), pp. 499–529; Patrick Wormald, *The Making of English Law: King Alfred to the Twelfth Century, Vol. 1: Legislation and its Limits* (Oxford: Blackwell, 1999; reprt. 2000); See, in this volume: Jay Paul Gates, 'Discursive Murders: The St Brice's Day Massacre, *Beowulf* and *Morðor*'.

[26] Jana K. Schulman, ed. and trans., *Jónsbók: The Laws of Later Iceland* (Saarbrucken: AQ Verlag, 2010); Ólafur Lárusson, *Grágás og lögbækurnar* (Árbók Háskóla Íslands, 1922; Reykjavík: Prentsmiðjan Gutenberg, 1923). See, in this volume: VanDonkelaar, 'Bringing Murder to Light'.

Beaumanoir (1283),[27] the treatise attributed to Henry Bracton *On the Laws and Customs of England* [*Bracton*] (c. 1240s–1250s),[28] among many others, provide ways in which their respective societies could define and adjudicate killing. After the Fourth Lateran Council (1215) legal systems, both ecclesiastical and secular, changed from accusatory to inquisitorial with the adoption of Roman law, but local customary laws were still applied. As Anthony Musson writes regarding English customary law, 'by emphasizing their laws' ancient origins and perhaps identifying a fundamental "law-giver", people could engender and further a sense of community and collective identity, whether it was the Christian Church or an individual kingdom'.[29] It was important for people to set the parameters by which they and their neighbours lived – or died – as a means of defining their sense of justice and injustice.

Law acts 'as a catalyst or dynamic to a consciousness of "nationality"'.[30] A clear and just practice of law helps give a sense of stability and cohesion to a community, and having a clear means of prosecuting those who threaten that stability through murder is a major component in the survival of any society. It was often meant to be one of the foundations that hold up society, preventing its fall into chaos; however, law and the governments that employed it could also be agents of murder. Laws could be applied unevenly or inconsistently and were certainly abused. Legal systems could be threatened by instability and war, and laws could be used as propaganda against enemies. By the nineteenth century, punishment ceased to be spectacle, as if the punishment 'was thought to equal, if not to exceed, in savagery the crime itself, to accustom the spectators to a ferocity from which one wished to divert them, to show them the frequency of crime, to make the executioner resemble a criminal, judges murderers, to reverse roles at the last moment, to make the tortured criminal an object of pity

---

[27] Philippe de Beaumanoir, *Coustumes de Beauvoisis* (Bourges: F. Toubeau, 1690). Philippe de Beaumanoir, *The Coutumes de Beauvaisis of Philippe de Beaumanoir*, trans. F. R. P. Akehurst (Philadelphia: University of Pennsylvania Press, 1992). See, in this volume: Jolanta N. Komornicka, 'Treacherous Murder: Language and Meaning in French Murder Trials', at p. 102.

[28] *Bracton: De Legibus et Consuetudinibus Angliæ* (*Bracton on the Laws and Customs of England attributed to Henry of Bratton, c. 1210–1268*), reproduced from the dual language critical edition by Samuel Thorne, with the Latin text of George Woodbine, 4 vols (Cambridge, MA: Harvard University Press, 1977). http://bracton.law.harvard.edu/Framed/mframe.htm (accessed: 20 May 2016); In this volume, see: Tracy, '"Mordre wol out": Murder and Justice in Chaucer'.

[29] Anthony Musson, *Medieval Law in Context: The Growth of Legal Consciousness from Magna Carta to the Peasants' Revolt* (Manchester: Manchester University Press, 2001), p. 25.

[30] Ibid.

or admiration'.[31] Medieval and early modern accounts of murder and the punishment of murderers grapple with the same concepts, punishing criminals but within certain boundaries, recognising the gravity of the crime but not perpetuating its atrocities in its adjudication. In *De laudibus legum Anglie* (1468–71), Sir John Fortescue, Lord Chief Justice of the Court of the King's Bench until his exile in 1461, compares the legal practice in France to that in England, condemning the French application of torture and, perhaps, criticising its potential introduction in England.[32] Fortescue argued that the major problem with France's criminal justice system was the ease with which innocents could be condemned, but English and Continental law shared certain precepts like the presumption of innocence.[33] In the introduction to *Crime in Medieval Europe*, Dean provides two accounts of homicide, comparing cases in Toulouse, France, and London, England. He argues that while there were similarities in the way these crimes were prosecuted, 'English law *was* clearly distinct from much continental law in many ways'.[34] From the twelfth century, English criminal law and procedure diverged from much of continental Europe and the 'resulting common-law system appeared erratic and strange to continental lawyers'.[35] As Dean explains, the key difference lies in the reception and influence of Roman law: 'without this as an anchor and inspiration, English law developed its own categories and methods, which vested much more influence in judges and custom, and much less in codified legislation or learned lawyers'.[36] However, though the divergence made real differences, it also 'conceals a broader convergence of general development'.[37]

In the medieval period, murder had very specific legal parameters depending on time, culture, geography and legal structures. This volume explores the variety of circumstances associated with murder in the Middle Ages including law, literature, punishments, justifications and prohibitions. By focusing specifically on murder, its various incarnations – assassination, infanticide, mariticide, regicide, tyrannicide or simple homicide – and its social impact, this volume explores the complexity of medieval jurisprudence regarding murder and social

---

[31] Foucault, *Discipline and Punish*, p. 9. See also: Alison Kinney, *Hood* (New York: Bloomsbury Academic, 2016).

[32] James Simpson, 'No Brainer: The Early Modern Tragedy of Torture', *Religion and Literature* 43.3 (2011): 1–23 at p. 4.

[33] Dean, *Crime in Medieval Europe*, p. 5.

[34] Ibid.

[35] Ibid.

[36] Ibid.

[37] Ibid.

responses to murder, as well as the implications of secret killing for medieval communities, that were recorded in various literary genres.

The volume is arranged in three sections, chronologically within each section, which integrate discussions of murder across genres, exploring the interdisciplinary aspects of this crime in the Middle Ages. The first provides the legal template for reading cases of murder in a variety of sources including trial documents, legal treatises and literary texts. It begins with the accounts of murder and magic in early Irish literature and law (Slavin), then considers the socio-political implications of mass murder embedded in literary discourse (Gates), the legal prohibitions of mourning murderers in medieval Jewish law as it was practised in France (Roth), treachery in French murder trials (Komornicka), and ends with the social and legal responses to murder in the works of Geoffrey Chaucer (Tracy). The second section examines the public hermeneutics of murder, especially the ways in which medieval societies interpreted and contextualised it in their textual traditions: Icelandic sagas (VanDonkelaar), Old French fabliaux (Latowsky), Arthuriana (Wood, Coleman) and accounts of assassination (Lubin, Hutchinson, McKenzie-McHarg). The final section focuses on the effects of murder within the community: murder as a social ill, especially in killing kin (Doolittle), the legal and literary implications of gender in the instigation and commission of murder (Gobbitt, Beynen, Turning), familial murder in Valencia (Ferragud), maternal infanticide in England (Berg) and murderers who are little more than children themselves (Parsons). Hannah Skoda concludes the conversation, analysing the disregard for the personhood of the victim and the public consequences of murder.

Murder can take many forms depending on both the method and the motive of the perpetrator. The chapters in the first part of this collection analyse the historical and legal parameters for defining and prosecuting murder, as well as literary responses to judicial practice. The early Irish *Cáin Adamnáin* (c. ninth century), a list of ecclesiastical regulations, includes specific provisions for classifying supernaturally-induced homicide as *duinetháide*, or secret murder, as Bridgette Slavin argues. Like legal texts, literature often explains how a society felt about murder, distinguishing between murder and other forms of killing. In the Old English elegiac poem, *The Wife's Lament*, the Wife bitterly recounts the murderous crime of her lord,[38] while the Old Norse *Völsungasaga* [*Saga of the Volsungs*] begins with a murder, a hidden crime, unclaimed and

---

[38] *The Wife's Lament*, trans. Roy Liuzza, in *The Broadview Anthology of British Literature: The Medieval Period* (Toronto: Broadview Press, 2006), p. 21.

uncompensated.[39] In *Beowulf* (c. 1000), Grendel, described as a *cwealmcuman* [murderous visitor] (792a), lives up to his lineage as a descendant of Cain:

> fifelcynnes eard
> wonsælī werweardode hwīle,
> siþðan him scyppen forscrifen hæfde
> in Cāines cynne – þone cwealm gewræc
> ēce drihten, þæs þe hē Ābel slōg;
> ne gefeah hē þære fæhðe, ac hē hine feor forwræc,
> metod for þy mane mancynne fram.

[this miserable man / lived for a time in the land of giants, / after the Creator had condemned him / among Cain's race – when he killed Abel / the eternal Lord avenged that death. / No joy in that feud – the Maker forced him / far from mankind for his foul crime] (104b–110).[40]

In his attacks on the hall Heorot, Grendel commits *morðbeala* [murder] (136a), a crime compounded by the fact that he does not follow the law; he would not make peace nor settle with money, and counsellors did not expect 'beorhtre bōte tō ban*an* folmum' [bright compensation from the killer's hands] (158). Murder makes 'monsters', and Cain's race is populated with ogres and giants (and Grendel) who violate the basic tenets of human conduct by killing their brethren. Grendel kills with *inwitþancum* [evil intent] (749). Murder is among the worst crimes that could mar even the most heroic life. At the end of the poem, as Beowulf dies, he rehearses his view of his duties to his nation: 'Ic ðās lēode hēold / fiftig wintra; næs sē folccyning, / ymbesittendra ænig ðāra, / þe mec gūðwinum grētan dorste, / egesan ðeon' [I held this people / fifty winters; there was no folk-king, / not any of the neighboring tribes, / who dared to face me with hostile forces / or threaten fear] (2732b–2736a). He is proud that, during his life, he 'ne sōhte searonīðas, nē mē swōr fela / āða on unriht' [sought no intrigues, nor swore many / false or wrongful oaths] (2738–2739a). Most importantly, Beowulf can say that he will not be reproached for the *morðörbealo māga* [murder of kinsmen] (2742a), unlike many of his Scandinavian counterparts who are detailed in Icelandic sagas. Beowulf has done his duty to his people, to his nation. Unlike his legendary predecessors who became embroiled in feuds that cost them everything, Beowulf has honoured his oaths and paid his debts

---

[39] *Saga of the Volsungs: The Norse Epic of Sigurd the Dragon Slayer*, trans. Jesse Byock (Berkeley: University of California Press, 1990).

[40] All Old English quotations from *Beowulf* are from *Klaeber's Beowulf*, ed. R. D. Fulk, Robert E. Bjork and John D. Niles, 4th edn (Toronto: University of Toronto Press, 2008); all translations are from *Beowulf*, trans. Roy Liuzza, in *The Broadview Anthology of British Literature: The Medieval Period* (Toronto: Broadview Press, 2006). Line numbers are given in parentheses.

and, at the same time, lived up to the ideals of justice without ever resorting to murder. Jay Paul Gates begins his chapter with *Beowulf*, exploring the concept of *morð* – defined as holding an entire ethnic group collectively accountable for a murder. Specifically, Gates analyses the intertextual elements in accounts of the St Brice's Day massacre (1002) and *Beowulf*, in which, he argues, there are overlapping concerns regarding lordship, ethnic identity and inter-ethnic violence.

Generally, in late twelfth- and thirteenth-century Europe, there were two movements of legal change: one regarding trial and proof and the other regarding punishment.[41] In various countries, ordeal gave way to denunciation and inquisition, which could, in certain cases, involve the use of torture to produce a confession. Pinchas Roth examines the contradictions in rabbinic law regarding mourning the death of murderers executed by the Christian state, specifically in southern France, and those executed by Jewish courts. Even though execution was rare in medieval Jewish law (Halakhah), openly mourning murderers convicted by rabbinic courts was potentially a subversive statement about the legitimacy of these courts in opposition to the secular (but still Christian) authorities. Jolanta N. Komornicka delves into the records of the Parlement of Paris, providing evidence that murder became equated with treason in the thirteenth and fourteenth centuries as courts valued human life over the loss of goods and property and treated murder as insidious and odious, especially when victims were betrayed by those closest to them.

English law moved away from monetary compensation towards juries that could denounce serious criminals, substituting jury verdicts for the ordeal but stopping short of implementing inquisitorial methods.[42] Torture never became part of medieval English legal procedure.[43] As Dean writes, the 'broadly common development was thus towards state prosecution of major crimes, in lists that varied from place to place, but might include homicide, house-breaking, rape and sodomy'.[44] Within the scope of his tales, Geoffrey Chaucer often employs comedy to satirise corrupt forces at play in English society and legal procedure, juxtaposing farcical narratives with more sombre ones. Drawing on *Bracton*, Larissa Tracy argues that Chaucer's tales of murder (*The Man of Law's Tale*, *The Prioress's Tale* and the comic *Nun's Priest's Tale*) punctuate the moral lessons of several of

---

[41] Dean, *Crime in Medieval Europe*, p. 5.

[42] Ibid., pp. 5–6.

[43] On the question of torture in English law, see: Edward Peters, *Torture* (Philadelphia: University of Pennsylvania Press, 1985); Tracy, *Torture and Brutality*; Bellamy, *Crime and Public Order*; J. G. Bellamy, *The Law of Treason in England in the Later Middle Ages* (Cambridge: Cambridge University Press, 1970); and W. R. J. Barron, 'The Penalties for Treason in Medieval Life and Literature', *Journal of Medieval History* 7 (1981): 187–202. In this volume, see: Tracy, '"Mordre wol out": Murder and Justice in Chaucer'.

[44] Dean, *Crime in Medieval Europe*, p. 6.

his *Canterbury Tales*, in which the application of torture in the judicial process is cause for concern and censure. According to Foucault, 'the tortured body is first inscribed in the legal ceremonial that must produce, open for all to see, the truth of the crime'.[45] But in Chaucer, the only 'truth' torture elicits is that of abuses which threaten social stability. He mocks those who rely on torture in *The Nun's Priest's Tale* and in the exaggerated portrait of the Prioress, who is juxtaposed against the staid legal persona of the Man of Law. These essays consider the social ramifications of murder cases in which the act of killing played into other concerns like property and status, and religious and temporal authority. Murder did not occur in a vacuum; it was often a symptom (or a product) of other societal unease or unrest.

The way medieval societies and audiences interpreted murder is the focus of the second section. Here, the essays assess the public hermeneutics of murder – how murder affected public impressions of both the victim and the perpetrator, and how communities internalised these crimes through comedy and idealised romance. Literature not only voices social condemnation of murder but also frequently records the laws by which murder and murderers were judged and dealt with. Following the legal evidence in the *Grágás*, Ilse Schweitzer VanDonkelaar highlights the intricacies of legal definitions of murder in Icelandic sagas, arguing that the saga-authors often reflect on both the successes and failures of such a system. Murder could provide comedy or, at least, comedic criticism of social abuses and institutional corruption. In her chapter on the Old French fabliaux, Anne Latowsky examines the comedy of murder in the tales of portable corpses in which unsuspecting fools *think* they have committed murder but are only abusing a dead body. She juxtaposes these tales with those of revenant priests, arguing that the consequences of murder are often ignored for comedic effect. Satire and comedy revel in outrageous acts like murder, but in their irreverent glee they also highlight the inequities within legal and social systems in the prosecution of serious crime.

Homicide denigrates the ideal of chivalric behaviour that governed, if not real society, then the fictional world populated by romance knights and ladies. In his examination of homicide in the *Queste del Saint Graal* (c. 1220–25), Lucas Wood argues that the personal piety of the *miles Christi* 'is exalted at the expense of the traditional, mutually reinforcing courtly-chivalric values of erotic love and glory-hungry martial prowess'.[46] This emphasis on the struggle between good and evil, in part, condemns aspects of the chivalric ethos for valorising senseless violence that often leads to murder. Echoing Wood's analysis of the French Gauvain as an inveterate killer of men, Dwayne Coleman interrogates the limits

---

[45] Foucault, *Discipline and Punish*, p. 35.
[46] Lucas Wood, '"Chevaliers ocirre": Manslaughter, Morality and Meaning in the *Queste del Saint Graal*', at p. 180.

of justice in the proliferation of murder in Thomas Malory's *Morte Darthur* (c. 1471), drawing sharp distinctions between murder and manslaughter and the implications of unlawful killing for the court of King Arthur, especially Gawain. Ultimately, while the chivalric ethos often necessitated killing, that violence had to be conducted within a set of acceptable social and religious parameters; those who transgressed those boundaries – who commit murder – find themselves on the wrong side of literary justice and law.

Assassination, the murder of political figures and heads of state, is the most destabilising form of homicide because it strikes at the head of government or its close allies; equally, state-sponsored assassination could undermine public confidence in the exercise of justice. Orchestrating the murder of political leaders or political enemies appears in several medieval contexts, including the killing of kings (regicide) or tyrants (tyrannicide). In this volume, Matthew Lubin surveys the history of poisoning in medieval and early modern Venice, contextualising the practice of state-sanctioned assassination for which poisoners might be employed for the good of the state. The assassination of the French King Charles VI's brother, Louis, duke of Orleans (d. 1407), led to a government crisis, which manifested in competing narratives of homicide or tyrannicide when his cousin (and murderer) John, duke of Burgundy, attempted to legitimise his crime, as Emily Hutchison explains. She reconsiders the physical murder of the Duke of Orleans and the social slander by which the Duke of Burgundy justified committing it, defamation that was branded a 'second murder' by Louis's house and deemed more heinous than the actual homicide. She investigates the entwined principles of a two-body system – the physical body and the body that was composed of memory and reputation – and how it was used in this case of fifteenth-century French murder. *Fama* or 'reputation' heavily influenced the way in which murders or murderers were portrayed in the variety of surviving records and circulating literatures. *Fama* plays a central role as evidence with 'strong probative value'; it was one of the half-proofs necessary to proceed to the use of torture in extracting a confession, 'the Queen of Proofs'.[47] But the *fama* of a crime could inspire 'rumors about the possible author of the deed',[48] which were enough to spark the public imagination. In the early modern period, assassins assumed exaggerated proportions as shadowy figures who participated in great plots to destabilise religious and political institutions. Andrew McKenzie-McHarg analyses the anti-Jesuit propaganda of the sixteenth century that imagines the Jesuit order as a massive, secret conspiracy tied to the assassination of monarchs and other major figures throughout early modern Europe. In each

---

[47] Vallerani, *Medieval Public Justice*, pp. 56–57.
[48] Ibid., p. 57.

instance, assassination (or the fear of it) elevates murder from an individual act to a political tool wielded for a much larger purpose.

But murder does not always occur on such a monumental or even notable scale. The essays in the third part of this collection provide insight into individual instances of murder, the legal and social implications of these crimes for their communities as well as the institutional and popular responses to murderers and their victims: family that murders family, mothers who kill their children, adolescents who kill, husbands who kill wives, wives who kill husbands and women who encourage men to commit murder on their behalf. Murder is often the product of private disputes and personal vendettas; family members are often the most likely suspects and the motives amount to issues of money, greed, sex, love and jealousy rather than complex psychopathy. Here, Jeffrey Doolittle analyses the conflicting terminology of *homicida* and *parricida* in the sixth-century *Historiae* of Gregory of Tours (c. 538–94) in terms of the social position of murderers and the sense of shame attached to their crimes: Gregory uses *homicida* as a critical label for members of the elite or their agents who delight in slaughter of innocent people while he reserves *parricida* mainly for offenders of royal status who have taken the lives of family members through shame-worthy motives.[49] The motives for murder have not changed, nor have most of the methods: poison, sharp force trauma (knives, axes, swords or other bladed weapons), blunt force trauma (cudgels, stones or bricks), suffocation, strangulation and, eventually, gunpowder projectiles. In his essay, Thomas Gobbitt focuses on the treacherous nature of poisoning in the Lombard laws (643), and the specifically gendered applications of certain laws that gave women legal standing where they normally would not have it.

Murder was not always condemned; authors often drew sharp distinctions between homicide carried out for the 'right' reasons and the 'wrong' ones. Some poets argued that murder served a greater good and, thus, was a rational and valid act. Focusing on the medieval Georgian text, *The Man in the Panther Skin*, G. Koolemans Beynen explains that the poet Rustaveli justifies murder in certain circumstances, especially when it is carried out rationally and with a logical and necessary end. In this context, the end justifies the means – even if it means murder. At the same time, the text reveals a certain unease with female rule by making the women the primary instigators of murder.

Killing within families was among the most heinous crimes, as Doolittle points out, but it was also among the most common forms of murder. Carmel Ferragud considers the unusual fifteenth-century court case of Sanxo Calbó, accused by his son-in-law of poisoning multiple members of their family, including Sanxo's daughter Isabel, and the horror it inspired in late-medieval Valencia. Patricia Turning examines the fifteenth-century case of Clare de Portet and the

---

[49] Jeffrey Doolittle, 'Negotiating Murder in the *Historiae* of Gregory of Tours', at p. 325.

intersections of gender, murder and the spectacle of public execution in the city of Toulouse. She argues that, in cases where the crime is grievous enough, the gender of the perpetrator becomes irrelevant in the exercise of justice. In her study of Margaret Vincent, the Catholic convert who murdered her own children in a bid to save their souls, Dianne Berg argues that the discourse of infanticide in many of the sixteenth-century accounts demonise Vincent, making and unmaking her into a monstrous mother as a form of Protestant propaganda. Ben Parsons delves into the motivations and social reaction to young murderers in sixteenth- and seventeenth-century pamphlets, revealing an unsettling lack of horror, or even concern, at the accounts of adolescents who kill. He argues that 'in most reports, youngsters who kill do not register as anomalous offenders who need to be interpreted along new lines but are readily drawn into given categories of killer'.[50] Accounts of murder and the swift punishment of the perpetrators circulated as popular literature, especially in the early modern period, and often served as a social register as well as entertainment, capturing the imagination and providing a lens for reading social reactions to murder in pre-modern society.

Murder tears at the very fabric of society, ripping it at the seams. The murder of outsiders or foreigners suggests underlying elements of darkness within a community; these elements can be justified by the need to protect or preserve a society. But murderers within the confines of family, or the boundaries of a township, threaten the stability of the delicate social order, which must be restored in the process and enactment of justice. When mothers kill children (Berg), fathers kill sons or daughters (Ferragud), adolescents kill parents or caretakers (Parsons), the parameters and expectations of natural order are tested and can only be restored through the sense that 'murder will out' and the guilty be brought to justice. Assassination strikes at the head of nations (Hutchison), is wielded by the state (Lubin) and can be employed in creating narratives of vast conspiracies (McKenzie-McHarg). Murder has always been present. While court records, chronicles, literature, art and law attempt to come to terms with these 'violent transgressions',[51] the accounts of medieval and early-modern murder in this volume register both approval and disapproval, sympathy and censure, deterrents and inspiration, justice and injustice (Doolittle, Gobbitt, Slavin, Komornicka, Turning and Roth). Murder can tarnish an entire ethnic group (Gates), sully chivalric reputations (Wood, Coleman) or reinforce them (Beynen). It can be funny (Latowsky) or it can be a sobering satirical commentary on the failures of society (VanDonkelaar, Tracy). Ultimately, this collection seeks to provide a more complex picture of one of humanity's most persistent crimes. Thus, the individual articles often share sources and have tried to

---

[50] Ben Parsons, 'Imps of Hell: Young People, Murder and the Early English Press', p. 442.
[51] Halttunen, *Murder Most Foul*, p. 2.

communicate with each other as much as possible. We have, therefore, compiled a select bibliography of secondary texts, which focuses on the various aspects of murder. Because murder crosses all boundaries, it is necessary to look at murder in the medieval period and its continuity into the early-modern era as a series of pictures, traversing geographical borders to piece together how pre-modern cultures responded to murder in law and imagined it in fiction. The aim of this volume is to investigate, where possible, the ways in which medieval and early modern societies viewed murder and dealt with murderers, praxes that are part of a much longer historical trajectory that stretches back to the ancient world and well into a regrettably infinite future.

PART I
MURDER ON TRIAL: JUSTICE, LAW AND SOCIETY

CHAPTER 1

Secret Killing and Murder by Magic in the Law of Adomnán

Bridgette Slavin

OLD IRISH LEGAL TEXTS, dating from the seventh and eighth centuries, recognise four types of killing: kinslaying, illegal homicide, legal killing and secret murder.[1] The term for secret killing, *duinetháide*, is comprised of *duine* [person] and *táide* [theft], which implies kidnapping, with or without a connection to murder; however, legal commentary classifies a murder as *duinetháide* if the victim's body is hidden or left in the open and the killer does not acknowledge the crime.[2] It is an offence that involves not only homicide (one person killing another) but also secrecy and intent. *Duinetháide* is directly associated with killing by means of magic in *Cáin Adamnáin* [*Law of Adomnán*], an early medieval Irish list of ecclesiastical regulations.[3] Section 46 of *Cáin Adamnáin* requires a person who kills another by the use of a charm to pay the penalty of secret murder: 'Mát epthai día n-apallar dabera nech do alailiu, féich dunetáiti ind' [If it be charms from which death ensues that any one give to another, the

---

[1] Fergus Kelly, *A Guide to Early Irish Law* (Dublin: Dublin Institute for Advanced Studies, 2005), pp. 125–29.

[2] For an edition, see: Daniel A. Binchy, ed., *Corpus Iuris Hibernici*, 6 vols (Dublin: Dublin Institute for Advanced Studies, 1978), p. 252.16–20 (*CIH*); for a translation, see: William N. Hancock et al., eds. and trans., *The Ancient Laws of Ireland*, 6 vols (Dublin: Commissioners for the Publishing of the Ancient Laws and Institutes of Ireland, 1865–1901), III:99 (*AL*). Fergus Kelly points out that while the literal meaning of *duinetháide* appears to be kidnapping or abduction without killing, the sources reveal that secret murder is always involved, particularly the hiding of a corpse on a mountain or in the wilderness (Kelly, *A Guide to Early Irish Law*, p. 128).

[3] Although not a penitential, *Cáin Adamnáin* is an Old Irish text of religious regulations directed at offences against women, children and clerics. The text dates to the ninth century but contains material from the late seventh or early eighth century; see: Kuno Meyer, ed. and trans., *Cáin Adamnáin* (Oxford: Clarendon Press, 1905), p. 246 (*CA*). For a more recent translation, see: Máirín Ní Dhonnchadha, 'The Law of Adomnán: a Translation', in *Adomnán at Birr, AD 697: Essays in Commemoration of the Law of the Innocents*, ed. Thomas O'Loughlin (Dublin: Four Courts Press, 2001), pp. 53–71.

fines of murder followed by concealment of the corpse (are to be paid) for it].⁴ Early Irish legal and ecclesiastical penalties for magic and murder suggest that the direct association between *duintheháide* and supernaturally-induced homicide is unique to *Cáin Adamnáin*. The majority of penalties associated with supernatural practices in these sources relate to drawing the affections of another to oneself and the purposeful or unintentional obstruction of procreation, indicating insecurity over the potentially harmful, and even lethal, consequences of love magic.⁵ Further analysis of the early Irish legal penalties required for both secret murder and magical practices reveals that with the exception of using supernatural methods to hinder reproduction, and therefore inhibit the potential of life, there is no explicit punishment for taking the life of another human by magic in early Irish secular law. Indeed, extant early Irish law appears less troubled about murder by magic than certain other medieval legal cultures. Rather, the lethal effects of magic appear as a particular anxiety of the Church in the early Irish penitentials.

Cáin Adamnáin straddles the ecclesiastical concerns of the penitentials and the fiscal reparation for crimes required of secular law. The severe penalty for murder by magic in *Cáin Adamnáin* demonstrates the intention of the author(s) to align Irish law with contemporary ecclesiastical attitudes towards the use of illicit supernatural practices. Early medieval Christendom differentiated between supernatural acts perceived as the intervention of God and those whose origins lay in demonic powers and pagan rituals or beliefs. The distinction of murder by magic in *Cáin Adamnáin* signifies the importance of this text in both early Irish and early medieval contexts. While extant Irish law does not distinguish the crime of murder by magic from other forms of homicide, *Cáin Adamnáin* remedies this by not only identifying magical homicide but also distinguishing it from other means of killing by doubling the punitive fine and including it under the purview of secret murder. From a wider perspective, *Cáin Adamnáin* stands among other early medieval legal traditions, particularly Anglo-Saxon and Carolingian, in drawing ecclesiastical concerns about non-Christian beliefs and practices into the realm of secular law by identifying and severely punishing supernaturally-induced homicide.

In many early medieval societies, including Irish, homicide could lead to feuding, creating potentially long-term instability; compensative fines were set in place to provide restitution and re-establish social balance. Because recompense for homicide could be acquired through compensation to the victim's family, several early medieval societies considered individuals who concealed

---

⁴ CA §46.30–31.
⁵ For a full discussion of love charms in medieval Ireland, see: Jaqueline Borsje, 'Rules and Legislation on Love Charms in Early Medieval Ireland', *Peritia* 21 (2010): 172–90.

the act of killing particularly disdainful, and they specifically separated the crime of secret murder from other forms of homicide. Icelandic law makes a distinction between a publicly acknowledged killing, *víg*, and the more grievous crime of secret murder, *morð*.[6] Anglo-Saxon law also differentiates between openly-declared homicide and the covert nature of murder.[7] Early Irish legal material demonstrates the heinous nature of *duinethaíde* by the heavy fines the accused is expected to pay and the extended length of distraint – the seizure of the accused's property to ensure such fines are paid – allowed for these payments to be made. A standard case of homicide, in which the killer openly acknowledges the crime, requires the perpetrator to compensate the victim's family with two fines. The first, known as *éraic* and later *cró*, is a fixed penalty of seven *cumala* (pl. of *cumal*), a unit of value that is worth three milking cows, for every free man, regardless of rank.[8] The killer is also expected to pay *lóg n-enech*, the victim's honour-price, which varies based on the individual's status.[9]

Bretha Étgid [*Judgments of Inadvertence*], an eighth-century text concerning criminal law, states that people guilty of secret murder must pay double this amount due to the degree of *ferg* [wrath] in their actions.[10] The commentary explains that for *duinethaíde* the standard penalties of seven *cumala* and honour-price are due for murder, while the same amount is added for the

---

[6] Kelly, *A Guide to Early Irish Law*, p. 128, fn. 23. For more on the significance of public acknowledgement of killing in Icelandic law and literature, see in this volume: Ilse Schweitzer VanDonkelaar, 'Bringing Murder to Light: Death, Publishing and Performance in Icelandic Sagas'.

[7] Bruce R. O'Brien discusses the development of the murder fine in Anglo-Saxon law in 'From *Morðor* to *Murdrum*: The Preconquest Origin and Norman Revival of the Murder Fine', *Speculum* 71 (1996): 321–57. For further discussion on murder, particularly in relation to intent, in medieval England, see: J. M. Kaye, 'Early History of Murder and Manslaughter', *Law Quarterly Review* 83 (1967): 365–95, 569–601; Thomas A. Green, 'The Jury and the English Law of Homicide, 1200–1600', *Michigan Law Review* 74 (1976): 413–99; idem, 'Societal Concepts of Criminal Liability for Homicide in Medieval England', *Speculum* 47 (1972): 669–95; John Bellamy, *Crime and Public Order in England in the Later Middle Ages* (London and Toronto: Routledge & Kegan Paul, 1973). In this volume, see: Jay Paul Gates, 'Discursive Murders: The St Brice's Day Massacre, *Beowulf*, and *Morðor*', and Larissa Tracy, '"Mordre wol out": Murder and Justice in Chaucer'.

[8] *Electronic Dictionary of the Irish Language* (*eDIL*) s.v.1 *cumal* (pl. *cumala*): http://edil.qub.ac.uk/search?q=cumal&search_in=headword (accessed 28 November 2016).

[9] *eDIL* s.v 1 *enech, ainech*: http://edil.qub.ac.uk/search?q=enech&search_in=headword (accessed 28 November 2016); Kelly, *A Guide to Early Irish Law*, pp. 125–26; Neil McLeod, 'Assault and Attempted Murder in Brehon Law', *The Irish Jurist* 33 (1998): 351–91 at p. 351.

[10] 'Diablad fiach ferg', *CIH*, p. 252.16; translated in Hancock et al. as 'fines are doubled by malice aforethought', *AL* III, pp. 99.

concealment of the body.[11] The severity of *duinetháide* also affects the process by which the victim's family acquires compensation. *Di Cethairshlicht Athgabálae* [*The Four Divisions of Distraint*] states that secret murder receives a distraint of five days due to the heinousness of the crime and large fine.[12] The extreme penalty for *duinethaide* suggests that Irish lawmakers considered it one of the most offensive crimes against the stability of medieval Irish society. The association between *duinethaide* and magic in *Cáin Adamnáin* extends this abhorrence and apprehension about social stability to the use of supernatural practices to commit homicide.

While the penalty for killing someone by the use of a charm in *Cáin Adamnáin* demonstrates repulsion at practices perceived as magical by the author or authors of *Cáin Adamnáin*, the enforcement of this fine is more difficult to determine. Known as *Cáin Adamnáin* in Old Irish, the text was more widely referred to as *Lex Innocentium* [*Law of Innocents*]. The title *Lex Innocentium* reflects the humanitarian emphasis of *Cáin Adamnáin*, which focuses primarily on the protection of women, but also safeguards clerics, youths and Church property.[13] Saint Adomnán, abbot of Iona, at the Synod of Birr in County Offaly, promulgated *Cáin Adamnáin* in 697 CE on the centennial of the death of Saint Columba, Iona's founding saint. The term *cáin* has two meanings: primarily, it refers to 'regulation'; secondly, to 'punishment (by fine or otherwise) for breach of regulation'.[14] Such laws were promulgated in Ireland in the eighth century and, to a lesser degree, in the ninth.[15] While religious houses promoted these regulations, they were heavily influenced by secular legal language and maxims, and often, though not always, enacted by a king on a provincial level or throughout

---

[11] *CIH*, p. 252.23–25 = *AL* III, pp. 99. This doubled fine is required even if the victim is still alive when found because it was the intention of the killer to murder and hide the body. If the killer and the concealer are different people, then they each pay the penalty for their own part in the crime, be it the murder or the concealment.

[12] *CIH*, p. 1694.9–11 = *AL*, I, pp. 176–77.

[13] Colin Smith and James Gallen argue for *Cáin Adamnáin*'s place in the history of international humanitarian law in '*Cáin Adamnáin* and the Law of War', *Journal of the History of International Law* 16 (2014): 63–81.

[14] eDIL s.v. *cáin*: http://edil.qub.ac.uk/search?q=cain&search_in=headword (accessed 28 November 2016); Máirín Ní Dhonnchadha, 'Birr and the Law of the Innocents', in *Adomnán at Birr*, ed. O'Loughlin, pp. 13–32 at p. 20.

[15] With the exception of the Laws of Adomnán, Patrick (*Cáin Phátraic*) and Sunday (*Cáin Domnaig*), many of the *cánai* were enacted at a local level. For example, according to the *Annals of Ulster* (AU), the *Law of Patrick* was enforced in 737, 767, 783, 799, 806, 811, 823 and 836 CE. Provincial *cánai* listed in AU include: the Law of Ciarán: 744, 788 and 814 CE; the Law of Comán: 772 and 793 CE; and the Law of Colum Cille (Columba): 753, 757 and 778 CE.

all of Ireland by an assembly of kings (*rígdál*).[16] Adomnán found support for his *Cáin* throughout Ireland. Section 28 contains a list of ninety-one signatories that includes representatives of every major Irish monastic centre and kingship, who all pledge to uphold Adomnán's law until doom.[17] Due to the lack of case law from the period, it is difficult to discern the degree to which these signatories and their successors enforced *Cáin Adamnáin*. Unlike *Cáin Phátraic* [*Law of Patrick*], which was re-promulgated numerous times, the *Annals of Ulster* mention the re-enactment of *Cáin Adamnáin* only once, in 727 CE.[18] Thus, *Cáin Adamnáin* requires a specific and severe penalty for the crime of magical homicide; however, the implementation of this law may not have extended beyond the early eighth century. It is likely, therefore, that individuals accused of murder by magic faced different charges than those presented in *Cáin Adamnáin* for much of the medieval period; unfortunately, extant legal texts remain silent on the matter.

While the association between *duinethaide* and magic in *Cáin Adamnáin* indicates an adverse attitude and severe approach to killing another by magical practices, it does not reveal the frequency of accusations for this crime. Nevertheless, though not directly linked, Irish annals do record homicide by both *duinethaide* and magic.[19] While extant sources do not provide specific legal cases of individuals prosecuted for murder by magic, the *Annals of the Four Masters* record such a crime and, therefore, the potential that such cases came before the enforcers of *Cáin Adamnáin* while it was in favour. Despite the lack of a quantitative record for murder by supernatural means in early medieval Ireland, considered together, the annalistic account of murder by magic and the legal maxim in *Cáin Adamnáin* that severely penalises this crime bear evidence that a belief in supernaturally-induced homicide prevailed in early medieval Ireland and that murders perceived as such existed. *Cáin Adamnáin* is significant in this regard as it secularises a fear

---

[16] Thomas Charles-Edwards, *The Medieval Gaelic Lawyer* (Cambridge: University of Cambridge, Department of Anglo-Saxon, Norse and Celtic, 1999), pp. 43–53.

[17] *CA* §28.14–21.

[18] AU 727.5 CE; The *Annals of the Four Masters* (M) refer to Caencomhrac, the abbot and bishop of Doire-Chalgaigh, as the 'steward of Adamnán's Law' in 727 CE, suggesting that the law was in use at this time.

[19] Both the *Annals of Ulster* and the *Annals of the Four Masters* record incidents of *duinethaide*. Ecclesiastical: AU 879 CE, M 876 CE and AU 885 CE; Secular: M 891 CE and M 1349 CE. The *Annals of the Four Masters* records a death caused by magic for the year 734: 'Fergus Glutt toisech Cobha d'ecc. At-ces dosidhe aes ulc & aidhmhillti ag tealgad graintseligh in ro laitis iopadha ina aighidh fair, conad é fochann a bhais' [Fearghus Glut, chief of Cobha, died. It appeared to him that wicked and destructive people used to cast spits, in which they put charms, in his face, which was the cause of his death].

of the mortal consequences of illicit supernatural practices, considered demonic and pagan by the Church, by requiring a legal fine for the crime.

Cáin Adamnáin is particularly interesting in relation to homicide as it raises the legal value of vulnerable members of society by increasing the fines for numerous homicides. The text particularly stresses the protection of women. Máirín Ní Dhonnchadha points out that *Cáin Adamnáin* demonstrates Marian devotion as it emphasises the role of women as life-givers and draws a connection between them and Mary, the mother of Jesus.[20] The text elevates the status of women by significantly altering the penalty required for the killing of a woman. The accused has a hand and a foot cut off before being executed, and his kin must pay the standard *éraic* fine for a free man, which is seven *cumala*.[21] As an alternative, the culprit can undergo fourteen years' penance and pay double the fine, or fourteen *cumala*.[22] The entirety of the fine is paid to the head of Iona's *familia*; however, the final clause in this regulation (§29) states that Adomnán does not take the fine owed to the kin, lord or church of the victim, which suggests that the full doubled fine is not kept entirely by Iona.[23] Section 41 similarly indicates that one-third of the fine for every woman who has been slain is given to whomever it belongs according to traditional law; therefore, the portion of the additional fine owed to the Ionan *familia* can be understood as a tax or superlevy.[24]

Cáin Adamnáin also addresses the killing of clerics and the young. Any person who participates in, or idly stands by and allows, the slaying of a clerical student or youth must pay eight *cumala* and undergo eight years of penance,[25] and the *familia* of Iona receives a superlevy of one-eighth for the murder of every cleric or youth.[26] As Julianna Grigg argues, 'Rather than appropriating the prerogatives of Irish traditional law, these fines were in effect a tax added to personal injury cases that were dealt with under the *Cáin*'.[27] Thus, *Cáin Adamnáin* alters the status of vulnerable members of society by adjusting the compensatory punishment required for homicide in certain instances. These alterations to traditional law have a twofold effect: in addition to addressing the humanitarian interests of

---

[20] Ní Dhonnchadha, 'Birr and the Law of the Innocents', pp. 22–27.
[21] Women are also penalised for murder in *Cáin Adamnáin*. Such a woman is set adrift in a boat so that God can determine her fate, CA §45.30–31.
[22] Ibid. §33.22–25.
[23] The text claims that the *éraic* fine will be paid to Adomnán or any *coarb* [successor of the founding saint; leader of a religious community] that fills his position until doom, ibid. §29.20–21.
[24] Ibid. §41.26–29. Ní Dhonnchadha, 'Birr and the Law of the Innocents', p. 27.
[25] CA §35.24–27. The regulation reduces the fine for inadvertence and ignorance.
[26] Ibid. §44.28–29.
[27] Julianna Grigg, 'Aspects of the Cáin: Adomnán's *Lex Innocentium*', *Journal of the Australian Early Medieval Association* 1 (2005): 41–50 at p. 45.

Cáin Adamnáin by making the murder of defenceless members of society more expensive and, therefore, more inhibiting, it also offers a financial benefit to the Ionan *familia*. Traditional murder cases require compensation offered directly to the victim's family, unless enforcement is necessary, which requires an enforcer's fine.[28] Although a unique addition to standard procedure in secular law, acquiring wealth by adding taxes to pre-existing fines should not be interpreted as the sole purpose of *Cáin Adamnáin*. Financial gain is certainly a bonus, and even an incentive; however, the humanitarian interests are clearly the focus of the text. Section 46 of *Cáin Adamnáin*, which penalises the killing of another by use of a charm, does not raise the status of a particular demographic, yet by demanding the double fine for *duinethaide* in cases where death ensues from the use of magic, the promulgation of this law put pressure on the public to refrain from supernatural practices, lest they lead to taking the life of another. The murder creates social upheaval, while the use of magic is an ecclesiastical concern. *Cáin Adamnáin* uses the doubled-fine of *duinethaide* to forward a Christian agenda of suppressing practices considered illicit and threatening to the Church and to society at large. Thus, while *Cáin Adamnáin* aims to protect women, youths and clerics from physical violence by increasing the punishment for the murders of these individuals, it seeks to protect all members of society from the occult nature of non-physical, magical attack by equating the penalties for secret murder and supernaturally-induced homicide. *Cáin Adamnáin* demonstrates a perception that some members of society are defenceless against the violence of a war-driven culture and require protection: however, all members are threatened by the inherent evil of magic.

Early Christianity inherited from the Classical and Judaic traditions a view that magic was foreign, illicit and inherently evil.[29] With the official Christianisation of the Roman Empire in the fourth century, Christians sought to define themselves, to separate their religion from its Jewish origins and the other non-Christian religions around them. The concept of magic played a significant role in this process and underwent a deep-seated shift with the rise of Christianity in Late Antiquity. Early Christian thinkers continued to separate illicit from accepted supernatural practices; however, the qualification of magic changed. This alteration took place on an ideological level and is linked to an increased focus on the figure of the devil as the supreme enemy and opposition of God in later apocalyptic Judaism. From this framework, early Christian intellectuals modified the traditional *daimones* of the Classical era,

---

[28] Kelly, *A Guide to Early Irish Law*, p. 125.

[29] For further discussion on the origins of medieval thoughts on magic, see: Michael Bailey, 'The Meanings of Magic', *Magic, Ritual, and Witchcraft* 1.1 (2006): 1–23; Valerie Flint, *The Rise of Magic in Early Medieval Europe* (Princeton: Princeton University Press, 1991); and Richard Kieckhefer, *Magic in the Middle Ages* (Cambridge: Cambridge University Press, 1989; reprt 2000).

who were customarily morally ambiguous supernatural beings, into Christian demons, inherently evil creatures that serve the devil with the aim of leading Christians astray.[30] Christian thinkers frequently cited Pauline writings, such as I Corinthians 10:20–1, which states that pagans sacrifice to demons in support of the 'demonisation of magic'.[31]

Another inherent aspect of the early Christian interpretation of magic was its close connection to the classical concept of superstition and the process of Christianisation. Early Christians adopted the Roman term *religio* to refer to the true religion of Christ. They also embraced *superstitio*, which non-Christians once used to indicate extreme or unwarranted religious dedication or ritual activity. Christian authorities designated all devotion and cultic practices dedicated to pagan entities as demonic and superstitious. This stipulation included magic but also encompassed all non-Christian rituals.[32] Consequently, in the early conversion period, the late antique synthesis of biblical, early Christian and classical concepts of magic merged with the folk beliefs and rituals of various cultures: Celtic, Germanic, Scandinavian and Slavic. During the Christianisation process, pagan gods were demonised and pre-Christian religious practices were considered superstition and often regarded as magic.[33]

Augustine of Hippo (354–430 CE) was the most outspoken of the Church Fathers against demons and their connection to magic. In his *De Doctrina Christiana*, Augustine combines the concepts of magic, demons and superstition. He regards human activity superstitious if:

> […] idola pertinens, vel ad colendam sicuti Deum creaturam partemve
> ullam creaturae; vel ad consultationes et pacta quaedam significationum cum
> daemonibus placita atque foederata, qualia sunt molimina magicarum artium,
> quae quidem commemorare potius quam docere assolent poetae. Ex quo genere
> sunt, sed quasi licentiore vanitate, aruspicum et augurum libri.
>
> [It concerns the making and worshipping of idols, or the worshipping of the
> created order or part of it as if it were God, or if it involves certain kinds of

---

[30] Valerie Flint, 'The Demonization of Magic and Sorcery in Late Antiquity: Christian Redefinitions of Pagan Religions', in *Witchcraft and Magic in Europe: Ancient Greece and Rome*, ed. Bengt Ankarloo and Stuart Clark (Philadelphia: University of Pennsylvania Press, 2002), pp. 277–348; Jeffrey Burton Russell, *The Devil: Perceptions of Evil from Antiquity to Primitive Christianity* (Ithaca: Cornell University Press, 1977); idem, *Satan: The Early Christian Tradition* (Ithaca: Cornell University Press, 1981); Elaine Pagels, *The Origin of Satan* (New York: Vintage, 1995); Bailey, 'The Meanings of Magic', p. 8.
[31] Flint, 'The Demonisation of Magic', p. 297.
[32] Bailey, 'The Meanings of Magic', p. 8.
[33] Edward Peters, 'The Medieval Church', in *Witchcraft and Magic in Europe: The Middle Ages*, ed. Bengt Ankarloo and Stuart Clark (Philadelphia: University of Pennsylvania Press, 2001), pp. 173–238 at p. 187.

consultations or contracts about meaning arranged and ratified with demons, such as the enterprises involved in the art of magic, which poets tend to mention rather than to teach. From this category – only their vanity is even more reckless – come the books of the haruspices and augurs].[34]

Augustine put forth four particular arguments about demonic magic that continued to influence thoughts on the subject into the early modern period: that pagan gods are really demons (Psalms 95:5); pagan religions are superstitious (*De Doctrina Christiana* 75, *De Civitate Dei* IV.30–34); demons enter into pacts with humans, each for the sake of vainglory (Isaiah 28:15); and that all Christians should be aware of the difference between Christian miracles and demonic wonders (*De Civitate Dei* VIII 21.7, 21.8, 22.2).[35] Isidore of Seville (c. 560–636 CE) also had a lasting influence on medieval thoughts on magic. In his *Etymologies* (Book VIII, Chapter 9), Isidore provides a reference to various supernatural practitioners, including: *magi, malefici, auspices, augures, haruspices, arioli, necromancers, hydromantii, divini, genethliaci* and *mathematici*, citing Greco-Roman, Judaic and biblical sources. In Book VIII, 9:31, Isidore claims that all of the supernatural practices listed in his reference are demonic arts and the result of the association of men and bad angels, which all Christians must avoid.[36] Thus, as Karen Jolly points out, 'the essential divide for these Church writers is between Christian/religion/divine miracle and pagan/magic/demonic illusion'.[37] While the early medieval Church perpetuated the belief that all non-Christian supernatural practices are demonic, the terminology used to refer to magic in many early medieval Latin and vernacular texts is rather vague, as is the case with *Cáin Adamnáin*.

The penalty for supernaturally-induced homicide is clear in §46 of *Cáin Adamnáin*; however, the regulation is less specific as to the nature of the magical practice that caused the death in question. *Cáin Adamnáin* requires the accused to pay the doubled fine specifically for a homicide that results from the use of an *epaid*.[38] According to the *Dictionary of the Irish Language*, *epaid* (pl. *aipthi*) refers to a charm or spell.[39] Jacqueline Borsje suggests that, similar to the Greek term *pharmakon* (φάρμακον), '*epaid* is a supernatural instrument that can destroy,

---

[34] *De Doctrina Christiana* II §20.30 (*PL*, 34.0050), translated in *Magic and Witchcraft in Europe 400–1700: A Documentary History*, ed. Alan Charles Kors and Edward Peters, 2nd edn (Philadelphia: University of Pennsylvania Press, 2000), pp. 44–5.
[35] Ibid., p. 43.
[36] *Etymologies*, Book VIII, Chapter 9 (*PL*, 82.0310–0314), translated in ibid., pp. 50–54.
[37] Karen Jolly, 'Medieval Magic: Definitions, Beliefs, Practices', in *Witchcraft and Magic in Europe: The Middle Ages*, ed. Ankarloo and Clark, pp. 1–66 at p. 15.
[38] CA §46.30–31.
[39] eDIL s.v. *epaid*: http://edil.qub.ac.uk/search?q=epaid&search_in=headword (accessed 28 November 2016).

poison, create and heal and that may be accompanied by or consist of words of power'.⁴⁰ Thus, the term *epaid* encompasses a variety of functions and supernatural practices, including those that are ingested, worn or spoken. Further on, §46 offers either an example of, or an alternative term for, such an *epaid*. After listing the penalty for killing another with an *epaid*, §46 discusses the process for determining and paying the fines for other secretive killings, particularly *dubchrecha* [dark/secret raids]⁴¹ and *chnáimchrói* [bone/body -wounds, -blood, -death/dismemberments],⁴² that are found in one of the four nearest mountainous areas. Gilbert Márkus points out that while *chnáimchrói*, comprised of *cnáim* [bone] and *cró* [blood], has been translated to mean some form of bloody demise, in modern Irish folklore, *chnáimchrói* refers to a charm or an enchantment that can lead to death, which fits the supernatural context of §46.⁴³ Whether the author(s) and audience of *Cáin Adamnáin* understood *chnáimchrói* as a specific type of charm or a more general example of potentially lethal magic is not clear from the present text; however, taken in this wider context, *Cáin Adamnáin* links killing by supernatural practices to secrecy. *Dubchrecha* and *chnáimchrói* are examples of secret murder because they refer to unacknowledged murders found in the countryside. The individual who kills another by the use of an *epaid* also conceals himself or herself through the occult nature of the act.

Although concern over the harmful effects of an *epaid* appears in the secular legal material, these sources are silent concerning killing another person through magic. The Old Irish tract on distraint (*Di Cethairshlicht Athgabálae*) states that *imarchor auptha*, the carrying or casting of an *epaid*, is an offence:⁴⁴

IMARCHOR AUPTHA (b)
¹ .i. cipe dogne (b)

---

⁴⁰ Borsje, 'Rules and Legislation', p. 176.
⁴¹ Borsje translates *Dubchrecha* as 'dark raids', ibid., p. 177; Meyer translates it as 'secret plunderings', *CA*, p. 31; Ní Dhonnchadha, suggests 'dire mutilations', in 'The Law of Adomnán', p. 66.
⁴² *Chnáimchrói* is more challenging to interpret. Meyer does not offer a translation but suggests that it is a compound of *cnáim-chró*, at *CA*, p. 31, fn. 2; Ní Dhonnchadha chooses 'dismemberment', in 'The Law of Adomnán', p. 66; Borsje suggests 'bone -wounds, -blood, -death', in 'Rules and Legislation', p. 177.
⁴³ Gilbert Márkus, ed. and trans., *Adomnán's 'Law of Innocents': Cáin Adomnáin* (Kilmartin, Argyll: Kilmartin House Trust, 2008), p. 23 n. 46.
⁴⁴ The edition and translation for all items from *Di Cethairshlicht Athgabálae* referred to in this essay belong to Borsje, 'Rules and Legislation'. Borsje has arranged the original text in capitals, while the gloss and commentary are in miniscule: (a) refers to the earliest manuscript version of *Cethairshlicht Athgabálae*, containing Old Irish text and gloss found in Dublin, Trinity College, MS 1337 (H.3.18). For an edition, see: *CIH*, pp. 890.38–891.4, and for a commentary, see: Liam Breatnach, *A Companion to the Corpus Iuris Hibernici* (Dublin: Dublin Institute for Advanced Studies, 2005), pp. 272, 287; (b) refers to London, British Library, Harley MS 432, which contains a continuous

² .i. letfiach ann o tiucfa fogal, j anfot sin uili (b).

[CARRYING/CASTING CHARMS/SPELLS
¹ i.e. whoever does so
² i.e. [he shall pay] half fine for it where injury results: and all this is without evil intent].⁴⁵

The glossators state that anyone who carries an *epaid* is culpable; however, they do not refer to the accused's intent in using the charm or spell. Rather, the second gloss requires a fine for only half the honour-price of the victim, and this only if the accused's actions do not indicate an intent to harm though they do result in injury.⁴⁶ Because the previous two legal regulations relate to love magic, it is possible that the purpose for using the *epaid* referred to in *imarchor auptha* is to induce or diminish intimacy.⁴⁷ An obvious concern for impairment is present; however, the partial fine indicates that death is not taken into account in this instance.

Mimir do cor do coin [putting/casting a bad/dangerous morsel for/to a dog], the entry immediately following *imarchor auptha*, points to the potentially lethal danger of such charms.

MIMIR DO CHOR DO CHOIN (a), MIMIR DO COR DO COIN (b),
    MIMIR DO
CHOR DO CHUIN (c)
¹ .i. promad auptha son dus i mbia aithi j a mbiat aminsi (a) i. da promad (b)
² .i. im smacht in coin ł ineclainn (b) .i. im smacht in coin, ł in eneclann (c)
³ .i. froma uptha dus inbud amainsi; lethdiri ind, uair ni fo fath marbtha (b) i. fromha uptha inbu amhainsin, lethdire inn uair ni fo fath marbtha (c)

---

copy of a portion of the tract. For the law text, see: *CIH*, p. 387.30–33, for the glosses, see: *CIH*, pp. 387.34–388.17, and for the commentary, see: Breatnach, *A Companion*, p. 287; and (c) refers to a longer extract with later glosses that are provided in Dublin, Trinity College, MS 1336 (H. 3. 17). See: *CIH*, p. 1692.15–37 for edition and Breatnach, *A Companion*, p. 287 for commentary.

⁴⁵ b=*CIH*, p. 387.32 (original text), p. 388.12–13 (gloss); Borsje, 'Rules and Legislation', p. 185.
⁴⁶ Borsje, 'Rules and Legislation', p. 185.
⁴⁷ The previous two entries are: *fuba n-imda* [supernatural attack of a bed], *CIH*, pp. 891.2, 387.31–32, 1692.31, and *collud mbrethi* [destruction of a birth], *CIH*, pp. 387.32, 1692.33. An example of using a charm for love can be found in the following Heptad: *bean di-a tabair a ceile upta oc a guide co mbeir for druius* [A woman to whom her mate has given charms at soliciting her so that he brings on fornication]; *CIH*, p. 48.11= *AL* V, p. 292. *Upta* refers to *aipthi*, the accusative plural of *epaid*: *eDIL* s.v. *epaid*. The Heptads include legal material and commentary on a variety of topics in early Irish law. Kelly, *A Guide to Early Irish Law*, p. 266; Breatnach, *A Companion*, pp. 291–2. For an edition of the Heptads, see: *CIH*, pp. 1.1–64.5, 537.16–549.18, 1821.28–1854.36, 1881.9–1896.22. For a translation, see: *AL* V, pp. 119–351.

⁴ .i. from*ad* felmais (b) .i. *froma* felmuis (c)
⁵ .i. from*ad* na pisoc, ⁊ anfot indethb*iri* he (b) .i. *froma* na pisog, ⁊ anfot indetb*ire* e (c).

[PUTTING/CASTING A BAD/DANGEROUS MORSEL FOR/TO A DOG
¹ i.e. to test a charm (*epaid*), namely to find out whether there is swiftness in it and if there are supernatural crafts (*amainsi*) in it (a) i.e. to test it (b);
² i.e. concerning the smacht-fine [for] the dog or the honour-price (b, c);
³ i.e. to test a charm/spell (*epaid*) to find out whether it has supernatural craft (*amainse*); half *díre*-fine for it, because it was not intentional that he was killed (b, c);
⁴ i.e. to test an enchantment (*felmas*, b, c);
⁵ i.e. to test the sorcery (*pisóca*), and it is the inadvertence of an unnecessary act (b, c)].⁴⁸

The object given to the dog is likely edible, and the glossators interpret the morsel as dangerous because it has been affected by something supernatural, referring to *amainse* [supernatural cunning or craft] in gloss 1 and gloss 3; *epaid* [charm, spell] in gloss 1 and gloss 3; *felmas* [enchantment, sorcery; a spell or a charm] in gloss 4; and *pisóca* [sorcery] in gloss 5.⁴⁹ Although the purpose of the charm is unclear in this item, the glosses indicate that the testing of the *epaid* is intentional but the lethal affect is not. The charm given to the dog connects to the previous item, *imarchor auptha*, as certain glossators of *mimir do cor do coin* refer back to it. An Old Irish gloss refers specifically to *epaid*: '. i. pro*mad* auptha son dus i mbia aithi j a mbiat am*insi*', [i.e. 'to test a charm (*epaid*), namely to find out whether there is swiftness in it and if there are supernatural crafts (*amainsi*) in it'].⁵⁰ Another glossator states that the purpose of giving the morsel to a dog is 'to test it' [*da promad*], with 'it' referring to the *epaid* that is the transgression considered in *imarchor auptha*.⁵¹ Later glosses state that half of the *díre* [honour-price, penalty]⁵² is to be paid to the owner of the dog because its death was inadvertent. Thus, while secular law penalises inadvertent injury and the death of another person's dog through the use of an *epaid*, there is no direct association between homicide and magic.

The double fine for killing another with an *epaid* found in *Cáin Adamnáin* has no precedent in early Irish law. The lack of a reference to murder by supernatural

---

⁴⁸ a = *CIH*, p. 891.2–3 (original text and gloss); b = *CIH*, p. 387.32 (original text); *CIH*, p. 388.13–15 (gloss); c=*CIH*, p. 1692.35–37 (original text and gloss); Borsje, 'Rules and Legislation', p. 186.
⁴⁹ Borsje, 'Rules and Legislation', p. 186.
⁵⁰ Ibid.
⁵¹ Ibid.
⁵² eDIL s.v. *díre*. http://edil.qub.ac.uk/search?q=dire&search_in=headword (accessed 28 November 2016).

means in extant early Irish legal sources suggests at least two possibilities: that secular law penalised murder by magic in the same manner as other homicides, or there was, at one time, a law text that did incorporate this crime. Although a lack of textual evidence leads only to conjecture, the fact that *Cáin Adamnáin* purposefully increased the traditional legal penalties for murdering women, clerics and the young in order to inhibit the killing of these individuals indicates that the same approach was taken with regard to murder by magic: in order to discourage the use of supernatural practices, particularly with the intent to harm another, *Cáin Adamnáin* expanded the standard penalty for murder to equal that of secret murder.

While extant secular Irish law does not offer a specific penalty for killing a person through supernatural practices, other early medieval legal institutions require the death penalty for murder through magic. Like Irish law, Anglo-Saxon law required compensation to the victim's family in cases of homicide. However, in contrast to Irish legislation – a corpus created and regulated by a professional class of lawyers and judges – Anglo-Saxon law includes royal decrees. Late ninth- and early tenth-century Anglo-Saxon law demonstrates a rise in use of the death penalty as opposed to financial compensation for certain crimes. For example, the legislation of King Æthelstan (d. 939 CE) emphasises capital punishment for some offences, including *wiccecræftum* [witchcraft].[53] Similarly, the Capitulary of Paderborn, issued by Charlemagne in 785 CE to regulate the newly conquered and forcibly converted Saxons, states that any man or woman who has been deceived by the devil and eaten another person will be put to death.[54] More generally, Charlemagne's *Admonitio Generalis* [*General Admonition*] of 789 CE requires the death penalty for anyone who practises magic and does not amend their ways, regardless of whether it leads to the death of another.[55] Charlemagne's lethal punishment for the practice of magic echoes earlier Roman

---

[53] *II Æthelstan* 6; Felix Liebermann, ed., *Die Gesetze Angelsachsen*, 3 vols (Halle: Niemeyer, 1903–1916), 1:150–166 at p. 152. For further discussion on murder in Anglo-Saxon law, see in this volume: Jay Paul Gates, 'Discursive Murders: The St Brice's Day Massacre, *Beowulf* and *Morðor*'.

[54] 'Paderborn, 785 (Capitulary concerning the parts of Saxony)', in *Readings in Medieval History*, ed. Patrick J. Geary, 2 vols (North York: University of Toronto Press, 2016), 1:249–51 at p. 250 (§ 6).

[55] Chapter 18 of the *Admonitio Generalis* bans people from becoming sorcerers, magicians and enchanters, while chapter 65 condemns to death those who practise augury and necromancy if they do not conform. See: P. D. King, *Charlemagne: Translated Sources* (Lancaster: University of Lancaster, 1987), p. 211 (§18), p. 215 (§65); Edward Peters, 'Early Canon Law and Carolingian Legislation to 1100', in *Witchcraft and Magic in Europe: The Middle Ages*, ed. Ankarloo and Clark, pp. 194–206 at p. 198.

law, particularly the Theodosian Code, which dates to the early Christian period of the empire.[56]

The laws of Charlemagne and Æthelstan postdate the documentation of secular laws in Ireland as well as *Cáin Adamnáin* and demonstrate a particular interest of these monarchs in consolidating royal and judicial power while bringing secular law more into alignment with ecclesiastical concerns.[57] Ireland at this time did not have one king, but many kingdoms; however, secular law was generally universal throughout the island. While Irish law stands in contrast to these other early medieval legal institutions in being issued by legal specialists rather than a king, *Cáin Adamnáin* is comparable in its aspiration to bring secular law more into alignment with the Church's desire to eradicate magical practices.

Two Old Irish penitentials also associate magic and *duinetháide*, indicating that *Cáin Adamnáin* is not unique in its severe resolve against the use of magic in early Irish religious regulations. The eighth-century *Old Irish Table of Commutations* situates magic, in this instance *druídecht* [magic, druidry],[58] in the same context as homicide and *duinetháide*, sins considered so destructive that only the intervention of God or excessive self-mortification can reduce the terms of atonement.[59] Not all penitentials are so severe in the atonement of such sins. For example, the following canon (§7) from the eighth-century *Old Irish Penitential* requires seven years for the atonement of supernaturally-induced

---

[56] *Codex Theodosianus* 9.16.4. Clyde Pharr, trans., *The Theodosian Code* (Princeton: Princeton University Press, 1952), p. 237.

[57] Andrew Rabin argues that Æthelstan's increased use of capital punishment was an attempt to consolidate judicial power; Andrew Rabin, 'Capital Punishment and the Anglo-Saxon Judicial Apparatus: A Maximum View?', in *Capital and Corporal Punishment in Anglo-Saxon England*, ed. Jay Paul Gates and Nicole Marafioti (Woodbridge: Boydell Press, 2014), pp. 181–99 at p. 189. Peters points out that the increased penalties for practising magic during Charlemagne's reign demonstrate the close alliance between the Frankish, particularly Carolingian, dynasty and reform-minded Frankish clergy. See: Peters, 'Early Canon Law and Carolingian Legislation to 1100', p. 197.

[58] 'Secret lore and arts of the druids; in a wider sense occult science, wizardry', *eDIL* s.v. *druídecht*: http://edil.qub.ac.uk/search?q=druidecht&search_in=headword (accessed 28 November 2016). For further exploration of *druídecht*, see my forthcoming monograph, *Druídecht: Perceptions of Magic and Druidry in Early Irish Texts* (Cardiff: University of Wales Press).

[59] D. A. Binchy, 'The Old Irish Penitential', in *The Irish Penitentials*, ed. Ludwig Bieler (Dublin: Dublin Institute for Advanced Studies, 1963), pp. 258–77 at §5 p. 278; E. J. Gwynn, 'An Irish Penitential', *Ériu* 7 (1913): 121–95. The connection between homicide and magic may have New Testament origins. In the Vulgate Bible, Revelations 21:8 declares that those guilty of *homicidium* [homicide] and *veneficium* [poison, magic] among other sins will burn in fire and brimstone. For a discussion of these distinctions in medieval Venice, in this volume, see: Matthew Lubin, 'Poisoning as a Means of State Assassination in Early Modern Venice'.

murder:⁶⁰ 'Nech tober ẹpthai nó dogni arracht nó tober tonnuath conidapail nech de .uii. anni pendite amail cach dunorcuin. Manib marb nech de tri bliadna pendite' [Anyone who gives *aipthi*⁶¹ or makes an apparition/a spectre⁶² or gives a poisonous drink so that someone dies of it, seven years' penance, as for a homicide. If no one dies of it, three years' penance].⁶³ According to the *Old Irish Penitential*, and unlike *Cáin Adamnáin*, death ensuing from supernatural practices requires no more atonement than that allotted for standard murder by a layperson, which is seven years.⁶⁴

While the *Old Irish Penitential* does not state the particulars of the penance for homicide, the canon claims that the payment of legal fines reduces the proportion of the penance. Contrition is qualified based on the results of the transgression: magic resulting in death requires the penance of homicide, as opposed to causing a non-lethal consequence, which requires slightly less than half the years of atonement (three years). There is a distinction in the mechanisms used for supernatural means in the Old Irish canon. In addition to the use of charms [*epaid*], necromancy or the creation of (and presumably interaction with) an apparition [*arracht*],⁶⁵ poison [*tonnad*] is also threatening.⁶⁶ *Cáin Adamnáin* separates the use of charms from poison [*neim*], which is linked particularly with female offenders in §45; however, it contains no reference to necromancy.⁶⁷ The *Old Irish Penitential*, on the other hand, clearly maintains the connection to early medieval theological arguments concerning demonic magic with the specific mention of communing with spirits. Furthermore, similar to

---

⁶⁰ Gwynn, 'An Irish Penitential', pp. 130–31; Binchy, 'The Old Irish Penitential', p. 272.

⁶¹ Gwynn translates 'drugs'; however, I choose to follow Borsje's rendering to leave *aipthi* untranslated in this context; Borsje, 'Rules and Legislation', p. 176.

⁶² Gwynn translates 'a bogey'. I adhere to Borsje's interpretation of 'an apparition/a spectre' in 'Rules and Legislation', p. 176.

⁶³ Gwynn, 'An Irish Penitential', §7.168–69.

⁶⁴ Canons 1–11 in Section V, which deals with matters of *ira* [anger], contain the penitential requirements for a variety of homicides, including kinslaying, killing another in revenge, in a brawl and with magic. Some of these sins require more penance, such as kinslaying; however, homicides that do not fit into a specific category that are committed by laymen require seven years of penance; Bieler, *The Irish Penitentials*, pp. 271–72.

⁶⁵ *eDIL* s.v.1 *arracht*: 'idol, idolatrous image, apparition, spectre, monster': http://edil.qub.ac.uk/search?q=arracht&search_in=headword (accessed 28 November 2016).

⁶⁶ *eDIL* s.v. *tonnad*: 'death, draught of death, a kenning for blood, poison': http://edil.qub.ac.uk/search?q=tonnad&search_in=headword (accessed 28 November 2016).

⁶⁷ CA §45.30–31; *eDIL* s.v. *neim*: http://edil.qub.ac.uk/search?q=neim&search_in=headword (accessed 28 November 2016). Poison is frequently associated with female murderers in medieval legal sources. In this volume, see: Carmel Ferragud, 'A Multiple Poisoning in the City of Valencia: Sanxo Calbó's Crime (1442)'; Lubin, 'Poisoning as a Means of State Assassination'; Thomas Gobbitt, 'Poisoning, Killing and Murder in the *Edictus Rothari*'; and Dianne Berg, 'Monstrous Un-Making: Maternal Infanticide and Female Agency in Early Modern England'.

Bretha Étgid's claim that secret murder receives a double penalty on account of *ferg* [anger], the compiler of the *Old Irish Penitential* considers the use of magic in the harming of another to be motivated by malice. The penitential lists this canon (§7) under the vice of *ira* [anger] together with other regulations against homicide and against wounding and verbally abusing another. Although the *Old Irish Penitential* does not add to the punishment for murder by magic on account of anger, the compiler associates supernatural practices with harm.

All three Old Irish religious regulations demonstrate a clear repulsion at magical practices and contextually link these acts to homicide. However, the atonement for a murder resulting from magic varies between them. The *Old Irish Table of Commutations* does not identify the specific crime of killing another by magical practices, yet it claims that commutation – compensation – cannot reduce the penance for either the sin of practising magic [*druídecht*] or secret murder [*duinetháide*]. While the *Old Irish Penitential* claims that the payment of fines can reduce the accused's penance, atonement for killing another by magic is the same seven years that is delineated for homicide. To practise magic requires penance, but to kill another by supernatural means is no more serious than a standard homicide. *Cáin Adamnáin* requires legal compensation for murder plus a punitive tax paid to the Ionan *familia*. Finally, it is the only text among the Old Irish religious regulations to equate supernaturally-induced death directly to secret murder. Sharing the concern over the practice of magic, and even the lethal effects of such activities, with the other Old Irish ecclesiastical regulations, *Cáin Adamnáin* requires the most severe punishment for those accused of killing another by supernatural methods. The severity of this penalty in *Cáin Adomnáin* comes not from the penitential measures required by other ecclesiastical regulations to purge the sin of murder but from punitive compensation aligned to traditional Irish law. Although limited textual evidence prevents a clear view of the actual enforcement of *Cáin Adomnáin*, the strong regnal support for the law indicated by the ninety-one signatories in §28 stresses the far-reaching intention for its administration.

Old Irish ecclesiastical regulations clearly resonate with the concerns of the early medieval Church about practices perceived as magic. Irish sources composed in Latin demonstrate that anxiety over supernatural practices leading to death, either intentionally or inadvertently, predates the Old Irish penitential material and *Cáin Adamnáin*. Unlike the Old Irish religious regulations, Latin penitentials composed by Irish ecclesiastics display a more specific concern for homicides produced by magic in a clerical context, particularly sexual scandal. There is a clear concern for killing another by means of magic. Some of the Latin penitentials also link magic and homicide in relation to abortion. The penance for causing abortion by such means is considerably low when compared with the penance for murder by magic. Thus, while considered a form of homicide, abortion does not fully equate to the killing of a living member of society in these texts.

The Latin *Penitentialis Vinniani* [*Penitential of Finnian*] and *Paenitentiale S. Columbani* [*Penitential of Saint Columbanus*], both written in the sixth or seventh century, share an arrangement of three transgressions connected to the concern for supernaturally-induced homicide: *maleficium* [evil deed] – that is, love magic – abortion.[68] Canon 18 of the *Penitential of Finnian* requires atonement from a cleric or woman who has harmed or deceived another by *maleficium* [evil deed]:

> Si quis clericus uel si qua mulier malifica uel malificus si aliquem maleficio suo deciperat, inmane peccatum est sed per penitentiam redimi potest; sex annis peniteat, tribus cum pane et aqua per mensura et in residuis .iii. annis abstineat a uino et a carnibus.

> [If any cleric or woman who practices magic have led astray anyone by their magic, it is a monstrous sin, but it can be expiated by penance. (Such an offender) shall do penance for six years, three years on an allowance of bread and water, and during the remaining three years shall abstain from wine and meat].[69]

The next transgression, canon 19, pertains to love magic: 'Si autem non deciperat aliquem sed pro inlecebroso amore dederat alicui, annum integrum peniteat cum pane et aqua per mensura' [If, however, such a person has not led astray anyone but has given [something][70] for the sake of wanton love to someone, he shall do penance for an entire year on an allowance of bread and water].[71] Canon 20, connected to canon 19, relates to abortion: 'Si mulier maleficio suo partum alicuius perdiderit, dimedium annum cum pane et aqua peniteat per mensura et duobus annis abstineat a uino et a carnibus et sex quadragissimas <ieiunet> cum

---

[68] The oldest of the Irish penitentials, the *Penitential of Finnian*, is dated in relation to the *Paenitentiale S. Columbani* (*Penitential of Columbanus*), which draws heavily upon Finnian's text and was composed by Columbanus on the Continent sometime after 591 CE. See: Bieler, *The Irish Penitentials*, pp. 3–4.

[69] Bieler, *The Irish Penitentials*, §18.78–79. The translation is Bieler's, based upon Vienna, National Library, MS Lat. 2233 (Theol. Lat. 725). The opening sentence to the Vienna version of the text literally reads *clericus uel si quia mulier malificacus*. Jacqueline Borsje points out that *malificacus* is a non-existent word. It is a form of scribal shorthand intending *malefi -ca, -cus*. See: 'Rules and Legislation', p. 174, fn. 8. Variations of this text include: *clericus maleficus uel si qua mulier malefica* (St Gall, MS Stiftsbibliothek 150, saec. IX); *clericus maleficus uel si qua mulier malefica* (Paris, Bibliothèque nationale, MS lat. 12021 [Sangermanensis 121], saec. X); *clericus uel si qua mulier malefica* (Paris, Bibliothèque nationale. MS lat. 3182 [Codex Bigotianus], saec. X).

[70] Bieler translates 'a potion'; however, in this instance, I choose to follow Borsje's rendering of 'something', as the Latin text does not specify what is given. See: 'Rules and Legislation', p. 174.

[71] Bieler, *The Irish Penitentials*, §19.78–79.

pane et aqua' [If a woman by her magic destroys the child she has conceived of somebody, she shall do penance for half a year with an allowance of bread and water, and abstain for two years from wine and meat and fast for six forty-day periods with bread and water].[72]

Examined together, §§18–20 connect through the association of *maleficium*.[73] Much as the Irish term *epaid* incorporates any number of magical items or actions, late antique and early medieval authors often use *maleficium* to imply supernatural practices in a general sense.[74] Similarly, the specific form of *maleficium* in Finnian's penitential is unclear and should be read, like *epaid*, to relate to a number of possible supernaturally-related actions and substances, such as: spoken words of power and ritualistic behaviour; items that are worn on the body or placed in a certain area; and the ingestion of particular food or drink. Fear over the fatal consequences of *maleficium* predates the Irish penitentials and reflects the widespread concerns of the Early Christian Church over the use of practices considered to be supernatural. The Synod of Elvira condemned the lethal effect of *maleficium* in the early fourth century, while later penitentials distinguish between different types of *maleficium*, such as love magic and the creation of storms.[75] The penitentials of Finnian and Columbanus both clearly link *maleficium* to abortion; however, they differ slightly in relation to the potentially lethal consequences of magical practices. Nevertheless, neither of these penitentials penalises murder by magic as severely as *Cáin Adamnáin*.

Differences in language between the two authors demonstrate that while both associate abortion with supernatural practices, Finnian places a stronger emphasis on sexual scandal than Columbanus, who more explicitly refers to homicide resulting from *maleficium*. According to §18 in the *Penitential of Finnian*, the use of *maleficium* to cheat or beguile another is redeemable and requires the greatest penance of the three canons related to magic. The penitent must fast on bread and

---

[72] Ibid., §§20–21.78–81.

[73] Bieler suggests the aphrodisiac is a potion, which is certainly possible, yet Finnian provides no clear indication in his text. Similar to the vague definition of *maleficium*, the implied object or compound intended to induce love remains unclear: however, any number of substances – animal, plant or human – or combinations of these were considered aphrodisiacs. See: Eleanor Long, 'Aphrodisiacs, Charms, and Philtres', *Western Folklore* 32.3 (1973): 153–63.

[74] Flint, *The Rise of Magic*, pp. 13–21, 51–54; Hans P. Broedel, *The Malleus Maleficarum and the Construction of Witchcraft: Theology and Popular Belief* (Manchester: Manchester University Press, 2003), pp. 131–34; Zubin Mistry, 'Alienated from the Womb: Abortion in the Early Medieval West, c. 500–900', PhD dissertation (University College, London, 2011), p. 107, and see also, idem, *Abortion in the Early Middle Ages, c.500–900* (York: York Medieval Press, 2015).

[75] Yitzhak Hen, *Culture and Religion in Merovingian Gaul, A.D. 481–751* (Leiden: Brill, 1995), pp. 180–89.

water for three years, followed by another three years abstaining from meat and wine. The particular outcome of *maleficium* is ambiguous in this canon. This lack of clarity comes from Finnian's use of *decipere*: 'Si quis clericus uel si qua mulier malifica uel malificus si aliquem maleficio suo deciperat'. Ludwig Bieler translates *decipere* to mean 'lead astray', but additional translations include 'to catch, ensnare, entrap, beguile, elude, deceive, cheat'.[76] Thus, to lead astray by *maleficium* may mean the use of any supernatural art to deceive another, or *decipere* may refer to 'leading astray' from a moral viewpoint. Canons 18–20 are listed among those focused on clerical sins (§§10–29), most directly to moral transgressions related to sexual scandal (§§10–16, 19–21). As §§19–20 clearly involve love magic, it is possible to read *decipere* there to refer to a man or woman who leads another astray from clerical vows of chastity. However, reading canon 18 in a slightly wider context, this section of Finnian's Penitential also refers to homicide committed by clerics (§§12, 23, 24).[77] It is, therefore, also possible that *decipere* includes a lethal use of *maleficium*. While the penance of six years for leading another astray, or possibly for murder through *maleficium*, is relatively harsh, it is considerably less exacting than the atonement for clerical murder, which is to be an exile for ten years, with seven years of penance in another region.[78] That Finnian clearly refers to homicide committed by clerics and not laity in this section of his penitential, and because §18 specifically mentions evil-doing clerics and women and only requires six years of penance (as opposed to the ten required for clerical homicide), it is possible that Finnian chose *decipere* to refer to deceiving or harming someone, as opposed to murder in relation to magic. Rather, the three canons that follow §18 indicate that Finnian is concerned more with the sexual scandal associated with clerics and women who use *maleficium* for love magic and abortion. For Finnian, the exposure of a sexual digression, particularly the manifestation of a nun's fornication through the birth of a child, requires a greater penance than hiding the sin through abortion by supernatural means.

The connection between sexual scandal in §19, concerning love magic, and §20, dealing with abortion, is obvious, but the degree of atonement differs. The penance for love magic (§19), which is to fast on bread and water for a year, is considerably less than the punishment for harming or cheating another by *maleficium* (six years). Abortion through *maleficium* (§20) also receives a comparatively light penance of half a year of fasting on bread and water, followed by two years abstaining from meat and wine while fasting on bread and water for six forty-day

---

[76] s.v. 'decipio' in Charleton T. Lewis and Charles Short, *A Latin Dictionary Founded of Andrews' Edition of Freund's Latin Dictionary* (Oxford: Oxford University Press, 1956), p. 520.
[77] Bieler, *The Irish Penitentials*, §§10–24.76–83.
[78] Ibid., §23.80–81.

periods during the ecclesiastical year. Once again, the exact nature of the *maleficium* is ambiguous; however, the effect is clear: 'Si mulier maleficio suo partum alicuius perdiderit' [If a woman may have destroyed the child of someone by her *maleficium*]; *partum* is the subject of *perdere* [to destroy] and, thus, the foetus is destroyed.[79] While there is no direct precedent for this grouping of canons (*maleficium* – that is, love magic – abortion), the association between lethal, aphrodisiac and abortifacient magic exists in Roman law and literature, particularly the use of poisons or potions.[80] Concern over the use of potions and poisons in relation to abortion is found in the texts of the early medieval period, including *Sermo* 19 and *Sermo* 200 by Caesarius of Arles (c. 470–542 CE),[81] a canon from the mid sixth-century Council of Lérida[82] and the seventh-century *Lex Visigothorum* [*Law of the Visigoths*].[83] Similarly, a British canonical text, *Excerpta Quedam de Libro Dauidis* [*Excerpts from a Book of David*], dating from the early sixth century, requires three years of penance for anyone who *uenenis hominem occidere* [plans to kill a man with poisons].[84] While *maleficium* is a general term referring to magical practices, based on the history of concern over abortifacient poisons in Roman and early ecclesiastical texts, Finnian may have had some form of poison in mind when compiling §20 on abortion. Furthermore, similar to *Cáin Adamnáin*, which specifically punishes women for the use of poison (§45), Finnian's language in §20 clearly targets women in this matter.

According to the *Penitential of Finnian*, the practitioners of *maleficium* in §18 are evil-doing clerics and evil-doing women: 'clericus uel si qua mulier malifica uel malificus' [a cleric or woman who practices *maleficium* (evil deed)].[85] *Maleficium* in §19 is implied by the clause, 'Si autem non deciperat aliquem' [If, however, such a person (an evil-doing cleric or evil-doing woman) has not led

---

[79] St Gall, Stiftsbibliothek MS 150, saec. IX, uses *decipere* instead of *perdere*. See: Bieler, *The Irish Penitentials*, p. 79. My translation.

[80] For example, in the third century, the Roman jurist Paulus' *Sententia* on *Lex Cornelia de sicariis et veneficis* dealt with abortion in relation to poison. See: Paulus, *Sententiae*, V.23.14, an edition of which can be found in Enzo Nardi, *Procurato Aborto Nel Mondo Greco Romano* (Milan: A. Guiffrè, 1971), pp. 433–37. For discussion on Roman views of abortion, see: Mistry, 'Alienated from the Womb', pp. 33–41.

[81] Germain Morin, ed., *Sancti Caesarii Arelantensis Sermones*, Corpus Christianorum Series Latina 103–104 (Turnhout: Brepols, 1953), pp. 91, 810.

[82] Gonzalo Martínez Díez and Félix Rodríguez, eds., *La Colección Canónica Hispana 4: Concilios Galos, Concilios Hispanos: Primera Parte* (Madrid: Consejo Superior de Investigaciones Cientificas, 1984), p. 300.

[83] Karl Zeumer, ed., *Lex Visigothorum* VI.3.1, MGH *Leges Nationum Germanicarum I* (Hanover: Hannoverae Impensis Bibliopolii Hahniani, 1902), p. 260. VI.2.3 stipulates against the use of poison in general, p. 259.

[84] Bieler, *The Irish Penitentials*, §11.70–71; for dating information, see p. 3.

[85] Bieler refers to the general sense of *maleficium* signifying magic in *The Irish Penitentials*, §18.78–79.

astray anyone]. However, §20, relating to abortion, is gender specific: 'Si mulier maleficio suo partum alicuius perdiderit', which Bieler interprets as, 'If a woman by her magic destroys the child she has conceived of somebody', choosing *alicuius*, the genitive singular of *aliquis* [someone], to refer to the father.[86] *Aliquis*, however, could refer to a woman or a man, which would offer a translation such as, 'If a woman may have destroyed the child of someone by her *maleficium*', suggesting that it may not be her own pregnancy, but that of another. However, reading §20 as a sequence with §21 supports Bieler's interpretation. Canon 21 reads: 'Si autem genuerit, ut diximus, filium et manifestum peccatum eius fuerit, ui. annis, sicut iudicatum est de clerico, et in septimo iungatur altario, et tunc dicimus posse renouare coronam et induere uestimentum album debere et uirginem nuncupare' [But if, as we have said, she bears a child and her sin is manifest, <she shall do penance> for six years <with bread and water>, as in the judgment in the case of a cleric, and in the seventh year she shall be joined to the altar, and then we say her crown can be restored and she may don a white robe and be pronounced a virgin].[87] While the abortion canon (§20) does not specify exactly what form *maleficium* takes, canon 21 gives further indication as to who is performing and receiving the abortion, as well as an explanation for the relatively easy penance for it. Read in sequence, canon 21 suggests that the woman referred to in canon 20 may be a fornicating nun who aborts her offspring. It is possible that Finnian is referring to a lay woman; however, the immediate connection with clerical fornication in the preceding digression of canons (particularly §§10–17, 19–20), lends considerable weight to the likelihood that Finnian is here particularly concerned about the moral digressions of a nun.

Finnian proclaims that laity require less penance.[88] This woman's penance equals that of a cleric who has fallen into *maxima ruina* by fornicating and then killing the child of that union after birth (§12). The penance for such a cleric is to fast on bread and water for three years, '[i]n fletu et <lacrimis atque> orationibus die ac nocte postulet de Domini misericordia' [in weeping and tears, and prayers by day and night, and shall implore the mercy of the Lord].[89] He must abstain from meat and wine for a further three years, be deprived of his clerical office and remain an exile for the period of seven years, after which time, the cleric can be restored to his office by the judgment of a bishop or priest.[90] Understood in this context of sexual scandal, it is a greater offence to allow the sin of clerical fornication to be manifest in society through the birth of a child (whether

---

[86] s.v. *aliquis*, Lewis and Short, *A Latin Dictionary*, p. 89.
[87] Bieler, *The Irish Penitentials*, §21.80–81.
[88] Ibid., §6.76–77.
[89] Ibid., §12.76–79.
[90] Ibid.

subsequently killed or not) than to seek love or perform an abortion through acts deemed supernatural.[91] Finnian appears to be more concerned with the sexual status of holy men and women than their use of magic to harm another, to obtain love or to end a pregnancy. Columbanus, on the other hand, is more explicit in linking murder to magic.

The *Penitential of Saint Columbanus*, which is dependent on Finnian's text, also includes the *maleficium* – love magic – abortion arrangement of transgressions, yet there is variation between the two penitentials. Columbanus inserts Finnian's use of *decipere* in §18 concerning *maleficium* with *perdere* and thereby intensifies the first transgression of *maleficium* with clearer language: 'Si quis maleficio suo aliquem perdiderit' [If anyone has destroyed someone by his magic art].[92] While the exact type of *maleficium* remains unclear in this canon, the effect is clear: *maleficium* is lethal. The wording between the two penitentials differs. The penance is the same: six years. Based on word choice, Columbanus more clearly condemns the lethal potential of magical practices. Furthermore, in contrast to Finnian, he delineates the difference between the length of penance for homicide by a cleric and a layman. A cleric who kills another must do penance for ten years.[93] The penance of a lay murderer is the same as one who destroys another by magic: six years.[94] While Columbanus shares an anxiety over supernaturally-induced homicide with *Cáin Adamnáin*, his penalty remains less harsh and is equal to that of a standard homicide.

The *Penitential of Saint Columbanus* also shows a concern over the lethal outcome of *maleficium* in relation to love magic and abortion; however, unlike Finnian, Columbanus does not limit this practice to women: 'Si autem pro amore quis maleficus sit et neminem perdiderit, annum integrum cum pane et aqua clericus ille paeniteat, laicus dimidium, diaconus duos, sacerdos tres; maxime, si per hoc mulieris partum quis[que] deceperit, ideo vi quadragesimas unus quisque insuper augeat, ne homicidii reus sit' [But if anyone has used magic to excite love, and has destroyed no one, let him do penance on bread and water for a whole year, if a cleric, for half a year, if a layman, if a deacon for two, if a priest for three; especially if anyone has thus produced abortion, on that account let each add on six extra forty-day periods, lest he be guilty of murder].[95] While Finnian refers to women who use *maleficium* to perform abortion on themselves, Columbanus uses *quisque* [whoever], which in this context refers

---

[91] Mistry, 'Alienated from the Womb', pp. 106–09.
[92] Bieler, *The Irish Penitentials*, §6.100–101.
[93] Ibid., §1.98–99.
[94] Ibid., §13.102–103.
[95] Ibid., §6.100–101.

to the clerics, laymen, deacons and priests mentioned in relation to love magic.[96] Columbanus considers the love magic condemned earlier in the passage to be responsible for ending the pregnancy: 'si per hoc mulieris partum quis[que] deceperit' [especially if anyone thus (on account of love magic) produced abortion].[97] Furthermore, Columbanus uses *decipere* in relation to abortion [*partum ... deceperit*] and adds the clause 'ne homicidii reus sit' [lest he be guilty of homicide].[98] The additional clause and the implication that abortion occurred as a *result* of love magic indicate that Columbanus left room for ambiguity in the intention of this sin. The original intent of the offender may not have been abortion; rather, the pregnancy might have terminated as a result of the supernatural practices involved in the appropriation of love.[99] If understood in this milieu, the final clause, 'lest he be guilty of murder', signals the potentially lethal side effects of magic.

Penalties against abortion exist in the secular legal material as well wherein it is penalised as an act of homicide. According to *Bretha Étgid*, a woman who starves herself to kill her unborn child is expected to pay the entire fine for homicide, which includes *éraic*, the standard body fine of seven *cumala* for a freeman, and full honour-price. The woman pays the fine for homicide to the family of the father, a *cumal* to her own family, and if she is married, she is also expected to pay *coibche*, her bride-price and full honour-price to her husband.[100] A man may also be held accountable for instigating an abortion by withholding food from a pregnant woman, and, therefore, her unborn child. In such cases, the man is also expected to pay *éraic* and full honour-price to the father's family, a *cumal* to the mother's family and *coibche* and honour-price to the woman.[101] According to a heptad that is quoted in a gloss on *Gúbretha Caratniad* [*The False Judgments of Caratnia*], abortion is also considered grounds for a husband to divorce his wife.[102] These examples do not mention the use of supernatural practices. They do indicate the serious crime against both life, in terms of the intention to kill an unborn child, and kin, in relation to divorce and the loss of a potential family member. Both of these violations can be extended to a crime

---

[96] Borsje, 'Rules and Legislation', pp. 175–76. *The Old Irish Penitential* also lists abortion as a transgression; however, there is no reference to supernatural means as the manner in which is it performed. See: Gwynn, 'An Irish Penitential', pp. 166–67.
[97] Bieler, *The Irish Penitentials*, §6.100–101. The text in parentheses is my own.
[98] Ibid., §6.100–101. *Mulieris partum quis[que] deceperit* can alternatively be read, 'anyone has harmed the child of a woman'; see: Mistry, 'Alienated from the Womb', p. 112; see also: Borsje, 'Rules and Legislation', p. 178.
[99] Mistry, 'Alienated from the Womb', p. 113.
[100] CIH, p. 270.30–32 = AL III, pp. 204–05.
[101] CIH, p. 270.37–40 = AL III, pp. 206–07.
[102] CIH, p. 2198.24–26; Kelly, *A Guide to Early Irish Law*, p. 75.

against the community and interpreted as holding both Christian and secular values of the period.[103] As *Bretha Étgid* treats abortion as homicide through starvation, one would expect that the destruction of a foetus through supernatural practices would likewise require the penalty for homicide. Old Irish legal texts, however, do not connect the use of magic to abortion directly; rather, they display a concern for inhibiting intercourse and, therefore, the birth of a child, by supernatural means. Similar to the penalties for using an *epaid* in early Irish law, these transgressions relate to love magic and the potential to cause harm; in this case, harm to one's honour, to the marital relationship, and, in a wider context, the community through the prevention of creating a future generation.

Two regulations listed in *Di Cethairshlicht Athgabálae* suggest negative love magic that prohibits procreation. According to the text, *fuba n-imda* [the (supernatural) attack of the bed] may lead to *collud mbrethi* [the destruction of a birth]. The gloss of *fuba n-imda* indicates an attempt to estrange marital partners from each other through supernatural means:

FUBA NIMDA (a), FUBA NIMDA (b), FUBAE NDIMDA (c)
[1] .i. pisoca isin lep*aid* (b) .i. pisog*a* isin lepuidh (c)
[2] .i. a ndlegar en*eclann* (b) .i. i ndlegur ein*eclann* (c)
[3] .i. a ben do breith uad (b) .i. a ben do br*eith* uad*a* (c)
[4] [*followed by* .i. froma uptha dus *crossed out* (b).i. in folusc (?) lige (?) (c)
[5] .i. conabi tualaing nacha setchi (a) .i. co*n*abi tualaing lanamnus (b) .i. cunabitualuing lanamnus (c)
[6] .i. cnamcosait (b) .i. cnam cosuit (c).

[THE [SUPERNATURAL] ATTACK OF A BED
[1] i.e. sorcery in the bed
[2] i.e. for which honour-price is due
[3] i.e. to take away a person's wife from him
[4] i.e. the testing of a charm/spell to find out] (b); i.e. the *folusc*-lying ? (c)
[5] i.e. so that he is not able [to have sex with] any partner (a) i.e. so that he is not able to have sexual intercourse (b, c)
[6] i.e. the *cosait*-bone].[104]

The implied intention in this item is to use supernatural practices to create marital strife, particularly by inducing impotence in the husband [gloss 5: 'so that he

---

[103] The protection of unborn family members serves the long-term benefit of the kin group as well as the moral obligation set forth in the commandment, *non occides* [Thou shalt not kill], found in Exodus 20:13. See: Wallace Johnson, '*Bretha Étgid, Duinetháide* and the Bible: Religion, Morality and Secret Murder in Eighth-Century Ireland', MPhil thesis (University of Wales, Lampeter, 2003), pp. 7–8.
[104] a = *CIH*, p. 891.2 (original text and gloss); b = *CIH*, p. 387.31–32 (original text), *CIH*, p. 388.10 (gloss); c=*CIH*, p. 1692.31 (original text and gloss). The edition and translation belong to Borsje, 'Rules and Legislation', p. 180.

is not able (to have sex with) any partner'], or stealing the wife of another man [gloss 3: 'to take away a person's wife from him'].[105] Thus, men appear to be the intended recipients of *fuba n-imda*. According to the second gloss, the victim receives a slight to his honour and, therefore, should collect full honour-price.[106] The oldest of the glosses (gloss 5) remains neutral as to who performs *fuba n-imda*, relating only its purpose: impotence.[107] Later glosses (particularly gloss 3) suggest the transgressor is a third party. Other possible interpretations suggest the wife's responsibility.[108] The sixth and final gloss offers *cnam cosait* as an example of *fuba n-imda*.[109] *Cnáim* means bone[110] and *cosaít* is the verbal noun of *con-saídi*, which means 'complaint, dispute, or strife',[111] all of which indicates the use of a bone in such a way as to create conflict or conspiracy. It is possible that *cnam cosait* refers to some kind of 'bone of contention',[112] a verbal dispute as opposed to a physical object; however, other references to the use of bones and body parts for magical purposes in both Irish and Continental sources suggest that the 'cosaít bone' is actually an object that supposedly imbued supernatural properties or was used to create some sort of charm.[113]

---

[105] Borsje, 'Rules and Legislation', p. 181.
[106] Ibid., p. 180.
[107] '.i. conabi tualaing nacha setchi', *CIH*, p. 891.2; Old Irish text and gloss is found in Trinity College MS 1337 (H.3.18).
[108] A law tract on marriage and divorce cites *O'Davoren's Glossary* entry on *fuba*, which suggests the wife's responsibility: 'Fuba .i. fubthad nó fodiubadh. Feis .i. druis, ut est fuba co fessaib .i. a fubthad co fesaib .i. a leamad nó pisoga do [dénum dó]', '*Fuba* .i.e. terrifying or undermining. *Feis*, i.e. lust, ut est '*fuba co fessaib*', i.e. terrifying him with charms, i.e. rendering him impotent, or to practise enchantments upon him'. See: W. Stokes, ed. and trans., 'O'Davoren's Glossary', *Archiv für celtische Lexikographie* 2 (1904): §930.355; *CIH*, p. 1502.12–13; Breatnach, *A Companion*, p. 136, fn 142, 306; Borsje, 'Rules and Legislation', p. 180.
[109] *Cnam cosait* is present in both Harley MS 432 at *CIH*, p. 388.10 (*cnamcosait*) and Trinity College MS 1336 (H. 3. 17) at *CIH*, p. 1692.31 (*cnam cosuit*), but is absent from the Old Irish material in Trinity College MS 1337 (H. 3. 18).
[110] *eDIL* s.v. *cnáim*: http://edil.qub.ac.uk/search?q=cnaim&search_in=headword (accessed 28 November 2016).
[111] *eDIL* s.v. *cosaít*: http://edil.qub.ac.uk/search?q=cosait&search_in=headword (accessed 28 November 2016).
[112] Borsje, 'Rules and Legislation', p. 181.
[113] An example of such use may be found in another regulation listed in *Di Cethairshlicht Athgabálae*. The commentary for *Im comorguin cnama*, 'for the breaking of a bone', offers insight into the appropriation of human bones for supernatural purposes. The glossator explains that the bones are retrieved from a churchyard without permission for the following purpose: 'ac tabairt a smera eisib do upaib, .i. am*ail* ata c*om*cen*n* for ochtorach' (*CIH*, p. 395.14–15 =*AL* I p. 202.30–31), which Hancock et al. translate in *AL* I as 'i.e. to take their marrow out of them for sorcerers, such as the "comchenn for ochtarach"' (*AL* I p. 203). *Cáin Adamnáin* §45 states that a woman caught digging under a church should be set adrift in a boat; the same punishment is required for a woman who commits

Fuba n-imda is considered to be responsible for the supernatural practice directly following *collud mbrethi* [the destruction of a birth].

— (a) COLLUD MBRETHI (b) COLLUG MBRE*ITH*E (c)
¹ .i. iss *ed* asas de-side (b) .i. is edh fhasus de-side (c)
² .i. gab*ail* cu*m*aing l clainde (b) .i. gab*ul* cumung no clain*n*e (c)
³ .i. na .s.47 uriata coi*m*perta (b) .i. na .s. uairiata coimpert*a* (c)
⁴ .i. a lemadh (b) .i. a lemad (c)
⁵ .i. ne*m*dul cuice 'na imda (b) .i. nemdol chuice 'na imda (c).

[THE DESTRUCTION OF A BIRTH
¹ i.e. this results from the just-mentioned thing;
² i.e. the taking of power or of [the ability to have] offspring (?);
³ i.e. the fines for the barring of procreation;
⁴ i.e. to render him impotent.
⁵ i.e. not going to her in her bed].¹¹⁴

The name *collud mbrethi* [the destruction of a birth] brings to mind the association between supernatural arts and abortion so present in the Latin penitentials, but the glosses to this excerpt relate *collud mbrethi* to the previous item concerning impotence, claiming that 'this results from the just-mentioned thing'.¹¹⁵ Thus, the glossators discuss the destruction of a birth in a sexual and marital context rather than as aborting a foetus; *collud mbrethi* results from the inability to procreate due to impotence or lack of intercourse, presumably by supernatural means [gloss 2: 'the taking of power or of (the ability to have) offspring'; gloss 4: 'to render him impotent'; gloss 5: 'not going to her in her bed'].¹¹⁶ Intention plays a vital role in the requirement of fines, as does the outcome of the transgression. There is an implied action in these penalties: one is using a charm, spell or potion on another person, which requires a penalty related to the victim's honour-price. While not directly responsible for death, the supernatural practices related to these two examples of love magic inhibit procreation and, therefore, reveal concerns over the use of magic and the hindrance to new life.¹¹⁷ The lower penalties for these crimes reflect the loss of a potential life, as opposed

---

murder (including by poison) or arson, *CA* §45.30–31. It is possible that there is a connection between this transgression and *Im comorguin cnama*; however, this cannot be said with certainty.

¹¹⁴ b = *CIH*, p. 387.32 (original text), *CIH*, p. 388.10–12 (gloss); c=*CIH*, p. 1692.33–34 (original text and gloss); Borsje, 'Rules and Legislation', p. 183.
¹¹⁵ Borsje, 'Rules and Legislation', p. 183.
¹¹⁶ Ibid.
¹¹⁷ For a full discussion on the impact of impotence on early Irish society, see: Brónagh Ní Chonaill, 'Impotence, Disclosure and Outcome: Some Medieval Irish Legal Comment', online at: http://www.arts.gla.ac.uk/scottishstudies/earticles/LegalConcern.pdf (accessed 26 June 2016).

to the greater fine for the death of a living person or developing foetus, such as the fine for murder required for killing an unborn child through starvation in *Bretha Étgid*. The stipulations against *fuba n-imda* and *collud mbrethi* reflect a belief in the potential harm that can result from supernatural practices. They do not explicitly refer to murder or abortion by magic. Thus, similar to the crime of murder by magic, early Irish ecclesiastical regulations contain the only extant evidence for sanctions against supernaturally-induced abortion.

Cáin Adamnáin is the only extant legal source from medieval Ireland to require punitive restitution for murder by magic. It combines both common thoughts on supernatural practices throughout Christendom in this period and the practice of fiscal compensation for crimes required by traditional Irish law. The late antique and early medieval Church sought to eradicate its members' participation in non-Christian practices and beliefs, many of which were perceived as being inspired by demons. Early Irish penitentials directly align with the wider concerns of the Church at this time. Christian theologians in the seventh century, both abroad and in Ireland, speak out against non-Christian belief systems and practices in terms of magic.[118] Early Irish ecclesiastic regulations written in both Irish and Latin penalise the lethal consequences of supernatural practices. The penance for killing a non-clerical person by means of magic in the penitentials equals that of a standard homicide. The Irish penitentials also link illicit supernatural practices to abortion; however, the penance for this sin is less than that of a homicide and, indeed, less than the penance required for the birth of an illegitimate child to a woman connected to a monastic house. This suggests that, at least in the eyes of the penitential compilers, the use of supernatural aids to abort a foetus is less offensive in the eyes of God than the manifestation of illicit fornication.

The sanctions against murder by magic in the penitentials often contrast the penalties against the use of supernatural practices for homicide and abortion in early Irish secular law. While *Bretha Étgid* equates the fiscal retribution for aborting a foetus through starvation to murder, there is no mention of abortion

---

[118] For example, in Ireland, Muirchú pitted Saint Patrick against pagan druids in supernatural contests that mirrored biblical accounts of the prophets and apostles. See: Muirchú, *Vita Sancti Patricii* I.10 (9) 2–3, the edition and translation of which can be found in Ludwig Bieler, ed. and trans., *The Patrician Texts in the Book of Armagh* (Dublin: Dublin Institute for Advanced Studies, 1979), pp. 74–75. A seventh-century Irish theologian, Augustinus Hibernicus, criticised the druidic doctrine of transmigration in his *De mirabilibus sacrae scripturae* [On the Miracles of Scripture] (*PL*, 35.2149–2202) i.17 (*PL*, 35.2164). Composed in 655 CE, *De mirabilibus sacrae scripturae* is separated into three books concerning: the Pentateuch, the Old Testament and the New Testament. John Carey has translated portions of Book I and all of Book III in *King of Mysteries: Early Irish Religious Writings* (Dublin: Four Courts Press, 1998), pp. 51–74. For the section on druidic doctrine, see p. 58.

caused by methods perceived as magical in the secular legal corpus. These laws punish the use of magic only when it results in injury, the death of a dog or the inhibition of procreation. Indeed, early Irish legal texts contain no reference to supernaturally-induced homicide, nor do the fines for magical practices equate either those of homicide or secret murder, which requires double the fine of murder due to its secretive nature and premeditated intent. This evidence suggests at least two possibilities: that secular law penalised cases of murder by magic in the same fashion as homicide, as opposed to secret murder, or that there was, previously in existence, a legal text on illicit killing that incorporated this particular crime.

The extant material clearly demonstrates that the double fine for killing another through supernatural means found in *Cáin Adamnáin* is unique in early Irish secular law. In addition, the punishment for murder by magic that is outlined in *Cáin Adamnáin* can be compared to later Carolingian and Anglo-Saxon legal texts that also emphasise regnal support for the eradication of supernatural practices condemned by the Church. The laws of Charlemagne and Æthelstan demonstrate the interest of these kings in consolidating royal power – in part witnessed through the use of capital punishment for certain crimes, including the use of magic – while strengthening their alliances with the Church. The author(s) of *Cáin Adamnáin* sought regnal support for the humanitarian interest of protecting vulnerable members of society, particularly women, clerics and youths, from physical violence. *Cáin Adamnáin* extends this protection to all members of society, who are perceived as susceptible to the occult and nefarious dangers of supernatural attack, by equating murder by magic to secret murder. Although the extent to which the laws set forth in *Cáin Adamnáin* were enacted remains elusive due to a lack of case records, *Cáin Adamnáin* remains a significant document in the study of both homicide and magic in medieval Ireland as it demonstrates contemporary Christian beliefs about supernatural practices and demands the punishment for *duinetháide*, regarded as one of the most heinous crimes against society, in cases of murder by magic, a crime that has no precedent in early Irish traditional law.

CHAPTER 2

Discursive Murders: The St Brice's Day Massacre, *Beowulf* and *Morðor**

Jay Paul Gates

THE ANGLO-SAXON CHRONICLE records that, in 1002, King Æthelred II called for the wholesale slaughter of the Danes living in England, resulting in the so-called St Brice's Day massacre:

> Hēr on þissum geare sē cyng gerædde and his witan þet man sceolde gafol gyldon þām flotan, and frið wið hī geniman wið þon þe hī heora yfeles geswican sceoldan. Ðā sende sē cyng to þam flotan Leofsig ealdorman, and he þā þæs cynges worde and his witena grið wið hī gesætte and þet hī to metsunge fengon and to gafle; and hī þā þet underfengon, and him man þā geald .xxiiii. þusend punda [...] and on ðām geare sē cyng hēt ofslean ealle ða deniscan men þe on Angelcynne wæron on Bricius messedæg, forþon þām cynge wæs gecydd þet hī woldon hine besyrewian æt his life and syððan ealle his witan and habban syþðan his rīce.[1]

> [Here in this year the king and his councillors decided that they should pay tax to the fleet and make peace with them, on condition they should leave off from their evil deeds. Then the king sent Ealdorman Leofsige to the fleet and then he, at the command of the king and his councillors, arranged a truce with them, and that they should receive provisions and tax. And they undertook that, and they were paid 24 thousand pounds [...] and in that year the king ordered all the Danish men who were among the English race to be killed on Brice's Day, because it was made known to the king that they wanted to ensnare his life – and afterwards all his councillors – and have his kingdom afterwards].

---

* I owe thanks to Brian O'Camb, Kathleen Smith, Charlotte Thurston and Larissa Tracy for reading and commenting on drafts of this chapter. All errors remain my own.

[1] The massacre is recorded in the CDE texts of the Chronicle. All references to the Anglo-Saxon Chronicle are taken from *The Anglo-Saxon Chronicle: A Collaborative Edition, Vol. 7: MS E*, ed. Susan Irvine (Cambridge: D. S. Brewer, 2004), and all translations of the Anglo-Saxon Chronicle are taken from *The Anglo-Saxon Chronicle*, ed. and trans. Michael Swanton (New York: Routledge, 1998).

In the midst of an account of peace-making, it would seem, is presented a pair of murder plots: one the assassination of a king, the other the extermination of a people.

The Chronicle account of what appears to be an ethnic pogrom has proved unsettling for modern scholars and how such a policy was even conceived confounding. Yet, as Simon Keynes has observed, the narrative elaboration of the massacre by later medieval historians, emphasising ethnically-grounded violence and the brutal murder of women and children, as well as the modern application of the term 'massacre' to describe the events, have likely distorted readings of the historical events the Chronicle records.[2] Nonetheless, it is clear that Æthelred and his *witan* viewed the murder plot against them as a threat to the English community itself. However, some of the discourses in non-chronicle texts that are roughly contemporary with the events of St Brice's Day uncover implicit discourses in the Chronicle account that offer insight into how Æthelred and his *witan* conceived of the response to an assassination plot with what appears to be a coordinated murder of an ethnic population. Understanding the presence of those discourses in the Chronicle's account of the massacre also makes sense of why later accounts of the massacre shift to emphasising it as a genocide. Standing out to nearly all readers of the Chronicle account (medieval and modern) is the violence against a defined ethnic group living amongst another. Jonathan Wilcox suggests that the massacre may have initially been conceived as equivalent to a royal ravaging, aimed not at a region but at an ethnic population.[3] However, it is not at all clear how the Anglo-Saxons perceived 'ethnicity' or how that population was identified.[4] Wilcox does show that the Christian English, particularly the politically influential Archbishop Wulfstan, struggled mightily with how to deal morally with the Vikings, developing a logic rooted in scripture that allowed them to justify the massacre by focusing on a distinction between those inside and outside of the community. Yet a number of scholars have suggested that the early medieval *gens* [people] was limited to rulers and the warrior elite that

---

[2] Simon Keynes, 'The Massacre of St Brice's Day (13 November 1002)', in *Beretning fra seksogtyvende tværfaglige vikingesymposium*, ed. Niels Lund (Højbjerg: Hikuin, 2007), pp. 32–67.

[3] Ravaging was short-term political warfare for the purposes of asserting authority over and, often, punishing a rebellious region. On political violence, see: Ryan Lavelle, 'Towards a Political Contextualization of Peacemaking and Peace Agreements in Anglo-Saxon England', in *Peace and Negotiation: Strategies for Coexistence in the Middle Ages and the Renaissance*, ed. Diane Wolfthal (Turnhout: Brepols, 2000), pp. 39–55.

[4] On the difficulty of distinguishing even the Anglo-Saxons on their own terms, see, for example: Susan Reynolds, 'What Do We Mean by "Anglo-Saxon" and "Anglo-Saxons"?', *Journal of British Studies* 24 (1985): 395–414.

pledged allegiance to them, and 'ethnic' identification was primarily political.[5] Thus, only those who were political actors and those who participated in the economy of violence would have been considered full members of the 'ethnic' community.[6] However, the unprecedented English order to kill 'all the Danish men who were among the English race' demands a logic beyond inclusion and exclusion.[7] Even if political actors like those who plotted the murder of Æthelred and his counsellors defined the community, their actions had consequences for the larger community that was identified with them. Much of the confusion – and horror – regarding the intended targets of the massacre stem from examples of Norman and post-Conquest chroniclers picking up, elaborating on and, apparently, confusing the events. William of Jumièges, John of Worcester and William of Malmesbury all record the murder of women and children, the two Williams giving vivid descriptions of cruel murders. The two Williams and Henry of Huntingdon all claim that the massacre was the impetus for the Danish conquest of England by Swein 'Forkbeard' that took place in 1013. Keynes suggests that these later narratives are responsible for shifting the tone from one of political reprisal to one of genocide, not least because they were constructing a literary narrative.[8] Keynes's concerns are, of course, with uncovering history,[9] yet the distinction between historical and literary narrative is tenuous.[10] Keynes himself has observed that the Anglo-Saxon Chronicle annals recorded in the

---

[5] Patrick Geary, 'Ethnic Identity as a Situational Construct in the Early Middle Ages', *Mitteilungen der Anthropologischen Gesellschaft in Wien* 113 (1983): 15–26; John Moreland, 'Ethnicity, Power and the English', in *Social Identity in Early Medieval Britain*, ed. William O. Frazer and William Tyrell (London: Leicester University Press, 2000), pp. 23–51.

[6] N. J. Higham, *An English Empire: Bede, the Britons, and the Early Anglo-Saxon Kings* (Manchester: Manchester University Press, 1995), pp. 218–19.

[7] The Old English *menn* may confuse matters here since it can mean both 'men' and 'people of either sex'.

[8] Simon Keynes, *The Diplomas of King Æthelred 'The Unready' 978–1016: A Study in Their Use as Historical Evidence* (Cambridge: Cambridge University Press, 1980), p. 204; idem, 'The Massacre of St Brice's Day'. In his excellent article, Keynes traces the development of the St Brice's Day massacre story through its extensive developments, carrying out a case study of how history becomes legend and how such a legend may be used.

[9] Keynes takes the development of the story as an 'object-lesson, or case-study' in how to examine historical sources 'and dispose of the legendary accretions, in the hope of reaching the historical core' ('The Massacre of St Brice's Day', p. 33). Keynes's work is primarily historical whereas the concern here is the value of the intersection of story and history.

[10] Harold Scheub, *Story* (Madison: University of Wisconsin Press, 1998), p. 3. On narrative in the Anglo-Saxon Chronicle, see in Alice Jorgensen, ed., *Reading the Anglo-Saxon Chronicle: Language, Literature, History* (Turnhout: Brepols, 2010): Alice Jorgensen, 'Rewriting the Æthelredian Chronicle: Narrative Style and Identity in Anglo-Saxon

CDE manuscripts *s.a.* 983–1016 were composed after the fact as a political analysis of the events that led to the Danish conquest.[11] Thus, the Chronicle account should be taken with a grain of salt and is perhaps best read for the story it wants to tell, albeit about historical events.[12]

The developments of the St Brice's Day massacre as a historically inflected story invite comparison with other narrative sources and contemporary discourses because story, whether in historical or poetic narrative, provides a space for a community to reflect on consequential issues and to identify the common values and goals that bind them together as a community.[13] It also records a discourse that justifies or critiques the actions narrated. Yet the discourses that were evident to contemporary audiences may only emerge for a modern reader when a text is read with contemporary intertexts. After all, when a narrative is copied down as a text, the manuscript artefact represents 'a unified object of apprehension for reception in its own time'[14] that circulates with others in a textual community and, as Carol Braun Pasternack argues, should be read 'as treating issues of concern contemporary to the era of their manuscript production'.[15] Producing a common, relatively fixed artefact means that the textual community is mediated by the common ideologies and modes of thought shared by the texts.[16] As such, Wilcox is right that the St Brice's Day massacre is a 'flashpoint for examining the values of English society at the turn of the first millennium', but perhaps more because of the concerns highlighted by accounts of the events through the discourses employed than because of a sudden genocidal turn.[17] As narrative

---

Chronicle MS F', pp. 113–38 and Jacqueline Stodnick, 'Sentence to Story: Reading the Anglo-Saxon Chronicle as Formulary', pp. 91–112.

[11] Keynes, 'A Tale of Two Kings', *Transactions of the Royal Historical Society*, Fifth Series 36 (1986): 195–217 at p. 201.

[12] Courtney Konshuh, '*Anraed* in Their *Unraed*: The Æthelredian Annals (983–1016) and Their Presentation of King and Advisors', *English Studies* 97 (2016): 140–62 has recently revised the political analysis that Keynes originally argued for but without contesting the partiality of the chronicler.

[13] Scheub, *Story*, pp. 3–17.

[14] A. N. Doane, '"Beowulf" and Scribal Performance', in *Unlocking the Wordhord: Anglo-Saxon Studies in Memory of Edward B. Irving, Jr.*, ed. Mark Amodio and Katherine O'Brien O'Keeffe (Toronto: University of Toronto Press, 2003), pp. 62–75 at p. 63.

[15] Carol Braun Pasternack, *The Textuality of Old English Poetry* (Cambridge: Cambridge University Press, 1995), p. 200; Nicholas Howe, 'The Uses of Uncertainty', in *The Dating of Beowulf*, ed. Colin Chase (Toronto: University of Toronto Press, 1997), pp. 213–20 at p. 215–16.

[16] Brian Stock, *The Implications of Literacy: Written Language and Models of Interpretation in the Eleventh and Twelfth Centuries* (Princeton: Princeton University Press, 1983), pp. 1–10.

[17] Jonathan Wilcox, 'The St. Brice's Day Massacre and Archbishop Wulfstan', in *Peace and Negotiation: Strategies for Coexistence in the Middle Ages and the Renaissance*, ed. Diane Wolfthal (Turnhout: Brepols, 2000), pp. 79–91 at p. 91.

can draw communities into discussion, the textual community represents, as Renée Trilling puts it, 'literature's mediation of history, both as a reflection of contemporary modes of thought and as a tool for shaping a reader's perception of the world'.[18] Thus, reading narratives from the Anglo-Saxon Chronicle together with contemporary 'non-Chronicle intertexts' that are representative of major cultural domains, including law, heroic verse and later historiography, offers not only a more complete understanding of the community's worldview but also insight into its political and cultural discourses.[19]

Two intertexts frame the various accounts of the St Brice's Day massacre: a murder law known as *morð* (or *morðor*), which provides a roughly contemporary model of holding not just a group but an ethnic group responsible for a legal or political violation; and *Beowulf*, a poem working in a heroic discourse whose narrative is hung on the history of Scandinavian intertribal violence and contains the extermination of at least three peoples, and whose sole witness is roughly contemporary with the massacre.[20] Working within different discourses, these intertexts share with the Chronicle and other early medieval accounts of St Brice's Day overlapping concerns with lordship, ethnic identity and inter-ethnic violence. What emerges is an increasing focus on legal understandings of lordship and collective ethnic responsibility around the millennium, and the decision to order the massacre, if not the event itself, may be understood as far less shocking than it was perceived to be in hindsight, very much in line with the development of existing English policies, and part of a broader historical narrative concerning community, violence and good rule. In short, the order for the massacre appears to have been a limited political response to an assassination plot that resembles ethnically-grounded murder laws instituted by Cnut and the Normans but interpreted by later historians through discourses concerned with the destruction of peoples. And yet, that later accounts emphasised the horror of

---

[18] Renée Trilling, *The Aesthetics of Nostalgia: Historical Representation in Old English Verse* (Toronto: University of Toronto Press, 2009), p. 8.

[19] Alice Jorgensen, 'Introduction', *Reading the Anglo-Saxon Chronicle*, pp. 1–28 at p. 27.

[20] On the discursive role of heroic poetry, see: John D. Niles, 'Locating *Beowulf* in Literary History', *Exemplaria* 5 (1993): 79–109. The conscious shaping of English law and legal tradition as a discourse to promote royal authority is perhaps best attested in Alfred's laws, including his extensive prologue which traces the history of law-giving through both Christian and English traditions. See various chapters in Timothy Reuter, ed., *Alfred the Great* (Aldershot: Ashgate, 2003), especially: Allen J. Frantzen, 'The Form and Function of the Preface in the Poetry and Prose of Alfred's reign', pp. 121–36, and Simon Keynes, 'The Power of the Written Word: Alfredian England 871–899', pp. 175–98; see also: Scott Preston, *King Alfred's Book of Laws* (Jefferson, NC: McFarland, 2012); Lisi Oliver, 'Legal Documentation and the Practice of English Law', *The Cambridge History of Early English Literature*, ed. Clare A. Lees (Cambridge: Cambridge University Press, 2013), pp. 499–529.

ethnic conflict demonstrates on-going anxieties about community stability and the effects of inter-ethnic violence, on a small or large scale.

The St Brice's Day massacre may be an early formulation, earlier than previously thought, of the legal concept of *morð*, in which an ethnic group was held collectively accountable for a murder. This impression is bolstered in comparing the accounts of the massacre together with the poetic vocabulary of *morð* and the narration of the consequences for killing in *Beowulf*. The status of *morð* as a crime remains a bit obscure, and the term carried different meanings at different periods and in diverse discursive contexts. The word *morð* appears in early poetry indicating violence ranging from homicide to large-scale destruction;[21] it is often conflated with the Old Norse *morð*, which was associated with outlawry and indicates murder, unannounced killing or night-killing.[22] However, Bruce O'Brien demonstrates that in English there was a development from the tenth-century reign of Æthelstan where the interchangeable terms '*morð* and *morðor* became a matter of lordship and, under Cnut and afterwards, of corporate liability'.[23] Although this sense of *morð* is not included in Cnut's laws, the twelfth-century *Leges Edwardi Confessoris* relate that, after his conquest of England in 1016, Cnut instituted a murder fine that made English nobles stand 'as sureties for any of their men who might slay one of Cnut's Danes'.[24] Such a policy acknowledges ethnic tensions after the Danish conquest of England, but it provides a tidy solution to challenges of authority: Cnut maintained some of the English lords, presumably gaining their support, and they ensured the loyalty of their English followers. However, the murder fine described by the *Leges* is in contrast to the laws drafted in 1021x1022 in Cnut's name by Wulfstan,

---

[21] Joseph Bosworth and T. Northcote Toller, eds., *An Anglo-Saxon Dictionary* (Oxford: Oxford University Press, 1954), s.v. 'morþ'.

[22] Bruce R. O'Brien, 'From *Morðor* to *Murdrum*: The Preconquest Origin and Norman Revival of the Murder Fine', *Speculum* 71 (1996): 321–57 at p. 337. Cf. Richard Cleasby and Gudbrand Vigfusson, eds., *An Icelandic-English Dictionary* (Oxford: Clarendon Press, 1957), s.v. *morð*. See also in this volume: Ilse Schweitzer VanDonkelaar, 'Bringing Murder to Light: Death, Publishing and Performance in Icelandic Sagas'. O'Brien also notes that French *mordre*, while cognate with Old English *morð*, carried a different meaning and was taken into English as 'murder', pp. 330–31. The French word carried a meaning more like that of Modern English 'murder', 'indicating murder, assassination, intentional killing, cruel mistreatment, or smothering'. See also: Alan Hindley, Frederick W. Langley and Brian J. Levy, eds., *Old French-English Dictionary* (Cambridge: Cambridge University Press, 2000), s.v. *mordre*; Algirdas Julien Greimas, ed., *Dictionnaire de l'ancien français* (Ligugé: Larousse, 1997), s.v. *mordrir*. See also in this volume: Jolanta N. Komornicka, 'Treacherous Murder: Language and Meaning in French Murder Trials'.

[23] O'Brien, 'From *Morðor* to *Murdrum*', p. 325.

[24] Ibid.; See also: *Leges Edwardi Confessoris*, in *Die Gesetze der Angelsachsen*, ed. Felix Liebermann (Halle: Max Niemeyer, 1903–1916; rpt. Clark: The Lawbook Exchange, 2008), p. 16. All cited laws are from Liebermann's edition.

archbishop of York, where he includes *morð* in a list of *botleas* crimes (crimes that could not be compensated by payment of wergild or a fine).[25] O'Brien suggests that Wulfstan revived the word *morð* specifically in opposition to Cnut making *morð* compensable, possibly in line with Danish law. Despite the differences in these records, in both cases, *morð* is linked with violation of lordship. Under the Normans, the crime of *morð* developed into *murdrum*, where the English of an entire area were held responsible for the murder of a Norman if the killer was not known.[26]

Broadly speaking, in English, *morð* appears to have developed two general senses: 'A killing with no hope of effective compensation or a betrayal of one's lord',[27] and from the Danish and the Norman conquests, it increasingly developed into collective responsibility for an ethnic (English) community. In these, *morð* discursively connects lordship, violence and community, all issues prevalent both in *Beowulf* and in all of the early medieval accounts of the St Brice's Day massacre. Although not directly related to either the St Brice's Day massacre or to murder law, *Beowulf* posits a collective ethnic accountability for violence that corresponds to collective accountability for violations of lordship, if not outright treason, that *morð* came to hold after Cnut's conquest. If these issues were already present in millennial poetic discourse, they almost certainly circulated in political discourse. Even if it does not use the word *morð*, the Chronicle account of the St Brice's Day massacre indicates that the concept of holding an ethnic group collectively accountable for a legal or political violation was available to Æthelred and his counsellors. What the consequences of that were, however, are perhaps made clearest by *Beowulf*.

Although the dating of *Beowulf* has long proved contentious, in its manuscript context the poem is a product of the period of millennial Viking invasions in England, and more than a few scholars have interpreted the manuscript's contemporary purpose as cultural and political commentary. In its extant form, *Beowulf* appears in the London, British Library, Cotton Vitellius A.xv manuscript, dated by N. R. Ker to sometime between 975 and 1025, and dated on palaeographical grounds by David Dumville to between 997 and 1016.[28] Many

---

[25] *Husbryce 7 bærnet 7 open þyfð 7 æbære morð 7 hlafordswyce æfter woruldlage is botleas* [According to secular law, attacks on houses, arson, open theft, murder that cannot be denied, and betrayal of one's lord are uncompensable] (II Cnut 64).

[26] *Leis Willelmi* 22; *Willelmi I. Articuli X* 3.

[27] O'Brien, 'From *Morðor* to *Murdrum*', p. 347.

[28] N. R. Ker, *Catalogue of Manuscripts Containing Anglo-Saxon* (Oxford: Clarendon Press, 1957) dated the *Beowulf* manuscript to s. X/XI. Later, he dated it more closely to 990–1040, in Dorothy Whitelock, *The Will of Æthelgifu, A Tenth-Century Anglo-Saxon Manuscript* (Oxford: Oxford University Press, 1968), pp. 45–46. Based on script, David Dumville restricted the dates to 997–1016 in '*Beowulf* Come Lately: Some Notes

scholars have seen the poem reflecting on political issues and English identity, particularly identifying monsters, monstrosity, Otherness and their threat to community as the themes unifying the texts of the manuscript.[29] Susan Kim argues that the monsters explore the tension between English identity as Christian and as barbarian.[30] Kathryn Powell proposes that the monsters of the manuscript point to a concern with 'monstrous foreign aggression as a particular problem for rulers'.[31] Others have focused specifically on *Beowulf* and made more functionalist political claims. Leonard Neidorf contends that 'English leaders were fully aware of the ways in which cultural products could assist their efforts'.[32] Reading *Beowulf* in conjunction with the 1013 royal decree of national penance known as VII Æthelred, Neidorf further argues that *Beowulf*, concerned with the themes of loyalty and disloyalty, invoked nostalgia for a by-gone age of peace and unity and was intended as an example to the English in the face of the Viking crisis.[33] Helen Damico makes a more radical version of the historically specific argument, claiming composition for the poem in the eleventh century. She posits that *Beowulf* specifically alludes to politics, and with the *Encomium Emmae Reginae*, acted as propaganda in the succession controversy between Cnut's sons, Harthacnut and Harald.[34]

on Paleography of the Nowell Codex', *Archiv für das Studium der neuern Sprachen und Literaturen* 225 (1988): 49–63. For a discussion of the debate over the dating of the manuscript, see the 'Re-visions' preface in Kevin Kiernan, *Beowulf and the Beowulf Manuscript* (Ann Arbor: University of Michigan Press, 1996), pp. xv–xxviii. For a discussion of the history of scholarship on the dating of the poem, as opposed to the manuscript, see: Robert E. Bjork and Anita Obermeier, 'Date, Provenance, Author, Audiences', in *A Beowulf Handbook*, ed. Robert E. Bjork and John D. Niles (Lincoln: University of Nebraska Press, 1997), pp. 13–34; Roberta Frank, 'A Scandal in Toronto: The Dating of "Beowulf" a Quarter Century On', *Speculum* 82 (2007): 843–64; Leonard Neidorf, ed., *The Dating of Beowulf: A Reassessment* (Cambridge: D. S. Brewer, 2014), pp. 1–18.

[29] Kenneth Sisam, 'The Compilation of the Beowulf Manuscript', in *Studies in the History of Old English Literature* (Oxford: Clarendon Press, 1953), pp. 65–96. See also: Andy Orchard, *Pride and Prodigies: Studies in the Monsters of the Beowulf-Manuscript* (Cambridge: D. S. Brewer, 1995).

[30] Susan Kim, 'Man-Eating Monsters and Ants as Big as Dogs: The Alienated Language of the Cotton Vitellius A.xv "Wonders of the East"', in *Animals and the Symbolic in Mediaeval Art and Literature*, ed. Reinier Munk and L. A. J. R. Houwen (Groningen: Egbert Forsten, 1997), pp. 38–51.

[31] Kathryn Powell, 'Meditating on Men and Monsters: A Reconsideration of the Thematic Unity of the *Beowulf* Manuscript', *Review of English Studies*, New Series 57 (2006): 1–15 at p. 1.

[32] Leonard Neidorf, 'VII Æthelred and the Genesis of the *Beowulf* Mansucript', *Philological Quarterly* 89 (2010): 119–39 at p. 121.

[33] Ibid., p. 135.

[34] Helen Damico, *Beowulf and the Grendel-Kin: Politics and Poetry in Eleventh-Century England* (Morgantown: West Virginia University Press, 2014). Damico acknowledges the problem of the manuscript's date for her reading of *Beowulf* as an eleventh-century

However appealing it may be to read *Beowulf* as engaging directly with the politics of its day, the period of between two and five decades during which the *Beowulf* manuscript may have been produced, as well as Neidorf's work on the poem's early presence in England, suggest that it participated in a more fluid narrative tradition, speaking to different audiences at different times, holding meanings and addressing concerns for each, so interpretation of the poem should not be limited to such specific moments.[35] Nonetheless, *Beowulf*, in its manuscript context, is a millennial English 'cultural product'. As such, anxieties expressed in the poem may very well reflect millennial English anxieties, and it may have acted as one site among many for the English community to reflect on the history of English policy toward the Vikings and to consider political options, including pogroms of ethnic cleansing.[36]

From its opening, *Beowulf* invokes heroic discourse and invites reflection on community and deeds through memory:[37]

Hwæt, wē Gār-Dena   in geārdagum
þēodcyninga   þrym gefrūnon,
hū ðā æþelingas   ellen fremedon. (1–3)[38]

[Truly, we have heard of the spear-Danes in days gone by, of the might of the people-kings, how those nobles did great deeds].

---

production (pp. 4–8). Damico previously argued for the *Beowulf* poet's interweaving of real and fictive events in the Grendel episode and the direct incorporation of his judgements on the Danish attacks in England between 1003 and 1016. See: 'Grendel's Reign of Terror: From History to Vernacular Epic', in *Myths, Legends, and Heroes: Essays on Old Norse and Old English Literature in Honour of John McKinnell*, ed. Daniel Anlezark (Toronto: University of Toronto Press, 2011), pp. 150–66.

[35] Neidorf, *The Dating of Beowulf*, pp. 1–18; see also: Frank Battaglia, 'Not Christianity versus Paganism, but Hall versus Bog: The Great Shift in Early Scandinavian Religion and its Implications for *Beowulf*', in *Anglo-Saxons and the North: Essays Reflecting the Theme of the 10th Meeting of the International Society of Anglo-Saxonists in Helskinki, August 2001*, ed. Matti Kilpiö, Leena Kahlas-Tarkka, Jane Roberts and Olga Timofeeva (Tempe: Arizona Center for Medieval and Renaissance Studies, 2009), pp. 47–68. On the poem having different meanings at different times, see: Niles, 'Locating *Beowulf* in Literary History'.

[36] On the context for a fear of treachery and millennial social stresses to economic motives, see: Ryan Lavelle, 'Ethnic Cleansing in Anglo-Saxon England', *BBC History* (2002): 42–44.

[37] Roy M. Liuzza, '*Beowulf*: Monuments, Memory, History', in *Readings in Medieval Texts: Interpreting Old and Middle English Literature*, ed. David F. Johnson and Elaine Treharne (Oxford: Oxford University Press, 2005), pp. 91–108 at p. 92.

[38] All quotations from *Beowulf* are taken from R. D. Fulk, Robert E. Bjork and John D. Niles, eds., *Klaeber's Beowulf and the Fight at Finnsburg* (Toronto: University of Toronto Press, 2008). All translations are my own.

The audience is presented with statements of familiar matter expressed through the traditional poetic formula *wē gefrūnon*, grounded in a first-person plural pronoun that assumes a common identity with its audience.[39] However, if *Beowulf* is read as a millennial text composed before Cnut's conquest, the heroic Scandinavian matter of the poem seems to be at odds with the audience invoked through the English *wē*, a point Dorothy Whitelock raises in dating the poem to no later than the eighth century.[40] The question becomes, what *wē*, as a community, are supposed to recall about the stories *wē* know about the Danes, and what interpretations the poem itself encourages. After all, as Roy Liuzza states, 'The author of *Beowulf* is mindful of the differences as well as the connections between the past and the present, and is concerned with difficult questions of the continuing relevance of those *geārdagum* to the present.'[41] But, as Michael Lapidge observes, the poem does not present history linearly: instead, it jumps backward and forward in time, demanding that the audience assemble the narrative by remembering what has already been told, both about what has happened in the past and what will happen in the future, and, consequently, shaping its audience through 'the processes of acquisition and evaluation of knowledge, of the mental perception of an event rather than the event itself, and the arrangement of these mental perceptions in a narrative structure.'[42]

If *Beowulf* opens by invoking the memory of heroic deeds and reflection on community identity, the very structure of the poem sets its audience up to anticipate disaster for individuals and peoples due to inter-ethnic violence.[43] Within the first hundred lines, the poem presents the unification of the Danes under Scyld Scefing, the development of a successful royal line, the building of Hēorot as a place for the people, its downfall, and the immediate appearance of Grendel. In this quick historical summary may be seen the confluence of Kim's and Powell's arguments for concerns with monsters, identity, rulers and foreigners. It introduces Scyld's foreign fighting as the foundation of the Danes as a people and their prosperity but also shows violent conflict as their downfall.[44]

---

[39] Lavelle, 'Peacemaking', p. 40.
[40] Dorothy Whitelock, *The Audience of Beowulf* (Oxford: Clarendon Press, 1951).
[41] Liuzza, '*Beowulf*: Monuments, Memory, History', p. 100. Cf. Trilling above, n. 18.
[42] Michael Lapidge, '*Beowulf* and Perception', *Proceedings of the British Academy* 111 (2001): 61–97 at p. 81.
[43] J. R. R. Tolkien, '*Beowulf*: The Monsters and the Critics', Sir Israel Gollancz Memorial Lecture, *Proceedings of the British Academy* 22 (1936): 245–95; Roberta Frank, 'The *Beowulf* Poet's Sense of History', in *The Wisdom of Poetry: Essays in Early English Literature in Honor of Morton W. Bloomfield*, ed. Larry D. Benson and Siegfried Wenzel (Kalamazoo: Medieval Institute Publications, 1982), pp. 53–65 at p. 64–65; Fulk et al., *Klæber's Beowulf*, pp. cxxiii; Frantzen, 'Form and Function', pp. 124–25.
[44] Kathryn Hume, 'The Theme and Structure of *Beowulf*', *Studies in Philology* 72 (1975): 1–27 at pp. 11–12.

The narrative juxtaposition of Hēorot's construction and destruction demands a recollection of historical knowledge that offers a space for reflection on contemporary events similar, perhaps, to the Chronicle account of the payment of tribute to the Danes, their subsequent treachery and the order for the St Brice's Day massacre. And when the poem returns to present events, Grendel appears, beginning a series of episodes in which the three monsters fix the audience's attention on problems and ambiguities concerning the legitimacy and consequences of violence within the heroic discourse.

Scyld securing peace for his community through violent inter-ethnic conflict presents a familiar heroic discourse that would have had a particular resonance for an English audience facing on-going Viking attacks:

Oft Scyld Scēfing   sceaþena þrēatum,
monegum mǣġþum   meodosetla oftēah,
eġsode eorlas [...]
wēox under wolcnum, weorðmyndum þāh,
oð þæt him ǣghwylċ   þāra ymbsittendra
ofer hronrāde   hȳran scolde
gomban ġyldan. (4a–11a)

[Often Scyld Scefing terrorised nobles, took away the mead-benches from troops of enemies, from many peoples [...] He grew under the heavens, prospered in honour, until every one of those surrounding peoples over the sea had to obey him, give tribute].

While presented in the language of praise, the core image is of the subjugation and destruction of others' communities, represented in the image of the mead benches. Certainly a millennial English audience must have had mixed feelings about the heroic discourse in light of their own violent encounters with the Danes and the forced payment of tribute.[45] *Beowulf* teaches its audience not only to read the events of the poem through historical reflection but to engage with contemporary events through a 'retrospective mode'.[46] It presents murderous vengeance, even to the point of collective destruction, as the consequence of establishing community through violence, and reflects on and provides possible models for how communities manage violent threats. The introduction of

---

[45] John D. Niles argues that *The Battle of Maldon* is a mythopoetic text which shows that conflicted English views about the heroic discourse were developing by the end of the tenth century. *Old English Heroic Poems and the Social Life of Texts* (Turnhout: Brepols, 2007), pp. 203–52. Responding to Niles, Leonard Neidorf argues that *Maldon* is self-consciously responding to its political context. See: 'II Æthelred and the Politics of *The Battle of Maldon*', *Journal of English and Germanic Philology* 111 (2012): 451–73.

[46] Lapidge, '*Beowulf* and Perception', p. 81; F. C. Robinson, *Beowulf and the Appositive Style* (Knoxville: University of Tennessee Press, 1985), p. 7.

Hēorot as the *folcstede*, an image of stability and prosperity for the people, also anticipates its destruction:

> Ðā iċ wīde gefræġn   weorc ġebannan
> maniġre mæġþe   ġeond þisne middanġeard,
> folcstede frætwan.   Him on fyrste ġelomp,
> ædre mid yldum,   þæt hit wearð eal ġearo,
> healærna mæst;   scōp him Heort naman
> sē þe his wordes ġeweald   wīde hæfde.
> Hē bēot ne ālēh: bēagas dælde,
> sinċ æt symle.   Sele hlīfade
> hēah ond hornġēap;   heaðowylma bād,
> lāðan līġes —   ne wæs hit lenġe þā ġēn
> þæt se ecghete   āþumswēoran
> æfter wælnīðe   wæcnan scolde. (74a–85b)

> [Then, I have heard, the work was imposed on many a people far and wide in this middle-earth, the dwelling place decorated. In time it came to pass for them, quickly among men, that it was completed, the greatest of hall-dwellings. He whose word had wide authority created for it the name Hēorot. He did not fail to fulfil his boast: shared out rings, treasure at feasts. The hall towered high and wide-gabled, awaited waves of battle, hostile flame. Nor was it very long until the hatred of swords should awake between those sworn in oath because of deadly hostility].

Not only are Hēorot's construction and destruction narrated together but the audience is expected to know the history that led to its fall, to understand that 'those sworn in oath' refers to the failed marriage alliance of Hrothgar's daughter Freawaru with the Heathobard Ingeld.[47] Moreover, although the effect is delayed, the audience is expected to assemble the passing historical allusion with Beowulf's later political analysis concerning exogamous marriage as doomed to failure in his account of Hēorot to Hygelac. As Beowulf observes, no matter how good the bride, men's memories of hostility will be revived when they see the swords of their slain fathers worn by their now-allies and peace will fail (2020–69). Following Beowulf's interpretive model, what *wē* have heard about past deeds *wē* must use to understand the present. Embedded in this historical narrative is conflict among peoples and anxiety about the potential of achieving peace, encouraging the English audience to consider both the history of the Danes and how to maintain peace for themselves.

---

[47] Such familiarity with history and legend is similarly assumed in *Widsith*. See: Rolf H. Bremmer, Jr., 'Across Borders: Anglo-Saxon England and the Germanic World', in *The Cambridge History*, ed. Lees, pp. 185–206 at p. 199.

With the question of peace-making in the air, the poem returns to the present, introducing Grendel, the first monster to focus the audience's attention on the Danes' own responses to violence. The poem maintains the heroic discourse, but also makes some uncomfortable associations between the Danes and the Grendel-kin, calling into question the legitimacy of any inter-ethnic violence. Repetitions of language bring events into dialogue and lead to a certain ambiguity of meaning. The Danes often performed *ellen* [great deeds] (3b), and Grendel is introduced as *se ellengæst* in his first appearance in the poem (86a). Although frequently emended to *ellorgæst* [alien spirit], agreeing with later references to the Grendel-kin (807b, 1349a, 1617a, 1621b),[48] *ellen* introduces two peoples and draws a connection between them. The very term that is used in a presumably positive light when invoking the Danes' deeds at the beginning of the poem takes on a more sinister quality when it is compounded with *gæst*. Unmarked for vowel length in the manuscript, the meaning of *gæst* is ambiguous:[49] if read as *gǣst*, it indicates a 'spirit', 'ghost' or something like the Old Norse *draugr*;[50] but *gæst* would indicate 'guest', 'stranger' or 'enemy'.[51] Scyld himself was a foreign enemy to those he conquered, and Grendel is an unwelcome and hostile outsider who performs great deeds like the Danes, indeed echoing Scyld's deeds when he denies to the Danes the mead-hall as a place of community.

This is not to suggest that the poem presents the Danes as inherently wicked, nor that the Danes and the Grendel-kin are one and the same nor even necessarily parallel. The quality of their deeds is distinguished. Whereas Scyld is identified as a good king (11b) for forcing the neighbouring tribes to pay tribute, Grendel 'gefremede / morðbeala māre, ond nō mearn fore, / fæhðe ond fyrene' [performed more wicked murders, feuding and crimes, and did not mourn on account of that] (135a–137a). His killing is the first appearance of *morð* in the poem, in the early sense of murder or night-killing; it is explicitly wicked and criminal, and it drives further violence.[52] While the killings by Grendel and his

---

[48] See: Fulk et al., *Klaeber's Beowulf*, n. 86a.

[49] Antonette DiPaolo Healy, ed., *Dictionary of Old English* (Toronto: University of Toronto Press, 2007–), s.v. 'gāst': 'Wordplay on the senses of *gyst* "visitor, stranger" and *gāst* "spirit, soul, demon" is common in poetry; some poetic examples spelled *gæst-* or *gast-* which have been treated s.v. *gyst* (q.v.), may alternatively be read as forms of *gāst*. *Gæst-* and *gast-* are left unmarked for length throughout'.

[50] Bosworth-Toller, s.v. 'gæst'. Michael Lapidge, '*Beowulf* and the Psychology of Terror', in *Heroic Poetry in the Anglo-Saxon Period: Studies in Honor of Jess B. Bessinger, Jr.*, ed. Helen Damico and John Leyerle (Kalamazoo: Medieval Institute Publications, 1993), pp. 373–402 at p. 375.

[51] Bosworth-Toller, s.v. 'gæst', I and II.

[52] *Morð(or)* appears alone or in compounds ten times in the poem. Of these, two define killing by Grendel (136a, 1683a), one refers to Cain killing Abel (1264a), one refers to the accidental and uncompensable killing of Herebeald by his brother Hæðcyn (2436b),

mother are *morð* as used generically in heroic discourse, the poem's emphasis on collective accountability for inter-ethnic violence indicates that a newer sense of *morð* may already have been developing. By introducing Grendel and his disruption of community stability, the poem begins a reflection not only on violence but also on violence as murder and how peace is established and maintained. Daniel Anlezark stresses how Grendel's association with Cain (105–108) and the subsequent line of post-diluvian monsters drives how the audience interprets his killing: 'Cain's killing of Abel, mentioned twice in the poem, seems to have held a special place in the Anglo-Saxon poetic imagination, and the *Beowulf* poet is not alone in dwelling on this mythic fratricide as an important moment in the descent of human society into murderous hate'.[53] There is a fine line between heroic deeds in support of a community and murderous, destructive feud. Thus, the poem presents alternative perspectives on violence largely determined by its effects on the community and the perpetuation of conflict.

Moreover, the possibility of peace is grounded in inter-ethnic conflict and raises questions about community and ethnic identity. Scyld pursued violence but offered peace in exchange for tribute. Grendel, however, refuses all of the recognised ways of making peace:

> sibbe ne wolde
> wið manna hwone   mægenes Deniġa,
> feorhbealo feorran,   fēa þingian,
> nē þǣr nǣnig witena   wēnan þorfte
> beorhtre bōte   tō banan folmum. (154b–158b)

[he did not want peace with any of the men of the Danish people, nor to cease his deadly attack, nor to settle with tribute, nor did any of the counsellors need to expect bright compensation from the hands of the killer].

Grendel refuses to make a settlement with the Danes or to make amends for the killing. But more strikingly, Grendel rejects *sibb*; that is, he refuses not only to make peace but also to make the Danes in some way part of his kin group, presumably through an exogamous marriage.[54] The poem has already raised the issue of inter-ethnic marriage as a means of peace-making and reflects on it repeatedly: Hrothgar's unnamed sister was married to the Swedish Onela (62a–63b), a figure who plays a significant role in the Swedish wars later in the

---

three relate to the events in Finnsburg (1079a, 1105a, 2055a), two refer to the killing of dragons by Sigemund and Beowulf (892b 2782b) and Beowulf denies being guilty of murder in one (2742a).

[53] Daniel Anlezark, *Water and Fire: The Myth of the Flood in Anglo-Saxon England* (Manchester: Manchester University Press, 2006), p. 296.

[54] Fulk et al., *Klaeber's Beowulf*, s.v. 'sibbe'. Bosworth-Toller s.v. 'sib', 'I. relationship; II. friendliness; III. peace; IV. peace, concord, unity'.

poem; Hrothgar's queen is Wealhtheow, whose very name suggests that she was herself a foreign bride;[55] and the destruction of Hēorot, invoked fewer than seventy lines earlier, will be brought about by deadly hostility between the Danes and the Heathobards, joined through the marriage of Freawaru to Ingeld. Grendel's refusal of *sibb* highlights the challenges of inter-ethnic conflict, but the failures of marriage alliances between peoples do not offer much hope. Indeed, the Finnsburg episode that follows suggests that the only solution to on-going inter-ethnic violence is the destruction of a people, like that ordered for the St Brice's Day massacre.

After Grendel's death, the celebration in Hēorot is a return of the Danes to their mead benches, a brief reclamation of community stability before the appearance of Grendel's mother. Recounting in detail a failed marriage alliance, the aftermath of conflict and the tragedy of broken faith,[56] the Finnsburg episode presents the Danes' heroic self-perception.

> Bugon þā tō benċe   blǣdāgande,
> fylle ġefǣgon;   fæġere ġeþǣgon
> medoful maniġ   māgas þāra
> swīðhicgende   on sele þām hēan,
> Hrōðgār ond Hrōþulf.   Hēorot innan wæs
> frēondum āfylled;   nalles fācenstafas
> Þēod-Scyldingas   þenden fremedon. (1013a–1019b)

[The men in glory turned to their benches, taking pleasure in the feast; fittingly the kinsmen drank many cups full of mead, courageous in the high hall, Hrothgar and Hrothulf. Hēorot was filled with friends; the people of the Scyldings did not perform any acts of malice at that time.]

The Danes have re-established community. They are at peace, free both from internal threats and from threatening others (as far as they know). However, the narrator gestures to their future of internal strife (Hrothulf will betray Hrethric and usurp the throne) and sets up the Danes' treachery as the filter through which to understand the Finnsburg story. The scop, *æfter medubence* [among the mead benches], the image of community stability, tells a tale of the Frisian ambush of the Danes in Finn's hall, the peace established, the Danes' violation of that peace and the subsequent slaughter of the Frisians.[57]

---

[55] Bosworth-Toller, *s.v.*, 'wealh', I. 'a foreigner, properly a Celt', II. 'a slave, a servant'; *s.v.* 'þeow', 'a servant, often with the stronger sense of slave'.

[56] Andy Orchard, *A Critical Companion to Beowulf* (Cambridge: D. S. Brewer, 2001), p. 171.

[57] For a summary of the rather confusing events of the story, see: *Beowulf*, ed. Federico Olivieri (Torino, 1934), pp. lii–liii; quoted in Nicola Zocco, 'The *Episode of Finn* in *Beowulf*. Discharging Hengest', *Linguistica e Filologia* 24 (2007): 65–83 at p. 67.

While ostensibly a tale of Danish heroism, the poem challenges the heroic discourse by presenting a personal and mournful account of the effects of the slaughter for Hildeburh, a Danish princess who had been married to the Frisian Finn as a part of a treaty. If political agency is a requirement of ethnic identification, women's status in the ethnic community is at best questionable.[58] Hildeburh attempts to be a political agent, but it is not clear that *Beowulf* permits her – or any of the female characters in the poem – full agency and so does not permit full ethnic identification. Historically, there were certainly powerful and politically influential women, like Emma, the Norman princess who was married first to Æthelred II and subsequently to Cnut. The fact that Cnut would marry Emma not only as a means of allying himself with Normandy but also, presumably, of shoring up the legitimacy of his rule in England, is evidence of a noble woman's ability to be a political actor and a full member of an ethnic community, and possibly of more than one.[59] However, as will become clear, *Beowulf* presents women's status as rather more tenuous. Noble women are identified in terms of their marriages and their children, their identification with the new community is ambiguous and, while they attempt to affect politics, their authority is circumscribed.[60]

---

[58] Stacy Klein, *Ruling Women: Queenship and Gender in Anglo-Saxon Literature* (Notre Dame: University of Notre Dame Press, 2006).

[59] It is worth noting that Emma's marriage to Cnut and the degree of autonomy she is granted differ greatly between the Anglo-Saxon Chronicle account, in which Cnut has her fetched to him (*s.a.* 1017), and the *Encomium Emmae Reginae* (a propaganda piece that Emma commissioned) in which Cnut desires her for her political stature. In the encomiast's narration, Emma carefully negotiates the terms of her marriage and her children's place in dynastic succession (II.16). Alistair Campbell, ed., *Encomium Emmae Reginae* (Cambridge: Cambridge University Press, 1998), pp. 32–33.

[60] On Emma and *Beowulf*, see: Damico, *Beowulf and the Grendel-Kin*, ch. 4; Joyce Hill, '"Þæt wæs Geomoru Ides!" A Female Stereotype Examined', in *New Readings on Women in Old English Literature*, ed. Helen Damico and Alexandra Hennessey Olsen (Bloomington: University of Indiana Press, 1990), pp. 235–47 makes a compelling argument that women in politically motivated royal marriages did, in fact, wield significant, but informal, power. She goes on to argue, however, that in heroic poetry, the emphasis on men's deeds on the battlefield necessarily diminished (if not erased) women's political influence. Cf. L. John Sklute, 'Freoðuwebbe in Old English Poetry', in *New Readings on Women*, ed. Damico and Olsen, pp. 204–10. It should be noted, however, that *Beowulf* is a notoriously slippery object of interpretation and there are quite a few scholars who have found that women play much more successful roles in the poem. For summaries of alternative readings of women's political agency in *Beowulf*, see, for example: Alexandra Hennessey Olsen, 'Gender Roles', in *A Beowulf Handbook*, ed. Bjork and Niles, pp. 311–24; Klein, *Ruling Women*, pp. 87–124; and Nathan A. Breen, 'The King's Closest Counselor: The Legal Basis of Wealhtheow's Comments to Hrothgar, *Beowulf* 1169–87', *The Heroic Age* 14 (2010).

The Finnsburg account extends the reflection on inter-ethnic violence beyond its effects on the warrior elite as Hildeburh sees both her son and her brother killed:

> þæt wæs ġeōmuru ides!
> Nalles hōlinga   Hōces dohtor
> meotodsceaft bemearn   syþðan morgen cōm,
> ðā hēo under sweġle   ġesēon meahte
> morþorbealo māga,   þǣr hēo ǣr mǣste hēold
> worolde wynne. (1075b–1080a)

[That was a mournful lady! Not at all without cause did Hōc's daughter mourn the decree of fate after morning came, when under heaven she could see the wicked murder of kinsmen, where she had previously held the greatest joy in the world].

Hildeburh, intended as a peace-weaver between two peoples, suffers losses described in the same vocabulary as Grendel's initial attack on Hēorot: *morþorbealo māga*. The inter-ethnic violence has brought about wicked murders of kinsmen. If, with Grendel, *morþorbealo māga* was equated with feud and crimes, it should be here as well. While the repetition of language may have originally operated structurally as thesis-antithesis,[61] the killing here, like Grendel's, is wicked and drives further violence. But *morþorbealo māga* may also highlight Hildeburh's ambiguous ethnic status – a Danish princess married off to become the wife of a Frisian king to bind the two peoples together in peace and, presumably, blood through their son, she sees the wicked murder of kinsmen on both sides, losing son and brother. Yet she still attempts to perform her role as peace-weaver, ordering the bodies of her son and brother to be burned together on the same funeral pyre. As Shari Horner interprets the scene, Hildeburh 'orders a visual symbol of the destroyed peace accord, and the pyre signals not only the breakdown in the alliance at Finnsburg, but also the impossibility of creating peace out of hostility'.[62] Indeed, Hildeburh's agency itself will be curtailed when she is carried home with the Danes after the slaughter of the Frisians. Horner goes on to argue that, throughout the poem, women's efforts to insert their voices into the political realm and assert their power, or even their own narratives, are universally curtailed.

As to the warrior elite that defines the ethnic group, the poem suggests that there is no peaceful resolution to *morþorbealo māga* and the Danes cannot be

---

[61] John D. Niles, *Beowulf: The Poem and Its Tradition* (Cambridge, MA: Harvard University Press, 1983), p. 157.
[62] Shari Horner, 'Voices from the Margins: Women and Textual Enclosure in *Beowulf*, *Postmodern Beowulf: A Critical Casebook* (Morgantown: West Virginia University Press, 2006), pp. 467–500 at p. 473.

trusted. Finn attempts to establish a truce, even to the extent that he debases himself and the rest of the Frisians:

> Fin Henġeste
> elne unflitme   āðum benemde
> þæt hē þā wēalāfe   weotena dōme
> ārum hēolde,   þæt ðǣr ǣniġ mon
> wordum nē worcum   wǣre ne brǣce,
> nē þurh inwitsearo   ǣfre ġemǣnden,
> ðēah hīe hira bēagġyfan   banan folgedon
> ðēodlēase,   þā him swā ġeþearfod wæs;
> ġyf þonne Frȳsna hwylċ   frēcnen sprǣċe
> ðæs morþorhetes   myndġiend wǣre,
> þonne hit sweordes ecg   syððan scēde. (1096b–1106b)

[Finn affirmed to Hengest with oaths resolutely and without dispute that, on the advice of his counsellors, he would rule the survivors of calamity honourably, so that no man there with words or deeds would break the truce, nor through secret treachery would they, lordless, ever say that they followed their ring-giver's killer when the necessity was imposed on them. If, then, any of the Frisians should with bold speech call to mind that murderous hate, then the sword's edge should settle it thereafter].

Almost from the moment of peace, even as Finn promises to keep the Frisians from invoking the murderous hate (ðæs morþorhetes) at the risk of resuming the feud, Hengest, the Danish leader, 'to gyrnwræce / swiðor þohte [...] gif he torngemot þurhteon mihte' [thought of stern vengeance [...] how he might arrange a hostile meeting] (1138b–40b). The Danes' treachery is no better than Grendel's refusal of *sibb*, and may well be worse because it is dishonest.[63] What is, however, clear is that *morð*, in old and new senses, is at the centre of the conflict in Finnsburg. The slaughter and the murderous hatred fall into the traditional heroic discourse where *morð* indicates homicide generally; but the loss of the Danish lord, Hnæf, the betrayal of the Frisian lord, Finn, and the collective accountability all bring the conflict into the later sense of *morð*, suggesting that once *morð* is committed there is no resolution but through destruction.

Whereas the Finnsburg episode presents ethnic destruction as being applied only to men, there are clear consequences for women: the appearance of Grendel's mother begins a cycle of violence that results in the only case of

---

[63] Zocco argues that Hengest is not actually treacherous in this scene and that he exactly keeps to the language of the agreement. While Zocco's larger argument, that the *scop* is suggesting to Hrothgar that he should pay particular attention to his words, is compelling, her defence of Hengest requires special pleading and provides him with quite the lawyerly mind. 'The *Episode of Finn* in *Beowulf*, pp. 65–83.

complete and successful genocide narrated in the poem, that of the Grendel-kin. While Grendel effectively carries out successful attacks against Hēorot, disrupting the Danish society, once he is dead, it seems that there is no further male figure in the line to avenge his death, as is evident from Grendel's mother taking vengeance. However, once she is killed, the whole line is extinguished:

> wǣron ȳðgebland   eal ġefǣlsod,
> ēacne eardas,   þā se ellorgast
> oflēt līfdagas   ond þās lǣnan ġesceaft. (1620a–1622b)

[the blending waves were completely cleansed, the vast lands, when the alien spirit relinquished life-days and this loaned creation].

The solution to the Danes' troubles appears to be a successful, if unwitting, destruction of an entire people, male and female. Moreover, with their destruction, all the monsters that inhabit the landscape go away and spaces again become habitable for the community. As Hēorot is cleansed (*gefælsod*) when Beowulf defeats Grendel (825a), so with the death of Grendel's mother the world the men inhabit is cleansed (*gefælsod*). Where the poem previously engaged with violence among the male warrior-elite, even if reflecting on the effects of that violence on the larger community, with the death of Grendel's mother, the violence is extended in new ways and raises questions about whether and when women could become the targets of violence.

Lest the audience be uncomfortable with the killing of women in ethnic conflict, the poem offers biblical parallels. Where Grendel is associated initially with the fratricidal Cain and the origin of monsters,[64] Daniel Anlezark argues that the cleansing of the mere is a reference 'to the destruction of the giants in the primeval deluge',[65] a point punctuated by the presentation to Hrothgar of the giant-sword hilt on which the story is written (1687a–93b). Looking forward to the Danes and the Geats, the poem continues the pattern of creating associations between peoples and elaborating interpretation of those associations through the invocation of scripture. As the biblical narrative goes, God will not destroy the Earth again with flood, but rather with fire. So the fate of Hēorot by treachery and flame is foretold, and the flames of the dragon that will attack the Geats and burn Beowulf's hall is anticipated.[66]

Beowulf opens by invoking the audience's memory of a heroic past and closes with the political implications of a heroic past on the present for the Geats.

---

[64] Malcolm Godden, 'Biblical Literature: The Old Testament', *The Cambridge Companion to Old English Literature*, ed. Malcolm Godden and Michael Lapidge (Cambridge: Cambridge University Press, 1991), pp. 206–26 at p. 216.
[65] Anlezark, *Water and Fire*, p. 293.
[66] Ibid., pp. 336–37.

Overshadowing the Geats' reasonable anticipation of impending tribal extinction upon Beowulf's death is the image of the dragon that squats on the treasure of another people long since extinct. The dragon is not responsible for the destruction of that people and will not be responsible for the destruction of the Geats, but the monster's appearance in the poem demands particular attention. Although it is not clear exactly what destroyed the people, the 'Lay of the Last Survivor' states that they were dispatched by *guðdeað* (2249b), indicating death by warfare. Thus, the poem advances to its conclusion with a reflection on all the conflicts throughout the poem, highlighting that the political conflicts of the warrior-elite have led to the impending destruction of the whole community in the future, but offering no solution.

On the death of Beowulf, two voices predict the collective consequences for the Geats. In their statements, they clearly draw connections between the loss of their lord and the anticipated destruction of the people. The messenger says,

> Nū ys lēodum wēn
> orleghwīle, syððan underne
> Froncum ond Frȳsum   fyll cyninges
> wīde weorðeð. (2910b–2913a)

[Now this people must expect a time of war when the fall of the king becomes known widely, apparent to the Franks and the Frisians].

He goes on to narrate the origins of the feuds that will be renewed. His message is followed by the unnamed Geatish woman's lament:

> swylce giōmorgyd   Gēatisc meowle
> æfter Bīowulfe   bundenheorde
> sang sorgcearig,   sæide geneahhe
> þæt hīo hyre hereġeongas   hearde ondrēde
> wælfylle worn,   werudes egesan,
> hȳnðo ond hæftnȳd. (3150a–3155a)

[and a Geatish woman, with hair bound up, sang a song of lamentation, full of sorrowful cares, for Beowulf, earnestly said that she dreaded hard days ahead, invasions, great slaughter, the terror of the host, harm and captivity].

The two voices tell of a fear of resumed foreign conflict, but what stands out is the expression of fear of the consequences of war, not just for the warriors but for all the people. And it is in this moment of fear of resumed conflict that they are afraid not only of war but of annihilation, demonstrating that both the legitimacy of violence and the possibility of ethnic destruction were circulating in heroic discourse.

Over the course of the poem, events consistently develop violently, but kings and their peoples are always pursuing peace and stability for themselves.

Inter-ethnic violence is the norm; the pattern of war succeeding feud throughout the poem conforms to actual practice, and the stability of community is maintained only through successful foreign fighting.[67] Yet Beowulf returns attention to good rule, positing an unusual understanding of violence as necessary but restrained:

> Iċ ðās lēode hēold
> fiftiġ wintra;   næs sē folccyning
> ymbesittendra   ǣniġ ðāra
> þe meċ gūðwinum   grētan dorste,
> eġesan ðēon.   Iċ on earde bād
> mǣġesceafta,   hēold mīn tela,
> ne sōhte searonīðas,   nē mē swōr fela
> āða on unriht.   Iċ ðæs ealles mæġ
> feorhbennum sēoc   ġefēan habban;
> forðām mē wītan ne ðearf   waldend fira
> morðorbealo māga   þonne mīn sceaceð
> līf of līċe. (2732a–2743a)

[I ruled this people fifty winters. There was no king of any of the surrounding peoples who dared to attack me with war-friends, advance terror. I awaited at home what fate measured out, ruled well what was mine, did not seek to contrive hostility, did not swear many oaths unjustly. I, sick with mortal wounds, can rejoice in all of that because the ruler of men need not accuse me of the wicked murder of kinsmen when my life flees the body].

Beowulf presents an image of kingship that recognises the necessity of violence but attempts to minimise it. He defines the peace he maintained by what he did not do, and his vocabulary persistently evokes comparisons with earlier scenes. He did not start wars (like Scyld). He did not make false treaties (like the Danes). He is not guilty of *morðorbealo māga* [the wicked murder of kinsmen]. In this, Beowulf may be claiming that he did not bring about the deaths of any of his people by entering into unnecessary conflicts. However, he may also be claiming that he did not promote cycles of violence, unlike Grendel, whose actions promoted the continuation of violence, *fǣhðe ond fyrene* [feuding and crimes]. Yet, not even this relatively peaceable rule can free the Geats from hostility after his death because he did participate in aggressive inter-ethnic violence under Hygelac's rule and in *fǣhðe ond fyrene* during the Swedish wars (2480a). This is what the messenger and the Geatish woman recall. If inter-ethnic violence is inevitable and the consequence for participating in it is the possible destruction of the people, the poem is grim; but more importantly, it offers a space for its audience to discuss their own attitudes to community stability. With

---

[67] Hume, 'The Theme and Structure of *Beowulf*', p. 12.

the messenger's prophecy and the Geatish woman's lament, the present moment hangs in suspension. For the moment, the Geatish community is stable, but future consequences are predicted through the recollection of the past. Similarly, an English audience would be left to ponder their own past in relation to on-going conflict with the Danes and the security of their community. *Beowulf* shows that there were multiple ways of receiving traditional heroic discourse and that narrative interpretation is open to a community's context. While great deeds are clearly admirable in *Beowulf*, they also have consequences that affect not just those who perform deeds but the rest of the community. To protect one's own community against those consequences requires an awareness of history. Once inter-ethnic conflict has commenced, the possibilities of ending it, not just in the present, but going forward, may require tribute (an option the English had already pursued in the face of Viking attacks), a blending of the peoples through marriage (a course of action the Scandinavians pursued in England)[68] or, failing those options, the annihilation of a people.

It is remarkable just how much the Anglo-Saxon Chronicle account of the St Brice's Day massacre invokes these very points. The English pay tribute, the Danes immediately violate the treaty and plot against the king and his counsellors and Æthelred orders the extermination of one ethnic population living amongst another. It would not be unreasonable to imagine Æthelred and his counsellors reflecting on *Beowulf* or other heroic stories as they weighed their political options in 1002. Although the Chronicle's account of the plot and the massacre could be the imposition of the later legal concept of *morð* as collective accountability for a murder since it was composed after Cnut's conquest, the evidence of *Beowulf* indicates that a political discourse that considered the possibility of destroying treacherous ethnic groups to halt cycles of violence was already circulating around the time of the millennium. Yet, no matter how treacherous the Danes may have been, it is difficult to imagine the English ordering a pogrom rather than targeting the violence toward those most likely to be responsible for the plot that violated the treaty and threatened the lives of king and counsellors.

Resisting the idea of a genocidal massacre, Keynes suggests that the violence of St Brice's Day 'was probably aimed not at all inhabitants of the Danelaw, but at mercenaries, traders and other Danes whose trustworthiness the king and his counsellors had good reason to suspect'.[69] Dawn Hadley makes a similar suggestion about the target of Æthelred's order based on the vocabulary of the account: '[I]t is not the descendants of Danish immigrants of the late ninth century who are generally known as Danes in written sources of the later tenth and eleventh

---

[68] D. M. Hadley, 'Viking and Native: Re-Thinking Identity in the Danelaw', *Early Medieval Europe* 11 (2002): 45–70.

[69] Keynes, 'A Tale of Two Kings', p. 211.

centuries, but rather recent arrivals: merchants, disaffected Danish noblemen, mercenaries, troublemakers and enemies, individuals who were "out of place" or causing trouble".[70] Moreover, Susan Reynolds observes that the chroniclers generally held the attitude that 'Danes were invaders and enemies, not subjects of the kingdom'.[71] And Matthew Innes has shown that English kings carefully avoided ethnicising regional politics, preferring instead to draw all of the regions into the English kingdom.[72] Nor is it clear what the Chronicle's phrase *on Angelcynne* means. Hadley stresses that historians have used law codes to distinguish ethnic groups, but that the vocabulary 'may be more likely to be indicative of the limitations of regional interests placed on tenth-century royal authority'[73] as in the vocabulary of *Dena lagu* and *Engla lagu* contained in Anglo-Saxon laws from the tenth and eleventh centuries. And referring to a charter from the monastery of St Frideswide, she observes that 'in contemporary sources it is only in Oxford, remote from the main regions of earlier Scandinavian settlement, that the order can be shown to have been effected'.[74] From these perspectives, Æthelred's order was a response to an assassination plot targeting those suspected; whatever violence was carried out may have been limited to areas under English law (i.e. not the Danelaw), and those targeted were recognisably foreign men who should have been covered by the terms of the original peace. In this sense, the violation would have been seen as something akin to a regional rebellion and the response, as Wilcox suggests, something like a royal ravaging aimed at an ethnic population within regions under English law. Thus, it was not a genocide but a limited and legitimate, if violent, political response.[75]

---

[70] Hadley, 'Viking and Native', p. 53; Keynes, 'A Tale of Two Kings', p. 212. Cf. Reynolds, 'What Do We Mean By "Anglo-Saxon"?', pp. 409–10.
[71] Reynolds, 'What Do We Mean By "Anglo-Saxon"?', p. 409.
[72] Matthew Innes, 'Danelaw Identities: Ethnicity, Regionalism, and Political Allegiance', in *Cultures in Contact: Scandinavian Settlement in England in the Ninth and Tenth Centuries*, ed. Dawn M. Hadley and Julian D. Richards (Turnhout: Brepols, 2000), pp. 65–88.
[73] D. M. Hadley, 'Ethnicity and Acculturation', in *A Social History of England, 900–1200*, ed. Julia Crick and Elisabeth van Houts (Cambridge: Cambridge University Press, 2011), pp. 235–46 at p. 238.
[74] S 909 in P. H. Sawyer, *Anglo-Saxon Charters: An Annotated List and Bibliography* (London: Royal Historical Society, 1968); Hadley, 'Ethnicity and Acculturation', p. 239.
[75] Archaeologists have very tentatively drawn a possible association between a recently discovered mass burial in Oxford and the events of St Brice's Day narrated in the cartulary. Whether or not it is direct evidence of the massacre, the authors conclude 'that the execution of a captured raiding party is more likely than the slaughter of Oxford inhabitants of Danish descent'. A. M. Pollard, P. Ditchfield, E. Piva, S. Wallis, C. Falys and S. Ford, '"Sprouting Like Cockle Amongst the Wheat": The St Brice's Day Massacre and the Isotopic Analysis of Human Bones from St John's College, Oxford', *Oxford Journal of Archaeology* 31 (2012): 83–102 at p.83.

While events almost certainly played out as Hadley and Keynes describe them, there are challenges to such a muted reading of the story of the St Brice's Day massacre and how the events of the day were understood by contemporaries and later chroniclers. It is clear that acts of violence were carried out on St Brice's Day and met with approval from various commentators; Keynes goes so far as to say that 'it is easy to understand why in its day it might have been one of King Æthelred's more popular decisions'.[76] It also entered into historical narrative as a pogrom and not as a simple political ravaging. Æthelred faced rebellions and betrayals through much of his reign but never responded with anything comparable to the St Brice's Day massacre. Targeting an ethnic group for the betrayal, rather than just the plotters or the leaders of the Danish army, suggests that he viewed the plot as akin to the later understanding of the crime of *morð* – an uncompensable killing or a betrayal of one's lord for which an ethnic group was held collectively accountable. As Julia Barrow has shown, 'rebellion in Anglo-Saxon England […] was clearly a breach of the oath of loyalty to the ruler; moreover major acts of wrong-doing counted as a breach of loyalty and, if repeated often enough, made the accused notorious and thus un-lawworthy and liable to outlawry, while lands which he held from the king would be removed from him […] but evidently compromises were possible and sometimes necessary.'[77] Charter S 939 recounts Æthelred's granting of a request by a widow to drop an accusation of treason (a plot to receive the Danish Swein 'Forkbeard') against her dead (English) husband and to allow his will's disposal of property to the Church to stand.[78] Æthelred also forgave his son, Edmund 'Ironside', for raising an army and rebelling against him, as well as repeatedly receiving back Eadric *streona* after betrayals of varying degrees.[79] The focus of the Chronicle on all the 'densican men þe on Angelcynne wæron' suggests that the violation of the terms of the peace was not seen as comparable to a betrayal by an English nobleman or the rebellion of a region. Nor does the violation of peace explain Æthelred's response since renewed hostility immediately after peace-making

---

[76] Keynes, 'A Tale of Two Kings', p. 212.

[77] Julia Barrow, 'Demonstrative Behaviour and Political Communication in Later Anglo-Saxon England', *Anglo-Saxon England* 36 (2007): 127–50 at p. 136; see also: Ryan Lavelle, 'Representing Authority in an Early Medieval Chronicle: Submission, Rebellion and the Limits of the *Anglo-Saxon Chronicle*, c. 899–1065', in *Authority and Gender in Medieval and Renaissance Chronicles*, ed. J. Dresvina and N. Sparks (Newcastle-upon-Tyne: Cambridge Scholars, 2012), pp. 62–101 at p. 67.

[78] Edited and translated in N. P. Brooks and S. E. Kelly, *Anglo-Saxon Charters 18: Charters of Christ Church Canterbury, Part 2* (Oxford: Oxford University Press, 2013), pp. 1003–08. See: Lavelle, 'Representing Authority', p. 69.

[79] The most contemporary and complete record of his betrayals is the Anglo-Saxon Chronicle s.a. 1007–1017, but on the dating of the Chronicle CDE s.a. 983–1016, see: Keynes, 'A Tale of Two Kings'.

was fairly common.⁸⁰ Rather, the discourse that the Chronicle participates in emphasises that the crime violated lordship and the whole ethnic group was culpable. Indeed, these emphases on violated lordship and ethnicity are forcefully presented in the only relatively contemporary record of the St Brice's Day massacre. The charter from the monastery of St Frideswide, mentioned by Hadley, is the base line for analysis of the narrative, framing the events in ethnic terms and justifying them through a biblical parallel:⁸¹

> Omnibus enim in hac patria degentibus satis constat fore notissimum quoniam dum a me decretum cum consilio optimatum satrapumque meorum exiuit vt cuncti Dani, qui in hac insula velut lollium inter triticum pululando emerserant, iustissima examinacione necarentur, hoc que decretum morte tenus ad effectum perduceretur, ipsi qui in prefata vrbe morabantur Dani, mortem euadere nitentes, hoc Xpi sacrarium, fractis per vim valuis ac pessulis, intrantes asilum sibi repugnaculum que contra vrbanos suburbanos que inibi fieri decreuerunt, set cum populus omnis insequens, necessitate compulsus, eos eiicere niteretur nec valeret, igne tabulis iniecto, hanc Ecclesiam, vt liquet, cum ornamentis ac libris combusserunt.⁸²

> [For it is fully agreed that to all dwelling in this country it will be well known that, since a decree was sent out by me with the counsel of my leading men and magnates, to the effect that all the Danes who had sprung up in this island, like cockle amongst the wheat, were to be destroyed by a most just extermination, and this decree was to be put into effect even as far as death, those Danes who dwelt in the afore-mentioned town [Oxford], striving to escape death, entered this sanctuary of Christ, having broken by force the doors and bolts, and resolved to make a refuge and defence for themselves therein against the people of the town and suburbs; but when all the people in pursuit strove, forced by necessity, to drive them out, and could not, they set fire to the planks and burnt, as it seems, this church with its ornaments and its books].⁸³

While it is unclear how many people were affected at Oxford or who among the Danes was killed, the image is clearly of a mob set against a recognisable ethnic population. Yet in this earliest record is a literarily crafted narrative and, whether

---

⁸⁰ Lavelle, 'Representing Authority', p. 76.
⁸¹ The charter is dated to 1004, and although the extant copies of the cartulary are from much later, Stenton demonstrated its authenticity as a reliable contemporary witness. See: F. M. Stenton, 'St Frideswide and Her Times', *Oxoniensia* 1 (1936): 105–06; on the reliability of the document, cf. Keynes, 'The Massacre of St. Brice's Day', pp. 34–35.
⁸² Spencer Robert Wigram, ed., *The Cartulary of the Monastery of St. Frideswide at Oxford*, 2 vols (Oxford: Clarendon Press, 1895–1896), 1:2–3.
⁸³ Dorothy Whitelock, ed., *English Historical Documents* (London: Eyre & Spottiswoode, 1968), nos 127 and 545.

the massacre itself happened as claimed, there was already a discourse in play to recognise an ethnic problem and a justification to act on that.

The account also invokes a scriptural reference that offers a frame for interpreting the events. The charter's language of 'lollium inter triticum' is reminiscent of Matthew 13:25, 'zizania in medio tritici' [cockle amongst the wheat]. Moreover, the specific image in the charter of Æthelred's command to exterminate the 'Dani', followed by them gathering together in a church and being burned, correlates strongly with the lord's command in Matthew to gather and burn the cockle. The account associates the English with Christianity and operates within an English tradition of growing a heroic Christian history.[84] The destruction of the 'Dani' in a church may be indicative of a claim to an English Christian society as against a non-English, non-Christian population that was disrupting them. And although the burning of those in the church violates legal protections of sanctuary and the mention of the burning of the church with its ornaments and books implies a sense of loss, if not condemnation, the scriptural parallel guides interpretation of the image in the same way that, in *Beowulf*, Grendel's association with Cain defines the quality of his murders and the Flood imagery overwhelms the significance of killing a woman. While the charter account, dated to 1004, may follow the actual events at a remove of two years, it records a discourse that defines national identity by faith and fidelity to the lord. Moreover, as Niles suggests that in 'an act of poetic imagination' there are political implications, the charter provides a sense of how an act of historical imagination might draw on a recognisable narrative discourse to drive present political discourse.[85] The charter is evidence that the English did massacre a group of Scandinavians, at least in Oxford, on the order of King Æthelred and that they had a discourse to hand that not only legitimised the brutal murder of a group of foreigners but that also framed English and Danish ethnicities in terms of religion and lordship.

Considering the charter of St Frideswide as a point of comparison, elements of the Chronicle account stand out as concerned specifically with lordship, community and ethnic violence. The charter shapes a sense of English identity as distinct from Danish through their Christian faith, and Æthelred models his royal authority on the lord in Matthew. While only an echo, the grammatical parallel

---

[84] Robert Hanning, *The Vision of History in Early Britain* (New York: Columbia University Press, 1966), pp. 64–65. Nicholas Howe, *Migration and Mythmaking in Anglo-Saxon England* (New Haven: Yale University Press, 1989), argues that migration and conversion are the two dominant and repeated frames for discussing Anglo-Saxon historical memory and through these, 'Anglo-Saxon England found its myth of the past and the future. This myth may be thought of as a map of the imagination, as an ordering of experience into an evocative image by which the culture could sustain itself' (pp. 5–7).

[85] John D. Niles, *Homo Narrans: The Poetics and Anthropology of Oral Literature* (Philadelphia: University of Pennsylvania Press, 1999), p. 86.

of *Deniscan men þe on Angelcynne wæron* [the Danish men who were among the English race] with *lollium inter triticum* [cockle amongst the wheat] certainly raises concerns of lordship and community – the lord (*dominus*) orders the foreign plants to be separated from the wheat and destroyed. And Alice Sheppard has argued that the annals 978–1016 are a reflection on English identity as bound up with lordship.[86] As such, the record of the plot to assassinate Æthelred and all his counsellors after may present events as rebellion against the king; the massacre then takes on a specific 'ethnicised' quality that may be read against the later laws on *morð*, which held an ethnic group accountable for a violation of lordship. The plot against the king is itself a crime that could carry collective accountability, but the plot against a lord by a foreign people would be perceived as a plot against English identity itself.

It is likely that the events of the massacre were remembered by later historians as a pogrom because of the combination of a discourse of ethnic identities, collective responsibility for the plot and the tendency of Norman and post-Conquest historians to attribute the conquests of England by the Danes and the Normans to the moral failings of the English. These authors looked for ways to advocate for peace between peoples and to represent the St Brice's Day massacre as an example of the English exacerbating ethnic hostilities, not as defending against foreign invaders. As such, an early development of the legal concept of *morð* may have been elaborated into genocide in support of an idea of ethnic inclusion.[87] The accounts develop a narrative of Æthelred's violation of his own royal responsibilities, undermining the English nation but leaving the post-Conquest English redeemable under good lordship.

One text may stand as an example for all. In his *Gesta Normannorum Ducum*, probably composed over the course of the 1050s,[88] the Norman William of Jumièges takes up the St Brice's Day massacre and is the earliest author to express horror at it, elaborating the details of the massacre to portray it as a pogrom. But while William retains the emphases on lordship and ethnic violence that are present in the earlier accounts, his story is not that of a group held responsible

---

[86] Alice Sheppard, *Families of the King: Writing Identity in the Anglo-Saxon Chronicle* (Toronto: University of Toronto Press, 2004), pp. 88–92; see also: Lavelle, 'Representing Authority', p. 69.

[87] I discuss post-Conquest historians' use of Anglo-Saxon history to make political claims in their context in 'The "Worcester" Historians and Eadric *Streona*'s Execution', in *Capital and Corporal Punishment in Anglo-Saxon England*, ed. Jay Paul Gates and Nicole Marafioti (Woodbridge: Boydell Press, 2014), pp. 165–80.

[88] Elisabeth van Houts argues that William likely completed the *Gesta Normannorum Ducum* just before 1060 and then revised elements and added the account of the Norman conquest of England up to c. 1070: *The Gesta Normannorum Ducum of William of Jumièges, Orderic Vitalis, and Robert of Torigni*, ed. and trans. Elisabeth M. C. van Houts, vol. 1 (Oxford: Clarendon Press, 1992), pp. xx and xlvi–l.

for a violation; rather, he portrays community stability disrupted by the king and he establishes a redemptive model for the English people that would be picked up by later authors:[89]

> Cum in statu supra intellecto tam preclaro sub rectore Normannie felicitas polleret, rex Anglorum Edelredus regnum, quod sub magna potentissimorum regum gloria diu floruerat, tanto nefarie proditionis scelere sui regiminis tempore polluit, ut et pagani tam execrabile nefas horrendum iudicarent. Nam Danos per omne regnum unanimi concordia secum pacifice coabitantes, mortis periculum minime suspicantes, subito furore sub una die perimi, mulieres quoque aluo tenus terre esse defossas, et ferocissimis canibus concitatis mamillas ab earum pectoribus crudeliter extorqueri, lactentes uero pueros ad domorum postes allisos excerebrari iussit, nullis criminum existentibus culpis.

> [But while, as we learnt above, under such a famous ruler [i.e. Richard] the prosperity of Normandy grew, Æthelred, king of the English, defiled a kingdom that had long flourished under the great glory of most powerful kings with such a dreadful crime that in his own reign even the heathens judged it as a detestable, shocking deed. For in a single day he had murdered, in a sudden fury and without charging them with any crime, the Danes who lived peacefully and quite harmoniously throughout the kingdom and who did not at all fear for their lives. He ordered women to be buried up to the waists and the nipples to be torn from their breasts by ferocious mastiffs set upon them. He also gave orders to crush little children against door-posts].[90]

Although this account gives the most elaborate list of horrors of any of the early medieval authors that recounted the St Brice's Day massacre, it is to contrast Æthelred as a wicked lord with the good Norman Richard II (Æthelred's brother-in-law) and to justify the Danish conquest of England under Swein 'Forkbeard' in 1013. In this, William appears to collapse events more than a decade apart to explain a causal connection that sets up the flight of Æthelred,

---

[89] John of Worcester, *The Chronicle of John of Worcester, vol. II, The Annals from 450 to 1066*, ed. R. R. Darlington and P. McGurk, trans. Jennifer Bray and P. McGurk (Oxford: Clarendon Press, 1995), s.a. 1002, pp. 452–53; Henry, Archdeacon of Huntingdon, *Historia Anglorum: The History of the English People*, ed. and trans. Diana Greenway (Oxford: Clarendon Press, 1996), sect. VI.1, pp. 338–39; and William of Malmesbury, *Gesta Regum Anglorum Volume I*, II.165.12, ed. and trans. R. A. B. Mynors, R. M. Thomson and M. Winterbottom (Oxford: Clarendon Press, 1998), pp. 276–77. All pick up on aspects of William of Jumièges's version of the St Brice's Day massacre and use them to shape their own arguments for ethnic inclusion in post-Conquest England. Keynes, 'The Massacre of St Brice's Day', provides a full discussion of these accounts.

[90] William of Jumièges, *The Gesta Normannorum Ducum of William of Jumièges, Orderic Vitalis, and Robert of Torigni, Volume II, Books V–VIII*, ed. and trans. Elisabeth M. C. van Houts (Oxford: Clarendon Press, 1995), pp. 14–17.

and more importantly his sons, to Richard's court and the subsequent path of a Norman duke to the English throne.

Contrary to the charter of St Frideswide, in which the rhetoric drew on a familiar biblical parable to emphasise English ethnic and religious unity guided by Æthelred's good lordship, William's account presents the heathen Danes as living peaceably among the English and Æthelred as destroying England. There is no hint of law or justice here: the Danes have committed no crime and there is no assassination plot; rather, there is just a pogrom driven by a king's sudden fury. William's act of historical imagination focuses on the criminality of the massacre, making no clear reference to men, let alone warriors, as victims, and emphasising the brutal murders of women and children. Indeed, this is the first mention of women and children as victims in the massacre, and it makes the events even more horrible. However, William does permit the possibility of redemption: the crimes are the fault of a wicked and criminal king, not the English as a people. It is Æthelred who devises cruel means of murdering the women and children, not the English generally. For William, the English kingdom was once great and, it is implied, could be again under a good king. Indeed, at the time of writing, there was again a good English king, Edward 'the Confessor', who (so William recounts), had also appointed the Norman Duke William as his heir to the English throne.[91] Thus, in his account of the St Brice's Day massacre, William of Jumièges puts the whole of the responsibility on Æthelred and absolves the English people, giving them the opportunity to accept good and just rule, first of Edward and in anticipation of Duke William. The themes of failed lordship, possible English redemption and ethnic inclusion that William of Jumièges elaborated drive the post-Conquest English accounts of the St Brice's Day massacre. The authors largely share William's horror at the events – whether or not they choose to narrate the murders in detail – and reject large-scale ethnic pogroms. Of course, the English were, by the early twelfth century, a people conquered – but not exterminated – and the ethnic group that would be held collectively accountable for killing under the Norman *murdrum* laws. And yet, they, like William of Jumièges, seem to have held onto the core issues contained in the pre-Conquest English accounts of the St Brice's Day massacre: lordship, inter-ethnic violence and collective ethnic responsibility. However, by the time these authors took up the account, the discourses implicit in the Anglo-Saxon Chronicle and the St Frideswide charter were no longer current or relevant and so the accounts of the massacre shifted to accommodate new discourses and, in doing so, modified the events themselves.

Together, the accounts of the St Brice's Day massacre and *Beowulf* reveal a millennial political discourse connecting lordship, ethnic identity and community

[91] Ibid., pp. 158–159.

stability. *Beowulf* suggests that foreign aggression is monstrous, that inter-ethnic conflict carries dire consequences for the community beyond the warriors and that even good rule cannot ensure the long-term security of the community. In turn, it invites reflection on how to respond to violence and maintain community stability, including justifying by way of scriptural parallels the possibility of annihilating the foreign enemy. The St Frideswide charter includes a similar use of scripture to present the order by Æthelred and his counsellors to exterminate an ethnically distinct enemy as a just means of defending the English community. Yet, holding the ethnic group as a whole responsible for a plot against the king's life may also show an early instantiation of the legal concept of *morð* as 'corporate liability' for a violation of lordship. As lordship and English identity were increasingly linked discursively over the course of the tenth century, the murder plot appears as a threat to the English community itself. The association of the massacre with *morð* must have been an easy one for the Anglo-Saxon Chronicle's audience since *morð* as a legal policy was instituted after Cnut's conquest, and the chronicler may easily have retained an earlier ethnicising discourse comparable to that of the charter. However, for the chroniclers after the Norman Conquest, the tables had been turned and ethnicising discourse worked against the English. Later accounts of the massacre were also engaged with questions of inter-ethnic conflict and the relationships between lordship and community stability, but they were looking for a way to harmonise the peoples. Although *murdrum* was fully in place under the Normans in England, to represent the massacre as such would simply have exacerbated conflict. The post-Conquest English chroniclers who addressed the St Brice's Day massacre were looking for a way to resist claims of ethnic difference and so presented the massacre as a failure of lordship and the English as redeemable under a good king. The elaboration of the events of the St Brice's Day massacre into a literary narrative by chroniclers is the reason that the St Brice's Day massacre was remembered as a genocide rather than what it likely was, a political response to a treaty violation and a betrayal of the king through an assassination plot – something that very much resembles the murder laws of *morð* and *murdrum*.

CHAPTER 3

Mourning Murderers in Medieval Jewish Law

Pinchas Roth

MEDIEVAL JEWISH LAW (Halakhah) followed closely in the wake of the classic period of rabbinic jurisprudence, as recorded in the Talmudic corpus of Late Antiquity (c. 100–500 CE). Although the rabbis of the Talmud ostensibly recognised the Bible as their foundational source, profound differences between the biblical and rabbinic legal systems abound and do not elicit any particular anxiety in the Talmud. While the Bible repeatedly declared that a murderer should be punished by death, it did not spell out the form or procedure of that punishment.[1] By contrast, Talmudic law sets out very detailed rules for capital punishment, including decapitation for murderers.[2] The Mishnah (a classic rabbinic text redacted in Palestine around 200 CE) recognises four forms of capital punishment – stoning, burning, strangulation and decapitation. Decapitation is referred to by the generic term 'killing' (*hereg*):

מצוות הנהרגין. היו מתיזים את ראשו בסייף כדרך שהמלכות עושה.

[The law of those who are executed by killing – they would remove his head with a sword, as the [Roman] empire does] (mSanhedrin 7, 3).[3]

The Mishnah lists only two crimes punished by decapitation:[4]

---

[1] Pamela Barmash, *Homicide in the Biblical World* (Cambridge: Cambridge University Press, 2005).
[2] Victor Aptowitzer, 'Observations on the Criminal Law of the Jews', *Jewish Quarterly Review* 15 (1924): 55–118, esp. pp. 82–85; Aharon Shemesh, *Punishments and Sins: From Scripture to the Rabbis* (Jerusalem: Magnes Press, 2003), pp. 127–45; Devora Steinmetz, *Punishment and Freedom: The Rabbinic Construction of Criminal Law* (Philadelphia: University of Pennsylvania Press, 2008), pp. 53–68; Yair Lorberbaum, *In God's Image: Myth, Theology, and Law in Classical Judaism* (Cambridge: Cambridge University Press, 2015), pp. 124–34.
[3] Following Parma, Biblioteca Palatina (BP), MS 3173. All translations are mine unless otherwise noted.
[4] The enumeration of the four categories of capital punishment occupies chapters 7–9 and 11 of tractate Sanhedrin of the Mishnah.

ואלו הן הנהרגים – הרוצח ואנשי עיר הנדחת

[These are the ones who are executed by killing – the murderer, and the people of the idolatrous city] (mSanhedrin 9, 1).

All the laws of capital punishment in the Mishnah were probably already unenforceable at the time they were formulated in late-antique Palestine, then part of the Roman empire.[5] Roman law accepted the possibility of Jewish religious or national leaders functioning as legal authorities, but this was explicitly limited to civil law and treated as a form of arbitration, without full legal authority.[6] In the centuries that followed, Jewish legal autonomy became even more curtailed as communities scattered throughout the Diaspora and found themselves in different, often precarious, situations in Asia, North Africa and Europe.[7] But although capital punishment was not physically meted out by Jewish courts, as part of the rabbinic legal corpus, the laws pertaining to execution were studied, elaborated and debated. While strictly theoretical, this body of law continued to occupy the attention of rabbinic scholars for centuries and to influence the ways in which they conceptualised judicial violence. The ambivalence of many classic rabbinic texts regarding the justice and morality of capital punishment reverberates within later discussions, from the Middle Ages and beyond. Among those texts, a particularly striking theme is the problematisation of mourning for executed criminals.

The state of Jewish legal autonomy differed from place to place in respect to local attitudes towards Jewish communities and their rights and according to the state of local non-Jewish court systems. The Jews of medieval Iberia had a fairly high opinion of the non-Jewish courts at their disposal and often made use of them.[8] At the same time, at least until the late fourteenth century, Jewish

---

[5] Beth Berkowitz, *Execution and Invention: Death Penalty Discourse in Early Rabbinic and Christian Cultures* (Oxford: Oxford University Press, 2006). On Jewish legal autonomy during the rabbinic period, see: H. P. Chajes, 'Les juges juifs en Palestine de l'an 70 à l'an 500', *Revue des etudes juives* 39 (1899): 39–52 (updated Hebrew translation in *Shenaton ha-Mishpat ha-Ivri* 20 (1997): 429–43); Jill Harries, 'Courts and the Judicial System', in *Oxford Handbook of Jewish Daily Life in Roman Palestine*, ed. Catherine Hezser (Oxford: Oxford University Press, 2010), pp. 85–101.

[6] Amnon Linder, *The Jews in Roman Imperial Legislation* (Detroit: Wayne State University Press, 1987), pp. 204–11.

[7] Generally, see: Simhah Assaf, *Ha-Onashin ahare hatimat ha-Talmud* [*Punishments after the Close of the Talmud*] (Tel Aviv: Ha-Poel ha-Zair, 1922); Simhah Assaf, *Bate ha-din ve-sidrehem ahar hatimat ha-Talmud* [*The Courts and their Procedures after the Close of the Talmud*] (Jerusalem: Defus-ha-po'alim, 1924). For specific regions, see below.

[8] Yom Tov Assis, 'Jewish Attitudes to Christian Power in Medieval Spain', *Sefarad* 52 (1992): 291–304; Elka Klein, *Jews, Christian Society, and Royal Power in Medieval Barcelona* (Ann Arbor: University of Michigan Press, 2006), pp. 49–50; Alexandra Eni Paiva

communities maintained the right to execute their own criminals.[9] That punishment, however, was reserved for people whose actions harmed the community as a whole – especially informers.[10] Capital, or even corporal, punishment of murderers by the Jewish community was a rare occurrence.[11] In any case, it was decreed and carried out by Jewish lay leaders according to their political needs and not by religious judges following the rabbinic penal code.

In Northern Europe as well, Jews sometimes availed themselves of Christian courts.[12] However, that use was more circumspect and was perceived within the community as a negative, potentially dangerous phenomenon.[13] When a dispute arose between Jews, the communal expectation was that they would resolve the dispute within the bounds of the community, whether through a local Jewish court, an *ad hoc* local Jewish arbitrator or a regional Jewish authority. That said, Jews had the right to turn to non-Jewish legal authorities, and at times they did so in the hope of achieving results that they had not managed to achieve through Jewish tribunals. However, involving gentile courts was perceived as undermining the authority of communal leadership and possibly opening up internal Jewish practices and norms to outside scrutiny and control. Communal rules from Northern Europe spelled out the punishment for Jews who crossed the line

---

Guerson de Oliviera, 'Coping with Crises: Christian-Jewish Relations in Catalonia and Aragon, 1380–1391', PhD dissertation (University of Toronto, 2012), pp. 109–117.

[9] Yom Tov Assis, *The Golden Age of Aragonese Jewry: Community and Society in the Crown of Aragon, 1213–1327* (London: Littman Library, 1997), pp. 288–96; Yom Tov Assis, 'Crime and Violence among the Jews of Spain (13th–14th Centuries)', *Zion* 50 (1985): 221–240; Itzhak Brand, 'Religious Recognition of Autonomous Secular Law: The Sitz im Leben of R. Nissim of Girona's Homily (no. 11)', *Harvard Theological Review* 105 (2012): 163–88; Marc Saperstein, *Leadership and Conflict: Tensions in Medieval and Early Modern Jewish History and Culture* (Oxford: Littman Library, 2014), pp. 31–42.

[10] David Kaufmann, 'Jewish Informers in the Middle Ages', *Jewish Quarterly Review* 8 (1896): 217–38; Ilana Lourie, 'Mafiosi and Malsines: Violence, Fear and Faction in the Jewish Aljamas of Valencias in the Fourteenth Century', *Actas del III congreso internacional encuentro de las tres culturas*, ed. Carlos Carrete Parrondo (Toledo: Ayuntamiento de Toledo, 1988), pp. 69–102, republished in Elena Lourie, *Crusade and Colonisation: Muslims, Christians and Jews in Medieval Aragon* (Aldershot: Variorum, 1990), essay XII.

[11] Saperstein, *Leadership and Conflict*, pp. 37–40; Assis, 'Crime and Violence', pp. 236–38.

[12] Rachel Furst, 'Striving for Justice: A History of Women and Litigation in the Jewish Courts of Medieval Ashkenaz', PhD dissertation (Hebrew University of Jerusalem, 2014), pp. 57–66.

[13] Moses Frank, *Kehilot Ashkenaz u-bate dinehen* [*The Communities of Ashkenaz and Their Courts*] (Tel Aviv: Devir, 1938), pp. 117–23; Leo Landman, *Jewish Law in the Diaspora: Confrontation and Accommodation* (Philadelphia: Dropsie College, 1968), pp. 86–103; Esriel Hildesheimer, 'The Provision against Gentile Courts in Late Medieval Ashkenaz: Halacha and Practice', in *Proceedings of the Tenth World Congress of Jewish Studies*, 3 vols (Jerusalem: World Union of Jewish Studies, 1989), 1:217–24; Birgit Klein, 'Jewish Legal Autonomy in the Middle Ages: An Unchallenged Institution?', *Zutot* 3 (2003): 121–34.

by involving non-Jewish authorities in internal disagreements.[14] Nevertheless, there were Jews who chose to run that risk, and there were many more who used it as leverage, threatening to turn to non-Jewish courts if their demands were not met by Jewish authorities.

Southern France, in this respect as in many others, appears similar to Northern Europe in the twelfth century but later shifted closer to Iberia.[15] According to records from the thirteenth century onwards, Jews often used non-Jewish courts for civil and criminal cases against Jews and against Christians.[16] That shift seems to be linked to the spread of Roman law throughout the Western Mediterranean during the twelfth and thirteenth centuries.[17] Roman law, with its codified rules and procedures, was perceived (by Jews and Christians alike) as being more rational and trustworthy than customary law and, therefore, worth using.[18] In Southern France, at least, that period marks the decline of Jewish civil courts dealing with monetary matters, as the non-Jewish alternative was more efficient and accessible, and, henceforth, Jews turned to rabbinic courts only for matters of personal status (marriage and divorce).[19]

Moving from civil to criminal law, the situation becomes more complex since the Roman legal tradition that made room for autonomous Jewish courts of

---

[14] Louis Finkelstein, *Jewish Self-Government in the Middle Ages*, 2nd edn (New York: Philipp Feldheim, 1964), pp. 150–160.

[15] On Jewish culture in southern France and its shifting northern-southern orientation, see: Isadore Twersky, 'Aspects of the Social and Cultural History of Provençal Jewry', *Journal of World History* 11 (1968): 185–207; reprinted in I. Twersky, *Studies in Jewish Law and Philosophy* (New York: Ktav, 1982), pp. 180–202.

[16] Joseph Shatzmiller, *Recherches sur la communauté juive de Manosque au Moyen Age, 1241–1329* (Paris: Mouton, 1973), pp. 65–118.

[17] On the spread of Roman law from Italy into southern France during the twelfth and thirteenth centuries, see: André Gouron, *La science du droit dans le Midi de la France au Moyen Âge* (London: Variorum, 1984); Jean-Pierre Poly, 'Les légistes Provençaux et la diffusion du droit romain dans le Midi', *Mélanges Roger Aubenas* (Montpellier: Université, 1974), pp. 613–35; John H. Pryor, *Business Contracts of Medieval Provence: Selected Notulae from the Cartulary of Giraud Amalric of Marseilles, 1248* (Toronto: Pontifical Institute of Medieval Studies, 1981), pp. 22–26. For a reflection of this shift from within rabbinic literature, see: Haym Soloveitchik, 'A Note on the Penetration of Roman Law in Provence', *Tijdschrift voor Rechtsgeschiedenis* 40 (1972): 227–29.

[18] Daniel Lord Smail, *The Consumption of Justice: Emotions, Publicity, and Legal Culture in Marseiile, 1264–1423* (Ithaca: Cornell University Press, 2003), pp. 29–88; Landman, *Jewish Law in the Diaspora*, pp. 104–14; Haym Soloveitchik, 'Rabad of Posquieres: A Programmatic Essay', in *Studies in the History of Jewish Society in the Middle Ages and in the Modern Period*, ed. E. Etkes and Y. Salmon (Jerusalem: Magnes Press, 1980), pp. 31–34.

[19] I hope to expand upon this point in the near future. For now, see: Shlomo H. Pick, 'The Jewish Communities of Provence Before the Expulsion in 1306', PhD dissertation (Bar-Ilan University, Ramat-Gan 1996), pp. 250–62; Pinchas Roth, 'Legal Strategy and Legal Culture in Medieval Jewish Courts of Southern France', *AJS Review* 38.2 (2014): 375–93.

arbitration also explicitly deprived Jewish courts of authority in criminal cases.[20] Nevertheless, some medieval Jewish communities did possess the power to punish Jewish offenders corporally, although it is not always clear whether this power was *de jure* or *de facto*, or indeed to what degree this power was used.[21] However, whether Jewish courts were empowered to punish them or not, violent Jewish criminals did exist in medieval Europe, as recent scholarship has demonstrated.[22] In practice, Jewish courts often simply ignored murderers or dealt with them in non-legal ways.[23] Murderers could be placed under ban or excommunication by the court. More often, though, murder was dealt with as a religious violation concerning the individual murderer's standing before God and requiring repentance rather than social sanction – thus entirely sidestepping problems of jurisdiction and legal procedure.[24] The murder did not need to be investigated, witnesses need not be called and cross-examined, laws both civic and Talmudic could be overlooked and the perpetrator's confession was sufficient to brand him guilty.[25] Prescriptions of penance for murderers can be found in a number of medieval rabbinic sources, and one version may date back

---

[20] See above.
[21] Assaf, *Ha-onashin*; Israel Ta-Shma, 'Rabbi Isaac of Dampierre's Responsum Concerning Informers', *Zion* 68 (2003): 167–74; Stephen M. Passamaneck, *Modalities in Medieval Jewish Law for Public Order and Safety* (Cincinnati: Hebrew Union College Press, 2009).
[22] Elliott Horowitz, *Reckless Rites: Purim and the Legacy of Jewish Violence* (Princeton: Princeton University Press, 2006); Israel J. Yuval, *Two Nations in Your Womb: Perceptions of Jews and Christians in Late Antiquity and the Middle Ages*, trans. B. Harshav and J. Chipman (Berkeley: University of California Press, 2006); Ephraim Shoham-Steiner, 'The Medieval Jewish Underworld: Jewish Involvement in Crime in Medieval Europe', Tikvah Working Paper 08/11: http://www.nyutikvah.org/pubs/1011/0811Steiner.html (accessed 6 September 2015); Ephraim Shoham-Steiner, *The Medieval Jewish Underworld: Jews and Crime in Medieval Europe* (Detroit, MI: Wayne State University Press, forthcoming); Simcha Emanuel, 'Fires and Crimes in the Late Middle Ages: Testimonies from the Halachic Literature', in *Asufa le-Yosef: Studies in Jewish History Presented to Joseph Hacker*, ed. Yaron Ben-Naeh et al. (Jerusalem: Zalman Shazar Center, 2014), pp. 157–69; Alexandra Guerson, 'Death in the Aljama of Huesca: The Jews and Royal Taxation in Fourteenth-Century Aragon', *Sefarad* 75 (2015): 35–63. See also: Michael Stanislawski, *A Murder in Lemberg: Politics, Religion and Violence in Modern Jewish History* (Princeton: Princeton University Press, 2007).
[23] Furst, 'Striving for Justice', pp. 33–35; Aaron Kirschenbaum, *Jewish Penology: The Theory and Development of Criminal Punishment among the Jews Throughout the Ages* (Jerusalem: Magnes Press, 2013), pp. 494–502.
[24] Shlomo Eidelberg, *Jewish Life in Austria in the XVth Century* (Philadelphia: Dropsie College, 1962), pp. 87–91.
[25] Aaron Kirschenbaum, *Self-Incrimination in Jewish Law* (New York: Burning Bush Press, 1970).

to the Geonic period (i.e. eighth- to tenth-century Iraq).²⁶ Those prescriptions emphasise their voluntary nature as distinct from formal court procedure:

ההורג נפש בזמן הזה אין בידינו לעשות לו מאומה, לא להורגו ולא לחובשו ולא להגלותו, אלא לימנע ממנו שלא להתערב עמו... במה דברים אמורים במסרב כנגד הקהילות ואינו מתנחם ומקבל דין, אבל אם ניחם אחרי שפכו דם אחיו, ורוצה לקבל דין, דנים אותו ברצונו כדמיית קין.

[Someone who kills a person in the present day, there is nothing that we can do to him – neither to kill him, nor to imprison him nor to exile him, but simply to avoid interacting with him … This is true of someone who defies the communities, does not show remorse and will not accept judgment. But if he is remorseful after spilling his brother's blood and he wants to be judged, we judge him as he asks like Cain].²⁷

More often, medieval Jews accused of crimes came before non-Jewish courts. On the whole, rabbinic law adopted the Talmudic adage of Samuel (from third-century Iraq): 'The law of the kingdom is the law', meaning that the surrounding legal system was recognised as authoritative by Jewish courts.²⁸ This adage was applied quite routinely to civil law, and rules governing taxation and other monetary areas imposed by whichever form of authority held sway in a particular region would be recognised by Jewish judges as binding even within the system of Halakhah.²⁹ As Ron S. Kleinman writes, 'According to Jewish law, in monetary matters the parties to a transaction may stipulate their own conditions, and local custom is regarded as an implied condition in the transaction'.³⁰ Thus, local law could be recognised and upheld even if it contradicted Talmudic law since both

---

26 Moshe Hershler, 'Teshuvot Geonim ve-Kadmonim (Responsa of Geonim and Ancient Authorities)', *Sinai* 66 (1970): 173–77; Jacob Elbaum, *Repentance and Self-Flagellation in the Writings of the Sages of Germany and Poland 1348–1648* (Jerusalem: Magnes Press, 1992), p. 19 n. 3; Avishai Bar-Asher, 'Penance and Fasting in the Writings of Rabbi Moshe de León and the Zoharic Polemic with Contemporary Christian Monasticism', *Kabbalah* 25 (2012): 306.

27 Hershler, 'Teshuvot Geonim', pp. 173–74. The first sentence is cited, in the name of Sherira Gaon, by Rabbi Isaac ben Moses of Vienna (mid thirteenth century) in *Or Zarua*, ed. Yaakov Farbstein (Jerusalem: Machon Yerushalayim, 2010), 1:112 and 1:105, and the entire passage is also found in Parma, BP, MS 2092 (de Rossi no. 1237), fol. 168v.

28 Babylonian Talmud, Baba Kamma 113a; Baba Batra 55a.

29 Landman, *Jewish Law in the Diaspora*; Shmuel Shilo, *Dina de-Malkhuta Dina: The Law of the State is Law* (Jerusalem: Jerusalem Academic Press, 1974); Gil Graff, *Separation of Church and State: Dina de-Malkhuta Dina in Jewish Law, 1750–1848* (Birmingham, AL: University of Alabama Press, 1985); Sylvie Ann Goldberg, 'Common Law and Jewish Law: The Diasporic Principle of dina de-malkhuta dina', *Behemoth: A Journal on Civilisation* 2 (2008): 39–53; Ron S. Kleinman, 'Civil Law as Custom: Jewish Law and Secular Law – Do They Diverge or Converge?', *Review of Rabbinic Judaism* 14 (2011): 11–36.

30 Kleinman, 'Civil Law as Custom', p. 13.

parties to the suit shared their acceptance of prevailing local legal conditions. By contrast, the right of a regime to impose corporal or capital punishment upon a Jew lacked this legal basis and was more difficult (though not impossible) to justify in Jewish terms.[31] However, when the punishment was already *fait accompli*, Halakhists could reflect upon it in a less prescriptive and more revealing way. Their attitude to the punishment would reflect whether they felt that the punishing court was fundamentally prejudiced against Jews and could not judge them fairly, or, conversely, that they expected Jewish murderers to be punished in the same way as a non-Jew accused of the same crime. This range of attitudes colours Jewish legal sources that discuss whether or not to mourn a Jewish murderer who was executed by Christian justice. Mourning executed Jewish murderers in the normal manner could stem from an underlying suspicion that their execution was unjust. Treating such dead Jews in an abnormal way, by refraining from formal mourning customs, could be an expression of solidarity with the justice system that took their lives. By contrast, observing their deaths in the normal manner was not only a way of embracing them, in death, back into the circles of family and community but also of protesting their loss. The Rabbis of the Mishnah, who were consumed by their own fear that the penal system they had devised might lead to the erroneous execution of innocent people, interpreted even the ostensibly standard mourning ritual as an accusatory statement by the relatives of the dead criminals. When the medieval heirs of those rabbis prescribed normative mourning for executed Jews, they were essentially expressing their lack of responsibility for those deaths. If the rabbis felt implicated by the execution, and if they identified with the authoritative system that imposed it, they would at least raise the possibility that the dead should not be mourned.

According to Talmudic law, grieving (as an internal emotional process) is unregulated, but formal mourning begins only after burial and then continues for an intense period of seven days (often referred to as *shiva*, seven) followed by more relaxed mourning periods of thirty days and one year.[32] Jewish burial in late antique Palestine was performed in two stages. First, the body was laid, wrapped in shrouds, in a cave; a year later, once the flesh had decayed, the bones were interred in an ossuary, a trough, or in a niche within the cave. Both stages

---

[31] Shilo, *Dina de-Malkhuta Dina*, pp. 264–75.

[32] See generally: Maurice Lamm, *The Jewish Way in Death and Mourning* (New York: David, 1969). According to bMoed Katan 27a, the mourning period begins only after the stone has been rolled over the cave entrance. Medieval rabbis considered different ways in which this ruling would apply in their times when corpses were buried in the ground and not in caves. See: Samson ben Abraham of Sens, commentary on mOhalot 2:1.

of burial were occasions of mourning and memorialisation by the family of the deceased.[33]

Not so for criminals. The Mishnah mandated a modified ritual for those executed by a rabbinic court:[34]

ולא היו קוברין אתן בקברות אבותיהן אלא שני קברות היו מותקנין לבית דין, אחד לניסקלין ולנשרפין ואחד לנהרגים ולנחנקים. נתאכל הבשר היו מלקטים את העצמות וקוברים אותן במקום. והקרובים באין ושואלים את שלום העדים ואת שלום הדיינים, כלומר דעו שאין בליבינו עליכם, שדין אמת דנתם. ולא היו מתאבלין אלא אוננין שאין אנינה אלא בלב.

[They would not bury them in the graves of their fathers. Rather, there were two graves allocated for the court – one for those [executed by] stoning and burning, and one for those by decapitation and strangling. When the flesh was consumed, they would collect the bones and bury them in that place. The relatives come and inquire after the welfare of the witnesses and of the judges, as if to say, 'Know that we have nothing in our hearts against you, for your judgment was true'. And they would not mourn, but would only grieve, for grief is only in the heart (mSanhedrin 6:5–6)].[35]

The principle was that executed criminals were not to be mourned by their families, and the implied rationale was that such mourning could be perceived as an accusation of injustice directed at those responsible for their deaths – namely, the rabbinic court.[36] The public mourning ceremony could become a political statement about the legitimacy of the rabbinic court, and, therefore, it was eliminated in order to uphold the public standing of the legal system.

The Babylonian Talmud (composed in Babylonia c. 200–500) extrapolated further insight from this rule by contrasting such criminals with people executed by agents of a (non-Jewish) political regime:

---

[33] Jodi Magness, *The Archaeology of the Holy Land* (Cambridge: Cambridge University Press, 2012), pp. 230–55; Gideon Avni, Uzi Dahari and Amos Kloner, *The Necropolis of Bet Guvrin-Eleutheropolis* (Jerusalem: Israel Antiquities Authority, 2008), pp. 209–16.

[34] As noted above, these laws were not a reflection of actual practice at the time of the Mishnah when the rabbis did not possess the power or authority to perform executions.

[35] For the Roman legal reality at the time, see: J. G. Cook, 'Crucifixion and Burial', *New Testament Studies* 57 (2011): 193–213.

[36] On rabbinic anxiety about the justice that could be achieved in rabbinic courts, see: Chaya Halberstam, 'The Impossibility of Judgement', in *Law and Truth in Biblical and Rabbinic Literature* (Bloomington: Indiana University Press, 2010), pp. 76–105. For a similar concern in medieval Christian thought, see: James Q. Whitman, *The Origins of Reasonable Doubt: Theological Roots of the Criminal Trial* (New Haven: Yale University Press, 2008). I am grateful to the anonymous reader for this reference.

אמ' ליה אביי – מאי קא מדמית הרוגי מלכות להרוגי בית דין? הרוגי מלכות כיון דשלא
כדין קא מיקטלי הויא להו כפרה. הרוגי בית דין כיון דכדין קא מיקטלי, לא הויא להו כפרה.
תידע דהא תנן לא היו קוברין אות' בקברו' אבותיהן.

[Abaye retorted: Would you compare those who are slain by a Kingdom[37] to those who are executed by the rabbinic court? The former, since their death is not in accordance with law, obtain forgiveness; but the latter, whose death is justly merited, are not forgiven. This can also be proved from what we learnt [in the Mishnah]: They would not bury them in the graves of their fathers'].[38]

For the Talmud, the ban on mourning criminals is not a measure to stifle anger against the justice system. It is an indication of ontological, or at least religious, reality – criminals are not mourned because they are not forgiven. They are also buried outside their patriarchal grounds because, as the Talmud explained, 'We do not bury the wicked with the righteous'.[39]

By stark contrast, people who were killed by government agents were perceived not as criminals but victims because the decision to execute them was 'not in accordance with law'. They were killed, not because they were found guilty in a (rabbinic) court of law, but as part of an arbitrary abuse of power by those in control. According to Solomon ben Isaac of Troyes (known by the acronym Rashi, d. 1105), the pre-eminent medieval exegete of the Talmud, the government in question here was a Gentile one.[40] The context of the Talmudic discussion, which invokes biblical verses about foreign violence against Israel,

---

[37] 'Kingdom' in rabbinic parlance is often a reference to the Roman empire. Beth Berkowitz, *Defining Jewish Difference: From Antiquity to the Present* (Cambridge: Cambridge University Press, 2012), pp. 102, 142.

[38] Babylonian Talmud, Sanhedrin 47a–b (Jerusalem, Yad ha-Rav Herzog, MS 1); translation adapted from *The Babylonian Talmud*, ed. I. Epstein (London: Soncino Press, 1935–1948). See also: *The Tractate Mourning (Semahot)*, chap. 2, sect. 6, trans. Dov Zlotnick (New Haven: Yale University Press, 1966), p. 34.

[39] bSanhedrin 47a. A similar attitude can be found in early medieval Christianity in Northern Europe. Andrew Reynolds, *Anglo-Saxon Deviant Burial Customs* (Oxford: Oxford University Press, 2009); Duncan Sayer, 'Christian Burial Practice in the Early Middle Ages: Rethinking the Anglo-Saxon Funerary Sphere', *History Compass* 11 (2013): 133–46; Anne Iren Riisøy, 'Deviant Burials: Societal Exclusion of Dead Outlaws in Medieval Norway', in *Cultures of Death and Dying in Medieval and Early Modern Europe* ed. Mia Korpiola and Anu Lahtinen (Helsinki: University of Helsinki, 2015) pp. 49–81. For a similar policy in late medieval France, see: Esther Cohen, *The Crossroads of Justice: Law and Culture in Late Medieval France* (Leiden: Brill, 1993), pp. 195–201.

[40] Rashi ad loc. (Tractate Sanhedrin, Daniel Bomberg: Venice, 1520), s.v. *Haruge malkhut*: 'Those of the nations' (הני דאומות). Later printings of the Talmud were censored, and Rashi's words were changed to 'Those of the idol worshippers' (הני דעובדי כוכבים). As mentioned above (n. 37), the Talmud was probably referring to the Roman empire.

strongly supports his explanation.[41] But Moses Maimonides (d. Egypt 1204) understood the term to refer to agents of a Jewish king:

כל הרוגי מלכות, אף על פי שבדין המלך נהרגו והתורה נתנה לו רשות להורגן, הרי אלו מתאבלין עליהן ואין מונעין מהן כל דבר, וממונם למלך ונקברין בקברי אבותיהן. אבל כל הרוגי בית דין, אין מתאבלין עליהן אבל אוננין, שאין אנינות אלא בלב, ואין נקברין עם אבותיהן עד שיתאכל הבשר, וממונם ליורשיהם.

> [In the case of those who are executed by the State, although they are put to death by order of the king, who is empowered by Scripture to do so, their relatives observe mourning for them and do not deny them any of the rites (performed for the dead); their property goes to the king, and they are buried in their ancestral tombs.
>
> For those, however, who are executed by order of the court, no mourning rites are observed; but the relatives grieve for them, for grief is a matter of the heart; they are not buried with their ancestors until their flesh has wasted away; and their property passes to their heirs].[42]

For Maimonides, the distinction is not between Jewish and non-Jewish authority but between justice and power. People sentenced to death by (Jewish) courts die justly, while those killed by (Jewish) royal mandate do not. Although the Jewish monarchy that Maimonides had in mind was a utopian ideal, it was still a political institution whose goal was public order and stability – not justice. As Aviezer Ravitzky, an expert on medieval Jewish political thought, explains:

> Maimonides ... allowed the king to act beyond the accepted halakhic context if the circumstances so required, but only in matters involving bloodshed (e.g. pronouncing a death sentence on a murderer even if the strict laws of evidence did not allow this). It is the judges of Israel, not the king, who are allowed to deviate from the law in broad spheres, whereas the king's authority to deviate is confined to a well-defined domain. In this matter the law of the king is prevented from expanding and developing into a system of laws parallel to, and competing with, the 'law of the Torah'.[43]

---

[41] The immediate context of Abaye's statement on bSanhedrin 47a is Psalms 79: 'O God, the heathen are come into thine inheritance; they have defiled Thy holy temple; they have made Jerusalem into heaps. They have given the dead bodies of thy servants to be food unto the fowls of the heaven, the flesh of thy saints unto the beasts of the earth.' The Talmud explains that 'thy saints' are those who are truly holy, but 'thy servants' are criminals who were in fact liable for death but were killed by 'the heathen'.

[42] *The Code of Maimonides: Book Fourteen: The Book of Judges*, trans. Abraham M. Hershman (New Haven: Yale University Press, 1949), p. 165.

[43] Aviezer Ravitzky, *History and Faith: Studies in Jewish Philosophy* (Amsterdam: J. C. Gieben, 1996), pp. 51–52. See further: Gerald J. Blidstein, '"Ideal" and "Real" in Classical Jewish Political Theory: From the Talmud to Abrabanel', *The Quest for Utopia: Jewish Political Ideas and Institutions Through the Ages*, ed. Zvi Gitelman (Armonk: M. E.

Thus, the important question is not one of legitimacy, but of legality. A person found guilty in a court of law and subsequently executed was a criminal and was not to be mourned. Maimonides recognised that considerations of public order and stability often led kings to kill people they considered dangerous, and he sketched out the constitutional grounds and limits of royal power within a utopian Jewish kingdom. But execution by a king, even by the divinely endorsed King David or his descendant of Messianic times, was still the result of non-legal considerations of public policy, and the victim must be mourned.

Maimonides was particularly influential among the Jews of medieval Provence and Languedoc, and much of the rabbinic literature in that region was written in his wake.[44] One of those legal works composed in Southern France is a now-lost book titled *Zot Ḥukat ha-Torah* [*This is the Law of the Torah*].[45] The identity of its author is unknown, but he was a recognised rabbinic authority in late thirteenth-century Provence.[46] In one of the surviving fragments of *Zot Ḥukat ha-Torah*, the author quoted Maimonides' ruling on mourning the victims of (Jewish) royal execution but not those of (Jewish) judicial execution, and added:

ואומ' אני כי ה"ה נמי בהרוגי אומות העולם אם בדין הרגוהו. דאין קוברי' אותם בקברי אבותיהם דומי' דרשע אצל צדיק

[And I say that this is also true of those executed by Gentiles, if they were killed justly. They are not buried in the graves of their fathers, just like the wicked with the righteous].[47]

The distinction drawn by Maimonides between the violence of kings and judges allowed this Provençal rabbi to liberate this law entirely from its ethnic context. Jews executed by order of non-Jewish courts were considered 'wicked' and unworthy of standard burial, just like criminals executed by a Jewish court, because their punishment was prescribed by a legal entity. By contrast, following Maimonides, he would say that Jews killed by royal mandate deserved full

Sharpe, 1992), pp. 47–53; Gerald J. Blidstein, *Political Concepts in Maimonidean Halakha* (Ramat-Gan: Bar Ilan University Press, 2001).

[44] James T. Robinson, 'We Drink Only from the Master's Water: Maimonides and Maimonideanism in Southern France, 1200–1306', *Studia Rosenthaliana* 40 (2007–2008): 27–60.

[45] cf. Numbers 19:2.

[46] Pinchas Roth, 'Later Provençal Sages – Jewish Law (Halakhah) and Rabbis in Southern France, 1215–1348', PhD dissertation (Hebrew University of Jerusalem, 2012), pp. 117–20.

[47] New York, Jewish Theological Seminary of America (JTSA), MS Rab. 653, fol. 64r; St Petersburg, Russian National Library (RNL), MS Evr. IV 6, fol. 55v. In both manuscripts, the comment is found as a gloss in the margins of Sefer Mitzvot Katan and is identified at the end of the gloss as originating in *Zot Ḥukat ha-Torah*.

mourning whether the king who ordered their death was Jewish or not. In other words, while a Jewish king would not practise 'justice', a Gentile court could.

It is hard to say whether this ruling was ever carried out in practice by the relatives of Provençal Jewish criminals, and, in any case, the idea was not expressed so starkly by any other rabbi, in Provence or elsewhere. Whatever Maimonides and his European acolytes may have thought about the question, the need to mourn a relative, even a violent one, would have been quite strong. In one story, found in several sources including a different fragment of the same *Zot Ḥukat ha-Torah*, the family of a Jewish murderer did not refrain from mourning their relative's death at the hands of local courts. The story is told of a Jewish murderer executed in Lunel, near Montpellier in eastern Languedoc:[48]

מעשה היה בלוניל בכה[ן] שהרג את הנפש ונהרג הוא עליו. ולא ניתן לקבורה עד עשרים יום כי עכבו מושל העיר בביתו של נהרג. והסכימו דלא מי[קרי] סתימ[ת] גולל עד שנקבר, ולא התחילו למנות אבלות עד שנקבר. ולא אכלו בשר ולא שתו יין האבלים כל אותם עשרים יום. זאת חקת התו ר'.

> [There was a case in Lunel of a priest (Cohen) who murdered someone and he was killed for it. [His body] was not released for burial for twenty days because the town governor kept it in the victim's home. They agreed that 'moving the covering stone' did not begin until burial, and they did not begin counting their mourning [period of seven days] until he was buried. The mourners did not eat meat or drink wine for the duration of those twenty days].

The relatives of the Lunel murderer performed the normal mourning ritual even though their kinsman had been executed for his crime.[49] The seven-day mourning period was delayed, however, since mourning could begin only after the burial was completed. In this case, the murderer was executed, but his body was kept in the home of the victim for two weeks, and, therefore, mourning did not commence until two weeks had passed.

This account of a Jewish murderer executed by the governor of Lunel, whose body was subsequently kept under 'house arrest', is somewhat surprising, and

---

[48] New York, JTSA, MS Rab. 653, fol. 64v; RNL, MS Evr. IV 6, fol. 56r; Amsterdam, Portugees Israelitisch Seminarium, MS Ets Haim 47 A 31/6, fol. 18v. The story is also found in Moscow, Russian State Library, MS Guenzburg 73, fol. 14v, and a possible reference is found in the glosses of Moses ha-Cohen of Lunel on Maimonides, Mishneh Torah, Laws of Mourning 1, 3.

[49] The fact that the murderer was a priest does not play an explicit role in the story, but it may have been mentioned to deepen the shock the story would evoke. In rabbinic sources, priests represent peace, and a priest who killed a person, even accidentally, could not recite the priestly blessing, which ends with the words (Numbers 6:26) 'May God grant you peace' (Babylonian Talmud, Berachot 32b).

no other documents seem to describe it or similar cases.⁵⁰ To be sure, municipal officials in France administered the death penalty under certain circumstances.⁵¹ Although European legal thinking had begun to shift towards a more aggressive and inquisitorial attitude to crime during the thirteenth century,⁵² it was not until the fourteenth century that homicide was fully criminalised in European societies.⁵³ In practice, murderers usually either fled the city or reconciled with the relatives of the victim – an attitude that stemmed, at least partially, from the assumption that many murders were the result of feuds or family disputes.⁵⁴ Perhaps the policy regarding Jewish murderers was different because, owing to

---

⁵⁰ In medieval France and Germany, Jews who died in captivity were sometimes held for ransom before being released for burial. The most famous example is that of Rabbi Meir of Rothenburg, who was captured in 1286 while trying to flee the Holy Roman Empire, died in prison in Ensisheim in 1293 and was buried in Worms in 1307. For this, and a similar case from the twelfth century, see: Simcha Emanuel, 'Did Rabbi Meir of Rothenburg Refuse Redemption from Prison?', *Netuim: A Journal for the Study of Torah she-Be'al Peh* 19 (2014): 155–69. Accounts of these two northern cases emphasise the malicious and pecuniary justification for the ruler holding on to the body, in stark contrast to the Lunel text that presents it as a routine component of the legal system.

⁵¹ Roger Grand, 'Justice criminelle, procedures et peines dans les villes aux XIIIe et XIVe siècles', *Bibliothèque de l'École des chartes* 102 (1941): 51–108; Susan L'Engle, 'Justice in the Margins: Punishment in Medieval Toulouse', *Viator* 33 (2002): 133–65; Sebastien Hamel, 'L'application de la peine de mort par les justices municipals: l'affaire Berthe du Jardin au parlement de Paris (1369–1398)', *Violences souveraines au Moyen Âge: Travaux d'une École historique*, ed. François Foronda, Christine Barralis and Bénédicte Sère (Paris: Presses universitaires de France, 2010), pp. 29–37; Patricia Turning, *Municipal Officials, Their Public and the Negotiation of Justice in Medieval Languedoc: 'Fear Not the Madness of the Raging Mob'* (Leiden: Brill, 2012).

⁵² Richard M. Fraher, 'The Theoretical Justification for the New Criminal Law of the High Middle Ages: "Rei publicae interest, ne criminal remaneant impunita"', *University of Illinois Law Review* (1984): 577–95; Sarah Rubin Blanshei, 'Crime and Law Enforcement in Medieval Bologna', *Journal of Social History* 16 (1982): 121–38; Trevor Dean, *Crime in Medieval Europe 1200–1550* (Harlow: Pearson Education, 2001), pp. 5–11.

⁵³ Claude Gauvard, *'De grace especial': Crime, état et société en France à la fin du Moyen Age* (Paris: Publications de la Sorbonne, 1991), pp. 798–806; Pieter Spierenburg, *A History of Murder: Personal Violence in Europe from the Middle Ages to the Present* (Cambridge: Polity, 2008), pp. 43–64; Steven Bednarski, *A Poisoned Past: The Life and Times of Margraida de Portu, a Fourteenth-Century Accused Poisoner* (Toronto: University of Toronto Press, 2014), p. 91. In this volume see: Patricia Turning, 'A Case of Mariticide in Late Medieval France', among others. Developments in England followed a different trajectory. Dean, *Crime in Medieval Europe*, pp. 5–6; Naomi D. Hurnard, *The King's Pardon for Homicide before A.D. 1307* (Oxford: Clarendon Press, 1969); Thomas Andrew Green, 'The Jury and the English Law of Homicide', *Michigan Law Review* 74 (1976): 413–99; idem, *Verdict According to Conscience: Perspectives on the English Criminal Trial Jury, 1200–1800* (Chicago: University of Chicago Press, 1985), pp. 28–32.

⁵⁴ Kathryn L. Reyerson, 'Flight from Prosecution: The Search for Religious Asylum in Medieval Montpellier', *French Historical Studies* 17 (1992): 603–26; Smail, *The Consumption of Justice*, pp. 185–90.

their status as property of the king's chamber (*servi camerae regis*), Jews were barred from taking part in feuds.[55] Similarly, in Aragon, the punishment for murdering or wounding a Jew differed from punishment for violence towards Christians because Jews were royal property.[56] Therefore, even homicide committed in the context of a feud, which would normally be ignored by the authorities, was prosecuted when perpetrated by a Jew.

The Lunel customary from 1367, detailing municipal legislation for the town, does not deal with homicide, so it does not explain why the murderer's body was kept in the victim's house.[57] In other parts of Languedoc, however, the prescribed punishment was burial alive underneath the body of the victim.[58] Perhaps the peculiar situation described in this passage reflects an application of this punishment. The Jewish murderer may have been killed by being buried alive underneath his victim, who was buried within the grounds of his own home. After two weeks, the murderer was assumed to be well and truly dead and was then exhumed and reburied in his own plot.

The first ruling from *Zot Ḥukat ha-Torah*, that criminals executed by a non-Jewish court should not be mourned, expressed what might be a strong endorsement of the Provençal court system as an agent of justice, comparable

---

[55] Guido Kisch, *The Jews in Medieval Germany: A Study of Their Legal and Social Status*, 2nd edn (New York: Ktav Publishing House, 1970), pp. 119–28; David Nirenberg, *Communities of Violence: Persecution of Minorities in the Middle Ages* (Princeton: Princeton University Press, 1996), pp. 31–32. Despite this law, there is some evidence for feuding Jews. See: Mark D. Meyerson, 'The Murder of Pau de Sant Martí: Jews, Conversos, and the Feud in Fifteenth-Century Valencia', in *'A Great Effusion of Blood'? Interpreting Medieval Violence*, ed. Mark. D. Meyerson, Daniel Thiery and Oren Falk (Toronto: University of Toronto Press, 2004), pp. 57–78; François Soyer, 'Living in Fear of Revenge: Religious Minorities and the Right to Bear Arms in Fifteenth-Century Portugal', in *Vengeance in the Middle Ages: Emotion, Religion and Feud*, ed. Susanna A. Throop and Paul R. Hyams (Farnham: Ashgate, 2010), pp. 85–103. The category of *servi camerae regis* has elicited a large amount of scholarship. See recently: David Abulafia, 'The Servitude of Jews and Muslims in the Medieval Mediterranean: Origins and Diffusion', *Mélanges de l'École française de Rome: Moyen Âge* 112 (2000): 687–714; Anna Sapir Abulafia, *Christian-Jewish Relations 1000–1300: Jews in the Service of Medieval Christendom* (Harlow: Longmans, 2011); Ilan Shoval, 'Servi regis Re-examined: On the Significance of the Earliest Appearance of the Term in Aragon, 1176', *Hispania Judaica Bulletin* 4 (2004): 22–70; Ilan Shoval, *Jews and Muslims as Servi Regis in the Kingdom of Aragon, 1076–1176: A Comparative Study of Minorities in a Medieval Frontier Society* (Jerusalem: Ben-Zvi Institute, 2010).

[56] Thomas W. Barton, *Contested Treasure: Jews and Authority in the Crown of Aragon* (University Park: Pennsylvania State University Press, 2015), pp. 29–30.

[57] Edouard Bondurand, 'Les coutumes de Lunel: Texte de 1367', *Memoires de l'Academie de Nîmes* 8 (1885): 35–78.

[58] L'Engle, 'Justice in the Margins', pp. 147–47; *The Costuma d'Agen: A Thirteenth-Century Customary Compilation in Old Occitan Transcribed from the Livre Juratoire*, trans. F. R. P. Akehurst (Turnhout: Brepols, 2010), pp. 36–39.

to Jewish courts of yore. The second paragraph, which was merely recorded by *Zot Ḥukat ha-Torah* and was not necessarily the opinion of its author, preserved the memory of a Jewish murderer actually executed by authorities in Lunel. But the focus of the account was the technical question of when mourning should commence. The fundamental question of whether mourning was appropriate at all for an executed murderer was not taken up, but taken for granted. This can be seen as a rejection of the first position and of the legality of the execution. More likely, though, it was a case of ritual instinct – in this case, the need to mourn the dead – overriding legal distinctions.[59] Although his reading of the sources led the author of *Zot Ḥukat ha-Torah* to the conclusion that executed murderers should not be mourned, he or his community could not bring themselves to follow through in practice and restrain themselves from mourning their dead. The legitimacy of the Lunel judiciary's actions was not in question; indeed, the Jews of Languedoc and Provence acknowledged that legitimacy even when they chose not to withhold mourning rites from those who met their deaths through it.

This legitimacy was dependent on the confidence that Jews felt towards the court system in southern France; namely, that it was a system that was equipped and inclined to deal with Jews as individuals and in accordance with codified law. Jews in other regions experienced the court system differently and responded in kind. In late medieval Germany, the legal position of Jews was much more precarious than that of their Provençal coreligionists, and their negative attitude towards gentile execution of Jewish murderers was expressed in a responsum by Rabbi Jacob Weil. Weil (often referred to by the acronym Mahari, מהר"י, 'our teacher rabbi Jacob') was an important rabbinic decisor in fifteenth-century Germany where he served in the communities of Augsburg and Erfurt.[60] He sent a responsum to a learned Jewish man, Simon, whose brother had been tried and executed for killing another person, apparently another Jew. The murderer's family had observed the normal mourning rites after his death, and Rabbi Simon now asked whether their decision to mourn him had been the right one.

המקום יהא בעזרך אהו' הר"ר שמעון י"ץ. שפיר עבדת שהתאבלת על אחיך, כיון דלאו בדין סנהדרין איקטיל, לא גרע ממי שנהרג בדין המלך, אע"ג שחייב מיתה מדינ ה.

[May the Lord be your Help, my beloved Rabbi Simon. You did well in mourning your brother, because he was not executed by order of the Sanhedrin

---

[59] For a striking and well-known example of ritual instinct overriding rabbinic legal distinctions to condone murder (in the context of religious persecution), see: Haym Soloveitchik, 'Religious Law and Change: The Medieval Ashkenazic Example', *AJS Review* 12 (1987): 205–21.

[60] Bernard Rosenzweig, *Ashkenazic Jewry in Transition* (Waterloo: Wilfrid Laurier University Press, 1975), pp. 11–18.

and is no worse than those executed by order of the king, even though he was legally deserving of death].[61]

Weil quoted the ruling of Maimonides mandating mourning for the victims of Jewish royal justice. He emphasised that Maimonides refers to a case where the action of the (Jewish) king was legally justified, and, in the case of *lèse-majesté*, might even be religiously mandated in order to maintain the king's honour, which is in itself a religious value. Thus, although royal execution was not, strictly speaking, justice, it was still religiously justified. Execution by a non-Jewish court, on the other hand, had nothing to do with law as Weil saw it. Furthermore, the way in which Simon's brother had been killed was cruel and painful. In Weil's mind, this made it even clearer that the execution was unjust, that he had died the way he did only because he was a Jew and not because of his crimes and, therefore, that mourning was appropriate.

A more troublesome point for Weil in the case of Simon's brother was the concern that the brother might be considered a suicide and, thus, unworthy of mourning.[62] This concern stems from an aspect of the story preserved towards the end of the responsum,

שאמר לו מאן דהוא תלך לחוץ מן החירות ומסור עצמך כדי שיהא לך כפרה, וכן עשה

[that someone told him 'leave the freedom (*herut*) and give yourself up so that you can achieve expiation (*kapparah*)', and so he did].[63]

Nonetheless, Weil speculated that the murderer may still have thought he could escape and, therefore, turning himself in to the authorities who subsequently killed him should not be considered suicide:

ועוד הכא לא הוי איבד עצמו לדעת, דשמא סבור היה לברוח למקום שלא יוכלו לרדוף אחריו לתופשו, ודמיא למצאוהו תלוי באילן, דאין זה בכלל איבד עצמו לדעת, אע"ג דמוכח מילתא שהוא עצמו עשה, אמרינן דילמא רוח רעה מבעתתו.

[Furthermore, he is not considered a suicide, because perhaps he planned to flee to a place where they could not pursue him and capture him. It is similar to a

---

[61] Ya'akov Weil, *She'elot u-Teshuvot Mahari Weil*, ed. Yonatan Shraga Domb (Jerusalem: Makhon Yerushalayim, 2001), pp. 142–43, no. 114. The responsum was also published in Moses Mintz, *She'elot u-Teshuvot Maharam Mintz*, ed. Yonatan Shraga Domb (Jerusalem: Makhon Yerushalayim, 1991), pp. 518–19, no. 106.

[62] Semakhot 2:1–4 (*The Tractate Mourning*, trans. Zlotnick, pp. 33–34); Benjamin Gesundheit, 'Suicide: A Halakhic and Moral Anaylsis of Masekhet Semahot, chapter 2, laws 1–6', *Tradition: A Journal of Orthodox Jewish Thought* 35 (2001): 34–51. On this section of the responsum, see: Yechezkel Lichtenshtein, 'Suicide as an Act of Atonement', *Jewish Law Annual* 16 (2006): 51–91 at p. 79.

[63] Weil, *She'elot u-Teshuvot Mahari Weil*, p. 143.

person found hanging from a tree, who is not considered a suicide,[64] even when it is evident that he did it himself, because we say that perhaps he was driven by an evil spirit].[65]

Weil's account describes the murderer as having fled to 'the freedom', where he was protected from punishment. This is almost certainly a reference to sanctuary, such as a church, where medieval murderers often fled to seek refuge.[66] According to Roman, canon and German law, Jews were ineligible for legal asylum since the religious status of the church was not considered relevant to non-Christians.[67] This case, then, may point to the gap between law and practice, suggesting that Jews did, on occasion, take advantage of the law of sanctuary and that this was respected by their pursuers, despite being unsupported by codified law.

Despite the possibility that Simon's brother may have received the right of asylum that was normally denied to Jews, it is clear that in Rabbi Weil's eyes the murderer was dealt with cruelly because he was a Jew. Late medieval German laws indeed prescribed specific forms of execution for Jews, which included hanging the condemned upside down with dogs hanging beside him, intended to be both painful and humiliating.[68] Mourning the victim of such treatment was more than ritual performance; it was a protest against the injustice perpetrated against a Jew who deserved to have been executed by a Jewish court. In a hypothetical Jewish court, he might well have been found guilty and executed for his crimes, but this would have been in accordance with the law and in a way that preserved his human dignity.

The problem of how a Jewish community should relate to the execution of Jewish murderers by Christian authorities continued to reverberate beyond the late Middle Ages, as evidenced by a fascinating account from early modern Italy. In 1590, a Jew in Ferrara named Manasso was sentenced to death for conspiring with a Christian woman, Madonna Lavinia Bendadei, to murder her brother-in-law. According to a contemporary description written by Giulio Cesare Croce (who also composed a poem celebrating the execution), Manasso 'was put on

---

[64] *The Tractate Mourning*, trans. Dov Zlotnick, p. 33.
[65] Weil, *She'elot u-Teshuvot Mahari Weil*, p. 143.
[66] Karl Shoemaker, *Sanctuary and Crime in the Middle Ages, 400–1500* (New York: Fordham University Press, 2011); William Chester Jordan, *From England to France: Felony and Exile in the High Middle Ages* (Princeton: Princeton University Press, 2015).
[67] Kisch, *The Jews in Medieval Germany*, p. 188.
[68] Guido Kisch, 'The "Jewish Execution" in Mediaeval Germany', *Historia Judaica* 5 (1943): 103–32; Kisch, *The Jews in Medieval Germany*, pp. 186–87; Mitchell B. Merback, *The Thief, the Cross, and the Wheel: Pain and the Spectacle of Punishment in Medieval and Renaissance Europe* (Chicago: University of Chicago Press, 1999), pp. 187–88; Mitchell B. Merback, *Beyond the Jewish Badge: Anti-Judaism and Antisemitism in Medieval and Early Modern Visual Culture* (Leiden: Brill, 2007), p. 263.

a wagon, surrounded by rabbis who comforted him'.[69] Comforting those condemned to death was a common element in executions in Renaissance Italy, but no other examples of Jewish participation in the practice are known.[70] Croce's description should probably be read in light of his verse account of Manasso's execution, which places in Manasso's mouth the following line: 'But soon I was rushed away from the Jews, who had not wanted me to suffer such abuse, for they loved me fervently'.[71]

If the Jews loved Manasso 'fervently', it seems safe to assume that they did not believe he was guilty of the heinous crimes of which he was accused, or at least did not deserve the cruel series of punishments to which he was condemned by the Ferraran court. The Jewish community had its own reasons for preventing the execution of Jewish criminals – leaders feared that 'when one Jew is guilty, all are blamed'.[72] Their fear, that the execution of a Jewish murderer by Christian society was an event that boded ill for the community as a whole, led the rabbis to show solidarity with Manasso as he was led to his death. At the same time, the specific way in which the rabbis expressed that solidarity was moulded by that same Christian society. Jewish pious confraternities rose in Ferrara and Venice during the course of the sixteenth century.[73] One of their declared goals was tending to the dying and dead, and new rituals and texts were composed for this purpose.[74] The establishment of these Jewish confraternities and their emphasis on death rituals were both influenced by contemporary developments

[69] Meryl Bailey, 'Public Executions in Popular Verse: The Poems of Giulio Cesare Croce', in *The Art of Executing Well: Rituals of Execution in Renaissance Italy*, ed. Nicholas Terpstra (Kirksville, MO: Truman State University Press, 2008), p. 329.

[70] Nicholas Terpstra, 'Theory into Practice: Executions, Comforting, and Comforters in Renaissance Italy', ibid., p. 132.

[71] Bailey, 'Public Executions', p. 338.

[72] Statement by Rabbi Leone Modena (Venice, 1571–1648), as quoted by David Malkiel, *A Separate Republic: The Mechanics and Dynamics of Venetian Jewish Self-Government, 1607–1624* (Jerusalem: Magnes Press, 1991), p. 149.

[73] Elliott Horowitz, 'Jewish Confraternal Piety in Sixteenth-Century Ferrara: Continuity and Change', in *The Politics of Ritual Kinship: Confraternities and Social Order in Early Modern Italy*, ed. Nicholas Terpstra (Cambridge: Cambridge University Press, 2000), pp. 150–71; Elliott Horowitz, 'Processions, Piety and Jewish Confraternities', in *The Jews of Early Modern Venice*, ed. Robert C. Davis and Benjamin Ravid (Baltimore: Johns Hopkins University Press, 2001), pp. 231–47; Elliott Horowitz, 'Jewish Confraternal Piety in the Veneto in the Sixteenth and Seventeenth Centuries', in *Gli Ebrei e Venezia: Secoli XIV-XVIII*, ed. Gaetano Cozzi (Milano: Edizioni Comunita, 1987), pp. 301–13.

[74] Elliott Horowitz, 'The Jews of Europe and the Moment of Death in Medieval and Modern Times', *Judaism: A Journal of Jewish Life and Thought* 44 (1995): 271–81; Avriel Bar-Levav, 'Leon Modena and the Invention of the Jewish Death Tradition', in *The Lion Shall Roar: Leon Modena and His World*, ed. David Malkiel (Jerusalem: Magnes Press, 2003), pp. 85–101; Avriel Bar-Levav, 'Ritualisation of Jewish Life and Death in the Early Modern Period', *Leo Baeck Institute Year Book* 47 (2002): 69–82.

among Italian Christians, and it seems evident that the rabbis, who joined the procession in order to offer Manasso consolation, knew that they were offering precisely the same assistance that prominent and pious Christians in Ferrara would have done for a condemned Christian criminal.

Jewish ritual responses to the deaths of Jewish criminals at the hands of Christian officials provide glimpses of the experiences of Jews – rabbis, murderers and their relatives – living as a minority under Christian rule. As their experiences and their perception of Jewish murderers differed over time and place, so their religious response adapted. In Late Antiquity, under imperial Roman rule, the rabbis of the Mishnah reserved their moral qualms about capital punishment for their own, theoretical penal code. People executed under that system were not to be mourned lest the mourning ritual become the accusation that they were, in fact, innocent. But Jews who were tried and executed by Roman authorities were assumed to be innocent and their deaths unjust, and, therefore, they were to be mourned. For Maimonides in the thirteenth century, this ethnic and political distinction became one between religious and temporal power. Political violence carried no guise of justice, whether imposed on Jews by Jewish or non-Jewish powers. But judicial violence could and ought to be just, and mourning its victims could be construed as questioning that justice. Over the course of the Middle Ages, the practice of Jewish communities and their religious leaders was to mourn all their dead, whether they believed them to have been executed justly or unjustly. Yet the underlying concern of the Talmudic practice, that capital punishment carried with it the acute danger of killing the innocent, continued to reverberate. The fault lines of this reverberation were the borders that Jews perceived around their community. For some communities, particularly in Southern Europe, the surrounding non-Jewish court system seemed fundamentally trustworthy even when it carried out death sentences against Jewish miscreants. In other places, particularly in Northern Europe, non-Jewish courts were seen as prejudiced against Jews, and any execution they carried out was assumed to be motivated by hatred.

CHAPTER 4

Treacherous Murder: Language and Meaning in French Murder Trials

Jolanta N. Komornicka

UNDER COVER OF DARKNESS in 1262, an escaped prisoner snuck into the town of Montdidier, France, knocked at the first door he came to and when a woman answered, he struck her with a knife.[1]

In 1290, Judoco Reston was arrested in the town of Roye in northern France on suspicion of murder and acting treacherously.[2]

In 1312, the abbot of Saint-Nicolas-sous-Ribemont hired assassins who waylaid the clerk Robert de Suzanne as he headed for an appearance at court against the abbot, mortally wounding him.[3]

In 1320, Robin de La Fontaine brutally attacked a valet of the king, cutting off his nose before killing him.[4]

This is a small sample of the murder cases heard by the Parlement of Paris from 1254 to 1320. The diversity of victims and perpetrators displays a range of motives, and the cases also feature multiple times and locations – during the day, at night, in the home, on the public road – with an even greater variety to be had within the full set of 667 extant wrongful death cases tried in this sixty-seven-year period. The variety was such that the records show little by way of a pattern with regard to murder in late thirteenth- to early fourteenth-century France, though studies of the fourteenth and fifteenth centuries tend to evince clear trends and patterns, especially those focused on specific towns and small-scale localities.[5] Although the records of the Parlement of Paris from 1254 to 1320

---

[1] Auguste-Arthur Beugnot, ed., *Les olim ou registres des arrêts rendus par la cour du roi sous les règnes de Saint Louis, de Philippe le Hardi, de Philippe le Bel, de Louis le Hutin et de Philippe le Long*, vols 1–3 (Paris: Imprimerie Royale, 1839–48), 1:544–45.

[2] Ibid., 2:298–99.

[3] Paris, Archives nationales (AN), X2a 1, fol. 38v, 8 March 1313; fol. 141r, 30 July 1312.

[4] AN, X2a 2, fol. 89v, 12 February 1320.

[5] For example, see: Esther Cohen, 'Patterns of Crime in Fourteenth-Century Paris', *French Historical Studies* 11 (1980): 307–27 at pp. 317–18; Barbara Hanawalt, 'Violent

(inclusive) chiefly record incidents in northern France, the reach of royal jurisdiction was gradually expanding due to successful royal claims on non-domain territories, the development of an organised and increasingly autonomous court system, and the piecemeal negotiation of royal rights versus local privileges in lands beyond the Ile-de-France. Cases from Gascony and Languedoc are not uncommon, increasing the diversity of material in the court's records. Moreover, historical studies that focus on a single region rarely have to contend with a judicial system in flux, yet, in the second decade of the fourteenth century, Parlement not only extended its reach but also began operating independently from the king. The Capetian rulers had established an administrative network of *baillis* and seneschals that encouraged a governing and fiscal structure with Paris at the centre, though, in reality, France retained many centrifugal forces. The Parlement of Paris came to have charge over a large segment of these officials and was the institution to confront the jurisdictional hurdles that municipalities and lords threw up to protect their traditional privileges and autonomy. As a result, the very nature of the court and the records was changing in this period.

However, Parlement's records from these sixty-seven years do reveal one very clear pattern: more and more, murder was becoming identified with treason and described as treacherous. The fact that the turn of the fourteenth century was not a time of uniformity or consistency in record keeping raises a question as to the reliability of any identifiable trend. Much of the variety in the court registers can be ascribed to the wealth of factors that prompt human beings to kill one another and to the prevalence of violence in medieval Europe as a whole.[6] This variety also has roots in the composition style of the records themselves. These take the form not of depositions but of extracts, summaries of the inquests and the various documents submitted by the litigants. The extracts are short on criminal details and long on procedure, betraying the interests of a judicial body slowly attempting to expand judicial authority and to cut to the heart of the matter.[7] The scribes who performed this work did not greatly concern themselves with issues of precision when it came to summarising the nature or circumstances of the

---

Death in Fourteenth- and Early Fifteenth-Century England', *Comparative Studies in Society and History* 18 (1976): 297–320 at p. 298; Carl Hammer, 'Patterns of Homicide in a Medieval University Town: Fourteenth-Century Oxford', *Past and Present* 78 (1978): 3–23 at pp. 14–18.

[6] Hanawalt, 'Violent Death', p. 317; Hammer, 'Patterns of Homicide', pp. 22–23; D. M. Nicholas, 'Crime and Punishment in Fourteenth-Century Ghent (first part)', *Revue belge de philologie et d'histoire* 48 (1970): 289–334 at p. 310; Xavier Rousseaux, 'La repression de l'homicide en Europe occidentale (Moyen Age et Temps modernes)', *Geneses* 19 (1995): 122–47 at pp. 125–26.

[7] Elizabeth M. Hallam, *Capetian France 987–1328* (Harlow: Longman, 1980), pp. 135, 296–97, 328.

offences. The death of a person at the hands of another might just as readily be called *homicidio* as *multro, interfecio, occisione, facte mortiis* or half a dozen other things, with none inherently indicating anything other than a wrongful death. As other scholars have noted, one prominent result of the study of medieval French murder is that, despite distinctions between murder and homicide present in the work of contemporary jurists and canonists, trial and pardon records reveal little interest in consistently differentiating between the two.[8] Linguistic precision and vocabulary choices simply cannot be reliable guides for the evaluation of criminal behaviour and its prosecution at this particular moment in time.

Despite such caveats regarding the unreliability of court scribes' writing style, the association of murder – that is, wrongful deaths perpetrated intentionally – with treason clearly emerges. Xavier Rousseaux argues that cases of murder can teach historians about social tensions and contemporaries' collective methods of knowing and understanding their culture.[9] Examination of treacherous murder reveals the contemporary structures that made murder treacherous, regardless of the precise circumstances. Treacherous murder was fundamentally a violent, non-accidental death through which the murderer violated a culture shared with the victim. Because its essence concerned murder's violation of social norms surrounding violence and death, the circumstances of the early fourteenth century underlay the rhetorical shift.

While the rhetoric of high treason (often rendered as *lèse-majesté*) had been a part of French political thought since the end of the eleventh century, it was not until the reign of King Philip IV (r. 1285–1314) that monarchs began to make serious, if limited, use of it.[10] Territorial rebellions and the royal affirmation of sovereignty made the charge of *lèse-majesté* newly useful, and even productive. The wars in Flanders (1297–1305) and Gascony (1294–1303), as well as continued unrest in both regions after the conclusion of peace treaties, involved issues of lordship and the French king's claims to sovereignty in those regions, issues

---

[8] Rousseaux, 'Repression de l'homicide', pp. 130–31; Claude Gauvard, *'De grace especial': Crime, état et société en France à la fin du Moyen Âge* (Paris: Publications de la Sorbonne, 1991), pp. 800–1; Hanawalt, 'Violent Death', p. 299. Cf. Thomas A. Green, 'Societal Concepts of Criminal Liability for Homicide in Medieval England', *Speculum* 47 (1972): 669–94 on the distinction in England.

[9] Rousseaux, 'Repression de l'homicide', p. 125.

[10] Franck Collard, *The Crime of Poison in the Middle Ages*, trans. Deborah Nelson-Campbell (Westport, CT: Praeger, 2008), p. 128; Jacques Chiffoleau, 'Sur le crime de majesté médiéval', in *Genèse de l'état moderne en méditerranée: Approches historique et anthropologique des pratiques et des representations*, Actes des tables rondes internationals tenues à Paris les 24, 25 et 26 septembre 1987 et les 18 et 19 mars 1988 (Rome: École Française de Rome, 1993), pp. 184, 192; Simon Hirsch Cuttler, *The Law of Treason and Treason Trials in Later Medieval France* (Cambridge: Cambridge University Press, 1981), p. 8.

the Crown addressed with legal manoeuvres as well as military ones. Gascony was particularly troublesome for the French, and four times over the course of forty-five years (1293–1337) the population changed allegiances.[11] The many wars by their nature lent themselves to concerns over betrayal and treason; indeed, the perpetually shifting alliances between both the petty lords and great nobles increased the king's work of cementing loyalty.[12] The political divisions in France – fiefs, provinces, *appanages*, counties and *seigniories*, all at least nominally subject to the king – exacerbated the situation as loyalty was put to the test.[13] Crimes of *lèse-majesté* struck at the integrity of the king's relationships and claims to sovereignty, severing bonds and, in the process, threatening the ability of the king to claim to be more than one among many territorial lords. The opening decades of the fourteenth century reaffirmed the dangerous position of the French king if ever his throne were at risk, as Philip II Augustus (1180–1223) foresaw and began to rectify through a slow programme of centralisation. The concept of *lèse-majesté* was one method of shoring up, with a practicable strategy of enforcement, the Roman law doctrines of sovereignty that had preoccupied French kings since the mid thirteenth century. For such a strategy to work, the idea of treason that underlay charges of *lèse-majesté* had to be intelligible and relevant to the broader society. Where *lèse-majesté* was primarily a learned expression, infrequently encountered in the vernacular literature before the fifteenth century and seldom recorded as employed by litigants at trial even in the late fourteenth, 'treason' was a part of the broader society's ideas about social order.

While the negative vision of treason and the traitor were not unique or new to the late Middle Ages, the threat that traitors presented changed around the turn of the fourteenth century. In part, this was due to the elevated political attention paid to high treason. Additionally, this period witnessed changes to the judicial and social construction of what constituted a crime. In this period of political strife, and in light of a concerted effort on the part of the monarchy to reconstruct denizens of French territories into subjects of the French Crown, crime was increasingly a matter of public concern and a threat to the common good,

---

[11] Howard Kaminsky, 'The Noble Feud in the Later Middle Ages', *Past and Present* 177 (2002): 55–83 at p. 73; Jan Dumolyn and Jelle Haemers, 'Patterns of Urban Rebellion in Medieval Flanders', *Journal of Medieval History* 31 (2005): 369–93 at p. 374; Yvonne Lanhers, 'Crimes et criminels au XIVe siècle', *Revue historique* 240 (1968): 325–38 at pp. 332–33.

[12] Craig Taylor, ed., *Debating the Hundred Years War*, vol. 29, *Pour ce que plusieurs (La Loy Salicque) and A declaration of the trew and dewe title of Henrie VIII* (Cambridge: Royal Historical Society, 2006), pp. 9, 99; Rhys Jones, 'Mann and Men in a Medieval State: The Geographies of Power in the Middle Ages', *Transactions of the Institute of British Geographers*, New Series 24 (1999): 66.

[13] Dumolyn and Haemers, 'Patterns of Urban Rebellion', pp. 372–77; Robert Knecht, *The Valois: Kings of France 1328–1589* (New York: Hambledon, 2006), p. 24.

assimilable to high treason.[14] Worse, it was capable of corrupting the entire society. According to the fourteenth-century chronicler Richard Lescot, crime was a disease, a miasma that affected the public, while his contemporary Jean Froissart envisioned political unrest as a contagion.[15] The contagion metaphor spoke to popular conceptions of society, particularly that of the *corpus rei publicae*, as well as to the ramifications of unchecked criminality on the lives of individuals.[16] For the concept of the traitor, this framework of disease threatening the common good meant that regardless of the personal motives that spurred the betrayal, the breach of trust became a violation of communal bonds. Like the leper, another reviled character, the traitor's disorder could not remain contained within himself and, with time, would undo an entire community.[17]

If treasonous activities offended the behavioural norms at the heart of a society and threatened to introduce a wave of similar offences, then labelling particular actions treasonous and prosecuting offenders was a method of asserting what those norms were for the community. Treason came to act as a modifier

---

[14] This idea was first fully articulated by Panormitanus in the fifteenth century, who was building off a long-running conversation between canonists, secular jurists, popes and kings about the nature of the common good. On the development of the idea of crime as a public matter, see: Michael Jones, 'Trahison et l'idée de lèse-majesté dans la Bretagne du XVe siècle', in *La faute, la répression et le pardon: actes du 107e Congrès national des sociétés savantes, Brest, 1982, section de philologie et d'histoire jusqu'à 1610* (Paris: CTHS, 1984), pp. 105–06; Richard M. Fraher, 'Preventing Crime in the High Middle Ages: The Medieval Lawyers' Search for Deterrence', in *Popes, Teachers, and Canon Law in the Middle Ages*, ed. James Ross Sweeney and Stanley Chodorow (Ithaca: Cornell University Press, 1989), p. 219; Innocent IV, *In quinque libros decretalium Commentaria* (Venice, 1610), fol. 602; Kenneth Pennington, *The Prince and the Law, 1200–1600: Sovereignty and Rights in the Western Legal Tradition* (Berkeley: University of California Press, 1993), pp. 230–33.

[15] *Chronique de Richard Lescot, religieux de Saint-Denis (1344–1364)*, ed. Jean Lemoine (Paris: Renouard, 1896), p. 84; Jean Froissart, *Chroniques de Flandre, de Hainaut et d'Artois au temps de Cent Ans (1328–1390) de Jean Froissart*, trans. Denise Poulet (Troesnes, Laferte-Milon: Corps 9, 1986), p. 9.

[16] Claude Gauvard, 'Fear of Crime in Late Medieval France', in *Medieval Crime and Social Control*, ed. Barbara A. Hanawalt and David Wallace (Minneapolis: University of Minnesota Press, 1999), pp. 1–48 at p. 24; Joseph Canning, *Ideas of Power in the Late Middle Ages, 1296–1417* (Cambridge: Cambridge University Press, 2011), pp. 43, 51, 156; R. I. Moore, 'Heresy as Disease', in *The Concept of Heresy in the Middle Ages (11th–13th c.)*, ed. Willem Lourdaux and Daniël Verhelst (Leuven: University Press, 1976), pp. 1–11.

[17] See, for instance, the example of Simon de Montfort and the metaphor of leprosy infecting the realm: *Annales Monastici: Annales Monasterii de Oseneia, A.D. 1016–1347*, ed. Henry Richards Luard (London: Longman, 1869), pp. 176–77; R. I. Moore, *The Formation of a Persecuting Society: Power and Deviance in Western Europe, 950–1250* (Oxford: Blackwell, 1987), pp. 45–53; Alfonso, Rey de Castilla y Leon, *Las Siete Partidas*, Partida Septima (Madrid: Imprenta Real, 1807), Titulo II: Prologue.

that recast the crime of murder from one of violent death to one of betrayed cultural norms.

From 1254 to 1299, 5 per cent of wrongful death cases (and 8 per cent of cases clearly identifiable as murder) joined murder to treason. In contrast, from 1300 to 1320 that percentage rose to 27 per cent (49 per cent of murder cases). The scribal interest in connecting these ideas coincides with the aforementioned judicial, political and social developments co-occurring in France. Despite the differences between them, all four murder cases which began this article appear in Parlement's registers as having happened treacherously. The escaped prisoner in 1262 had 'postmodum hoc maleficium perpetrasset, quod videtur tangere proditionem' [committed his latest evil in such a way that it touched upon treason].[18] The authorities in Roye arrested Judoco 'pro suspicione insidiarum, et de presumacione occisionis' [on suspicion of plotting treachery and the presumption of murder] (*Olim* v. II, 298). The assassins hired by the abbot 'verbationis de nocte proditorem facte in personae Roberti' [beat him at night, doing treason to the person of Robert], and had 'insidiis ipsum Robertum lettaliter vulnerarunt' [mortally wounded this same Robert treacherously].[19] In 1320, Robin 'pensatis insidiis proditionaliter invasit verberunt et lettaliter vulnerarunt' [plotting treachery, treasonously beat and mortally wounded] the king's servant.[20] These and all the other cases of treacherous murder reveal more by what they do not have in common than what they do. There is no commonality of status or status relationships – social superiors treacherously murdered their inferiors just as often as the reverse. Such murders took place during the day and at night, at home and on the road. Weapons ranged from knives and swords to sticks and poison. Although the victims were initially unaware of the ensuing attack, many fought back, some even successfully defending themselves, which resulted in an attempted treacherous murder. Attackers worked alone and in groups, for hire and for themselves, victimising strangers as well as neighbours.

The result is a verbal linkage of murder to treason without clear indication of what makes one murder treasonous and another not. Yet, if the defining elements are unclear, the stigmatisation and moral condemnation of the violence are readily apparent. Few records from the localities survive, so it is impossible to say whether this outrage was limited to royal authorities, as Rousseaux suggests, or was part of the defining separation between murder and homicide later in the fourteenth and fifteenth centuries.[21] Certainly, local customary law codes

---

[18] Beugnot, ed. *Olim*, v. I, 544–45. For all subsequent in-text references, volume and page numbers follow in parentheses. Unless otherwise noted, all English translations are my own.
[19] AN, X2a 1, fol. 38v, 8 March 1313; fol. 141r, 30 July 1312.
[20] AN, X2a 2, fol. 89v, 12 February 1320.
[21] Rousseaux, 'Repression de l'homicide', p. 134.

and legal treatises associated treason and murder. The French jurist Philippe de Beaumanoir provides one of the most succinct formulations of this relationship in his 1283 *Coutumes de Beauvaisis*: 'Traison si est quant len ne monstre sembland de haine, et len het mortiement, si que par le haine lon tue, ou fet tuer, ou bat, ou fet batre dusques a afoleure cheli qui li het par traison' [Treachery is when you show no sign of hatred and yet you harbor a deadly hatred so that because of the hate you kill the person you hate treacherously (or have them killed) or you beat them (or have them beaten) until they are injured].[22] He immediately follows these words with: 'Nus murtre n'est sans traison' [No murder is without treachery].[23] Treatises like Beaumanoir's were well known to the judges in Parlement, who often served in local courts prior to their royal appointments, though examination of Parlement's treacherous murder cases shows that no one definition from the customaries applies. Instead, the repeated use of the language of treachery in almost 50 per cent of murder cases after 1300 conveys as much, if not more, in terms of moral opprobrium as judicial methodology, raising the questions of what prompted such outrage over murder at this time, and what caused court scribes to turn to treason as an intelligible means of conveying it.

The association between murder and treason begins with the deployment of a specialised terminology. While terms for sedition and *lèse-majesté* appear in a handful of cases, the vast majority use two terms, either in isolation or in combination: *insidias* (often found in the phrase *pensatis insidiis*) and *proditio* (usually in its adverbial form). Because the number of treacherous murder cases is so small for the thirteenth century (five such cases out of 102 instances of wrongful death, with sixty-one of those 102 clearly identifiable as murder), the following percentage breakdown comes from the 152 treacherous murder cases heard between 1300 and the end of 1320 (out of 565 wrongful deaths, 309 of them were murder): 83 per cent used a variant of *insidias*, 33 per cent *proditio* and 20 per cent used both. Translating *proditio* as 'treason' presents few complications, but *insidias*, particularly in the phrase *penastis insidiis*, has often been rendered in the literature as 'premeditation' or 'malice aforethought'.[24] Going back to the seventeenth century, Du Cange's glossary of medieval Latin offers 'premeditation' and 'obsession' for *insidiae*, while nineteenth- and twentieth-century French archivists provide the translation 'ambush' (*guet-apens*). More recently,

---

[22] Philippe de Beaumanoir, *Coustumes de Beauvoisis* (Bourges: F. Toubeau, 1690), p. 148; F. R. P. Akehurst, trans., Philippe de Beaumanoir, *The* Coutumes de Beauvaisis *of Philippe de Beaumanoir* (Philadelphia: University of Pennsylvania Press, 1992), p. 825.

[23] de Beaumanoir, *Coustumes de Beauvoisis*, p. 148; Akehurst, trans., *The* Coutumes de Beauvaisis, p. 825.

[24] The question of vernacular constructions must be left aside as all of Parlement's records from this period are in Latin.

Patricia Turning translates *pensatis insidiis* as 'with bad intentions'.[25] Yet premeditation, whether understood as malice aforethought, plotting or ambush, does not sufficiently convey the meaning and significance that *insidias* contributes to the records. Late medieval authors employed *insidias* to mean both an act carried out in secret and treason in the sense of a profound betrayal, ideas linked in descriptions of poisoning.[26] Canon law used the phrase *per insidias* to describe this inherently secretive crime; indeed, Thomas Aquinas classified death from poison as an occult offence.[27] Treatises of civil law similarly appealed to this secretive meaning in their descriptions of poisoning as *insidias venenosas*.[28] When designating treason, *insidias* more often appears in literary works and chronicles, rather than legal texts, as when one chronicler uses it to indicate the treasonous overtures the lord of Argenton made to the opposing side in advance of a battle.[29] An insidious act was more than one that was contemplated in advance. Its association with the hidden made it nefarious and its treasonous qualities made it odious. The choice to pair instances of murder with *insidias* was one that commented on the destructive nature of the crime at hand, not just its level of planning.

Secret murders and betrayals may well have had premeditation as an indispensible component, but not as the defining element. The trial records demonstrate that there were other ways to indicate premeditation and malicious intent without the connection to treachery. Most commonly, the scribes' basic descriptions of the events relate how an attack was pre-planned. There are also specific formulations used for malice aforethought, including *pensatis maleficium* and *ex cogitata malicis*. In 1312, a court scribe clearly differentiated between such premeditation and *pensatis insidiis* in a murder case, writing 'idem Theobaldus,

---

[25] Charles Du Fresne Du Cange, et al., eds., 'Insidiæ', *Glossarium mediae et infirmae latinitatis*, vol. 4 (Niort: L. Favre, 1885), col. 379a; Edgard Boutaric, Alphonse Grün and Léopold Delisle, eds., *Actes du Parlement de Paris*, vol. 2 (Paris: Henri Plon, 1867), p. 343; Brigitte Labat-Poussin, Monique Langlois and Yvonne Lanhers, eds., *Actes du Parlement de Paris: Parlement criminel règne de Philippe VI de Valois inventaire analytique des registres X²ᴬ 2 à 5* (Paris: Archives Nationales, 1987), p. 307; Patricia Turning, *Municipal Officials, Their Public, and the Negotiation of Justice in Medieval Languedoc* (Leiden: Brill, 2012), p. 144.

[26] Collard, *Crime of Poison*, pp. 127–55; *Statuta capitulorum generalium ordinis cisterciensis ab anno 1116 ad annum 1786*, ed. Josephus Maria Canivez, vol. 6 (Louven: Bureaux de la Revue, 1938), 15. Cf. in this volume: Thomas Gobbitt, 'Poisoning, Killing and Murder in the *Edictus Rothari*'.

[27] Thomas Aquinas, *Summa Theologiae*, Pt. II-II, q. 61, art. 3, in *Corpus Thomisticum: S. Thomae de Aquino Opera Omnia*, http://www.corpusthomisticum.org/iopera.html (accessed 21 December 2016).

[28] See: Collard, *Crime of Poison*, pp. 132–33.

[29] Charles Aubertin, *Histoire de la langue et de la littérature françaises au moyen âge d'apres les travaux les plus récents* (Paris: Eugene Belin, 1876), 2:285.

excogitata malicia ac pensatis insidiis, ipsum Philippum, evaginato gladio, invasisset ac de quodam baculo adeo crudeliter percussisset et vulnerasset quod ipse Philippus aliter mortis periculum evadere non poterat nisi vim repellendo' [said Thibaud, planning malice and also plotting treachery, fell upon the said Philippe and so cruelly struck him with his sword and also with a stick that the said Philippe could not escape the peril of death without driving him off] (*Olim* v. III, p. II, 726). Within the registers, the language of *pensatis insidiis* had meaning beyond simple premeditation. Associated with the secretive and treacherous, it served to modify 83 per cent of the murder cases between 1300 and 1320, connecting those murders to these same qualities of secrecy and treachery.

If *pensatis insidis* were meant as no more than premeditation, it would be natural to expect it to modify other types of crimes that required the same amount of planning and forethought, if not more. Yet unlike descriptions of intent and wilful malice, *pensatis insidiis* is not used in cases of burglary or forgery, and it is very rarely deployed in instances of kidnapping for ransom. Indeed, the only instance of treachery being mistakenly applied to a case comes from a kidnapping trial, in which the phrase *pensatis insidiis* has been crossed out.[30] That so few other crimes were done *pensatis insidiis*, and that those that were, like murder, were violent offences, is surprising in light of research on crime in the later Middle Ages. Barbara Hanawalt, studying England, and Esther Cohen, looking at France, separately conclude that property crime received the most and severest attention.[31] Both suggest that in a time of violence and high mortality rates, the enduring nature of property eclipsed the value of any human life, at least so far as the courts were concerned. Yet despite the clear interest the courts had in pursuing property crimes, the records in Parlement show no interest in associating such offences with treason, an idea that held enormous sway in a society predicated on bonds of loyalty and mutual obligation.[32] Thefts and other property crimes did not take place treacherously, though they did involve premeditation and even malice.[33] In other words, despite research that has suggested

---

[30] AN, X2a 1, fol. 125r, 18 October 1317.
[31] Hanawalt, 'Violent Death', p. 317; Cohen, 'Patterns of Crime', p. 327; Trevor Dean, *Crime in Medieval Europe 1200–1550* (Harlow: Pearson Education, 2001), pp. 65–68.
[32] Laurent Macé, 'La trahison soluble dans le pardon? Les comtes de Toulouse et la félonie (XIIe–XIIIe siècles)', in *La trahison au Moyen Âge: De la monstruosité au crime politique (Ve–XVe siècle)*, ed. Maïté Billoré and Myriam Soria (Rennes: Presses Universitaires de Rennes, 2009), p. 372.
[33] Except when the theft was committed through an act of violence or involved sacrilege, though even these instances are vanishingly rare. Valérie Toureille has argued that theft was considered a form of treason; however, the instances she cites, apart from beginning with the second half of the fourteenth century, largely concern pillage and brigandage, acts Parlement prosecuted as treasonous for their association with seigniorial

that goods were valued over human life, it is loss of human life that is repeatedly described in the records as tied to the worst of all crimes: treason.

Though enmeshed in the contemporary social discourse around crime, Parlement retained its own particular understanding of offences. Not only did the court emphasise the odious nature of murder over theft but it particularly loathed physically violent murders and applied the language of treason to them over other wrongful deaths, suggesting that the language of treason did more work than simply justify a harsh penalty.[34] An examination of Parlement's treatment of poisoning cases clarifies the distinction. Franck Collard persuasively argues that poison was strongly tied to contemporary ideas of treason.[35] He shows how the need for the poisoner to be in a position of intimacy and trust in order to administer the deadly dose was the essence of treasonous betrayal. Poison undermined the essential familial and political bonds that gave cohesion to medieval society.[36] A French poem from c. 1300 saw in poisoning 'trahison, tricherie, toute desleaute' [treason, trickery, complete disloyalty], while a case from the Holy Roman Empire in 1313 recriminates the poisoner as 'pejor Juda traditore ... traditor et insidiator pessimus, malignissimus traditor et infidelissimus' [worse than Judas the traitor ... the worst traitor and plotter, most malignant traitor and most unfaithful].[37] Italian jurists, many of who influenced French judicial thought, asserted that to poison was to conjoin betrayal with killing indelibly.[38] The argument was not that killing in itself was permissible but that the act of poisoning aggravated the degree of the offence by drawing in the crime of treason.

By the turn of the fourteenth century, poison and treason occupied a shared space in the hierarchy of despicable murders and crimes. Yet in the records of the Parlement of Paris, out of a total of twenty-four cases of poisoning (4 per cent of wrongful death cases, 8 per cent of murder), only one contains mention of treason. That lone case is instructive for understanding how Parlement understood the relationship between treason and murder. In 1312, Girbert de Podio Celsi accused Hugue Caric of having deposited, with Girbert's enemies, a variety of important documents that Girbert entrusted to Hugue for safe-keeping. Hugue

---

war and imperiling of the public roads. Valérie Toureille, *Vol et brigandage au Moyen Âge* (Paris: Presses Universitaires de France, 2006), pp. 13–14, 29–30.

[34] Ultimately, it is not possible to say whether cases of treacherous murder resulted in harsher punishments, as few of the records indicate the verdict.

[35] Collard, *Crime of Poison*, pp. 128, 130–31.

[36] Ibid., pp. 143–44, 270.

[37] Ibid., p. 131; *Imperator Heinricus: Ein Spätmittelalterlicher Text über Kaiser Heinrich VII. in kritischer Beleuchtung*, ed. Kurt-Ulrich Jäschke (Luxemburg: St.-Paulus-Druckerei, 1988), pp. 128–29.

[38] Collard, *Crime of Poison*, p. 130.

was thereby 'tradidit fraudulenter' [acting fraudulently] and, Girbert continued, 'par occidendo eumdem ipsi fecerat capitales insidias preparati bannitos a regno nostro occulte multociens' [machinating the highest treachery with men banned from the royal realm in order to kill him], and had 'falso et proditorie impocionavit et taliter quod ex hiis mortuus fuit' [falsely and treasonously poisoned him so as to kill him].[39] Like all other instances of fatal poisoning, victim and assailant had a relationship beyond casual acquaintance. Poisoning relied upon a pre-existing level of trust that could be exploited. Hugue had earned so much of Girbert's confidence that he was entrusted with keeping valuable documents out of the hands of Girbert's enemies. Hugue apparently kept his true intentions hidden until the end, even after conspiring with outlaws to ambush Girbert, for when that first attempt failed, he still remained close enough to administer (if unsuccessfully) the fatal poison.

The strife between Hugue and Girbert stands out for the complexity of the betrayal, in contrast to the other poisoning cases. Unlike the rest, Hugue's attempted poisoning of Girbert is only one out of several crimes and betrayals. It is also the only poisoning case to involve physical violence; the combination of betrayed trust and physical violence produced the treachery. As a counter-example, consider the case of a Jew accused of poisoning a Christian. Though the Jewish surgeon David supposedly poisoned numerous Christians in and around Saint-Quentin, including a priest, the trial record contains no language of treason.[40] It reads like all other non-violent poisoning cases, despite the prevalent idea that all Jews were poisoners, infected by Judas' treason.[41] Though Christian society generally regarded Jews as the arch-betrayers, and considered poisoning the pinnacle of murder-by-treason, David's crime was not treacherous murder

---

[39] AN, X2a 1, fol. 5r, March 1312.
[40] AN, X2a 1, fol. 83r, 12 October 1317. Note that in this case, just like all others, there is no way to know the truth of the allegations, only that they were made against the accused.
[41] 'De Symonia et Avaritia', in *The Poems of Walter Wimborne*, ed. A. G. Rigg (Toronto: Pontifical Institute of Medieval Studies, 1978); Canon 18 of the 1267 Council of Vienna depicted all Jews as poisoners. 'Item omnibus Christianis istius provinciae & civitatis & dioecesis Pragensis sub poena excommunicationis districtius inhibemus, ne Judaeos vel Judaeas secum ad convivandum recipiant, vel cumeis bibere vel manducare audeant ... nec Christiani carnes venales, seu alia cibaria a Judaeis emant, ne forte Judaei per hoc Christianos, quos hostes reputant, fraudulenta machinatione venenent' [Item: All Christians of this province and of the city and diocese of Prague, under the penalty of excommuication, we severely forbid from hospitably receiving any male or female Jew, whether to drink or to eat ... nor are the Jews to sell meat to Christians, or any food that comes from Jews, lest the Jews fraudulently plot the poisoning of the Christians, whom they regard as their enemies]. See: J. D. Mansi, *Sacrorum Conciliorum nova et amplissima collectio*, vol. 23 (Venice: Antionium Zatta, 1779), p. 1175.

because it was not violent. An omnipresent theme in Parlement's use of *proditio* and *insidias*, treacherous murder is violent murder.

One of the hallmarks of late medieval distinctions between types of killing was intentionality. Spontaneous violence did not engender the same degree of moral outrage or criminal culpability as did the premeditated. In fourteenth-century England, to commit a crime with malice aforethought elevated the severity of the offence, making it felonious.[42] In the case of a wrongful death, this meant the difference between homicide (committed without premeditation) and murder (committed with premeditation), though the distinction was still in its infancy and would not be recognised in statute until 1390.[43] Similar distinctions existed in France. The jurist Philippe de Beaumanoir and the anonymous author of *Le livre de justice et de plaid* both distinguish between homicide and murder on the basis of the attacker's intentions.[44] A brawl in a tavern that got out of hand and resulted in death was not of the same gravity as the blow dealt at night or from a place of hiding.[45] The canonist Guillaume Durand (1230–1296) underlines how much planning a murder *per insidias* took by linking the phrase with the term *per industriam*, underscoring its severity in comparison to other forms of wrongful death.[46] Treacherous murder could not be accidental and its intentionality – the willingness of the perpetrator to apply effort to undermining and betraying an established relationship – exacerbated the disgust it engendered in the members of the court.

Like *insidias*, *proditio* could indicate the overall repugnancy of murder, but it could also illuminate the character of murderers. By the mid fourteenth century, English statutes established that a wife who killed her husband or a servant who killed his master had committed treason. Such acts were not aggravated forms of murder. The Statute of Treasons (1351/52) made no less of a distinction between the killing of a superior by an inferior in the form of master–servant than in that of king–subject.[47] Similarly in France, three-quarters of a century earlier, *Le livre de justice et de plaid* characterised treason as failing to fulfil one's duties,

---

[42] See in this volume: Larissa Tracy, '"Mordre wol out": Murder and Justice in Chaucer'.

[43] Matthew Lockwood, 'From Treason to Homicide: Changing Conceptions of the Law of Petty Treason in Early Modern England', *Journal of Legal History* 34 (2013): 31–49 at p. 34; Hanawalt, 'Violent Death', p. 299.

[44] Note that most medieval writers did not consistently use 'homicide' to mean exclusively either manslaughter or murder, though some, like Beaumanoir, did.

[45] Beaumanoir, *Coustumes des Beauvoisis*, p. 148; *Li livres de justice et de plet*, ed. Louis Nicolas Rapetti, François Adrien Polycarpe Chabaille and Henri Klimrath (Paris: F. Didot, 1850), pp. 289–90; Rousseaux, 'Repression de l'homicide', pp. 130–33; Gauvard, 'De grace especial', p. 800.

[46] Guillaume Durand, *Tractatus de modo generalis concilii celebrandi* (London: Gregg Press, 1671), II:xlv:156.

[47] Lockwood, 'From Treason', p. 34.

obligations or vows.⁴⁸ Such legal formulations rested on shared conceptions of how treason marked the boundaries of moral behaviour and social order. Its importance was such that there were multiple terms available, many going in and out of favour as the centuries passed – *insidias* [treachery], *seditio* [sedition], *conspiratio* [conspiracy], *proditio* [treason] – and these are just a few from the Latin. These terms signal the importance of the offence; they do not describe the specific form the action took. Their purpose rests in the evocation of communal horror and irrevocable sanction.⁴⁹ Terms like sedition, conspiracy and infidelity highlight the problematic and grave moral status of both the act and the actor. To Beaumanoir, such acts are fundamentally perverse because they are committed in secret through trickery and deep-seated hatred. To his contemporary, the author of *Le livres de justice*, such acts reveal a dereliction of duty and obligation, the compromising of one's word in a society predicated on oaths, vows and mutual ties of obligation. In other words, more than any other type of criminal, traitors committed offences as much against the very fabric of society as against their targeted victim.⁵⁰ Loosed by their own deeds from the bonds of society, traitors (to the minds of jurists) rejected order for disorder, the natural structure of relationships and acceptable behaviours for unnatural and even inhuman ones.⁵¹ In linking treason to murder, along with all the attendant baggage that treason and traitors carried, jurists and court scribes associated the social condemnation of one crime with another. In using treason to modify murder, scribes increased the severity of the latter and transformed the very nature of murder itself.

Perhaps the use of *insidias* and *proditio* did not give murder the socially disruptive force treason had but was, instead, a means of designating a set of aggravating circumstances: done at night, in secret, from hiding or in violation of a sworn truce. In this sense, treacherous murder exists only for those cases that bear the language and does not tar the remaining murder cases with the same brush. However, the majority of treacherous murder cases do not contain such aggravating elements. To say that they do is to read *pensatis insidiis* as 'ambush' – despite contemporary evidence to the contrary – and to assume

---

⁴⁸ *Livres de jostice*, pp. 297–98.
⁴⁹ Maïté Billoré, 'Introduction', in *La trahison au Moyen Âge: De la monstruosité au crime politique (Ve–XVe siècle)*, ed. Maïté Billoré and Myriam Soria (Rennes: Presses Universitaires de Rennes, 2009), pp. 15–34; Stephen D. White, 'Alternative Constructions of Treason in the Angevin Political World: Traïson in the History of William Marshall', *e-spania* (2007), p. 13, http://e-spania.revues.org/document2233.html (accessed 18 November 2016); Collard, *Crime of Poison*, p. 128.
⁵⁰ Macé, 'La trahison soluble dans le pardon?', p. 372; Bruno Lemesle, 'Trahisons et idées de trahison sous les princes angevins et normands (1050–1150)', *La trahison au Moyen Âge*, ed. Billoré and Soria, pp. 229–38 at p. 232.
⁵¹ Jolanta N. Komornicka, 'Man as Rabid Beast: Criminals into Animals in Late Medieval France', *French History* 28 (2014): 157–71 at p. 167.

that *proditio* only indicates Beaumanoir's secret, deadly hatred over the range of associations given to treason at the time. Assuming the presence of aggravating circumstances is problematic. For most cases, the records do not permit us to know whether the victim had any foreknowledge of the assault as their deaths ensured silence on that score; yet, in the rare instances that the victim successfully fended off the attack, there is reason to believe that the sequence of events may have been finessed to best suit the plaintiff's needs. In 1309, for example, Estoud de Roquefort accused Guillaume Unaud of having treacherously invaded his home with twenty armed men in breach of a sworn peace. Estoud claimed that he and his friends had emerged unarmed but that Guillaume had attacked anyway, shutting them up in the local church and setting it on fire, in the process treacherously killing one of Estoud's friends.[52] Parlement ordered an investigation into the matter, only to discover that Estoud's friend was still very much alive. Moreover, Estoud was the one who violated the peace, and he was the one who attacked in arms and committed arson. Estoud confessed to all this and to lying to the court in order to procure a judgment of Guillaume's guilt. Had Estoud's friend done a better job of lying low, perhaps the deceit would never have come to light. Estoud sought to use the idea of treason to elevate the nature of Guillaume's supposed assault and murder in order to convict his enemy. Estoud's guilty admission revealed the lies he had told and clearly illustrated his understanding that the language of treason was an important means of making those lies believable and urgent enough to secure a (fraudulent) conviction. His story of the attack was a performance, with treason the key element designed to win the audience's sympathy.

Trials always represented an especially structured form of performance.[53] Everyone had a role to play, and the statements made in court were part of a script intended to persuade the listener, drawing upon legal and cultural tropes

---

[52] 'proditorie armari fecerat, in domo sua, viginti homines, qui dictum Estouldum et ejus comitivam, qui venerant sine armis, interficere conati fuerant et eos incluserant in ecclesia dicti loci, et postmodum ipsos in eorum domo voluerant ignis incendio concremare, quodque idem miles, pensatis incendiis, proditorie interfecerat Guillelmum de Mombeto, qui erat de familia et vestibus predicti Estoldi' [treacherously armed, there came into his home twenty men. They tried to kill Estoud and his companion, who had come unarmed, and they enclosed them in the church of that place. Afterwards they set fire to and burned down his home, and that knight, plotting treachery, treasonously killed Guillaume de Mombeto, who was part of Estoud's household]. Beugnot, ed., *Olim*, 3:I.381.

[53] On the development of source criticism and reading trials as performances, see: Caterina Bruschi, *The Wandering Heretics of Languedoc* (Cambridge: Cambridge University Press, 2009), pp. 3–5.

for their effectiveness.⁵⁴ Previous work in the history of emotions has illustrated how the court played a role in expressing the language of hatred, revenge, anger and honour.⁵⁵ As part of the structure of social relationships, the display of these emotions in a public venue involved a shared vocabulary and set of cultural expectations, along with norms for behaviour and legal display. It may be fair to say that trials provided an opportunity to claim, display and cement a variety of social relationships and status markers that were not directly relevant to the legal judgment of the criminal or civil infraction. The inverse also applies: the accusation of a particular crime could be used to show the accuser's participation in the correct relationships and the defendant's rupture of relationships, or ascription to the wrong ones. The commentary on relationships displayed at trial equally involved a shared discourse on enmity and honour and a shared cultural discourse of treason. A unique case in its level of detail, and in the presence of both victim and assailant, Guillaume Unaud's complaint against Estoud de Roquefort illustrates how little information most trials provide regarding the circumstances behind wrongful deaths. Arguing that the language of treason acted as a shorthand for aggravating circumstances makes assumptions both about the meaning of the terms used and about the reliability of the records themselves. Yet the evidence suggests that treacherous murder is an intentional application of treason's moral opprobrium and fundamental betrayal to the act of murder, thereby commenting on murder's own rupture of a fundamental set of relationships.

Scholars cannot expect consistency or uniformity in the redaction of trials. If some cases with aggravating circumstances have the language of treason while others do not, then either *insidias* and *proditio* are not inherently meaningful beyond acting as a substitute for 'at night', 'with malice aforethought', etc., or *insidias* and *proditio* draw on larger societal ideas regarding treason, violence and proper behaviour, indicating prevailing sentiments regarding murder as a whole, not as any individual case or murderer. Though not all instances of treacherous murder involve parties personally known to one another, to speak of murder done via treason is to speak of people sharing – or who are supposed to share – a common locality, culture and method of killing, yet one of them violates those shared norms, often in a manner that is inherently unequal, that denies the other party the ability to respond or act on an even playing field. As evident in cases of poisoning, violence was key to how Parlement united treason and murder, and it was the norms around violence that murder betrayed.

⁵⁴ Shannon McSheffrey and Julia Pope, 'Ravishment, Legal Narratives, and Chivalric Culture in Fifteenth-Century England', *Journal of British Studies* 48 (2009): 818–36 at p. 820; Derek Neal, *The Masculine Self in Late Medieval England* (Chicago: University of Chicago Press, 2008), p. 52.
⁵⁵ Daniel Lord Smail, 'Hatred as a Social Institution in Late-Medieval Society', *Speculum* 76 (2001): 90–126 at pp. 94–95, 113; Kaminsky, 'Noble Feud', p. 59.

Scholars in many fields of history and literary criticism have addressed the question of legitimate violence. It is part of current research into feud culture, the practice of revenge, the encroachment of royal power on traditional noble privileges and gendered performances and behaviours.[56] Howard Kaminsky, Richard Kaeuper and Justine Firnhaber-Baker, among others, show how concerns and contests over the control and practice of legitimate violence express the place of law and justice in society, envision society's proper order and offer alternative means of pursuing disputes and legislating decisions, as well as demonstrating status and power.[57] Violence *per se* was not a crime as it was part of established, expected mechanisms for settling disputes, but medieval society did regulate violence. However, certain places, classes of people and methods of engagement fell beyond the pale.[58] In the condemnations in cases of treacherous murder, the court particularly vilifies premeditated violence that remained secretive until the final moments.

Rousseaux argues that the growing interest in prosecuting certain offences as 'felony' and 'murder' was part of a royal desire to 'stigmatise' premeditated

---

[56] As just a few examples, see: Daniel Lord Smail, *The Consumption of Justice: Emotions, Publicity, and Legal Culture in Marseille, 1264–1423* (Ithaca: Cornell University Press, 2003), pp. 16, 167; Kate McGrath, 'The Politics of Chivalry: The Function of Anger and Shame in Eleventh- and Twelfth-Century Anglo-Norman Historical Narratives', in *Feud, Violence and Practice: Essays in Medieval Studies in Honor of Stephen D. White*, ed. Belle S. Tuten and Tracey L. Billado (Farnham: Ashgate, 2010), pp. 56–58; William Ian Miller, *Bloodtaking and Peacemaking: Feud, Law, and Society in Saga Iceland* (Chicago: University of Chicago Press, 1990), p. 219; Dianne Hall, 'Women and Violence in Late Medieval Ireland', in *Studies on Medieval and Early Modern Women: Pawns or Players?*, ed. Christine Meek and Catherine Lawless (Dublin: Four Courts Press, 2003), pp. 138–40; Miriam Müller, 'Social Control and the Hue and Cry in Two Fourteenth-Century Villages', *Journal of Medieval History* 31 (2005): 29–53 at p. 31. As Larissa Tracy has noted, violence was not perceived equally by all sectors of late medieval society, though her focus is primarily on the use and abuse of official violence in the form of judicial torture and brutality and not the social performance of violence. Larissa Tracy, *Torture and Brutality in Medieval Literature: Negotiations of National Identity* (Cambridge: D. S. Brewer, 2012), pp. 1–2, 4–5.

[57] Kaminsky, 'Noble Feud', pp. 63, 67, 79; Richard W. Kaeuper, 'The King and the Fox: Reaction to the Role of Kingship in Tales of Reynard the Fox', in *Expectations of the Law in the Middle Ages*, ed. Anthony Musson (Woodbridge: Boydell Press, 2001), p. 12; Justine Firnhaber-Baker, 'Techniques of Seigneurial War in the Fourteenth Century', *Journal of Medieval History* 36 (2010): 90–103 at p. 96; Esther Cohen, 'Violence Control in Late Medieval France: The Social Transformation of the Asseurement', *Tijdschrift voor Rechtsgeschiedenis* 51 (1983): 111–22 at pp. 120–21.

[58] Müller, 'Social Control', p. 30; Cohen, 'Violence Control', pp. 119–20; Nicholas, 'Crime and Punishment', pp. 289–90; Karen Jones, *Gender and Petty Crime in Late Medieval England: The Local Courts in Kent, 1460–1560* (Woodbridge: Boydell Press, 2006), pp. 63–69.

violence.⁵⁹ In Parlement's records, however, it is less the premeditation than the secrecy and dissimulation that provoke the court's ire. Several cases of treacherous murder hinge on this aspect of pretence, such as when the murderers of Jean l'Anglais's father entered his home under the claim of friendship, only to attack and murder him treasonously once inside.⁶⁰ The pretence came with an attendant denial of a formal challenge, refusing the victim the opportunity to respond to the threat or prepare a good death.⁶¹ Just as Jean l'Anglais's father expected no ill of his friends, Raimond de Sine-gradu rightfully anticipated a reprieve from hostilities after concluding a peace agreement with Pierre d'Avene. But as l'Anglais's father was deceived, so was Raimond, for no sooner had he and Pierre ritually embraced than Pierre attacked, binding his hands, striking him about the head and body and leaving him for dead.⁶² In a society heavily invested in forms of ritual, there were established means for announcing hostile intent, just as there were for ending it. Engaging in violence without going through the proper motions was, in itself, treasonous. In 1316, Eustache de Boves had come at the head of an armed band and attacked Mathieu du Rieu just as Mathieu was returning home, leaving him for dead. In detailing the crime, the scribe takes time to note that the attack was not preceded by any challenge, in contravention of the custom between nobles, and, therefore, Eustache had committed treason against Mathieu.⁶³ In contrast, when Robert de Fiennes killed Johannier de Hedigneul in the course of an open and declared feud, the choice of language and ruling reflects the more acceptable nature of the violence. Robert was summoned *super morte* 'over the death' of Johannier, whose killing (*interfecisse*) received no qualifications or modifiers; he was granted his liberty while the case was still on-going and received a pardon from the king soon thereafter.⁶⁴ Eustache, however, had

⁵⁹ Rousseaux, 'Repression de l'homicide', p. 134.
⁶⁰ 'videter ut amici ... patrem summ proditionaliter ceperunt et murtro interfecerunt' [appearing as a friend ... he treasonously grabbed his father and murdered him]. AN, X2a 2, fol. 134r, 28 March 1317.
⁶¹ Collard, *Crime of Poison*, p. 134.
⁶² 'in quo eundem amicabiliter receperat et amplexatus fuerat, proditorie cum armis invaserat, violenter ceperat, et ligatis manibus, ipsum in capite et aliis membris sui corporis atrociter vulnerarat, ipsumque sic vulneratum, quasi mortuum reliquerat' [and while he received him amicably and embraced him, he treacherously and in arms attacked and violently grabbed him, and binding his hands he grievously wounded him in his head and other parts of his body, and so wounded he left him for dead]. Beugnot, ed., *Olim*, 3:I.626–27.
⁶³ 'nulla precedente sint diffidatore ... aliqua diffidatione precedente et propter hoc cum partes fuit nobiles debent de consuetudine nobilium dicto Matheum ad proditionem imputam' [without having first offered challenge ... a preceding challenge is necessary between noble parties according to the noble custom and because of this Mathieu had treason committed against him]. AN, X2a 1, fol. 89r, 28 January 1316.
⁶⁴ AN, X2a 1, fol. 124v, 3 June 1317; fol. 180v, n.d. 1317.

'inhumaniter et proditorie invaserunt eundem insidiis extriquitatis et eundem interfecunt' [inhumanely and treasonously attacked him, treacherously pulled him out and killed him].[65] The words for the deaths are practically the same, *interfecisse/interfecunt, super morte/strata publica mortuum*, but the valuation of the deeds could not be more different. Though Johannier died, Robert acted within the sphere of acceptable, even honourable, violence. Eustache did not, and, as a result, he fled the pursuit of the law, as opposed to Robert whose confidence in the legitimacy of his violence brought him without constraint to court.

The importance of regulating violence manifests itself in commitments to the inviolability of the various types of truces and peace accords made between individuals at all levels of society, not just those between nobles. Parlement's approach to the *asseurement*, a form of guaranteed peace between two parties and their families, shows how the ideas of legitimate violence, murder and treason were all of a piece in late medieval France. In two different cases from the thirteenth century, the court, which at the time still met under the guidance of the king, had ruled that the breach of an *asseurement* was equivalent to murder.[66] Breaches of *asseurement* were, thus, always matters of high justice reserved to the king. The *Établissements de Saint Louis*, a compilation of legal codes from the Orléanais between 1272 and 1273, characterise the breach of an *asseurement* as 'one of the greatest treacheries there is'.[67] Court rulings and law codes joined this offence, which invariably took the form of a violent attack, to treason and murder, showcasing in statute form how murder's treachery was indelibly linked to questions of legitimate violence and the normative behaviours regulating it.

The language for treason embodied the fears of late medieval society. By combining treason with murder, court scribes (whether intentionally or not) indicated that, in a society in which violence was common, some forms of killing exceeded social norms. Society had a right to place limits on the nature and expression of violence, while violation of those limits (*asseurements*, challenges) caused injury beyond the sphere of the victim and the victim's family. Moreover, a society predicated on honour valued the right of everyone to an honourable death, which murder stole from the victim.

Murder became treacherous when its violence exceeded social bounds. Over the first quarter of the fourteenth century, the relationship between murder

---

[65] AN, X2a 1, fol. 89r, 28 January 1316.
[66] 'cum fraccio assecuracionis sit sequela multri', 'fraccio assecuracionis sit de pertinenciis multri' [with breaking of the asseurements, which is like murder ... breaking of the asseurements let it be pertaining to murder]. Beugnot, ed., *Olim*, 1:718, 728.
[67] 'car ce est appellé *trive enfrainte*, qui est une des grans traisons qui soit' [because it is called breach of truce, which is one of the greatest treasons there is]. *Établissements de Saint Louis, Roi de France, suivant le texte original, et rendus dans le langage actuel, avec des notes*, ed. M. l'Abbé de Saint-Martin (Paris: Nyon l'aîné, 1786), I:xxviii: 55.

and treason proliferated in court records, reflecting judicial and social concerns about a breakdown in proper behaviour at a time of political strife and heightened judicial awareness of the high treason known as *lèse-majesté*. The language of treason was a language of moral opprobrium directed against certain forms of violence, applicable throughout all levels of French society. It was also a language bound by social norms governing those whom it perceived as capable of treacherous murder. Domestic disputes that resulted in death were never treacherous, regardless of whether it was a husband killing his wife or a wife her husband. On the other hand, certain victims were almost assured the language of having been murdered treacherously, as was the case for pregnant women. Charges of *pensatis insidiis* or *proditio* gave voice to the belief that it was the very culture the murderer shared with the victim, and not any personal relationship, that had been betrayed through a secret hatred, enacted in uncountenanced, premeditated and, ultimately, illegitimate violence.

CHAPTER 5

'Mordre wol out': Murder and Justice in Chaucer*

Larissa Tracy

IN MODERN PARLANCE, the phrase 'murder will out' means that any secret will eventually be revealed, that murder cannot go undetected.¹ The roots of this idiom can be traced back to Geoffrey Chaucer's *Nun's Priest's Tale*, part of his fourteenth-century *Canterbury Tales* (c. 1388–1392),² in which the hysterical Chaunticleer (a well-known rooster of French fable) dreams of murder in his sleep, imagining it as a portent of his own death in the jaws of the ever-present, preying fox Reynard. But Chaunticleer and his (primary) wife Pertelote bicker like hens over its significance, and she dismisses his fear, telling him "'For Goddes love, as taak som laxatyf'" (2943). On the surface, murder seems a side note to the greater concerns of the narrative: the pride of Chaunticleer and his willingness to listen to Pertelote that lands him in mortal danger, the very danger that he imagined from the beginning. And yet, amidst the humour and satire, this episode reveals a distinct desire for justice in the discovery and prosecution of murder, while at the same time cautioning against the application of judicial torture in the process of law. When Chaucer composed his version of the Chanticleer/Reynard fable, England was embroiled in civil unrest, which manifested in uprisings and rebellions like the Peasants' Revolt in 1381, as well

---

* This essay is an expansion of some material in *Torture and Brutality in Medieval Literature: Negotiations of National Identity* (Cambridge: D. S. Brewer, 2012), especially chapter 4, which deals extensively with the *Prioress's Tale*. The *Nun's Priest's Tale* and the *Man of Law's Tale* receive a much fuller treatment here, with a specific focus on murder (as well as torture) in fourteenth-century English law. My deepest gratitude goes to Jeff Massey for his comments and suggestions on this chapter, and to Asa Simon Mittman for his encouraging input.

¹ 'murder will out'. Dictionary.com. Online Etymology Dictionary. Douglas Harper, Historian. http://www.dictionary.com/browse/murder--will--out (accessed 20 May 2016). Also see: John Ayto, *The Oxford Dictionary of English Idioms* (Oxford: Oxford University Press, 2010), p. 236.

² Larry D. Benson, 'Introduction', *The Riverside Chaucer*, 3rd edn (Boston: Houghton Mifflin, 1987), p. xxix. All quotations from the various texts of the *Canterbury Tales* are taken from this edition. Line numbers are given in parentheses.

as royal intrigue and dissent that led to the deposition of King Richard II in 1399 and his murder (through starvation) in 1400 – the same year of Chaucer's death.[3] Murder, treason and violence were prominent features of the late fourteenth-century political and social landscape, often echoed in Chaucer's *Canterbury Tales*.[4] Ultimately, in this seemingly silly beast fable and other tales of murder in the *Canterbury Tales*, Chaucer draws sharp distinctions between illicit murder, mob violence and justice, thus suggesting that overstepping legal boundaries in the application of torture, even in the correct prosecution of murder, has a destabilising effect and potentially leads to further violence and bloodshed.

Murder occurs in many of Chaucer's tales. The *Physician's Tale* describes the murder of Virginia by her father to save her from the sexual attentions of an unjust judge; the *Prioress's Tale* centres around the murder of a young Christian *clergeon* and the subsequent torture and execution of an entire Jewish population in a Turkish ghetto; and the *Man of Law's Tale* features massacre, murder, betrayal and, finally, restitution and redemption. There are murders recounted in the *Monk's Tale*, some gruesome and tragic (like that of Hugelino of Pisa) and others just and epic (like those of Nero and Holofernes). The *Tale of Melibee* opens with the assault on Melibee's wife and the mortal injury (via five wounds) of his daughter. The *Pardoner's Tale* chastises the sins of blasphemy and greed that lead to murder. But murder is one thing; torture is a bird of a different feather. Chaucer generally makes torture an unpleasant thorn in the judicial side; legal in rare circumstances, but not advisable and certainly not laudable. The *Man of Law's Tale* (hereafter *MoLT*), *Prioress's Tale* (hereafter *PT*) and *Nun's Priest's Tale* (hereafter *NPT*) are tales of murder, which also include singular references to interrogatory torture, a practice that ran contrary to English common law of the fourteenth century. Chaucer's fictions thus include traces of historical fact that gauge and adjudicate the realities of English law and justice, including the prosecution of murder.

MoLT appears in Fragment II (Group B^1), while *PT* occurs in Fragment VII (Group B^2) of the *Canterbury Tales* before *NPT* in the same fragment and group. *NPT* has been read as a response to *PT* either as a mockery of the pretentious

---

[3] In fact, in *Who Murdered Chaucer? A Medieval Mystery* (New York: Thomas Dunne, 2003), Terry Jones, Robert Yeager, Terry Dolan, Alan Fletcher and Juliette Dor argue that Chaucer may have been caught up in the court politics of Richard II. They analyse the suspicious circumstances regarding Chaucer's death around the time the king was murdered.

[4] John Scattergood, 'Social and Political Issues in Chaucer: An Approach to *Lak of Stedfastnesse*', in *Reading the Past: Essays on Medieval and Renaissance Literature* (Dublin: Four Courts Press, 1996), pp. 192–214 at p. 192. See: Rory McTurk, *Chaucer and the Norse and Celtic Worlds* (Aldershot: Ashgate, 2005); Frances McCormack, *Chaucer and the Culture of Dissent: The Lollard Context and Subtext of the* Parson's Tale (Dublin: Four Courts Press, 2007); and Alastair Minnis, *Fallible Authors: Chaucer's Pardoner and Wife of Bath* (Philadelphia: University of Pennsylvania Press, 2008).

Prioress by her priest, an attempt to match her tale or as a validation of the brutality of the Prioress.[5] So the references to murder and torture in the humorous *NPT* may simply echo the more serious ones made in *PT*. Or *NPT* may inject serious issues into a farcical tale to criticise the Prioress's serious – and apparently thoughtless – savagery. *MoLT* is told by a narrator supposedly steeped in the traditions of the English judicial system, one aware of the contemporary trend to associate late-medieval English justice with the ancient traditions of the Anglo-Saxons in the interests of promoting English national identity pre-Conquest. *NPT* narratively mimics the mob violence endorsed in *PT*, and *PT* mirrors the problematic application of justice in *MoLT*. The references to torture in these tales are brief, almost negligible. Each tale offers a different perspective on the prosecution of murder cases, the pursuit of the truth, the use of torture in discovery and the resulting punishment. Maura Nolan notes that there is a tension, which Chaucer recognised, between the 'concrete and the abstract in legal discourse, finding it both appropriable and threatening, both useful and dangerous'.[6] Throughout the *Canterbury Tales*, 'mordre wol out' (3052): secrets will be revealed and crimes will be punished. But, at times, Chaucer questions the limits to which justice should go.

Chaucer interrogates these limits throughout the *Canterbury Tales*: the absence of justice for crimes (like rape) committed against the peasant class (*Wife of Bath's Tale*), the imbalance of justice for the clergy (like Absolon) who commit grievous bodily harm (*Miller's Tale*), the abuse of power and the resulting injustice (like Walter against Griselda) (*Clerk's Tale*), the cuckoldry and triumph of lovers who scheme (*Shipman's Tale*) and the needless suffering of innocents (*Knight's Tale*). In short, Chaucer tests the boundaries of law, and he finds several chinks in the armour of English justice. But *murder*, which Chaucer often uses interchangeably with the word *homicide*, is of particular concern. The Pardoner associates it with the vices of gluttony, drunkenness and swearing: 'This fruyt cometh of the bicched bones two, / Forsweryng, ire, falsnesse, homycide' (*Pardoner's Tale*, 656–57). When the men inquire after a corpse carried past the tavern, they are told that he was an old friend of theirs and 'sodeynly he was yslayn to-nyght, / Fordronke, as he sat on his bench upright. / Ther can a privee theef men clepeth Deeth, / That in this contree al the peple sleeth, / And with his spere he smoot his herte atwo, / And wente his wey withouten wordes mo' (673–78). The three villains in his tale swear a drunken oath to 'sleen this false traytour

---

[5] Richard West, *Chaucer 1340–1400: The Life and Times of the First English Poet* (New York: Carroll and Graf, 2000), p. 72. See also: Tracy, *Torture and Brutality*, pp. 169–90.
[6] Maura Nolan, '"Acquiteth yow now": Textual Contradiction and Legal Discourse in the Man of Law's Introduction', in *The Letter of the Law: Legal Practice and Literary Production in Medieval England*, ed. Emily Steiner and Candace Barrington (Ithaca: Cornell University Press, 2002), pp. 136–53 at p. 137.

Deeth' (699). Death – inevitable, unavoidable, silent and secret – is described as a murderer who kills stealthily in the night. However, in the *Pardoner's Tale*, the justice of Death's homicide is unquestionable; each man who swears to slay Death falls victim to greed, conspiring to murder his fellows for gold. They all end up killing one another, and Death triumphs in their murders and betrayal: 'Thus ended been thise homycides two, / And eek the false empoysonere also. / O cursed synne of alle cursednesse! / O traytours homycide, O wikkednesse!' (893–96). The Pardoner is a corrupt messenger who follows his tale of greed and treachery with a request for donations and an offer of papal indulgences and relics for a good price. But Chaucer's moral regarding murder is clear: Murder is a crime of betrayal and deceit carried out in darkness with malice of intent, and, ultimately, murder will out.

During the tumult of the late fourteenth century, the law, and being on the right side of it, became increasingly important for both the king, in pursuing his ambitions at home and abroad, and for his opponents, in seeking to challenge his behaviour or his reading of legality.[7] As Anthony Musson points out, the English became more interested in the study of law and legal practice after the adoption of the *Magna Carta* in 1215. From the late twelfth century, education in the 'learned laws' was available at Oxford and, from the early thirteenth century, in canon law at Cambridge, though English students could also have studied at the law schools in Paris or Bologna.[8] Common law was not taught at the universities, it was learnt by watching and doing;[9] however, various legal tracts were copied and adapted to incorporate aspects of English law. *Tractatus de legibus et consuetudinibus regni Angliae* [*Treatise on the Laws and Customs of the Kingdom of England*], attributed to Ranulf de Glanvill and known simply as *Glanvill* (c. 1187–1189), was revised around 1229 and circulated widely.[10] Yet despite the availability of legal manuals, several officials operated without formal legal training. The treatise *On the Laws and Customs of England* (hereafter *Bracton* [c. 1240s–1250s]), attributed to Henry Bracton, criticises the judiciary of the day for being unlearned in law and 'for perverting the laws and customs by deciding cases more by their own will than

---

[7] Anthony Musson, *Medieval Law in Context: The Growth of Legal Consciousness from Magna Carta to the Peasants' Revolt* (Manchester: Manchester University Press, 2001), p. 232.

[8] Ibid., p. 38.

[9] As Morris Arnold writes, 'In the fourteenth century a man became a man of law the same way he learned to be a smith or a skinner or bowyer: he watched master craftsmen at work, sought their advice, and did his best to imitate them'. 'Law and Fact in the Medieval Jury Trial: Out of Sight, Out of Mind', *American Journal of Legal History* 18.4 (1974): 267–80 at p. 279.

[10] Musson, *Medieval Law*, p. 39.

by the authority of the laws'.[11] *Bracton* synthesises English law and Roman law, and late thirteenth- or early fourteenth-century texts – including *Mirror of Justices, Britton* and *Fleta* – are, in effect, revisions of *Bracton*.[12] In short, by the fourteenth century, there was a relatively large body of treatises that established a common English legal tradition. According to Musson, 'the survival of manuscript lectures and "do-it-yourself" manuals is symptomatic of a growing awareness of the need for oral and written instruction in law'.[13] The availability of these treatises in the thirteenth and fourteenth centuries implies a legal literacy among many different learned individuals, possibly even Chaucer, who displays a comprehensive knowledge of everything from surgical and astronomical treatises to continental romances and fables in his work.[14] So perhaps it is not surprising that many of Chaucer's tales deal with legal process and practice, or that one of his pilgrims is a Man of Law. But the specific episodes of violence and torture in the *Canterbury Tales*, an estates satire operating on multiple levels, suggest a more specific interest in the application of justice within a civil society and the destabilising potential of those processes when they are subverted or abused, especially in cases of murder.

In England, the word *murder* (c. 1300), from Old English *morðor* (plural *morþras*), meant 'secret killing of a person, unlawful killing', as well as 'mortal sin, crime; punishment, torment, misery'.[15] The Latin *Bracton*, which predates the Middle English appearance of *murder*, distinguishes between 'homicide committed openly and in the presence of many bystanders; and of homicide committed in the absence of witnesses, which is called murder'.[16]

> Murdrum vero est occulta extraneorum et notorum hominum occisio a manu hominum nequiter perpetrata, et quæ nullo sciente vel vidente facta est præter solum interfectorem et suos coadiutores et fautores, et ita quod non statim assequatur clamor popularis. Occulta dicitur quia occisor ignoratur, nec scitur quis ille fuerit qui occidit. Item extraneorum et notorum hominum, ut

---

[11] Ibid., p. 37.
[12] Ibid., p. 40.
[13] Ibid., p. 39.
[14] For more on Chaucer's knowledge of surgical texts, see: Larissa Tracy, 'Wounds and Wound Repair: The Medieval Literary Surgeon in Text and Cultural Tradition', in *Medizin und Militär–Soldiers and Surgeons: Beiträge zur Wundversorgung und Verwundetenfürsorge im Altertum*, ed. R. Breitwieser, F. Humer, E. Pollhammer, Robert Arnott (Archäologischer Park Carnuntum: Neue Forschungen Bd. 15), forthcoming.
[15] 'murder will out'. Dictionary.com. See n.1 above.
[16] The Latin text and English translation of *Bracton* are from Bracton Online: *Bracton: De Legibus et Consuetudinibus Angliæ (Bracton on the Laws and Customs of England attributed to Henry of Bratton, c. 1210–1268)*, reproduced from the dual language critical edition by Samuel Thorne, with the Latin text of George Woodbine, 4 vols (Cambridge: Harvard University Press, 1977): http://bracton.law.harvard.edu/Framed/mframe.htm (accessed 20 May 2016), 2:378. Hereafter, page and line numbers are given parentheses.

comprehendatis tam masculum quam feminam, et sic excludatis animalia bruta quæ ratione carent.

[Murder is the secret slaying of man by the hand of man, [whether those slain are known or strangers,] [committed wickedly,] done out of the sight of and unknown to all except the slayer alone and his accomplices and abettors so that no public hue and cry immediately pursues them, and [where] who the slayer is cannot be ascertained. The word 'secret' is used because the slayer is unknown; 'of man,' so as to include male and female and exclude brute animals lacking reason]. (379.4–11)

In *Bracton* the primary penalty for murder is the payment of 'murder-fines', which (allegedly) date back to the days of King Cnut (c. 990–1035) (379.15–16).[17] *Bracton* clarifies that it is *not* murder when someone is slain or devoured by animals because animals lack reason; nor is it murder when someone dies by misadventure, like drowning; nor *per infortunium ubi nulla subset felonia* (379.36–37) [by misadventure where there is no concealed felony] (379.35–36).

But when it does occur, murder is a crime against the king's peace:

Est etiam inter alia crimina crimen capitale quod in parte tangit ipsum regem, cuius pax infringitur, et in parte privatam personam, quæ nequiter et contra pacem domini regis occiditur. [...] Et est homicidium hominis occisio ab homine facta. [...] Est enim dictum homicidium ab homine et cædo, cædis, quasi hominis cædium. [...] (340.12–14, 16–18)

[Among other crimes there is a capital crime [called homicide], which partly concerns the king, whose peace is broken, and partly the private individual who is slain wickedly and in breach of the king's peace. ... Homicide is the slaying of man by man. ... For it is called 'homicide' from 'homo' and 'caedo, caedis,' 'man-killing,' so to speak]. (340.12–14, 17–18)

Bracton further specifies that there are several kinds of homicide, including spiritual and corporal (340.18–19); corporal homicide, *homo occiditur corporaliter* [where a man is bodily slain] (340.20) can be committed in two ways, *lingua vel facto* [by word or by deed] (340.21–22): 'Lingua tribus modis, scilicet præcepto, consilio, defensione sive tentione. Facto quatuor modis, scilicet iustitia, necessitate, casu et voluntate' [By word in three ways, that is, by precept, by counsel, and by denial or restraint. By deed in four ways, that is, in the administration of justice, of necessity, by chance and by intention] (340.22–23; 21–24). For *Bracton*, then, even lawful execution by judges or officers of those who were guilty could be considered a form of murder (340.24; 24–25). However, the intent of the killing is the defining feature:

---

[17] See, in this volume: Jay Paul Gates, 'Discursive Murders: The St Brice's Day Massacre, *Beowulf* and *Morðor*'.

Istud autem homicidium si sit ex livore vel delectatione effundendi humanum sanguinem, licet ille iuste occidatur, iste tamen peccat mortaliter propter intentionem corruptam. Si vero hoc fiat ex amore iustitiæ, nec peccat iudex ipsum condemnando ad mortem, et præcipiendo ministro ut occidat eum, nec minister si missus a iudice occidit condemnatum. Et peccat uterque si hoc fecerint iuris ordine non servato. (340.25–31)

[But it is homicide if done out of malice or from pleasure in the shedding of human blood [and] though the accused is lawfully slain, he who does the act commits a mortal sin because of his evil purpose. But if it is done from a love of justice, the judge does not sin in condemning him to death, nor in ordering an officer to slay him, nor does the officer sin if when sent by the judge he kills the condemned man. But both sin if they act in this way when proper legal procedures have not been observed]. (340.25–31)

The motivation and openness of a homicide determined whether a killing qualified as *murder* (341.22), a felony rather than a misadventure. All murder is homicide, but not all homicide is murder.

Once the nature of the homicide – felonious murder or simple misadventure – was established, then proper punishments could be exacted. There were two kinds of punishment for either spiritual or corporal homicide (341.23–24; 22–23). Spiritual homicide was generally punished with penance, while corporal homicide was punished in a variety of ways (341.27; 28–29). Justifiable homicide ('committed in doing justice, with a proper and lawful intention') was not punished (341.28; 28–30). Non-premeditated murder was most likely punished by the murder fines outlined in *Bracton*, while premeditated murder – and accessory to such murder – was punished more harshly. Homicide could be punished with hanging, especially if it occurred in conjunction with other crimes of *lese-majesty* (French: *lèse-majesté*), the rights of the king:

Sicut videri poterit, ut si quis accusatus fuerit de furti crimine vel homicidii, et similiter de crimine læsæ maiestatis, et convictus, gravius punitur crimen læsæ maiestatis quam crimen furti vel homicidii, quia ex uno sequitur quod criminosus trahitur, frangitur et suspenditur, ex alio non sequitur nisi tantum suspensio. (318.30–34).

[As may be seen where one has been accused of the crime of theft or homicide and also of lese-majesty; [if it is] proved the crime of lese-majesty is punished more severely than theft or homicide, for in the former case the criminal is drawn, broken and hanged and from the others nothing follows but simple hanging]. (318.28–32)

Significantly, English law focuses on the position of the king and his peace in determining certain murder cases, and it was within the king's jurisdiction to employ torture, though few of them did.

Torture took a variety of forms in medieval discourse. According to the *Oxford English Dictionary*, its English origins come from 'late Middle English (in the sense "distortion, twisting", or a physical disorder characterized by this): via French from late-Latin *tortura* "twisting, torment", from Latin *torquere* "to twist"'.[18] But in English texts, those subjected to torture are described as being 'put in harde pine'. The *Middle English Dictionary* gives the primary definition of 'pine' as: 'Pain or injury resulting from punishment; punishment; torture, torment; persecution; a punishment, kind or instance of torment'.[19] Generally, as medieval society understood it, torture meant the infliction of pain in a legal interrogation as means of extracting a confession: the 'Queen of Proofs'.[20] As Patricia Turning points out elsewhere in this volume as part of her analysis of murder trials in France and Ireland, torture was applied by several secular courts as a means of 'discovery' to determine the guilt of the accused.[21] But torture was not part of the English judicial procedure, except in rare cases and only under the rights of the king.[22] *Lese-majesty* left open the potential for abuse in the judicial procedure, even when it was used in the interests of discovering the truth behind murder.

The court of the king was also where corporal punishment was imposed (297.36), for '[v]ita vero et membra hominum sunt in manu regis, vel ad tuitionem vel ad pœnam cum deliquerint, nisi ita sit forte quod aliquis gaudeat speciali libertate, quod habeat tol et them etcetera ut infra' [Power over the lives and members of men is in the king's hand, to protect or to punish when they do wrong, unless some private person enjoys the special liberty of having toll and

---

[18] http://www.oxforddictionaries.com/us/definition/american_english/torture (accessed 20 May 2016).

[19] *The Middle English Dictionary*, http://quod.lib.umich.edu/cgi/m/mec/med-idx?-type=id&id=MED33414 (accessed 21 April 2014).

[20] Edward Peters, *Torture* (Philadelphia: University of Pennsylvania Press, 1985), p. 7. Peters further points out that, to the medieval mind, *torture* meant something very specific; judicial torture was the *only* kind of torture, however it was administered, and any other form of punishment not designed to elicit a confession should not be called torture (p. 7).

[21] Patricia Turning, 'A Case of Mariticide in Late Medieval France', in this volume. See also: Bridgette Slavin, 'Secret Killing and Murder by Magic in the Law of Adomnán'.

[22] On the question of torture in English law, see: Tracy, *Torture and Brutality*; John Bellamy, *Crime and Public Order in England in the Later Middle Ages* (London and Toronto: Routledge and Kegan Paul, 1973); J. G. Bellamy, *The Law of Treason in England in the Later Middle Ages* (Cambridge: Cambridge University Press, 1970); W. R. J. Barron, 'The Penalties for Treason in Medieval Life and Literature', *Journal of Medieval History* 7 (1981): 187–202; and Emanuel J. Mickel, *Ganelon, Treason, and the 'Chanson de Roland'* (University Park: The Pennsylvania State University Press, 1989). John Bellamy points out that torture was, essentially, a Tudor development, with its formative years most likely in the 1520s and 1530s, though common lawyers claimed it was never practised under common law except on the fiat of the monarch. *Strange, Inhuman Deaths: Murder in Tudor England* (Stroud: Sutton, 2005), p. 186.

team etc.] (298.2–5; 2–4). *Bracton* does include provisions for the use of torture under *lese-majesty*: 'Ad dominum regem pertinet et coronam suam cognoscendi de crimine læsæ maiestatis, ut de nece vel seditione personæ suæ vel regni vel exercitus sui' [Cognisance of the crime of lese-majesty belongs to the lord king and his crown, as an attempt on his life or the betrayal of his person, his realm or his army] (298.5–7). All forms of murder, as well as rape, arson, robbery and false imprisonment, fell under this designation and all involved 'pœnam corporalem [...] et secundum quod fuerint maiora vel minora gravem inducunt pœnam vel minus gravem' [corporal punishment, heavy or light depending upon whether the crimes are major or minor] (298.21–22; 20–21).[23] Torture was a potential facet of some of these punishments, not in the interrogative sense, but as part of the actual punishment once the accused was found guilty and sentenced:

> Inducunt enim quædam ultimum supplicium cum pœna graviori et tormentis, ne statim deficiant, quandoque sine tormentis. Item quædam inducunt membrorum truncationem, quædam exilium perpetuum vel ad tempus, et eodem modo imprisonamentum. Pœnæ autem ad correctionem hominum sunt inventæ, ut quos divinus timor non revocat, temporalis saltem pœna cohibeat a peccato. Ipse enim deus propter iniquitatem corripit homines. (298.22–28)

> [Some involve the ultimate penalty, with greater pain and torture lest they die at once; sometimes that same penalty without torture. Some entail mutilation of members, some exile, permanent or temporary, [or] permanent or temporary imprisonment. Punishments were devised for the correction of men, so that those whom the fear of God cannot turn from evil may at least be restrained by a temporal penalty. For God himself punishes men for their iniquity]. (298.21–26)

However, in this sense, torture (*tormentis*) is more correctly translated as *torment*, describing the gravity of the punishment rather than the practice by which a confession is extracted. Still other punishments include cudgeling, flogging,

---

[23] Other crimes that fell under *lese-majesty* included various kinds of forgery: counterfeiting the royal seal or coins, or making bad money out of good, as well as concealing a treasure trove and breaking the plea of the king's peace (298.7–1). These were considered more serious crimes than murder and rape, for example, because they principally affected the person of the king. *Glanvill* defines crimes of *lese majesty* in similar terms: 'Crimen quod in legibus dicitur crimen lese maiestatis, ut de nece uel sedition persone domini regis uel regni uel exercitus; occultation inuenti thesauri fraudulosa; placitum de pace domini regis infracta; homicidium; incendium; roberia; raptus; crimen falsi, et si qua sunt similia: que scilicet ultimo puniuntur supplicio aut membrorum truncation' [The crime which civil lawyers call *lèse-majesté*, namely the killing of the lord king or the betrayal of the realm or the army; fraudulent concealment of treasure trove; the pleas of breach of the lord king's peace; homicide; arson; robbery; rape; the crime of falsifying and other similar crimes: all these are punished by death or cutting off of limbs] (p. 3). *The Treatise of the Laws and Customs of the Realm of England Commonly Called* Glanvill, ed. and trans. G. D. G Hall (Oxford: Clarendon Press, 1993).

pillorying and ducking (298–99.34, 1–2). Other punishments were not physical but involved the pronouncement of a judgment with infamy: the ruin of someone's legal reputation. In fact, *Bracton* is clear that those who have already been sentenced, especially to execution, cannot be punished excessively:

> Et non alio modo puniatur quis quam secundum quod se habeat condemnatio, ut si gladio animadverti debeat in aliquem, tunc non securi neque telo neque fustibus vel laqueo alio quove modo. Item qui vivi exuri debent non eis verberibus noceatur, nec virgis, nec tormentis: quia plerique deficiunt dum torquentur, et hoc nisi aliter exigat enormitas delicti.
>
> [One is not punished in any way other than that provided in his condemnation, as where he ought to be executed by the sword he shall not be put to death in any other way, neither by the axe nor the spear, by cudgels nor by the rope. Similarly, those condemned to be burned alive ought not to be injured by floggings, whippings, or tortures, since many perish while under torture; this [is so] unless the enormity of the offence demands otherwise]. (299.3–8)

Unnecessary violence against prisoners was strictly forbidden (299.8–12).

Based on the interpretation of the mix of English and Roman law in *Bracton*,[24] judges and legal authorities in fourteenth-century England had a responsibility to be lenient and benign and to mitigate rather than increase punishments (299.11–16; 13–16). And yet, Chaucer includes torture as an interrogatory tool in at least three of his murder tales, usually as part of the process of discovery, even when guilt has been previously established by other means, suggesting that the application of torture circumvents the legal procedure. The crime of murder in Chaucer's work offers a variety of opportunities for interrogating the boundaries of justice in England: at times, murder is prosecuted and punished according to correct legal procedures; at times, authorities test the acceptable parameters of law by applying torture. In the context of his other accounts of murder in the *Canterbury Tales*, the episodes of torture undermine the efficacy of justice and cast doubt upon the absolute authority of monarchs who resort to it. While texts like *Bracton* outline circumstances where torture *could* be used, Chaucer's examples question whether it *should*.

MoLT describes a king's love for his wife and the false accusations against her that lead to their separation. The beautiful Custance, daughter of the Roman emperor, is set adrift by her Syrian mother-in-law-to-be who prefers to slaughter her son and his wedding guests rather than accept his conversion and

---

[24] Because of this mix, it is difficult at times to entirely trust *Bracton* because it is often contradictory. See: Jonathan Rose, 'The Legal Profession in Medieval England: A History of Regulation', *Syracuse Law Review* 48.1 (1998): 1–154. Available at: https://papers.ssrn.com/sol3/papers.cfm?abstract_id=1422764 (accessed 30 April 2017). My thanks to the anonymous reader for this reference.

marriage to the Christian Custance. Shipwrecked on the Northumberland coast, Custance is taken in by a constable and his wife Hermengyld. When Custance refuses the attentions of a young knight dwelling in that town, he plots to murder Hermengyld and frame Custance: 'for despit he compassed in his thought / to maken hire on shameful deeth to deye' (591–92). He carries out his nefarious plan and 'Kitte the throte of Hermengyld atwo, / And leyde the blody knyf by dame Custance / And wente his wey' (600–02). Custance, blamed by the constable for his wife's death, is taken before the English king Alla who is noted for his wisdom and just rule. He sentences Custance to death, but the people (and Chaucer) affirm her innocence and her devotion to Hermengyld. Moved by the will of the people, Alla orders further investigation into the alleged crime rather than automatically executing Custance, 'a trouthe for to lere' (630). Custance maintains her composure and her innocence, praying to God and Mary: 'If I be giltlees of this *felonye*, / My socour be, for ellis shal I dye' (643–44, my emphasis). Chaucer clarifies that this is a case of felony murder: homicide done in secret and with malicious intent, as defined by *Bracton*. To further his investigation, Alla has the treacherous knight swear to her guilt on a Bible – an *English* Bible, 'A Britoun book, written with Evaungiles' (666) – and he perjures himself, swearing that 'She gilty was' (668). As a result, 'An hand hym smoot upon the nekke-boon, / That doun he fil atones as a stoon / And bother his eyen broste out of his face / in sighte of every body in that place' (669–72). He is struck down for bearing false witness: Chaucer thus invokes divine justice in the exercise of temporal justice.[25] Custance is exonerated by the divine revelation, and all the pagans convert, a religious transformation brought about via the application of correct legal procedure as much as by virtue of apparent miracle. The divinely blinded and innately false knight is then 'slayn for his untrouthe / By juggement of Alla hastily' (687–88).

But Custance's trials – literal and figurative – are not over yet. Alla and Custance fall in love, but his mother, Donegild (who is 'ful of tirannye' [696]) plots to spoil his marriage to 'so strange a creature' (700). Once they are married, Alla goes away to war against the Scots and, in his absence, Custance gives birth to a baby boy. The evil Donegild intercepts letters announcing the birth of his son, instead telling Alla that the child was born 'so horrible a feendly creature' (751), because Custance is secretly 'an elf' (754) summoned by charms and sorcery. Despite his mother's claims, Alla writes to Custance that he will accept the child, but Donegild intercepts that letter from the drunken messenger as well

---

[25] Bursting eyes is a favourite punishment meted out by Irish saints to punish various sacrilege and transgressions. See: Máire Johnson, 'In the Bursting of an Eye: Blinding and Blindness in Ireland's Medieval Hagiography', in *Wounds and Wound Repair*, ed. Larissa Tracy and Kelly DeVries (Leiden: Brill, 2015), pp. 448–70.

and replaces it with a forged order that Custance and her child be cast away in the same boat that brought her to England (799–800). Exiled, Custance leaves with her son; her ship is intercepted by a senator (her uncle) sent to find her in Syria after news of the earlier massacre reaches her father. Although he fails to recognise her, he takes her home to his family out of Christian pity. There she stays, living in pious obscurity until the grief-stricken Alla – seeking penance after executing his mother for her part in the since-revealed plot against Custance – sees their son in a papal audience with the senator. They are reunited and Alla explains his innocence in her exile. Then Custance reveals herself to her father (the emperor), and the pope declares their son, Maurice, the next emperor. Custance and Alla return to England where they live in love for a year until Alla dies; Custance returns to Rome and lives out the rest of her virtuous life. Everything ends well, despite the fact that Alla ends up dead. In his virtuous death, at least, Alla is redeemed for the injustices he commits.

Throughout the tale, the repeated motif of murder and intrigue highlights the significance of legal procedure, which seems an appropriate subject for a man of law. Torture appears once, but not in the murder trial against Custance; rather, it is unjustly applied against the drunken messenger after the discovery of the deceptive exchange of letters that results in Custance's exile. Donegild uses legal language to forge the letter ordering Custance's banishment, threatening the constable upon 'peyne of hangyng, and on heigh juyse' (795) that he must put Custance in the same ship in which she arrived. When Alla returns and finds her gone, the constable tells him all but he still resorts to torture to force a confession. Torture is out of place here and excessive, especially since it is used against a witless participant who becomes a victim of Donegild's plot. The messenger cannot be held responsible for the counterfeit letters, and the only things to which he can confess are being drunk and careless: 'He drank, and wel his girdle underpighte; / He slepeth, and he fnorteth in hyse / Al nyght, til the sonne gan aryse' (789–91). When he delivers his missive, the Constable bemoans the contents, lamenting that the king could be so cruel to the innocent Custance. The messenger seems completely unaware that the letter has been switched (806–19).

Applying torture is uncharacteristic of Alla, who is patterned after Ælle, one of the best-known Northumbrian kings in both pre- and post-Conquest English tradition.[26] In the *Historia Ecclesiastica*, Bede establishes the sixth-century Ælle's reputation as a founding father of early English Christian civilisation, a

---

[26] John Frankis, 'King Ælle and the Conversion of the English: The Development of a Legend from Bede to Chaucer', in *Literary Appropriations of the Anglo-Saxons from the Thirteenth to the Twentieth Century*, ed. Donald Scragg and Carole Weinberg (Cambridge: Cambridge University Press, 2000): pp. 74–92 at p. 80.

reputation that endured in later Middle English chronicles like Matthew Paris' thirteenth-century *Chronica Majora*.[27] Resorting to torture undermines Alla's association with English justice and 'gode olde lawe' because there was no provision for it in pre-Conquest law or practice.[28] Alla transforms from a fair, just and law-abiding king into one who uses torture in desperation against a man who was too drunk to know he was deceived: 'This messager tormented was til he/ Moste biknowe and tellen, plat and pleyn' (885–86).[29] All he can tell is that Donegild got him drunk and that he passed out in her castle; he is not really guilty of anything except being manipulated. While Alla is entitled to apply torture, his decision to use it is problematic because it contradicts the cultural reputation of this early Christian king, and it results in a clear miscarriage of justice. Chaucer says nothing about the methods employed in 'tormenting' the messenger, only that it provides the first clue to the truth: 'And thus, by wit and sotil enquerynge,/ Ymagined was by whom this harm gan sprynge' (888–89). The use of 'sotil' suggests deceptive, shadowy means, implying that, while understandable in the context of the tale, the use of torture potentially taints the reputation of an otherwise admirable king. It casts a shadow on Alla's capacity to exercise true justice, revealing flaws in the judicial systems that allow it.

With the information obtained through torture in hand, Alla ferrets out the family plot and 'out of drede,/ his mooder slow – that may men pleynly rede – / For that she traitour was to hire ligeance' (893–95). She violates her allegiance to Alla as her king, not just as his mother, a crime of *lese-majesty*. But Alla later repents his action (legal as it may be) by taking a pilgrimage to Rome, which positions him to be briefly reunited with Custance: 'Kyng Alla, which that hadde his moder slayn, / Upon a day fil in swich repentance / That, if I shortly tellen shal and playn, / To Rome he comth to receyven his penance' (988–91). His

---

[27] Ibid., pp. 81–83.
[28] Tracy, *Torture and Brutality*, pp. 169–72.
[29] 'Torment', or more specifically the verb 'tormenten', has several meanings in Middle English, but the primary one is associated with torture or punishment: '1. (a) To inflict physical pain deliberately and systematically on (sb., a part of the body), esp. for coercion or punishment, torture (sb.); — also without obj. [quot. c1384]; (b) to inflict physical or spiritual pain unremittingly on (sb., a part of the body, a soul) for punishment, subject to the torments of hell or its equivalent; (c) to inflict pain on (oneself, one's body), esp. for self-mortification; *ppl.* tormented, in pain [last quot.].' *Middle English Dictionary*, http://quod.lib.umich.edu/cgi/m/mec/med-idx?type=id&id=MED46371 (accessed 5 May 2014). In *The Riverside Chaucer*, Larry Benson notes twenty-seven occurrences in all of Chaucer's works for *tormente*, *turmente* or some variant, such as *tormenten* or *turmented*, or the noun *tormentour*. But not all of these instances refer to torture in the judicial or interrogative sense, and many do not refer to the infliction of physical pain at all. Benson defines *tormente*, *turmente* as the verb 'torment, torture' in *Troilus* and the *Knight's Tale*, but in these texts, it refers to the mental suffering of the character, not literal torture. Benson, ed., *The Riverside Chaucer*, p. 1299.

willing repentance suggests that he recognises his transgressions of both law and morality, for while the text does not explicitly state that he regrets resorting to torture against the messenger, he puts himself in the pope's hands, seeking from Christ to 'Foryeve his wikked werkes that he wroght' (994). Torture is an instrument of unstable power; Chaucer, who omits details of the torture and says that Alla repents his previous actions, signals his disapproval of the brutality enacted by kings, even when it is for a good end and even if they have the right to do it. As a soldier and servant of the crown, Chaucer would have been intimately familiar with royal prerogative and its consequences; through *MoLT*, then, Chaucer may be urging Richard II, embroiled in his own wars and intrigues, to consider the lesson of Alla's repentance as a model for kingly behaviour.

While *MoLT* probes the boundaries of English justice, the tale told by the lively Prioress tries to justify torture and mob violence as valid responses to murder.[30] She tells of a virtuous Christian boy brutally slain in a Jewish ghetto in a far-away part of 'Asye' for singing a religious hymn in praise of the Virgin Mary, and she details the subsequent summary execution of those held responsible. As I have argued elsewhere, this tale is problematic not solely because of the murder of the boy, whose throat is cut savagely before he is tossed into a privy, but because of the anti-Judaic[31] treatment of the murderers who 'with torment and with shameful deeth echon' (628) are dragged behind horses (or quartered), and then hanged without trial or inquiry.[32] The word 'torment' in this context means torture, but in a punitive sense rather than an interrogative one, an explicit contravention of law outlined in *Bracton*. In *PT*, judicial brutality is enacted by legal authority, but there is no formal trial, no process of law, just summary execution carried out by the civil authority at the first suspicion of a crime and the discovery of a body. As Sheila Delany says, the Jews are 'condemned, tortured, and executed on circumstantial evidence supported by a miracle' like the unjustly

---

[30] Greg Wilsbacher, 'Lumiansky's Paradox: Ethics, Aesthetics and Chaucer's "Prioress's Tale"', *College Literature* 32.4 (2005): 1–28 at p. 2.

[31] In using the term anti-Judaic rather than anti-Semitic, I am referring specifically to medieval attitudes, as Michael Calabrese does in his article 'Performing the Prioress: "Conscience" and Responsibility in Studies of Chaucer's Prioress's Tale', *Texas Studies in Literature and Language* 44.1 (2002): 66–91 at p. 85. For a fuller discussion of torture in the context of the Prioress's character and her tale, see: *Torture and Brutality*, pp. 169–90.

[32] Being dragged to the gallows and hanged was the prescribed punishment for traitors in medieval Europe, though rarely, in some places such as France, the traitor might also be flayed. According to Bellamy, in general, the punishment of traitors, like the scope of high treason, was similar all over Europe at this time (*The Law of Treason in England*, p. 13).

tortured messenger in *MoLT*.[33] Greg Wilsbacher argues that the Jews are tried, convicted and punished within the space of a stanza, 'in part because the goal of a unified Christian community requires their immediate disappearance.'[34] Miri Rubin recounts multiple instances of Christian mob violence against Jews in the fourteenth and fifteenth centuries where crowds, incensed by tales of host desecration, did not stop long to think, acting on a simple set of 'signs and prompts, almost like an animal lacking reason.'[35] In these instances, Jews were often thrown into fire, 'not at the ordered stake of secular punishment, but fires lit by townspeople or groups of people who assembled for the task of revenge',[36] or tortured in punitive spectacles. It may be these displays of mob rule to which Chaucer responds in *PT*, just as he does in *NPT* in his singular reference to the Peasants' Revolt of 1381 (3394–96). The Christians in *PT* act *en masse* in calling for the provost, and Chaucer condemns this barely legal prelude to lynching; indeed, his fourteenth-century audience – nobles, burghers and clerics all too familiar with such spectacles of themselves – would likely have felt similarly uncomfortable with the effects of mob violence.

In Chaucer's version of the tale (there are numerous analogues),[37] the seven-year-old child is raised in a society (a 'greet citee' in 'Asye' [488]) where different religious communities coexist, where civil authorities have given the Jews licence to live only because they are financially necessary: 'Amonges Cristene folk a Jewerye, / Sustened by a lord of that contree / For foule usure and lucre of vileynye, / Hateful to Crist and to his compaignye' (489–92). Helen Cooper argues that setting the tale in 'Asye' removes any need for adhering to European legal procedures; it 'allows the law to inflict a particularly horrific punishment; God's enemies come to a miserable end on this earth, the murdered child has his end not in the cesspit but in the procession before the Lamb. The Jews, like the Saracen mother-in-law of the *Man of Law's Tale*, are cast by definition as enemies of God.'[38] Yet Delany refutes Cooper's reading, offering a more compelling connection between the setting and the question of justice, further noting that there is no confession extracted in the text: the actual murderer is never appre-

---

[33] Sheila Delany, 'Chaucer's Prioress, the Jews, and the Muslims', *Medieval Encounters* 5.2 (1999): 198–213 at p. 205. Many of these arguments are also made in Sheila Delany, 'Asia in the Prioress's Tale', in *Chaucer and the Jews: Sources, Contexts, Meanings*, ed. Sheila Delany (London: Routledge, 2002), pp. 43–68.
[34] Wilsbacher, 'Lumiansky's Paradox', p. 13.
[35] Miri Rubin, *Gentile Tales: The Narrative Assault on Late Medieval Jews* (Philadelphia: University of Pennsylvania Press, 2004), p. 88.
[36] Ibid., p. 89.
[37] For a brief discussion of Chaucer's sources, see: Florence H. Ridley's explanatory notes to the *Prioress's Prologue and Tale*, *The Riverside Chaucer*, ed. Benson, pp. 913–16 at p. 913.
[38] Helen Cooper, *Oxford Guides to Chaucer: The Canterbury Tales* (Oxford: Oxford University Press, 1989), p. 293.

hended, and those punished are punished only for knowing about the murder, not for carrying it out.[39] If the tale is meant to take place in Islamic territory, as Delany suggests, then Islamic law 'would normally have required a rigorous court proceeding, in which the Jews would probably have won'.[40] Louise O. Fradenburg questions the reality of justice in the tale,[41] and the absence of law is a major point either way. Whether Chaucer's audience was familiar with Islamic or Judaic law or not, they knew that English custom required a jury trial and a verdict, and that summary execution was neither valid nor just. Authorities that resort to such brutality only undermine their own rule and destabilise the local power structure. By including episodes of torture applied unjustly and against relative innocents, Chaucer advocates an adherence to law and justice particular to England and absent outside its borders. The Jews are not alien – neither to the fictional setting of *PT*, nor to the well-travelled Chaucer – even if their presence would have seemed alien in fourteenth-century England and to the Prioress in her isolated ignorance.[42] The alien 'Other' are the Christian authorities who flout the legal process familiar to Chaucer's English audience and who engage in unnecessary wholesale brutality.

The Prioress points out that the clergeon's school is at the far end of the street, presumably requiring dozens of Christian children to walk through the Jewish ghetto every day, which they do unmolested until the devil supposedly convinces the Jews that this particular child must be exterminated:

> Our firste foo, the serpent Sathanas,
> That hath in Jues herte his waspes nest,
> Up swal, and seide, 'O Hebrayk peple, allas!
> Is this to yow a thyng that is honest,
> That swich a boy shal walken as hym lest
> In youre despit, and synge of swich sentence,
> Which is agayn youre lawes reverence?' (558–64)

Satan's appeal to the Jews' adherence to religious law in his efforts to turn them to murder is a striking contrast to the absence of civil law at the end of the tale when the Jews are punished before the child has miraculously spoken and revealed the truth of his murder. The Prioress describes the child's death in detail: the hired 'homycide' (567) waits in an alley, grabs the child, holds him fast, 'kitte his throte, and in a pit hym caste' (571). This 'homycide' – used as a noun describing the perpetrator as well as the crime, just as in *PT* – lurks much like Reynard

---

[39] Delany 'Chaucer's Prioress', p. 205.
[40] Ibid.
[41] Louise O. Fradenburg, 'Criticism, Anti-Semitism, and the *Prioress's Tale*', *Exemplaria* 1 (1989): 69–115 at p. 76.
[42] The Jews were officially expelled from England by Edward I in 1290.

in the *NPT* who waits for Chaunticleer, 'As gladly doon thise homycides alle / That in await liggen to mordre men. O false mordrour, lurkynge in thy den!' (3224–26). Murderers – whether human or animal – plot in the dark, in secret, stalking their prey. To add insult to injury, the Prioress elaborates on the kind of pit: 'I seye that in a wardrobe they hym threwe/ Where as thise Jewes purgen hire entraille' (572–73). Any audience shocked by the brutality of the murder would be further disgusted by the image of the child's body being thrown into a privy among the excrement and waste.

In traditional saints' lives or miracles of the Virgin, the evildoers realise their error and are converted.[43] If *PT* followed its traditional conclusion, evident in other extant versions,[44] that is what *should* happen, but it does not. No one is converted; in fact, no one is even given the opportunity to convert because the Jews are tortured and executed before they can fully witness the extent of the miracle. The Prioress explains that the widowed mother, desperate in her search for her son, goes to the ghetto and confronts the Jews who lie and say that they have not seen the child. With their lie, 'Jhesu of his grace/ Yaf in hir thoght inwith a litel space/ That in that place after hir sone she cryde,/ Where he was casten in a pit bisyde' (603–06), and the child's voice rings out from the cesspit 'with throte ykorven' (611) with a resounding chorus of *Alma redemptoris*. The actions of the crowd are immediate: they send for the provost. He comes without tarrying and 'after that the Jewes leet he bynde' (620). There is no inquisition into the guilt of the accused and no threat of torture; only its application matters, and no questions are asked at all. Any pretence of law has been shattered and all the legal structures circumvented. Their guilt is assumed and proclaimed with the arrival of the civil authority. The child's singing body is carried to the abbey and placed on the bier, where his mother, this 'newe Rachel' (627), weeps inconsolate.

With the punishment of the Jews, no one particular person is singled out; they are all condemned to death for their assumed part in hiring the murderer or their supposed knowledge of it:

With torment and with shameful deeth echon,
This provost dooth thise Jewes for to sterve
That of this mordre wiste, and that anon.
He holde no swich cursednesse observe.
'Yvele shal have that yvele wol deserve';

---

[43] Daniel F. Pigg notes that it is unclear whether others are converted by the singing, which would have been expected in a miracle tale. See: 'The Semiotics of Comedy in Chaucer's Religious Tales', in *Chaucer's Humor: Critical Essays*, ed. Jean E. Jost (New York: Garland, 1994), pp. 321–48 at p. 339.

[44] Dahood, 'The Punishment of the Jews', p. 482. On sources, see: Ridley, notes to the *Prioress's Prologue and Tale*, p. 913.

Therfore with wilde hors he dide hem drawe,
And after that he heng hem by the lawe. (lines 628–34)

The Jews are subjected to torture (*torment*) based on an assumption of guilt – not in the interest of 'discovery' – and then executed. Many critics have argued that *drawe* means torn apart by wild horses (equine quartering), but Roger Dahood effectively explains that it means being dragged by horses to the place of execution.[45] This may not *seem* as brutal as being torn asunder by horses; criminals were often dragged to the gallows. But as it is, equine dragging, which involves being tied behind a horse and pulled along the ground, 'is harsh indeed'.[46] However, the injustice of a mass execution without recourse to law is brutal enough, despite the Prioress's assertion that 'he heng hem by the lawe' (634). They have not been tried; they have been rounded up and lynched after being tortured. It is still a humiliating and unnecessarily excessive punishment for an entire group of people. Dahood suggests that this only seems excessive 'at first blush' because the crime is murder, not treason, but he concludes that the Jews executed for the murder of Hugh of Lincoln in 1255 suffered the same fate and that Chaucer saw 'nothing offensive in it'.[47] Even though it is clear that Hugh was not murdered by Jews,[48] ninety-one were rounded up and held in the Tower of London for their part in the alleged blood ritual after a certain Copin (or Jopin) admitted, under threat of torture, to murdering the boy.[49] Copin was then executed, despite being promised protection if he confessed. Of those imprisoned, eighteen were hanged, their property confiscated by Henry III, while the rest were pardoned and set free.[50] The gruesome details of the mass execution are

---

[45] Roger Dahood focuses on the punishment of the Jews in his article 'The Punishment of the Jews, Hugh of Lincoln, and the Question of Satire in Chaucer's *Prioress's Tale*', *Viator* 36 (2005): 465–91. Dahood also chronicles other English accounts of child-murder in his article 'English Historical Narratives of Jewish Child-Murder, Chaucer's *Prioress's Tale*, and the Date of Chaucer's Unknown Source', *Studies in the Age of Chaucer* 31 (2009): 125–40. There is a critical debate about whether the Jews were equine quartered and then hanged or simply dragged behind horses to be hanged. Dahood discusses the nature of this punishment at length, reviewing each of the possibilities for defining *drawe*, concluding that it means dragging along the ground rather than equine dismemberment or quartering. 'The Punishment of the Jews', pp. 466–69. This interpretation is logical because, for them to be hanged, there must be an intact body; they are drawn to the place of execution by horses and then hanged.

[46] Dahood, 'The Punishment of the Jews', p. 470.

[47] Ibid., pp. 472, 473.

[48] Ridley, notes to the *Prioress's Prologue and Tale*, pp. 913–16.

[49] Gavin I. Langmuir, 'The Knight's Tale of Young Hugh of Lincoln', *Speculum* 47.3 (1972): 459–82 at p. 477. Also see: Florence H. Ridley, 'A Tale Told Too Often', *Western Folklore* 26.3 (1967): 153–56; and Dahood, 'The Punishment of the Jews', pp. 465–91.

[50] There is some question as to whether anything would have been done at all had the royal authorities not intervened; since there is no evidence of prior secular action, 'one

present in the Burton annals that record the events surrounding the murder of Hugh of Lincoln, and Chaucer's omission of those details suggests that he refused to fully participate in glorifying the wrongful execution of a group of people and the perpetuation of the mythology surrounding blood libel and ritual murder.[51] If Chaucer was not offended by the mass execution of the Jews because they were Jews (as Dahood contends), then he may have been offended by the contravention of law alien to an English sense of justice.[52] Chaucer inhabited a political climate that abhorred social abuse, and even though torture was institutionally illegal, brutality was not uncommon; 'the perversion of justice by the very men expected to uphold the law – the judges, sheriffs, and juries who were taking bribes or extorting money for their own profit – was of particular concern to the political community of late medieval England'.[53] According to texts like *Bracton*, there is no provision for this kind of judicial brutality in English law: not even in cases of *lese-majesty*. While the execution of the Jews in *PT* (and London) is suspect, and the anti-Judaic sentiment in the tale deplorable to a modern audience (if not fully to a contemporary one), the punishment constitutes civil judicial brutality that would have been problematic for an English audience. Regard for the law has been subverted either by sectarian hatred or financial concerns. Chaucer may not be satirising the Prioress, but he does satirise the mindset that created her and that she perpetuates in her own ignorance.

Part of that satire may lie in the Nun's Priest's response to *PT*, urged by the Host after the Knight interrupts the Monk's ponderously long recitation of the disastrous fate of great men and kings (2767–79). Denied a description in the *General Prologue*, and passed over in his own prologue in favour of the Host's mockery of his horse, 'a jade' (2812) that is 'bothe foul and lene' (2813), the Nun's Priest seems comical with a puffed-up chest that resembles that of the foul protagonist of his tale. In the *Epilogue* to *NPT*, Harry Bailly wryly praises the priest's fable as somewhat autobiographical: 'by my trouthe, if thou were seculer, / Thou woldest ben a trede-foul aright' (3450–51). In 'nede of hennes' (3453) indeed 'moo than seven tymes seventene' (3454), the Host points out 'whiche braunes

---

may wonder sadly whether the miscarriage of justice would have occurred had Henry III not passed through Lincoln that autumn with John de Lexinton'. See: Langmuir, 'The Knight's Tale of Young Hugh of Lincoln', p. 477.

[51] Compared to the Burton annals, which may have been one of Chaucer's sources for this material, the Prioress's tale is restrained and matter-of-fact, focusing on the 'justice of the punishment', keeping the description spare. See: Dahood, 'The Punishment of the Jews', p. 482.

[52] Dahood argues that Chaucer's connections to Lincoln and his loyalty to John of Gaunt, a direct descendant of Henry III, 'inclines against the likelihood of Chaucer's detachment from the prevailing anti-semitism [sic] of his time'. Ibid., pp. 483, 490.

[53] John Aberth, *A Knight at the Movies: Medieval History on Film* (New York: Routledge, 2003), p. 156.

hath this gentil preest, / So gret a nekke, and swich a large breest! / He loketh as a sperhauk with his yen' (3455–57). The priest is so red in the face that he 'nedeth nat his colour for to dyen / With brasile ne with greyn of Portyngale' (3458–59). Clearly worked up by the power of his own tale of murder, the Nun's Priest parallels the exaggerated delight the Prioress takes in the gruesome subject of her tale. Torture appears briefly in *NPT* as part of Chaunticleer's exposition on the power of dreams. Relating a tale taken from Cicero or Valerius Maximus,[54] Chaunticleer gives the example of a man who dreams of his fellow pilgrim's murder, ignoring the portent only to discover his companion's body in a dung cart as the apparition foretold. The companion receives warning of his fellow's death twice, and in the third dream his friend – now slain – appears: 'I am now slawe. / Bihoold my bloody woundes depe and wyde!' (3014–15). Like the wounds of Henry VI in *Richard III* that Shakespeare says 'Open their congeal'd mouths and bleed afresh' (I.ii.230), the victim's ghostly wounded corpse gives evidence of murder. The pilgrim, murdered for his gold (as he explains in his fellow's dream), tells him 'every point how he was slayn, / with a ful pitous face, pale of hewe' (3023–24). Much like Shakespeare's ghostly King Hamlet, the victim gives his own testimony, providing the testimony designed to indict his murderers. When the victim's companion wakes, he remembers his dream. Echoing the Prioress's account of the child in the cesspit, Chaunticleer says the man began to cry, '"Vengeance and justice of this felonye: / 'My felawe mordred is this same nyght, / And in this carte he lith gapyng upright. / I crye out oon the ministres"' (3040–43). However, he appeals to the magistrates to ferret out the culprits and bring them to justice, not to the mob violence of *PT*, though, ultimately, it is the community that reveals the murder by upending the dung cart and uncovering the body.

The Nun's Priest parodies the violence of *PT*.[55] His Chaunticleer is a flamboyant echo of the Prioress's *clergeon* whose clear singing in praise of the Virgin Mary becomes the motive (along with Satanic intervention) for his murder. Chaunticleer praises the justice of God for revealing the deed and explains the swift civil actions of the magistrates:

> Mordre wol out; that se we day by day.
> Mordre is so wlatsom and abhomynable
> To God, that is so just and resonable,
> That he ne wol nat suffre it heled be,
> Though it abyde a yeer, or two, or thre
> Mordre wol out, this my conclusioun.
> And right anon, ministres of that toun

---

[54] Susan H. Cavanaugh, notes to the *Nun's Priest's Tale*, *The Riverside Chaucer*, ed. Benson, pp. 935–41 at p. 938.
[55] Ibid., p. 935.

> Han hent the carter and so soore hym pyned,
> And eek the hostiler so soore engyned,
> That they biknewe hire wikkednesse anon,
> And were an hanged by the nekke-bon. (3052–62)

This reference to torture, 'so soore hym pyned' and 'so soore engyned', does not have a direct bearing on the tale except in the context of Chaunticleer's preoccupation with the possibility of his own murder. Richard West contends that the Nun's Priest repeats and endorses the Prioress's 'savage thoughts on crime and punishment',[56] which, in turn, suggests that Chaucer does as well. But the presence of torture is problematic in an English context; what Chaunticleer lauds is what he ('king of his roost') sees as the correct application of justice through legitimate authority, not the mob violence and mass slaughter of *PT*. However, there is no reference to a trial, nor to a jury, the function of which is a primary facet of English common law outlined in *Bracton*. Juries were cautious and aware of their responsibility. According to Musson, depending on the 'nature and level of the offense they were trying, jury members, either individually or collectively, had to take cognizance of the legal, social and even political ramifications of their decisions'.[57] In cases of homicide, the jury's deliberations and 'ability to import their understanding of the incident to the final verdict … suggests there were societal forces which the law could not penetrate'.[58] But in *NPT*, as in *PT*, there is no jury, no recourse to social knowledge or understanding; instead, in *NPT*, both the carter and the hosteler are tortured to reveal their part in the crime, not their motivation – theft – which has already been revealed in the dream. In fact, their confessions seem hardly necessary at all. Chaunticleer expounds on the stigma murder holds in English society – 'abhomynable' and 'wlatson' – a disgusting crime committed by horrible people; but he, like the Prioress, discusses torture as a means to an end at the hands of authorities (magistrates in *NPT* and the provost in *PT*) who act alone. Chaunticleer, though justifiably paranoid, is a parody; he is a caricature of those who accept most things at face value and ask few questions.

In the context of the Peasant's Revolt, to which the Nun's Priest alludes by comparing the chaotic farmyard melee against the fox to 'Jakke Straw and his meynee' (3394) who certainly never made 'shoutes half so shrille / whan that they wolden any Flemyng kille' (3395–6), the juxtaposition of murder swiftly and justly adjudicated to the secret stalking of Reynard and subsequent mob violence would have been an uncomfortable association. As Musson writes, over a fortnight, the Peasant's Revolt contributed a period of 'misrule': the public burning of documents, the targeting of government and shire officials (designed to paralyse administrative operations) and the beheading of 'traitors' on Tower

---

[56] West, *Chaucer 1340–1400*, p. 72.
[57] Musson, *Medieval Law*, p. 115.
[58] Ibid.

Hill, essentially turning society upside down and attempting to give an air of legitimacy to the rebellion.[59] According to Musson, the 'involvement of people drawn from all social levels (including members of the lesser clergy) with their own experiences of justice and royal administration would have created an interesting mixture of ideas, grudges and complaints'.[60] The murder dream in *NPT* highlights the correct exercise of justice in an era of chaos, misrule and rebellion, but an exercise that seems to exist only in a dream and is tainted by the use of torture in discovering the truth, perhaps an echo of the tyranny that inspired the Peasant's Revolt in the first place.

Throughout the *Canterbury Tales*, murder reveals the worst tendencies of humanity: the desire to secretly kill other human beings out of greed or malice. While each murder narrative delves into the heinous nature of the crime, in *MoLT*, *PT* and *NPT* specifically, Chaucer exposes the contradictions and potential for abuse in a system whose authorities act autonomously without employing the jury system, a mainstay of English law. In each instance, a singular judicial authority – magistrate, provost or king – resorts to interrogatory torture and acts with impunity. While these tales emphasise the restoration of justice in the prosecution of the crime, the methods potentially undermine the very justice they enact. The Man of Law speaks with gravity and legal authority of the regret Alla feels for exercising his *lese-majesty*. By contrast, the Prioress and the Nun's Priest are laughable narrators, and their exaggerated tales are excessive and ridiculous. Each tale seems to indicate the need for torture in 'proving' murder cases, even though it was *not* permissible under English law, except in cases of *lese-majesty*. In *MoLT* it is a regrettable, excessive transgression; in *PT* it is a symptom of misrule and tyranny; and in *NPT* it signals a tendency towards authoritarian action. Most of Chaucer's murder tales focus on the application of justice without resorting to torture; murderers are condemned by the treachery of their actions as the crime is brought to light through divine intervention or proper legal authorities: 'mordre wol out'. Perhaps the emphasis on the foulness of murder in these three stories is meant to justify the use of torture in its adjudication. Perhaps the fallibility of the Nun's Priest and Chaunticleer, or the fact that the *NPT*'s whole exposition is in aid of proving the efficacy of dreams, diminishes the credibility of authorities that use torture. Or perhaps these episodes simply point out that torture *was* used despite the protests and prohibitions laid out in English legal tradition by texts like *Bracton*. In any of these interpretations, the use of torture to reveal the truth of murder suggests that the authorities – then as now – were just as susceptible to the violent tendencies that propelled murderers in times of unrest and misrule.

[59] Ibid., pp. 242, 246.
[60] Ibid., p. 247.

PART II

THE PUBLIC HERMENEUTICS OF MURDER: INTERPRETATION AND CONTEXT

CHAPTER 6

Bringing Murder to Light: Death, Publishing and Performance in Icelandic Sagas

Ilse Schweitzer VanDonkelaar

THE MEDIEVAL SAGAS of Iceland (*Íslendinga sögur*) capture a world at once fantastic and familiar to modern audiences – a world in which individuals and families fought to survive in a frontier landscape, navigating threats natural and supernatural, political and economic, ultimately creating a complex social organisation unlike any other in the medieval world. Composed during the thirteenth and fourteenth centuries, the sagas reflect a vision of the past lives of Iceland's farmers (*bondi*) and chieftains (*goði*) in the tenth- to eleventh-century Icelandic Commonwealth, around and after the time of the country's settlement and conversion to Christianity (c. 1000). A second textual legacy of medieval Iceland is the culture's highly intricate set of legal codes, adopted and maintained at the annual national assembly and regulating conduct in areas ranging from inheritance to slander, from marriage to property disputes over driftwood. Together, the literary and legal texts of Iceland establish the law codes as a shared means of regulating behaviour and of strengthening familial and political connections within communities. Concurrently, the legal and literary texts offer glimpses of the gaps between theory and practice. While the law requires that individuals keep themselves open in their deeds and honest in their reputations, the sagas reveal that the force of the law, in fact, depends upon one's reputation, and that legal rituals meant to bring foul deeds to light could, in turn, be used by characters to conceal guilt and to escape social responsibility.

For cases of homicide, both legal and saga texts provide formulae (verbal and non-verbal) to enable the public pursuit of justice by bringing the act of killing into the open. Yet the Icelandic sagas rarely reproduce the detailed script that legally transforms murder to manslaughter; in most cases, the saga-authors create their own language for bringing murder to light. While saga-characters employ various modes of legal and poetic performance to declare and conceal their own crimes, the saga-authors use these dramatic moments to critique the repurposing and circumvention of Icelandic law by the powerful, revealing the importance of reputation in securing justice and exploring how narrow the space between honour and dishonour might be.

According to Icelandic law, the act that distinguishes manslaughter from murder occurs in the performative act of 'publishing' a killing. The *Grágás* law codes of the Icelandic Commonwealth, memorised and recited orally from around 930 CE and recorded around 1117–18 CE, preserve the procedures by which one should declare a killing by his own hand in early Icelandic society.[1] The later law codes preserved in *Jónsbók* (adopted in 1281) reflect a revision of Icelandic law after the country's loss of independence to Norway in 1262; even so, *Jónsbók* draws over half of its content (43 per cent of its chapters are replicated directly) from *Grágás*,[2] hence a level of continuity in the law of the land. In the detailed formulae of *Grágás* and *Jónsbók*, the act of publishing a killing ensured the prosecution of the correct party, guaranteed that homicides would be reported within a reasonable amount of time, and encouraged an open exchange of information between plaintiff and defendant. Conversely, the act of concealing a crime changed the nature of the crime itself.[3] In *Grágás*, murder and killing are two distinct concepts; murder involves some act of secrecy or concealment:

---

[1] Icelandic law, in general, was characteristically performative; the Law-Speaker, an elected and paid position of office in Iceland, was required to recite from memory one-third of the extant law code at annual meetings of the Althing (the yearly assembly at which suits were brought and cases heard). As William Ian Miller explains, 'in a preliterate and oral culture he was the society's statute book'. William Ian Miller, 'Of Outlaws, Christians, Horsemeat, and Writing: Uniform Laws and Saga Iceland', *Michigan Law Review* 89 (1991): 2081–95 at p. 2084.

[2] Jana K. Schulman, ed. and trans., 'Introduction', in *Jónsbók: The Laws of Later Iceland* (Saarbrucken: AQ Verlag, 2010), p. xv. Schulman cites Ólafur Lárusson, *Grágás og lögbækurnar* (Árbók Háskóla Íslands, 1922; Reykjavík: Prentsmiðjan Gutenberg, 1923), pp. 45–65.

[3] Regarding the manner in which secrecy could change the nature of a crime or irreparably damage the reputation of the one responsible, in his analysis of the character of the thief in *Beowulf*, Theodore Andersson examines differences in how Icelandic law treated theft and seizure of property. Though both warrant full outlawry as punishment, Andersson notes that charging someone with theft, which entails a concealment of stolen goods, causes more injury to the person's honour. Andersson places this crime in the larger context of Germanic law, which afforded equal disgrace to those who committed crimes furtively; he suggests that in Icelandic law, secret theft is even layered with additional connotations of cowardice, femininity or sexual perversion. Accusations of cowardice or shameful behaviour (*níð*) were considered so damaging to one's reputation in Icelandic society that *Grágrás* stipulates a penalty of lesser outlawry to anyone who creates such slander, and full outlawry if one composed slanderous poetry. Theodore Andersson, 'The Thief in *Beowulf*, *Speculum* 59 (1984): 493–508 at p. 505; see also: *Grágás: Islændernes lovbog i fristatens tid, udgivet efter den kongelige Bibliotheks Haandskrift*, ed. Vilhjálmur Finsen, 2 vols (Copenhagen, 1852; reprint, Odense: Odense University Press, 1974): II, chaps. 237 and 238, p. 197.

'þat er mælt. ef maðr myrþir man oc varðar þat scog gang. en þa er *morð* ef maðr leynir eða hylr hræ eða gengr eigi i gegn' [it is prescribed that if a man murders a man, the penalty is outlawry. And it is *murder* if a man hides it or conceals the corpse or does not admit it].[4] The term *morð*, indicating 'murder', is obviously not unique to Icelandic law; the same term signifies an unforgivable homicide in early English law as well.[5] *Morð* for the Normans and English 'impli[ed] concealment, in particular the hiding away of the dead body'.[6] Medieval Irish law also distinguishes between concealed and acknowledged killing; as Bridgette Slavin states in this collection, seventh- and eighth-century Irish legal texts designate four different kinds of killing, with a special category for *duintetháide*, 'secret murder'.[7]

Concealment (and the dishonourable reputation such behaviour brings) can take several forms, including not only the murderer's failure to publish the crime but also his or her commission of the crime at night. There is a distinction, for example, between *víg* and *náttvíg* – night killing – in the thirteenth-century *Egil's Saga*, when Queen Gunnhild of Norway calls for Egil's death:

> Gunnhildur mælti: 'Vér viljum ekki lof hans heyra. Láttu konungur leiða Egil út og höggva hann. Vil eg eigi heyra orð hans og eigi sjá hann'. Þá mælti Arinbjörn: 'Eigi mun konungur láta að eggjast um öll níðingsverk þín. Eigi mun hann láta Egil drepa í nótt því að náttvíg eru morðvíg'.
>
> [Gunnhild spoke, 'We do not want to hear his praise. Let him be led out and kill him, King. I do not want to hear his words nor see him'. Then Arinbjorn spoke, 'the king will not yield to incitement concerning all your shameful work. He will not have Egil killed at night because night-killings are murder']. (60)[8]

---

[4] Italics mine. Finsen, *Grágás*, I.88. All modern English quotations from *Grágás* taken from *Laws of Early Iceland: Grágás, the Codex Regius of Grágás, with Material from other Manuscripts*, trans. Andrew Dennis, Peter Foote and Richard Perkins, 2 vols (Winnipeg: University of Manitoba Press, 1980): II:146. Additional material, ibid. at I.78:220, stipulates 'and it is murder if a man hides it from the majority of the people in the commune'.

[5] Several chapters in this collection address additional provisions for murder in thirteenth- and fourteenth-century English law. See: Jay Paul Gates, 'Discursive Murders: The St Brice's Day Massacre, *Beowulf* and *Morðor*' and Larissa Tracy '"Mordre wol out": Murder and Justice in Chaucer'.

[6] Frederick Pollock and Frederic William Maitland, *The History of English Law Before the Time of Edward I*, 2nd edn, 2 vols (Cambridge: Cambridge University Press, 1968), II:468. Also cited in William Ian Miller, 'Choosing the Avenger: Some Aspects of the Bloodfeud in Medieval Iceland and England', *Law and History Review* 1.2 (1983): 159.

[7] Bridgette Slavin, 'Secret Killing and Murder by Magic in the Law of Adomnán', in this volume.

[8] All quotations in Old Norse come from *Íslendinga Sögur: Orðstöðulykill og texti* (CD-ROM) (Reykjavik, 1998). Unless otherwise attributed, modern English translations are my own. Chapter numbers are given in parentheses in the text.

Arinbjorn's reaction, calling Gunnhild's machinations *níðingsverk* [shameful work], indicates the dishonour inherent in committing homicide at night when it could be shielded from public view; the terminology for the crime changes and *víg* [killing] becomes *morðvíg* [murder-killing]. The power of shame and the weight of an individual's reputation as a source of social and political capital in Icelandic society (as in other medieval cultures) cannot be underestimated. Power and position in society 'depended on retention of wealth as well as on retention of reputation';[9] thus, a reputation for shameful behaviour, cowardice or dishonesty meant not only a lack of credibility but likely also a lack of supporters and advocates in a legal or social setting. Moreover, in wider medieval culture, an individual created and maintained his or her reputation by 'managing one's own behavior with nearly exclusive attention to its mirroring in the public perception of it'.[10] In this cyclical process, reputation determined how an individual would act and be perceived in public, and that public performance also determined reputation. This is relevant to legal proceedings, as, in general, 'medieval legal systems readily acknowledged the force of common opinion', admitting 'common knowledge' about one's actions and reputation as reliable forms of evidence.[11] This symbiotic relationship between reputation and performance meant that the shame or illegality of any given act was not only defined by *the act itself* but also by the reputation and subsequent performance of the person who committed the act.

Individual reputation and the ability to perform according to a legal script were elements essential to determining the nature of a killing. As no state apparatus existed to seek out and investigate 'the non-publishing wrongdoer', the Icelandic system of law depended on people either admitting their crimes or committing them in 'an open and notorious manner'[12] – metaphorically, in the clear light of day. In Icelandic society, bringing a homicide from the secret and shameful legal space of 'murder' to the open and prosecutable space of 'killing' required a specific verbal and situational performance. For the verbal admission of guilt, *Grágás* stipulates that 'laga losto þessa alla er her ero talþir um vig oc

---

[9] Jesse L. Byock, *Feud in the Icelandic Saga* (Berkeley: University of California Press, 1982), p. 234.

[10] Thelma Fenster and Daniel Lord Smail, 'Introduction', in *Fama: The Politics of Talk and Reputation in Medieval Europe* (Ithaca: Cornell University Press, 2003), pp. 1–11 at p. 4.

[11] Ibid., p. 3; Thomas Kuehn, 'Fama as a Legal Status in Renaissance Florence', in *Fama: The Politics of Talk and Reputation in Medieval Europe* (Ithaca: Cornell University Press, 2003), pp. 27–46 esp. p. 28. Though this collection focuses on the concept of *fama* in continental European and English contexts, the Icelandic law codes and textual evidence from the sagas show similar weights placed on reputation and public knowledge in Icelandic legal proceedings.

[12] William Ian Miller, 'Dreams, Prophecy and Sorcery: Blaming the Secret Offender in Medieval Iceland', *Scandinavian Studies* 58 (1986): 101–23 at p. 101.

um sár oc drep oc um frum hlaup oll scal lysa fyrir v. hvom þeir er allir se rettir at leiðar lengð i ix bua quið fra vetvangi' [publishing of all these lawbreakings here told, killings, wounds, and blows and all assaults, is to be done before five neighbours qualified in terms of distance from the place of action to serve on a panel of nine neighbours].[13] The formula supplied for this publishing involves witnesses and a specific verbiage – *lýsa víg* [to declare / make known / publish / report the killing] – in the act of bringing the crime to light. In the event that a killing takes place on the outskirts of a community, and all survivors are on one side, the killer

> scal ganga til böiar þess er næstr er þeirra er hann hygi ohaett fiorve sino af þeim af söcom oc segia lögfostom manne einom eþa fleirom oc queða a þessa lund at. Fundr occar var hann scal queða oc nefna hin oc segia hvar var. Ec *lysi* sár þau mer ahond. oc þan a verka allan er a honom er unin. ec *lysi* sár ef at sárom geriz. en *vig* ef at *vigi* geriz. (Italics mine)
>
> [is to go to the first house where he thinks his life is in no danger on that account and tell one or more men legally resident there and state it in this way: 'There was an encounter between us', he is to state, and name the other man and say where it was. 'I *publish* those wounds as my work and all the injury done to him; I *publish* wounds if wounds are the outcome and *killing* if *killing* is the outcome'].[14]

The procedure for publication as preserved in *Jónsbók* replicates many of these elements. The later law code establishes,

> Ef maðr er af tekínn þa aa sa at wera baní er *vigi lýsír* aa hendur ser. En *lýst* skal *vigi* samdæguris innan heraðs. ok nefna sik aa nafn ok náttstað sínn ok herað þat er hann er our. ok *lysa* fyrir frialsum manni ok fulltiða. (italics mine)
>
> [If someone is killed, then the killer is the one who *declares* himself to be the cause of the *other's death*. And the *killing* shall be *published* on the same day in the district and the killer shall state his name, his lodgings for the night, and the district from which he comes, and he shall *report* the killing to a man, free and of age].[15]

Again, as in *Grágás*, *Jónsbók* utilises the formula *lýsa víg* for publication and sets forth a framework for timely declaration and proximity to the place of the crime, as well as a necessary 'audience' to witness the publishing. The successful performance of this script ensures that, in a culture lacking a process for criminal investigation, the killer involves objective witnesses who can testify to the veracity of his claims and, more importantly, that the killer creates (or maintains) a

---

[13] Finsen, *Grágás*, I.87:150; trans. Dennis et al., *Grágás*, I.87:143.
[14] Finsen, *Grágás*, I.87:153–54; trans. Dennis et al., *Grágás*, I.87:146.
[15] Schulman, *Jónsbók*, chap. IV.10: 48–49.

reputation for honesty. Further, the legal weight of this act indicates an intimate connection between words and deeds; a person 'owned' what he or she did by speaking it. Thus, the destructive act of killing is taken into the body of the killer through the creative act of speech and concurrently transformed into an act that is, if not socially acceptable, at least socially negotiable.[16]

Obviously, speech is essential to this process, though the laws also provide instructions in cases where the killer is unable to speak: 'þat er mælt. ef maðr er omale oc scal sa maðr lysa er adile væri vigsacarinar ef hin væri veginn ef sa er þar' [It is prescribed that if a man has lost his power of speech, publishing is to be undertaken by the man, if at hand, who would be the principal in the killing case if the man in question had been killed].[17] That Icelandic laws made stipulations for people who lacked the power to verbalise what they had done demonstrates the communicable nature of individual transgressions. If the killer *cannot* verbalise his own guilt, the responsibility for publication falls upon his 'principal' or representative in the killing case, and some responsibility for the act (or, at least, the responsibility of making the killing 'lawful') resides within the killer's representative. In this way, an acknowledgement of responsibility and embodiment of guilt can spread beyond the first actor and involve his closest kin, friends and family.

This web of shared responsibility is borne out in the sagas in the famously complicated genealogies the authors provide to introduce a new character, chapter or event. Jesse Byock observes that 'the introduction of a major character often includes genealogical ties that determine inheritance, blood vengeance, and kinship responsibilities. Such information is also often a clue to issues and alliances in the coming feud'.[18] Though, in this case, Byock cites the kin-lists as indicative of the characters who may be pulled into an incipient feud, these interpersonal webs also demonstrate the extent to which an individual's reputation may spread beyond himself to his kin and how one's reputation may be influenced by his

---

[16] The necessary weight afforded to speech in Icelandic culture and the performative nature of law parallels J. L. Austin's concept of 'performative utterances', wherein a person's speech becomes an action, and the meaning is greater than the utterance itself. In such instances as naming, betting or apologising, a person performs an action in which the weight of meaning is in the words themselves, and not an internal act of which the words are representative. Applied to moments of declaration of killing in the sagas, the concept of the performative utterance suggests that the meaning of the declaration is not in reporting the *incident* but in claiming responsibility. See: J. L. Austin, *How To Do Things With Words*, 2nd edn (Cambridge, MA: Harvard University Press, 1975). For an analysis of the practice of announcing crimes in medieval Sweden, as well as the impact of gender on crime and punishment, see: Christine Ekholst, *A Punishment for Each Criminal: Gender and Crime in Swedish Medieval Law* (Leiden: Brill, 2014).

[17] Finsen, *Grágás*, I.87:151; trans. Dennis et al., *Grágás*, I.87:144.

[18] Byock, *Feud in the Icelandic Saga*, p. 67.

kin-group. Thus, an individual with an honourable reputation (and, perhaps, attendant wealth and power) would be supported in his suit by kin and neighbours and have more capability to negotiate a settlement or a peaceful resolution to his case (or to rely on his kin and connections to secure a skilled advocate or 'broker' to negotiate for him, as Byock observes).[19] Conversely, an individual with an unsavoury reputation as a liar, thief, troublemaker or worse might be unable to muster the support of kin, friends or even an advocate. Without the financial, physical and reputational protection of a kin-group, he or she would be unlikely to receive a favourable ruling in any case, regardless of the truth of his or her testimony.

Beyond providing a script for verbalising responsibility, the law codes require a timely performance. Publication must take place twelve hours from the time of the killing[20] or before the third sunrise from the time of the incident, depending on the circumstances.[21] The law even provides instructions for the treatment of the corpse, preventing any possibility of concealment. While the corpse must not be hidden or destroyed, *Grágás* stipulates that either the principal in the killing case or the dead person's companions must take the corpse to church; if the killer is the only person present, 'hann scal hylia hræ ef hann gengr fra manne dauðom. sva at hvarke æte fuglar ne dýr. hann scal segia hvar þat er' [if he leaves a man dead, he is to cover his corpse so that neither birds nor beasts may eat it. He is to say where it is].[22] Though covering up a corpse may be (linguistically *and* literally) just a shade away from physically concealing it, by acknowledging the location of the body and making his actions public, the killer uses the powers of performance and reputation to avoid any suggestion of concealment.

The distinction between killing and murder carries additional legal ramifications relating to self-defence in Icelandic law; by failing to admit his action openly, a murderer lost any right to an affirmative defence whereby he might justify the killing.[23] Yet looking to the punishments for killing versus murder in the law codes yields an ambiguous result: according to *Grágás*, the penalty for conviction of both killing and murder is the same – a sentence of outlawry, which entailed a loss of all personal property, exile from Iceland and a loss of all rights of provision or

---

[19] Ibid., pp. 37–39, 41–43.
[20] Finsen, *Grágás*, I.87:153; Dennis et al., *Grágás*, I.87:146.
[21] Finsen, *Grágás*, I.87:150, 153; Dennis et al., *Grágás*, I.87:143, 145. For example, if a homicide takes place in the mountains or fjords, the survivors have until the third sunrise to publish the incident.
[22] Finsen, *Grágás*, I.87: 154; Dennis et al., *Grágás*, I.87: 146. Additional material in Dennis et al., stipulates that 'he is to cover the corpse with stones or turf or clothing or snow if nothing else is available', *Grágás*, I.80:220.
[23] Miller, 'Dreams, Prophecy and Sorcery', p. 101.

protection against further violence.²⁴ *Jónsbók* provides a similar condemnation of unacknowledged killing, promising a loss of property and peace: 'en ef hann lýsir æigi sua vigi. þa er hann mordíngi réttr. ok fyrir gert fe ok friði' [If he does not declare the killing in this manner, then he is a true murderer and he has forfeited his property and peace].²⁵ The loss of 'property and peace' carries the implication of outlawry – a sentence of social death. While Icelandic law and government had no official mechanism to hand down or carry out capital punishment, for an individual to find himself outside the law left him open to retributive violence. As Theodore Andersson and William Ian Miller observe, 'law enforcement was a private matter, and the ultimate sanction behind the law and all legal judgments was the blood feud or the fear of it'.²⁶ Of course, as the sagas detail, many of these settlements did escalate into feud, pulling wider and wider communities into unending cycles of retributive killing. As Byock argues, however, this system of lawfully conducted feud was not, as Andersson and Miller suggest, a deterrent to violence, but instead a 'socially stabilizing process' into which violence was directed, regulated and contained.²⁷ This process relied upon public knowledge of acts of violence, as well as knowledge of the social and familiar connections of victim and aggressor, so that the community knew who had the right to avenge a death or other violation. An individual and kin-group could be insulated from a feud through strong social links, political and economic power and reputations for honesty, wisdom, strength and lawful behaviour.

While the law codes allow that acknowledging violent actions would leave an individual open to legally sanctioned, privately executed punishments, the laws themselves and the sagas suggest that Icelanders found ways to avoid such lethal spirals of violence. In practice, such feuds could be avoided through legal arbitration, settlement and compensation of the victim's kin.²⁸ Byock observes that resorting to retributive violence to avenge a manslaughter would fall to the

---

²⁴ The laws distinguish between full (*skóggangr*) and lesser outlawry (*fjörbaugsgarðr*), which involved a payment to the chieftain and banishment from Iceland for three years.
²⁵ Schulman, *Jónsbók*, chap. IV.10:50–51.
²⁶ Theodore M. Andersson and William Ian Miller, *Law and Literature in Medieval Iceland: Ljósvetninga Saga and Valla-Ljóts Saga* (Stanford, CA: Stanford University Press, 1989), p. 8. Further, in instances of vengeance killing, 'the target [...] need not be the wrongdoer himself, but one of his kin'. In cases where members of the victim's family are unsatisfied with a legal judgment, they might repay the killer *or those closest to him* with violence anyway. Thus, while reputation and safety dictate that a kin-group should monitor the behaviour of relatives and to encourage each other to be forthcoming in publication of wrongdoings, it is still incumbent upon the individual to acknowledge his own actions, and to risk a heavy judgment. Ibid., p. 17.
²⁷ Byock, *Feud in the Icelandic Saga*, p. 2.
²⁸ The *vígsbœtr*, the 'killing compensation', which *Grágás* sets as equivalent to forty-eight ounces (one mark) of silver for a free man. See: Dennis et al., *Grágás*, I: 254.

slain individual's kin, who might choose to pursue the claim in other ways if there was no one willing or able to avenge the death, or if they sensed not much support among their community.²⁹ Further, not all killings were equal; in the case of a slain servant, compensation by the killer might suffice for punishment. The thirteenth-century *Eyrbyggja Saga* provides an example of such a situation when the Breidavik brothers put the slave Egil to death. The narrator explains,

> Það voru lög í þann tíma ef maður drap þræl fyrir manni að sá maður skyldi færa heim þrælsgjöld og hefja ferð sína fyrir hina þriðju sól eftir víg þrælsins. Það skyldu vera tólf aurar silfurs. Og er þrælsgjöld voru að lögum færð þá var eigi sókn til um víg þrælsins.
>
> [Then was the law at that time that if a man killed a slave before him that this man should bring to [his] home the slave's wergild and set out himself before the third day after the killing of the slave. Then should [the payment] be twelve ounces of silver. And when the wergild was lawfully paid, then there was no recourse for the killing of his slave]. (43)

In the case of a slain thrall, the victim amounts to mere property, and the killer acknowledges his accountability for the homicide by paying the slave's owner.

Thus, punishment for a crime is not necessarily meant to reflect one's place in a moral hierarchy or to punish for perceived guilt or sin. The fact that murder and killing are *both* punishable by outlawry indicates that the goal of such sentences is to rid the community of 'troublemakers',³⁰ and 'to return the community to a workable arrangement [...]; harmony within the community was more important than justice to the individual'.³¹ The distinction between murder and killing, therefore, rests on the concept of individual shame and the danger of a negative reputation to one's life and the lives of his family. But beyond this, given the apparent reliance of the Icelandic legal system on voluntary and immediate disclosure of actions, and the weight of one's reputation to influence standing in society and the likelihood of receiving justice, murder disrupted these systems in a way that killing could not. An individual was expected to publicise a killing, bringing the act itself to common knowledge but also creating his own reputation as a lawful individual, a kind of capital that would strengthen his case in court. In this situation, with strong support from one's kin and advocates at the assembly, the killer might even be able to justify his actions and 'buy off' the family of the deceased. Murder, conversely, endangers an individual's reputation as well as those related to him, weakening a system that depends upon kinship

---

²⁹ Jesse Byock, *Medieval Iceland: Society, Sagas, and Power* (Berkeley: University of California Press, 1988), pp. 69–70.

³⁰ Ibid., p. 29.

³¹ Ibid., p. 102.

ties and advocacy to reach legal compromises. In cases where the killer does not publish, the family of the slain cannot seek redress, compensation or even retributive violence, breaking down the system of justice. Even beyond this, looking to the function of feud as a system that stabilises and centralises violence, murder disrupts this system by taking violent actions out of the light of day and the public knowledge, thus making it impossible for violence to be contained, redressed or returned within a legally-sanctioned system. By introducing shame and concealment into a system that depends upon open commission of violent acts and clear communication of one's reasons for committing said acts, murder destabilises the process whereby individuals can use brutality and violence in a 'lawful' manner.

Reconstructing the realities of life in a long-gone culture from the remnants of literature, art, chronicles and law is always a tricky process, and mining the sagas for evidence of 'life as it was' in medieval Iceland should be done with care. The disparity between the time at which the texts were written and that in which the histories they memorialise occurred suggests that the tenth-century society preserved there is, in part, a reflection of the mindsets and perspectives of thirteenth-century authors. As these texts blend literary achievement with social history, they are not lenses through which the actual function of law and order in medieval Iceland can be observed.[32] However, though the existence of a written law does not signify a law-abiding populace, medieval Icelanders were by no means legally illiterate.[33] The saga-authors were well versed in the law codes of *Grágás* and *Jónsbók*, as well in as the histories and genealogies of the families and feuds of Iceland,[34] which clearly provided a wealth of examples of historical law-making and law-breaking. Yet the narrative agency afforded these authors also gave them space to adapt, elide or reproduce the legal rituals, placing them in the mouths and bodies of characters of varied reputations, power and emotions. In these moments, saga-authors demonstrate how the legal script actually fails to distinguish between killing and murder in a way that brings dishonourable acts to light, nor does it prevent further acts of bloodshed. Instead, the distinction between these two crimes and their punishments depends heavily upon the killer, the victim and their respective reputations.

---

[32] See: Hugh Firth's fascinating use of the family sagas and contemporary sagas to estimate numbers of homicides in medieval Iceland, as well as his analysis of the role of socioeconomic and political power dynamics in the enactment of justice or retribution in these killings. Firth, 'Coercion, Vengeance, Feud, and Accommodation: Homicide in Medieval Iceland', *Early Medieval Europe* 20 (2012): 139–75.

[33] While the population may not have always followed the law, this does not mean that there were legally illiterate; *Jónsbók* itself was used for reading instruction in early modern Iceland.

[34] Byock, *Feud in the Icelandic Saga*, p. 26.

Indeed, the sagas rarely reflect the publication process being carried out according to the specific legal script; instead, authors manoeuvre around the *lýsing* process, using formulaic constructions such as 'news of the killing spread' or 'someone went to tell about the killing' to indicate that the event becomes public knowledge (the verb *lýsa* does not appear in these instances). Yet they also provide instances in which bodies are concealed and murders not published; in these moments, the sagas reveal the law's inadequacies in ensuring public knowledge of crimes, as well as the law's failure to ensure just treatment of all individuals. Two episodes from the mid thirteenth-century *Laxdæla Saga* and *Eyrbyggja Saga* exemplify the narrative formulae that replaces publication. These episodes also elucidate the difficulties of ascertaining whether characters have actually behaved lawfully and the extent to which lawful behavior is inseparable from reputation.

In *Eyrbyggja Saga*, news of Thorbjorn's death is circulated by Odd Katlason: 'Hann fór þar til er hann kom til Fróðár og sagði þar tíðindin' [He went to the place where he came to Fróðár and spoke there the news] (18). After Odd Katlason delivers news of the killing, 'lét Þuríður húsfreyja safna þá mönnum og fara eftir líkunum en flytja heim sára menn. Þorbjörn var í haug lagður' [the wife Thurid gathered the men to go and fetch the corpses and convey home the wounded men. Thorbjorn was laid in a mound] (18). Shortly thereafter, when Katla (a woman suspected of witchcraft) is stoned to death by Arnkel and his men, 'spurðust nú þessi tíðindi öll jafnsaman og var engum harmsaga í' [now all together heard of these events but it was sad news to no one] (20). Later, when Arnkel slays Hauk, 'spurðust nú þessi tíðindi. Stóð allt kyrrt þessi misseri' [now (people) heard of these events. All remained calm for the season] (35). From these examples, the audience cannot know whether the murders were published in legal fashion. From a structural standpoint, recreating the performance of the legal formula is not crucial to the overall narrative; the forward momentum of the narrative only requires the spread of information so that characters and communities can be aware of the slayings and may involve themselves or seek redress, as appropriate.[35]

Beyond serving a structural function, though, the example of Katla's stoning suggests that, even if a murder is committed and goes unpublicised, if the victim is not worthy of sympathy or lacks social standing, the murderer is unlikely to

---

[35] In Byock's analysis of the structural elements of the feud in Iceland sagas, he breaks the feud itself into discrete 'feudemes' of conflict, advocacy and resolution. The passing of information about a killing falls into the category of the advocacy feudeme: 'if a person is involved in a dispute only because someone informed him about the killing, such giving of information would be advocacy (information passing). Only if a killing takes place "on the scene", that is, as an action, is it conflict or resolution, depending upon the circumstances.' *Feud in the Icelandic Saga*, p. 58.

be held to account and punished for his actions. Thus, reputation, even more than lawful action or performance, determines who is worthy of receiving justice. Within the same saga, when men kill the wretched Spa-Gils, who himself has just murdered a character (for pay) and fled the scene, they dispose of him without publishing his death: 'tóku þeir hann af lífi og kösuðu hann þar við klifið' [they took his life and heaped earth over his body by the cliff] (32). In the earlier case of Thorbjorn, the reference to burial in a mound implies that his corpse is disposed of lawfully; for Spa-Gils, the outcome is not so charitable. The deposition of Spa-Gils's body by the cliff – in the same location where he has been killed and at a distance from settlement – is an act of concealment. Spa-Gils's lack of social standing, allies and protectors means that his killers have no fear of injuring their own reputations by not publishing his death (nor any fear of reprisal); thus, the murder goes unacknowledged.[36] For Katla and Spa-Gils, characters without support or honourable reputations, their unmourned and nearly unmarked murders are, in fact, tacitly accepted, perhaps as beneficial to the larger, law-abiding and honourable community.

Likewise, one episode from *Laxdæla Saga* poses a challenge for the audience to ascertain whether a body has been buried or hidden, reflecting the power of an individual's reputation to determine whether or not his actions can be called honourable. In this episode, Eldgrim threatens and attempts to steal horses from Thorleik Hoskuldsson; he is caught in the act of thievery by Thorleik's uncle, Hrut Herjolfsson, who attempts to calm the matter by bribing Eldgrim with his own horses. Eldgrim brandishes a weapon and attempts to flee; Hrut kills Eldgrim with a single blow: 'féll Eldgrímur dauður af hestinum sem von var. Síðan huldi Hrútur hræ hans. Þar heitir Eldgrímsholt, suður frá Kambsnesi' [Eldgrim fell down dead from his horse, as was to be expected. Hrut then concealed the body. There it is called Eldgrimsholt, to the south of Kambsness] (37). After the killing, Hrut rides to Kambsness to his nephew, 'og segir Þorleiki þessi tíðindi' [and told Thorleik about these events] (37). Though Hrut tells Thorleik what transpired (he, in turn, opines that Hrut's motives were ill and that no good would come of the deed), the precise legal terminology of publication is absent. Furthermore, there is some question as to whether Hrut actually follows lawful procedure or conceals the killing. The word *huldi* (inf. *hulda*) means 'to cover' in modern English, but it carries additional shades of meaning that indicate

---

[36] Michael Irlenbusch Reynard pays specific attention to the tragic situation and end of Spa-Gils and the ways that the 'slow-witted' caricature of the þræll, the slave or impoverished freeman, could be used by more powerful characters to achieve their ends in the sagas. See: Irlandbusch Reynard, 'Killing to Qualify: The Underprivileged Assassins of *Eyrbyggja Saga*', *Nordica Bergensia* 33 (2006): 75–95 esp. pp. 77, 85.

veiling, hiding or secrecy.[37] Yet the very next statement – that the landscape now bears Eldgrim's name (*Eldgrimsholt*, 'Eldgrim's Woods') – makes it clear that the character's death at this spot is public knowledge, though the narrator never clarifies at what point the knowledge *became* public. Despite the absence of the *lýsing* formula, the saga draws on other aspects of Hrut's character to 'excuse him' from any hint of shameful behaviour. First, Hrut attempts to resolve the matter reasonably with Eldgrim and to prevent an act of thievery; secondly, the narrator explains that the eighty-year-old Hrut 'þótti hann mikið hafa vaxið af þessu verki' [was thought to have grown much from this deed] (37). Hrut's established reputation and the increased respect this killing earns him outweighs any suggestion of unlawful or secretive behaviour in the treatment of the body. While this episode shows that literary texts tend to develop codes and motifs of their own, separate from the very precise language set forth in *Grágás* and *Jónsbók*, it also reflects the extent to which legality relies as much upon the power of the aggressor and victim as it does on the law itself. Thus, the legal formula – even when used in its entirety – is hollow without the reputation of the speaker and the communal acceptance of the worth of a victim's life.

Although the sagas often elide the complete performance of publication in favour of the 'news spread' formula, when the *lýsing* process *does* occur, saga characters use the script for cynical and dishonest purposes, or to further a chain of violence and assert their own aggressive reputations.[38] In this way, while the legal script does successfully function as a means of 'bringing murder to light', it also becomes a parody of itself, allowing characters to use violence to further their reputations rather than relying on one's reputation to legitimise or justify violence. The ritual of publishing occurs relatively often in the late-thirteenth-century *Njal's Saga*. During the spate of vengeance-killings that envelops the families of Njal and Gunnar, Brynjolf kills Atli and *sagði víg* [reported the killing] (38). Brynjolf is then killed by Thord in retaliation for the death of Atli; afterwards, 'Þórður fann smalamann Hallgerðar og *lýsti vígi* á hönd sér og sagði hvar Brynjólfur lá og bað hann segja Hallgerði vígið' [Thord met one of Hallgerd's shepherds and *declared the killing* done by his own hand and said where Brynjolf

---

[37] In their translation of *Laxdæla Saga*, Magnus Magnusson and Hermann Pálsson have translated a section thus: 'Eldgrim fell dead from his horse, as was only to be expected. Hrut then covered up the body; the place is called Eldgrimsholt'. Their use here of 'covered' instead of 'concealed' leaves the legality of Hrut's actions here a bit more open. Magnusson and Pálsson, *Laxdæla Saga* (New York: Penguin, 1969), p. 134.

[38] Obviously, this is not always the case. In *Laxdæla Saga*, the procedure appears to be carried out lawfully when Thorgils and his men kill Helgi Hardbeinsson: 'eftir þessi tíðindi ríða þeir Þorgils í brott og yfir hálsinn til Reykjardals og *lýstu* þar *vígum* þessum' [After these events, Thorgils and his men rode away over the ridge into Reykjardale and there they published the killings] (65). Italics mine.

lay and asked him to inform Hallgerd of the killing] (39).³⁹ Thord is then killed by Skjold and Sigmund, after which 'Hallgerður sendi mann til Bergþórshvols að segja vígið' [Hallgerd sent a man to Bergthorsknoll to report the killing] (42). Finally, Skarp-Hedin and his brothers attack Sigmund and Skjold, with the outcome that '*lýsti* Skarphéðinn *vígi* Sigmundar á hendur sér en þeir Grímur og Helgi vígi Skjaldar sér á hendur' [Skarp-Hedin declared that he had killed Sigmund and that Grim and Helgi had killed Skjold] (45).⁴⁰

Two of these examples contain specific language of publication (*lýsti vígi*), while the others imply that the killings were made known. The frequency of this action is connected to the characters' motivations for killing. The murders are not committed in self-defence nor to resolve arguments between specific men; rather, they are manifestations of the rivalry between the families of Njal and Gunnar. The retributive killings are each committed in response to a previous act of violence by one family or the other. As these homicides are *meant* to be public (killing Gunnar's servant has no meaning if Gunnar and Hallgerd do not find out about it), the publication process ensures that there is no doubt as to personal responsibility. Further, by publishing a killing, a person gains recognition for that deed, thus increasing his reputation for strength and prowess in the community. The prevalence of legal publishing in *Njal's Saga* demonstrates that both the commission and the declaration of crimes are crucial to the communication between the families – there is no misunderstanding of who is repaying violence with violence. Killing and *lýsing* are part of a performance intended to assert power over the individuals of the opposing 'clan', to grow the reputations of individuals and their kin-groups and to bring acts of violence into a public (and defensible) arena. In this case, killing becomes accepted, and even sanctioned, as a part of this public performance of family honour and power.

While *Njal's Saga* supplies this powerful example of how publishing can legitimise violence and grow an individual's reputation for just and honest behaviour, the saga also provides a glaring example of how the legal formulae were exploited for cynical purposes. In a bid to increase his own power, Mord Valgardsson incites Skarp-Hedin and the Njalssons to kill Hoskuld Hvitanessgodi, a political rival of Mord's. While Mord does not accept blame in this specific homicide, his shepherd informs Hildigunn, Hoskuld's wife, that "'kallaði Skarphéðinn á mig og lýsti víginu á hönd sér'" ['Skarp-Hedin called to me and declared the killing by his own hand'] (112). Having established Skarp-Hedin as the killer, Mord continues the act of publishing:

---

³⁹ Italics mine.
⁴⁰ Italics mine.

Fór Mörður þá ofan í Ossabæ. Þangað komu níu búar þeir er næstir bjuggu vettvangi. Mörður hafði tíu menn með sér. Hann sýnir búum sár Höskulds og nefnir votta að benjum og nefnir mann til hvers sárs nema eins. Það lét hann eigi sem hann vissi hver því hefði sært en því hafði hann sjálfur sært. En hann lýsti víginu á hendur Skarphéðni en sárum á hendur bræðrum hans og Kára. Síðan kvaddi hann heiman vettvangsbúa níu til alþingis. Eftir það reið hann heim.

[Then Mord went down to Ossaby. To that place came nine neighbours who were nearest the place of manslaughter. Mord had ten men with him. He showed the neighbors Hoskuld's wounds and named witnesses to the mortal wounds and named the man (who had inflicted) each wound except for one. Then he made as if he did not know who had made that wound, but he himself had made that wound. And he published the killing against Skarp-Hedin, and (other) wounds against his brothers and Kari. Then he called from home nine neighbors to the scene of action to the Althing. After that, he rode home]. (112)

Mord's performance exemplifies the code of behaviour required by the laws, but it is tainted by his omission and his own self-interest. He performs the publication in the place of the killing and within the stipulated amount of time, he calls witnesses, he ensures that the body is observable, identifies wounds and names the killer. This performance, perfectly following the letter of the law, is unique among murder publications due to its completeness. As it is uncommon to find a character who takes such great pains to follow every regulation, Mord's close adherence to the legal script casts suspicion on his motives; indeed, his performance masks his own guilt in the act as he does not admit responsibility for the wounds he caused. In his commentary on Mord's character in the saga overall, Byock observes the morally ambiguous nature of this figure: Mord 'is not an honourable character, he is not a clearly delineated villain. Within the world of the sagas he is a man who skillfully uses the political tools of his society to his own advantage'.[41] The character's fluency with the law and his exploitation of the legal formula in its complexity and completeness serves as illustration and critique of how the ambitious in Icelandic society might escape a damaged reputation, legal fines or punishments, and continue to accrue power.

While *Njal's Saga* provides situations wherein characters use their knowledge of the law to improve their own social positions or a family's reputation, *Laxdæla Saga* creates another tableau wherein a performance of legal ritual fails to make clear the distinction between shame and honour. The mortal combat and final words between cousins Kjartan Óláfsson and Bolli Þorleiksson exemplify a killing that is, by its nature, shameful, and yet appears to be legitimised by a lawful performance. Goaded to fight his kinsman by his wife, Guðrún, and her brothers the Osvifssons, whom Kjartan has bested, Bolli advances upon Kjartan with his

[41] Byock, *Feud in the Icelandic Saga*, p. 200.

sword drawn. Kjartan remarks, '"víst ætlar þú nú frændi *níðingsverk* að gera en miklu þykir mér betra að þiggja banorð af þér frændi en veita þér það"' ['certainly you now intend, kinsman, to do *shameful work* but it seems much better to me to be killed by you, kinsman, than to give you that (death)'] (49).[42] The implication of shame in this situation stems from the familial relationship between Bolli and Kjartan; for Bolli to kill a kinsman would be dishonourable and would damage the system wherein one kinsman may avenge the death of another. Casting aside his weapons, Kjartan refuses to fight his cousin any longer. Unmoved by Kjartan's words or actions, 'engi veitti Bolli svör máli Kjartans en þó veitti hann honum banasár. Bolli settist þegar undir herðar honum og andaðist Kjartan í knjám Bolla' [Bolli gave no answer to Kjartan's words but nevertheless gave him his death-wound. At once Bolli caught him under his shoulders and Kjartan died at Bolli's knees] (49). Just as Kjartan warns him of the implicit shame in what he is about to do, Bolli further endangers his own honour by killing an unarmed man. Finally, the scene ends as 'iðraðist Bolli þegar verksins og *lýsti vígi* á hendur sér' [immediately Bolli repented of his act and *declared that he* had done the killing himself] (49). This sudden shift is part of a set of circumstances that allows Bolli to walk away from this crime with some aspect of his good reputation intact. Although his deed is 'shameful', Bolli nearly receives permission from Kjartan to deal the death-blow. Additionally, as soon as he kills his cousin, Bolli demonstrates remorse, holds Kjartan's body at his knees – in a kneeling and penitent posture – and acknowledges legal responsibility for the killing. In this situation, the special use of legal terminology for publication ensures that Bolli has acted according to law, even if his crime is reprehensible and destructive to his own family.

Bolli's declaration, taking place just moments after the killing and in the same place that Kjartan has fallen, is witnessed in the text by the Osvifssons (who aid Bolli in the attack). The tragedy of this situation and the emotional impact upon Bolli is given shape through his physical closeness to his victim and his immediate verbal acknowledgement and ownership of his own guilt. Though the author establishes him as a sympathetic character due to his willingness to publish the killing legally, he is made even more sympathetic through his physical performance of regret. Although Miller characterises expressions of emotion in Icelandic sagas as stylised or extremely ambiguous at times, he observes that

> Emotions (or at least their display) form an important part of the work
> of legitimizing and justifying our actions. The more obviously public
> the performance, the more the performance might tend to take on a

---

[42] Italics mine. As discussed earlier, in *Egil's Saga*, the term *níðingsverk* appears in relation to a planned night-killing and indicates the shameful work of killing under cover of darkness.

quasi-formalized style, to have an almost ritualized aspect to it. Mourning customs are an obvious example, but there are others.[43]

This moment of fused confession and remorse is one such performance that legitimises and justifies Bolli's actions. Despite all of these factors – the legal ritual, the audience, the sympathetic and emotional performance of regret and even Kjartan's pre-mortem forgiveness – Kjartan's charge of *níðingsverk* still resonates in the aftermath of his killing. Following the slaying, Bolli acts lawfully and takes what actions he can to legitimise his actions and salvage his reputation in the eyes of the law, community and saga-audience, but he has still committed a shameful act *twice over* in the killing of an unarmed kinsman. While he makes his guilt public and pays for his crime,[44] his killing of a kinsman causes a rift in his family that ultimately results in his slaying by Kjartan's brothers. His initial shameful act of killing a kinsman is thus repaid by more kin-slaying, starting a cycle of intra-familial violence wherein kinsmen who should defend each other are instead incited to kill each other to protect their individual reputations. This particular episode emphasises that while one might perform a legal ritual to change the nature of murder, shame extends beyond simple concealment or dishonesty to encompass the danger that an individual can pose to his entire kin-group.

While the act of publication at times humanises individuals – especially those who commit unforgivable acts of violence in the sagas – composing poetry functions in a similar way. Though certainly not a legal act of declaration, the 'versification' of a killing happens frequently (and much more often than publication), notably in *Eyrbyggja Saga*. In Icelandic society, the ability to craft poetry was a skill celebrated as much as a person's prowess in battle; therefore, to kill a person and then compose a verse about the deed demonstrates that the killer is doubly skilled. For these reasons, reciting a poem after a killing would earn a character more respect and recognition than simply publishing the death.

Just as publishing is a kind of performance in which a destructive act is acknowledged and verbalised, thus bringing the killer's actions 'to order', so is the composition and recitation of a poem a similarly 'orderly performance', producing a strict arrangement of words that brings something unspoken or unperceived to light. In *Eyrbyggja Saga*, Thorarin kills Thorbjorn and his companions to avenge an insult. While there is no evidence that Thorarin publishes

---

[43] William Ian Miller, 'Emotions and the Sagas', in *From Sagas to Society: Comparative Approaches to Early Iceland*, ed. Gísli Pálsson (Enfield Lock, Middlesex, UK: Hisarlik Press, 1992), pp. 89–109 at p. 104.

[44] Guðrún's brothers receive a sentence of outlawry for their attack on Kjartan, while Bolli receives a lighter sentence of a fine due to the intervention of Kjartan's father Óláf, Bolli's foster-father.

this murder, when he returns home, Geirrid asks him what has happened. He responds:

> Varði eg mig þar er myrðir
> morðfárs vega þorði,
> hlaut örn af ná neyta
> nýjum, kvenna frýju.
> Barkat vægð að vígi
> valnaðrs í styr þaðra.
> Mæli eg hól fyr hæli
> hjaldrsgoðs af því sjaldan.

> [In the court of weapons / they called me a coward: / I defended my honour, / Fought, fed the eagles. / My sword bears witness, / Put to the war-test: / But I don't care to boast – / Bloodshed's not my business].[45]

Geirrid responds by asking more directly, "'segið þér víg Þorbjarnar?'" ['are you declaring the killing of Thorbjorn?'] (18:54), to which Thorarin responds by composing another verse about the killing. Certainly, Thorarin's language does not follow the scripted legal formula for declaring a killing – when directly confronted about his lack of a forthright declaration, he evades the charge with further poetics. The choice to write his own script for ownership of a deed instead of using the *lýsing* formula indicates a desire to own the notoriety for his violent deed, but not necessarily to pay for it.

A similar performance occurs in *Eyrbyggja Saga* when Styr kills two berserks in a bathhouse. At their burial, he recites:

> Sýndist mér sem myndi
> móteflandar spjóta
> Ála ekki dælir
> él-herðöndum verða.
> Uggi eg eigi seggja
> ofrgang of mig strangan.
> Nú hefr bilgrönduðr brandi
> berserkjum stað merktan.

> [I knew that these berserks, / unbending in battle, / would prove a fierce pair / to me and my friends. / But I'm not afraid / Of the fury of the fight: / I've buried those berserks' / Bodies in a pit]. (28:79)

There is no textual indication that he had previously published the killings, yet his performance at a burial (indicating venue and ensuring an audience) involves some of the same elements. These poetic performances evidence a desire for

---

[45] *Eyrbyggja Saga*, chap. 18; English translation by Hermann Pálsson and Paul Edwards, *Eyrbyggja Saga* (New York: Penguin, 1989), p. 53. Hereafter, chapter and page numbers are given in parentheses in the text.

public acknowledgement of one's reputation as a fierce killer, but more so, they show a desire for recognition of the poet's wit and ability to reveal his own character as he chooses.

Finally, another killing in *Eyrbyggja Saga* is followed by the recitation of a verse: when Bjorn kills Thorodd, he begins his poem with an assertion that he committed the deed:

> Munat hyrlesti hraustum
> hríðar mér að stríða,
> heldr hef eg vígi valdið
> Viðleggs sona tveggja
> sem vígbalkar válki
> valdr geymi-Bil falda
> eða dalsveigi deigum
> Draupnis skatt að kaupa.

[Sword-skilled, I slaughtered / the sons of Wood-Leg. / It was harder for Thorodd / to thrust me through, / than to lie making love / to his elegant lady / or rob the Earl's traders / and take their taxes]. (29: 82)

Arguably, as composing a poem entails a greater personal effort (and creative energy) than reciting a legal formula, the versification of a killing creates an even stronger connection between the killer and his deed. Beyond this, such poetry forms a nexus between creative and destructive forces. It is perhaps unsurprising that such a location of antithesis would also be the site of another oppositional relationship: in composing a verse about a killing, the poet both reveals and conceals his deed. The extreme rigidity of form and heavily metaphorical and abstract content required of the skaldic poetry preserved in the sagas ensures that any 'confession' of a crime in verse form will be veiled by poetics. In instances of versifying killings, therefore, information is brought to light *and* concealed, allowing the killer to keep his honour, life and property intact; beyond this, he strengthens his reputation as a fighter and in the highly-valued arena of poetic composition.

And therein lies a larger problem with the definitions of murder and the function of publication. The communal and social value of publication is that the ritual brings one's acts into the public sphere so that they may be judged and redressed openly; the value of *lýsing* for the individual is to avoid the shame assumed to be attached to concealment. However, when saga-characters versify their killings, they problematise the idea of concealment as equivalent to shame. Versification, a performance of both revelation and concealment, creates a space wherein the antithetical concepts of prestige and shame must coexist. Beyond this, as poetry is an act of personal creation in which the poet reworks his own thoughts and deeds into a form that, in its clever obscurity, increases his own renown, these kinds of 'declarations' cannot function in making acts of killing open or public. Thus, the killings they describe remain personal riddles for the killers and do not allow victims or claimants to pursue damages or justice for the slain. While versification shares many of the performative elements of the legal declaration formula, on both an individual and a social level, it turns the performance inward and obscures as much as it reveals. The killer claims his deed and adds to his own renown but denies knowledge to the public and justice to the victim's kin; on a larger scale, the poet prevents a system of laws based upon open declaration of one's acts from functioning properly and removes himself from social responsibility.

Speaking to the challenges of life in the saga-world, Miller describes a society obsessed with the fear of shame, where 'one's honour was at stake almost every second. There was no relief. One was always, so to speak, performing.'[46] Certainly, it is essential to draw a boundary between this saga-world, a literary world of outlaws, law-abiders, heroes and anti-heroes alike, and the medieval Icelandic culture that produced and intoned the laws of *Grágás* and *Jónsbók*. Both Icelandic law and literature built themselves around the concept of performance: in the recitation of the law before it was committed to writing; in the high social status enjoyed by poets and the value placed upon poetry; in the necessity of declaring one's actions in public and in the omnipresent concern with reputation. Yet even given this shared foundation of performance between law and literature, the saga-authors (and the characters they create) subtly employ, manipulate and question the power of the legal script to ensure peace and justice within the saga-world. The specific legal ritual of *lýsing*, a performance wherein the killer not only declares his deeds for all to hear but determines the very nature of his own act – killing and not murder – is a moment of great power in both a legal and a narrative sense. Legal publication can save one's life and reputation; publication (or a failure to do so) in the sagas can be a moment of great emotional revelation. Of course, as the sagas show, this performance does not always bring foul deeds to light and, in fact, the definition of murder may depend just as much upon one's social standing and reputation as on his ability to perform the ritual. Whether embodied in the practice of *lýsing* or in the versification of a killing, a character's declaration of guilt and agency may allow for a redemption that is both legal and emotional. This kind of redemptive performance is often necessary in texts such as the sagas, in which the reader is asked so often to sympathise with violent, marginalised or tragic individuals. In such cases, the most believable performances unite the linguistic precision of the law with the creative agility of the poet, giving full force to the emotions of saga-characters and making the saga-world a richer and more immediate one.

---

[46] William Ian Miller, 'Deep Inner Lives, Individualism and People of Honor', *History of Political Thought* 16.2 (1995): 190–207 at p. 206.

CHAPTER 7

'I Think This Bacon is Wearing Shoes': Comedy and Murder in the Old French Fabliaux

Anne Latowsky

IN ONE OF THE THREE VERSIONS of the thirteenth-century Old French comic tale of the sacristan, *Le Sacristain II*, a servant woman in a tavern opens a bag supposed to contain a side of bacon. Instead, it contains the fully-dressed dead body of a monk. She pulls the corpse out by the boot and struggles to cut the 'meat' as she endures heckling from rowdy guests. Fed up, she finally responds: 'Par seint Leonart,/ Cist bacons est plus dur que hart/ Si est chauciez, ce m'est avis!' [In the name of Saint Leonard, this bacon is harder than a rope, and I think it is wearing shoes!] (624–7). At first, this might seem like a simple joke about what a fool she is, but the servant's failure to recognise what she is cutting, or to consider that a person might have been murdered, is typical of the characters who encounter dead bodies in the fabliaux.[1] All of the fabliaux that deal with murder involve the violent death of men, primarily priests, most of whom are pursuing married women. Murder is not the main subject, however, but rather the precondition for the humorous adventures of a potentially incriminating corpse. In all of the murder fabliaux, the narrator and the audience share knowledge of the murderous circumstances that created the corpse, but these details are never available to the characters within the story who must dispose of the body. The conspiracy between narrator and audience, when juxtaposed with the antics of those who deal with the dead body, produces a narrative experience that is unique to the murder fabliaux. As corpse comedy combined with social satire, these comic tales play out in their own special moral universe. The world of the murder fabliaux tolerates, and even celebrates, vengeance against adulterous

---

[1] *Le Sacristain II*. The references to the fabliaux texts throughout are from *Le Nouveau recueil complet des fabliaux*, ed. Willem Noomen and Nico van den Boogaard, 10 vols (Assen and Maastricht: Van Gorcum, 1983–1998). *Les trois Boçus*, 5:191–208; *Le Prestre comporté*, 9:1–66; *Le Sacristain I-III*, 7:1–190; *Le Chapelain*, 6:79–99; *Estormi*, 1:1–28; and *Les quatre Prestres*, 8:135–40. All translations are mine.

priests, not because they deserve to die, but because successful corpse comedy needs a murdered body that fails to elicit sympathy.

An accusation of murder in thirteenth-century France would have been no laughing matter, as one might expect, so the fervent desire not to get caught with a murdered body would have certainly resonated with any audience, no matter how unlikely such an occurrence might have seemed. If the *Coutumes de Beauvaisis* (1283) offer an accurate portrait, the accused would have faced punishment by hanging. Murder would have incurred capital punishment alongside three other crimes: treason, homicide (killing someone in a melee) and rape (*murtre, traïson, homicide* and *fame esforcier*).[2] For these crimes, 'il doit estre trainés et pendus' [he must be dragged and hanged].[3] In spite of the severity of the crime, the approach to murder in the fabliaux is strikingly blithe.[4] What matters is the ability of the person burdened with the corpse to get rid of it. The treatment of murder is not simple disregard, however. Since the main goal of the fabliaux is humorous and witty entertainment, something must be done to get past the gravity of murder in order to produce a comedic corpse story.[5] For the adventures of the murdered body to be funny, a fabliau must adhere to a set of conventions, a moral code even, that permits this sort of murder to be taken lightly. The audience needs to remain on the side of those trying to dispose of the body, even if those people are guilty of murder.[6] These conventions include the creation of an unsympathetic victim, repeated sight gags based on misperception, serial parallel scenes marked by ironic dialogue and failed conversations with corpses and, finally, incongruous moralising by the narrator. The humour

---

[2] For further cases of murder in France, especially as treason, see in this volume: Patricia Turning, 'A Case of Mariticide in Late Medieval France'; Emily J. Hutchison, 'Defamation, a Murder *More* Foul?: The "Second Murder" of Louis, Duke of Orleans (d. 1407) Reconsidered'; and Jolanta N. Komornicka, 'Treacherous Murder: Language and Meaning in French Murder Trials'.

[3] Philippe de Beaumanoir, *Coutumes de Beauvaisis* (Paris: Alphonse Picard et fils, 1899), 1:429; Nicole Gonthier, *Le châtiment du crime au Moyen Âge: XIIe-XVIe siècles* (Rennes: Presses Universitaires de Rennes, 1998), pp. 20–1.

[4] Evelyn Birge Vitz observes that *Le Sacristain* seems rather immoral, but also slightly Christian, in that God helps those who pray to him and the wicked are punished. *Medieval Narrative and Modern Narratology: Subjects and Objects of Desire* (New York: New York University Press, 1989), p. 206.

[5] Logan Whalen, 'Modern Dirty Jokes and the Old French Fabliaux', in *The Old French Fabliaux: Essays on Comedy and Context*, ed. Kristin L. Burr, John F. Moran and Norris J. Lacy (Jefferson, NC: McFarland, 2007), pp. 147–59 at p. 158; Willem Noomen, 'Performance et mouvance: À propos de l'oralité des fabliaux', *Reinardus* 3 (1990): 127–42 at p. 131.

[6] For Marie-Thérèse Lorcin, the fabliaux have their own conventions and 'mythologie sociale' in which the people trying to get rid of bodies are sympathetic heroes. See: 'Les Revenants dans les fabliaux', *Reinardus* 2 (1989): 91–101 at p. 101.

derives from the narrator's dramatic, yet irony-laced, presentation of the confusions and misperceptions of the characters within the story to a set of listeners who are aware that the corpse in question is the body of a murdered priest. He is not just any priest, however, but a lusty man with a taste for married women and an established record of predatory sexual behaviour. The murdered priest in the fabliaux, therefore, deserves (at least in this comedic context) whatever initial murderous violence and subsequent corpse abuse has befallen him.

Murder is relatively rare in the fabliaux, with perhaps fifteen instances in the corpus of plus or minus 150 tales that date from the end of the twelfth century into the early decades of the fourteenth century.[7] The victims of murder are priests, with the exception of some singing hunchbacks in *Les trois Boçus*.[8] The murderers are either a jealous husband, often working in tandem with his wife, or a dupe hired by the couple to get rid of the bodies, who then kills an innocent bystander. Within that group, there are only two basic storylines: the multiple killings of similar-looking people, and the single battered corpse transported around. In the former, the victims all look alike (they are all hooded priests and monks, or corpses stuffed in similar bags or, in the one case, hunchbacks), so the fool charged with getting rid of one body believes that the other bodies are revenants.[9] This group includes *Les trois Boçus* [*The Three Hunchbacks*], *Estormi* and the *Les quatre Prestres* [*The Four Priests*]. The fabliaux involving a single dead body passed around include the highly popular *Sacristain I, II* and *III* [*The Sacristan*], *Le Prestre comporté* [*The Priest Who Was Carried Around*] and *Le Chapelain* [*The Chaplain*].[10] These tales are longer and feature a variety of characters who encounter the body in increasingly outlandish situations, such as propped on a horse or on an outhouse toilet.[11]

---

[7] François Suard, 'Les Trois cadavres encombrants', in *Épopée animale, fable, fabliau: Actes du IVe Colloque de la Société Internationale Reinardienne, Evreux, 7–11 septembre 1981* (Paris: Presses Universitaires de France, 1984), p. 611. For the dating, see: Per Nykrog, *Les Fabliaux: Nouvelle édition* (Geneva: Droz, 1973), p. xxii. Killings are more common than castration and torture, which are fairly rare, but still relatively unusual. See: Larissa Tracy, 'The Uses of Torture and Violence in the Fabliaux: When Comedy Crosses the Line', *Florilegium* 23 (2006): 143–68 at p. 165.

[8] Nykrog called secular priests 'les bêtes noires des fabliaux' (*Les Fabliaux*, p. 133). See also: Philippe Ménard, *Les Fabliaux: Contes à rire du moyen âge* (Paris: Presses Universitaires de France, 1983), pp. 122–25; Suard, 'Les trois cadavres encombrants', p. 61; Nykrog, *Les Fabliaux*, p. 65.

[9] For superstition related to the walking dead, see: Brian J. Levy, *The Comic Text: Patterns and Images in the Old French Fabliaux* (Amsterdam: Rodopi, 2000), pp. 188–92.

[10] For the popularity of the murder fabliaux, see: ibid., p. 191.

[11] Roy J. Pearcy calls these 'multiple *narreme*' or 'episodic' fabliaux in *Logic and Humour in the Fabliaux: An Essay in Applied Narratology* (Cambridge: D. S. Brewer, 2007), pp. 194–6.

The basic patterns that characterise the murder fabliaux can be traced to folkloric motifs found in multiple oral traditions. Stith Thompson's catalogue of motifs describes both 'the corpse handed around' and 'the thrice dead corpse', both of which occur in the K Section of the catalogue devoted to 'Deception'.[12] The 'Unresponsive corpse' is another listed by Thompson (K2152), in which the 'Corpse is set up so that dupe addresses it and when it does not respond knocks it over. He is accused of murder.'[13] D. L. Ashliman's collection of folktales in the English language lists #1536 as 'disposing of a corpse' in which inadvertent theft takes the burden off one person and passes it on.[14] All of these scenarios occur in some form in the fabliaux, but although popular motifs explain certain fundamental and predictable elements, they do not account for the narrative complexity of the fabliaux that feature the corpse of the lecherous priest, a stock character of the genre.

The murder fabliaux, with their physical and verbal humour surrounding dressed-up and misidentified corpses, are especially theatrical, and meant to be performed with different voices for the different characters, gestures using the whole body, and props.[15] Norris Lacy has observed: '[W]e will not fully appreciate the comedic potential until we begin thinking of these works as much in terms of performance as of textuality'.[16] Brian J. Levy even singles out the transferred-corpse stories as occasions wherein such performances would have been especially likely.[17] What is more, the performer of a murder fabliau would have to embody the narrator's combined omniscience and faux didacticism while

---

[12] Stith Thompson, *Motif-Index of Folk-Literature, Vol. 1: A Classification of Narrative Elements in Folk Tales, Ballads, Myths, Fables, Mediaeval Romances, Exempla, Fabliaux, Jest-Books, and Local Legends* (Bloomington: Indiana University Press, 1960), K2152. See also: Aurelio M. Espinosa, 'Hispanic Versions of the Tale of the Corpse Many Times Killed', *Journal of American Folklore* 49 (1936): 181–93 at p. 181 and Archer Taylor, 'Dane Hew, Munk of Leicestre', *Modern Philology* 15 (1917): 221–46 at p. 221.

[13] Mikel Koven, 'Traditional Narrative, Popular Aesthetics, *Weekend at Bernie's*, and Vernacular Cinema', in *Of Corpse: Death and Humor in Folklore and Popular Culture*, ed. Peter Narváez (Logan: Utah State University Press, 2003), p. 297.

[14] Ibid., p. 298.

[15] My use of the term 'theatrical' resembles what John M. Ganim describes as 'a governing sense of performance, an interplay among the author's voice, the fictional characters, and his immediate audience', in *Chaucerian Theatricality* (Princeton: Princeton University Press, 1990), p. 5. See also: Brian J. Levy, 'Performing Fabliaux', in *Performing Medieval Narrative*, ed. Evelyn Birge Vitz, Nancy Freeman Regalado and Marilyn Lawrence (Cambridge: D. S. Brewer, 2005), pp. 123–140 at pp. 124–25; Anne Cobby, 'Rhyme or Reason: *Le Prestre comporté* and *Le Prestre et le chevalier*', in *The Old French Fabliaux*, ed. Burr, Moran and Lacy, pp. 107–33 at pp. 107–10.

[16] Norris J. Lacy, 'Subject to Object: Performance and Observation in the Fabliaux', *Symposium* 56 (2002): 17–23 at p. 17.

[17] Levy, 'Performing Fabliaux', p. 140; Lacy, 'Subject to Object', p. 17.

effectively conveying the wild misperceptions of the characters within the story. The murder fabliaux are also best understood in terms of the narrative event. For each tale, the adventures of the corpse are recalled as a series of occurrences tied together by the narrator/storyteller with explicit, if absurd, didactic intent.[18] The recounting of the entire story then becomes its own new narrative event, combining the recalled adventures of the corpse with the narrative interventions and interactions between narrator and audience, all of which has been handed down as a text.[19] Lacy observes that the reader's attention is often drawn to the narrator's relationship to his material, to his craft and to his public, meaning that the subject of many fabliaux, is 'as much storytelling as it is the story being told'.[20] This recognition of the self-aware narrator is essential for appreciating how the triangulation between moralising narrator, sometimes gruesome corpse stories, and the imagined audience intended to 'learn' from the experience makes laughing at priestly murder possible.

Often the pleasure and humour of the murder fabliaux derive from the discrepancies between what is known by some and perceived by others, as in the above case of the servant in the tavern. One character's tough cut of meat is the external audience's and narrator's murdered body. Or, in *Le Sacristain I*, one character's unresponsive hooded figure on a toilet with straw stuffed in his wiping hand is the audience's recently-murdered adulterous priest.[21] The circumstances that the characters within the story believe to be true then allow for permissible violence against the dead body. This is especially true if the person appears to be dangerous, crazy, a wild animal, a thief or an incarnation of the Devil. For example, the monk in the outhouse finds the behaviour of his silent colleague to be unacceptably rude, so he punches his slumped, hooded head. In the case of *Le Prestre comporté*, the violence against a corpse is justifiable because the club-wielding bishop believes there is a wild dog under his covers. Here, the drunken bishop wakes up and yells at the dog: "'Par foi', [fait il], "ce n'est pas doute/ Que li prieus ne m'ait dit voir!/ Or me pora mestier avoir/ Cheste machue que j'ai cha./ Alés, fait il, fuiés, vescha!/ Que vis dyables vous emport!'"

---

[18] For the moral aspect of the fabliaux, see: Mary Jane Schenck, *The Fabliaux: Tales of Wit and Deception* (Amsterdam: Benjamins, 1987), pp. 103–04.

[19] Richard Bauman, *Story, Performance, and Event: Contextual Studies of Oral Narrative* (Cambridge: Cambridge University Press, 1986), p. 112. Bauman cites Roman Jakobson and Mikhail Bakhtin on the existence of both the event that is narrated and the narration as event.

[20] Norris J. Lacy, *Reading Fabliaux*, 2nd edn (Vestavia Hills, AL: Summa Publications, 1999), p. 111.

[21] It was commonplace to associate toilets with the work of the Devil. See: Martha Bayless, *Sin and Filth in Medieval Culture: The Devil in the Latrine* (New York: Routledge, 2012), p. 178.

['I swear', [he said], 'there is no doubt that the prior was telling the truth, for he will have done me a great service by giving me this club that I have here. Go on, get out. Be off with you! Get the hell out of here!'] (1029–34). Amazed at the lack of reaction, he decides to investigate: 'Si sent et taste le mort prestre' [So he feels and touches the dead priest] (1055). He proclaims, '"Dont n'esse pas lisse ne wains, / Ains est hons ou femme sans doute"' ['This is not a dog, but rather a man or a woman, no doubt'] (1058–9). He then calls for a lantern and discovers the body. The bishop is innocent, though, since he thought he was protecting himself from a savage dog, while the audience is entertained by the idea of a dead priest being taken for a wild dog in bed with an abbot. The bed scene is the final adventure in the *Le Prestre comporté*, but earlier, when the body is left perched on a grazing horse, the peasant charged with guarding the animal feels a tug on the rein around his wrist, awakens and then beats the alleged thief for trying to steal his horse. In both cases, the violence against the body is acceptable because of what the character believes is happening, while the external audience knows that the victim was already dead.

The central misperception in the murder fabliaux occurs in the minds of the people who inflict violence on an already dead body and then believe they are guilty of murder.[22] This realisation prompts them to hide the body, which results in the performative comedy of the portable priest. When the monk in *Le Sacristain* angrily punches the man on the toilet and gets no reaction, he lifts the hood to discover that he is dead and cries out: '"Dius, com m'a encombré peciés. / Or sui jou de murdre enteciés/ Ke ferai, las, se c'est seü?"' ['God has burdened me with sin/ Now I'm on the hook for murder!/ What will I do if this is found out?'] (249–51). Likewise, in *Le Chapelain*, which contains episodes borrowed from other fabliaux, a couple stares at the slumped body of a priest at their front door.[23] Since the manuscript is incomplete, the modern reader learns only later that an angry sheep killed the priest, and the animal's adulterous female owner ditched the body at the couple's door. Looking down on the body in the doorway, the wife believes she has killed him, but in her own defence, she tells her husband that she recognised the priest as a well-known madman, a *fol prové* [proven crazy man] (7), so she hit him so hard that he died. Here again, there is an excuse for the violence as well as no reason to suspect that the priest was already dead. The humour lies in the fact that she believes she has just beaten a crazy man to death in self-defence, while the audience knows

[22] Vitz discusses competing causalities in the *Sacristain*, such as what is desired, what is random or what characters believe to be the reason for events, such as the work of the Devil (*Medieval Narrative*, pp. 202–03).

[23] Henri Platelle, 'La voix du sang: Le cadavre qui saigne en présence de son meurtrier', in *La piété populaire au moyen âge: Actes du 99e Congrès national des sociétés savantes, Besançon, 1974* (Paris: Bibliothèque nationale, 1977), 1:166.

she was pounding on a dead body. In keeping with the folkloric motif, her main concern is to get rid of the body, which they stuff in a bag and send down the river. The wife scolds her worried husband: "'Taisiez! Ja de ce ne vos esmaiez,/ Que bien nos en deliverons!'" ['Shut up! Don't get all worried about this. We will get ourselves out of this!'] (26–28). In another example of this mistaken sense of guilt, early in the *Le Prestre comporté*, a woman finds her priest/lover strangled to death in her bathtub. The servant who had run the bath before the jealous husband came back to strangle the lover believes she is somehow responsible for the man's death and swiftly comes up with a plan to get rid of the body and free themselves of the whole affair: "'Que cuites serons de cest plait'" ['We will be cooked for this thing'] (377); consequently, she worries and immediately thinks about how to get rid of the body. Indeed, characters must feel they are at risk of being accused of murder so they will try to dispose of the body in ways that will place the corpse in the possession of other surprised non-murderers, thus allowing the same scenario to replay itself in a new context.

In some cases, the death appears to be an accident, which elicits a sense of communal relief rather than any regret. In *Le Sacristain I*, the villagers believe that the dead monk in question was armed and out of his mind before he died.[24] The townspeople react in horror as the corpse, propped on a war horse and looking very much alive, rides into the church, right up to the altar: "'Ci vient uns moines tous armés'" ['Look! There is an armed monk coming!'] (462).[25] A frightened peasant then warns the abbot that the monk is planning to do harm, at which point the narrator intervenes:

> Et saciés que li secretains
> Fu encore sor le palefroi.
> Por le noise et por l'esfroi
> Ke la jent aloient menant,
> S'en va vers le moustier bruant;
> Mais si basse i estoit l'entrée,
> Si comme i vient de randonee
> Fiert la teste al lintel desus:
> Ronpent cordes et el ciet jus
> Trestous envers, janbes ouvertes.

[And be aware that the sacristan was still on the palfrey. Because of the noise and ruckus that the people were making, he [the horse] went towards the noisy church, but the entry was so low, and he came in so quickly, that he [the priest]

---

[24] Levy notes the importance of narrative asides conveying 'good riddance' after the murder of the lecherous priest ('Performing Fabliaux', p. 133).

[25] This is parody of epic. See: Levy, *The Comic Text*, p. 35. For the motif of the corpse mounted on a horse that runs wild, see: Taylor, 'Dane Hew', p. 246.

smashed his head on the lintel above, the cords broke, and he fell flat, totally upside-down with his legs wide open]. (480–87)

When the townspeople lift his bloody cape and realise he is dead, they assume he died from smashing his head and then falling off his horse. They lament his passing, but the narrator quickly celebrates the fact that the murderous couple is now free from worry. He adds that the woman even gets to keep the money from the priest's initial offer of sex as well as the bacon for which he had been mistaken earlier. To all but the narrator, the audience and the original killers, the monk bumped his head while seeming to terrorise villagers. Thanks to the narrative construction of the murder fabliaux, two perceived realities based on a single scene, the already dead man riding in on a warhorse and the crazy monk who dies when he bumps his head, can coexist within the same narrative event.

The interplay of competing narratives surrounding a single corpse is particularly complex in Le Prestre comporté in the scene with the abbot and the alleged wild dog in the bed. After they pull back the blankets to reveal the corpse, the narrator allows that no one stood up to condemn the abbot for his murderous actions. He weighs in sympathetically, though, stating: 'Mes il est lor maistre et lor sire, / Si ne l'i oserent sus metre; / Il ne s'en ossent entremetre, / Car bien sevent qu'il lor puet nuire / Et lor abeïe destruire: / Pour che ont la chose celee' [But he was their master and their lord, thus they did not dare accuse him, they did not dare get involved, for they knew well that he could hurt them and destroy their abbey. For this reason, they kept the affair covered up] (1092–97). The narrator's commentary appears to decry earnestly the power relations that conspire to protect the mighty, even when they murder, but his ironic outrage is deflated by the fact that the audience knows that the bishop is innocent, and not just because he thought he was beating a wild beast. In the strange moral universe of the fabliaux, thanks to the play of misperception, the witnesses are guilty of letting the abbot get away with a murder he did not commit.

The murder fabliaux include a significant amount of dialogue in direct speech, which often takes the form of ironic conversations highlighting the failure or refusal to recognise that someone is dead.[26] In a one-sided conversation with a corpse, the adulterous woman in Le Prestre comporté speaks to her strangled lover in the bathtub, assuming he is just resting. She beseeches him to respond and to open his eyes, then complains to her servant: '"Ha, Bourghet, il me tient si vil / Que il ne me daigne respondre; / Bien cuic morir et de duel fondre / Quant je li ai m'amour donnée, / N'encor ne m'a nes esgardee"' ['Oh Bourget, he holds me in such disdain that he doesn't even deign to respond to me. I could just die

---

[26] Pearcy unfairly finds a lack of verbal humour in the transported corpse stories in *Logic and Humour*, p. 196.

and collapse in grief over it. For ever since I gave him my love, he won't even look at me'] (181–83). The wife is, of course, pleading with a dead body to show her some affection. When she swears that *she* will die if he does not respond, the irony is intended for comic effect as part of a theatrical scene designed for verbal and physical humour.

For these scenes to work, the actors in the story must remain ignorant of the murder, while knowledge of the crime constitutes the bond of complicity between the narrator and the audience. Later on in *Le Prestre comporté*, the wife and her servant leave the dead priest/lover at another couple's front door, a scene that also occurs in *Le Chapelain*. When the husband gets up to answer the door naked, he trips and lands on top of the corpse lying in the doorway. The physical humour is explicit here, but it is the verbal play that escalates as they fail to realise that the visitor is dead, choosing to focus instead on more frivolous issues such as whether or not he is a real priest. The husband looks down and suggests that perhaps: "'Ou il par sa genglerie / Ceste noire cape emprontee'" ['Or by his trickery, he borrowed this black cape'] (413–14). The idea that the priest might be an impostor then gives way to their displeasure at his mode of entry, so they berate him: "'Mieus vous venist iestre a l'hostel!'" ['You would be better off at an inn!'] (423) and "'Nous tenés vous ore pour bestes?'" ['Do you take us for animals?'] (426). The wife then wonders whether he is sleeping, at which point the husband finally realises that the man is dead and insists that he must have died while falling into their house, for he is sure he heard him knocking at the door. The more absurd the theory, the funnier it is that murder is never anyone's initial suspicion. As this scene reveals, the murder fabliaux are deceptively complex in that they combine multiple comedic elements from different registers: the farcical physical humour of falling through doorways mixed with the verbal incongruity found in the dialogue between people who misperceive what they see before their eyes, all of which is narrated in an ironic voice with frequent asides.

One of the central comic strategies of murder fabliaux involves failed dialogue between a passerby and a corpse that seems to be a living person failing to respond. Frustration with a non-responsive corpse leads to escalating violence against the dead body, as in the above-mentioned toilet scene in *Le Sacristain*. In *Le Prestre comporté*, when the presumed horse thief does not cry out in pain, the peasant guarding the horse hits harder, exhausting himself. Finally, the peasant looks under the hood and finds to his horror that the man is dead. Although he feels terrible, he is far more concerned about the trouble he may be in. Then he wonders aloud what the priest was doing on his horse in the first place. His question reminds the audience that they already have the answer to the man's question, but it also highlights the complicity between the storyteller and his listeners.

Those who encounter a priest, whether cloaked and still alive or already dead and stuffed in a bag, at times fear that he is a revenant or the work of the Devil. The stories with multiple dead bodies feature the revenant theme more prominently since the dupe (who really has multiple bodies to bury) falls for the ploy of a penny-pinching couple who convince him that the one body they paid him to get rid of keeps coming back. In both *Les quatre Prestres* and *Estormi*, in addition to the three priests killed by the couple, the dupe also kills a passerby because he mistakes him for the one he just buried. The fourth priest is an innocent bystander, but the fear that he is a revenant or the Devil invites sympathy for the killer's desperate actions. The killing is then played as an unfortunate misunderstanding to be blamed on the Devil, with the tone remaining light and humorous.[27] In *Les quatre Prestres*, the narrator invites the audience to share in a *merveille* that he has heard regarding a married woman loved by three priests. The woman lures the three men to her home, telling them to wait out back in the bakehouse, which her husband has rigged to collapse when he pulls out the keystone. They all die instantly, although it is unclear whether he intended to kill them. The husband feels a sense of remorse, but his wife's immediate concern is to get rid of the bodies. She summons a local ruffian, hoping to trick him into dealing with all three bodies for the price of just one. Each time he manages to hurl a body into the marl pit, she scolds him, yelling '"revenuz est"' ['He is back'] (42), thereby playing on the fool's fear of revenants.[28] When a fourth priest stops to warm his hands by the fire, the terrified fool wrestles him into the pit. Only this time he falls in with his victim, making five deaths in all.

The comic violence perpetrated against apparent, yet false, revenants in the fabliaux is a satirical response to the ghost and revenant stories from oral and written sources that permeated the culture of thirteenth-century France. The rise of the fabliau genre at the turn of the thirteenth century coincided with the development of popular preaching that involved sermons peppered with short didactic stories known as moral *exempla*.[29] Revenants, or the walking dead, made frequent appearances in these tales, so much so that Jean-Claude Schmitt describes the ghostly material gathered by the mendicant orders in the

---

[27] See: Levy, *The Comic Text*, p. 189, and more generally pp. 192–96, for belief in the work of the Devil and understanding the fear it would have provoked.

[28] Maria Cristina Azuela Bernal, 'Del espanto a la hilaridad en el relate cómico medieval', *Acta Poetica* 30 (2009): 61–83 at p. 83.

[29] Brian J. Levy, 'Le Fabliau et l'exemple: étude sur les recueils moralisants anglo-normands', in *Épopée animale*, p. 313. Stephen Gordon, 'Domestic Magic and the Walking Dead in Medieval England: A Diachronic Approach', in *The Materiality of Magic*, ed. Ceri Houlbrook and Natalie Armitage (Oxford: Oxbow, 2015), pp. 65–84 at p. 66.

thirteenth century as too copious to quantify.[30] Clerics who adapted anecdotes and popular ghost stories for the *exempla* tended to adhere to the oral sources, keeping them in a form familiar to their audiences.[31] The belief in the presence of the walking dead in both clerical and popular culture at the time was well attested and explains the presence of faux revenants in the often pseudo-didactic fabliaux.[32] The fabliaux are clearly far more comic than the *exempla*, but edifying morality tales could also be amusing and accessible.[33] Some of the violence against dead bodies in the fabliaux can also be tied to the rise of the *exempla*. Often revenants wanted absolution or a favour of some kind, but, as Esther Cohen argues, a revenant was frequently a malignant power whose appearance presaged bad things to come. Destruction of a revenant could sometimes require extreme measures such as dismemberment, decapitation and burning of the corpse before reburial.[34] The growing popularity of such tales helps to explain the sometimes surprising, yet obviously satirical, violence against priestly bodies in the fabliaux, which can also be read as criticism or mockery of popular fears of the walking dead.

The fact that monks were common in revenant lore provides a useful explanation for the prominence of the priest as travelling corpse in the fabliaux.[35] Nancy Caciola writes that these were men of the cloth who had, in her words, 'abdicated their sacred duties and become embroiled in pursuits that were properly the preserve of the laity: sex and violence'.[36] This characterisation of sinful churchmen certainly applies to the priests in the fabliaux. Culturally speaking, the prevalence of monks in revenant tales suggests that there was ample exposure to the concept of justifiable violence against a sinful dead priest, a concept ripe for parody. Of particular concern was a person who had experienced a bad death, like murder,

---

[30] Jean-Claude Schmitt, *Les Revenants: Les Vivants et les morts dans la société médiévale* (Paris: Gallimard, 1994), p. 158.

[31] Hans Peter Broedel, 'Gratuitous Examples and the Grateful Dead: Appropriation and Negotiation of Traditional Narratives in Medieval Exemplary Ghost Stories', in *Translatio or the Transmission of Culture in the Middle Ages and the Renaissance Modes and Messages*, ed. L. H. Hollengreen (Turnout: Brepols, 2009), pp. 97–112 at p. 101.

[32] Lorcin, 'Les Revenants', p. 91; R. C. Finucane, *Appearances of the Dead: A Cultural History of Ghosts* (Buffalo: Prometheus Books, 1984), pp. 59–60; Levy, 'Le Fabliau', pp. 311–12.

[33] Levy, 'Le Fabliau', p. 311; Miri Rubin, *Charity and Community in Medieval Cambridge* (Cambridge: Cambridge University Press, 2002), pp. 80–81.

[34] Nancy Caciola, 'Wraiths, Revenants, and Ritual in Medieval Culture', *Past & Present* 152 (1996): 3–45 at p. 21; Schmitt, *Les Revenants*, p. 103; Esther Cohen, *The Crossroads of Justice: Law and Culture in Late Medieval France* (Leiden: Brill, 1993), pp. 135–36; Danielle Westerhof, *Death and the Noble Body in Medieval England* (Woodbridge: Boydell Press, 2008), p. 25; Gordon, 'Domestic Magic', p. 66.

[35] Schmitt, *Les Revenants*, p. 151.

[36] Caciola, 'Wraiths', p. 28.

and who had been an especially malicious person in life, which again applies to most of the priests in the murder fabliaux.[37] To give an example of a fear-inspiring anecdote, a story from the late thirteenth-century *Chronicle of Lanercost* describes a monk who lived perversely and came back wearing his habit. He terrorised the community by waiting in attics and storehouses, savagely beating and even killing people.[38] There are no actual revenants in the fabliaux, but the fear of them governs many of the reactions of characters who encounter a murdered monk. Without the shared cultural baggage of the sinful monk as revenant, the scenes in the fabliaux that parody this phenomenon cease to function as social satire. The fabliaux audience can enjoy knowing the truth about the dead body while laughing at the characters who believe they are seeing ghosts.

The belief that one has come face to face with a revenant seems somewhat banal next to the possibility that the Devil himself has stolen the bacon meant for dinner and replaced it with an incarnation of himself in the form of a dead, or, at least very quiet and motionless, monk. In keeping with the failure to see a dead body as a sign that a murder has occurred, the internal characters in the murder fabliaux are less troubled by the Devil hanging from a hook in the tavern than they are by the absence of pork for dinner.[39] In both *Le Sacristain* and the *Le Prestre comporté*, thieves accidentally grab a bag with a body in it from a dung heap instead of a bag filled with a promised side of bacon. In *Le Sacristian II*, a man grabs what he thinks is a pig's foot from the bottom of the bag, but gets the heel of a shoe instead. The dry and burnt cord from which the bag hangs then breaks and the whole thing falls on his head, sending them both tumbling backwards into a wooden box. Like the servant girl in the tavern, he too assumes he has encountered strange pork rather than a dead man and cries out: "'Li bacons est cheüz sor moi!'" ['The bacon fell on me!'] (730). His wife, Martinet, brings a lantern and stares at the monk:

> Par la foi que doi seint Martin
> N'est pas bacons, ainz est malfez
> Qui sanble moine coronez!
> Si est chauciez, se Dieus me salt!

---

[37] Stephen Gordon, 'Disease, Sin, and the Walking Dead in Medieval England, c. 1100–1350', in *Medicine, Healing and Performance*, ed. Effie Gemi-Iordanou et al. (Oxford: Oxbow Books, 2014), pp. 55–70 at pp. 56–57. See also: Claude Lecouteux, *The Return of the Dead: Ghosts, Ancestors, and the Transparent Veil of the Pagan Mind*, trans. Jon E. Graham (Rochester, VT: Inner Traditions, 1996), p. 45; Caciola, 'Wraiths', p. 29 and Scott G. Bruce, *The Penguin Book of the Undead* (New York: Penguin Books, 2016), particularly the section 'Night is the Dead's Dominion', pp. 119–40.

[38] Caciola, 'Wraiths', p. 26.

[39] For food in the fabliaux, see: Sarah Gordon, *Culinary Comedy in Medieval French Literature* (West Lafayette, IN: Purdue University Press, 2006), pp. 129–32.

Li bacons qui pendoit en halt
N'i est mie, perdu l'avons:
Nous avons moine por bacon.

['Holy Saint Martin! That's not bacon, that's the Devil looking like a tonsured monk, and he is wearing shoes, God help me. The bacon that was hanging up there is no longer there. We have lost it. We have a monk for bacon']. (736–42)

They blame demonic possession for the switch, but the presence of the Devil is of no concern next to the loss of the bacon. Here, the corpse humour relies on the incongruity and absurdity of the non-reactions of the tavern-dwellers to the presence of a dead body. These people do not see a corpse and think murder; they see a corpse and think the Devil stole their bacon. The fact that a priest has been murdered and his body abused remains knowledge reserved for the audience. The actual explanation, the truth, will occur to no one, while the wild misperceptions of the characters within the story allow for multiple levels of symbolic play surrounding food and demons. The complexity of the murder fabliaux allows for the narrator to mediate between the bizarre world of those who misperceive what they see and the truth that he shares with the audience. Moreover, when the characters in the story wonder whether the Devil stole their dinner and replaced it with an incarnation of himself in the guise of a monk hanging in a meat sack, the fableor succeeds in raising questions about the kind of influence that ghostly sermons may be having on the community.

Later in the *Le Prestre comporté*, the comedy of non-recognition escalates into a literary parody as the host in the tavern perceives the switch from pork to dead monk as a marvel or wonder in need of interpretation:

Li ostes, ki plus n'i areste,
Monte la ou li prestres pent;
Molt s'esmerveille quant il sent
Le sourpliç et le cape noire.
'Dius', dist il, 'c'est cape a prevoire
Que je senc chi entre mes mains!
U ce est faarie au mains,
U c'est autre senefiance:
Ains ne fui mais en tel balanche
De nule riens jour de ma vie.
Par mon chief, bacons n'es ce mie!
Quels dyables l'eüst viestu?'
Son brach estent, si a sentu
Ses pies et tous cauciés les treuve.
'Hé, Dius', dist il, 'iceste treuve
M'a de mon sens si destourné!'

[The host, who waited no more, climbed up where the priest was hanging. He was amazed when he sensed the surplice and the black cape. 'God,' he said, 'This is the cape of a priest that I feel here in my hands! Either this is magic in my hands or there is some other explanation. Never a day in my life have I been in such peril. By God, this not bacon at all! What the devil dressed it up?' He extended his arm and then felt his feet and found them to have shoes on. 'Oh, God,' he said. 'I think I am losing my mind!'] (813–28)

The appearance of the body is deemed a *merveille*, an instance of 'féerie', of the sort one hears about in Brittany, he proclaims. The passage plays on the terms *sens* and *sentir* to describe the act of feeling and touching the mysterious body as he ponders whether there might be magic in his hands, and then he wonders whether he is losing his mind, his *sens*. The use of the term *senefiance* parodies the language of higher-register genres, such as romance, by treating the transformation of bacon into a dead human body as a marvellous and meaningful occurrence. The rather mundane truth that evades the speaker, that this is simply a man who has been murdered and stuffed in a bag, makes the invitation to contemplation all the more humourous.

These scenes involving missing pork are undeniably rich in symbolism, but the confusion always stops before there is any real risk of accidental consumption or any such transgression of the limits of comedy, even by fabliau standards.[40] For Jean-Claude Aubailly, the laughter born of these substitutions remains ambiguous, neither pagan nor Christian, but rather a more universal fear of the divine as it intrudes upon daily life.[41] Even Levy, whose focus is comedy, describes these sequences in terms of metamorphoses in which 'the degradation of the man transformed into beast reaches the uttermost point of sick, as a newly slain corpse mutates into a cured pig'.[42] Mutation is too strong a term, though, since the two objects are never anything but switched, and nothing is consumed despite the disturbing potential for cannibalism. There is a tacit understanding between narrator and audience that these stories feature macabre corpse humour, but never go too far. A body will be abused, but it will not be eaten.

While fabliaux narrators do not concern themselves much with murder as a crime, they have plenty to say about lesser vices in tones that echo the teachings

---

[40] For sexual connotations relating to bacon, see: Gary D. Mole, 'Du Bacon et de la femme: Pour une relecture de *Barat et Haimet* de Jean Bodel', *Neophilologus* 86 (2002): 17–31 at p. 25.

[41] Jean-Claude Aubailly, 'Le fabliau et les sources inconscientes du rire médiéval', *Cahiers de civilisation médiévale* 118 (1987): 105–17 at pp. 116–17. Pearcy speaks here of humour dependent on confusion in *Logic and Humour*, pp. 194–95.

[42] Levy, *The Comic Text*, p. 72.

of popular preaching.⁴³ For instance, *Les quatre Prestres* features a narrator who is strikingly blasé about the deaths of the four priests and the foolish ruffian. His only comment at the end is: 'Ce puet on bien dire du prestre: / Mieux li venist au moustier ester!' [One can rightly say of the priest that he would have been better off staying at the church!] (76). He then refers to a familiar proverb: 'Soventes foiz avient a court / Que tieus ne peche qui encourt' [Often it happens that he who has not sinned pays the price] (79–80). Essentially, his message is 'sometimes bad things happen to good people'. He also implies that any priest out walking at night is likely up to no good. Despite the five dead bodies, he has nothing but banalities to offer, which creates both humour based on incongruity and the potential to see the tale as a satirical commentary on the more traditional didactic genres that were growing in popularity at the time.

Incongruent morals are a common element of the fabliaux in general, but they are especially significant when they are part of the tacit refusal to acknowledge the presence of murder.⁴⁴ The explicit moral of the *Les trois Boçus*, which is more an involuntary manslaughter fabliau than a murder tale, is even more incongruent since it deals with money, a theme barely broached in the story. The tale follows the same model as the bakehouse story, with no concern for the multiple victims, who, in this story, have no predatory intentions and are not violently murdered but die of suffocation while being hidden from the jealous husband in a drawer. Despite the multiple deaths, the narrator is only interested in the rich hunchback's ability to lure a beautiful wife despite his ugliness. At the end of the story, the narrator utters a jarring *non sequitur* about money: 'Honiz soit li hom, quels qu'il soit, / Qui trop prise mauvés deniers, / Et qui les fist fere premiers!' [Shame on the man, whoever he may be, who esteems evil money too much and shame on the man who first created it!] (294–6). The poet also laments that anyone and anything can be bought. For Lacy, this moral is 'thoroughly inappropriate and illogical', but the illogical nature of the moral is the humour itself.⁴⁵ The moral is not just illogical, however, since it highlights the refusal to acknowledge that innocent people have been killed by focusing on something unrelated. Given that the fabliaux reflect awareness of contemporary moralising discourses, their nonchalant treatment of murder must therefore be taken as essential to the genre's upside-down moral code, which is designed for comedy.

---

⁴³ See generally Levy, 'Le Fabliau'; Brent A. Pitts, 'Truth-Seeking Discourse in the Old French Fabliaux', *Medievalia et Humanistica* 15 (1987): 95–117 at p. 108; Erik Hertog, *Chaucer's Fabliaux as Analogues* (Leuven: Leuven University Press, 1991), p. 215.

⁴⁴ Noomen, 'Performance et mouvance', p. 134.

⁴⁵ Lacy, *Reading Fabliaux*, p. 147.

As a genre, the fabliaux are frequently both self-referential and intertextual, traits that are particularly evident in the murder fabliaux, which are based on a small set of established and predictable patterns. In *Le Sacristain I*, for instance, the couple plans to lure the sacristan with the promise to trade sex for money. The wife warns: '"Par foi, sire, li moines vient; / Mais une riens vous veul je dire; / Por Diu, gardés vous de l'ocire!"' ['I'm telling you, my lord, the monk is coming. One thing I want to say to you is, for God's sake, be careful not to kill him!'] (146–48). Her statement can be taken at face value but also as a nod to the fact that the audience knows that this will not be a travelling corpse tale unless there is a body. The husband has to kill the monk, but her statement also points to other similar stories. Her warning proves fruitless, as expected, and the husband, incensed by the sight of the sacristan lifting up his wife's *chemise*, jumps out from his assigned hiding place and yells: '"Venus estes a vostre jor!"' ['Your day has come!'] (173). The monk tries to escape, but the husband gets him by the hair and delivers a blow to the back of his head. The monk jumps up again, so the enraged husband bashes him on the head until it shatters in pieces and the brains spill out. The wife feels guilty of *grans peciés* [a great sin] (188), but her husband assures her with a meaningful proclamation: '"Dame", dist il, "ne doutés mie,/ Ke vous n'en serés ja blasmee!"' ['My lady', he said, 'have no doubt whatsoever that you will ever be blamed for this!'] (192–93). On one level, the husband is simply trying to reassure his wife, but on a metanarrative level, the dialogue here reinforces the tacit understanding that couples who are victims of adulterous priests never pay a price for their murderous revenge.

Even within the relatively small corpus of murder fabliaux, there are exceptions that prove the rules. *Le Chapelain* offers the sole exception to the unspoken rule that nobody, or rather no human being, gets caught for killing an adulterous priest. Its parodic approach involving the anger-prone sheep ultimately reinforces the centrality of allowing murderers to walk away unscathed. In this case, the priest-lover is mortally wounded when the sheep reacts angrily to catching the adulterous lovers in the act. The identity of the murderer is only revealed, however, when the two men who accidently dredge up the body accuse one another of the crime and are sentenced to a judicial duel.[46] They are not guilty, the narrator reminds the audience: 'Mes nus d'aus deus n'en a lo tort' [but neither of the two is in the wrong] (265). What follows is a parody of hagiography in which God intervenes to save the innocent men.[47] As they battle, the guilty animal happens to walk by in a flock on the way to market. In the presence of the

---

[46] For judicial duels in the fabliaux, see: Mary Jane Schenck, 'Orality, Literacy and the Law: Judicial Scenes in the Fabliau', *Reinardus* 8 (1995): 63–75.

[47] Brent A. Pitts, '*Merveilleux*, Mirage, and Comic Ambiguity in the Old French Fabliaux', *Assays* 4 (1987): 39–50 at p. 42.

real murderer, the wounds of the dead man miraculously begin to bleed again.[48] To test the evidence, the provost waits until the bleeding has stopped and then recreates the parade of passersby, human and animal, that coincided with the bleeding. When the guilty sheep goes by, the wounds begin to bleed and the provost has the animal seized. He then summons the animal's owner, informing her that she can no longer hide him. She admits that the chaplain had been in her bed when the sheep went into a rage and knocked him flat and killed him.

The end of the sheep story contains a surprising expression of explicit frustration, 'Que li murtres fu tant celez' [that the murder had to be so covered up] (410). This is unusual for a murder fabliau, since sympathy is supposed to lie with the murderers, but the statement makes more sense coming from the man who was framed for the crime. The narrator then tells of how the adulterous priest was buried in great shame and then reassures the audience: 'Par cest conte savoir poez / Que nus murtres n'iert ja celez' [With this story you can know that no murder will remain covered up] (430–31). This is ironic to anyone who knows other comic tales of murdered priests. Charles Muscatine singles out *Le Chapelain* as being unique in its pious conclusion and condemnation of vice, citing the fact that the narrator affirms that the guilty always get caught.[49] The opposite is the case, however. The one time a priest-lover is murdered and the community learns the truth, it is not the husband or the complicit wife who is responsible, but a farm animal that is then set free. The murderous husband in the *Le Sacristain I* speaks for the larger corpus of murder fabliaux when he tells his worried wife that she has absolutely nothing to worry about; she will never be found out.[50]

Another exception that reinforces the moral and aesthetic code of the murder fabliaux is *Estormi*, a tale that breaks the implicit rules regarding the need to turn a blind eye to murder. *Estormi* follows the multiple-body pattern, but fails to kill the priests quickly and move swiftly to the corpse disposal narrative. Instead, the narrator draws out the planning and execution of the murders, and is plodding and deliberate in the burial sequence. He then drones on, appropriately rather than incongruently, about how the couple was greedy and the priests should have stayed out of trouble. It takes the narrator 250 verses of 630 to announce that he knows he needs to get to the part about the long night dealing with the bodies. Corpse disposal is supposed to comprise the majority of the story, so the proportions are off. Rather than a comedy of errors peppered with ironic commentary that refuses to acknowledge murder, *Estormi* focuses on the murder. In

---

[48] Broedel, 'Gratuitous Examples', p. 139; Platelle, 'La voix du sang', p. 166.
[49] Charles Muscatine, *The Old French Fabliaux* (New Haven: Yale University Press, 1986), p. 103.
[50] Suard sees sympathy for the women in these tales. See: 'Les trois cadavres', p. 622.

fact, *Estormi* is so long and unwieldy that Lacy even suggests, although not with regard to murder in particular, that the author is trying to demonstrate inept storytelling. This may well be the case given how inexpertly he adapts the corpse motif.[51] For instance, the murders are excessively graphic. The jealous husband strikes the third priest so hard that his mouth fills up with a mixture of blood and brains, and the man falls dead, his body trembling on the ground. Although the scene is a parody of epic, the violence is still shocking.[52] The narrator even says that Jehan brandishes his club *felonessement* [wickedly] (172). After the gratuitously violent bludgeoning, the narrator interjects that 'li fabliaus seroit corrompus' [the fabliau would be corrupted] (255) if he neglected to tell of how they managed to get rid of the bodies. This aside proves, at the very least, that he was thinking about the conventions to which he was supposed to adhere. Yet, even the appointed dupe, Estormi, is a far more violent murderer than his counterparts in other tales. When he kills the requisite innocent bystander, he drives a pick into the back of a priest's head causing his brains to spill out. To be fair, the dupe believes he is dealing with a demonic presence, whom he tells to go back to Hell where he came from, but this is a far cry from dragging a passerby into a marl pit. *Estormi* is too gruesome to be funny and lacks the interplay between narrator, actors and audience that enlivens the other murder fabliaux.

Either the author of *Estormi* did not know the rules surrounding how to be funny with dead bodies or, more likely, he broke them on purpose. Either way, his murder fabliau is markedly less clever than the others. He even breaks the rule of incongruent moralising by blaming the greedy couple for the murders: 'Qu'il ont porchacié laidement/ Lor mort et lor definement' [For they pursued in an ugly way their death and destruction] (133–34). Yet, ultimately, he says the priests deserved what they got for trying to take Yfame's honour, 'ainz furent paié a lor droit' [Thus they were paid what they were owed] (605). This unexpected example of direct commentary on the murder itself dampens the spirit of the story, revealing a narrator who does not use irony or perpetuate the topsy-turvy moral code of murder fabliaux in which moralising is either strikingly lax or off topic. The result is an unfunny fabliau. Yet despite its failures, *Estormi* succeeds as a commentary on its own genre by shedding light on the successes of the other murder fabliaux that are funny.

Unlike certain more respectable killings that happen during feuds or public fighting, murder, when carried out under cover of darkness, without warning

---

[51] Lacy, *Reading Fabliaux*, pp. 96–97.
[52] See: Tracy, 'The Uses of Torture and Violence', for the argument that going beyond the limits of comedy with violence and brutality was sometimes intentional as a form of cultural criticism.

and with attempts to hide the body, was seen as a particularly grievous crime.[53] This is exactly what happens to priests in the fabliaux, and yet no one seems troubled by anything but the thought of getting caught or being falsely accused. Daron Burrows asks why modern critics seem to find the murder of priests less shocking than the scenes of castration and maiming in the fabliaux, positing that perhaps the murder scenes seem less like sadism and torture.[54] Burrows is correct that the murders are presented more lightly, but this is because the refusal to acknowledge the murders is essential to the larger architecture of the humorous corpse story.[55] The predatory priest who abuses his power, lives like an aristocrat, and sleeps with other men's wives is the stock character of choice for these stories, but this does not mean there was any particular intention to condone priestly murder.

The increasing presence of ghost stories about revenant monks within sermons offers a better explanation for the playful treatment of murder in the fabliaux. What is more, there was precedent in didactic literature for downplaying murder, even when it was supposed to be the primary focus. In the 30,000-line *Vie des Peres*, a popular collection of morality tales from the early thirteenth century with eight tales devoted to the sixth commandment against murder, the actual topic of murder remains secondary to the discussion of the consequences for the perpetrator, such as repentance and penance. Adrian Tudor writes: 'Upon close inspection, it becomes clear that although murder is a motif which adds to the interest and excitement of these tales, it is not absolutely central to their moral teachings'.[56] The murder fabliaux function similarly insofar as they feature murder, but they employ the act as a stepping stone to discuss its aftermath. If there were any actual moralising subtext to be gleaned from the murder

---

[53] Pieter Spierenburg, *A History of Murder: Personal Violence in Europe from the Middle Ages to the Present* (Cambridge: Polity, 2008), p. 58; Bernard Ribémont, 'Le "crime épique" et sa punition: quelques exemples (XIIe-XIIIe siècles)', in *Crime and Punishment in the Middle Ages and Early Modern Age: Mental-Historical Investigations of Basic Human Problems and Social Responses*, ed. Albrecht Classen and Connie Scarborough (Berlin: De Gruyter, 2012), pp. 29–42 at p. 35.

[54] Daron Burrows, *The Stereotype of the Priest in the Old French Fabliaux: Anticlerical Satire and Lay Identity* (Bern: Peter Lang, 2005), pp. 193, 200. See also: R. Howard Bloch, *The Scandal of the Fabliaux* (Chicago: University of Chicago Press, 1986), pp. 190–93. For Lacy, they are anti-priest but not anticlerical, in *Reading Fabliaux*, p. xix. Huguette Le Gros argues that the fabliaux are not against the vocation, but individuals, 'Parodie et représentations sociales dans les fabliaux', in *Comique, satire et parodie dans la tradition renardienne et les fabliaux*, ed. Danielle Buschinger and André Crépin (Göppingen: Kümmerle, 1983), p. 31.

[55] Lorcin, 'Les revenants', pp. 99–101; Burrows, *The Stereotype*, pp. 67–68.

[56] Adrian Tudor, *Tales of Vice and Virtue: The First Old French 'Vie des Pères'* (Amsterdam: Rodopi, 2005), p. 183. See also: Elisabeth Pinto-Mathieu, *La 'Vie des Pères': Genèse de contes religieux du XIIIe siècle* (Paris: Honoré Champion, 2009), pp. 246–52.

fabliaux, beyond warning priests to stay home and keep their hands off married women, it might be the dangers of accidentally killing someone in a jealous rage; however, unlike in the morality tales, there is no penance and little repentance in the murder fabliaux. Murder functions in the service of comedy, not moral instruction. Without lusty priests and the jealous rages they inspire, there would be no corpse comedy, and that would be no fun.

CHAPTER 8

'Chevaliers ocirre':
Manslaughter, Morality and Meaning
in the *Queste del Saint Graal*

Lucas Wood

MANY EXTRAORDINARY AND PORTENTOUS events unfold in the *Queste del Saint Graal* (c. 1220–25), which follows the *Lancelot* (c. 1215–20) and precedes the *Mort le roi Artu* (c. 1225–30) in the Vulgate Cycle of Old French Arthurian prose romances, but one of the most quietly striking things to occur in the *Queste* is – nothing. In the world of chivalric romance, the absence of adventures is the greatest surprise of all, as an indignant Gauvain grouses to his companion Hestor des Mares:

> Par foi, […] de ceste chose me voloie je complaindre a vos. Car, se Dex me conselt, onques puis que je me parti de la cité de Kamaalot ne trovai je aventure nule. Si ne sai pas coment ce est alé : car por aler en estranges terres et en lointains païs […] et por chevauchier de nuiz et de jorz ne remeist il pas. Car ge vos creant loiaument […] que por aler seul, sanz autre besoigne fere, ai je puis ocis plus de .x. chevaliers dont li pires valoit assez, ne aventure ne trovai nule.[1]

> [By my faith, … I wanted to complain to you about that very thing, for I haven't found a single adventure, God help me, since I left the city of Camelot. I don't know how or why, but it wasn't for lack of travelling to foreign lands and far countries … and riding night and day. For I assure you truthfully … that travelling alone, on no other mission, I have since killed more than ten knights, the worst of whom was of no mean worth, without finding a single adventure].

The unwonted absence of adventures assumes here the function of the conventional romance *merveille*, which induces wonder or bewilderment and the desire for an explanation.[2] As usual in the *Queste*, this desire is soon gratified by one

---

[1] *La Quête du Saint-Graal*, ed. Fanni Bogdanow, trans. Anne Berrie (Paris: Livre de Poche, 2006), §179.22–31. Hereafter, section and line numbers will be given in parentheses. All English translations of Old and modern French texts are my own.

[2] See, among many scholarly accounts of the marvellous in Old French literature: Jean-René Valette, 'La Merveille et son interprétation: L'exemple du *Lancelot* propre', *Revue des langues romanes* 100.2 (1997): 163–208.

of the ubiquitous *preudomes* – wise, righteous hermits or monks endowed with preternatural hermeneutic expertise – who appear throughout the text to interpret the questing knights' adventures and offer spiritual guidance.[3] Gauvain's frustration turns out to be a source of insight into the state of his own soul and the nature of the Grail quest, which is nothing like the secular tests of valour and prowess that were formerly the Round Table fellowship's bread and butter. The hermit explains that, as Hestor and Gauvain have been shown in an allegorical vision, their 'povre foi' [weak faith] and lack of 'charité, abstinence, [et] verité' [charity, abstinence and truth] (§195.24–25) preclude them from encountering worthwhile adventures because

> Les aventures qui ore avienent sont les demostrances et li signe del Saint Graal, ne li signe del Saint Vessel n'aparront ja a pecheor n'a home qui soit envolepez de terriens vices. Dont il ne vos aparront ja ; car vos estes trop desloial pecheor. Si ne devez pas quidier que cez aventures qui or corent soient de chevaliers ocirre et mehaignier, ainçois sont des choses esperitex qui sont graindres et meuz valent assés. (§195.32–40)

> [The adventures now taking place are the signs and showings of the Holy Grail, and the signs of the Holy Vessel will never appear to sinners or to men wrapped up in earthly vices. Therefore, they will never appear to you, for you are most reprehensible sinners. And do not think that the adventures now underway involve killing and maiming knights; rather, they are spiritual things, which are greater and far worthier].

The gist of this speech comes as no surprise to the audience, nor even, it seems, to Gauvain, who takes no offence and decides with little evident regret (and to the chagrin of the hermit, who was trying to induce contrition rather than acceptance) that he may as well return home to Camelot to wait out the conclusion of an enterprise for which he is obviously ill-suited. Indeed, despite being framed as an ad hominem denunciation of Gauvain's and Hestor's individual iniquity, the hermit's recriminations also testify more abstractly to what other *preudomes* have spelled out rhetorically and the structure of the Grail quest inherently implies: the supersession of secular 'chevalerie terriene' [worldly chivalry] by the sublime ideal of 'chevalerie celestiel' [heavenly chivalry] (§140.21; §52.29–30).[4] Within this frame, the personal piety of the *miles Christi* (soldier or knight of Christ), defined principally by chastity, humility and unshakable faith in divine providence, is exalted at the expense of the traditional, mutually reinforcing courtly-chivalric values of erotic love and glory-hungry martial prowess.

---

[3] These figures are discussed and contextualised by Paul Bretel, *Les Ermites et les moines dans la littérature française du Moyen Âge* (Paris: Champion, 1995).

[4] On this opposition, see: Jean-René Valette, *La Pensée du Graal: Fiction littéraire et théologie (XIIe–XIIIe siècle)* (Paris: Champion, 2008), pp. 682–708.

The Vulgate Cycle's paragon of secular virtue is Lancelot, the champion of ennobling eros whose complicated paternal relationship with the saintly Grail Knight, Galaad, is central to the *Queste*, but Gauvain is the real personification of *chevalerie terriene* in the text. Whereas the paradoxical Lancelot is alternately berated for his worldliness and shown how close his love-fueled excellence has already brought him to religious illumination, to the point that he eventually earns a partial vision of the Grail's theophanic secrets, Gauvain typifies a secular ideal that cannot or will not be converted into spiritual currency. The *Queste* plays on multiple levels with Gauvain's conventional literary image in the verse romance tradition, evoking in a negative light his status as an unusually changeless stock character, his function in Chrétien de Troyes as a normative touchstone of the establishment values of prowess and courtesy, and his portrayal in subsequent verse romances as a swashbuckling serial seducer who simultaneously exemplifies and parodies the chivalric ideal.[5] By harshly condemning Arthur's nephew as an unrepentant sinner for the very qualities that usually make him beloved and respected, the *Queste* critiques chivalric romance as both ideological system and literary genre. At the heart of this agenda lies the text's insistent but nuanced representation of Gauvain as an inveterate killer of men. Unable to dispense with knightly violence (as it does with *fine amor*) without ceasing entirely to speak the language of knighthood and its literature, the *Queste* articulates, through the problem of homicide, an ambition to be simultaneously romance and 'anti-romance',[6] reforming or transforming both the ethical and the aesthetic paradigms of the tradition it appropriates and turns against itself. As the whipping boy for *chevalerie terriene*, Gauvain commits a string of licit but painfully pointless homicides that denounce the vanity and self-destructiveness of secular chivalric culture. At the same time, the *preudomes*' authoritative religious discourse links these killings to personal moral turpitude, but as consequences and signifiers – that is, as indices rather than instances – of sin. Indeed, the very tangible guilt always associated with homicide from a Christian standpoint accrues precisely to those too spiritually blind to perceive either the real immorality of homicidal

---

[5] Gauvain's evolving place in the romance tradition is surveyed by Keith Busby, *Gauvain in Old French Literature* (Rodopi: Amsterdam, 1980), and Jean Larmat, 'Le Personnage de Gauvain dans quelques romans arthuriens du XIIe et du XIIIe siècle', in *Études de langue et de littérature françaises offertes à André Lanly* (Nancy: Université Nancy II, 1980), pp. 185–202. For a discussion of the English Gawain's murderous reputation in Thomas Malory, see, in this volume: Dwayne Coleman, 'Murder, Manslaughter and Reputation: Killing in Malory's *Le Morte Darthur*'.

[6] Daniel Poirion, 'Semblance du Graal dans la *Queste*', in *Écriture poétique et composition romanesque* (Orléans: Paradigme, 1994), pp. 201–215; G. R. Simes, '*La Queste del Saint Graal* as Chivalric Anti-Romance', *Parergon* 5 (1987): 54–70; Francis Dubost, *Aspects fantastiques de la littérature narrative médiévale (XIIème–XIIIème siècles): L'Autre, l'Ailleurs, l'Autrefois* (Paris: Champion, 1991), 2:761–62.

violence or the more abstract, bloodless ways in which the struggle between good and evil is constantly waged and symbolically staged all around them in the *Queste*'s heavily allegorised world.

The condemnation of unredeemed chivalry as an ethos that valorises senseless violence for its own sake is yoked, then, to a critique of romance heroes ignorant of the significance that God (or his anonymous amanuensis, the *Queste* author) has inscribed in the 'letter' of material reality and romance readers disinclined to look past the surface of historical or narrative events for their higher, spiritual import. In its very capacity as a powerful metonym for sin, however, homicide is one of the few kinds of literal events that the *Queste* resolutely refuses to interpret metaphorically. Whether deploring deaths or using crusade ideology and rhetoric to exonerate good Christians who take life, it treats the fundamental fact of killing in emphatically non-allegorical terms that insist on the moral personhood of both slayers and slain. The spectacle of homicide in the *Queste* thus challenges knights and readers to interpret differently in order to live more righteously, but it also ultimately warns against giving too free a rein to allegory's 'semiotic imperialism',[7] its tendency to dominate and reductively devalue diegetic events viewed as mere vehicles or pretexts for the communication of totalising, extra-narrative meaning, obscuring the moral truth that interpretation is meant to proclaim.

However the symbolic scope of the Grail quest should be understood – whether it is a figure of universal human striving toward knowledge and experience of God, or a 'class gospel' exclusively targeted at the real or theoretical sanctification of the warrior aristocracy, or an essentially literary exploitation of Christian themes and motifs in the service of romance fiction, or something of all three[8] – the *Queste* treats the key tenets of *chevalerie celestiel* in a perfectly consistent and entirely literal fashion. While cultivating ambiguous, imbricated allegorical senses, the text wears its moral theology sincerely on its sleeve. Even in narrative episodes that the *preudomes* interpret allegorically, lust and vainglory are always sins, and chastity and self-abnegation are always virtues.

---

[7] John F. Plummer, 'The Quest for Significance in *La Queste del Saint Graal* and Malory's *Tale of the Sankgreal*', in *Continuations: Essays on Medieval French Literature and Language in Honor of John L. Grigsby*, ed. Norris J. Lacy and Gloria Torrini-Roblin (Birmingham, AL: Summa, 1989), p. 109.

[8] Albert Pauphilet, *Études sur la* Queste del Saint Graal *attribuée à Gautier Map* (Paris: Champion, 1921), p. 25; Emmanuèle Baumgartner, *L'Arbre et le Pain: Essai sur 'La Queste del Saint Graal'* (Paris: SEDES, 1981); E. Jane Burns, *Arthurian Fictions: Rereading the Vulgate Cycle* (Columbus: Ohio State University Press, 1985); Nancy Freeman Regalado, '*La Chevalerie Celestiel*: Spiritual Transformations of Secular Romance in *La Queste del Saint Graal*', in *Romance: Generic Transformations from Chrétien de Troyes to Cervantes*, ed. Kevin Brownlee and Marina Scordilis Brownlee (Hanover, NH: University Press of New England, 1985), pp. 91–113.

They are not signifiers to be decoded but moral values that guide interpretation. When Gauvain's would-be confessor tells him that he has been excluded from participating in the Grail adventures for want of personal virtue, therefore, the lesson is clear: Gauvain can either cultivate faith, charity and chastity or he can resign ignominiously from the quest. The remark about killing and maiming knights awkwardly appended to the holy man's edifying exegesis, however, offers an apparent critique of violence equivocally related to the moral code of *chevalerie celestiel*. The assertion that Grail adventures are not *de chevaliers ocirre* could mean that the Grail quest is not 'about' killing insofar as its stakes and meaning do not derive from the simple demonstration of physical prowess upon the bodies of human opponents. On the other hand, the *preudome* could be stating in much stronger terms that Grail adventures do not involve killing at all, although it would be uncertain even then whether death-dealing is fundamentally incompatible with the spiritualised quest or merely immaterial to it. Slaying knights (*chevaliers ocirre*) is certainly not a primary objective or essential feature of chivalric activity in the context of the Grail quest, but the hermit stops short of stating explicitly that no Grail adventure will ever result in casualties, let alone that all killing is proscribed under heavenly chivalry's new dispensation as it is according to the sixth commandment's 'Non occides' [Thou shalt not kill] (Ex. 20:13).

This ambivalence is sustained throughout a text otherwise pedantically liberal with categorical ethical statements. A distinct *mansuétude* [gentleness] modelled on that of the infinitely forgiving God is exemplarily exhibited by Galaad and imitated by Lancelot and by the lesser Grail hero, Boort, on various occasions,[9] while gratuitous violence is rarely represented and is roundly condemned when it does occur. Still, in line with the *Queste*'s overarching strategy of critiquing and reforming chivalric romance from within romance's own discourse, combat remains an accepted, albeit decreasingly essential, means of manifesting virtue, with martial excellence redefined as evidence of rectitude and divine favour. Galaad's invincible prowess, in particular, is demonstrated and praised throughout the quest. If Lancelot is reprimanded by God for drawing his sword to fight two lions who guard the Grail castle, then 'remet s'espee el fuerre et dit que par lui n'en sera ja mes ostee, ainz se metra en la merci Nostre Seignor' [resheathes his sword and says that he will never again draw it, instead throwing himself on Our Lord's mercy] (§304.1–3), the point is less that Lancelot has become a pacifist than that he has finally exchanged proud self-reliance for the humility of faith.

Thus, the *Queste* displays little interest in developing a typology of 'authorized' and 'unauthorized' forms of violence along the lines proposed by Nancy

[9] Pauphilet, *Études*, pp. 34–36, 41–42.

Black.[10] Instead, it thematises and theorises what violence, especially homicidal violence, can *mean*. In the context of Gauvain's complaint that he has killed (*ocis*) more than ten worthy knights without encountering any adventures to speak of, *chevaliers ocirre* defines the ugly essence of secular chivalry and secular romance viewed both from the perspective of eternity through the lens of religious faith and from a utilitarian standpoint immune to the flamboyant charms that typically mask the socially, as well as spiritually, pernicious qualities of the warrior aristocracy and its self-aggrandising mythologies. Like the chivalric ideal they help to construct, romance's narrative form and conventions privilege 'marvellous adventures' that frequently amount to orgies of untrammelled aggression, sometimes embellished with a veneer of social utility, as when heroes slay monsters or human oppressors or abolish 'evil customs',[11] but more often enjoyed and glamourised in their own right. By juxtaposing Gauvain's inability to 'aventure trover qui face a ramentevoir en conte' [find any adventure worth recounting in a tale] (§179.3–4) with his ten disappointing – and unrecounted, because unworthy of narration – homicides, the *Queste* forces apart two terms that romance habitually equates: on the one hand, bloody victory in combat, and, on the other, the *aventure* as a source of personal honour confirmed by public approbation (*henor, pris* or *los*). At the same time, the image of Gauvain's aimless wandering through an evacuated narrative space offers a God's-eye view of what secular romance is, ontologically speaking, even when it appears marvellously eventful on its own terms: a non-narrative, 'a vacation of meaning … because it is emptied of redemptive discourse, a language turned away from its extralinguistic reference'[12] – that is, from truth both literal and spiritual – and cut off, like its vainglorious heroes, from the plenitude of the divine. Gauvain's *horror vacui* at the apparently inexplicable absence of meaningful events, which is really a sign of his inadequacy as an interpreter of his own biography insofar as he does not see that adventure deprivation is itself a significant (non-)event, ironically coincides with the way the *Queste*'s ideal reader looks back on the knight errant's action-packed romance career.

Homicide, so often the subject and substance of romance narrative, thus occurs here *instead* of narrative, in place of and in opposition to true substance or

---

[10] Nancy B. Black, 'Violence in *La Queste del Saint Graal* and *La Mort le roi Artu* (Yale 229)', in *Violence in Medieval Courtly Literature: A Casebook*, ed. Albrecht Classen (New York: Routledge, 2004), pp. 143–57.

[11] See: Norris J. Lacy, 'On Customs in Medieval French Romance', *Revue belge de philologie et d'histoire* 83.3 (2005): 977–86.

[12] Matilda Tomaryn Bruckner, *Shaping Romance: Interpretation, Truth, and Closure in Twelfth-Century French Fictions* (Philadelphia: University of Pennsylvania Press, 1993), p. 105. Cf. Douglas Kelly, 'Romance and the Vanity of Chrétien de Troyes', in *Romance*, ed. Brownlee and Brownlee, pp. 74–90.

value, as even Gauvain seems dimly to recognise. In fact, in rebuking Gauvain for thinking that legitimate Grail adventures consist of killing and maiming knights, the hermit may seem to criticise rather unfairly. After all, Gauvain's complaint to Hestor is precisely that he has slain ten men but encountered no adventures to speak of. Yet the power of the *Queste*'s critique of chivalry depends on this point of apparent incoherence. The spokesman for worldly knighthood must be vilified despite remaining, by the normal standards of medieval laymen, a decent and even praiseworthy man because the text shows how, in Richard Kaeuper's words, the problem of violence is 'built into some of the very ideals of chivalry, not merely in the lamentable inability of fallible men to attain them'.[13]

The specificity and the stakes of the *Queste*'s treatment of chivalric homicide emerge more clearly in the context of the literary predecessors and contemporaries to which the text demands comparison. By outing romance as a genre of murderous tales not worth the telling, the *Queste* does not cut all ties with the tradition so much as it appropriates and continues, while reorienting and radicalising, a self-critical discourse present in the romance tradition from its inception. Chrétien de Troyes' foundational works, particularly *Erec et Enide* (c. 1165–70) and most especially the *Chevalier au lion* (c. 1177–81), are deeply concerned with recruiting the knight as privileged practitioner of violence into a politically stable and personally fulfilling social order. That said, Chrétien grants combat a central role in chivalric identity-formation and romance aesthetics,[14] and his reflections on the ethics of violence indulge in playful casuistry regarding when, why and how courtly knights should kill without disputing the basic acceptability of slaying one's opponent in fair combat. Respect for the proprieties takes precedence over, and largely takes the place of, concern for human life in the inculcation of knightly discipline. In the *Chevalier de la charrete* (c. 1177–81), for instance, Lancelot finds himself bound by a vanquished opponent's formal request for mercy but unwilling to disappoint the damsel who has requested the helpless knight's head as a boon. After struggling to reconcile the demands of pity and largesse, Lancelot decides to resume the duel so that he can behead his opponent with a clear conscience, ignoring the latter's renewed pleas for mercy.[15] To the extent that neither other characters nor the narrator take any real issue with the deed, the *Charrete*'s limited consideration of the ethics of honourable killing represents the kind of pseudo-morality that the *Queste*

---

[13] Richard W. Kaeuper, *Chivalry and Violence in Medieval Europe* (Oxford: Oxford University Press, 1999), p. 3.

[14] See, e.g., Alvaro Barbieri, 'Ferire, gioire, patire: I lemmi della violenza nei romanzi di Chrétien de Troyes', in *Parole e temi del romanzo medievale*, ed. Anatole Pierre Fuksas (Rome: Viella, 2007), pp. 101–37.

[15] Chrétien de Troyes, *Le Chevalier de la Charrette*, ed. and trans. Charles Méla, in *Romans* (Paris: Livre de Poche, 1994), vv. 2734–2939.

forcefully exposes and condemns. Still, Chrétien's characteristic irony, which leaves undecided the poet's (and the alert reader's) ultimate attitude toward Lancelot's decision, preserves the possibility of a different interpretation that the *Queste* perhaps pursues in the same way that it develops, to edifying ends, a number of Chrétien's playful flirtations with the allegorical interpretability of adventure narrative.

Without offering much in the way of an alternative ethical system, several second-wave verse romances of the late twelfth and thirteenth centuries, many starring a Gauvain whose reputation outstrips his performance, parody the excesses of romance violence (without necessarily ceasing to enjoy them) and explode the myths that knightly status implies personal virtue and that right makes might rather than vice versa.[16] In this way, they echo some of the *Queste*'s non-religious criticisms of chivalry even if they do not quite justify the comical, but perhaps telling, fear of knights exhibited by a peasant crone from whom Lancelot requests a night's shelter in the relatively late *Merveilles de Rigomer* (c. 1250–68):

Mil ans a que j'ai oï dire
que li armé chevalier sunt
les plus males coses del mont,
ne ja chevaliers haubergiés
par moi ne sera herbergiés;
car il ne se doutent ne duelent,
ains ocïent quanques il voelent.
Se jou t'avoie herbergié,
le matin au prendre congié,
sai jou bien, que tu m'ociroies,
ja autre bien ne me feroies.[17]

[I heard a thousand years ago / that armed knights are / the worst things in the world, / and no armoured knight / will find lodging with me; / for, feeling no doubt or regret, / they kill whomever they want. / If I did lodge you, / the next

---

[16] See, for example: Kristin L. Burr, 'The Point of Revenge: Questioning Chivalry in *La Vengeance Raguidel* and *Les Merveilles de Rigomer*', in *Vendetta: Essays on Honor and Revenge*, ed. Giovanna Summerfield (Newcastle upon Tyne: Cambridge Scholars Publishing, 2010), pp. 13–33; Annie Combes, 'Sens et abolition de la violence dans *L'Âtre Périlleux*', in *La Violence dans le monde médiéval* (Aix-en-Provence: CUERMA, 1994), pp. 151–64; and, on the 'epigonal' romances more generally, Beate Schmolke-Hasselmann, *The Evolution of Arthurian Romance: The Verse Tradition from Chrétien to Froissart*, trans. Margaret Middleton and Roger Middleton (Cambridge: Cambridge University Press, 1998).

[17] *Les Mervelles de Rigomer von Jehan*, ed. Wendelin Foerster and Hermann Breuer, 2 vols (Dresden: Gesellschaft für romanische Literatur, 1908 and 1915), vv. 3520–30. My translation.

morning, at leave-taking, / I know that you would kill me / and do me no other favours].

Meanwhile, the prose *Lancelot*, which precedes the *Queste* in the Vulgate Cycle, generally endorses the pursuit of worldly honour through combat. While the text attaches no particular positive value to dispatching opponents rather than simply defeating them – indeed, the *Lancelot*'s abundant non-fatal combats in and beyond a tournament context are crucial both for measuring knights against each other so as to establish a hierarchy (as in the *Queste*) and for cementing homosocial friendships and communities (as in Chrétien's *Erec et Enide* and *Chevalier au lion*) – it does not stigmatise lethal violence either. The *Mort le roi Artu*, on the other hand, picks up the *Queste*'s narrative and steers it toward the implosion of the Arthurian world in a way that largely reinstates the ethical ideals of the *Lancelot*'s secular chivalry even while foregrounding the suffering inflicted on individuals and societies by the self-perpetuating cycles of killing that irrational commitments to honour and vengeance set in motion when a feud erupts between the lineages of Gauvain and Lancelot.[18] Overall, if certain ideas and themes – the often symbolic, almost ritual function of combat in the *Lancelot*, the meaningless destructiveness of sociopolitical ideologies in the *Mort* – connect the *Queste* to its cyclical prequel and sequel, the Grail romance nevertheless presents a deliberately, radically distinct vision of chivalric violence's semiotic and moral status.

Within a decade or so of the Vulgate Cycle's composition, the prose *Tristan* (c. 1225–45), a compendious *summa* of the *matière de Bretagne* that amalgamates the Tristan legend with the Vulgate stories of Lancelot and the Grail, responds more directly (albeit selectively and rather reductively) to the indictment of sanguinary, morally bankrupt chivalry embodied in the *Queste*'s Gauvain. The *Tristan* constructs 'Gauvain l'assassin' [Gauvain the murderer], in the company of his brothers (except for Gaheriet) and the aptly named Brehus sans Pitié [Brehus the Pitiless], as an antitype of the chivalric ideal modelled by the romance's heroes, a ruthless villain goaded by prickly pride, envy and vengeful wrath to

---

[18] Several decades later, in a context of Franco-Italian cultural exchange, Brunetto Latini's allegorical poem *Il Tesoretto* (c. 1267) likewise acknowledges the excessive, disruptive violence engendered by prickly chivalric honour and advocates wholly secular reform based on the ideal of 'fortitude tempered by restraint and prudence', emphasising the social utility of the knightly class – as, indeed, does the young Lancelot's mentor, the Lady of the Lake, early in his eponymous Vulgate romance. See Peter W. Sposato, 'Reforming the Chivalric Elite in Thirteenth-Century Florence: The Evidence of Brunetto Latini's *Il Tesoretto*', *Viator* 46.1 (2015): 218–19; and *Lancelot: Roman en prose du XIIIe siècle*, ed. Alexandre Micha (Geneva: Droz, 1978–1983), 7:XXIa.7–21.

multiple counts of treason and cold-blooded murder.[19] Since Gauvain is also the homicidal anti-hero of the *Queste*, comparison with the prose *Tristan* brings into relief a crucial feature of the killings attributed to him in the Vulgate text: they are, without exception, perfectly legitimate slayings with which no secular witness could find fault. Feudal justice's conceptual framework for classifying and evaluating instances of homicide features extensively in the prose *Tristan* and, as Howard Bloch has shown, in the *Mort le roi Artu*,[20] as well as in the sociopolitically realistic introductory section of the Vulgate *Lancelot*. By contrast, the *Queste* declines even to exploit the readily available motif, originated in Chrétien's *Conte du Graal* (c. 1180–92) and already recalled in the Vulgate *Lancelot*, of the accusation of treacherous murder levelled against Gauvain by enemies whose plaint may or may not be justified.[21] In fact, the Vulgate Grail narrative never introduces the basic distinction between licit and 'treacherous' or 'felonious' homicide (*ocirre en traïson, par felonie* or *desloiaument*), that is, a fatal attack deliberately undertaken without a challenge having been issued, or in a situation in which the victim is unable or unprepared to defend himself properly. This is a strategic move and not an oversight, for crime is irreducibly individual; as a concept, it singles out infractions of a system's rules without inviting reflection on the essential validity of the rules themselves. By showing some knights wantonly violating, often with impunity, the loosely codified but affectively charged dictates of feudal law and chivalric honour, a text like the prose *Tristan* may impugn the integrity of knighthood as a social body and question the ability or desire of individuals to put into practice the self-glorifying ideals preached by their class, but it does not pose a theoretical challenge to those ideals as such. Many verse romances likewise employ reprehensible characters for circumscribed ideological subversion, showing that knights *can* be wicked despite their immaculate genealogies, high rank and avowed principles of conduct, but not that all knights, let alone knighthood itself, are fundamentally flawed. The *Queste*, on the other hand, strikes at romance's courtly-chivalric ideal itself precisely by insisting that Gauvain is *not* a criminal, not a murderous maniac, not even (except in nebulous spiritual terms) a bad man, and that the deaths he nevertheless deals out to his

---

[19] Laurence Harf-Lancner, 'Gauvain l'assassin: La récurrence d'un schéma narratif dans le *Tristan en prose*', in *Tristan — Tristrant: Mélanges en l'honneur de Danielle Buschinger*, ed. André Crépin and Wolfgang Spiewok (Greifswald: Reineke, 1996), pp. 219–30; Fanni Bogdanow, 'The Character of Gauvain in the Thirteenth-Century Prose Romances', *Medium Aevum* 27 (1958): 154–61; Keith Busby, 'Gauvain in the Prose *Tristan*', *Tristania* 2.2 (1977): 12–28.

[20] R. Howard Bloch, *Medieval French Literature and Law* (Berkeley: University of California Press, 1977), pp. 13–62.

[21] See: Chrétien de Troyes, *Le Conte du Graal*, ed. and trans. Charles Méla, in *Romans*, vv. 4688–4726; *Lancelot*, ed. Micha, 1:XIV.2.

own companions are the tragic consequences of perfectly practised *chevalerie terriene*.²²

This conclusion imposes itself most forcefully when, between meeting Hestor and conversing with the hermit, Gauvain claims his eleventh victim. Encountering an unidentified armed knight who challenges him to a joust, Gauvain senses a potential adventure in the offing, or at least an end to the monotony of his uneventful travels. 'Par foi', he declares, 'puis que je parti de Camaalot ne trovai je mes qui joste me demandast, et puis que cist la demande, il n'i faudra pas' [By my faith ... since leaving Camelot, I have found nobody who has challenged me to a joust, and since this man wants one, he will not be denied it] (§185.17–19). The challenger unhorses Gauvain, suffering a fatal wound in the process, and asks his vanquisher to carry him to a nearby monastery where he can receive the last rites. Only there does Gauvain finally ask the stranger's identity and learn, to his horror, that he has killed a fellow Grail quester and companion of the Round Table, Yvain l'Avoutre [Yvain the Bastard]. Occurring as it does during a fair, open engagement in which the laws governing violence are held in abeyance by the tacit mutual consent of two combatants well aware of the joust's inherent risks, this slaying is clearly not a murder, nor even an actionable form of manslaughter. Furthermore, Yvain's death is manifestly accidental – the unhorsed Gauvain leaps up, totally unaware that he has dealt a killing blow, and readies his sword before realising that his challenger is no longer game – and quite undesired by his opponent. For his part, the mortally wounded man is remarkably sanguine about his fate, especially once he discovers his killer's identity. 'Donc ne me chaut,' he declares, 'se je sui ocis par la main de si preudome com vos estes' [Then I do not mind ... dying by the hand of so noble a man as you] (§188.7–8). Beyond coolly accepting his own death as an occupational hazard, Yvain rejoices that he has been slain by a famous hero, as though Gauvain's status conferred meaning and value on his victim's unnecessary demise.

In the context of the *preudomes*' speeches, Yvain's attitude elicits a mixture of admiration for his nobility and dismay at his willing self-sacrifice for what the *Queste* shows to be so unworthy a creed. Yvain has literally been killed by his own ideal, which Gauvain traditionally embodies, during an utterly pointless combat undertaken without the slightest ill will on either side, simply because jousting is the thing to do when two (romance) knights run across each other in the countryside. As much as Gauvain himself, whose inarticulate distress at the blood on his hands clashes with his victim's serenity to produce a destabilising moment of affective dissonance for the audience, secular chivalric ideology is the killer here,

²² Richard Trachsler, *Clôtures du cycle arthurien: Étude et textes* (Geneva: Droz, 1996), pp. 75–76.

one that cannot be exculpated – any more than Gauvain can – by Yvain's ready pardon. The sparing, tightly controlled staging of death in combat in the *Queste* thus symbolically condenses all the self-destructive excesses of 'une chevalerie qui s'est donné(e) (à) de fausses idoles' [a chivalry that has given itself (over to) false idols],[23] the golden calves of worldly honour and glory, ever thirsty for sacrificial blood. Going beyond a critique of individual misdeeds or even of abuses endemic to the knightly class, the *Queste* condemns a chivalric culture that kills its own adepts by propagating the idea that adventures, as means of achieving personal self-realisation and public status, ultimately are *de chevaliers ocirre*. The poignant irony is that, as the romance tradition repeats over and over, Gauvain, or his reputation, the dream he represents, is beloved wherever he goes. Yvain is pleased to die by his lance; much later, when Gauvain is wounded by Galaad in a mêlée (a sure sign of divine disfavour for those with eyes to see) and left bleeding among his erstwhile antagonists, they bear no grudge: 'Et com il conurent monseignor Gauvain et il virent qu'il fu blecié, si en furent molt corrocié li plusor d'els, car c'estoit l'ome del monde qui plus estoit coneuz d'estranges jenz' [And when they recognised my lord Gauvain and saw that he was wounded, most of them were very vexed, for of all men he was the best known to foreigners] (§241.2–5). Touchingly, but also horrifyingly, the Arthurian world in which the *Queste* is and is not set – for Gauvain and Hestor inhabit a reality that Galaad, for one, largely transcends – loves, and cannot stop loving, the agent of its own destruction, the personification of its own lethal illusions and absurd, self-massacring drives.

From the clerical perspective that dominates the *Queste*'s analysis of secular chivalry, the kind of combat that causes Yvain's death is not only tragic but also sinful. For Bernard of Clairvaux, the great twelfth-century Cistercian reformer whose profound influence on the *Queste*'s spirituality has been qualified but never persuasively disputed, the tournaments beloved of the knightly class – 'maledictas illas nundinas' [those accursed fairs],[24] as Bernard calls them in a letter to Abbot Suger of Saint-Denis – are offences that cry to heaven, brazen celebrations of gratuitous, aestheticised violence that risk lives and souls for the sake of spectators' pleasure and a vacuous glory lacking even the paltry justification of secular political objectives. Indeed, the canons promulgated at the Second and Third Lateran Councils in 1139 and 1179 include bans (to be lifted only in 1316) on tournaments framed in precisely these terms, going so far as to

---

[23] Paul Bretel, 'Galaad, héros et passeur dans la *Queste del Saint Graal*', in *Figures du passeur*, ed. Paul Carmignani (Perpignan: Presses universitaires de Perpignan, 2002), p. 230.

[24] *Opere di San Bernardo*, ed. Ferruccio Gastaldelli, vol, VI.2, *Lettere: Parte seconda (211–548)*, trans. Ettore Paratore (Milan: Scriptorium Claravallense/Fondazione di Studi Cistercensi, 1987), §376. My translation. The evidence for Cistercian thought's role in the *Queste* is reviewed by Karen Pratt, 'The Cistercians and the *Queste del Saint Graal*', *Reading Medieval Studies* 21 (1995): 69–96.

stipulate that those mortally wounded in such contests – the slain rather than the slayers only by the luck of the draw, as Bernard says – should be granted absolution if it is requested, but must be denied a church burial. The implicit suggestion that death in tourney necessarily finds the combatant in a state of mortal sin, in the same way as suicide, resonates with Yvain l'Avoutre's willing acquiescence to his own honourable death.[25]

At the same time, and more concertedly, clerics like the hermit who chastises Gauvain after Yvain's death implicitly equate the knight errant's pursuit of glorious violence with at least semi-conscious homicidal intent.[26] If, without expressly setting out to kill anyone, the *Queste*'s antihero-elect repeatedly finds himself on the winning side of armed conflict and (therefore) the losing side of the quest, it is because the text stigmatises in him 'la sanglante erreur de cette société chevaleresque qui, sous prétexte de prouesse, se détruisait elle-même et se damnait' [the bloody error of the chivalric society that, under the pretext of cultivating prowess, destroyed and damned itself].[27] This corrupting error is more explicitly denounced at the level of customary social practice in a strange narratorial aside on the alleged customs of the Welsh aristocracy that parodies thirteenth-century reality to demonstrate the ease with which the logic of

---

[25] Lateran III's canon 20 reiterates, largely verbatim, Lateran II's canon 14; see: *Decrees of the Ecumenical Councils*, ed. Norman P. Tanner (London: Sheed & Ward, 1990), 1:200 and 1:221. The *Queste* contains two important tournaments (§16–18 and §170–176), and while neither of them is condemned as such, both work in different ways precisely to subvert the values that tournaments typically put on display, substituting the worship of God for the rites of 'the demi-god prowess' (Kaeuper, *Chivalry and Violence*, p. 129 ff.), or at least appropriating prowess as a remotivated signifier of sanctity. On literal and allegorical tournaments as motifs central to the interpretation of violence in chivalric literature, see: Catalina Girbea, 'Rapport introductif: L'imaginaire du tournoi', in *Armes et jeux militaires dans l'imaginaire: XIIe-XVe siècles*, ed. Girbea (Paris: Classiques Garnier, 2016), pp. 7–33.

[26] Medieval canon law accords a prominent place to the issue of intent quite early on. Burchard of Worms' influential *Decretum*, for example, carefully distinguishes between homicides committed wilfully (*sponte*), and less serious ones committed involuntarily (*non sponte*) the latter being subdivided into accidental homicides involving negligence and purely accidental homicides. See: Greta Austin, *Shaping Church Law Around the Year 1000: The* Decretum *of Burchard of Worms* (Farnham: Ashgate, 2009), pp. 166–74. By the thirteenth century, secular justice also applies the notion of *mens rea*, but it jostles awkwardly with older models of guilt. See: Bloch, *Medieval French Literature and Law*, pp. 13–62. The *Établissements de saint Louis* for the Touraine-Anjou region (compiled c. 1270–73) state in §1.40 that unrealised homicidal intent ('volenté d'omicide sans plus faire') is not a punishable offence. See: *Les Établissements de saint Louis*, ed. Paul Viollet (Paris: Renouard, 1881), 2:55–56, or *The Établissements de Saint Louis: Thirteenth-Century Law Texts from Tours, Orléans, and Paris*, trans. F. R. P. Akehurst (Philadephia: University of Pennsylvania Press, 1996), p. 28.

[27] Pauphilet, *Études*, p. 42.

warrior honour can be twisted into ideologically-sanctioned insanity, if it is not already such:

> ... a cel tens estoient si desreé jenz et si sanz mesure par tot lo roiaume de Gales que se li fiz trovast lo pere gisant en son lit par acheson d'enfermeté, il le tressist hors par la teste ou par les braz, si l'oceist erraument, car a viltance et a reproche li fust atorné se ses peres moreust en son lit. Mes quant il avenoit que li peres ocioit le fil ou li filz lo pere, et toz li lignages moreust d'armes, lors disoient la jent del païs qu'il estoient de haut lignaje. (§116.23-30)

> [... at that time, such mad, immoderate people lived throughout the kingdom of Wales that if a son found his father lying sick in bed, he would drag him out by the head or the arms and kill him immediately, for he would be shamed and reproached if his father died in his bed. But when a father killed his son or a son killed his father, and the whole lineage died in combat, then the people of that country said their lineage was noble].

In portraying secular chivalry as a dangerous, disruptive institution, the romance is heir to numerous clerical complaints about the knightly aristocracy's propensity for disorderly, wanton destructiveness that proliferated in France in the wake of the late tenth-century *Pax Dei* [Peace of God] movement, which strove to protect both religious and lay noncombatants and their property from the depredations of the warrior class.[28] Pope Urban II's call for the First Crusade at the Council of Clermont in 1095, as reconstructed in Fulcher of Chartres' *Historia Hierosolymitana*, directly links the crusading project to the peace movement's still-unfulfilled goals:

> Procedant [...] contra infideles [...] qui abusive privatum certamen contra fideles etiam consuescebant distendere quondam. Nunc fiant Christi milites, qui dudum exstiterunt raptores; nunc iure contra barbaros pugnent, qui olim adversus fratres et consanguineos dimicabant.[29]

> [Let those who were once accustomed improperly to wage private war against the faithful ... go forth ... against the infidels. Let those who recently appeared as robbers now become soldiers of Christ; let those who formerly battled their brothers and kinsmen now fight justly against the barbarians].

Some forty years later, Bernard of Clairvaux mobilises the same contrastive rhetoric in his panegyric apology for the nascent Templar order, *De laude novae militiae* [*In Praise of the New Knighthood*]. As hybrid products of monastic asceticism

---

[28] Diverse perspectives on this movement are collected in *The Peace of God: Social Violence and Religious Response in France around the Year 1000*, ed. Thomas Head and Richard Landes (Ithaca: Cornell University Press, 1992).

[29] *Fulcheri Carnotensis Historia Hierosolymitana (1095–1127)*, ed. Heinrich Hagenmeyer (Heidelberg: Carl Winters Verlag, 1913), I.iii.7. My translation.

and warrior training, the Templars represent a much-needed innovation capable of repurposing the military prowess of a materialistic and quarrelsome secular aristocracy whose brand of chivalry is hardly worthy of the name, let alone of carrying out God's will on earth. Punning scornfully, Bernard asks,

> Quis igitur finis fructusve, saecularis huius, non dico, militiae, sed malitiae? [...] Non sane aliud inter vos bella movet litesque suscitat, nisi aut irrationabilis iracundiae motus, aut inanis gloriae appetitus, aut terrenae qualiscumque possessionis cupiditas. Talibus certe ex causis neque occidere, neque occumbere tutum est.[30]

> [What, then, is the end or fruit of this worldly knighthood, or rather knavery, as I should call it? ... What else is the cause of wars and the root of disputes among you, except unreasonable flashes of anger, the thirst for empty glory, or the hankering after some earthly possessions? It certainly is not safe to kill or to be killed for such causes as these].

Both Urban II and Bernard are interested in harnessing the concept of the *miles Christi* to channel and discipline violence, rendering it socially and theologically useful rather than anarchic, disruptive and even sacrilegious.[31] However, where the pope proposes a simple substitution of just, foreign war against legitimate ('infidel') enemies for internecine strife in Europe, Bernard is also, and more fundamentally, concerned with the morality of homicide as such.[32] While

---

[30] Bernard of Clairvaux, *De laude novae militiae*, in *Oeuvres complètes*, vol. 31: *Éloge de la nouvelle chevalerie; Vie de saint Malachie; Épitaphe, hymne, lettres*, trans. Pierre-Yves Emery (Paris: Cerf, 1990), §3.1–2, 3.26–31. Translation taken from Bernard of Clairvaux, *In Praise of the New Knighthood*, trans. Conrad Greenia, in *The Works of Bernard of Clairvaux*, vol. 7, *Treatises III* (Kalamazoo: Cistercian Publications, 1977), pp. 132–33. Bernard is far from the only twelfth-century cleric to excoriate misbehaving knights, as discussed by Kaeuper, *Chivalry and Violence*, pp. 73–81; Aryeh Grabois, 'Militia and Malitia: The Bernardine Vision of Chivalry', in *The Second Crusade and the Cistercians*, ed. Michael Gervers (New York: St Martin's, 1992), pp. 49–56; and Matthew Strickland, *War and Chivalry: The Conduct and Perceptions of War in England and Normandy, 1066–1217* (Cambridge: Cambridge University Press, 1996), pp. 70–97.

[31] This theme returns in Bernard of Clairvaux, *De laude novae militiae*, §10 (*In Praise of the New Knighthood*, 143–44). For an overview of contemporary discourses on Christian chivalry, see: Jean Flori, 'De la chevalerie terrienne à la chevalerie celestielle: La mutation idéologique du XIIe siècle', *Études médiévales* 3 (2001): 341–55.

[32] So too is a family of narratives, including Marcus' *Visio Tnugdali* (1149), the English Cistercian Henry of Saltrey's *Tractatus de purgatorio sancti Patricii* (c. 1184) and the latter's French translation by Marie de France, the *Espurgatoire seint Patriz* (c. 1190), that ascribe monitory visions of the afterlife to knightly protagonists and explicitly critique chivalric violence. Tnugdalus, an excellent but spiritually unawakened young knight not unlike Gauvain, sees an undifferentiated multitude of homicides, parricides and fratricides suffering torments that, according to his angelic guide, he himself has well deserved because 'licet enim non sis parricida aut matricida aut fratricida, es tamen

endorsing the concept of holy violence enacted by Christians serving as God's blameless tools, Bernard resists issuing crusaders a blank cheque to commit all sorts of abuses with impunity, stressing that killing is an inherently sinful act regardless of context unless the individual responsible is genuinely and exclusively committed to God's service. Even where violence erupts in the heat of passion or is motivated by a desire for glory, conquest, revenge or plunder rather than a murderous intent to kill, ensuing deaths damn the man responsible, which makes any unsanctified combat a spiritually risky business:

> Quoties namque congrederis tu, qui militiam militas saecularem, timendum omnino, ne [...] occidas hostem quidem in corpore, te vero in anima [...]. Si in voluntate alterum occidendi te potius occidi contigerit, moreris homicida. Quod si praevales, et voluntate superandi vel vindicandi forte occidis hominem, vivis homicida.[33]
>
> [Whenever you go forth, O worldly warrior, you must fear lest the bodily death of your foe should mean your own spiritual death ... If you happen to be killed while you are seeking only to kill another, you die a murderer. If you succeed, and by your will to overcome and to conquer you perchance kill a man, you live a murderer].

A Bernardine understanding of secular combat as a double bind from which neither victor nor victim emerges with an unscathed soul informs the *Queste*'s representation of homicide. However, this moral viewpoint does not fully account for the romance's complex use of homicide as both an instance and, often more importantly, a signifier of sin – specifically, and circularly, the sin of

---

homicida' [while you may not be a patricide, a matricide or a fratricide, you are a homicide]. *L'Au-delà au Moyen Âge: 'Les Visions du chevalier Tondal' de David Aubert et sa source la 'Visio Tnugdali' de Marcus*, ed. and trans. Yolande de Pontfarcy (Bern: Peter Lang, 2010), p. 32; my translation. In the story of Saint Patrick that begins Marie's *Espurgatoire*, the saint confesses and then chastises an old man – seemingly a knight, though he is not identified as such – who initially fails to mention having slain five men, 'quel que ço seit u dreiz u torz' [whether rightly or wrongly], because, he says, 'ne quidai pas ... que ço fust dampnables pechiez' [I did not think ... it was a damnable sin]; this otherwise irrelevant anecdote seems to exemplify the wrong-headed secular warrior attitude that will be corrected when Owein, the Purgatory-bound knight, exchanges the earthly weapons he used against men for the allegorical arms of faith, which can defeat demons, and becomes 'li chevaliers Ihesucrist' [the knight of Christ]. Marie de France, *Saint Patrick's Purgatory*, ed. and trans. Michael J. Curley (Binghamton, NY: Medieval & Renaissance Texts & Studies, 1993), vv. 241–46, 879; my translation. Cf. vv. 651–58 and 787–808. Compare the Latin *Tractatus*, which Marie follows closely on these points, in *Saint Patrick's Purgatory*, ed. Robert Easting, EETS o.s. 298 (Oxford: Oxford University Press, 1991), pp. 121–54.

[33] Bernard of Clairvaux, *De laude novae militiae*, §2.10–21; *In Praise of the New Knighthood*, p. 131.

wilful blindness to the ways in which the material, historical world ought to be interpreted to edifying and even salvific effect. Gauvain's case is once again paradigmatic because his stubborn commitment to the morally problematic ethics of *chevalerie terriene* is also a literalist resistance to the hermeneutic programme promulgated by the text, which systematically redefines linguistic and narrative signs, including *chevalerie* and the act of *chevaliers ocirre*, in newly spiritual terms.

Overcome with grief after slaying Yvain l'Avoutre, Gauvain declares the whole affair a 'grant mesaventure' [great misadventure] (§188.3) – a stroke of ill luck, but also, as the term suggests, a kind of anti-adventure that confers no honour and conveys no marvellous meaning. Yet even in its negativity, *mesaventure* is somehow on a par with *aventure*, its tragic double. Gauvain and Hestor are upset about 'ceste aventure qui avenue lor estoit, car il voient bien que ç'a esté droite mesaventure' [this adventure that had happened to them, for they saw clearly that it had been a pure misfortune] (§189.2–4), an unwelcome but still consequential and vaguely portentous gift of the same chance or destiny responsible for bringing them other, happier occasions for performing the prowess that defines them as chivalric subjects and as the protagonists of romance narrative. To a limited extent, of course, Gauvain and Hestor are correct: Yvain's death is indeed darkly significant. By this point in the *Queste*, it has been established that nothing happens at random in the Grail's environs. When what looks like 'ill luck' befalls someone in the romance plot whose stage management has been taken over by a meticulous providence, it is nearly always a consequence of that character's spiritual failings, as the dying Yvain emphasises by remarking that Gauvain must have struck him down 'par la volenté de Nostre Seignor ou par mon pechié' [by the will of Our Lord or because of my own sins] (§187.25).[34] This is the key connection that Gauvain and Hestor have missed and continue, despite Yvain's timely reminder, to overlook: Grail adventures occur in order to be interpreted, to have their surface appearances (*semblances*) exchanged for their meanings (*senefiances*), normally in moral terms where the imperfect questers are concerned.[35]

---

[34] Compare, for example, the case of Meliant (§46–52), who commits the sins of pride – expressed as, and to some extent consisting of, an act of misreading – and covetousness, receives a near-fatal wound and is told by a monk that 'ceste meschaance vos est avenue par vostre pechié' [your sin brought this misfortune upon you] (§51.19–20).

[35] The adventures of Galaad, who needs no moral guidance, produce different kinds of *senefiances* or *demostrances* (revelatory 'showings') focusing mostly on his figural relationship to Christ and on the history of the Grail lineage. See: Baumgartner, *L'Arbre et le Pain*, pp. 97–107. On the different levels of interpretation operative in the *Queste*, cf. Armand Strubel, *La Rose, Renart et le Graal: La littérature allégorique en France au XIIIe siècle* (Geneva: Slatkine, 1989), pp. 269–90.

Without exactly believing that the point of the Grail quest is to ride around slaughtering knights, then, Gauvain does make the error of assuming that Grail adventures are *de chevaliers ocirre* in that he imagines events like the slaying of Yvain to bespeak no higher logic and to consist only of their literal, superficial elements. Faithful to the secular romance tradition, as Emmanuèle Baumgartner writes, Gauvain 's'oppose à toute prise en compte autre que littérale des aventures rencontrées, refusant ainsi [...] la glose, la quête du sens, la seule aventure pourtant qui, dans cet univers, reste encore ouverte et féconde' [opposes any way but the literal one of understanding the adventures he encounters, thus rejecting ... the gloss, the search for meaning, although it is the only adventure that, in this universe, remains open and fruitful].[36] The gravity of his mistake is reflected in the weight of bloodguilt that Gauvain will assume by the end of the quest, when, as Arthur's court takes stock of its losses in the first pages of the *Mort le roi Artu*, he is forced to confess that he has personally killed eighteen of his peers: 'non mie', he asserts, 'por ce que je fusse meillor chevalier que uns autres, mes la mescheance se torna plus par devers moi que vers nus de mes compaignons. Et sachiez que ce n'est pas par ma chevalerie, mais par mon pechié' [not because I was a better knight than any other, but because ill fortune bore more heavily on me than on any of my companions; and this was due not to my knightly prowess, but to my sinfulness].[37] Here and in the *Queste*, Gauvain is perfectly willing to pay lip service to the *preudomes*' ideas about sin and its causal logic, but he remains constitutionally incapable of really understanding or internalising them.[38] Tellingly, when the hermit who has dismissed him from the quest calls him back in a last-ditch effort to make him understand that repentance and redemptive conversion are still and always possible, Gauvain politely declines to pursue the topic on the grounds that he must attend to more urgent business. Just as the knight cannot interpret his experiences as spiritual signifiers, he will not apply the moral lessons they teach even when they are spelled out for him, and his intransigence saps the therapeutic value of what ought to serve as corrective

---

[36] Emmanuèle Baumgartner, 'Retour des personnages et mise en prose de la fiction arthurienne au XIIIe siècle', in her *De l'histoire de Troie au livre du Graal: Le temps, le récit (XIIe–XIIIe siècles)* (Orléans: Paradigme, 1994), pp. 472–73.

[37] *La Mort du roi Arthur*, ed. and trans. Emmanuèle Baumgartner and Marie-Thérèse de Medeiros (Paris: Champion, 2007), §2.23–26.

[38] See the instructive comparison between Gauvain and Lancelot, the most important intradiegetic addressee of the *Queste*'s statements on the power of conversion and repentance, in Jean-Charles Payen, 'Le Sens du péché dans la littérature cistercienne en langue d'oïl', in *Les Chemins de la* Queste, ed. Denis Hüe and Silvère Menegaldo (Orléans: Paradigme, 2004), pp. 62–64.

'contre-aventures (comme on dit un contre-poison)' [counter-adventures (as one says a counter-poison)].[39]

Beyond a simple misconception about where the meaning of adventures lies, Gauvain's attitude amounts to a rejection of God's grace. This, more than the sin inherent in the act of killing, is what situates his slaying of Yvain outside the frame of the Grail adventures, which consist essentially of homiletic experiences that become meaningless if their subject will not participate in the process of edification and personal transformation. The knight does not so much sin by killing as kill because he is already a sinner and is committed to remaining such. Homicide thus functions as 'le signe extérieur et comme social de la perversité' [the external and, as it were, social sign of perversity][40] and as the material manifestation of a refusal to interpret romance reality in symbolic terms. By the same token, homicide becomes the distinguishing mark of the culpably literal reader, the appropriately concretised death stroke of misguided fidelity to the letter that, as Paul says, kills where the spirit gives life (2 Cor. 3:6). Anyone spiritually enlightened enough to profit from a metaphorical understanding of homicide is necessarily too virtuous to commit the legible deed, while those in sufficiently bad odour with God that He would allow them to be responsible for another's death must be hardened reprobates who can think about, and must therefore be taught, right and wrong in only the most basic literal terms.

This circular logic preserves a balance between literal and figurative (sins and virtues, but also readings) that many critics perceive as threatened, or even abandoned, in a text where 'la prévalence du sens spirituel provoque la dévaluation de l'aventure et du niveau littéral qui en rend compte' [the prevalence of spiritual meaning devalues the adventure and the literal level on which it is related].[41] It is dramatically demonstrated early in the quest by the contrasting ways in which a group of seven cruel brothers is construed, almost in the same breath, by the hermit who interprets the adventure(s) in which they feature. The seven set upon Galaad when he tries to enter the mysterious *Chastel as Puceles* [Castle of Maidens], but after a long combat, the Grail knight's preternatural strength and prowess prevail against the odds and the brothers take flight, unpursued by their adversary, who proceeds to liberate the castle's imprisoned damsels. Meanwhile, the brothers run into Gauvain and two of his worldly comrades, attack them and are slain in what is, by all normal standards, a clear-cut case of legitimate self-defence. Although the seven are 'las et traveillié' [weary and worn out] (§62.15–16) from their recent defeat, they have a significant numerical advantage

---

[39] Poirion, 'Semblance du Graal', p. 203.
[40] Pauphilet, *Études*, p. 43.
[41] Michel Stanesco, *D'armes et d'amours: Études de littérature arthurienne* (Orléans: Paradigme, 2002), p. 252.

and advertise their intent to kill Gauvain and his friends because they are knights errant like Galaad. When Gauvain arrives at a hermitage, however, the resident *preudome* urges him to make confession and then chastises him for his part in the day's events:

> Et certes, se vos ne fussiez si pechierres com vos estes, ja li .vii. frere ne fussent ocis par vos ne par vostre aide, ainz feissent encore lor penitance de la male costume qu'il avoient maintenue el Chastel as Puceles, et s'acordassent a Deu. Einsi nel fist mie Galaaz, li Bons Chevaliers, [...] ainz les conquist sanz ocirre. (§64.18–24)

> [And indeed, if you were not so great a sinner as you are, the seven brothers would never have been slain by your hand or with your help; instead, they might yet have done penance for the evil custom they upheld in the Castle of Maidens, and been reconciled with God. Galaad, the Good Knight, did nothing of the sort ... but rather defeated them without killing them].

The hermit then goes on to expound an elaborate figural analogy between Galaad's adventure and the Harrowing of Hell, explaining to Gauvain that 'par les .vii. chevaliers doiz tu entendre les .vii. pechiez mortels' [by the seven knights you should understand the seven deadly sins] (§65.3–4) that enslaved the world prior to Christ's advent. The juxtaposition of these two interpretive modes is jarring, but instructive regarding the patterns of interaction between moral and figural interpretation in the text. Galaad, in battling evil personified, stays his hand, apparently out of regard for the humanity of the real men who stand for Satan's slave-masters,[42] even if the evidence of other passages links the Good Knight's mercy less to charitable neighbour-love (a Christian virtue little emphasised in the *Queste*) than to respect for God's providential plans. Meanwhile, Gauvain, in fighting merely human adversaries, slaughters them without compunction, which is at least partly why his battle does not deserve to become a *figura* of sacred things.[43]

---

[42] The hermit never asserts that the seven brothers *are* the deadly sins, any more than Galaad *is* Christ. He says only that the real characters should be identified with their theological counterparts so the structural resemblance between the two episodes becomes visible. 'Typological analogy lies not between person and person, but between act and act', as noted by Pauline Matarasso, *The Redemption of Chivalry: A Study of the Queste del Saint Graal* (Geneva: Droz, 1979), p. 80; see also pp. 60–61 and Erich Auerbach, 'Figura', trans. Ralph Manheim, in *Scenes from the Drama of European Literature* (New York: Meridian, 1959), pp. 11–76. It is perhaps worth noting, although the hermit does not, that the death of the 'deadly sins' at the hands of Galaad-Christ would have detracted from the coherence of the figural analogy given the sins' robust presence in the post-Incarnational world.

[43] Cf. the much later episode (§239–41) wherein Galaad comes upon a tournament gone wrong in which the numerically inferior losing side, having been put to rout, is being

The basic reasonableness of Gauvain's actions from a secular perspective only underscores the way in which his all-too-literal homicides offer an interpretive key to the condition of the secular chivalric Everyman's badly stained, but still salvageable, soul. In the very brute fact of their humanity, the seven sinful brothers are monitory mirror images of Gauvain himself, the man whom the hermit hopes to convince of his own inalienable capacity and urgent need for redemption. Such is the homiletic gambit subtending Gauvain's unfavourable comparison to Galaad, one that the hermit spells out:

> Gauvain Gauvain, se tu voloies lessier ta male vie que tu as si longuement maintenue, encor te porroies tu acorder a Deu, car l'Escriture dit que nus n'est si pechierres, por qu'il requiere de buen cuer misericorde a Deu, qu'il ne l'ait. Por ce te loeroie je [...] a fere penitance de ce que tu as fet. (§65.19–24)
>
> [Gauvain, Gauvain, if you chose to leave the evil life you have led for so long, you could still be reconciled with God, for Scripture says that no man is so great a sinner that, if he makes a heartfelt plea for God's mercy, he may not receive it. Therefore, I would advise you ... to do penance for what you have done].

The repetition of numerous key words from the hermit's reproach for the killing of the brothers suggests that if Galaad's adventure has a figural parallel in the biblical past, Gauvain's homicidal exploits have their own analogue closer to home. He is the victim of his own sins, the wayward soul who needs a stay of execution to discover contrition and turn from the long-inhabited darkness. At the same time, he is the one responsible for slaying or sparing himself in the spirit by choosing or refusing to repent of his deeds – his recent homicides but also, by extension, his whole life's history of squandered potential – and so to reform the sinful inner disposition of which his rising body count is the outward sign. His situation is dire, but all is not yet lost, for the bitterly ironic fact that the brothers attacked Gauvain for his superficial likeness to Galaad holds out the hopeful promise of a spiritual awakening that might bring the sinner truly to resemble the Christ-like Grail hero. But Gauvain cannot spare himself any more than he did the seven brothers. Bad exegete that he is, he fails to recognise himself either in their deaths or in the hypothetical promise of their projected futures, cuts his abortive confession short and departs unabsolved.

> slaughtered by the victors, for whom Gauvain and Hestor are fighting. Galaad joins the underdogs, deals Gauvain an incapacitating blow, and turns the tide of the mêlée. For once, no *preudome* appears to interpret the event according to any of the available and, by this point, rather painfully obvious allegorical schemata (the Old Law versus the New Law, the mass of sinners against the virtuous minority, *chevalerie terriene* versus *chevalerie celestiel*, etc.). It is as though Gauvain's very participation diminishes the significance of the event – or an explicit interpretation is unnecessary since the reader already knows, more or less, what it would say, while Gauvain once again fails to listen.

Vociferously though the *preudomes* proclaim otherwise, on a narrative level, Gauvain's refusal to be redeemed is inevitable because of his allotted structural role as the incarnation of the *chevalerie terriene* that is, by definition, unilluminated by grace and impervious to the Grail's transformation of the romance world. The reader alone ultimately can and must profit from the moral and hermeneutic instruction that falls on Gauvain's deaf ears, and from that which is proffered through his story. Yet the lessons to be drawn from Gauvain's exemplary homicides are not entirely obvious, for if the comparison between his and Galaad's interactions with the seven evil brothers indicates that the actions of the virtuous signify on an allegorical level and ought to be understood accordingly, it also suggests that, where killing is concerned, the most important moral interpretation of events coincides with their literal sense. The problem of homicide, in other words, acts as a check on the *Queste*'s often overpowering drive to allegorise, working to preserve the 'épaisseur ontologique' [ontological depth][44] of the romance narrative and the moral integrity of the text.

How it does so is demonstrated in two unusually and disturbingly violent episodes in which the virtuous Grail questers, not the guilty Gauvain, take centre stage. One of these occurs near the end of the quest when Galaad and his companions, the secondary Grail heroes Perceval and Boort, enter a Scottish castle called Qarceloi.[45] The trio is warned that the inhabitants hate King Arthur and his knights, but Boort assures Galaad and Perceval that God will protect his own just before the locals attack and the questers respond with uncharacteristic savagery, slaughtering everyone in the castle 'ausi come bestes mues' [like dumb animals] (§276.6). When their blood cools, the questers are horrified by what they have done, but Boort proposes a pious explanation, only to be contradicted by Galaad:

> Certes, fet Boorz, je ne quit mie que se Nostre Sires les amast de riens, que il fussent si martirié com il sont. Mes il ont esté par aventure aucune jent renoiee et malooite et ont tant mesfet vers Nostre Seignor qu'il ne voloit pas que il regnassent plus. Por ce, si nos i envoia ça Nostre Sires por els destruire. Vos ne dites mie bien, fet Galaaz. Por ce, s'il mesfirent a Nostre Seignor, n'en estoit mie nostre la venjance a prendre, mes a Celui qui tant atent que li pechierres se reconoisse. Por ce vos di je que je ne serai ja mes aese devant que g'en sache veraies noveles de ceste ovre que nos avons fete, s'il plest a Nostre Seignor. (§276.18–29)

---

[44] Stanesco, *D'armes et d'amours*, p. 252.
[45] The implications of this episode, including some of the points explored below, are more extensively analysed in Lucas Wood, 'The Ethics of Election in the *Queste del Saint Graal*', *New Medieval Literatures* 15 (2013): 183–224.

['Indeed', said Boort, 'I really don't think they would have been massacred like that if Our Lord loved them at all. Perhaps they were cursed apostates who had sinned so greatly against Our Lord that he did not want them to reign any longer. That's why Our Lord sent us here to destroy them'. 'That was ill spoken', said Galaad. 'If they did sin against Our Lord, the vengeance for it was not ours to take; it belonged to Him who stays his hand until the sinner recognises himself as such. Therefore, I tell you that I will have no peace until I know the truth about this deed we've done, if it please Our Lord'].

Unsurprisingly, Boort is right. The resident priest attests that Galaad and his companions have performed 'la meillor ovre que onques chevalier feissent' [the best deed ever done by knights] (§277.21–22), namely, the prophesied, divinely ordained punishment of a band of godless, church-razing, priest-murdering, sister-raping renegades who are 'paior que Sarrazin' [worse than Saracens] (§277.28–29). Pauline Matarasso suggests that the Qarceloi massacre reenacts the Old Testament model of 'God's avenging justice', forming a diptych with the subsequent episode in which Perceval's sister willingly sacrifices her life to cure a leprous lady in a somewhat awkward *figura* of Christ's Passion. It is clear in any case that, as Matarasso also notes, the Lord's own vengeance has indeed been exacted here through his unwitting human tools.[46]

According to both Boort and the priest, then, there is no need for God's pawns to feel human guilt for the blood on their hands. As Bernard of Clairvaux asserts in *De laude novae militiae*,

> vero Christi milites securi praeliantur praelia Domini sui, nequaquam metuentes [...] de hostium caede peccatum, [...] quandoquidem mors pro Christo vel ferenda, vel inferenda, et nihil habet criminis, et plurimum gloriae mereatur [...] Sane cum occidit malefactorem, non homicida, sed [...] malicida, et plane Christi vindex in his qui male agunt, et defensor christianorum reputatur.[47]
>
> [the knights of Christ may safely fight the battles of their Lord, fearing [no] sin if they smite the enemy, ... since to inflict death or to die for Christ is no sin, but rather, an abundant claim to glory ... If he kills an evildoer, he is not a mankiller, but ... a killer of evil. He is evidently the avenger of Christ toward evildoers and he is rightly considered a defender of Christians].

The description of the Grail knights' victims as *paior que Sarrazin* is a conspicuous nod toward the crusading context in which Bernard writes, and although the Qarceloi episode is not part of an organised holy war, the same theological premises apply. Yet if the *Queste* is evidently willing to countenance divinely

---

[46] Matarasso, *The Redemption of Chivalry*, p. 176; see also pp. 67–69.
[47] Bernard of Clairvaux, *De laude novae militiae*, §4.1–15; *In Praise of the New Knighthood*, p. 134.

sanctioned slaughter on a large scale, it is also anxious – like Bernard, who goes on to emphasise that infidels should not be killed unless there is no other way to prevent them from harming Christians – about how the *miles Christi*'s licence to kill might be misapplied. The *Queste* champions the New Law far less militantly than does the roughly contemporary, or somewhat earlier, Grail romance of *Perlesvaus*, for example. That text's eponymous hero believes that 'on doit faire guerre encontre guerroieur et pais encontre paissible' [one must make war against the warlike and peace with the peaceful] and upholds a pitiless *lex talionis* that leads him, on one representatively grisly occasion, to drown a particularly violent enemy in the gore of his own beheaded followers, quipping that the warmonger's thirst for blood will finally be satisfied.[48] In the *Queste*, by contrast, Galaad may be wrong to feel guilty about eliminating the inhabitants of Qarceloi on God's behalf, but it is no accident that the robotically perfect Christian knight is, for once, the one to 'err' in his grasp of divine providence. Recalling the same theological point about the limits of human knowledge and the ever-present possibility of any sinner's redemption used to condemn Gauvain's slaying of the seven brothers, Galaad emphasises precisely his own humanity and his humility, confirming the personal virtue that fits him to act as a killer of evil. For homicide on God's behalf is not an allegorical gesture, a mere *senefiance*. It is a literal deed with real and dire consequences for both victims and perpetrators, and the doctrine of guiltless 'malicide' can therefore function only if it is grounded in a contingent, human moral reality constantly open to questioning and revision, in the 'good' knight's ongoing struggle to be good and the 'bad' victim's freely sustained commitment to evil.

The Qarceloi incident thus exploits the problem of homicide to stage a reminder of interpretation's necessary open-endedness within a reassuringly closed narrative frame. A more enigmatic and, in many ways, more troubling challenge to grapple with the meaning of manslaughter confronts the reader in an earlier episode where Boort's elder brother Lyonel nearly slays his saintly sibling. Lyonel is enraged because Boort previously chose – correctly, according to the *preudomes*, though his moral logic may not be self-evident – to rescue a maiden from being raped rather than saving his brother from two knights who were beating him while dragging him off, as Boort thought, to his death. Lyonel's dissatisfaction with this decision is perhaps understandable in human terms, but he takes it to an extreme, declaring the failure to render assistance

---

[48] *Le Haut Livre du Graal (Perlesvaus)*, ed. and trans. Armand Strubel (Paris: Livre de Poche, 2007), p. 608; the episode in question is on p. 614. See, alongside the editor's extensive introduction, Anne Berthelot, 'Violence et Passion, ou le christianisme sauvage de *Perlesvaus: Le haut Livre du Graal*', and Francis Dubost, 'Le *Perlesvaus*, livre de haute violence', both in *La Violence dans le monde médiéval* (Aix-en-Provence: CUERMA, 1994), pp. 21–36 and 181–99.

a crime against family and fellowship, for which he intends to exact the death penalty: 'Onques nus freres ne fist tel desloiauté, et por ce ne vos asseur je fors de la mort, car bien l'avez deservie' [No brother ever committed such disloyalty, and, therefore, I guarantee you nothing other than death, for you well deserve it] (§230.34–36). Boort begs his brother's pardon on bended knee, but Lyonel refuses and demands a judicial duel, then, acting 'come cil que li anemis avoit eschaufé jusqu'a volonté d'ocirre son frere' [as one whom the devil had inflamed with desire to kill his brother] (§232.14–16), disregards Boort's continued pleas for peace and renewed fraternal love, runs him over with his horse and prepares to behead him.

At this point, however, the local hermit runs up, tries to bring Lyonel to his senses, and, failing, declares himself ready to die for Boort, whose body he covers with his own. Lyonel obligingly kills the hermit and again prepares to dispatch Boort, only to be stopped a second time by another passerby, the Round Table knight Calogrenant, who first reasons, then fights with Lyonel, only to be cut down in his turn. Out of defenders, Boort, 'en qui humilitez estoit aussi comme naturelment enracinee' [in whom humility was rooted as though by nature] (§235.23–24), begs his brother one last time to let the matter be, 'car se il avient, biau frere, que je vos occie ou vos moi, nos serons mort de pechié' [for if I kill you, dear brother, or you kill me, we will die the death of sin] (§235.26–27). Of course, Lyonel again refuses and, amid tears and prayers for divine forgiveness, Boort finally draws his sword to defend himself, only to be saved from committing fratricide by a fireball from heaven that knocks both brothers to the ground. A voice instructs Boort to depart his brother's company, which he does after again requesting, and this time receiving, Lyonel's pardon, then leaving his would-be executioner with a mild reprimand – 'Biau frere, vos avez trop mal esploitié de cel chevalier qe vos avez ocis, qui estoit nostre compainz, et de cest hermite ausi' [Dear brother, you acted very badly in killing this knight, who was our companion, and this hermit also] (§237.5–7) – and a reminder to bury his victims' bodies.

Legally speaking (as the text again does not), Lyonel's totally unwarranted slaying of the unarmed hermit is the only unequivocal, premeditated murder graphically narrated in the *Queste*, but what is surprising about the episode is not so much this exceptionally heinous violence as its bizarrely noncommittal reception by Boort, God and the narrator. Beyond the obvious indications that Lyonel behaves wrongfully under the influence of evil impulses, no explicit moralising frame makes sense of the scene. Of course, this does not mean that none is available. The fact that Lyonel vindicates his wrath by referring to Boort's perceived (and, from a purely secular perspective, not wholly imaginary) neglect of his responsibilities as a fellow knight and brother, representing his own murderous actions as a perverted, excessive, selfish form of justice, suggests an extension of the critique of *chevalerie terriene* advanced through Gauvain's homicidal adventures. Lyonel's attempted fratricide, associated with accusations of treason and disloyalty, may also hint at figural linkages with the primordial slaying of Abel by Cain, which the *Queste* will rehearse slightly later in another context: 'Et Caÿn, qui de lonc tens ot la traïson porpensee, [...] vint aprés, si le quida ocirre si sodeinement qu'il ne s'en aperceust... Einsi reçut Abel la mort par la main de son desloial frere' [And Cain, who had been plotting the treason for a long time ... approached, planning to surprise and kill him before he knew what was happening ... Thus, Abel died by the hand of his disloyal brother] (§259.11–260.2). In the romance, however, neither brother dies, while Calogrenant and the hermit, who do, seem merely to be collateral damage – unless, as intercessors who sacrifice themselves to keep both brothers free of the mortal sin of fratricide, they become two more of the Christ-figures who proliferate in the *Queste*. In any case, unglossed as they are, the victims of Lyonel's wrath are not absorbed into any allegorical system, any interpretive grid that would read out of existence the raw reality of their senseless deaths, even as their killer goes unpunished and virtually uncondemned, in this life at least.

Rather than being absolved by some odd amnesty, the guilty Lyonel and his presumable spiritual depravity seem simply to be sidelined by the narrator's primary focus on Boort. Like most of Boort's adventures, his brother's assault is a test of moral logic and fortitude that he must pass, in this case by resisting wrath and pride, refusing to risk fratricide and turning the other cheek with Job-like patience and *humilitez*. Yet the idea that heroic 'humility' is demonstrated by watching an aged hermit and a close friend be butchered, then letting their killer depart with a gentle rebuke, is hard to take, even in the world of the *Queste*. Further complicating the issue, Boort's religious reasons for refusing to fight his brother are doubled by personal, secular concerns, notably during Lyonel's combat with Calogrenant, when Boort vacillates helplessly between reluctance to kill his beloved brother and shame (not guilt) at the idea that Calogrenant should die on his behalf while he sits idly by. Throughout the episode, in fact, the often complacent Boort acts less like a saintly 'sergent Jhesucrist' [servant of Jesus Christ] (§229.11), secure in his dogmatic certainty that God's will is always done, than like a confused, anxious man torn between the imperatives of theology and emotion, between monastic, chivalric and human values, reduced to blindly hoping that everything will somehow be all right in the end. But perhaps this is exactly the point. Faith, of which the *preudomes* speak so eloquently in their homilies, is hard to understand, harder to practise, and harder still to write convincingly into a romance plot; right and wrong, so clearly and rigorously explainable in the abstract terms of moral theology, so persuasively allegorised in the convolutions of exegesis, are things with which individuals must continually grapple on the level of messy, opaque, literal reality, especially when human lives are on the line.

In the *Queste del Saint Graal*, then, *chevaliers ocirre* names the morally and semiotically ambiguous terrain that lies on either side of allegorical reading. As a key term in the romance's reformist critique of *chevalerie terriene*, it stands for allegory's antithesis: worldly chivalry's brutally, blindly literal investment in the hack and slash of the gorily glorious mêlée. Used to spur reflection on the moral value and limits of allegoresis, it either becomes the site of interpretation's apotheosis, wherein individual actions cease merely to signify sacred truth and cross over into the concrete enactment, the perfectly literal execution of God's will, or else offers the occasion for interpretation's salutary arrest in the face of a life's irreducible eradication. From both angles, violence imposes on its privileged knightly practitioners a corresponding obligation to ask questions. The first line of questioning casts doubt on the true meaning of the visible, the obvious, the beautiful but spiritually empty surfaces of secular knightly culture and the romance narratives that sing its praises. The second directs the flower of Christian chivalry back from spiritual abstractions toward the material, historical reality of the human world in which the *Queste*'s readers, like its heroes, are called to strive toward becoming the vessels of providence – always beneficially uncertain, in the absence of the text's helpful hermits, where exactly they stand.

CHAPTER 9

Murder, Manslaughter and Reputation: Killing in Malory's *Le Morte Darthur*

Dwayne C. Coleman

IN THE ARTHURIAN SOCIETY of Sir Thomas Malory's *Le Morte Darthur* (c. 1471), both the enforcement of social order and the accrual of social status are largely achieved by means of violence. Living in fifteenth-century England, Malory no doubt witnessed, and may have participated in, the familial feuds of that century that culminated with the Wars of the Roses in the 1460s and 1470s. Malory himself was charged with several crimes and was often incarcerated, and it is likely that he had some familiarity with English law.[1] As Larissa Tracy explains in the introduction to this collection, throughout the medieval period, 'murder' (or unpardonable homicide) referred to intentional homicide committed from ambush or in secret, and Malory's treatment of the crime reflects that definition in his conception of the Arthurian past. Those who murder in Malory's work are usually motivated by pride and reputation, the defence of family honour or an individual knight's sense of 'worship'. When the satisfaction of honour cannot be achieved by lawful means, King Arthur's knights will at times resort to murder, giving rise to the potential for an escalating cycle of fatal vengeance and posing a threat to the cohesiveness of the Round Table. To counter that threat and encourage adherence to the law, King Arthur formulates the Pentecost oath, the only formally expressed code defining chivalric behaviour in the *Morte*. The oath prohibits Arthur's knights from resorting to murder and requires them to grant mercy to whomever asks it, but the pledge proves an insufficient deterrent. However, King Arthur's prominent knights are rarely tried for murder, while Queen Guinevere is, and murder in Malory's work becomes not so much a legal charge as an appellation, a name that adversely affects the level of worship an individual knight may reach within his career. Gawain's reputation as a murderer, which Malory chooses to construct, creates factionalism within the Round Table, and when many knights reject him on that

---

[1] Jacqueline Stuhmiller, '*Iudicium Dei, iudicium fortunae*: Trial by Combat in Malory's le Morte Darthur', *Speculum* 81.2 (2006): 427–62 at p. 432.

basis in favour of Lancelot, their final feud over the death of Sir Gareth and the resulting division among Arthur's knights plays a crucial role in the destruction of Arthur's kingdom. Malory creates an imagined version of Arthurian chivalry, which relies upon a system of ritualised violence, and in creating it, he must negotiate whether law can be impartially and consistently applied in that society.

In 'The Tale of Sir Gareth of Orkney', Malory relates Sir Gareth's future alienation from his elder brother Sir Gawain: 'For evir aftir sir Gareth had aspyed sir Gawaynes conducions, he wythdrewe hymselfe fro his brother sir Gawaynes felyshyp, for he was evir vengeable, and where he hated he wolde be avenged with murther' (7.360.32–35).[2] Malory is obviously referring to the murders of Sir Pellinore and Sir Lamorak that Gawain and his other brothers will commit later in 'The Book of Sir Tristram'. He portrays these murders as being among the more destructive events in the history of the Round Table, and although Gawain tries to use the justification of blood feud, the killings are murder and a betrayal of the Pentecost oath sworn at the ordination of the Round Table. As Gareth's reaction illustrates, Gawain gains a persistent reputation as a murderer. Malory follows the tradition of his French sources in giving Gawain this reputation rather than following the English tradition in which Gawain appears much more sympathetic. In doing so, he juxtaposes two imperfect knights, Gawain the murderer and Lancelot the adulterer, who become the chief leaders of opposing factions within the Round Table. Sir Lancelot's later killing of Sir Mellyagaunt, after denying his plea for mercy, appears as a counterpoint to Gawain's murderous acts. The killing comes as part of trial by combat and, therefore, is not murder – and the duplicitous Mellyagaunt garners little sympathy. However, Lancelot's determination to 'be revenged' upon him pushes the boundaries of justice and creates an undercurrent of moral ambiguity (19.1138.28). Because Lancelot has already amassed a solid name as a chivalric archetype, no authoritative voice ever questions the righteousness of Lancelot's action just as Gawain is never really made to answer for Lamorak's death. Before their deaths, both knights seek atonement for their moral failures, but no formal charges or trials are ever pursued against either of them specifically for these killings. For Malory, the impact on a knight's worship and the communal reaction to a murder, culminating with the fracturing of the Table, become the most serious consequence. Eventually, Gawain will have no choice, and he will have no way to maintain his honour without duelling Lancelot; thus, Malory must negotiate what he laments and what he admires in both characters while still confronting the murder.

---

[2] All quotations of Malory's text are from Thomas Malory, *The Works of Sir Thomas Malory*, ed. Eugène Vinaver, rev. P. J. C. Field, 3 vols, 3rd edn (Oxford: Oxford University Press, 1990). Book, page and line numbers are given in parentheses.

Judicial combat emerges as the most significant legal process in *Le Morte Darthur*. Although the practice had become less prominent by Malory's time, it retained important functions well into the fifteenth century.³ Both Laura K. Bedwell and Beverly Kennedy cite Malory's presentation of trial by combat as the primary means of dealing with murder or treason; Kennedy calls it 'the only judicial process in King Arthur's realm'.⁴ While judicial combat was ostensibly a vindication of God's judgment in legal affairs, Malory does not clearly present it as such. Jacqueline Stuhmiller affirms: 'Malory … was as fascinated by the idea of judicial combat as he was appalled by the suggestion that such combat could provide a just ruling'.⁵ As Lancelot's judicial duel with Mellyagaunt in 'The Knight of the Cart' episode and the duels of Lancelot and Gawain demonstrate, true justice, in the legal and not the poetic sense, is not always the actual outcome. Bedwell asserts: 'And herein lies the problem with trial by battle – right does not always prevail'.⁶ Nevertheless, as Stuhmiller explains, in the *Morte* '[j]udicial battles fulfill a number of practical objectives: they release community tensions, appease the public's desire for spectacle, punish known offenders who can be brought to justice in no other way, resolve conflicts with minimal bloodshed, and force a divided community to accept a single verdict'.⁷ Judicial combats also decide matters of honour and, at times, help to regulate the level of violence within the Round Table order. When Gawain and Lancelot fight their final honour duel, however, no release of tension or satisfactory verdict results, and the destabilising effect provides Mordred his opportunity to pursue his final revolt against Arthur.

Chivalry bears within its own structure the potential for producing cycles of vendettas. However, chivalry is not law or a governing principle but an ideal mode of behaviour that applies to a particular social class. It cannot itself enforce law, and its most coercive aspect – force of arms – often becomes a catalyst for revenge. In his historical study of chivalry and violence, Richard W. Kaeuper delineates the problem with chivalry as an agent of public order in the Middle Ages: 'the right and personal practice of warlike violence has fused with honour, high status, religious piety, and claims about love, so that those knights who are inclined, or who see opportunity, will be likely to act with whatever force they

---

³ Stuhmiller, '*Iudicium Dei*', pp. 428–29.
⁴ Laura K. Bedwell, 'The Failure of Justice, The Failure of Arthur', *Arthuriana* 21.3 (2011): 3–22 at p. 13; Beverly Kennedy, *Knighthood in the* Morte d'Arthur (Cambridge: D. S. Brewer, 1985), p. 39.
⁵ Stuhmiller, '*Iudicium Dei*', p. 435.
⁶ Bedwell, 'The Failure of Justice', p. 13.
⁷ Stuhmiller, '*Iudicium Dei*', p. 435.

can muster, confident in their course of action'.[8] According to Kaeuper, Malory's work belongs in a tradition of medieval romances that, for a knightly audience, engage in self-criticism, debate and efforts to reform chivalry. Chivalric romances like Malory's work illustrate medieval society's recognition that chivalry had not become the satisfactory means of restraining violence and maintaining public order.[9] Gawain's expression of intent toward Pellinore expresses not only the desire for vengeance but also a jealousy over the favour implied by Arthur's and Merlyn's granting of precedence to Pellinore and Torre. In this incident, Malory introduces the competitive nature of the quest for 'worship' among Arthur's knights: 'Envy, at least in the sense of fierce competition, was inherent to the system'.[10] Kaeuper adds that in Malory's work martial prowess is 'probably the highest human good ... and a chief ingredient in nobility'.[11] Unfortunately, in the quest to display prowess and achieve a name for it, Malory's knights believe that worship is a zero-sum concept, and there simply is not enough to go around. As Andrew Lynch puts it, the Arthurian system of chivalry is an 'honour economy' in which the kin and followers of the prominent knights 'are like shareholders whose stocks are devalued when another centre of worship – for "worship" read "power" – grows stronger'.[12] When Gawain or Gaheris feel devalued, as in their feud with King Pellinore's family, they will turn to murder to eliminate their competition. As kinsmen of King Arthur, their reputation as murderers conflicts with the king's ability to enforce the law impartially and threatens the stability of the community.

Many knights die at the hands of others, but in highlighting the failings of individual knights and the collective flaws of the Arthurian order, Malory focuses on numerous thematically crucial murders. A quick tally of these murders shows the following: Gawain and his brothers (except Gareth) kill both Pellinore and Lamorak; on his own, Gaheris murders his mother Morgause; King Mark kills Tristram and Alisander le Orphelin; and in the episode of 'The Poisoned Apple', Sir Pynell le Saveayge kills Sir Patryse of Ireland, intending to murder Gawain, for which Guinevere is tried. All of these murders, with the exception of the killing of Patryse, take place within 'The Book of Tristram', and all take place for reasons of jealousy or family rivalry. Knights are permitted to fight over their disputes and settle them through violent means, but these killings violate both the Pentecost oath and the law. As Bedwell clarifies, murderers in Malory's text

---

[8] Richard W. Kaeuper, *Chivalry and Violence in Medieval Europe* (Oxford: Oxford University Press, 1999), p. 9.
[9] Ibid., pp. 35–39.
[10] Andrew Lynch, *Malory's Book of Arms: The Narrative of Combat in* Le Morte Darthur (Cambridge: D. S. Brewer, 1997), p. 93.
[11] Kaeuper, *Chivalry and Violence*, p. 290.
[12] Lynch, *Malory's Book of Arms*, p. 97.

are 'those who kill through trickery, who ensure that their victims are at a disadvantage, or who take others by surprise'.[13] For instance, Gawain and his brothers kill Lamorak in a secluded place, ambushing him and leaving little opportunity for a fair fight. Furthermore, in the competition to prove knightly prowess, as Lynch argues, fights must be fair, and '"worship" must be attached to the superior fighter beyond any suspicion of foul play or improper advantage'.[14] The identity and standing of the slain party is also crucial. Because Lamorak is called a worthy knight of great prowess, the ruthless method employed by Gawain and his brothers makes his death the most heinous of crimes. Lynch says of characters like Gawain and King Mark: 'Their closure of another's potential for more adventures is the worst crime such a narrative can imagine, especially when the potential is great'.[15] Later, in contrast to the communal indignation at the deaths of Lamorak or Tristram, good knights, the death of Mellyagaunt, a dishonourable coward, causes little outrage and passes with only muted public reaction.[16] Lancelot's killing of Mellyagaunt does not draw a charge of murder because of its context within the judicial duel, but, as Dorsey Armstrong argues, the lack of public approval suggests that the outcome is not unambiguously just.[17] Under the guise of judicial combat, Lancelot removes someone who nearly exposes his affair with the queen. Malory's ambivalence results from trying to maintain sympathy for Lancelot while trying, perhaps with limited success, not to portray him as being above the law.

Very early in the *Morte*, Malory introduces the internecine strife driven by the assertion of family honour, which will form the Arthurian order's most crucial weakness and give rise to a cycle of murderous revenge. In 'The Tale of Balyn and Balan', King Pellinore slays King Lott, Gawain's father, during the rebellion against the newly crowned King Arthur. Upon Lott's death, Malory remarks, '[K]ynge Pellynore bare the wyte of the dethe of Kynge Lott, wherefore Sir Gawayne revenged the deth of hys fadir the tenthe yere aftir he was made knight, and slew Kynge Pellynor hys owne hondis' (2.77.19–22). Interestingly, Malory's choice of words – that Pellinore 'bare the wyte', that is, the responsibility for Lott's death – emphasises how large a role reputation plays in incidents of homicidal violence in both Malory's imaginary past and the historical legal setting. Soon after, in 'The Weddynge of Kynge Arthur', Sir Torre and Sir Gawain are knighted and go on their first quest along with King Pellinore, and another discordant note is

---

[13] Bedwell, 'The Failure of Justice', p. 8.
[14] Lynch, *Malory's Book of Arms*, p. 44.
[15] Andret is one of King Mark's henchmen, complicit in the death of Tristram. See: ibid., pp. 88–89.
[16] Lynch calls Mellyagaunt 'worthless in fighting', ibid., p. 44.
[17] Dorsey Armstrong, *Gender and the Chivalric Community in Malory's* Morte Darthur (Gainesville: University Press of Florida, 2003), p. 187.

struck when Gawain first reveals his vengeful nature. As Merlin gives Pellinore one of the more respected seats at the Round Table, Gawain tells his brother Gaheris, "'Yondir knight ys putte to grete worship, whych grevith me sore, for he slewe oure fadir kynge Lott. Therefore I woll sle hym'" (3.102.12–4). Gawain's enmity toward Pellinore seems to be based on the faulty premise that Pellinore's killing of King Lott was wrongful and should be subject to vengeance; however, Pellinore killed Lott in open warfare. If anything, Lott is in the wrong because, as Kennedy points out, 'Lott was in rebellion against his liege lord, Arthur, when Pellynore killed him'.[18] Therefore, Pellinore is not guilty of murder in having killed Lott. Significantly, Gawain does not distinguish between a slaying that happens during open warfare from that which occurs during the personal blood feud; what was a fight with honour will lead, at least once, to what Malory considers murder. In the early days of Arthur's rule, little distinguishes warfare from blood feud, and one of the defects of the Pentecost oath, which Arthur's knights will later swear, resides in its failure to clearly delineate the difference. As Lynch points out, 'The Lott-Pellinore family feud is a dark thread throughout the text, and such affairs must have been perfectly familiar to a man of Malory's experience'.[19] The feud highlights Gawain's tragic flaw, his tendency toward vengeance, and the role it will play in the destruction of the Round Table becomes clear even before Arthur has firmly established his Order.

Malory attempts to place mercy as the societal deterrent to fatal violence, and he uses Gawain's initial career to establish it as part of Arthur's chivalric code. On his first quest, Gawain accidentally slays a maiden who throws herself over a knight to whom Gawain has denied the courtesy of mercy. Instead of killing the knight she is defending, he beheads her, and shame, rebuke and swift punishment abound for Gawain. This act is not murder, but its unfortunate nature highlights the necessity of mercy within Arthurian chivalry. Gaheris begins by telling him: "'that ys fowle and shamefully done, for that shame shall never frome you. Also ye sholde gyff mercy unto them that aske mercy, for a knyght withoute mercy ys withoute worship'" (3.106.22–25). Considering Lynch's observation on the importance of worship, Gaheris' comment should cut him to the quick. Immediately, four knights attack Gawain and Gaheris in punishment, telling Gawain, "'thou haste shamed thy knyghthode, for a knight withoute mercy ys dishonoured. Also thou haste slayne a fayre lady to thy grete shame unto the worldys ende, and doute the nat thou shalt have grete nede of mercy or thou departe frome us'" (3.107.18–22). Besides hammering home the lesson about mercy, the knights' warning frames the attack as retribution for Gawain's deed and shows the need for an enforceable code. However, when enforcement of

---

[18] Kennedy, *Knighthood in the* Morte d'Arthur, p. 164.
[19] Lynch, *Malory's Book of Arms*, p. 62.

the law relies upon knights policing themselves, certain crimes will go unpunished, equating to a failure of justice through consensual inaction. Gawain's quest catalyses the establishment of the Pentecost oath for the entire order and leads directly to its primary clauses, decreeing before all else the prohibition of murder and offering the granting of mercy as a counter to homicide.

The critical conversation, especially since Vinaver's edition first appeared, has long considered the code to be central to understanding Malory's formulation of chivalry and the implications of the narrative that follows. Vinaver writes that the oath is 'perhaps the most complete and authentic record of Malory's conception of chivalry'.[20] As Armstrong points out, the Pentecost oath, though imperfect, becomes the central ordering principle of the Arthurian order in Malory's work.[21] In response, Robert L. Kelly issues a dissenting view: 'its syntactic awkwardness and lack of apparent logic suggest the author's lack of care in composing it, a fact which lessens the probability that it was intended to bear the deep interpretive significance many critics have assigned to it'.[22] Bonnie Wheeler agrees somewhat with Kelly about the oath's difficult syntax, but points out that the oath reacts to issues raised by the Gawain-Torre-Pellinore quests and 'reveals the gap between the best-intentioned language and the reality it is meant to order'.[23] In Kelly's view, the oath is intended to serve as a binding contract between the king as the supreme authority of his realm and his knights as sworn liegemen, but it is not meant to serve as a pledge to adhere to honourable behaviour.[24]

In the first articles of the oath, the knights swear 'never to do outerage nothir mourthir, and allwayes to fle treson, and to gyff mercy unto hym that askith mercy, uppon payne of forfeiture [of their] worship and lordship of kynge Arthure for evirmore' (3.120.17–20). Malory gives primacy to murder, mentioning it as the first crime to avoid. Considering all the killing that happens in the course of Malory's narrative, the problem for him is to define when the use of deadly force is righteous and when it is not, seeking to reach a non-lethal resolution among opposing parties once a combat proves decisive. Malory's concern for restraining factional violence may stem from the events of his own time,

---

[20] Vinaver, *The Works of Sir Thomas Malory*, p. 1335. Stephen H. A. Shepherd also quotes this statement in his edition of Malory, *Le Morte Darthur* (New York: W. W. Norton, 2004), p. 77 n. 6.

[21] Armstrong, *Gender and the Chivalric Community*, pp. 29–44.

[22] Robert L. Kelly, 'Royal Policy and Malory's Round Table', *Arthuriana* 14.1 (2004): 43–71 at p. 45. Kelly presents a thorough analysis of the language of the oath as it appears in the Winchester MS (pp. 51–53).

[23] Bonnie Wheeler, 'Romance and Parataxis and Malory: The Case of Sir Gawain's Reputation', in *Arthurian Literature XII*, ed. James P. Carley and Felicity Riddy (Cambridge: D. S. Brewer, 1993), pp. 109–32 at pp. 117–18.

[24] Kelly, 'Royal Policy', pp. 44–51.

namely, according to John Bellamy, the crisis of public order spanning the years 1450–1464.[25] Unfortunately, the oath still fails to deter knights from resorting to questionable means to pursue grievances. When Gawain and his brothers later attack Lamorak 'in a privy place', the secret nature of the attack shows a willingness to commit murder.

The second part of the Pentecost oath charges 'that no man take no batayles in a wrongefull quarell for no love ne for no worldis goodis' (3.120.23–24). Lancelot will find himself at variance with this clause, for it will conflict with his devotion to Queen Guinevere when he fights as her champion. In 'The Poisoned Apple' episode, he righteously defends her against a wrongful murder accusation in trial by combat, but he kills numerous knights in judicial duels and other combat in defending her against accusations of infidelity that are actually true. The oath does not and cannot replace the rule of law. It is too broad and much too vague to do so successfully. None of the clauses include any qualifications or speak of mitigating circumstances, and, thus, the code does little to address the conflicting loyalties that become one of the chief themes of Malory's later tales. As Laura Finke and Martin Shichtman argue, the oath is merely intended to control violence but not to eliminate it altogether: 'Arthur's Round Table coopts [sic] disruptive violence in an attempt to neutralize it, without ever entirely succeeding in banishing the random, impulsive, or chaotic elements that haunt the institutions of organised warfare'.[26] Arthur's knights can use fatal violence, but murder, secret or stealthy killing, is prohibited by law and by the oath. Those knights who resort to murder break the law and threaten the solidarity of the order.

For Gawain, his first quest will shape the rest of his career as a knight, as the queen charges Gawain from then on 'never to refuse mercy to hym that askith mercy' (3.108.35). Indeed, as Tracy points out, 'Malory endows Gawain with a sense of realization and remorse at his unchivalrous deed.'[27] Tracy also observes that Gawain is a manifestation of the cultural anxiety that Raluca L. Radulescu finds in Malory's work.[28] Moreover, he comes to embody the potential for vio-

---

[25] John Bellamy, *Crime and Public Order in England in the Later Middle Ages* (London and Toronto: Routledge and Kegan Paul, 1973), p. 9.

[26] Laurie A. Finke and Martin B. Shichtman, 'No Pain, No Gain: Violence as Symbolic Capital in Malory's *Morte d'Arthur*', *Arthuriana* 8.2 (1998): 115–34 at p. 126.

[27] Larissa Tracy, '"So He Smote of Hir Hede by Myssefortune": The Real Price of the Beheading Game in *SGGK* and Malory', in *Heads Will Roll: Decapitation in the Medieval and Early Modern Imagination*, ed. Tracy and Jeff Massey (Leiden: Brill, 2012), pp. 207–31 at p. 227. Raluca L. Radulescu, '"Oute of mesure": Violence and Knighthood in Malory's *Morte Darthur*', in *Re-Viewing* Le Morte Darthur, ed. K. S. Whetter and Raluca L. Radulescu (Cambridge: D. S. Brewer, 2005), pp. 119–31.

[28] Tracy, '"So He Smote of Hir Hede"', p. 227.

lent urges to overwhelm rational adherence to an oath or an ideal of behaviour. As events will prove, though, even Lancelot will be unable to pass the rest of his career without running afoul of the implications of the oath's mercy clause. Although Lancelot does not commit a clear act of murder, he does challenge the bounds of what is ethically acceptable in denying mercy to Mellyagaunt in order to silence him, showing the lengths he will go to hide his own betrayal of King Arthur. Despite Lancelot's breaking of the oath, Malory still attempts to treat him sympathetically.

Both Wheeler and K. S. Whetter advance the argument that Gawain's reputation as a murderer and destroyer of good knights is undeserved. Wheeler reacts to the statement in 'The Tale of Sir Gareth' that explains Gareth's shunning of Gawain, and, in the process, labels Gawain a murderer, saying that the text of the tale 'provides no proof of deviancy or vengeful character'.[29] She goes on to posit that 'Sir Gawain is the victim of reputation-robbing conspiracy perpetrated as a result of King Arthur's inattention and Sir Gareth's preference for Sir Lancelot. The narrator, who with the sole exception of this intrusion effaces himself from this tale, validates Sir Gawain's unworthiness without any demonstrated cause.'[30] Whetter seconds Wheeler's argument: 'Malory was no doubt influenced by the Prose *Tristan* in labeling Gawain a murderer in "Gareth," but it cannot be stressed enough that, within the "Tale of Gareth," there is in fact nothing to support this characterization.'[31] Concerning the text of 'The Tale of Sir Gareth' specifically, Wheeler and Whetter are, strictly speaking, correct, but the statement that Gawain 'was evir vengeable, and where he hated he wolde be avenged with murther' has implications beyond the tale and can be read in the larger context of the *Morte* (7.360.34–5). It looks back to Gawain's promise to avenge his father's death on Pellinore in 'The Tale of King Arthur', and it looks forward to the fulfilment of that promise and most emphatically to his role in killing Lamorak in 'The Book of Sir Tristram'. The reference to Gareth's shunning his brother here in 'The Tale of Gareth' ties closely to Gareth's reaction to Lamorak's death in the next section: 'And for cause that I undirstonde they be murtherars of good knyghtes I lefte there company, and wolde God I had bene besyde sir Gawayne whan that moste noble knyght sir Lamorake was slayne!' (10.699.5–9). Malory repeatedly refers to Gawain's murderous nature throughout the *Morte*, and, by repetition, he places the murder of Lamorak and the internal strife it precipitates as one of the central tragic acts that cause the dissolution of the Round Table. Malory clearly thinks of Gawain as a murderer, diminishing him while elevating

---

[29] Wheeler, 'Romance and Parataxis', p. 129.
[30] Ibid.
[31] K. S. Whetter, 'Characterization in Malory and Bonnie', *Arthuriana* 19.3 (2009): 123–35 at p. 127.

Lancelot. In favouring Lancelot, he expresses more affinity for Lancelot's motive of love for Guinevere than Gawain's motive of vengeance, drawing clear distinctions between the motives for killing – some are more acceptable to Malory than others.

The familial blood feud that Gawain and his brothers (except Gareth) pursue against King Pellinore and his son Sir Lamorak shows how a cycle of vengeance leads to murder. Lamorak's death aggravates the factionalism among Arthur's knights when King Arthur appears ineffectual in his efforts to prevent the killings. Furthermore, the killings of Queen Morgause, Pellinore and Lamorak are the critical actions from which the brothers' reputations as murderers arise. Gaheris begins the series of murders by the sons of Lott in 'The Book of Sir Trystram', beheading his mother as she and Lamorak lay in bed: 'So whan sir Gaherys sawe his tyme he cam to there beddis side all armed, wyth his swerde naked, and suddaynly he gate his modir by the heyre and strake of here hede' (10.612.9–11). As it is an ambush in the bed-chamber, the slaying meets the medieval definition of murder. From Gaheris' perspective, the slaying is a matter of family honour; it is shameful for their mother to sleep with the son of their father's enemy: '"... and thou to ly by oure modir is to muche shame foir us to suffir"' (10.612.25–26). Gaheris is sensitive to the potential for dishonour in this situation, forbearing to kill Lamorak at this time: '"... bycause thou arte naked I am ashamed to sle the!"' (10.612.32–33). However, his focus on shame does not equal sensitivity to law, and he and his brothers commit a shameful act in killing Lamorak by ambushing him in secret. When the death of the Queen of Orkney becomes known, Lancelot certainly believes that it is felonious, as he tells Arthur: '"Sir", seyde sir Launcelot, "here is a grete myschefff fallyn by fellony and by forecaste [treason], that your syster is thus shamfully islayne. And I dare say hit was wrought by treson, and I dare say also that ye shall lose that good knight sir Lamerok"' (10.613.13–17).[32] Lancelot's warning that Gawain and his brothers will attempt to kill Lamorak illustrates that public opinion now considers them capable of murder, and they are a threat to the king's peace. As a result, many knights turn against Gawain and, by extension, against Arthur when Lancelot breaks from the king, fracturing the fellowship and the institutional idea of justice.

At this point in 'The Book of Sir Trystram', the account of Pellinore's death surfaces again, and the questionable way in which Gawain and Gaheris kill Pellinore represents their first murder. Although Lamorak claims that Balyn le Saveage, not Pellinore, killed Lott, Gawain holds him responsible for his father's death (10.612.28–29). Revenge itself is not murder, yet it is not *why* but *how* Gawain and Gaheris slay Pellinore that may make it felonious. If, as Percival's mother attests, 'they slew hym nat manly, but by treson', then it becomes murder because

---

[32] Brackets appear in Vinaver's original text.

it implies that they resorted to treachery to carry out the killing (11.810.13). Her account of Pellinore's death is the only one that labels it 'treson', and, logically, she might be suspected of familial bias. Malory never directly explains how Gawain kills Pellinore, and with only Percival's mother's testimony as evidence, there is nothing else upon which to base a charge of murder. However, *publica fama* applies here. In the context of English legal tradition, *publica fama* exists when two or more reputable people testify that a suspect is widely believed to be guilty, or capable of being guilty, of a crime and can be used as probable cause to charge someone with a crime.[33] If others believe Pellinore's death to be treasonous as she does, then it would be possible to charge Gawain with murder. The method that Gawain and his brothers use in slaying Lamorak supports her belief that they are capable of felonious homicide.

Lamorak's death is a clear case of murder, and it stands as Gawain's clearest violation of the law. In this instance, they also compound unchivalric methods against Lamorak, when four brothers take on Lamorak alone. Sir Palomydes gives the fullest account of the murder:

> And that day that sir Lamorak was slayne he ded the moste dedis of armys that ever I saw knight do in my lyeff, and whan he was gyvyn the gre be my lorde kynge Arthure, sir Gawayne and his three bretherne, sir Aggrvayne, sir Gaherys and sir Mordred, sette upon sir Lamorak in a pryvy place, and there they slew his horse. And so they faught with hym on foote more than three owrys bothe before hym and behynde hym, and so sir Mordrede gaff hym his dethis wounde byhynde hym at his bakke, and all to-hewe hym: for one of his squyers tolde me that sawe hit. (10.699.17–27)

The violations of chivalry in this one attack are numerous. More than any other detail, the fact that they attack Lamorak 'in a privy place' makes it a secret killing and meets the primary definition of murder in English legal tradition. They outnumber him four to one, they attack him in a private place, slaying his horse (a tactic later confirmed as unchivalric by Mellyagaunt's use of it) and then they increase the dishonour by stabbing Lamorak in the back and mutilating his body. Their conduct shows that where family honour (or the perception of it) is concerned, Gawain and his brothers prioritise vengeance above chivalry and the law, and a significant number of respected knights now believe them to be murderers.

---

[33] Henry Ansgar Kelly, 'Inquisition, Public Fame and Confession: General Rules and English Practice', in *The Culture of Inquisition in Medieval England*, ed. Mary C. Flannery and Katie L. Walter (Cambridge: D. S. Brewer, 2013), p. 11. This essay is also cited in Larissa Tracy, 'Wounded Bodies: Kingship, National Identity, and Illegitimate Torture in the English Arthurian Tradition', *Arthurian Literature* 32 (2015): 1–29.

The murders of Pellinore and Lamorak are the most tragic in Malory's work for the way in which they critically damage the reputation of Gawain and hang as a persistent shame over the entire order. In 'The Book of Sir Trystram', Trystram tells Gaheris to his face that he, Gawain, Aggravain and Mordred are now known primarily for their murderous reputation: '"But hit is shame," seyde sir Trystram, "that sir Gawayne and ye be commyne of so grete blood, that ye four bretherne be so named as ye be: for ye be called the grettyste distroyers and murtherars of good knyghtes that is now in the realme of Ingelonde"' (10.691.25–29). The words 'ye be called' show that Trystram, a man who will himself be murdered, is only one among many of Arthur's knights who consider them murderers. By the time Percival's mother describes Pellinore's murder, Lancelot, Tristram, Palomides and Gareth have all expressed their belief that Gawain and his brothers are capable of these murders. The sheer number of times that various characters recount Lamorak's murder (around eleven times) demonstrates the infamy of the crime and builds a case against the brothers. Nevertheless, kinship to Arthur shields Gawain and his brothers from prosecution and underscores how Arthur's selective application of the law becomes a source of conflict among his knights.

Although critics have often cited familial rivalries as a source of instability in Arthur's kingdom, that factor alone does not account for the total cause for its destruction. The combination of Gawain's insatiable anger and the blood feud, along with Lancelot and Guinevere's affair, help push the volatility of the Arthurian order toward critical mass. As Kennedy points out, family feuds do not have to end in fatal violence, and Arthur, as uncle and king to Gawain, might have stopped the feud from escalating. In Kennedy's example, when Lancelot hears that his brethren have formed an envious enmity toward Sir Tristram, he forbids them from harming him upon pain of death (10.785.7–13).[34] King Arthur should have issued a similar order, and he actually does express his intent to prevent Lamorak's murder when Lancelot warns him: '"That. shall I lette", seyde kynge Arthur' (10.613.25). Of course, he then fails to give that order, and Lamorak dies at his nephews' hands. Since Gawain is willing to ignore the law, there could equally be some question whether Gawain, in his rage, would have respected his king's authority and obeyed. Arthur's position as king meets its greatest challenge in the need to curb the relentless passions of his nephews and best knights. His knights act in their own self-interests, and when Arthur tries to deal equitably, justly and legally with knights who break the law, he often has to act *against* his own self-interest. Arthur *would* be just if only his knights would follow his *laws*. The law defining murder already exists for Arthur's knights, and has for some time. They fail to obey, however, and he fails to prosecute them. In the case of Morgause's death, Arthur banishes Gaheris from court, but later

---

[34] Kennedy, *Knighthood in the* Morte d'Arthur, pp. 208–09.

he shows leniency and acts out of family pride in allowing him to return for the tournament at Surluse.³⁵ Gawain and his brothers are never formally charged or tried for Lamorak's murder. When it comes to his nephews, King Arthur fails to act as an impartial agent of the law, although he will attempt to be an impartial judge when Guinevere is tried for murder, to her great peril. His execution of justice is selective, and, therefore, it fails to be true justice.

In 'The Poisoned Apple' episode, murder and legal procedure become entwined; the death of Sir Patryse at the hands of Sir Pynell is a direct result of Gawain's feud with Lamorak. Malory invents the motive, which does not appear in his sources: 'thys sir Pyonell hated sir Gawayne bycause hys kynnesman sir Lamorakes dethe; and therefore, for pure envy and hate, sir Pyonell enpoysonde sertayn appylls for to empoysen sir Gawayne' (18.1049.2–5). Unlike his treatment of Lamorak's murder, recounted by various characters indirectly, Malory presents Patryse's death directly and explains the immediate reaction: 'Than every knyght lepe frome the bourde ashamed and araged for wratthe oute of hir wittis, for they wyst nat what to sey' (18.1049.13–15). The knights are speechless with rage and are offended by the cowardly nature of the murder, immediately believing that Guinevere is guilty. Poisoning as a means of murder was considered extremely dishonourable as it exceeds secret attack in its deviousness, affording the victim no opportunity for self-defence.³⁶ Adding to the tragic pathos of the moment, the murder claims an innocent victim in the form of Patryse, since Gawain was Pynell's intended target, and nearly claims Guinevere as another since she is accused of the crime, only narrowly escaping execution when she, too, is actually innocent. Malory clearly considers this murder most foul and also foul treason: 'For the custom was such at that tyme that all maner of [s]hamefull deth was called treson' (18.1050.2–3).³⁷ As Stuhmiller notes, Malory uses the term 'treason' to be roughly synonymous with premeditation, with 'first-degree murder of peers or superiors', with cowardice or with the sense of committing, or intending to commit, injury against the king.³⁸ By extension of the last sense, the prohibition of murder in the Pentecost oath makes these acts treason since those who commit murder are then disloyal to the king. The oath, as an article of continued service to King Arthur, ought to reinforce the law and provide an additional deterrent against murder. Not only have Arthur's knights defied his law but they have also resorted to a most shameful method. Furthermore, the label 'treason' highlights the ways in which Arthur's kingdom has begun to disintegrate along

---

³⁵ Bedwell, 'The Failure of Justice', pp. 11–12, 17.
³⁶ For more on the implications of poisoning, see the three essays by Thomas Gobbitt, Carmel Ferragud and Matthew Lubin in this collection.
³⁷ Brackets are in the text of Vinaver's edition.
³⁸ Stuhmiller, 'Iudicium Dei', p. 439.

factional lines. By inventing the motive for Patryse's murder, Malory blames the escalation of the Gawain-Lamorak feud and the resulting anger of Arthur's other knights as the cause. The accusation of Guinevere receives most of the focus, but Malory closes the incident by creating a reminder of the murder's true perpetrator that will be written in stone on Patryse's tomb, recorded for posterity: 'Here Lyeth sir Patryse of Irelonde, slayne by sir Pynell le Saveaige that enpoysynde appelis to have slayne sir Gawayne, and by myssefortune sir Patryse ete one of the applis, and than suddeynly he braste' (18.1059.27–31).[39] While Queen Guinevere's trial, Lancelot's defence of her and her acquittal are also recorded there, Malory emphasises Pynell's intent to kill Gawain, building the Gawain-Lamorak feud as a major theme of 'The Tale of Lancelot and Guinevere'. Mark Lambert points out how Malory brackets 'Lancelot and Guinevere' with references to the deadly feud: 'the poisoning in the first episode is connected with Gawain's killing of Sir Lamorak (18.1049.1–5), and in the final episode, we are reminded that Lamorak was *with treason* slain "by sir Gawayne and hys brethirn" (19.1149.34–35)'.[40] This places the feud – and Gawain's treasonous murders – in parallel with the treason of Lancelot and Guinevere. The treason of Gawain and that of Lancelot and Guinevere stand here in contrast; while Malory condemns Gawain's acts, he finds ways to mitigate those of Lancelot and the queen out of sympathy for their love.

The second judicial duel, Lancelot's combat with Mellyagaunt in 'Lancelot and Guinevere', illustrates how Lancelot, motivated by rage, violates the Pentecostal oath and commits murder. Of course, he is motivated by his love for and service to Queen Guinevere, which conflicts with his loyalty to Arthur. In contrast to the occasions when Lancelot seems to hold his emotions in check, here Lancelot arrives to deal with Mellyagaunt already 'wood wrothe oute of mesure' (19.1128.19). Notably, Malory calls Lancelot's anger both 'wood', that is, insane, and 'oute of mesure', excessive in nature. That he intends lethal revenge against Mellyagaunt becomes clear when Lancelot tells Guinevere, '"And there ys nother kynge, quene ne knyght that beryth the lyffe, excepte my Lorde kynge Arthur and you, madame, that shulde lette me but I shulde make sir Mellyagaunte harte full colde or ever I departed from hense"' (19.1129.14–17). Before his arrival, Guinevere made peace with Mellyagaunt, and Lancelot admits that she is one of the few agents who can act as a mitigating factor against his anger. However, the matter is far from resolved for Lancelot, as John Michael Walsh observes: 'It is apparent that he is still not reconciled, as is further shown by a remark he shortly afterwards makes to Sir Lavayne, who has followed him to Mellyaguant's castle:

---

[39] The statement appears in all capitals in Vinaver's text.
[40] Mark Lambert, *Malory: Style and Vision in 'Le Morte Darthur'* (New Haven: Yale University Press, 1975), pp. 142–43.

"lat this passe, and ryghte hit another tyme and we may'" (19.1130.17–18).[41] Within the structure of Arthurian society, Guinevere cannot act as her own champion, and, instead, the oath suggests that Lancelot *must* act in her defence. More importantly, her husband Arthur cannot act as her champion because, as king, he must be an impartial judge. Once Mellyagaunt makes his accusation of treason against Guinevere, she becomes the factor that moves Lancelot to kill, even (paradoxically) in violation of his Pentecost oath, if not in violation of the law. If his slaying of Mellyagaunt is not murder, it is only because it is done openly, not in secret, and because Mellyagaunt agrees to the provisions of the duel that lead to his death. At this point, Lancelot's disloyalty to the king equals that of Gawain, but Malory continues to excuse Lancelot's deeds out of preference, accepting what he admires while trying to minimise Lancelot's transgressions.

When Lancelot defeats Mellyagaunt in trial by combat, Mellyagaunt yields and asks for mercy, which he is aware Lancelot has to grant according to the oath. Lancelot finds himself in a dilemma, for while he is aware of the obligation to grant mercy, he still desires revenge: 'for he had lever that all the goode in the worlde that he might be revenged upon hym' (19.1138.27–29). The Pentecost oath should dictate what Lancelot does: 'mercy should be granted immediately'.[42] The oath does not appear to be foremost in Lancelot's thinking and, instead, as in most matters, he looks to the queen for his cue: 'And anone the quene wagged hir hede uppon sir Launcelot as ho seyth "sle hym". And full well knew sir Launcelot by her sygnys that she wolde have hym dede' (19.1138.31–1139.3). In pushing Lancelot toward the act, she, too, violates the oath and the law that her husband sets. As Armstrong points out,

> Lancelot is here caught between two articles of the Pentecostal Oath: if he grants mercy, he displeases – and more important, perhaps harms the reputation of – the lady to whom he has attempted to render 'soccour'; if he obeys the request of his lady and slays his opponent, he has disobeyed the mercy clause. Unable to decide which guideline to follow, Lancelot chooses to disobey both articles. He has run out of options.[43]

Despite Lancelot's somewhat absurd provisions for continuing the combat, clearly Mellyagaunt will not survive. Lancelot's actions here put him *twice* in

---

[41] John Michael Walsh, 'Malory's "Very Mater of La Cheualer du Charyot": Characterization and Structure', in *Studies in Malory*, ed. James W. Spisak (Kalamazoo, MI: Medieval Institute Publications, 1985), pp. 199–226 at p. 208. Walsh quotes Malory from James W. Spisak and William Matthews, eds., *Caxton's Malory: A New Edition of Sir Thomas Malory's* Le Morte Darthur *Based on the Pierpont Morgan Copy of William Caxton's Edition of 1485*, 2 vols (Berkeley: University of California, 1983).

[42] Armstrong, *Gender and the Chivalric Community*, p. 186.

[43] Ibid., p. 32.

violation of the Pentecost oath, for not only does he not grant mercy when asked, but he also fights in a wrongful quarrel. Mellyagaunt's accusation that Guinevere has been adulterous with one of her ten wounded knights is incorrect in its letter, though not its spirit.[44] Lancelot is motivated to violate a major article of the oath not only by his anger at Mellyagaunt but also by the desperate need to eliminate someone who has come too close to the truth about their affair.

Furthermore, Armstrong argues that 'the resolution is not celebrated by the community as was the case with the trial of "The Poisoned Apple"'.[45] The community may already suspect the affair between Lancelot and Guinevere, and so fails to celebrate his victory. As early as 'The Book of Sir Launcelot', characters refer to rumours of the relationship and in 'The Death of Arthur', Arthur himself is said to have 'a demyng of hit' (20.1163.22). Since the speculation seems common, witnesses to the duel might fail to applaud the outcome because they acknowledge that, while Mellyagaunt's charge is not technically correct in this instance, there is truth in the accusation of infidelity.[46] Still, while there is no celebration, neither is Lancelot condemned for Mellyagaunt's death in the same way that Gawain is rebuked for killing the lady on that early quest (when the oath had not yet been established), nor is there the same kind of talk that plagues Gawain and his brothers after the death of Lamorak. The failure to condemn Lancelot's lack of mercy may stem from the realisation that justice equates to whatever can be defended by Lancelot in trial by combat.

Tellingly, Lancelot does not earn the title of 'murderer' for killing Mellyagaunt. His reputation as Malory's paragon of Arthurian chivalry, and the fact that Mellyagaunt is a contemptible coward, may be the only elements that save him. Lynch explains: 'Lancelot's amazing resilience shows how a "name", once gained, strongly resists alteration in the eyes of others. ... One can either see Malory as inconsistent in characterization here, or, preferably as consistent in his own way in maintaining his hero's reputation.'[47] It may be that Malory sympathises more with what Lancelot does out of love and devotion to Guinevere – since the 'Knight of the Cart' episode opens with his attempt to define 'trew' love – than he does with knights such as Gawain, who kill out of anger or vengeance. Walsh argues that the outcome of 'The Knight of the Cart' connects to the following episode of 'The Healing of Sir Urry'. Lancelot's reaction to his ability to miraculously heal Sir Urry, weeping like a beaten child, shows that he has internalised the shame of having killed Mellygaunt, an abuse of his martial

---

[44] Ibid., pp. 185–87.
[45] Ibid., p. 187.
[46] See: Stuhmiller, 'Iudicium Dei', p. 450 about how Lancelot reshapes the charge against Guinevere.
[47] Lynch, *Malory's Book of Arms*, p. 6.

skill.⁴⁸ 'The Healing of Sir Urry' shows that Lancelot does not lose his status as the 'beste knight of the worlde' (19.1145.19–20); according to Lynch, '[T]he prize of great prowess is the ability to take and defend every action according to the dominant public modes'.⁴⁹ However, the moral dubiousness of his motive and his consequent inner shame mark a deepened sense of his fallibility. As Walsh astutely observes: 'Lancelot's voluntary disarming is Malory's own invention. He gives us a vivid indication of the intensity of the lovers' desire for vengeance by making Lancelot go to such spectacular lengths to secure it. We realize that what we have witnessed is no better than a kind of legalized murder.'⁵⁰ Stuhmiller asserts that 'a homicide is classifiable as "murder" … if it is premeditated'.⁵¹ Just as Guinevere in this case is technically innocent of the charge against her, Lancelot is only technically innocent of murder if premeditation and motive are less relevant in medieval English law.⁵²

Stuhmiller asserts that the deficiencies of judicial combat and the resultant violence do not cause the collapse of Arthurian society: 'Quite the opposite, in fact: the increasing ineffectiveness of the *duellum* is only a sign of societal degradation, not a cause of it. Indeed, Malory celebrates violence, as long as it is used by the right people, in the right ways.'⁵³ King Arthur himself fails to enforce the law or the Pentecost oath with his nephews because of family ties, or, with Lancelot, because Lancelot helps him consolidate his kingdom. By the time of Lancelot's trial with Mellyagaunt, the vengeful murder and judicial process have become muddled. Regarding the last tale, Radulescu observes, 'as passions are expressed more openly than ever before, action needs to be taken, and temperance, although advocated at every stage, is no longer an option.'⁵⁴ Even the quest for the fair application of law becomes motivated by hatred and anger, as Malory openly explains that Agravain and Mordred are motivated greatly by their envy and hatred for Lancelot in their insistence that Arthur do something about the Lancelot/Guinevere affair: 'For thys Sir Aggravayne and Sir Mordred had ever a prevy hate unto the quene, dame Gwenyver, and to Sir Lancelot' (20.1161.11–13). It is the right thing to do perhaps, but they do it for the wrong reasons. Their attempt to trap Lancelot in the queen's chamber qualifies as attempted murder since they take with them twelve knights in an

---

⁴⁸ Walsh, 'Malory's "Very Mater"', p. 219.
⁴⁹ Lynch, *Malory's Book of Arms*, p. 95.
⁵⁰ Walsh, 'Malory's "Very Mater"', p. 213.
⁵¹ Stuhmiller, 'Iudicium Dei', p. 439.
⁵² In a dissenting opinion, J. M. Kaye argues that premeditation probably did not become a factor in defining murder in England until the sixteenth century. See: 'The Early History of Murder and Manslaughter, Part I', *Law Quarterly Review* 83 (1967): 365–95.
⁵³ Stuhmiller, '*Judicium Dei*', p. 462.
⁵⁴ Radulescu, '"Oute of mesure"', p. 130.

ambush, striking first even after they assent to taking him alive: 'we shall save thy lyff untyll thou com to Kynge Arthur' (20.1167.16–17).[55] From that point on, the cycle of lethal violence becomes unstoppable. Lancelot's accidental killing of Gareth and Gaheris finishes any chance for the revival of the order. Interestingly, Kenneth Hodges claims that Lancelot kills Gareth and Gaheris in a state of 'moral and emotional blindness', which does not excuse his failure to recognise them, and he considers their deaths murders.[56] Concerning their death, Stuhmiller agrees that Gareth and Gaheris 'did die "shamefully" at his hands because they were unarmed bystanders when they were cut down during the queen's rescue. Technically, therefore, he is guilty by Arthurian law of murder and treason.'[57] According to these arguments, Lancelot commits three murders, those of Mellyagaunt, Gareth and Gaheris; however, Lancelot defends himself against Gawain's charges by claiming that it was accidental: '"And alas, that ever I was so unhappy", seyde sir Launcelot, "that I had nat seyne sir Gareth and sir Gaherys!"' (20.1189.20–21). His shame and contrition mirror that of Gawain killing the maiden earlier. In using the word 'unhappy', meaning 'unlucky' in fifteenth-century English, Lancelot maintains that their deaths are the result of misfortune, and, therefore, are excusable. Gawain, of course, does not forgive him, though, and he goads King Arthur into supporting his duel against him. Nevertheless, when Gawain predictably insists upon revenge, many knights side with Lancelot because they still hold the murder of Lamorak against Gawain, and the rifts in the Round Table are then irreparable forever after.

Looking at the strict letter of law, both Gawain and Lancelot are clearly guilty of unrighteous, unsanctioned killings. Gawain's repeated offences are much more heinous in their execution and frequency, at least in Malory's eyes. However, Lancelot's misdeeds are much more problematic since Malory tries to treat him sympathetically while only implicitly indicating his guilt as traitor to the king. In the end, the Pentecost oath can neither ensure that Arthur's knights will obey the law, nor ensure that the authorities (Arthur and his knights) will effectively enforce it since they stand to lose too much if the law is applied objectively and without exception. In Malory's own case, no extant records show that he was ever brought to trial for the charge of attempted murder – perhaps in an effort by his accusers to keep him incarcerated – and, as a result, he was apparently denied

---

[55] D. Thomas Hanks argues that Malory alters his sources to make Sir Collgrevaunce, one of Mordred and Aggravaine's cohorts, the aggressor in the incident in 'Malory, the Mort[e]s, and the Confrontation in Guinevere's Chamber', in *Sir Thomas Malory: Views and Re-Views*, ed. D. Thomas Hanks (New York: AMS Press, 1992), pp. 78–89 at pp. 82–83.

[56] Kenneth Hodges, *Forging Chivalric Communities in Malory's* Le Morte Darthur (New York: Palgrave Macmillan, 2005), p. 149.

[57] Stuhmiller, 'Iudicium Dei', p. 450.

the opportunity to defend himself.[58] In the *Morte*, Malory might be arguing for an adherence to and fair application of the law, or at least lamenting the absence of it, since both in his narrative, and his life, a fair legal determination of guilt does not always happen.

Malory constructs an Arthurian society in which legally defined guilt and innocence have less bearing on moral and ethical questions. Lambert builds upon Derek Brewer's observation that, for Malory, shame takes precedence over guilt, and his Arthurian society measures moral culpability in the dimensions of a shame-honour opposition rather than one of guilt-innocence.[59] The shame-honour culture can be traced back to Old French literature, the tradition from which Malory draws much of his source material. According to F. R. P. Akehurst, these Old French works, such as Chrétien de Troyes' *Chevalier de la charrete*, establish that a knight must seek honour and defend himself against shame, both of which are dependent upon what people say about him. What he believes about himself is less important in such a culture.[60] Malory's narrative reflects a shame-honour culture in which, up to this point, knights like Lancelot and Gawain have been competing to establish honour; now they must also defend themselves against what people say of them. Hodges cites the support of C. David Benson, who writes: 'Gawain's vengeance against Lancelot, though often condemned by modern commentators as wicked and obsessive, is equally demanded by honour'.[61] The real trial of Lancelot and Gawain occurs in their final conflict during which their most serious crimes against their Round Table peers are tragically disputed. Sir Gawain begins by recounting Sir Lancelot's most heinous act: '"what cause haddist thou to sle my good brother sir Gareth that loved the more than me and all my kynne?"' (20.1189.12–13). When Lancelot counters by reminding Gawain of his shameful killing of Lamorak, Gawain's reply exposes his violent nature:

'Well, well, sir Launcelot,' seyde sir Gawayne, 'sytthyn thou enbraydyst me of sir Lamorak, wyte thou well I shall never leve the tyll I have the at suche avayle that thou shalt not escape my hondis'.

'I truste you well inowgh,' seyde sir Launcelot. 'And ye may gete me, I gett but lytyll mercy'. (20.1190.11–16)

---

[58] P. J. C. Field, *The Life and Times of Sir Thomas Malory* (Cambridge: D. S. Brewer, 1993), pp. 99–110.

[59] Lambert, *Malory: Style and Vision*, pp. 176–94.

[60] F. R. P. Akehurst, 'Good Name, Reputation, and Notoriety in French Customary Law', in *'Fama': The Politics of Talk and Reputation in Medieval Europe*, ed. Thelma Fenster and Daniel Lord Smail (Ithaca: Cornell University Press, 2003), pp. 75–94 at pp. 77–79.

[61] C. David Benson, 'The Ending of the *Morte Darthur*', in *A Companion to Malory*, ed. Elizabeth Archibald and A. S. G. Edwards (Cambridge: D. S. Brewer, 1996), pp. 221–38 at p. 232.

Lancelot's charge that he expects little mercy from Gawain, which is somewhat hypocritical considering the former's denial of mercy for Mellyagaunt, recalls the failure of Gawain's first quest, brings his troubled career full circle and renews his name of murderer. When, in their fight at Benwick, Gawain calls Lancelot a traitor for killing his brothers, the Breton knight has to respond to Gawain's words, though he is not eager to do so: "'I am ryght hevy at sir Gawaynes wordys, for now he chargith me with a grete charge. And therefore I wote as well as ye I muste nedys deffende me, other ellis to be recreaunte'" (20.1215.22–25). They both stand here, again accused of murder, and their protracted battle may be seen as their final trial by combat. The outcome of the trial will be neither satisfying nor necessarily just. In the end, Malory rejects formal legal proceedings in favour of something that much more resembles the duels of chivalry, which he reveals are neither fair nor decisive. While Malory seems to argue that both knights must be held accountable for their crimes, he is reluctant to show them as guilty and worthy of punishment in sympathetic recognition of their pursuit of honour.

When earthly justice proves inadequate either to prosecute or to punish the crimes of these knights, Malory formulates a pragmatic, and, perhaps, overly convenient, form of spiritual redemption for them. After his death, Gawain appears by God's 'speciall grace' with the ladies for whom he did 'ryghteous quarrels' to warn Arthur, which suggests that God has granted him salvation (21.1234.1–19). Lancelot's salvation is more explicit when his death is heralded by the Bishop of Canterbury's dream, in which he sees 'angellys heve up syr Launcelot unto heven' (21.1258.9). Still, the repentance that leads to possible redemption is only indirectly related to their violations of the oath. On his death bed, Gawain regrets and repents his feud with Lancelot in a letter to him, indicting himself for his motivations – the urge for revenge which leads to all his deadly feuds – but not the specific act of killing Pellinore and Lamorak (21.1231.8–20). On the grave of King Arthur and Queen Guinevere, the monk Lancelot repents to his brother monks "'my defaute and myn orgule and my pryde'" (the circumstantial motivation for killing Mellyagaunt) but he does not repent the killing itself (21.1256.29–38). Although this late repentance can neither undo the harm done nor revive the order from what little is left after Mordred's treachery, to Malory's mind, this repentance fits with his tendency to forgive characters with whom he is sympathetic. If King Arthur cannot be made an impartial judge of his favourite knights, Malory mirrors that leniency in his own treatment of them.

Instead of being ruled by the oath and the letter of the law, the knights of Malory's Arthurian order are governed, judged and 'sentenced' through a system tacitly agreed upon among them. They are tried for murder, not by a jury trial but instead by a series of combats, which not only prove prowess but also bring forth the reputation – the identity – of killers for communal consideration and response. When Lancelot and Gawain exchange accusations and insults of one another's honour, it is both prosecution and verdict for their past crimes. Their punishment is to make former friends into mortal enemies, a final misuse of their prowess, and then to repent their sins to God and their peers. If it seems illogical, unsatisfying and tragically ineffective, it is because Malory creates a narrative of the imagined past of English chivalry dependent on ritualised violence; in doing so, he must balance what he admires with what he laments. In describing a system in which men must often prove their familial loyalty, their love and their self-worth by killing, his Arthuriad proves that the heroic cannot be had without the tragic.

CHAPTER 10

Poisoning as a Means of State Assassination in Early Modern Venice

Matthew Lubin

There was a king reigned in the East
There, when kings will sit to feast,
They get their fill before they think.
With poisoned meat and poisoned drink.
He gathered all that springs to birth
From the many-venomed earth;
First a little, thence to more,
He sampled all her killing store;
And easy, smiling, seasoned sound,
Sate the king when healths went round.
They put arsenic in his meat.
And stared aghast to watch him eat;
They poured strychnine in his cup
And shook to see him drink it up:
They shook, they stared as white's their shirt:
Them it was their poison hurt.
– I tell the tale that I heard told.
Mithridates, he died old.
    – A. E. Housman, 'Terence, this is stupid stuff', from
          A Shropshire Lad (1896)

POISONING IS NOT A SUBJECT that medieval and early modern legists were reluctant to discuss, and it is mentioned at length in so authoritative a source as the Justinianic *Digest*, in Chapter 48.8, *Ad legem Corneliam de sicariis et veneficiis* [*Pertaining to Sulla's Law Concerning Murderers and Poisoners*]. In medieval Venice, an emporium for herbs and spices for far-flung realms, it was a matter of ethics (not unlike the Hippocratic Oath) that learned herbalists would not administer poisons for any reason. In this period, Venice's *speziari*, those responsible for mixing herbs and spices in salutary ways to help palliate human ailments, had regulations drawn up for them, just as other guildsmen did. The earliest one that survives is a Capitulary (1268), with separate sections for physicians and for pharmacists, by the *Giustizieri Vecchi*.¹ Regulation VIII for pharmacists read, 'Item, non dabo neque dari faciam neque docebo aliquem aliquam medicinam venenosam seu abortivam dare' [In addition, I shall not give, nor cause to be given, nor shall I instruct someone to give someone any poisonous or abortifacient compound].² Specific political events sometimes dictated legislation on the subject. The Barbo poisoning of 1410, in which a Tatar slave girl was thought to have poisoned her master with arsenic,³ led to a law dated 22 June 1410 outlawing the sale of eight toxic substances: napellum, opium, cantharides, 'worms of Caffa',⁴ the arsenic 'curinum', arsenic sublimate, silver sublimate and red arsenic by all but two tightly-overseen pharmacies in Venice, that of *Due Rughe* [Two Wrinkles] and that of San Giuliano on the Rialto.⁵ Still, the documentation of state-sanctioned murders that the Republic of Venice not only presided over, but wrote down on parchment, set Venice apart from other Italian city-states for its relative openness, and its volume, from the fourteenth to the eighteenth centuries.

Between the alleged poisoning of Doge Pietro Gradenigo in 1311 and the end of the Venetian Republic in 1797, murder by poisoning was carried out for social, political and economic reasons. Lawyers disagreed about whether to regard killing with poison as especially heinous or not. From 1500 forward, a major subset of Venetian juristic literature concerned the use of telling signs and evidence, *indicia*; however, the examples used in this literature were old ones repeated endlessly, such as the example of Titius and the slave of Alexander that concerned murder with a sword and not poison. The eighteenth century – in Europe, more generally, and in Venice, in particular – saw a transition to the inclusion of *venenum* in its discussions of *indicia* even as writers continued to point out how difficult it was to prove. In Rome, Paolo Zacchia (1584–1659), a physician to popes Innocent X and Alexander VII, penned *Quaestiones Medico-Legales* [*Medico-Legal Questions*] (1657) in which he applied the most authoritative medical knowledge at his disposal to troublesome questions about what should be regarded as poisoning, and whether one's intention in administering a toxic substance, or the location where it was done, mattered. In *Liber II, Titulum*

---

[1] Judges who administered laws dealing with the guilds, or *arti*, in Venice. Their constitution into a *collegio*, however, is associated with the year 1565 and the efforts of Giorgio Melichio, a pharmacist at the Struzzo d'Oro pharmacy (see below).

[2] Renato Vecchiato, *Gli speziali a Venezia: Pagine di Storia* (Venice: Mazzanti Libri, 2013), p. 34. All English translations are mine.

[3] Dennis Romano, *Housecraft and Statecraft* (Baltimore: Johns Hopkins University Press, 1996), p. 52.

[4] I have not been able to find any further information about this substance. The law is in the Frari state archive of Venice, series *Compilazione leggi, busta 427*.

[5] Paolo Preto, *I Servizi Segreti di Venezia*, 2nd edn (Bologna: Il Mulino, 2004), p. 366.

II, of this work, for example, which is devoted strictly to the moral and ethical problems that attend poisoning, Zacchia considers whether any substance generated by the human body can be considered a poison or not.[6] However, Zacchia's questions deal fundamentally with murders committed by individuals, and not those organised by a branch of a government and carried out for reasons of ostensible public interest rather than private benefit or private revenge.

Venetian jurists between the Middle Ages and the end of the Republic did not necessarily distinguish between private and public cases of murder in the way that modern students of the law do. When the Venetian ruling council, the Council of Ten – founded in response to a conspiracy to overthrow the government in 1310 – took upon itself to kill an enemy of the state, it may have kept in mind the rather cheery observation of Gasparo Contarini that 'medicus arte medicinae, quae rationalis est potential, potest et pharmacum, et venenum miscere' [a doctor of medical art, whose ability is based upon reason, can mix toxins and poison].[7] In the ruthlessness of his advice, the Florentine Machiavelli shared something of the same outlook as the Venetian Council of Ten in his *De Principatibus* [*The Prince*], though it may be revealing that his *l'Arte della Guerra* [*The Art of War*], despite extreme attention to detail in forging armies into fighting machines, makes no mention of the use of poison as a weapon of war.

State assassinations with poison, many of which were documented and made public long after the end of the Venetian Republic in 1797, testify to the government's frequent willingness to resort to this practice when the survival of the Republic was deemed to be at stake, especially in times of war, primarily against the Ottomans. Consideration of the gravity of these 'government-sanctioned murders' depends, in part, on the legal status of poisoning, variously referred to in the texts as *venenum*, *veneficium* and *toxicatio*. A basic insight that holds true far beyond Venice is the continued association of poisoning in the Middle Ages and early modern period with heresy, treason, diabolical service and other evils of the gravest kind. Citing the Justinianic *Digest*, Zacchia justified his lengthy treatment of poisoning in *Quaestiones Medico-Legales*, remarking that 'non inutiliter ergo pro ipsis Iurisconsultis ad hoc de venenis argumentum pertractandum accedemus; praecipue quia apud illos venenandi crimen gravissimum delictum existimatur, ut vere est, et gravius homicidio ... immo venenantes ut proditores habent' [I have agreed, therefore, to some purpose, to prolong this discussion on poisons, for the sake of these juriconsults; especially since among them, the

---

[6] Paolo Zacchia, *Quaestiones Medico-Legales* (Avignon, 1657), pp. 57–88.
[7] *Ad Paulum III de potestate pontificis duae epistolae* (Florence: s.n., 1558), p. 26. It is a satisfying irony that Contarini was suspected of being poisoned himself, on the order of Pope Paul III no less. Enrico Solmi, 'La fuga di Bernardino Ochino', *Bollettino senese di storia patria* 15 (1908): 77.

crime of poisoning is adjudged the most serious of crimes, as in truth it is, and more serious than homicide ... indeed, poisoners are held to be traitors].[8] This association was made in a wide variety of European societies from Antiquity, yet some places came to be more heavily associated with knowledge of poisoning, as well as the use of antidotes, than others. Venice was one of these places, most particularly in the sixteenth and seventeenth centuries, when literary treatments such as John Webster's *White Devil* and *Duchess of Malfi*, and Shakespeare's *Othello*, associated poison and treachery with villainous Italians. In his 1614 series of sermons, *The Divells Blanket*, Thomas Adams intoned: '[It] is observed, that there are sinnes adherent to Nationes, proper, peculiar, genuine, as their flesh cleaveth to their bones ... If we should gather *Sinnes* to their particular Centers, wee would appoint ... Poysoning to *Italie*'.[9]

Poisoning was undertaken in every part of Eurasia in the medieval period, and this included government elimination of those deemed enemies of the state. It should be pointed out that Venice's rivals and enemies used poison against it more than once in the medieval centuries, so that its poisoning activities did not take place in a one-sided vacuum: a story that, in 1172, the Byzantines had poisoned the wine and water of Venetian forces on Chios was enshrined in the state historical record by Marc'Antonio Sabellico, Venice's historiographer.[10] The Carrara lordlings in Padua had (or Venetian popular opinion *thought* that they had) deliberately poisoned the wells of Venetian subjects in their struggle with the republic; even in 1478, rumours flew that a certain friar, at the behest of King Ferdinand I of Naples, had come to Venetian territory to poison wells.[11] Venice may have been unique among the Italian city-states in terms of the volume of documents it collected on the practice of poison, which were first published by Vladimir Lamansky in his *Secrets d'État de Venise* [*State Secrets of Venice*] (1884). Lamansky's volume indicates that the Council of Ten was charged with maintaining the regime in power against its enemies, both external and internal, and

---

[8] Paolo Zacchia, *Quaestiones Medico-Legales, Editio Secunda Veneta* (Venice: Simone Occhi, 1751), Liber II, Titulus II, p. 127. In the wake of the 1531 Roose poisoning case, King Henry VIII of England pushed the House of Lords to change the status of poisoning in English law from that of a felony to treason. See: Miranda Wilson, *Poison's Dark Works in Renaissance England* (Lanham, MD: Bucknell University Press, 2014), p. xvii.

[9] Wilson, *Poison's Dark Works*, p. xxxi. Italian historiography on poisoning has distinguished among the regions and city-states of Italy, and some, such as Alessandro Pastore and Paolo Preto, who refers to '*Italia e Venezia, le patrie dei veleni*' (*I Servizi Segreti*, p. 361), have stressed Venice's particularly lugubrious reputation on this subject.

[10] Donald M. Nicol, *Byzantium and Venice: A Study in Diplomatic and Cultural Relations* (Cambridge: Cambridge University Press, 1992), p. 99.

[11] Preto, *Servizi Segreti*, p. 315.

committing themselves (in writing) to the poisoning of perceived enemies of the state.[12]

In the 130 years since Lamansky's book was published, research has continued on Venice's use of state assassinations, above all, though far from exclusively, in the work of Paolo Preto of the University of Padua.[13] A geographical breakdown of Lamansky's and Preto's cases of poisoning shows a statistical predominance of the overseas territories, including Dalmatia and Albania, suggesting that such killing appears to have been most favoured in war against the Ottomans, whose influence abutted that of Venice. In recent decades, increased attention has been paid to the *Stato da Mar* (the Venetian overseas territories in the central and eastern Mediterranean), forming a picture of societies in which local rulers, whose realms extended between Ottoman lands and those of either Venice or other Christian states, including Matthias Corvinus of Hungary, Đurađ Branković of Serbia and Skanderbeg in Albania, played off the larger powers against each other or (in the case of Skanderbeg) changed sides themselves. These powers tended to pursue their own local interests while barely heeding, or even acknowledging, a 'bigger picture' in diplomacy. The language employed in some of the Venetian documents suggests that Balkan Christians may have taken the initiative to petition the Council of Ten to remove politically-inconvenient rebels, and other undesirables, by means of poison. The question is whether these were murders or whether they were state assassinations committed with an understanding of legal invulnerability. The legal categories that jurists in the Veneto would have understood were deeply embedded with moral and theological concepts, and the *Realpolitik,* sometimes associated with the political amorality and immorality of Machiavelli and the Jesuits, made little impression on the juristic language of Venice and its *Stato da Mar*, which was conservative and wedded to *auctoritates*.[14] The Council of Ten made no sustained effort in the documents to justify the morality of these poisonings. Perhaps there was a wider gap between theory and practice in medieval and early modern Venice, as willingness to resort to poison far outstripped an inclination to justify such extreme measures in legal or theological terms.

Interest in diplomatic history as a systematically pursued subject has waned, and the exploration into the circumstances of state-sanctioned poison has been co-opted largely by popular, rather than academic, historians. And yet there are innumerable connections to be made between poisoning and other forms of

---

[12] Vladimir Lamansky, *Secrets d'État de Venise* (St Petersburg, Russia: Imperial Press, 1884).

[13] Preto, *Servizi Segreti*, esp. pp. 247–56 and pp. 329–53.

[14] For an understanding of the authorities that governed Venetian legal thinking far past the Middle Ages, see: Lamberto Pansolli, *La gerarchia delle fonti di diritto nella legislazione medievale veneziana* (Milan: Giuffrè, 1970).

secret activities, such as cryptographic writing in diplomatic correspondence. This connection appears to have been made, even if only unconsciously, in the mind of Giovanni Battista della Porta, one of the most accomplished of sixteenth-century chemists, who, in addition to his *Magiae naturalis* [*Natural Magic*] (1558), wrote a work on secret forms of writing titled *De Furtivis Literarum Notis* [*On Hidden Sigla for Writing*] (1563). Poisoning was not a skill that was openly taught, but what was done *furtive* 'in secret' was another matter.

Definitions of murder that were current in early modern Venice are somewhat different from those used now. The principal early modern legal handbooks used in Venice that discuss poisoning connect it less often with *homicidium*, killing another person, than with *maleficium*, the working of evil on someone, often with a supernatural implication. These handbooks stress the connections between poisoning, magic and, very often, wicked women and their wiles.[15] The Justinianic *Digest*, Chapter 50, describes *veneficium* as a synonym of the Greek word *pharmakon*, a word that could mean both poison and a remedy for poison – even a magic spell: 'Cum id quod nos "venenum" appellemus, Graeci "farmakon" dicunt, apud illos quoque tam medicamenta quam quae nocent, hoc nomine continentur' [Since that which we call 'venenum', the Greeks call 'farmakon', among them also are embraced in this name both medicinal substances, and ones that wreak harm].[16] In the first century CE, Valerius Maximus had already associated the crime *veneficium* (with all its social valences) with wicked wives:[17]

> Veneficii quaestio, et moribus et legibus Romanis ignota, complurium matronarum patefacto scelere orta est. Quae, cum viros suos clandestinis insidiis veneno perimerent, unius ancillae indicio protractae, pars capitalis iudicio damnatae centum et septuaginta numerum expleverunt.[18]
>
> [The investigation of poisoning, a crime unknown to Roman laws and Roman morals, has begun as it emerged through the rascality of many matrons, who, when they slew their husbands, by secret devices, were, by the evidence of a

---

[15] For further connections between women and poisoning, see, in this volume: Thomas Gobbitt, 'Poisoning, Killing and Murder in the *Edictus Rothari*' and Carmel Ferragud, 'A Multiple Poisoning in the City of Valencia: Sanxo Calbó's Crime (1442)'.

[16] *Digesta* 50.16.236. This section of the *Digest* is drawn from Gaius' first-century commentary on the Twelve Tables, an ancient and authoritative source for Roman law only codified long after it was alleged to have been formed: http://droitromain.upmf-grenoble.fr/Corpus/d-50.htm (accessed 3 July 2015).

[17] Valerius Maximus, *Dicta et Facta Memorabilia*, 6.3.8, as quoted in Giunio Rizzelli, 'Note sul *veneficium*', *Mulier. Algunas Historias de derecho romano*, ed. Rosaria Lopez and Jose Bravo Bosch (Madrid: Dinkman, 2013), pp. 297–314.

[18] Maximus, *Dicta*, 2.5.3.

single servant girl, condemned to capital punishment, and one hundred and seventy were executed].

The endurance of legal traditions and concepts from ancient Rome helps clarify the knowledge of venom and its application. In the Middle Ages and Renaissance, epochs prone to thinking in terms of hierarchies of crime, of sin and of contrasting binaries among virtues and vices – each virtue had its opposite: industry contrasted with sloth, chastity with lust, sobriety with intemperance – just as white magic had its dark opposite, so early modern herbalism and pharmacopoeists enjoyed both a happy reputation and an inherently suspect one. People feared that venom was likely to be abused by malignant practitioners who could access it and apply it in the course of their daily activities.

Venice's political subordination to the Byzantine empire, from its founding to about the year 1000, and the cultural and theological influences that Byzantium exercised upon Venice meant that the Dioscoridean tradition of *materia medica* was transmitted to Venice by way of the Greek-speaking lands. In this famous work, generally known to early modern Europe as *De Materia Medica*, Dioscorides describes both the curative and the noxious properties of several herbs from many parts of Europe, as well as a few from Africa and southwest Asia, asserting that the Pontic region that encompassed the area surrounding the Black Sea was especially rich in medicinal herbs.[19]

Dioscorides' work was published repeatedly in early modern Venice,[20] and it was the object of learned commentary by botanists all over Europe including Fuchs, Gesner and Mattioli. The idea that it could be dangerous and immoral to know much about poisoning may explain the lack of references to poison in the surviving European medical textbooks before 1200. While the fear of severe legal consequences for using poison may have prevented people from writing about its preparation, it is important to note that detecting poisoning was far from easy. Rumours of poisoning were rife after the deaths of rulers who had earned the hatred of multitudes, but the reports were not easily proven.[21] Some medieval handbooks for pharmacists, such as the *Viaticum*, also known as *De morborum*

---

[19] Gilbert Watson, *Theriac and Mithridatium: A Study in Therapeutics* (London: Wellcome Historical Medical Library, 1966), p. 34.

[20] I have consulted the Wechel edition in the University of North Carolina library. The famous Vienna codex of Dioscorides (Vienna, Austrian National Library, MS *Codex Vindobonensis Medicus Graecus* 1) includes a depiction of *aconitus* or *Aconitum napellum* on fol. 67v, which may be viewed at the University of Chicago's website at http://penelope.uchicago.edu/~grout/encyclopaedia_romana/aconite/materiamedica.html (accessed 24 July 2015).

[21] The recent forensic investigation of the body of Cangrande della Scala (1291–1329), prince of Verona in the early fourteenth century, supplied an interesting example of the opposite scenario. His death was not widely suspected to be the result of poison, but

cognitione et curatione [*On the Recognition and Treatment of Diseases*], which was based upon a work by Ibn al-Jazzar (c. 980) and translated in the late eleventh century by Constantine the African, contain sections on concocting poisons like *De cavenda et medicinanda mortifera potione* [*On being Careful of Deadly Poison and Employing it as Medicine*]. As Franck Collard notes, this section is only a very small proportion of the entire work;[22] however, the passage does not provide instructions on how to detect these poisons or how to produce their antidotes. The author may have been concerned with social respectability, and thus omitted important details about the poisons, but he could have defended himself by arguing that there were benefits to spreading the knowledge of poisons.

Poisoning took place in the Italian peninsula in the seigniorial period when nobles jostled for power by several different means. It has recently been determined that Cangrande della Scala, lord of Verona in the age of Romeo and Juliet, consumed deadly foxglove before his death, bearing out one strand of rumour surrounding his demise and seemingly contradicting an alternate theory that claimed he died after drinking from a polluted spring.[23] The Borgia family are said to have had a penchant for using poison, though there is no conclusive evidence that Cesare, Lucrezia or their father, Pope Alexander VI, ever used it. Yet Venice, which is sometimes thought of as a *patria dei veleni* [homeland of poisons],[24] was also associated with a curative compound, often known as *teriaca veneta* [Venetian theriac], which was prepared and closely monitored by the Venetian state.

Venice was situated within a wider network of discourses about anatomy and the interaction of natural substances with human physiology and medico-legal questions. The most detailed and well-known work on poisons to circulate in medieval Italy was the *De Venenis* by Paduan astrologer and professor of medicine Pietro d'Abano (1257–1316). D'Abano lived in the Byzantine empire and studied in Constantinople for two decades;[25] it is likely that he saw the cele-

---

the digitalis found in his remains makes it likely that he was murdered with foxglove. See note 23.

[22] Franck Collard, 'Poison et empoisonnement dans quelques œuvres médicales latines antérieures à l'essor des *Tractatus de venenis*', in *Terapie e guarigioni*, ed. Agostino Paravicini Bagliani (Impruneta: SISMEL, 2010), pp. 363–93.

[23] Gino Fornaciari et al., 'A Medieval Case of Digitalis Poisoning: The Sudden Death of Cangrande della Scala (1291–1329)', *Journal of Archaeological Science* 54 (February 2015): 163–67; Gian Maria Varanini, 'La morte di Cangrande della Scala. Strategie di comunicazione intorno al cadavere', in *Cangrande della Scala. La morte e il corredo funebre di un principe nel medioevo*, ed. E. Marini, P. Napione and G. M. Varanini (Venice: Marsilio Editori, 2004), pp. 11–21.

[24] Preto, *Servizi Segreti*, p. 361.

[25] Sante Ferrari, *I tempi, la vita, le dottrine di Pietro d'Abano* (Genoa: Tipografia Reale Istituto Sordomuti, 1900), p. 98.

brated Vienna manuscript of Dioscorides while sojourning there, but even if he did not, his debt to Dioscorides is great. *De Venenis* describes the properties of many natural substances, some of which are not inherently poisonous or only poisonous in large doses or when mixed with other materials (including *ficus Pharaonis*, the fig, and *asurum*, a substance that d'Abano says is made out of *lapis lazuli*, a semiprecious blue stone in high demand by medieval and Renaissance painters,[26] and physicians).[27] D'Abano discusses numerous substances commonly used in Venice as poisons, including *aconitum napellum, hellebore* and *euphorbium*, commenting on their curative properties as well as the mechanisms that he sees (often related to their elemental natures) that govern the actions of poisons in the human body. The Paracelsian principle that dosage alone makes a substance a 'poison' is borne out by d'Abano's work. D'Abano's treatise *De Venenis* was published in Protestant Marburg by Johannes Eichmann, known as the Dryander redaction.[28] This version of the *De Venenis* was published that same year in Venice by Vittorio dei Ravani and again by Johannes Gryphius in 1550. Bergamo-born Guglielmo Gratarolo, who moved between Venice and Padua most of the time and was a friend and correspondent of Girolamo Cardano, also took an interest in poisons and produced a work about antidotes titled *Consilium de praeservatione de venenis*.[29] Similarly, there is evidence that Pier Francesco Passerini's and Zacchia's work on poisoning, though first published in Piacenza and Rome, respectively, circulated widely in Venice as well.

Juridical concerns rarely obtrude into the naturalistic works such as d'Abano's *De Venenis* and works modelled upon it, such as Gratarolo's *Consilium*.[30] Passerini's and Zacchia's works stand in contrast with the other writings on the crime of poisoning. Both men were interested in canon law. In *Tractatus legalis et moralis de pollutione Ecclesiarum* [hereafter, *Tractatus de Pollutione (On the Pollution of Churches)*], first published in Piacenza (1654), Passerini addresses

---

[26] Michael Baxandall, *Painting and Experience in Fifteenth-Century Italy* (Oxford: Oxford University Press, 1988), p. 11. As Baxandall notes, ultramarine from crushed lapis lazuli was far more desirable in the early fifteenth century than was German blue, an alternative available from northern Europe. Baxandall contends that this demand related to the rarity of ultramarine, still only available as an import from the East, ultimately coming from mining of the Blue Mountain of Badakhshan, in modern-day Afghanistan.

[27] Pietro d'Abano, *De Venenis atque eorundem commodis*, ed. Johannes Dryander (Marburg: Eucharius Cervicornus, 1537), p. 14.

[28] The 1537 Marburg edition of this work boasts that it was a 'Liber plane aureus, per Joannem Dryandrum medicum pristino suo nitori restitutum' [a thoroughly golden book, restored by the doctor Johannes Dryander to its original lustre].

[29] Guglielmo Gratarolo, *Consilium de praeservatione de venenis* (Basle, 1555).

[30] d'Abano takes as his *auctoritates* Galen, Avicenna and Dioscorides, not Azo and Ulpian.

ritual pollution, a praxis of interest since Antiquity,[31] including sections on whether an act of poisoning carried out in a church pollutes a church or not. For Passerini, the situation makes a great difference.[32] Passerini's dense and citation-heavy text shows just how many authors, including Jesuits such as Luis Suarez and Roman lay jurists such as Prospero Farinacci (1544–1618), included poisoning in their juridical works in the period leading up to Passerini's contribution. Passerini cites Jacobus Butrigarius (d. 1348), teacher of one of the most influential medieval Italian jurists, Baldus de Ubaldis of Perugia, together with Bartolomeo of Saliceto and several others, in order to support his argument that the statutes speaking of homicide do not extend to poison: 'Primo, quod venenare secundum aliquos non videtur occidere, nec venefici proprie dicuntur homicidae, unde statutum de homicidio loquens non extenditur ad mortem veneno, illatam secundum' [First, that to poison does not seem to be to kill, according to some, nor are poisoners correctly called homicides. Whence it results that a statute speaking of homicide does not extend to death by poison].[33]

In *Quaestiones Medico-Legales*, Zacchia concentrated on the medical properties and ethics of poisoning, adding a dimension to the more formal legal studies dominant in this period which were, to a great extent, concerned with the correct interpretation of the Roman jurists on the legal status of poisoning. But such ethical questions of the kind Zacchia raised need not have intruded upon the thinking of the Council of Ten and the Inquisitors in Venice. The Council of Ten did, however, draw upon the expertise of local botanists who instructed at the University of Padua. For example, Melchiorre Guilandino, who managed the botanical garden at Padua, was called upon in 1574 to supply poison to dispatch the renegade Mustafa degli Cordovani, but his knowledge of poison was imperfect, and his initial concoction failed.[34]

It was often difficult to determine whether poison was the cause of death, but it was more difficult to determine whether there was intent in its application or whether the poisoning was accidental. The experiments on corpses of Mondino de' Liuzzi in the early fourteenth century in Bologna represent an important shift, not only in Italy, but in all of western Europe, in favour of the dissection of corpses in investigating anatomy, leading eventually to research on,

---

[31] Pier Francesco Passerini, *Tractatus Legalis et Moralis De Pollutione Ecclesiarum* (Piacenza: Giovanni Bazachi, 1654).

[32] Ibid., p. 191.

[33] Ibid., p. 191. The first counter-example provided is that of obstetricians giving women poorly chosen medicaments to facilitate childbirth, and, unintentionally, bringing about their patients' death.

[34] On which, see: Paolo Preto, 'Un infortunio professionale di Melchiorre Guilandino, direttore dell'Orto Botanico di Padova', *Quaderni dell' Università di Padova* 22–23 (1989–90): 233–36.

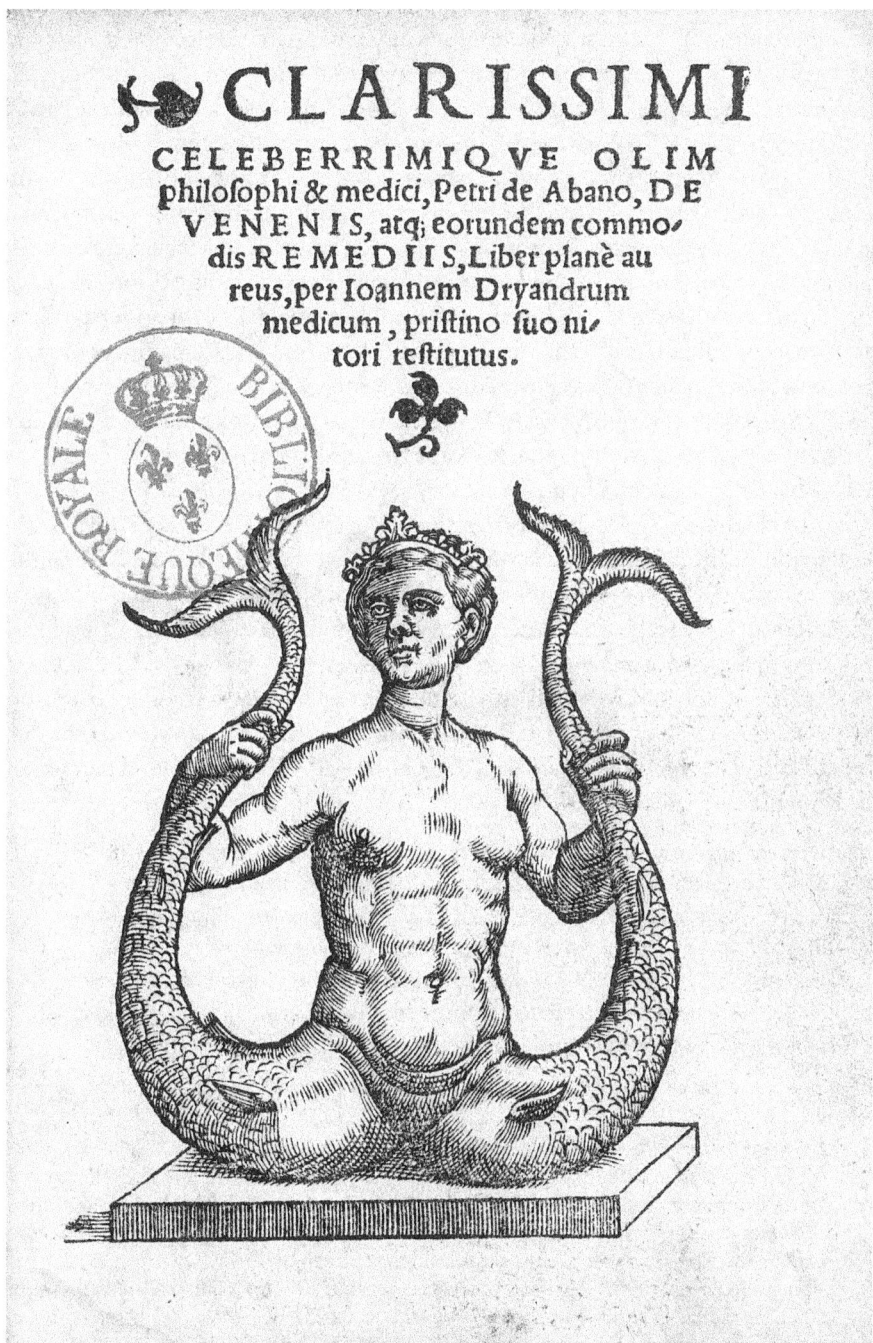

10.1 Title Page of Pietro d'Abano, *De Venenis*. Marburg: Johannes Dryander, 1537. Reproduced by kind permission of the Österreichische Nationalbibliothek, Vienna.

and dissection of, corpses to determine causes of death. However, knowledge of chemistry was spotty throughout the medieval and early modern periods. Richard Palmer argues that the Venetian state employed physicians in a capacity as coroners, men who could testify before the Inquisition concerning cause of death in suspected cases of magical curses.[35] But the extent of their diagnostic abilities was extremely limited. Some cases of murder carried out with poisoning in Venice were not recognised as such, while some deaths were erroneously attributed to poisoning (see Figure 10.1). Considering the superstition that eggs boiled for an excessively long time became poisonous, the level of understanding was clearly rudimentary.[36] The earliest reliable tests for identifying traces of arsenic, one of the main poisons commonly associated with the Venetian Republic, were carried out by the Scotsman James Marsh in the 1830s after his testimony failed to convict one Mr. Bodle, who was suspected of having administered arsenic to his father in a cup of coffee.[37]

Despite the lack of other contemporary evidence, Lamansky's invaluable collection drawn from secret archival documents of the old Venetian Republic demonstrates that in Venice there was a substantial number of officially approved instances of poisoning state enemies. For example, the Venetian Council of Ten approved a motion on 2 December 1450, asking what should be done if an intelligent and discreet person should present himself and offer to poison Duke Francesco Sforza of Milan. In what followed, the Council agreed that this would-be agent should be permitted to experiment with his intended poison on a criminal sentenced to death:

> [R]es est in punto parata, que est ballota parve rotunde, que iacte super ignem reddunt odorem suavissimum et delectabilem, quem quicumque odorat moritur, et quum, antequam detur extra, facienda est experientia, et in nostris carceribus presentialiter reperiatur unus latro, qui presentandus est legi, nec aliud sibi deest, quam audire sententiam suam, et omnes intelligunt, quam utilis et secura res esset statui nostro mors comitis [Francisci], vadit pars, quod auctoritate istius consilii capita consilii habeant libertatem practicandi cum

---

[35] Richard Palmer, 'Physicians and the Inquisition in Sixteenth-Century Venice: The Case of Girolamo Donzellini', in *Medicine and the Reformation*, ed. Ole Peter Grell and Andrew Cunningham (New York: Routledge, 1993), pp. 118–33. Palmer based his argument on cases in the archival series of records of trials by the Holy Office, the *Santo Uffizio*, in the Venice State Archive, generally involving witchcraft or heresy.

[36] On boiled eggs becoming poisonous, see: Davide Busato, *Venezia Criminale* (Venice: Helvetia, 2013): http://www.venezia.net/22/12/2013/veleni-e-magia-gli-veneziani-facevano-fuori-i-parenti-con-che-veleni.html (accessed 30 January 2015).

[37] James Marsh, 'Account of a Method of Separating Small Quantities of Arsenic from Substances with which it may be mixed', *Edinburgh New Philosophical Journal* 21 (1856): 229–36.

artifice huius operis, quod ipse faciat experimentum in homine illo carcerato, qui moriturus est pro furto...

[the substance has been prepared, to be precise, as a small and round ball, the which, when thrown upon a fire, give off a very subtle and pleasant smell. Whoever sniffs it, dies, and before this substance is administered out in the world, let an experiment be carried out. Let a robber be found in our prisons, who must be presented for selection, nor must another prevent him from hearing his sentence, and let all understand what a useful and safeguarding affair the death of Count Francesco would be to our state. Be it approved, that by the authority of this council, the heads of this council should have the freedom to practise with this invention in secrecy, so that the experiment itself may be carried out on this imprisoned man, who is scheduled to die for having committed theft...].[38]

Here, there is a lingering concern for doing the morally right thing: The condemned prisoner must understand his sentence, and the heads of the council must be granted the authority to undertake this lethal form of experimentation with legal immunity from responsibility. The document offers a rare reference to experimentation with poisons on humans, though Alessandro Pastore has found more such instances *in vili corpore* [in a wicked body], on the bodies of those who were already condemned to death, a practice that extended back to Antiquity.[39]

As the printing press enabled wider diffusion of knowledge about poisons and the subject became less taboo, poisoning came to feature more often in juristic works. Many early modern Italian jurists considered the ramifications of classifying death by poisoning as murder. Passerini's *Tractatus de pollutione* takes a measured note arguing that 'venenare secundum aliquos non videtur occidere' [to envenom, according to some, is not homicide].[40] Passerini's analysis suggests there was some speculation among legal authorities concerning the deliberateness of poisoning, whether it was considered *proditio* [betrayal or treason] and whether it was not a more nefarious act than a simple *homicidium*: 'dicendum est Veneficos non solere Homicidas dici, quia veneficium supra Homicidium addit qualitatem proditionis cuiusdam (si illud veneficus in aliam personam exerceat) longe abominabiliorem, quam sit simplex homicidii reatus' [It must be said that crimes of poison are not normally called homicides because the poisoning adds the quality of betrayal, beyond a homicide, which is a crime far more abominable (if the poisoner commits it against another person) than is the simple crime

---

[38] Lamansky, *Secrets d'État de Venise*, p. 9.
[39] Watson, *Theriac and Mithridatium*, p. 34.
[40] Passerini, *Tractatus de Pollutione*, p. 191.

of homicide].⁴¹ Passerini's discussion is brief but nuanced in its assessment of the hierarchy of crime, as well as of sin.

Together with Basel, Lyon and Paris, Venice was one of the principal European centres for publishing medical and botanical books.⁴² Venice's military outposts and trade contacts with the eastern Mediterranean made it possible for individuals to obtain poisonous materials such as Syrian bindweed, *Convolvulus scammonia*,⁴³ which could induce vomiting, purging and the appearance of intoxication, and local plants like belladonna, *Atropa belladonna*, which could be used as a cosmetic to dilate women's pupils. For those with the riches to pay for it, rarer substances like powdered diamond were also available, as in the case of Veneranda Porta who poisoned her husband, possibly with the help of a paramour (or more than one paramour) in June 1779. Porta first (unsuccessfully) employed boiled eggs, extract of toad and arsenic, but she finally succeeded in her attempts when she deployed powdered diamond as a poison. How such a poor woman got hold of such a costly material, and why she did not just use powdered glass, remains a mystery. There are few documentary sources to answer this question, but there was a longstanding written tradition about the potentially lethal effects of consuming powdered diamond. For example, in *De Pirotechnia* [*Of Metallurgy*] (1540), possibly written for his patron, Pandolfo Petrucci, Vannoccio Biringuccio writes: 'Physicians say, because of its effects, that it has the nature of cold and dry earth itself. Many have believed and do believe that if it is taken as food it is a deadly poison; but they are in error in this, although it is very true that it prepares for and brings about death if it is taken, not because it is a poison, but because of its contusion of the stomach'.⁴⁴ Powdered diamond was documented as a substance used by both private parties and Venetian officials as a method of poisoning. Referring to the late seventeenth century, Paolo Preto notes that powdered diamond was recorded as a poison in cases of state assassinations in 1683, 1685 and 1691.⁴⁵ Preto also suggests that Venetian agents reserved powdered diamond and scammony for persons of exalted social rank, and it is plausible that, in an age of hierarchical thinking

---

⁴¹ Ibid., p. 192.
⁴² Nancy Siraisi and Andrea Carlino, *Storia della Scienza* s.v. 'Il Rinascimento': http://www.treccani.it/enciclopedia/il-rinascimento-la-medicina_(Storia_della_Scienza)/ (accessed 23 February 2015).
⁴³ Siraisi and Carlino, *Storia della Scienza*, loc.cit. C.
⁴⁴ Vannoccio Biringuccio, *The Pirotechnia*, trans. Cyril Stanley Smith and Martha Teach Gnudi (Cambridge, MA: MIT Press, 1942; rpt 1966), p. 123.
⁴⁵ Preto, *Servizi Segreti*, p. 371.

about natural substances, they felt that people of higher social status should be dispatched in ways befitting their station.[46]

Curiously, diamond was widely considered to possess antidotal properties as well. In his *Speculum Lapidum* [*Mirror of Precious Stones*] (1502), Camillus Leonardus explains that:

> [D]iamond withstands poison, tho'ever so deadly, is a defense against the arts of sorcery, disperses vain fears, enables the quelling of quarrels and contentions, is a help to lunatics and such as are possessed of the devil: being bound to the left arm it gives victory over enemies, it tames wild beasts, it helps those who are troubled with phantasms and the nightmare and makes him that wears it bold and daring in his transactions.[47]

What experiences precisely convinced Venetians that certain substances worked well as antidotes remains open to question, but there is no doubt that some substances did enjoy that reputation. Saffron, mixed with other substances, is mentioned in legislation of the Great Council from 1288, and it was available in Venice from that date. In the *Terapeutica* [*Healing Matters*], published in Venice in 1554, Giovanni Attuario [John the Actuary] explains that a universal antidote could be composed of saffron, myrrh, cinnamon, euphorbium, mandrake root, poppy and several other, more minor, ingredients dissolved in honey.[48] In any case, the documents are plentiful enough to conclude that Venice deserves as much a reputation for disseminating knowledge regarding cures for poisons as for knowledge about poisons themselves.

Knowledge of noxious substances could be a dangerous thing if it were made public. In his *Magiae Naturalis*, Della Porta wrote that poisons were among the most abhorred means of killing known to man; indeed, it was with special bitterness that he complained that his enemies, mostly Frenchmen and others 'of the same flour', smeared his good name by calling him a 'poisoning mage' because he offered too many details about poisoning in his earlier works (although he had never dealt with topics that 'may not be contained within the boundary-walls of

---

[46] There is one aspect of state-sponsored poisonings that was not discussed by the ancient legists, nor by Aquinas, Machiavelli or other political theorists: industrial espionage. In at least two cases from 1754, State Inquisitors felt strongly enough to hire assassins to poison Friulan Piero de Vettor, for selling the secret of a certain glazing procedure, and Giovanni Vistosi, a pearl dealer who took knowledge of certain techniques with him to Florence. See: Preto, *Servizi Segreti*, p. 348.

[47] Quoted in Diana Scarisbrick, 'Forever Adamant: A Renaissance Diamond Ring', *Journal of the Walters Art Gallery* 40 (1982): 59.

[48] Pietro Perrone, *Storia prammatico-critica delle scienze naturali e mediche, parte terza* (Naples: Gerolamo Palma, 1834), p. 952.

Nature').⁴⁹ The conjoining of poison and spellcasting in certain medieval and Renaissance treatises may have also contributed to the association of poisoning with female behaviour. Pastore contends that a difference between *maleficae* and *veneficae* is that the former relied upon aid from the Devil while the latter did not.⁵⁰ No doubt thinking of the many domestic occupations that gave women the opportunity to administer poisons in food and drink, the Friulan jurist Tiberio Deciani, in his *Tractatus criminalis* [*Tract on Criminal Law*] (1579), expressed concern that poisons were too easy to obtain for those living in close proximity to their victims.⁵¹

Medieval and Renaissance students of poisons and their antidotes derived satisfaction from the thought that they were participating in a tradition that extended back to Andromachus, physician to Nero and contemporary of Dioscorides, as well as King Mithridates VI of Pontus and Bithynia (r. 120 BCE–63 BCE), one of the formidable opponents to Roman expansion during the Republic. Andromachus is credited as the source for a popular compound, the *teriaca di Andromaco*, composed of several ingredients culled from diverse locations. Like the traditions that bound doctors to Hippocrates and painters to Saint Luke, herbalists and pharmacists of medieval and Renaissance Venice rejoiced in their inheritance from Andromachus, Mithridates and other ancient savants of poisons and antidotes. The idea of a *teriaca*, the root of English treacle,⁵² derives from a Greek word for the viper, one of the key ingredients in that compound. Local tradition holds that Venetian pharmacists, under instructions from state officials, prepared the *teriaca di Andromaco* publicly, in front of the people, as a form of public instruction; how much they revealed about the crafting of lethal substances is less clear, for the documentary record is considerably less informative.⁵³ Another compound, the *teriaca di Mitridate,* took its name from the ancient narrative tradition that the long-lived King Mithridates gradually poisoned himself with low doses in order to build up a tolerance to some toxic substances. The sheer number of recipes for this substance – theriac – that survive in handbooks like that of Giorgio Melichio (1595), the Venetian pharma-

---

⁴⁹ Giovanni Battista della Porta, *Magia naturalis* (Naples: Orazio Salviani, 1589), *Praefatio*, iii: '*Gallus quidam in suo libro de oenomania me Magum veneficum putat ... Alios omitto eiusmodi farinae homines, qui me etiam Magum veneficum existimant, quum nil unquam hic, vel alibi a me tractatum sit, quod inter Naturae pomœria non contineatur.*'

⁵⁰ Alessandro Pastore, *Veleno: Credenze, crimini, sapere nell'Italia moderna* (Bologna: Il Mulino, 2010), p. 67.

⁵¹ Traiano Deciani, *Tractatus Criminalis* (Venice: Hieronymus and Johannes Zenarios, 1579), *Liber* IX, Cap. XXIII, p. 120.

⁵² Watson, *Theriac and Mithridatium*, pp. 111–12.

⁵³ Alessandro Pastore has found recipes for poison among the papers of the noble lady Pompilia Zambeccari in the Bologna state archive. *Veleno*, Plate 9, located between pp. 128 and 129.

cist, suggests that the compound was prepared in public, and in a festive atmosphere, as a sort of local specialty. Clearly, by the end of the sixteenth century, preparation of theriac had become a public occasion and organisers permitted public knowledge of its ingredients:[54] troches of vipers, long pepper,[55] cassia,[56] cinnamon, Florentine iris, costmary, gentian, birthwort, centaury, quinquefolium, athamanta,[57] great valerian,[58] lemon grass,[59] lavender,[60] turnip seeds, parsley, aniseed, hartwort,[61] fennel, field pennycress, wild carrot, amomum, a bit of myrrh (to keep the compound from sticking to the mortar), scordium, dittany of Crete, horehound, wild mint, polium, wall germander, cinnamon leaf,[62] St John's wort, gum, incense, troches of squills and hedycroum,[63] rose, saffron (exposed to the sun briefly), bastard-rhubarb, Lemnian earth, agaric, Malmsey wine and eastern acacia. Melichio was a pharmacist at the Struzzo d'Oro pharmacy, one that enjoyed high repute in Venice and throughout Europe. Even the Council of Ten left recipes for substances used for state-sponsored poisonings, including two detailed ones from 1540 and 1544, consisting of sublimate, arsenic, red arsenic or *risagallo*, orpiment (arsenic trisulfide), sal ammoniac, rock salt, verdigris and distillate of cyclamen, a common flower that blooms especially in December in Venice.[64] Thus, to uphold their reputation and to transmit accurately knowledge of the poisoning craft, Venice clearly had an interest in documenting, not destroying, its records of poisonings, including those that were state-sponsored.

[54] For the complete recipe, see: Giorgio Melichio, *Avertimenti*, quoted in Fumagalli, 'Storia e mirabili virtù': http://chifar.unipv.it/museo/Teriaca/Teriaca.htm (accessed 4 April 2015).
[55] *Piper longum*, smaller and more tightly clustered than black pepper.
[56] Probably *Cinnamomum aromaticum*.
[57] *Dizionario Botanico Italiano*, ed. Ottaviano Targioni Tozzetti (Florence: 1809), s.v. 'Athamanta cretensis', gives 'Meo' as one of the Italian names of this herb, now used to flavour liqueurs.
[58] Idem, s.v. 'Valeriana'.
[59] Probably *Helichrysum stoechas*.
[60] Probably *Lavandula latifolia*.
[61] According to John Hill, 'Seseli' is hartwort. *The History of the Materia Medica* (London: T. Longman, 1751), p. 524.
[62] Guy de Chauliac, *Inventarium sive Chirurgia Magna: Volume Two: Commentary*, ed. Michael R. McVaugh and Margaret S. Ogden (Leiden: Brill, 1997), p. 272, This is identified by McVaugh and Ogden as *folium indum* (a variant of *indicum*, from India); concurring with Guy in his geographical attribution, Targioni Tozzetti says in his *Dizionario Botanico Italiano* s.v. 'Folio' that *folio* is *laurum Malabatrum*, i.e. of Malabar.
[63] Nicholas Culpeper says of *trochischi hedicroi* that they are 'very seldom or never used but in other compositions; yet naturally they heat cold stomachs, help digestion, strengthen the heart and brain'. See: *A Physicall Directory, or, A Translation of the London Dispensatory Made by the Collegge of Physitians of London* (London: Peter Cole, 1651), p. 99.
[64] Preto, *Servizi Segreti*, p. 367.

While private murders through poisoning are documented throughout Italy in the Middle Ages and the Renaissance, the evidence for Venice being a centre of state assassinations via that method is based on an extensive series of government documents that outline plans for killing enemies of the state. Though these acts qualify as murder, the actual legal standing of the crime of poisoning – whether it was a subset of murder, *homicidium*, or whether it inevitably entailed treason as well – was the subject of long-standing debate. State assassinations were defensible, and no party within the Venetian municipality would be brought to trial due to the principle, attributed to Cicero, 'Salus populi suprema lex esto' [Let the safety of the people be the supreme law].[65] Alain Charbonnier suggests that in areas subject to Roman law, including Venice, the difference between state assassinations and murders is less pronounced than it is in Anglo-American law.[66] The first few generations of systematic historical research into the archives of the former Venetian republic – including Lamansky's collection and Louis de La Mas Latrie's treatise on the Venetian project to poison the Ottoman pasha of Bosnia and Sultan Mehmet II[67] – have led to the widespread belief that the early modern Venetian councils of state were willing to use poisoning. The premise is no longer dismissed as an untoward assault on the memory and political morals of that Republic. The entire first section of Lamansky's *Secrets d'État de Venise*, especially the *Miscellanea del Consiglio dei Dieci* [*Miscellaneous Documents of the Council of Ten*] and *Senato Mar* [*Senate: Overseas Territories Affairs*] series, concerns diplomatic activity related to poisoning. In the *Pacific Review* (1891), Irish pharmacist, barrister and historian J. C. McWalter wrote that the Council of Ten's resort to poison was fairly routine: '[they] seem to have regarded poisoning as a perfectly natural means of removing troublesome people, and kept a carefully detailed account of those persons who were to be poisoned.'[68] Archival records bear McWalter's conclusions out. Considering the destruction that the passage of time has wrought on many Venetian archival series, it is striking that so much documentation concerning cases of poisoning ordered by the Council of Ten still survives.

To name just a few examples: in 1311, it was suspected that Doge Piero Gradenigo's death was caused by poison; in the 1470s there was a coordinated attempt to poison both Ottoman Sultan Mehmet II (r. 1444–6 and 1451–81) and his pasha (or governor) of Bosnia. Venice's Council of Ten planned, or approved

---

[65] Cicero employed the formula in *De Legibus* (Leipzig: B. G. Teubner, 1928), III.iii.

[66] Alain Charbonnier, 'Il delitto di Stato come arte ai tempi della Serenissima', *Gnosis* 2 (2008): http://gnosis.aisi.gov.it/gnosis/Rivista15.nsf/ServNavig/21 (accessed 26 June 2015).

[67] Louis de la Mas Latrie, 'Projets d'empoisonnement de Mahomet II et du pacha de Bosnie accueillis par la république de Venise', *Archives de l'Orient* 1 (1881): 653–62.

[68] J. C. McWalter, 'On Some Historical Poisons', *Pacific Review* 6.1 (1891): 4–7.

plans, to poison several other Ottoman sultans, as well as King Sigismund of Hungary (r. 1387–1437) and King Charles VIII of France (r. 1483–98), whose invasion of the peninsula to press his claim to Naples in 1494 was momentous in Italian history. The 1512 death of Bayezid II was attributed to poisoning by his Jewish doctor, and Giovanni Maria Doglioni related the story in his *Historia Venetiana*.[69] Venetian archival documents amply validate Guido Ruggiero's observations; namely, that in the fourteenth, fifteenth, sixteenth and seventeenth centuries, the Council of Ten quickly suppressed internal and external threats to the state and was granted a good deal of flexibility in terms of how it brought about those outcomes.[70]

In January 1478, *more Veneto* [in the Venetian reckoning],[71] towards the end of the long Venetian-Ottoman war of 1463–79, one 'Lazarus the Turk', who, despite his name, was clearly aligned against the Ottomans at this time, was recorded in the vote tallies of the Council of Ten as having petitioned to poison the 'wells and waters' of the Turkish sultan.[72] Successive proposals for poisoning the Ottoman sultan survive in documents dating up to 1647, a time when the war over Crete raged; Preto has also recorded many proposals to poison Turkish troops far beyond that date.[73] Wartime saw the least resistance to the employment of ambitious poisoning projects, and surviving documents are unusually detailed, and numerous, for the period of the Cyprus War from 1570 to 1573. During that war, the *speziale* Nicolò Dalla Pigna sent a set of chemicals including verdigris, crystalline alum, black hellebore and an unspecified sublimate to the *provveditore generale* (a leading Venetian administrator) in Dalmatia, for the purpose of poisoning waters used by Ottoman forces. All waters used by Venetian subjects were to be left untouched, which was not an easy assignment. Plainly, the Venetian ruling councils did not regard such chemical warfare as beyond the moral pale.

Employing mass poisoning as a state weapon developed out of the (accurate) conviction that poisoning was difficult to detect and difficult to punish. Even Machiavelli, in the final book of his *Discourses on the First Decade of Titus Livy*, conveyed anxiety concerning the danger of mass poisoning in his analysis of the murder of Roman men by their wives, a practice well known in the Renaissance,

---

[69] Giovanni Maria Doglioni, *Historia Venetiana* (Venice: Damian Zenaro, 1598), pp. 611–12.

[70] Guido Ruggiero, *Violence in Early Renaissance Venice* (New Brunswick: Rutgers University Press, 1980), p. 19.

[71] The new year was celebrated in Venice on 1 March.

[72] *Quod Lazaro ... alias Turco, qui se obtulit capitibus huius consilii venenare puteos et aquas imperatoris Turcorum*, in Lamansky, *Secrets d'État de Venise*, pp. 26–27.

[73] Preto, *Servizi Segreti*, pp. 313–20.

which Livy associated with a prosecution in 331 BCE.[74] The *ius gentium*, the writers on the law of nations, were mixed in their opinions as to whether the use of poison on a large scale was defensible. Alberico Gentili, the north Italian Protestant jurist known for his analysis of the *ius gentium* in his *De Jure Belli Libri Tres* [*Three Books on the Law of War*], made the case in the segment titled *On Poisonings* (Book II, Chapter VI) that the amount of destruction wielded by a poisonous substance should be considered before it was used in war: '[e]st vero ille dolus facti, quum veneficiis uti volumus, qui contras hostes non probatur [there is deception in this deed, when we wish to use poisons, which have not been tried against an enemy].[75] Gentili only considers the deadliest poisons worthy of the name, arguing that their lethality should preclude mass poisoning in warfare; indeed, as mere contact with the toxin is enough to slay an enemy, the deadliness of the poison is more than the hostility of war can justify. Gentili's arguments in this section are based on ethical principles which, though influenced by Christian thinking, do not quote from, or even allude to, Scripture. He implicitly contrasts licit and civilised methods of warfare with those favoured by the barbarous enemies of the Romans such as the Parthians, the Getae and the Ethiopians, savage races who espoused the lowest forms of cruelty in wartime.

Throughout the Renaissance, non-Christian groups in Venice were repeatedly accused of poisoning, in some cases on a grand scale, such as the alleged conspiracies to poison the drinking water supplies of Venice during the Black Death of 1348–9.[76] Such a fear, however, was far from restricted to Venice. For example, in 1371, the Umbrian town of Narni promulgated a statute forbidding Jews from living near the municipal aqueduct or the fountains of the town. The preponderance of Jews in the medical profession exacerbated the perception of the viability of such a crime, which extended far beyond mass murder, and would have suggested a murderous hatred of Christians on the part of some Jews. Other sorts of murder, such as ritual murder of Christian boys – like that of Simon of Trent, a three-year-old who was said to have been abducted and murdered by Jews in 1475 – were (falsely) associated with Jews in the Veneto and elsewhere.[77] But poisoning, particularly on a large scale, of wells or other water supplies seems to have been a particular point of anxiety in many north Italian

---

[74] Livy, *Ab Urbe Condita*, ed. R. S. Conway and C. S. Walters (Oxford: Oxford Classical Texts, 1919), VIII.18. Online at: https://babel.hathitrust.org/cgi/pt?id=uc1.b000839455;view=1up;seq=207 (accessed 30 June 2017).

[75] Alberico Gentili, 'De veneficiis', *De Iure Belli Libri Tres* (Oxford: Clarendon Press, 1933), Capitulum VI: 249–62.

[76] See: Jacob R. Marcus, 'Confession of Agimet of Geneva, Châtel, Oct. 10, 1348', *The Jew in the Medieval World: A Sourcebook* (New York: Harper Torchbooks, 1965), pp. 43–47.

[77] Ronnie Po-Chia Hsia, *Trent 1475: Stories of a Ritual Murder Trial* (New Haven: Yale University Press, 1992), p. 17.

communities and elsewhere in the Middle Ages and Renaissance. Part of the reason for this anxiety was the difficulty in establishing a source of the poison and for producing an antidote. Renaissance medicine was far from helpless in the face of poison, but a patient needed to be properly diagnosed in order to be treated swiftly and successfully. In her work, Sheila Barker discusses tests of Florentine antidotes conducted in 1546 and 1660,[78] but in Venice, makeshift tests were carried out far earlier than those dates. Throughout pre-modern Europe, when poisoning of a consumable was suspected, it was not uncommon to test what remained of that material on animals, particularly pigs, chickens and dogs.[79]

The ability of medieval and Renaissance Venetian physicians to recognise poison as a cause of death was limited, but some practitioners had undergone training that would enable them to make that kind of prognosis. In 1368, Venetian members of the College of Surgeons were commanded by the Great Council to perform at least one annual demonstration on cadavers; two years later, the council made it mandatory for physicians of the city to contribute to the expenses of this demonstration, so that 'videndo ipsam notomiam, comuniter informari possunt de statu et condicionis humanae corporis' [by seeing this dissection, they might be collectively informed about the state and conditions of the human body].[80] Once a year for cadaver assessment was a paltry beginning, but it was an important step forward in the process of recognising the deployment of poison on the human body. Giuseppe Ongaro argues that medical doctors working for the courts were required, under the municipal statutes of Padua, to examine both the insides and the outsides of corpses.[81] Still, at this point, the chemical tests that would satisfy modern coroners as to the presence or absence of venom in the blood stream or organs remained beyond the ken of the Venetian coroners of the time.

The practical business of organising the government's store of poisons appears to have degenerated to a parlous state, according to a memo generated by the State Inquisitors from December 1755 which was unearthed by Lamansky. The document states: 'Fattasi osservatione, che le cose venefiche per servizio del Tribunale erano sparse per gli armadi delle scritture con rischio di qualche accidente, molte delle quali erano dal tempo corrotte e senza poi che si conoscesse di alcuna nè la qualità ne la dose' [it has been observed that the toxic substances in the service of the Tribunal are dispersed through the cabinets of documents, which carries a risk of some accident, [given that] many of them have become

---

[78] Sheila Barker, 'The Art of Poison', *The Medici Archives* 85 (2008): http://www.theflorentine.net/articles/article-view.asp?issuetocId=3464 (accessed 4 June 2015).
[79] Pastore, *Veleno*, pp. 191–205.
[80] Quoted in Giuseppe Ongaro, *Zooantropologia: Storia, Etica, e Pedagogia dell'interazione uomo/animale*, ed. Claudio Tugnoli (Milan: FrancoAngeli, 2003), p. 131.
[81] Ibid., pp. 115–64.

corrupted over time, and without anyone knowing of them either their properties, nor their correct dosing].[82]

There is, of course, still much work to be done on state-sponsored poisoning in Venice. The records of murder cases are incomplete for most of Europe in the medieval and early modern periods. However, archival research could disclose many more records of poisoning.[83] Accepting Preto's conclusion, or perhaps assumption, that Venetian 'secret services' not only existed but that *Realpolitik* placed them outside the regular legal channels of accountability from at least the fifteenth through to the eighteenth century, starting with the Council of Ten and extending much further, it is reasonable to conclude that the documents found by Lamansky and Mas Latrie are only part of a substantially larger corpus, much of which was deliberately destroyed. Clearly, the Venetian Republic would have taken steps to ensure that those committing the crimes – the perpetrators who actually administered the poison – were exonerated from blame. But argument *ex silentio* is both weak and dangerous. Venice's use of state-sponsored assassination seems to have been more frequent than that recorded by any Greek *polis* or by the Roman state. However, the quantitative disparity in the documentation that has survived from Greco-Roman antiquity and for Venice after 1400 is vast, and so drawing a firm conclusion is difficult. In the *Institutio Oratoria*, Quintilian cited *veneficium* for the ambiguity that the word could have in legal proceedings.[84] It was a word that, in some instances, connoted magical enchantments, and in others, poisonings without recourse to supernatural power.[85] This ambiguity persisted in the Middle Ages and the Renaissance. There are cases of *veneficia* that clearly did not involve magical spells, as in that of Veneranda Porta in 1779. Poisoning, though it might fall under the rubric of *homicidium*, and associated in the *Digest* with the more general concept of *sicarium* [violent killing], was, nonetheless, an exceptionally abhorrent and mysterious crime, which was

---

[82] Lamansky, *Secrets d'État de Venise*, p. 151.

[83] The *Necrologi* series in the *Provveditori alla Sanità* has yet to be systematically studied. With a team investigating the Venetian archives and the Marciana library, this is a project that could determine the extent to which Venice's reputation as the greatest practitioner of poisoning in Europe was deserved. Murder was generally defined throughout the Middle Ages as a killing carried out in secret; in this volume, see especially: Jeffrey Doolittle, 'Negotiating Murder in the *Historiae* of Gregory of Tours'; Bridgette Slavin, 'Secret Killing and Murder by Magic in the Law of Adomnán'; and Jolanta N. Komornicka, 'Treacherous Murder: Language and Meaning in French Murder Trials'.

[84] Quintilian, *Institutio Oratoria*, ed. Ludwig Radermacher, revised V. Buchheit (Leipzig: B. G. Teubner, 1971), VII.2.2.

[85] Matthew Dickie, *Magic and Magicians in the Greco-Roman World* (London: Routledge, 2003), p. 140.

all the more frightful for being difficult to prove.[86] The association of *veneficium* with incantations, with secrecy and with devious women all contributed to the horror with which the crime was viewed. The members of Council of Ten certainly understood the gravity attached to their orders. Statistics and itemisation of documented proposals for assassinations via poison by Venetian government councils shows that they were extremely common for the period after 1450 (See Table 10.1). The documentary record for poisoning is spotty before that, though the documentary record for the Council of Ten is quite full from about 1375 on, as it is for other law-enforcing bodies such as the *Quarantia*. Considering the dozens of documented cases in which the Council of Ten or the State Inquisitors recommend that their enemies be removed by 'secret, careful, and dextrous means', which undoubtedly implies poisoning in many cases, and including many cases of poisoning for which documentation could have been destroyed or never produced, Venice's reputation as a centre of state-sponsored poisoning from the period from 1400 to the end of the Republic seems amply deserved.

Table 10.1 Documented cases of proposed Venetian state-sponsored assassinations by poison, 1300–1797

Dates of documents on the subject	Target	Was the target killed?	Modern source	Contemporary source	Approving council of state
10 October 1431	Filippo Maria Visconti, duke of Milan	No	Preto, *SSV*, 367.	*Consiglio dei Dieci, Parti miste, registro* 11.	Council of Ten
2 December 1450; 4 August 1451	Francesco Sforza, duke of Milan	No	Preto, *SSV*, 367.	*Consiglio dei Dieci, Parti miste, reg.* 14, c. 15; Fulin, *Errori vecchi*, 1128–1133; Lamansky, *SEV*, 8–9.	Council of Ten
22 July 1477	Sultan Mehmet II	No	Mas Latrie, 'Projets', 654.	*Consiglio dei Dieci, Parti miste, filza* 1.	Council of Ten
5 November 1477	Ömer Bey, sanjakbey of Bosnia	No	Mas Latrie, 'Projets', 655.	*Consiglio dei Dieci, Parti miste, registro* 9; *filza* 1.	Council of Ten

[86] In an image published by Pastore, a chalice was inscribed in the margin of the record of one murder case to indicate the belief that it had involved poison. These examples can be found in a 1634 document from the series *Necrologi* of the archive of the *Provveditori alla Sanità: Veleno*, Plate 8, between pp. 128 and 129.

Dates of documents on the subject	Target	Was the target killed?	Modern source	Contemporary source	Approving council of state
27 January 1495	Barbeta, expert on sailing, Ottoman subject	Unknown	Preto, SSV, 338.	Consiglio dei Dieci, Parti miste, registro 27.	Council of Ten
23 January 1502	Sultan Bayezid II	No	Preto, SSV, 367.	Consiglio dei Dieci, Parti miste, registro 29.	Council of Ten
27 February 1515	Caramustafà	Unknown	Preto, SSV, 312.	Consiglio dei Dieci, Parti miste, registro 38.	Council of Ten
29 October 1521	Damian Clocovich, Croat chieftain	No; instead enlisted in the Venetian army	Preto, SSV, 309. Lamansky, SEV, 46–53.	Consiglio dei Dieci, Parti miste, registro 44; 46; 47.	Council of Ten
12 May 1545	Girolamo Adorno	Yes	Preto, SSV, 346; Lamansky, SEV, 65; G. Rizzi, 'Segreti di Medicina fra gli atti del Consiglio dei Dieci,' Il Friuli medico VI (1951) 7–31.	Consiglio dei Dieci, Parti secrete, registro 5.	Council of Ten
30 October 1562	Camillo Pechiari	Unknown	Preto, SSV, 334.	Consiglio dei Dieci, Parti secrete, registro 7, c. 94v.	Council of Ten
18 March 1563	Cernovich, dragoman in Constantinople	No	Preto, SSV, 113; Lamansky, SEV, 70–73; Lesure, Cernovic, 19; 121–62; 192; 216–30.	Capi del Consiglio dei Dieci, Lettere di ambasciatori Costantinopoli, busta 3; Consiglio dei Dieci, Parti secrete, registro 7.	Council of Ten, ordered of the Bailò in Constantinople
26 February 1571	Ottomans at Lake Urana (Dalmatia)	Unknown	Preto, SSV, 317.	Consiglio dei Dieci, Parti secrete, registro 9.	Council of Ten
25 September 1573	Domenico da Oderzo, renegade	Unknown	Preto, SSV, 349.	Consiglio dei Dieci, Parti secrete, registro 10.	Council of Ten

State Assassination in Early Modern Venice 251

Dates of documents on the subject	Target	Was the target killed?	Modern source	Contemporary source	Approving council of state
24 October 1574	Mustafa 'degli Cordoani' or 'Cordovani' (of the Cordwainers), renegade	Yes	Lamansky, *SEV*, 91.	*Consiglio dei Dieci, Parti secrete, registro* 11.	Council of Ten
22 February 1577	Marco Boldù	No; granted protection by Pope Pius V	Preto, *SSV*, 349.	*Capi del Consiglio dei Dieci*, Raccordi, 1480–1739, September 4, 1570; *Consiglio dei Dieci, Parti secrete, registro* 11.	Council of Ten
29 March 1583	Ottavio Avogadro, Veronese bandit	No	Preto, *SSV*, 344.	*Consiglio dei Dieci, Parti secrete*, reg. 13; ASV *Esposizione principi*, busta 6 of March 20, 1585.	Council of Ten
15 June 1630	Doctor Fasaneo, renegade	Yes; possibly not by poison	Preto, *SSV*, 349–50.	ASV, *Senato – Deliberazioni Costantinopoli*, registri 19, pt. II; 20; 21; 25; *Inquisitori di Stato* buste 274; 417; 472; Lamansky, *SEV*, 118–24.	State Inquisitors
30 May 1647	Sultan Ibrahim	No	Preto, *SSV*, 368.	*Inquisitori di Stato, buste* 527; 1215 n. 2.	State Inquisitors
15 April 1652	Unspecified Turkish commander on Albanian frontier	Unknown	Preto, *SSV*, 310.	*Inquisitori di Stato, buste* 258; 274. *Consiglio dei Dieci, Parti secrete, registro* 20.	Council of Ten
31 December 1653	Group of renegades in Constantinople	Yes	Preto, *SSV*, 351.	*Inquisitori di Stato, busta* 417.	Bailò of Constantinople

Dates of documents on the subject	Target	Was the target killed?	Modern source	Contemporary source	Approving council of state
26 January 1658	Domenico Battaia, pearl dealer	Yes	Preto, SSV, 348.	Inquisitori di Stato, busta 434.	State Inquisitors
10 November 1662	Two unnamed bandits	Unknown	Preto, SSV, 370.	Inquisitori di Stato, busta 61.	State Inquisitors
1662–1663	Antonio Gianotti, bandit in the Veronese region	Unknown; hired assassin claimed so.	Preto, SSV, 345.	ASV Stampe; Consiglio dei Dieci, buste e; 179; 506.	Council of Ten
April–June 1663	Beico bey	Unknown	Preto, SSV, 310.	Inquisitori di Stato, busta 46.	State Inquisitors
23 June 1668	Buglicibarà, a Turkish prisoner in Clis.	Unknown	Preto, SSV, 313.	Inquisitori di Stato, busta 274.	Suggested by the Venetian *Provveditore Generale* for Dalmatia and Albania, Antonio Priuli
28 June 1672	Andrea Barozzi, alleged Ottoman spy on Crete	Yes (in 1682)	Preto, SSV, 378–9.	Inquisitori di Stato, busta 148.	State Inquisitors
22 March 1682	Sanjakbey Durac (Zara)	Unknown	Preto, SSV, 320.	Inquisitori di Stato, busta 274.	State Inquisitors
10 March 1685	Suleyman aga, Ottoman official in Albania	Yes	Preto, SSV, 371.	Inquisitori di Stato, busta 36.	State Inquisitors
25 May 1702	Unknown	Unknown	Preto, SSV, 369.	Inquisitori di Stato, busta 667.	State Inquisitors, ordered of the captain general Giorgio Aliprandi.
19 Feburary and 9 June 1739	The 'uccello' (bird), a notorious bandit	Yes	Preto, SSV, 345.	Inquisitori di Stato, busta 186, to Carlo Coltran.	State Inquisitors

Dates of documents on the subject	Target	Was the target killed?	Modern source	Contemporary source	Approving council of state
7 September 1754	Piero de Vettor, trader in secrets of Venetian enamelling technique	Yes	Preto, SSV, 348.	Inquisitori di Stato, busta 534.	State Inquisitors
7 September 1754	Giovanni Antonio Vistosi, pearl trader	Yes	Preto, SSV, 348.	Inquisitori di Stato, busta 534.	State Inquisitors
1760-1767	Cristoforo Bullich	Yes, but possibly not by poison	Preto, SSV, 341.	Inquisitori di Stato, buste 49; 134; 162; 258; 277; 278; 394.	State Inquisitors
19 November 1767	Stefano 'the Little,' despot of Monte Negro	No	Preto, SSV, 370.	Inquisitori di Stato, busta 49.	State Inquisitors

Note: In compiling this chart, which is not comprehensive but an attempt, nonetheless, to list the surest documented cases of state-sponsored poisonings, I have followed Paolo Preto, *Servizi Segreti*, especially pp. 329–53 and pp. 361–71. I indicate whether the authorisation of poisoning is documented as having been carried out, or whether the assassination remains uncertain. I have included cases that were not planned as part of specific military manoeuvres, though they may have taken place during Venetian-Ottoman wars. Preto scarcely goes back before 1400, so that further cases may await discovery from earlier centuries, perhaps even before the constitution of the *Consiglio dei Dieci* in 1310. I have excluded proposals for the use of poison on a mass scale as a biological weapon of war, though these appear to have been plentiful during Ottoman-Venetian wars (e.g. Preto, *Servizi Segreti*, p. 320, on a proposal in 1650 to poison the fields in Crete that were used by the Ottomans to pasture their horses; and the April 1693 proposal by a *provveditore* for Dalmatia and Albania that eighty barrels of water be poisoned to use against Ottoman troops at Imoschi). I consider these examples to belong in a different category from 'assassination'.

Sources: Rinaldo Fulin, *Errori vecchi e documenti nuovi a proposito di una recente publicazione del conte Luigi de Mas Latrie* (Venice: G. Antonelli, 1882); Marino Sanudo, *I Diarii* (Florence: Rinaldo Fulin, 1886–1910); Vladimir Lamansky, *Secrets d'État de Venise* (St Petersburg: Imperial Press, 1884); Paolo Preto, *I Servizi Segreti di Venezia*, 2nd edition (Bologna: Il Mulino, 2004)

CHAPTER 11

Defamation, a Murder *More* Foul?: The 'Second Murder' of Louis, Duke of Orleans (d. 1407) Reconsidered

Emily J. Hutchison

ON 23 NOVEMBER 1407, LOUIS, duke of Orleans, was brutally murdered in the streets of Paris. The provost of Paris, Guillaume de Tignonville, reported that between ten and twenty men attacked Orleans and his valet with swords, axes and clubs, beating him even after he had fallen to the ground dead.[1] The surprise attack was gruesome, and every detail meticulously recorded by the chroniclers of the period, all of whom agreed that this was a shameful death for a royal body.[2] Many commented on the great effusion of blood, which was an important narrative strategy to emphasise Orleans' humanity, connecting

---

[1] Regarding the inquest and testimony, see: Jean-Marie Durand, *Heurs et malheurs des prévôts de Paris* (Paris: L'Harmattan, 2008), p. 111. See also: Richard Vaughan, *John the Fearless: The Growth of Burgundian Power* (Woodbridge: Boydell Press, new edn 2002), pp. 45–46. Apparently, only one woman witnessed the entire event. She was clear that she raised the hue by crying out 'Murder!' numerous times. Hence, there was absolutely no doubt about the nature of this crime. Indeed, she reported that numerous men jumped on the prince and hacked him to death with their swords and axes. Vaughan, *John the Fearless*, pp. 45–46.

[2] On the chroniclers' shock and moral judgement of the manner by which the duke was killed, see: Emily J. Hutchison, 'The Politics of Grief in the Outbreak of Civil War, 1407–1413', *Speculum* 61.2 (2016): 422–52 at pp. 422–23. For the details of the attack in the chronicles, see: Enguerran de Monstrelet, *La Chronique d'Enguerran de Monstrelet en deux livres avec pièces justificatives 1400–1444*, 6 vols (Paris, 1857), 2:157; Religieux de Saint-Denis, *Chronique du Religieux de Saint-Denys contenant le règne de Charles VI de 1380–1422*, trans. M. Bellaguet, 6 vols (Paris, 1852), 3:730–36, especially pp. 734 and 736 (hereafter RSD); Jean Juvénal, *Histoire de Charles VI, roy de France et de son règne, depuis 1380–1422. Nouvelle Collection des mémoires pour servir à l'histoire de France depuis le XIIIe siècle jusqu'à la fin du XVIIIe*, ed. Joseph François Michaud and Jean-Joseph-François Poujoulat, 32 vols (Paris, 1851), 2:437; Jean d'Orronville (dit Cabaret), *La chronique du bon duc Loys de Bourbon*, ed. A.-M. Chazaud (Paris: Librairie Renouard, 1876), p. 311.

his suffering to that of Christ.³ Their ultimate intention was to emphasise the heinousness of crime.⁴

After the provost of Paris launched his investigation into the killing and the funerary rites had been performed, John, duke of Burgundy, admitted his guilt to his uncles, the dukes of Berry and Bourbon. According to the chroniclers, when John of Burgundy first confessed, he claimed the devil had incited him. However, when he was given the chance to present his formal justification on 9 March 1408, he changed his refrain and refused to admit that he had committed murder.⁵ Rather, his spokesman, Jean Petit, claimed Burgundy had committed a lawful 'tyrannicide'. He argued that Orleans' crimes of tyranny, attempted usurpation (which, together, amounted to *lèse-majesté* [high treason]) and divine *lèse-majesté*, gave him legitimate cause to kill Louis without due judicial process or the king's express consent. Through the process of defamation, the legal narrative John of Burgundy and his team of experts (re)constructed this murder as a legitimate execution, akin to that of any other man convicted of treason. The next day he was formally pardoned for the crime.⁶

There are numerous points regarding this murder and the subsequent judicial process that make it a unique case. First, the two men involved were members of the royal family: the victim was the king's brother, and the killer their first cousin. Both were *princes of the blood*, a term used to identify and celebrate the most illustrious noblemen, the sons and grandsons of French kings. They were also extremely wealthy feudal peers of the crown and chivalrous warriors, which meant that they were above the regular legal procedures for homicide. Second,

---

³ See: Katherine Royer, *The English Execution Narrative, 1200–1700* (London: Pickering & Chatto 2014), pp. 33–48, n. 17.

⁴ Hutchison, 'The Politics of Grief', pp. 422, 429–36.

⁵ Petit's text is transcribed in full in Monstrelet, *Chronique* 1:177–242. Hereafter, volume and page numbers are given in parentheses. Unless otherwise indicated, all translations are my own. For more information on the extant manuscript copies, see: Emily J. Hutchison, '*Pour le roy et son royaulme*: Burgundian Propaganda under John the Fearless, Duke of Burgundy, 1405–1418', PhD Dissertation (University of York, 2006), pp. 13–14 nn. 50–51; Alfred Coville, 'Le véritable texte de la *Justification du duc de Bourgogne* par Jean Petit (8 mars 1408)', *Bibliothèque de l'École des chartes* 72 (1911): 57–91; and Alfred Coville, *Jean Petit et la question du tyrannicide au commencement du XVe siècle* (Paris: Picard, 1932).

⁶ For the pardon, published in March 1408, see: Lille, Archives départementales du Nord (hereafter ADN), B 656, no. 15.088; Urban Plancher, *Histoire générale et particulière de Bourgogne et Preuves*, vol. 3 (Dijon, 1748), p. 254, no. 256. I use Plancher's printed transcription for convenience [hereafter *Preuves*]. The pardon was republished in March 1409 after a peace treaty was made between Louis' sons and John of Burgundy. See: Dijon, Archives départementales de la Côte d'Or, B 11892, nos 18 and 18*bis*; Plancher, *Preuves*, pp. 256–58, no. 258. For his military retinue and the support he was given by the Parisians, see below, nn. 70–71.

the violent murder of a royal prince in the streets of Paris was highly anomalous, and it happened after years of tension between Louis of Orleans and John of Burgundy. Their hatred for each other was well known, yet the two had very recently entered into a formal friendship. They exchanged badges and the kiss of peace, shared in celebrations together and ate together – all of which were signs of fidelity and good will.[7] The assassination, therefore, was unexpected, and, by legal definition, a pre-mediated murder.[8] Third, King Charles VI had been suffering from bouts of mental illness since 1396. At the time of the duke of Burgundy's justification in March 1408, Charles was experiencing a lapse in cognition and was, therefore, unable to rule on his own; as a result, his regency council oversaw the pardon. In choosing this path, they were doubtless motivated by a desire to prevent war between the Houses of Burgundy and of Orleans. It is also likely that they were intimidated by Burgundy's intransigence and the large armed escort that had followed him to Paris.[9] Finally, there was no formal trial for John of Burgundy, nor for any of the assassins he hired. This was due to Burgundy's status as a member of the royal family, his coercive tactics and the king's mental health.

As a consequence of these unique conditions, the regular course of justice available to non-nobles if one of their kindred was murdered was not available to Louis' widow, Valentina Visconti, her children and their supporters.[10] Instead of a regular inquisitorial trial *in camera*, the House of Orleans' only recourse was to construct a public counter-narrative to try to achieve justice.[11] However, countermanding a formal pardon was not an easy task. Moreover, it was not strictly the murder of Louis' body that was of concern to their House. They also took a strong legal stance against his defamation. In their official refutation of 11 September 1408, the spokesman for the victim's family, Thomas de Bourg,

[7] Hutchison, 'Politics of Grief', pp. 428–29.
[8] See below, nn. 32 and 33.
[9] Hutchison, 'The Politics of Grief', pp. 435–36.
[10] Their children were: Charles, duke of Orleans, Philip, count of Vertus, John, count of Angoulême, and Marguerite. See Hutchison, 'The Politics of Grief', p. 437, n. 87.
[11] The inquisitorial trial required confession for a guilty verdict; therefore, the techniques deployed included secret trials that frequently involved torture in the pursuit of truth. See: Jean-Marie Carbasse, *Histoire du droit pénal et de la justice criminelle* (Paris: Presses Universitaires de France, 2000), pp. 188–91; Valérie Toureille, *Crime et châtiment au Moyen Âge, Ve-XVe siècle* (Paris: Éditions du Seuil, 2013), pp. 13–15, 192–210; Roger Grand, 'Justice criminelle, procedures et peines dans les villes aux XIIIe et XIVe siècles', *Bibliothèque de l'École des chartes*, 104 (1941): 51–108 at pp. 70–74. See also: Royer, *English Execution Narratives*, pp. 3–4. Unfortunately, because of their secret nature, there are very few surviving records of actual trials. To my knowledge, the only extant record that has survived for the reign of Charles VI (r. 1380–1422) is that published as *Régistre criminel du Châtelet de Paris, du 6 septembre 1389 au 18 mai 1392*, ed. Henri Duplès-Agier, 2 vols (Paris: Ch. Lahure, 1861 and 1864).

the abbot of Cérisy (hereafter Cérisy), argued that neither Louis of Orleans' death nor the subsequent defamation were excusable. Cérisy insisted that 'il ne souffist pas à partie adverse priver de vie Monseigneur d'Orléans, mais avec ce s'est efforcé de deshonnorer sa renommée par libelle diffamatoire, en occiant icellui par seconde mort' [it did not suffice for the adverse party to take the life of my lord of Orleans, but he also tried to dishonour his reputation by defamatory libel, in murdering him with a second death] (*Chronique* 1:292). In fact, he argued that Burgundy's *Justification* was an even greater crime than ordering the 1407 assassination. He claimed that, in refusing to accept punishment for the crime, Burgundy refused God's will and, therefore, maintained his sin.[12] Several years later, the House of Orleans restated that the defamation was Louis' second murder in the letter, justifying why they were about to challenge Burgundy to war. Addressing the king, they argued that

> non content d'avoir une fois tué et meurtri si dampnablement son cousin-germain, vostre seul frère, comme dit est; mais en perserverant en l'obstination de son trez disloyal, faux et mauvais courage, s'est efforcé de le tuer et meurtrir encores une autre fois; c'est assavoir de vouloir esteindre et damner et effacer entierement sa memoire et renommée par fausses mensonges et controuvées accusation, comme la Dieu grace, il vous est bien apparu notoirement et à tout le monde.
>
> [not satisfied with having killed and murdered so damnably his first cousin, your only brother, as it is said; but in persevering in his very disloyal, false and evil courage, he endeavoured to kill and murder him another time; that is to say (*assavoir*) [he] extinguished, damned, and entirely effaced his memory and reputation with false lies and contrived accusations, as it is well apparent to you and to everyone].[13]

Of course, Cérisy was speaking metaphorically when he called the defamation a 'second murder'. This was an essential rhetorical strategy, for just as the posthumous dismemberment of an executed traitor underscored the criminal's monstrous malfeasance, so too had the duke of Burgundy attempted to dismember the name, identity and legacy of Louis of Orleans to degrade him.[14] To refute

---

[12] Monstrelet, *Chronique*, 2: 312. See also: RSD, 4: 114. Bernard Guenée, *Un meurtre, une société: L'assassinat du duc d'Orléans 23 novembre 1407* (Paris: Gallimard, 1992), pp. 206–07.

[13] Paris, Archives nationales de France (hereafter AN), K 56, n. 18; ADN, B 657, 15.183. The document was transcribed by the chroniclers of the period: RSD, 4: 418–36; Juvénal, *Histoire de Charles VI*, 2: 456–64; and Monstrelet, *Chronique*, 1:124–53. The entire letter patent is also printed in Plancher, *Preuves*, pp. 278–85, no. 277. Hereafter, the source and page number are given in parentheses as *Jargeau*.

[14] On the dismemberment of bodies in English executions and the connection to dehumanisation, see: Royer, *English Execution Narratives*, pp. 37–40. It is important to note

and resist these spurious claims, Cérisy used the metaphor of murder to resuscitate his memory and his good reputation by humanising Louis anew. By the House of Orleans' reckoning, there were two violent deaths that needed to be punished: the murder of a body made of royal flesh and blood, and the murder of his living memory, his reputation. According to their judicial pursuit, his flesh and his reputation were equally important dimensions of Louis' identity and their family legacy. Both 'murders' demanded justice.

Ultimately, neither the king nor the Parlement of Paris, the highest court of the realm, ever publicly acknowledged that the defamation was equivalent to a bodily murder. Hence, this claim did not have much legal traction until the autumn of 1413 when the duke of Burgundy was unofficially exiled by the king for his support of the infamous 'Cabochiens' rebels. The pendulum then swung in favour of the House of Orleans, and they finally achieved some satisfaction in their quest for justice. It was at that point that they took control of the king and his council.[15] The duke of Burgundy was not retroactively found guilty of murder, but, in reversing the defamation, the 'second murder', the House of Orleans apparently achieved sufficient justice to put aside their legal claim. This suggests that Louis of Orleans' reputation was at least as important, and perhaps *more* important, than his body.

This was possible because reputation – *fama* – was crucial social capital while individuals were living, but it also held a significant place in the late medieval French legal system *post mortem*.[16] Indeed, it was an essential factor in determining guilt or innocence in a criminal investigation. The reputation of witnesses was crucial in establishing if they were appropriate for legal cases and, if a full royal pardon was granted, it was something that could be restored alongside other material things, such as a person's freedom or their goods and property.[17]

that in France, when men wrongly convicted of crimes that led to execution, such as treason, were posthumously found innocent and/or pardoned, they were taken down from the Montfaucon gibbet and had their names, titles and property restored. In so doing, their honour was equally restored. For example, Pierre des Essarts, the former provost of Paris, was executed in July 1413 and posthumously pardoned on 5 August 1413 (AN, JJ 167, fol. 269r-v).

[15] For his exile from Paris and the measures the Armagnac-led government initiated against the duke of Burgundy, see: Hutchison, 'Winning Hearts and Minds', pp. 22–23 and 'Politics of Grief', pp. 450–51; Bertrand Schnerb, *Jean sans Peur: le prince meurtrier* (Paris: Biographie Payot, 2005), pp. 577–602 and *Les Armagnacs et les bourguignons: la maudite guerre* (Paris: Perrin, 2001), pp. 144–46; Vaughan, *John the Fearless*, pp. 193–227; Alfred Coville, *Les cabochiens et l'ordonnance de 1413* (Paris: Librairie Hachette, 1888), pp. 335–406.

[16] Toureille, *Crime et châtiment*, p. 89.

[17] For the importance of honour and good reputation for both witnesses and the accused, see: Claude Gauvard, *'De grace especial': Crime, état et société à la fin du Moyen Âge* (Paris: Publications de la Sorbonne, 1991), pp. 124–30 and 130–35. Both witnesses

Moreover, an individual's reputation and their status determined if they could be subjected to torture in the inquest into their guilt.[18] As a consequence, punishment for slander could be severe.[19] Reputation was more than an abstract extension of the human it was connected to; rather, it had a physical and ideational role in producing the corporal body and in shaping that body's identity. Because name and reputation lived on indefinitely, a person's identity was still in the process of becoming even after the body expired. It was for this reason that the defamation and subsequent assaults on the duke of Orleans' living memory constituted more than mere slander; reputation was something of substance. Like any body, reputation was a thing that could be disfigured, a thing that could be attacked, harmed and even slain.[20]

---

and the accused endured a rigorous interrogation of their character and what was publicly known about them (their *fama*). Gauvard calls this the 'déclinaison d'identité'. She also argues directly that such practices illustrate the general assumption that reputation was a form of proof (pp. 137–39). See also: F. R. P. Akehurst, 'Name, Reputation, and Notoriety', in *Fama. The Politics of Talk and Reputation in Medieval Europe*, ed. Thelma Fenster and Daniel Lord Smail (Ithaca: Cornell University Press, 2003), pp. 75–94, esp. pp. 80–94. The restoration of a previously tarnished reputation was a constant in all *lettres de rémission* (pardon letters). For example, Philipot Richel, a vassal of Charles of Orleans who was 'forcé a faire guerre contre le roi' [forced to make war against the king], was formally pardoned and had his reputation restored (*renomee restitue*) (AN, JJ 167, fols 69v–70r). Likewise, Orleans' vassal Jean de Chaselle had his reputation restored (AN, JJ 167, fol. 70r).

[18] All the individuals who were submitted to 'the question' (torture) in the two volumes of the *Registre criminal du Châtelet* had dubious reputations regardless of status. See, for example, the case of Marion la Droiturière, dite l'Estallee, *Registre criminel du Châtelet*, 1: 331–35. For her execution by burning, see p. 363.

[19] For example, in 1411, Raoulet Vivien was accused by his 'enemies' of uttering words against the duke of Burgundy. He was imprisoned and only acquitted after an appeal to the Parlement of Paris (AN, X1a, fols 12v–13). Likewise, according to one chronicler, the anonymous *Bourgeois de Paris*, when the Orleanists had taken over the government in the autumn of 1413, they heavily policed the streets, taverns and other gathering places to prevent anyone from speaking ill of the so-called 'Armagnac' party. See: *Journal d'un bourgeois de Paris, 1405–1449*, ed. A. Tuetey (Paris, 1881), pp. 46, 48–49, 54, 64, and 66. For more details, consult Emily J. Hutchison, 'Knowing One's Place: Space, Violence and Legitimacy in Early Fifteenth-Century Paris', *The Medieval History Journal* 20.1 (2017): 44–45.

[20] For a discussion of the issues of reputation and *fama* in other medieval societies, see in this volume: Ilse Schweitzer VanDonkelaar, 'Bringing Murder to Light: Death, Publishing and Performance in Icelandic Sagas' and Jeffrey Doolittle, 'Negotiating Murder in the *Historiae* of Gregory of Tours'. For additional studies on murder as treason and a violation of *lèse-majesté*, see in this volume: Jolanta N. Komornicka, 'Treacherous Murder: Language and Meaning in French Murder Trials' and Andrew McKenzie-McHarg, '"A general murther, an universal slaughter": Strategies of Anti-Jesuit Defamation in Reporting Assassination in the Early Modern Period'.

Fama is not a private thing belonging to an individual. Because it belongs to the larger community within which it emerges, it is a public, material, yet fluid *thing* of significance. Its public constitution is evident in its semantic meaning. *Fama* is 'public opinion, idle talk, rumor, and reputation as well as fame; both a good name and a bad one were called *fama*; and while *fama* denoted information or news, at the same time it meant the image formed of a person by that information'.[21] Moreover, medieval *fama* was constructed through the moral binary of good and bad. A person's moral character was contingent on the reputation they had earned in the public mind, but which that same public constructed through its judgements of the individual's deeds. Thus, it was external to the individual. As Claude Gauvard demonstrates, reputation created two types of people: those who were considered susceptible and, thus, likely guilty of the crime for which they were accused, and all others.[22] Reputation spoke for the body, and it had a life of its own even while it was a vital part of an individual's personhood.

Hence, reputation constituted the bulk of a person's social capital in medieval society, which was analogous to economic capital. Because it derives from community talk, it played a critical role in French legal processes, most importantly regarding witness testimony, 'facts' and proofs.[23] According to F. R. P. Akehurst, 'having a good reputation might make it easier for a person to prevail in a lawsuit'.[24] Gauvard similarly contends that reputation was so powerful a force that it became 'indispensable' in the late medieval legal system. She explains that the sovereign's claim over the life or death of his subjects was not straightforward.[25] Rather, the right to punish crimes with death relied heavily upon the *fama* of a person, and, she argues, it is the 'opinion générale qui désigne par là-même le coupable' [the general opinion determines through it [*fama*] the guilty].[26] Reputation was a dynamic and concrete part of a person's identity but one that was also part of the collective. Indeed, although a reputation was directly attached to an individual, judicial documents reveal that it was produced by the community and, thus, belonged to it.[27]

The extraordinary ongoing legal battle between the two ducal houses between 1407 and 1413 attests to the importance of reputation in identity formation for individuals and families, reaffirming its significance as crucial social and political currency. The narratives the two parties produced to defend their

---

[21] Thelma Fenster and Daniel Lord Smail, 'Introduction', in *Fama: The Politics of Talk and Reputation*, p. 2.
[22] Gauvard, '*De grace especial*', pp. 140–42. See also: Toureille, *Crime et châtiment*, p. 89.
[23] Akehurst, 'Name, Reputation, and Notoriety', pp. 75–94, esp. pp. 80–94.
[24] Ibid., p. 80.
[25] Gauvard, '*De grace especial*', p. 142.
[26] Ibid., p. 142.
[27] Ibid., p. 137.

position are replete with evidence of the cultural value placed on justice, honour, identity and the flexible boundaries of the medieval body. Moreover, the case highlights that these dominant cultural norms, which connected honour and justice, were at times incongruent with institutional justice. This illustrates the complicated rhetorical landscape that the high-status nobility had to navigate in order to protect their reputation during a legal battle of this magnitude. Indeed, in striving for legitimacy, all parties had to play the dangerous game of appealing to the king, his Parlement and the king's subjects. A positive outcome was uncertain. Finally, the manner by which the narratives construct the murder and 'second murder' of Louis of Orleans reveal a great deal about the complexity and multidimensionality of the late medieval body. It was simultaneously bound by its flesh and blood, a material thing that could be murdered and unbound by its *fama*, an unstable, abstract thing connected to honour and shame that had concrete, material significance in late medieval France. It is for this reason that the defamation of Louis of Orleans was the murder *more* foul.

According to the laws of late medieval France, murder was the most serious crime people could commit against other subjects of the king. Physical murder was a capital crime in late medieval France, the equivalent to English felonies. These were crimes that violated the king's peace.[28] After treason and regicide, murder was the most serious crime. For this reason, there was a distinction drawn between homicide and murder even though both crimes could be punished with execution.[29] Homicide was defined as the result of a death that emerged spontaneously, typically the consequence a heated exchange. Anger and passion usually drove the accused to kill, and honour was the driving force.[30] As the early fifteenth-century pardon records (the *lettres de rémission*) indicate, the courts were more lenient on homicide than murder, especially when the reputations of both the assailant and the victim were weighed against one another.[31]

---

[28] Warren C. Brown, *Violence in Medieval Europe* (Harlow: Longman, 2011), pp. 20, 202, 205–07, 214. See also: Barbara A. Hanawalt, *'Of Good and Ill Repute': Gender and Social Control in Medieval England* (Oxford: Oxford University Press, 1998), p. 5. For the high crimes that were akin to English felonies, including murder, rape, arson and treason, see: Toureille, *Crime et châtiment*, pp. 23, 63–79.

[29] Carbasse, *Histoire du droit pénal*, pp. 369–72; Gauvard, 'De grace especial', pp. 800–06. For medieval definitions offered by Philippe de Beaumanoir, see: *The Coutumes de Beauvaisis of Philippe de Beaumanoir*, trans. F. R. P Akehurst (Philadelphia: University of Pennsylvania Press, 1992), p. 303.

[30] This is a theme throughout Gauvard's work, 'De grace especial'.

[31] An example was the pardon of a poor labourer named Perrin Milot who, in 1413, murdered a sergeant of the parish of St Eloy. The pardon stipulated that he was remitted in part because '[il] a este tout son temps homme de bonne vie renomme et honeste' [he had his entire life been a man of good life and reputation and honest], whereas his victim was 'homme de petite vie et roteux et de meschant gouvernement et qui laissoit sa

Murder, on the other hand, was a premeditated killing and considered the act of a 'secret hatred' – an enmity that was not made public and an act that was typically done in secret, under the cover of darkness or during a truce.[32] As Philippe de Beaumanoir famously wrote, 'No murder is without treachery'.[33] Likewise, individuals who hired assassins were equally guilty of murder because it indicated conspiracy. Such secret acts were exceedingly shameful. According to the legal categories differentiating the two forms of killing, it seems that extinguishing the victim's life was important, but it was not the most significant in determining the appropriate punishment. The reputations of the individuals involved, the reason for the killing, the killer's intention and whether his deeds during the act were honourable or shameful – such as openness or secrecy, honesty or deception – were more important factors in determining the legitimacy of the killing. Without doubt, physically harming a body was a grave offence; however, whether the body harmed was deserving of the act and whether the victim was a body of worth were two crucial legal dimensions of the case. They strongly influenced the outcome.[34]

These legal points explain why, in his legal narrative, Burgundy defended the assassination of Louis of Orleans as a tyrannicide rather than a murder. He needed to make a case for why the royal prince he killed was not a valued body and why he deserved to die without trial. Burgundy had to prove that his

    femme pour aler avec une autre femme quil maintenoit' [a man of low life and unfixed and of little self-control who left his wife to go with another woman that he supported] (AN, JJ 167, fol. 298r–v).

[32] Philippe de Beaumanoir explains, murder occurs 'when someone kills someone else (or has them killed) premeditatedly between sunset and sunrise, or when he kills someone or has them killed during a truce or a guaranteed peace' (*The* Coutumes de Beauvaisis, p. 303). See also: Carbasse, *Histoire du droit pénal*, pp. 369–372, and Gauvard, '*De grace especial*', pp. 800–06. For more on the shamefulness of secret hatred, see: Robert Bartlett, '"Mortal Enmities": The Legal Aspect of Hostility in the Middle Ages', in *Feud, Violence and Practice. Essays in Medieval Studies in Honor of Stephen D. White*, ed. Belle S. Tuten and Tracey L. Billado (Farnham: Ashgate, 2010), pp. 197–212, esp. pp. 201–02.

[33] Beaumanoir, *The* Coutumes de Beauvaisis, p. 303. See also: Gauvard, '*De grace especial*', p. 803 and Carbasse, *Histoire du droit pénal*, p. 370.

[34] For example, in one of the *lettres de rémission*, Estienne was pardoned for the homicide of Jehanne, an elderly widow between seventy and eighty years old, whom he tried unsuccessfully to rape while inebriated. The document explains that Estienne was pardoned because while he was an 'homme de bonne vie Renommee et conversacion honeste' [man of good life, reputation and honest conversation], Jehanne was 'faible et ancienne' [weak and old], 'Renommee davoir este de dissolu estat vie' [known for having been of a dissolute way of life], and who, apparently, was known to have had multiple sexual partners (AN, JJ 165, fol. 11v). I thank Allison Bailey for bringing this document to my attention. She discovered and analysed it in 'Policing Violence: Royal and Community Perspectives in Medieval France', undergraduate honours thesis (Mount Royal University, Calgary, AB, 2016).

intention was pure, had to overcome the secrecy of his plan to kill and the gruesomeness of the killing itself. All these facts had to fade into the background so that he could attempt to exculpate himself. Anything less, and he risked shaming himself into perpetuity. Therefore, he painted Louis as the worst of criminals, even denying him his right to his own name. Throughout the justification, he referred only to him as the 'criminal duke of Orleans'.[35]

Likewise, in refuting these claims, the House of Orleans had to be consistent in the labels they chose for defining both the killing and the man responsible for it in order to build their formal legal case against Burgundy. This four-year-long legal battle was not like any other regular trial, which would typically end within a few days. Both parties had to be very careful to rehearse the same points and deploy the same labels throughout the years. Consistency was the most crucial element in framing their legal case against the other. Unfortunately, the only source in which the formal refutation of Burgundy's defence is transcribed in full is in the pro-Burgundian chronicle written by Enguerran de Monstrelet, which means that there may have been some semantic variances from the real refutation text.[36] In Monstrelet's text, Cérisy falls short of calling the killing a murder; instead, he labels it a 'cruel homicide'. Perhaps Monstrelet was trying to soften his version to put Burgundy in the best possible light, but in adding the adjective 'cruel' even this author implicitly acknowledges murder over homicide. Certainly, in July 1411 when Louis' sons wrote their notorious *Jargeau Manifesto*, a very long letter patent to the king and to the *bonnes villes*, to justify challenging Burgundy to war, they were more direct. Here, they label him a *meurtrier* [murderer] (*Jargeau*, 280), and, for extra emphasis, they sometimes call him a *traistre meurtrier* [traitorous murderer] (*Jargeau*, 278, 280, 282, 284). Likewise, they insist that the body of Orleans was 'cruellement meurtry ou tué' [cruelly murdered or killed] (*Jargeau*, 284). They use the verbs *occire* [slay or kill], *tuer* [kill] and *meurtrir* [murder] to describe the action of killing. They also explain that 'par orreur et cruaulté' [by horror and cruelty], Burgundy committed the crime of parricide by killing such a close blood relative (his first cousin).[37] They explained, 'le crime de paricide [sic] auquel les droits ne savent imposer de peines assez grandes pour la trez horrible cruauté et abominable detestation dycellui' [the laws do not know how to impose serious enough penalties for the very horrible, cruel and abominable detestation of this man] (*Jargeau*, 278). These descriptions are not trivial hyperbole. The aim of the repeated emphasis

---

[35] For a full discussion on this label and its significance, see below.
[36] The Chronicler of Saint Denis, Michel Pintoin, included a fairly robust version of the text, but it is primarily a narrative of the presentation that includes lengthy, but not full, citations. See: RSD, 4: 92–128.
[37] For other discussions on parricide, see in this volume: Carmel Ferragud, 'A Multiple Poisoning in the City of Valencia: Sanxo Calbó's Crime (1442)'.

on the cruelty of Burgundy's act was to make a stronger legal case for its extreme immorality and to connect it to an irrational act of excessive and inhuman violence.[38] The depravity of the deed would, they hoped, nullify the claim that Burgundy made in his defence that he had been righteous in killing a tyrant whose body was not one of worth. They sought to invert his claim by positioning Burgundy as the man lacking all honour and worth, while repositioning Louis as the innocent victim who suffered death without cause, without trial. This tactic was a crucial legal manoeuvre to reinforce their position that this was murder rather than a justifiable homicide.

The claim was actually true. As the family rightly pointed out, the killing adhered to all the legal criteria of murder. For example, they argued that the death was the result of a secret hatred the duke of Burgundy had nurtured for a long time. The two men had declared a truce between them in 1405, swearing to be friends.[39] They exchanged badges, they ate together and they celebrated together. According to their complaint, only just before the murder, the men had pledged their love and loyalty, Burgundy visited him when he was ill and they spoke kindly to each other:

> [Le duc de Bourgogne] feignoit avoir avec vostredit frere, tout amour et loyauté, parce que dit est, conversoit souvent avec luy, et par especial en une maladie qu'il eut paravant ledit meurtre commis en sa personne, ycellui l'alla veoir et visiter, tant à Beauté comme à Paris, et luy monstroit tous signes d'amour, que freres, cousins, parents, et amis pouvoient et devoient porter et monstrer l'un à l'autre ... qui preuvent et monstre trop clairement que c'estoit une bien cruelle et mortelle trahison.
>
> [he feigned to have with your aforesaid brother love and loyalty, because as it is said, he conversed often with him, and in particular when [Louis] had an illness just before the aforesaid murder against his person, and this man [John of Burgundy] went to see and visit him at Beauté and in Paris, and showed him all the signs of love that brothers, cousins, relations, and friends can and should have and show to each other ... which proves all too clearly that this was a very cruel and deadly betrayal]. (*Jargeau*, 278)

These gestures signalled friendship and alliance. If he had refused to speak with Louis or treated him badly, he would have been publicly demonstrating his enmity with Louis. It was all the worse because he did these things just prior to the murder to cover his tracks, an act that, for the Orleanists, indicated betrayal and was the most important characteristic of the murder.

---

[38] Daniel Baraz explores this technique in depth in *Medieval Cruelty: Changing Perceptions, Late Antiquity to the Early Modern Period* (Ithaca: Cornell University Press, 2003), pp. 3–11.

[39] See: Hutchison, 'The Politics of Grief', p. 428.

They point out that, immediately following the murder, the duke of Burgundy also faked his grief, which made his betrayal even more heinous:

> Par les fausses, feintes et dampnables maniers tenuës par ledit traistre aprez l'accomplissement dudit trez horribles et trez detestable meurtre; car il vint au corps avec les Seigneurs de vostre Sang, se vestit de noir, fust à son enterrement, feignoit pleurer et faire deüil et avoir desplaisance de sa mort, cuidant par ce couvrir et celer et embler son mauvais peché...
>
> [By the false, faked and damnable undertakings by the aforesaid traitor after the accomplishment of the very horrible and very detestable murder; for he came with the body with the Princes of your Blood, he dressed himself in black, went to his burial, and feigned crying and mourning and displeasure for his death, thinking he would cover and hide and remove from sight his evil sin...]. (*Jargeau*, 279)

This was an egregious transaction, and all the chroniclers weigh in on this disgrace.[40] Only true friends could legitimately mourn their kindred. It was a sign of loyalty and duty. Their goal was to clearly identify the signs that Burgundy was responsible for the most serious crime, murder, to support their legal claim. Moreover, the details of the death were recounted in minute, visceral detail to impress upon the audience (the king, his Parlement and the citizens of the realm) just how this body was shamefully harmed.[41] They emphasise that no royal blood had ever been spilt in such a humiliating and cruel fashion. For this, the entire realm should grieve loudly and angrily, they added.[42] The point was to emphasise how the body of this royal prince, a man of nearly sacred blood, was shamefully destroyed. Such deeds could not go unpunished and, thus, they called the king to do his duty and punish his brother's murderer.

---

[40] For a complete discussion on this issue, see: ibid., pp. 429–36.

[41] 'et en oultre luy fendirent et aggravantirent toute la teste en divers lieux, et tant que la cervelle en cheyt presque toute en la bouë, là le renverserent, toüillerent et traignirent jusques à ce qu'ils virent qu'il estoit tout roide mort, qui est et seroit un trez grant horreur, pitié et douleur à oüir reciter du plus bas homme et du plus petit estat du monde ne oncques' [and also [he] separated and crushed his head in many places, and such that his brain fell almost entirely into the mud, and there threw, mixed and pulled him around until they saw that he was firmly dead, which is and would be a very great horror, pity and pain to hear recited even for the lowest man of the smallest estate of the world that ever was] (*Jargeau*, 279).

[42] 'mais le Sang de vostre noble Maison de France ne fust si crueusement ni si honteusement espandu, ne dont Vous, ne ceux de vostre, vos subjects tous et bienvaillans deussiez avoir tel deüil, courroux, et desplaisance ...' [but the Blood of your noble House of France was not so cruelly nor so shamefully shed that You and yours, and your subjects and all your supporters should not have mourning, anger and displeasure ...] (*Jargeau*, 279).

The emphasis on the materiality of the blood Cérisy describes here, and which is later rehearsed in the *Jargeau Manifesto*, had several purposes. The first was to elicit outrage at the extreme violence visited upon Louis, whose status and genetic identity as a *prince of the blood* should have naturally precluded him from such suffering. Cérisy explains, 'Car la condicion de sang royal doit estre de si grant pitié et loyaulté, que à peine pourroit elle souffrir cruaulté, homicide ou trahison quelconques. Et audit sang royal estoit moult prouchain mondit seigneur d'Orléans, car il estoit filz de roy et de royne' [For the condition of the royal blood should be of such great pity and loyalty that it could never suffer cruelty, homicide or betrayal at all. And to this royal blood was my aforesaid lord of Orleans very connected, for he was the son of a king and queen] (*Chronique* 1:281). He asserts that royal blood itself is a material thing to be protected and honoured; therefore, any body through which it flows demands loyalty. Moreover, Louis' blood is particularly important because French kings were given the great honour of the title, 'Most Christian King'. This ancient, regal lineage places him above other bodies. Murder of any body was a terrible crime; however, at a cellular level, the murder of this particular body was shameful in the extreme. It was the greatest act of disloyalty and betrayal, deserving of punishment.

The second reason for dedicating so much time and space to the issue of blood was its significance in performances of death and justice. As Katherine Royer argues, 'Blood flowing from a living body signifies life', but it also has multivalent meanings in narratives on death. For example, in execution narratives in medieval and early modern England, she observes that the absence of blood and pain in the descriptions of the deaths dehumanised the traitors being punished.[43] Similar patterns appear in France. For example, in the extant criminal registers of the Châtelet (1389–1391), there is no mention of any pain, suffering or spilling of blood during the inquisitorial torture or in the execution.[44] Likewise, the chroniclers' narratives of executions during Charles VI's reign were comparably silent in describing pain or suffering unless they were trying to illustrate that the execution was wrong, cruel and ignominious.[45] Royer argues that highlighting pain and suffering likens the victims to Christ. Conversely, the absence of pain and blood not only distances the criminal from their own human personhood but

---

[43] Royer, *English Execution Narratives*, pp. 34–37 and 44.
[44] This is true in every case recorded in the *Registre criminel du Châtelet*.
[45] This was the case for the Jean de Montaigu, the grand master of the king's household, who, in autumn 1409, was accused and found guilty of conspiring with Louis of Orleans. There is no mention of blood, but his pain and suffering, as well as his injuries from torture, are highlighted in Michel Pintoin's description of the execution (RSD, 4: 274–76). Pintoin's narrative of the execution of Louis of Orleans' former chamberlain, Jacques de la Rivière, includes some description of blood and pain. The chronicler refers to this execution as 'ignominious' (RSD, V: 54–56).

also distances them from Christ.[46] In Burgundy's justification of March 1408, Jean Petit accuses Orleans of high treason (*lèse-majesté*) and of tyranny, trying to dehumanise him entirely by effacing his name and status. In the *Justification*, Petit refuses to call Louis by name, instead referring to him only as 'le criminel duc d'Orléans' [the criminal duke of Orleans] throughout the text. Cérisy cleverly turns Petit's approach on its head. In emphasising over and over the spilling of his blood and the agony that he endured, Cérisy sought both to restore Louis' personhood and to connect his torment to Christ's.[47]

Furthermore, during the medieval period, the more blood that was shed in the enactment of a crime, the more serious it was. Bloodshed could serve as evidence that a serious capital crime had been committed. For example, in England proving that an assault caused 'effusion of blood' was a vital piece of evidence in the pursuit of a rape charge.[48] On both sides of the channel, too much blood could also be evidence of over-zealous, extreme and blameworthy spousal

---

[46] Royer, *English Execution Narratives*, pp. 35–36.

[47] Nowhere is this clearer than when he had Louis speak from beyond the grave to point out his wounds. Cérisy has him cry out, 'O Monseigneur mon frère! regarde comment pour toy j'ay recue mort. C'estoit pour la grant amour qui estoit entre nous. Regarde mes plaies, esquelles les cinq espécialement furent cruelles et mortelles. Regarde mon corps batu, soulé et envelope en la boe. Regarde mes bras coppez et ma cervelle espandue hors de mon chef. Regarde s'il est douleur pareille à ma douleur. Hélas! il ne souffist mie à partie adverse estaindre ma vie si cruellement et sans cause, mais si soudainement et traitreusement me sousprint, ainsi que je aloye de l'ostel de madame la Royne devers toy, par quoy il me mist en peril de dampnacion. Et après partie adverse s'est efforcé de diffamer moy et ma lignée, par son libelle mauvaise et diffamatoire' [My lord and brother! Look at the death I have suffered for you because of our strong love. Look at my wounds, five of which are especially cruel and mortal. Look at my body, beaten and mutilated (*foulé*) and covered in mud. Look at my arms cut off, and my brains leaking (*espandue*) from my head. Try to find pain that equals my pain. Alas! It did not suffice for the adverse party to extinguish my life so cruelly, but to do it so suddenly and treacherously by surprising me as I was on my way from the Queen's hotel to see you, for which he has put my soul in peril of damnation. And after, the adverse party endeavoured to defame me and my line with malicious and defamatory libel]. The rendering is reminiscent of Christ's stigmata. See: Monstrelet, *Chronique*, 1: 285.

[48] Hanawalt citing Ranulf Glanville's *Treatise on the Laws and Customs of the Kingdoms of England*, 'Whose Story Was This? Rape Narratives in Medieval English Courts', in '*Of Good and Ill-Repute*', p. 126. I have not yet found any specific reference to blood as evidence of rape in French laws. However, according to Valérie Toureille, the word *viol* [rape] stems from the Latin *violare* [to treat with violence, to force]. It retained its meaning as an excessive act of force and cruelty. Toureille, *Crime et châtiment*, p. 36. See also: Hannah Skoda, 'Violent Discipline or Disciplining Violence? Experience and Reception of Domestic Violence in Late Thirteenth- and Early Fourteenth-Century Paris and Picardy', *Cultural and Social History* 6.1 (2009): 9–27.

abuse.[49] Thus, Cérisy's attempts to prove that, rather than a dehumanised traitor and criminal, the illustrious duke of Orleans, a *prince of the blood*, was instead the victim of the excessively violent, cruel crime of premeditated murder.

Moreover, in a society that placed such strong importance on blood lineage to define patrimony and inheritance, family identity and authority, the Orleanists had to remind their intended audiences that Louis was his full-blooded brother. In the honour-based culture of the period, a harm against family or kindred demanded retaliation. Hence, Cérisy rails: 'Hélas! Ce seroit petit cuer et peu de bien, estre filz et frère de roy, se ceste mort si cruelle sans réparacion estoit mise en oubli, actendu que cellui qui le fist occire le devoit aymer comme son frère' [Alas! It would be a small heart and of little good to be the son and brother of kings, if this very cruel death without reparation is forgotten, given that he who had him killed should have loved him like a brother] (*Chronique* 1: 278). Building on the concept of bloodline, Cérisy also emphasises the king's relationship as the closest kin of Louis. He explains that 'fraternal love' should impel him to pursue justice.[50] To pressure the king and his royal council to punish Burgundy, Cérisy went as far as to argue that a lack of confidence in the project of monarchy was sure to follow if the king could not punish the man who illegally murdered his own brother (*Chronique*, 1:280). For the king to fail his brother was, in fact, to fail all his subjects. He had to demonstrate his respect for these ties by punishing Burgundy or risk, according to Cérisy, further tarnishing the illustrious reputation of the French crown.[51] Likewise, in 1411, Louis' sons echoed Cérisy's position in their 'Jargeau Manifesto' explaining their reason for challenging Burgundy to war. Regarding bloodline and the king's personal, familial tie to Orleans, they explained that they shuddered in horror to think of what was to come when

> ceux qui viendront aprez nous, lisent et trouvent en scriptures notables, qui soit party de bouche du Roy de France, qui est le plus grand Roy des Chrestiens, que en la mort de son seul frère germain, si honteuse, cruelle, si traistreuse et inhumaine mort, il n'ait point pris de desplaisance; lesquelles choses, nostre trez redoubté et souverain Seigneur, sont faites et redondent clerement en si trez grande lesion et vitupere de vostre proper honneur, de vostre Couronne et Majesté Royaule, qui y sont tellement foulez et blessiez que à peine est chose reparable.

---

[49] Philippe de Beaumanoir is clear that all discipline men give their wives should be moderate. See: *The* Coutumes de Beauvaisis, pp. 594–95.
[50] For this and what follows, see: *Chronique*, 1: 277–78.
[51] Cérisy claimed that rumours were already circulating around and outside the realm that the king was weak in his resolve to implement his chief duty as supreme justiciar. This, he argued, threatened the reputation of the crown (*Chronique*, 1:274, 277–78, 280).

[those who come after us read and find in our notable writings, that by his own tongue the king of France, who is the most Christian king, [said] that in the death of his only brother, a shameful, cruel and so treacherous and inhumane death, he had taken no displeasure. The things that have occurred ... are such a great lesion and condemnation (*vitupere*) of your personal honour, your Crown and royal majesty, which are terribly undermined (*foulez*) and injured (*blessiez*) that it is hardly possible to repair [them]]. (*Jargeau*, 281)

It is hard to ignore the physical dimension of the shame that the king and his royal crown allegedly endure as a result of inaction. Shame is characterised as a lesion that compromises not only the reputation of the man himself but also his metaphysical dimensions (his crown and royal majesty). Just as Orleans' body and his good name could both be murdered, the king's two bodies suffer materially in Cérisy's imagining. In this, Cérisy plays on the dualism of the king's two bodies – his person, which is finite, and the royal majesty, which is infinite – both of which are constructed by the good and righteous reputation he is able to sustain as king.[52] According to late medieval political thought, the king, as head of the body politic, was obligated to impose peace and harmony upon the 'body' he governed by ensuring that good justice prevailed.[53] In fact, political moralists and thinkers of the time agreed that a king's only right to authority was contingent on his ability to serve justice in this respect. However, justice for the Orleans family was complicated. They were not only intent, initially, on punishing Burgundy for the physical murder of the duke but their form of justice also hinged in the retraction of the defamation.

It is difficult to know with any certainty whether the king's own reputation was impugned or not in light of his inaction for there is little concrete evidence to prove anyone lost any respect for him or his authority within the realm or without. Regardless of the truth of the matter, such positions were important rhetorical devices for the legal case the Orleanists were trying to build even when (or if) they were hollow. Justice had to follow a different course for the high nobility. Both parties involved in such a high-profile dispute had to construct convincing narratives to lobby the king and his council, the Parlement of Paris, as well as the king's subjects in order to validate their cause. Hence, the Orleanists flagged the king's responsibilities to his subjects not only to remind the king and his judicial arm of their failure but to also reach a much broader audience. This, they hoped, would enable them to gain more moral support in

---

[52] Ernst Kantorowicz, *The King's Two Bodies: A Study in Mediaeval Political Theology* (Princeton: Princeton University Press, 1957, repr. 1997). See also: Victoria Kahn, 'Political Fiction and Theology in *The King's Two Bodies*', *Representations* 106.1 (Spring 2009): 77–101 and Steven Greenblatt, 'Fifty Years After *The King's Two Bodies*', *Representations* 106.1 (Spring, 2006): 63–66.

[53] Hutchison, 'Knowing One's Place', pp. 18–19, esp. nn. 60–62.

their pursuit, leading to financial and military reinforcement from the towns of the realm if required. This backing could, in turn, pressure the king and his council to respond favourably to their demands. The targets included the intellectual community and the king's subjects (for whom the *Jargeau Manifesto* was published). For the former group, the Orleanist narrative was congruent with current notions of sovereignty and moral rulership within the body politic; for the latter, their insistence on the right to vengeance corresponded to norms of family duty and obligation as much as it reflected popular perceptions of royal justice.[54] Ultimately, the Orleanists were looking for widespread support in their judicial case so that they would find strength in numbers to overcome the duke of Burgundy's control over the king and have the pardon overturned. This was no small task. Retracting a royal pardon could dishonour the king and weaken his authority. The House of Orleans had to try to make an airtight case without undermining their sovereign.

Typically, whether for homicide or murder, the accused was tried (and punished) through the king's court system, whether in the courts of the local *prévôts*, their superiors (the *baillis* and *sénéchaux*) or through the highest court of the realm, the Parlement of Paris.[55] In high profile cases for the highest nobility, the king (with his royal council) would try the individual himself, though this was typically reserved for the king's peers (like the duke of Burgundy).[56] In keeping with regular judicial procedure, the royal council met immediately after the assassination of Orleans on 22 November to decide how to proceed.[57] The provost of Paris was called upon and, on 24 November, initiated a formal investigation.[58]

The next day, Burgundy confessed to the crime and offered the names of his hired assassins.[59] However, these men had already escaped the city, taking

[54] For a concise synopsis of the prevailing ideas on good government and justice, and their widespread appeal, see: Emily J. Hutchison, 'Winning Hearts and Minds in Early Fifteenth-Century France: Burgundian Propaganda in Perspective', *French Historical Studies* 35.1 (2012): 3–30 at pp. 4–7.

[55] Carbasse, *L'histoire du droit pénale*, pp. 153–55; Simon Cuttler, *The Law of Treason and Treason Trials in Later Medieval France* (Cambridge: Cambridge University Press, 1981), pp. 89–92.

[56] Carbasse, *L'histoire du droit pénale*, pp. 164–65.

[57] RSD, 3:737.

[58] For details on these, see: Richard C. Famiglietti, *Royal Intrigue: Crisis at the Court of Charles VI, 1392–1420* (New York: AMS Press, 1986), pp. 61–65; Guenée, *Un meurtre*, pp. 178–79; Vaughan, *John the Fearless*, pp. 44–48. Ordinances were issued in the king's name shutting the gates of the city, mandating all hostels to declare if they had received strangers on 29 November 1407. See: *Ordonnances des rois de France de la troisième race*, ed. M. Secousse and M. de Vilevaut (1755) 9:261.

[59] Perhaps because the other great lords had agreed to allow the Provost to search their hotels. See: Famiglietti, *Royal Intrigue*, p. 63.

shelter in Burgundy's city of Bruges, where they were given annual pensions for the remainder of their lives.[60] Thus, the men were never punished for killing the duke of Orleans.[61] In the spring of 1411, Louis of Orleans' eldest son, Charles, now duke of Orleans, sent a letter to the king and the Parlement of Paris, which was copied and distributed across the realm for mass consumption. In it, he complained specifically that none of the assassins had been tried or punished for their crimes.[62] This ran counter to the proper course of justice, Charles argued, and he was right, at least in theory. Murderers were supposed to be tried and, if guilty, executed. For this reason, Charles insisted that the king and his judicial system do their duty to punish the guilty. He explained that the king was beholden to do justice 'à ung chascun indifférentement, tant au petit comme au grant' [to every person indifferently, as much to the little as to the great] (*Chronique*, 2:116). This meant punishing those guilty of bodily murder, which would include both the duke of Burgundy, for organising the conspiracy, and the men who did the foul deed. The king's negligence in pursuing these men was a further offence to their family's honour, and it compromised Louis' memory specifically because inaction was a tacit avowal that the assassination was indeed deemed legitimate. According to the House of Orleans, justice could only be served when all the men associated with it were tried and punished.

Knowing the importance of legal process, there are several reasons that explain why Burgundy went unpunished, and the first of these has nothing to do with the posthumous defamation of Louis of Orleans. Immediately following Burgundy's confession, there was much confusion that ultimately set the conditions for his pardon later in March 1408. When his peers did discover he was guilty, they told him not to join the royal council meeting on 26 November, and they urged him to leave Paris.[63] Enguerran de Monstrelet claims that the duke was apparently 'confus et en grant doubte' [troubled and in great doubt] (*Chronique*, 1:163–164) and fled at once. Once he arrived in his own territories, there was little the royal council could do to pursue him unless the king formally declared war upon him.

---

[60] They remained there, forbidden from leaving the city until their natural deaths. See: Vaughan, *John the Fearless*, p. 48.

[61] If Burgundy had not sheltered them, they would have been brought to trial either in the Châtelet (the court of the provost of Paris) or the Parlement of Paris, presumably for murder (not homicide). See: Guenée, *Un meurtre*, pp. 185–87.

[62] This letter was transcribed in *Chronique*, 2:116–21.

[63] Burgundy falsely participated in all the mourning rituals. This was an issue that caused even more distress amongst the royal family and council, and it was later used against him in the Orleanists' legal case against him. See: Hutchison, 'The Politics of Grief', pp. 429–36.

Additionally, the legal process for prosecuting of one of the highest peers of the crown for the murder of another was apparently more ambiguous than the prosecution of lesser noble subjects in the regional courts at this time. Custom dictated that when an individual committed an act like homicide, he was expected first to admit the crime, allowing his relatives to negotiate a peace act (stipulating the reparations for the death) with the family of the deceased.[64] Once this agreement was reached between the two parties, and the ritual of the 'amende honorable' [honourable amends] was complete, the king typically absolved him of wrongdoing,[65] and the guilty party's name and reputation were fully restored alongside his material possessions (his title and property). Apparently, this was how the royal council attempted to proceed in the aftermath of Louis of Orleans' murder. It is well known that the king's uncles (excluding Louis, duke of Bourbon, who refused to parley with Burgundy whatsoever),[66] went to Amiens in early December to convince Burgundy to acknowledge his guilt, negotiate with the House of Orleans and, thus, repair the king's honour.[67] They also insisted that he give up the assassins. Yet, as Enguerran de Monstrelet explains, to their great 'surprise' (*merveille*), Burgundy did not cooperate,[68] and he refused to take any responsibility for murder or to give up his men. In the refutation, Cérisy points to this problem specifically.[69] It mattered to the Orleanists because, in their judicial case, it stood as evidence of Burgundy's refusal to make amends, which indicated that this could not be a mere homicide.

In fact, Burgundy had brought with him a rather impressive cohort of at least 600–800 men-at-arms even though he had been expressly forbidden from doing so (*Chroniques* 1:173–174). Also, a huge crowd of Parisians met him at the gate of St Denis when he first arrived, and many more lined the streets cheering him as he entered and marched down the boulevard to his residence.[70] The duke's retinue was an overwhelming, threatening military parade.[71] Rather than showing humility and begging pardon, Burgundy showed only intransigence and aggression. These were bold and impudent acts that signalled he would not allow himself to be condemned for his act. Furthermore, he outright refused again to

[64] Guenée, *Un meurtre*, pp. 186–87.
[65] For the 'amende honorable', see: Claude Gauvard, *Violence et ordre public au Moyen Âge* (Paris: Picard, 2005), pp. 156–67.
[66] RSD, 3:742.
[67] Guenée, *Un meurtre*, pp. 186–87. For primary sources on this embassy, see: *Chronique*, 1:174–75 and Juvénal, *Histoire de Charles VI*, 3:438.
[68] *Chronique*, 1:174–75. For more discussion on this point, see Hutchison, 'The Politics of Grief', pp. 433–34.
[69] *Chronique* 1:289–90.
[70] See: RSD, 3: 754; Juvénal, *Histoire de Charles VI*, 438; and *Chronique*, 1:1:111.
[71] Coville, *Jean Petit et la question du tyrannicide*, pp. 105, 113.

give up the assassins and, rather than ask for pardon, he claimed that he had done the king a great favour.[72] His spokesman Jean Petit then spent two hours enumerating all ways in which Orleans had proven himself a tyrant, listing all his attempts on the king life (*Chronique* 1:185). These were important details for the legal case. To root his claims in contemporary jurisprudence, he had to try to prove that the king's own brother had committed corporal and divine *lèse-majesté*, and that it was, therefore, morally permissible and just to kill him without the monarch's permission (*Chronique* 1:206). Obviously, Burgundy was trying to skirt the fact that he had thwarted due process in condemning the king's brother without trial. There was no question that Burgundy's refusal to act as a humble supplicant confused the king and the royal council, which contributed substantially to his pardon. This was a surprising turn of events for all involved, especially the House of Orleans.

An important dimension of Burgundy's legal defence demands attention: his spokesman categorically refused to call Louis anything but the 'criminal duke of Orleans' throughout the text. Petit's tactic affirms the importance of reputation and its material consequences for individuals whose reputations are impugned. The term 'criminal' was rarely used in late medieval legal discourse; indeed, it was reserved only for the most significant of transgressions, in part because it carried substantial moral connotations.[73] Claude Gauvard explains that because the very word 'crime' was taboo, it could never be reversed or pardoned.[74] Therefore, it is never found in the *lettres de remissions* [remission letters] that granted full pardons to convicted felons. The learned men Burgundy hired to prepare the justification were expert in juristic thought and legal discourse; hence, they left no room for Louis' absolution of the fictional crimes they threw at him. Such tactics support Gauvard's argument that the moral and political gravity of the label made it a 'formidable weapon' in politics.[75] To be labelled thus damaged the accused beyond repair, permanently destroying their name – their *fama* – and alienating them from society. Toureille concurs, arguing that reputation is the most crucial ingredient in forming a person's honour. A negative reputation led to social exclusion at the very least.[76] The 'obliteration of honour' was, according to Gauvard, far worse than any physical pain inflicted upon a body.[77]

---

[72] Juvénal, *Histoire de Charles VI*, 2:438.
[73] 'L'emploi du mot "malefice" qui se substitue à celui de "crime" n'est pas insignifiant. Le méfait politique a, d'emblée, un contenu social et moral' [The usage of the word 'malefice' which can be substituted for 'crime' is not insignificant]. See: Gauvard, '*De grace especial*', pp. 111–22 at p. 120.
[74] Ibid.
[75] Ibid.
[76] Toureille, *Crime et châtiment*, p. 89.
[77] Gauvard, '*De grace especial*', p. 143.

The Burgundian narrative thus stripped Orleans of his name, his identity as a son and a brother of a king, his ducal titles and all his privileges. Through this process of estrangement, he became an anonymous criminal, a tyrant who deserved his vicious, premeditated death. Here, then, Orleans' body underwent a metamorphosis; it changed from a respectable royal body into something monstrous, yet something unknowable and unfamiliar, even to his family. The literal denial of his name had material consequences: Louis of Orleans became both a criminal and a *Nobody*. As a *Nobody* he had surrendered his very right to be mourned.[78]

This was an intolerable situation. In life, Orleans had been a very important man. Except for Burgundy, his peers apparently judged him to be an upstanding man of good repute. For example, when he died, the nobility wept deeply as a sign of their respect and friendship.[79] For Burgundy to erase this facet of Orleans' person posthumously was a shrewd legal tactic because a bad reputation, not shaken off easily in life, was virtually impossible to restore in death.[80] Indeed, during their lifetime, the nobility strove to build their *bona fama* for themselves through great deeds and feats of arms, through their charity and through their good manners so that their name would live on in perpetuity. All knew their bodies would not endure and that their souls would return to God, so the best a man could do to achieve honour was to preserve his living memory. As the fourteenth-century knight and standard-bearer of the Oriflamme, Geoffroi de Charny, explains: 'men of worth ... do not mind whether they live or die, provided that their life be good enough for them to die with honor'.[81] His point is that while fear certainly accompanies death, men should find respite in their courage and in preserving their good name. Otherwise, life is of little value. From Charny's point of view, the material significance of reputation is a *more* important dimension of the body than the flesh. Honour and reputation were the things that made the aristocratic man. According to all his peers, Orleans had indeed proven himself a man of worth; he had earned a mainly positive *fama* amongst the nobility. Yet his posthumous defamation eviscerated his *fama*, thereby effacing his person entirely, his 'second murder'. There was nothing left of the man they once knew and loved: neither his body nor his good name.

To counter Petit's points and restore Louis' *bona fama*, Cérisy first attacks the accusation that he is a nameless criminal. He argues that the label 'criminal' could not be legitimately applied to Orleans because it had not yet been formally

---

[78] *Chronique*, 1:242.
[79] See: Hutchison, 'Politics of Grief', pp. 429–33.
[80] Akehurst, 'Name, Reputation, and Notoriety', p. 82.
[81] Geoffroi de Charny, *A Knight's Own Book of Chivalry*, ed. Richard W. Kaeuper, trans. Elspeth Kennedy (Philadelphia: University of Pennsylvania Press, 2005), p. 70.

established through a trial nor that his deeds were worthy of execution.[82] Here, Cérisy draws on late medieval French law which stipulated that a man was innocent until proven guilty beyond any doubt. The legal adage stated 'les preuves doivent être plus claires que le jour à midi' [proofs had to be clearer than the day at noon].[83] This provision indicates that a simple presumption of guilt was insufficient evidence for punishment. Cérisy adds that while Burgundy falsely and precipitously called Louis a criminal, the 'cruel homicide' *was* actually a criminal act and was proven when Burgundy himself confessed to the deed.[84] That Burgundy had confessed to the killing on 25 November was a significant point in the judicial case against him because, in the legal system of late medieval France, as in the ecclesiastical courts, confession was considered the highest form of direct proof.[85] Ignoring the confession to the crime of murder was, therefore, unjust according to institutional law and practice.

After the formal refutation on 11 September 1408, the king's council rather vaguely declared that justice would be served and the House of Orleans would find satisfaction; however, none of the suggested punishments were ever carried out. In the autumn of 1408, negotiations opened between the House of Orleans and Burgundy. The basic demand for the Orleanists was that Burgundy publicly apologise for Louis' assassination.[86] This act would negate his spurious

---

[82] *Chronique* 1:273.

[83] Carbasse, *L'histoire du droit pénal*, p. 203.

[84] 'Car je repute icellui cruel homicide et par consequent criminal, non mie par souspeçon tant seulement, mais par la confession de sa propre bouche' [For I call this cruel homicide and by consequence it is criminal, not only because it is suspected, but because it was a confession from his own mouth] (*Chronique* 1:273). This point was later emphasised in the *Jargeau Manifesto*: 'l'énormité dudit meurtre, lequel on ne pourroit assez detester ne blasmer la notorieté d'ycellui, tant de droit comme de fait, la confession de partie qui l'a confessé notoirement et publiquement … la confession ainsy faite, selon toute raison escripte et tous droits et usages notoirement observez, vault et doit valoir en son prejudice, et jamais il ne doit estre recue à dire le contraire de sa confession, ne à la coulourer ou justifier autrement qu'il fit premierement; par laquelle confession, il Juge competent, se condamna luy-mesme de sa propre bouche, jetta sur luy sa Sentence…' [the enormity of the aforesaid murder, for which we cannot sufficiently detest or pass blame, as much by right as by deed, of the notoriety of the confession that he notoriously confessed publicly … the confession thus made, according to all reasonable writings and all the rights and customs notoriously observed, count and should count to his prejudice, and never should he have the opportunity to say anything contrary to his confession, or colour it or justify it otherwise than what he has already said; with the aforesaid confession he condemned himself by his own mouth, and a competent Judge [must] give him his sentence …] (*Jargeau*, 284).

[85] Even witness testimony was only considered a half proof. See: Carbasse, *L'histoire du droit pénal*, pp. 200–01.

[86] Lucien Merlet, 'Biographie de Jean de Montaigu, grand maître de France (1350–1409)', *Bibliothèque de l'École des chartes* 3.3 (1852): 273–79.

claims against Orleans, thereby restoring the latter's reputation fully and superficially make amends for the physical murder. Naturally, he refused, for to do otherwise would destroy his own reputation. Unfortunately for the Orleanists, Louis' widow, Valentina Visconti, died suddenly in early December 1408, which deflated their cause significantly. By 9 March 1409, the two parties signed the peace treaty of Chartres.[87] The articles of the treaty stipulated that Burgundy did not ever have to admit to any wrongdoing, and the Orleans children were hereafter forbidden from any retaliation for their father's death or defamation. It was a shameful legal outcome for their party for, thereafter, they had no righteous recourse to the law. This signifies a clash of cultural norms prioritising honour as the basic premise for justice with institutional, royal justice prioritising peace and harmony between the parties. So acute was this dissonance that the House of Orleans ultimately committed treason by disobeying the king and, in 1411, called the Peace of Chartres null and void because it was coerced and it contradicted reason and the rights of men to pursue those who harm them (*Jargeau*, 281).

Hence, in the spring of 1410, Charles, the new duke of Orleans, reaffirmed all his father's alliances with great princes.[88] The Armagnac party was officially formed at Gien, and, on 2 September 1410, their party sent a letter to the king, which they copied and distributed widely across the realm.[89] It explained that the perpetual failure of justice had harmed (*blecé*) their honour. While the letter was diplomatic throughout and stressed that their sole intention was to uphold the dignity of the crown, they nonetheless implicitly chastised the king for his inaction and rather arrogantly educated him in the norms of institutional justice. Indeed, the first third of the letter reminded the king (and thus his subjects) repeatedly of his sole obligation: 'les drois de vostre couronne, dominacion et majesté royale soient si noblement instituez, vous en eulx et iceulx en vous, fondez en justice' [the rights of your crown, authority and royal majesty are so nobly instituted, you in them and them in you, are founded on justice ...] (*Chronique*, 2: 82–86 and AN, X^{1a} 8602, fols 231–232v). As the months rolled on, the party became bolder in its pursuit of justice. In May 1411, Charles of Orleans

---

[87] For a discussion on the treaty, see: Léon Mirot, 'Autour la paix de Chartres', *Annales de Bourgogne* 3 (1931): 313–16. For a discussion on the emotional element of the treaty and its impact in the development of civil war, see: Hutchison, 'The Politics of Grief', pp. 443–44.

[88] For the various alliances between Charles of Orleans and Berry, Jacques of Bourbon, Jacques of Clermont, Bernard of Armagnac, Charles of Albret and Charles of Eu, see AN, K 56, nos 25$^{1-8}$, K 57, nos 1^{a-b}. Charles of Orleans also called upon all his vassals and made the necessary accommodations to pay his *gens de guerre*, including his knights, esquires, archers and crossbowmen (AN, K 57, nos 1–2$^{1-4}$, K 57 no. 6, and K 57 no. 9$^{1-36}$).

[89] The letter was drafted by the dukes of Berry, Orleans and Bourbon and the counts of Alençon and Armagnac (*Chronique*, 2:82–86 and AN, X^{1a} 8602, fols 231–32v).

wrote to the royal council in response to the king's earlier demands that he disband his troops and end his dispute with the duke of Burgundy. In it, Charles specifically named the murder and defamation as an ongoing issue not yet addressed. He explained that he would only comply with the king's request and retract his letters regarding 'les homicides, consentans, occiseurs et coulpables de la mort de mondit seigneur et père, et vostre frère' [the homicides, colluders (*consentans*), killers and guilty [men] of the murder of my aforesaid lord and father, your brother] (*Chroniques*, 2:116–22) if the king eliminated from his royal council numerous men who were impeding the king from punishing Burgundy and his hired assassins.[90]

On 18 July 1411, Louis' sons formally declared Burgundy their enemy and challenged him to war.[91] Four days before that, they wrote and circulated the *Jargeau Manifesto*, explaining that they wrote regarding the 'trez horribles et trez detestable meurtre' [very horrible and very detestable murder] (*Jargeau*, 279) of their father and emphasising the absolute necessity of restoring Louis' memory. In it, they shared their concern that the king had forgotten his only brother, but they insisted that, in the deep recesses of his mind, Orleans must still live on. Thus, they explained he simply needed to be reminded of who he was and what happened to him four years before (*Jargeau*, 278). Part of the purpose of this letter, then, was to reconstruct the living memory of the dead for the king and for the subjects of the realm. The letter also reminded the king of the failure of justice where both Louis' body and his reputation were concerned. Throughout this text, Louis rematerialises in the process of remembering. The tactic erased the lies and defamatory libel that had effaced Louis of Orleans, thereby 'murdering' him a second time. Clearly, the metaphor remained central to their narrative.

In the *Jargeau Manifesto*, Louis' sons also traced the trajectory of their legal case against Burgundy and pointed to the repeated failure of institutional justice (Jargeau, 279). Their narrative illustrates how incongruent that failure was with the cultural and social norms structuring family honour. As they themselves added, no man would abide the murder(s) of a father or brother without gathering a support network of friends and family to pursue him to the death (Jargeau, 284). They asked the king to support their cause, but they made it clear that they would pursue Burgundy regardless. And so they did challenge Burgundy to war, 'pour le trez horrible meurtre par toy faict en grand trahison d'aguet à pensé

---

[90] Addressing the king, Charles explained that the men were the king's enemies as well as his own, even though they were currently serving as his councillors. The list included the bishop of Tournai (Jean de Thoisy), the *vidame* of Amiens, Jean de Neelle, Jacques, lord of Heilly, Charles de Savoisy, Anthoine de Craon, Anthoine des Essars, Jehan de Courcelles, Pierre de Fontenay and Maurice de Ruilly (*Chronique*, 2:82–86 and AN, X^{1a} 8602, fols 231–22v).

[91] AN, K56, no. 18; ADN, B 657, 15.183; *Preuves*, 273 n.71.

par meurtriers affer' [for the very horrible murder done by you, with [the] great treason of aforethought (*d'aguet pensé*), by the hand of the murderers] (AN, K 56, no. 18; ADN, B 657, 15.183, and *Preuves*, 273 no. 71). In this, they adhere to the legal strictures of private warfare – their *right to war*.[92] According to this cultural convention, a formal and public denunciation of one's enemy and declaration of the enmity had to be published, as did a formal, public challenge to war.

It was not until 1413 that the Orleanist party could achieve satisfaction for the two 'murders', and then it was only because Burgundy had been alienated from the king as a result of the infamous Cabochien revolt in the capital (April–July) led by some of his associates.[93] After the rebellion was suppressed in August 1413, Burgundy fled the capital.[94] Significantly, while Burgundy remained formally unpunished for the murder of Louis of Orleans and thus avoided the odious label *murderer*, the Orleanists nonetheless achieved satisfaction for the defamation and agreed to put their legal case to rest. At their bidding, the Church officially condemned Jean Petit's defamatory justification, and there were several public book burnings of the circulating texts. Similarly, all defamatory letters issued against Louis and the Armagnacs since 1408 were officially repealed.[95] It was at this time that his family finally dropped their legal suit, they stopped wearing their mourning clothes, and Charles changed his personal motto from *Justice* to *Le droit chemin* and his colours from black to purple. These decisions suggest

---

[92] Richard W. Kaeuper, *War, Justice, and Public Order: England and France in the Later Middle Ages* (Oxford: Oxford Unversity Press, 1988), pp. 226–27; M. H. Keen, *The Laws of War in the Late Middle Ages* (Cambridge: Cambridge University Press, 1965), pp. 65–93. See also: Justine Firnhaber-Baker, 'Seigneurial War and Royal Power in Later Medieval Southern France', *Past and Present* 208 (2010): 37–76, and Howard Kaminski, 'The Noble Feud in the Later Middle Ages', *Past and Present* 177 (2002): 57–59.

[93] The leaders of the uprising and the architects of all the anti-Armagnac violence were fierce and loyal urban partisans of the duke of Burgundy. Some had received wine gifts or pensions from him. For the wine gifts to some of the Cabochien leaders, see: Dijon, Archives départementales de la Côte d'Or, B 1576, fols 193v, 194, 194v, 195. Denisot de Chaumont and Simmonet de Caboche also received payments from Burgundy for services rendered after the Cabochien uprising in September 1413 (B 1576, fol. 138v), October 1413 (B 1576, fol. 139), and in July 1414 (B 1576, fol. 139r–v). Several of the men listed as receiving wine gifts were on the official banishment lists.

[94] For the exile lists, see: *Ordonnances des rois de la troisième race*, ed. M. de Vilevaut and M. de Bréquiny (Paris: Imprimerie royale, 1763), 10:163–65; Louis Douët d'Arcq, *Choix des pieces inédites relatives au règne de Charles VI*, 2 vols (Paris, 1863–1864), 1:367–69.

[95] For the condemnation and the two book burnings of Petit's *Justification*, see: AN, K 58, nos 8iii–8iv and AN, K 60, no. 7); *Chartularium Universitatis Pariensis*, ed. H. Denifle et al., 5 vols (Paris, 1897), 4: no. 2014; and RSD 5: 270–78. For the retraction of letters against the Orleanist party, see: AN, K 58, no. 5 and RSD, 5: 190. Regarding the banishment and the restoration of the Orleanist princes' honour, see: RSD, 5: 184–94 and *Ordonnances des rois de la troisième race*, ed. Vilevaut and Bréquiny, 10:163–65, 167–70.

that the restoration of Louis' name was more than a mere consolation prize.[96] As Gauvard argues, punishment for a criminal guilty of a crime like murder was not the primary goal; rather, in defining the crime and restoring the good name of the victim, the family's own sense of honour was likewise restored.[97] This was, at least, due in part to their fulfilment of their duty as his kin.

This judicial case of double 'murder' demonstrates that the cultural and legal constructions of the body in late medieval France did not have a strict binary between the material and its ideational elements: in this case, a physical body and its public reputation. Rather, the two were so intimately interconnected and interdependent for their own interpellation that one could not be separated from the other. While reputation was a constructed abstraction of the physical body, the empirical evidence proves that reputation, nonetheless, had material substance; therefore, it could indeed be injured, wounded, exterminated and murdered. As Louis of Orleans' murder and defamation demonstrate, at the very base of the legal cases presented by both parties was a comparability between the two bodies. However, the ruin of good name emerges as the worse of the two murders according to the House of Orleans' legal position. It was also implicitly positioned in this way in the Burgundian legal defence for, in it, Orleans was transformed into a dehumanised criminal, a *Nobody* who was worthy of his shameful death. This was because, Burgundy claimed, during his life, Orleans had proven himself a tyrannical usurper who did not deserve the body he bore and the illustrious reputation that he enjoyed by mere virtue of the fact that he was a *prince of the blood*. For Burgundy, Orleans' true self dishonoured his genetic composition, and, thus, he had to be executed like any other man equally unworthy. The main problem was, however, that Burgundy did not go through the proper institutional channels to do so. Therefore, the Orleanists rightly pointed out that the extreme violence visited upon Louis' body was extraordinary and a great and painful assault. However, of greater importance was the subsequent effacement of Louis' memory in his posthumous defamation. They

---

[96] *Journal d'un bourgeois de Paris*, p. 44. See also: RSD, 5:150 and Juvénal, *Histoire de Charles VI*, p. 490. Charles of Orleans' accounts for September 1413 indicate that he paid 'cent seize livres cinq sols tournois' to a draper, goldsmith and embroiderer for 'douze aulnes de violet de Bruxelles pour faire quatre heuques brodées à la devise où est escript *le droit chemin*, à Vaillant [the goldsmith] pour avoir fait les feuilles et petites feuillettes dorées'. Léon, marquis de Laborde, *Les ducs de Bourgogne. Études sur les lettres, les arts et l'industrie pendant le XVe siècle*, 3 vols (Paris, 1852) 3: 262, no. 6229. Laurent Hablot, 'Devisier', in 'La devise, mise en signe du prince, mis en scène du pouvoir. L'emblématique des princes en Europe à la fin du Moyen Age', doctoral dissertation (Université de Poitiers, 2001), p. 545. See also: Hutchison, 'Partisan Identity in the French Civil War, 1405–1418: Reconsidering the Evidence on Livery Badges', *Journal of Medieval History* 33 (2007): 272.

[97] Gauvard, '*De grace especial*', p. 126.

framed this as terribly vile, likening it to the physical murder but placing the former above the latter within their scale of honour. In this way, Orleans' honour could be restored for the sake of his living memory, for the family's dignity and that of the royal House of France.

CHAPTER 12

'A general murther, an universal slaughter':
Strategies of Anti-Jesuit Defamation in
Reporting Assassination in the
Early Modern Period

Andrew McKenzie-McHarg

IN 1976 THE ASSASSINATION Information Bureau, a citizens' initiative attempting to mobilise support for renewed investigations into the series of assassinations beginning with Kennedy's murder in 1963, published a collection of essays with the title *Government by Gunplay: Assassination Conspiracy Theories from Dallas to Today*.[1] This was only the second time that the term 'conspiracy theory' had appeared in a book title, and its usage in this case is noteworthy due to the absence of any need felt by the editors to disavow conspiracy theories *per se*. In the wake of Watergate, with mistrust of official explanations running high, such non-official explanations were enjoying their moment in the sun. More generally, the phenomenon in question justified this attitude; in the initial attempts to understand an assassination, it is perfectly reasonable to countenance the possibility of a conspiracy. Yet it is not necessary even to open the book to catch a glimpse of those slippages in logic and affronts to plausibility that give conspiracy theories their bad reputation.[2] On the back cover of *Government by Gunplay*, a

---

[1] Sid Blumenthal and Harvey Yazijian, eds., *Government by Gunplay: Assassination Conspiracy Theories from Dallas to Today* (New York: Signet, 1976).

[2] Of course, this should not call into question the fact that there have been, on many occasions throughout history, organisations that have repeatedly used assassination as a means of achieving their goals; indeed, in this regard, one can think of the original Ismaili sect knowns as the Assassins who were so feared by the Crusaders. As a more modern example, Weimar Germany was beset by a series of assassination attempts targeting high profile, left-wing figures and traceable back to a shadowy right-wing organisation by the name of Consul. See: Martin Sabrow, *Die verdrängte Verschwörung. Der Rathenau-Mord und die deutsche Gegenrevolution* (Frankfurt am Main: Fischer Verlag, 1998). For a discussion of Venetian state-sponsored poisoning for the public good, see in this volume: Matthew Lubin, 'Poisoning as a Means of State Assassination in Early Modern Venice'.

blurb proclaims that the book explores 'Links in the Chain of Conspiracy'. Thus, in contrast to the title, which at least leaves open the possibility of a multitude of conspiracies, corresponding to a multitude of assassinations, this statement bears witness to a tendency to concatenate all the smaller conspiracies by positing one singular, all-encompassing conspiracy theory.

This tendency to imagine some broader, more encompassing subversion linking a series of assassinations was not specific to the political culture of the United States in the 1960s and 1970s. It was also at work in the early modern period, a period in which, on more than one occasion, the atmosphere of solemn respect induced by the presence of a dignitary dissolved as a result of a sudden act of violence undertaken by some previously inconspicuous commoner. Of course, every assertion of some commonality between two distinct periods can only be an invitation to refine further the observation by noting the pertinent differences. In this case, a significant point of contrast is discernible in the degree of certainty (or uncertainty) with which those claiming a conspiracy sought to identify and denounce the conspirators. In the case of the members of the AIB and the wider community of sceptics in the 1970s, the identity of the conspirators remained vague; speculation focused often on some shadowy cabal linking rogue members of the intelligence community with other figures whose backgrounds lay in organised crime. There was no such uncertainty in the early modern period. Many of those who were convinced that the assassinations emanated from one and the same source also felt very confident in naming that source: the Society of Jesus, the Catholic order founded by a Basque nobleman, Íñigo López de Loyola [Ignatius of Loyola], and granted official papal recognition in 1540.

By appealing to a typology introduced by the historian Geoffrey T. Cubitt, the distinction in the two cases can be expressed as one between 'plan-centred' and 'conspirator-centred' conspiracy theories.[3] According to this distinction, the point of departure is either the presumption that events unfold in accordance with a plan whose orchestrators (i.e. the conspirators) still need to be identified, or, alternatively, the point of departure is the presumption of guilt attached to an already-identified group whose proclivity for conspiratorial plans is treated as a given. For many Europeans, on both sides of the confessional divide, the Society of Jesus was this already-identified group. In the minds of its opponents, the order soon came to assume the character of an abiding source of subversion against the sovereign rights of European monarchs.

Prior to the early modern period, and predating the establishment of the Society of Jesus, the high and mighty had already been on the lookout for signs of

---

[3] Geoffrey T. Cubitt, 'Conspiracy Myths and Conspiracy Theories', *Journal of the Anthropological Society of Oxford* 20 (1989): 12–26, esp. pp. 19–24.

treachery within their retinue and at court. From the sixteenth century onwards, however, an unprecedented source of danger began to emerge. Now the powerful had also to entertain the prospect that lurking somewhere in the throng of those paying homage or in the succession of those submitting petitions was a subject with whom they had had no prior political dealings, who harboured no aspirations to usurp their power and who, instead, harkened to a divine calling to kill and be killed.[4] In those cases in which assassins did not lose their own lives in the course of carrying out the crime, the insistence with which interrogators tried to extract information about fellow conspirators seems to testify not only to an investigative thoroughness in ruling out conspiracy but also to a difficulty in accepting the notion of a lone assassin. A passage from the long chapter on conspiracies in Machiavelli's *Discorsi* (c. 1517) illustrates this prejudice. There he asserts 'that all conspiracies have been made by men of standing or else by men in immediate attendance on a prince, for other people, unless they be sheer lunatics, cannot form a conspiracy; since men without power and those who are not in touch with a prince are devoid alike of any hope and of any opportunity of carrying out a conspiracy successfully'.[5]

Machiavelli's characterisation of many early modern assassins as 'sheer lunatics' does not seem entirely off the mark. And yet his remark also reflects his predisposition to underestimate the potential for religion – and particularly religious difference – in compelling obscure commoners to undertake violent and unexpected interventions in high politics. Referring to the interrogations to which Raviallac, the assassin of Henri IV, was subjected, the historian Orest Ranum describes how 'it was obviously inconsistent with conventional political beliefs that anyone of so humble a station in society as he could come up with a plan to kill a king and have the courage to carry it out as an individual act'.[6] Thus, older presumptions about politics and power induced a tendency to suspect conspiracies behind assassinations. In addition to this, a prominent strand of anti-Jesuit polemic in the early modern period demonstrates a less conspicuous, but nevertheless still discernible, tendency to see in these conspiracies 'Links in

---

[4] Franklin Ford correctly draws attention to this point in his *Political Murder: From Tyrannicide to Terrorism* (Cambridge, MA: Harvard University Press, 1985), p. 146: 'In Europe the period between roughly the mid-1500s and the mid-1600s, variously referred to as that of the Wars of Religion, the Counter Reformation or the Catholic Reformation, occupies a special place in the history of political murder'. For other comments on the propensity of this period towards violence and conspiracy, see: Yves-Marie Bercé, 'Introduction', *Complots et conjurations dans l'Europe moderne*, ed. Yves-Marie Bercé and Elena Fasano Guarini (Rome: École française de Rome, 1996), pp. 1–5.
[5] Niccolò Machiavelli, *The Discourses* (London: Penguin, 2003), p. 402.
[6] Orest Ranum, 'The French Ritual of Tyrannicide in the Late Sixteenth Century', *Sixteenth Century Journal* 11.1 (1980): 63–82 at p. 71.

the Chain of a greater Conspiracy', to slightly paraphrase the blurb which, on the back cover of *Government by Gunplay*, fused together explanations of different assassinations in America in the 1960s and 1970s.

The task befalling early modern adherents of 'conspirator-centred', and more specifically 'Jesuit-centred', conspiracy theories was to show how known events, such as assassinations or assassination attempts, were the surface ripples emanating from the deeper cause of Jesuit conspiracy. Behind every assault upon a prince many suspected a conspiracy, and behind every conspiracy many were determined – for reasons often disingenuous and opportunistic – to discern the guiding hand of the Jesuits, no matter how implausible the charge or how flimsy the evidence supporting it. This repeated indictment of the Jesuits was the basis upon which the multiple conspiracies of early modern Europe were eventually fused into one all-encompassing conspiracy.

Such accusations and the more general antipathy aroused by the Jesuits testify, if nothing else, to the success of the order in staking out a prominent place on the religious and political map of early modern Europe. The order brought its distinctive methods and ethos to bear on the numerous fronts on which the Catholic Church sought to assert and re-assert its authority. Its persistence and its effectiveness guaranteed it vehement hostility from both within and without Catholic Europe. This hostility found expression in reams of printed materials, ranging from scurrilous pamphlets to learned treatises, all of which shared a common goal; namely, to convince the reader that the Jesuit order represented a perversion of true Christianity. By the eighteenth century, Catholic and Protestant opponents of the Jesuits had been joined by free-thinking *philosophes* and *Aufklärer*, who were convinced that the order represented an obstruction to the progress of enlightened reason.

Within the anti-Jesuit literature, one particular thematic strand concerns political doctrine and the attitude the Jesuits harboured – or were alleged to harbour – towards the secular authorities. The focus on this theme generated what, at first glance, might seem to deserve the epithet 'black chronicles'.[7] These chronicles revel in the enumeration of the acts of political violence allegedly perpetrated by the Jesuit order. An early example of this means of vilifying the Jesuits can be found in the immediate wake of Raviallac's murder of Henri IV, in a piece written by Henri's former advisor and one-time Protestant co-religionist Philippe Duplessis-Mornay: *Remonstrance à Messieurs de la Cour de Parliament*

---

[7] Christine Vogel writes of the '"schwarze" Ordensgeschichte' of the Jesuits in her *Der Untergang der Gesellschaft Jesu als Europäisches Medienereignis (1758–1773): Publizistische Debatten im Spannungsfeld von Aufklärung und Gegenaufklärung* (Mainz: P. von Zabern, 2006), pp. 166–73.

sur le Parricide commis en la personne du Roy Henry le Grand (1610).⁸ The subtitle of the English translation promises evidence *Manifestlie prooving the Jesuites to be the plotters and principal deviser of that horrible act.*⁹ The other end of the century saw the publication of *L'art d'assassiner les rois enseigné par les Jesuites à Louis XIV et Jacques II* (1696), a treatise that focused upon English affairs and prompted an English translation with the title: *The Art of Assassinating Kings, taught Lewis XIV. & James II. by the Jesuits.*¹⁰ The most exhaustive work in this vein, *Les Jésuites criminels de lèze-majesté dans la théorie et dans la pratique* [*The Jesuits, Criminals Guilty of Lèse-Majesté in Theory and in Practice*] (1758) appeared in the year following the attempt made on the life of Louis XV by Robert-François Damiens.¹¹ The text fed into the crescendo of anti-Jesuit sentiment that culminated in the expulsion of the Jesuits from France in 1763, a dramatic development that was itself only the harbinger of the suppression of the order ten years later.

Of course, as calumnious as these works were, even they had to admit that the Jesuits were not the direct perpetrators of the crimes they documented. The Bavarian historian Peter Philipp Wolf made the most direct admission of this fact in one of the many general histories of the Jesuits to appear in the eighteenth century:

---

⁸ This work, which appeared anonymously, finds its place in Duplessis-Mornay's collected works *Mémoires et Correspondance de Duplessis-Mornay* (Paris: Treuttel et Würtz, 1825), 11: 77–99. Raoul Patry provides some of the context in his study *Philippe Du Plessis-Mornay: Un huguenot homme d'état (1549-1623)* (Paris: Fischbacher, 1933), pp. 469–72. Nevertheless, Duplessis-Mornay's authorship has often been overlooked in other discussions of this piece. Thus, Roland Mousnier, in his classic *The Assassination of Henry IV: The Tyrannicide Problem and the Consolidation of the French Absolute Monarchy in the Early Seventeenth Century*, trans. Joan Spencer (London: Faber and Faber, 1973), gives an extended description of the contents of the tract without considering questions of authorship (pp. 54–56), and, more recently, Hélène Duccini, in her *Faire voir, faire croire: l'opinion publique sur Louis XIII* (Seyssel: Champ Vallon, 2003), has devoted some pages to the *Remonstrance* (pp. 90–92), also without linking it to Duplessis-Mornay. Duplessis-Mornay's condemnation of the king's murder takes on an ironic ring since he has long been considered as possibly involved in the authorship of one of the most notorious expositions of Huguenot monarchomach thought, *Vindiciae, contra tyrannos* (1579).

⁹ *A discourse to the lords of the Parliament: As touching the murther committed uppon the person of Henrie the Great, King of France*, trans. William Crashaw (London: Printed by T[homas]: P[urfoot], 1611).

¹⁰ The immediate event that inspired the piece was a conspiracy to kill William III in 1696. For details, see: Jane Garrett, *The Triumphs of Providence: The Assassination Plot, 1696* (Cambridge: Cambridge University Press, 1980).

¹¹ There were, apparently, two editions in 1758 (A la Haye), followed by a third in 1759 (A la Haye) and a fourth in 1760 (A Amsterdam), with each edition incorporating new material. This work seems never to have been translated into English, but a German translation appeared under the title *Gefahr der Majestäten auf Erden bey den abscheulichen Lehrsätzen und Thathandlungen der Jesuiten* (Frankfurt am Main and Leipzig,1761).

Es konnte freylich nie ihr Plan seyn, an Verschwörungen und Meutereien einen unmittelbaren und thätigen Antheil zu nehmen. Allein dieß war doch immer ihr Plan, vermittelst geheimer und verborgener Kunstgriffe, theils durch aufrührerische Schriften, theils durch mündliche Verbreitung gefährlicher Grundsätze, schreckenvolle Rebellionen und Verschwörungen zu veranlaßen.

[It could never be their plan to play a direct and active part in the conspiracies and mutinies. But it was always their plan to cause terrible rebellions and conspiracies, in part through secret hidden trickery, in part through seditious writings, in part through the verbal communication of dangerous principles].[12]

Indeed, making a case for Jesuit culpability in a way that did not contradict the known history too egregiously always remained a challenge for anti-Jesuit publicists. Yet the fabrication of such charges was facilitated by the hyper-vigilance and zeal at play in those murder cases that are treated as especially grievous because the victim is a state sovereign. Assassination is, after all, more than just homicide, and many distinctions in legal systems around the world still continue to attribute, if not a special sanctity, then certainly a special significance, to the life of the sovereign or the holder of the office invested with executive power.

Alleged Jesuit culpability was obviously the common denominator shared between events listed in the 'black chronicles', yet evidence substantiating such allegations was often embarrassingly elusive. In constructing (or rather fabricating) such a link, two main options presented themselves beyond the vague general reference to 'secret hidden trickery' made by Wolf. Wolf also speaks of 'verbal communication', and the classic context for such an exchange was the confessional. Yet the canard that imagined the confessionals as the secretive site at which the Jesuit confessor issued would-be assassins with their orders was too circumstantial to furnish a black chronicle with its leitmotif of Jesuit guilt. Ultimately, the other means mentioned by Wolf, namely 'seditious writings', proved itself to be the more viable option in gluing disparate events together. This meant that the chronicles came to be supplemented by a prefatory exposition of Jesuit political doctrine and, thus, took on a bipartite structure in explaining how Jesuit involvement remained one step removed from the bloodshed. Instead of a series of stories relating acts of violence and featuring scenes in which Jesuits issued instructions from within the confessional, there was a tendency to separate out an exposition of Jesuit doctrine and then follow it with a series of case studies documenting how this doctrine had been put into action

---

[12] *Allgemeine Geschichte der Jesuiten von dem Ursprunge ihres Ordens bis auf gegenwärtige Zeiten* (Zurich: Orell, Gessner, Füssli und Compag., 1789), p. 416. My translation. For some details on Wolf and his place within the context of the German Catholic Enlightenment, see: Michael Printy, *Enlightenment and the Creation of German Catholicism* (Cambridge: Cambridge University Press, 2009), pp. 131–35.

at certain junctures in the political history of various European states. Thus, the sequential logic of a chronicle was underscored by the implication that every event recorded in the chronicle was an outgrowth from the same root cause: a Jesuit doctrinal approbation of the killing of kings.

The doctrinal basis for the sinister 'verbal communication' referenced by Wolf can be traced back to the twenty-first canon of the Fourth Council of the Lateran (1215), which imposed on all members of the clergy the duty to observe the seal of confession.[13] What passed between penitent and priest under this seal was passed in the strictest confidence. As Jakob Keller, the Jesuit rector at the order's college in Munich, wrote over four centuries after this Council:

> Bey den Catholischen ist kein grössere obligation, zuschweigen / als die Beicht mit sich bringt: also daß in keinem zuefall / stehe darauf was es wöll / auch das Hayl des Vatterlands / nicht durchauß kan (nach aller Theologen Sententz) geoffenbart werden. Und dies billicher weiß: dann wer wolt sonst seine Sünde bekennen / wann er nit versichert wär?

> [Among the Catholics no other situation imposes a greater obligation of remaining silent than that imposed by the sacrament of confession: under no circumstances, even if the fate of the nation hangs in the balance, can the confession be revealed – thus the consensus among all theologians. And that with good reason because who would want to confess their sins if this security was not assured?][14]

As Keller saw it, the rule was, by its nature, sacrosanct and, in its application, unconditional. This remained true when a conflict emerged between the ecclesiastical and civil duties of the priest. The seal of confession could generate such a conflict if it covered the knowledge received by a priest not just of a sin but of a genuine crime. Confronted with such a conflict or prompted to consider its theoretical possibility, most Catholic authorities, such as Keller, were adamant in acknowledging the superiority of the religious office. The duties of the priest trumped those that the priest, as a subject or citizen beholden to secular

---

[13] Norman Tanner SJ, ed., *Nicaea I to Lateran*, vol, 1, *Decrees of the Ecumenical Councils*, 2 vols (Washington, DC: Georgetown University Press, 1990), 1:245, where the relevant provisions read as follows: 'Let [the priest] take the utmost care [...] not to betray the sinner at all by word or sign or in any other way. If the priest needs wise advice, let him seek it cautiously without any mention of the person concerned. For if anyone presumes to reveal a sin disclosed to him in confession, we decree that he is not only to be deposed from his priestly office but also to be confined to a strict monastery to do perpetual penance.'

[14] Jakob Keller, *Tyrannicidium oder lehr vom tyrannenmordt* (Munich: Getruckt durch Nicolaum Henricum, 1611), p. 48. My translation. For general comments on the history of the seal of confession, see: Bertrand Kurtscheid, *Das Beichtsiegel in seiner geschichtlichen Entwicklung* (Freiburg: Herder, 1912).

authorities, was otherwise compelled to observe, and this remained true even if the crime confided in the priest was as drastic as murder.[15]

But there were other cases that generated yet more controversy. There was, for example, the possibility that the penitent might confide in the priest the plan for an assassination that had not yet been committed. The possibility that an assassin might seek out a priest and request what might be called an 'advance' absolution arose as a result of the atmosphere of religious fervour and political instability characterising the early modern period.[16] The Reformation split Europe on religious grounds, and the ensuing conditions conjured up the scenario of a heretical king who professed a different faith from his subjects. It was conceivable that this king might force these subjects to abjure the true religion and thereby endanger their salvation. The extreme remedy in such a situation would be found in the subject who would not shirk from the obvious dangers in trying to kill the king. Because such an act could easily end in the death of the would-be assassin, it is not surprising that Catholic subjects would seek counsel with and absolution from a priest before embarking on such missions.

One such case occurred on 17 March 1582 when a young man from Biscay, Jean Jáuregui, approached the Dominican friar Antonin Temmermann in order to make such a confession. Two years prior to this, Philip II of Spain had issued a proclamation encouraging his subjects to murder William of Orange, the champion of the Protestant cause in the Netherlands. Philip promised a reward of 25,000 crowns to be given upon successful fulfilment of this request. Jáuregui was a servant and a bookkeeper in the house of a Spanish merchant. At the instigation of his master, he became the operative figure in a plan to kill William. Temmermann, according to the later official account, was willing to give absolution to Jáuregui, provided that he did not undertake the action for the base reason of pecuniary gain. Absolution would only be forthcoming if he was inspired by the glory of God and motivated by zeal for Roman Catholicism. Temmermann then apprised him of the dangers of his mission. The alleged spiritual sanction Temmermann gave to Jáuregui's plan was used to justify his execution, ten days after Jáuregui himself had been killed following the assassination attempt made upon William.

Although severely injured by the shot fired by Jáuregui, William survived.[17] Two years later, he was not so fortunate, succumbing to a bullet fired by the

---

[15] Walter Fischedick, *Die Zeugnisverweigerungsrechte von Geistlichen und kirchlichen Mitarbeitern* (Frankfurt am Main: Peter Lang, 2006).

[16] Henry Charles Lea, *A History of Auricular Confession and Indulgences in the Latin Church*, 3 vols (Philadelphia: Lea Brothers & Co., 1896), 1:445–46.

[17] For the official account, see: *Bref Recueil de l'assassinat, commis en la personne du très illustre Prince, Monseignur le Prince d'Orange* (Antwerp: Christophe Plantin, 1582). A recent account providing details of this first assassination attempt on William of Orange can

Catholic Balthasar Gérard. Gérard was apprehended and subsequently experienced the gruesome series of inflictions deemed appropriate for those guilty of killing a prince. If, in the early modern period, the state was keen to emphasise its claim to a monopoly of physical violence through the public spectacle of punishment, an attack upon the prince, as the fountainhead of state power and the personal embodiment of state sovereignty, demanded a particularly elaborate and gory desecration of the offender's body.[18] In Gérard's case, the punishment extended over four days and involved a grisly procession of torments that culminated in his quartering: His hands were cut off, salt was smeared in his wounds and red-hot pincers were applied to his body. Perversely enough, such excesses of violence helped elevate Gérard to the status of a martyr in the eyes of his sympathisers.[19]

An awareness of the dangers associated with attempts to kill a prince, along with a devotion to the Catholic religion, compelled men like Jáuregui and Gérard to seek out Catholic clergy before they put into action plans that, with a high degree of probability, would turn out to be not just murderous but also suicidal. In Jáuregui's case, Temmermann was implicated in the crime. However, Temmermann was a Dominican, so there was nothing specifically Jesuit about the predicament created by such foreknowledge. What distinguished the Society of Jesus from other religious orders was a tendency for such incidents to find a place in a generalised anti-Jesuit account of history. Thus, the 'black chronicle' entitled *The Art of Assassinating Kings, taught Lewis XIV. & James II. by the Jesuits* gives the following account of Jáuregui's attempt on William's life. On 18

    be found in Lisa Jardine, *The Awful End of Prince William the Silent: The First Assassination of a Head of State with a Handgun* (New York: HarperCollins, 2007), pp. 64–76. Jardine, however, perpetuates the tradition of falsely describing Temmermann as a Jesuit priest. An older study, which by examining the original court documents sought to absolve Temmermann of the charges and thereby elevate him to a 'martyr du silence de la confession' (p. 142), was provided by Albert de Meyer, *Le procès de l'attentat commis contre Guillaume le Taciturne, prince d'Orange, 18 mars 1582: Étude critique de documents inédits* (Brussels: L'Édition universelle, 1933).

[18] For the argument that through the spectacle of punishment the state reinforced its monopoly on violence, see: Pieter Spierenburg, *The Spectacle of Suffering. Executions and the Evolution of Repression: From a Preindustrial Metropolis to the European Experience* (Cambridge: Cambridge University Press, 1984), pp. 201–02. For a discussion of the bodily indignities suffered by Raviallac, see: Ranum, 'The French Ritual of Tyrannicide', pp. 70–73.

[19] As an example of a text eulogising Gérard in such a manner, see: *Les cruels et horribles tormens de Balthazar Gérard, Bourguignon, vrai martyr, souffertz en l'exécution de sa glorieuse et memorable mort: pour avoir tué Guillaume de Nassau, prince d'Orange, ennemy de son roy et de l'eglise Catholique* (Paris: Jean du Carroy, 1584) See also: Jardine, *The Awful End of Prince William the Silent*, which recounts the far more awful end of Gérard at pp. 58–60.

March 1582, after William rose from the Sunday dinner, Jáuregui was granted an audience with the prince: 'This wicked Ruffian [Jáuregui] discharg'd a Pocket-Pistol at the Prince, and wounded him in the Jaw below the Ear. Upon which, the Guard falling upon the Ruffian with their Swords and Halberds, kill'd him immediately ….'[20]

The description thus far is a predominantly factual account. However, continuing where the last sentence broke off, a two-tiered narrative form is introduced allowing for a far more sinister story to be grafted onto the factual account: '... the Guard falling upon the Ruffian with their Swords and Halberds, kill'd him immediately which was the reason that the Author of so black an attempt, could never be discover'd from the Mouth of the Murderer' (58). It was thus presumed that the crime originated in an 'Author' other than Jáuregui. Of course, such an assertion was not entirely groundless. Jáuregui was doing the bidding of his master who, in turn, was responding to the offer issued by Philip II. But Philip II and Jáuregui's Spanish master provided, at most, incentives and were hardly steering the course of action. The image of a more sinister orchestrator of events, operating at one step removed from visibility, was the source of inspiration for later chroniclers who, using this imaginative device, gave free rein to their own agendas in identifying the authors. Thus, the pamphleteer, writing of these events over a century after they occurred, no longer felt obliged to observe factual constraints in describing this deeper level of 'authorship'. He wrote that the 'the Marks that were shew'd upon Juvregni's Body, made it sufficiently apparent that the Jesuits were the Authors' (58).

Positing a deeper level of 'authorship' occurs in accordance with a principle that bifurcates agency, thereby annulling the simple presumption that behind each single act there is a single actor. Instead, causality is shared by differentiating between an instigator or 'author' on the one hand and an executor or perpetrator on the other.[21] In cases where a lone assassin is apprehended after carrying out an attack, much of the interrogation revolves around the question of accomplices: the investigators assume a conspiracy and seek to find out who else is involved. However, the imagination of the conspiracy theorist will often describe conspiracies not just as 'horizontal' egalitarian collusions sealed by the swearing of a common oath but will, rather, invoke a 'vertical' stratified order. In this way, the involvement of clerics and, more specifically, Jesuits could be elevated from the level of involuntary complicity to that of authorial instigation. On

---

[20] *The Art of Assassinating Kings: Taught Lewis XIV. and James II. by the Jesuites* (London: E. Whitlock, 1696), pp. 57–58. Hereafter, page numbers are given in parentheses.

[21] The role attributed to the Jesuits in these scenarios corresponds roughly to the category of an 'accessory before the fact' in Anglo-American law. In German law, the difference described here is closely aligned with that described by the legal theorist Claus Roxin in his classic *Täterschaft und Tatherrschaft*, 8th edn (Berlin: De Gruyter, 2006).

the basis of this alleged instigation, an underlying unity could be found linking disparate acts of political violence.

This situation is reflected in the differing evidential standards that were applied to cases of regicide. Bodin describes the extra vigilance of the community when it came to the prosecution of high treason: 'A subject is guilty of treason in the first degree not only for having killed a sovereign prince, but also for attempting it, advising it, or even wishing it'.[22] The gist of Bodin's statement is clear: concrete action was not necessary to elicit the charge of treason. Bodin then relates a story in which a subject of Francis I confided in a Franciscan friar that he had desired to kill the king but subsequently renounced this wish and now sought absolution for even having harboured it. The friar promptly broke the seal of confession, and the subject was then executed.[23] When it came to treason, the normal rules did not apply either in terms of evidential standards or, as Bodin's story seems to suggest, when it came to a rigid observance of the seal of confession. At the mere thought of an assault upon the king's life, a subject forfeited the right to his or her own life.

Similar provisions were codified in England when the Treason Act was passed by Parliament in 1351 during the reign of Edward III. This act declared the 'compassing and imagining' of the king's death to be a treasonous crime.[24] Later, in the seventeenth century, Sir Edward Coke expounded upon the significance of this provision in his *Institutes of the Laws of England*; whereas in most criminal cases culpability required an overt deed, merely 'compassing, machinating, counselling, &.c. to kill the king, though it have no other declaration thereof, was high treason by the common law'.[25] Thus, the lighter burden of proof justified by the gravity of the crime made it possible to condemn as treasonous mere speculation that seemed to challenge the authority of the king or, in particular,

---

[22] I take the translation from Jean Bodin, *On Sovereignty: Four Chapters from The Six Books of the Commonwealth*, ed. and trans. Julian H. Franklin (Cambridge: Cambridge University Press, 1996), p. 115. This is based on the French edition of *Six livres de la République* (Paris: Chez Jacques du Puis, 1583), where the equivalent passage is found on page 303: 'Or non seulement le subject est coulpable de lese majesté au premier chef, qui a tué le Prince souverain, ains aussi qui a attenté, qui a donné, conseil, qui l'a voulu, qui l'a pensé ...'. For a discussion of murder as treason and a violation of *lèse-majesté*, see in this volume: Jolanta N. Komornicka, 'Treacherous Murder: Language and Meaning in French Murder Trials' and Emily J. Hutchison, 'Defamation, a Murder More Foul?: The "Second Murder" of Louis, Duke of Orleans (d. 1407) Reconsidered'.

[23] Bodin, *On Sovereignty*, p. 116.

[24] See: John Bellamy, *The Law of Treason in England in the Later Middle Ages* (Cambridge: Cambridge University Press, 1970), and for the subsequent history of how the laws of treason were handled and expanded, see: John Bellamy, *The Tudor Law of Treason. An Introduction* (London: Routledge and Kegan Paul, 1979).

[25] Sir Edward Coke, *The Institutes of the Laws of England* (1628–1644) (London: E. & R. Brooke, 1798), III: pp. 5–6.

violate the special sanctity of his person. The attenuation of the normal burden of proof dovetailed into the bifurcation of agency. Where an actual attack upon the sacred person of the monarch had taken place, it was obviously possible to go beyond the perpetrator and consider a far wider circle of those linked to the crime by a more tenuous complicity. Thus, it required no great leap of the imagination to envisage how the office of a priest as a confessor – and, more specifically, a Jesuit priest or confessor – might connect the office-holder to the crime in virtue of the 'counselling' provided to the assassin and, thus, transform the priest into another guilty party.

Coke exploited the less exacting requirements of proof in a case where it had indeed been Jesuits – not Dominicans or Franciscans or members of another order – who were ensnared by the occupational hazard represented by the seal of confession. In late July 1605 the Jesuit priest Henry Garnet learned of a plan to blow up the Houses of Parliament in London.[26] Garnet's subsequent attempts to forestall the execution of the plotters' plan failed, as did the plan itself. At the end of January in 1606, a few days before the execution of Guy Fawkes, Garnet was discovered in hiding and arrested. No one disputed the fact that, in electing not to alert the civil authorities, Garnet was guilty of what was known as 'misprision of treason'. However, Coke was more ambitious in his prosecution. His aim was also to convict Garnet himself, and the order to which he belonged, of treason. This meant demonstrating that the Jesuits were not just hapless confidants or even willing accomplices; rather, they were the masterminds behind the plot. As such, this was a case in which, according to Coke, the principle 'plus peccat author, quam actor' applied: 'The Author or the procurer, offendeth more than the actor or executor'.[27]

---

[26] This information had been confided in him not by one of the men who had concocted the Gunpowder plot; rather, it had been relayed to him by another Jesuit priest, Oswald Tesimond, who had heard the confession of the man at the centre of the plot, Robert Catesby. For details, see: Antonia Fraser, *The Gunpowder Plot: Terror and Faith in 1605* (London: Phoenix, 2002).

[27] Coke's speech at Garnet's trial is reprinted ('as neere to his owne words, as the same could be taken') in *A true and perfect relation of the whole proceedings against the late most barbarous traitors, Garnet a Iesuite, and his confederats: contayning sundry speeches deliuered by the Lords Commissioners at their arraignments* (London: Robert Barker, 1606), O2v–U4r, here P1v. For more information on this compilation of documents, see: Frances E. Dolan, *True Relations: Reading, Literature, and Evidence in Seventeenth-Century England* (Philadelphia: University of Pennsylvania Press, 2013), pp. 29–51. Of course, as an attempt by the state to put forward the official narrative, this information is to be treated with scepticism in its claim to relate a 'true and perfect' account of what happened. This does not, however, diminish its value as an insight into the changing contours of anti-Jesuit sentiment.

Although the term 'author' here has the sense of instigator or primary agent, the more common meaning associated with the production of written texts is, in this instance, highly appropriate. Coke did not so much demonstrate that the Jesuits had actually instigated the plot to blow up Parliament; rather, he recounted the whole story of Jesuit infiltration into England, telling it as a series of attempts at high treason. He paralleled these attempts at treason with references to certain subversive publications, using phrases such as: 'And that Treason was likewise accompanied with a Booke ...'.[28]

Coke's speech marks one point in the history of anti-Jesuit discourse wherein the strategy of invoking the confessional to construct the link between the order on the one hand and an assault upon the life of the sovereign on the other was supplemented with references to written works of religious controversy; in this case, specifically those penned by the Jesuit Robert Persons.[29] There are also allusions to a specific Jesuit doctrine legitimising the killing of kings, though Coke seems less sure of himself in such matters. In a speech he gave following the arraignment of the surviving conspirators, Coke had declared that 'their [i.e. the Jesuits'] profession & doctrine is a Religion of distinction, the greatest part of them being without the text, and therefore in very deede, idle and vaine conceits of their owne braines'.[30] When Coke does submit textual proof for 'their Doctrine of deposing of Princes', he finds his main point of reference in the writings of the Spanish inquisitor Diego de Simancas, who was not a Jesuit.[31]

Despite the flimsy textual basis underpinning Coke's sense that the Jesuit position in such matters was an affront to notions of state sovereignty, he was, in actual fact, not so far off the mark. The right to resist and kill a king who abuses his power generated an inordinate amount of discussion in the history of

---

[28] *A true and perfect relation*, Q2r. Coke is referring here to Robert Persons' book, published under the pseudonym R. Doleman, *A Conference about the Next Succession to the Crown of Ingland* (Antwerp, 1594).

[29] Admittedly, at *A true and perfect relation*, Q1v–Q2r, Coke falsely attributes the work Persons published under a pseudonym, *Elizabethae Angliae Reginae haeresim Calvinianum propugnantis saevissimum in Catholicos sui regni Edictum cum responsione* (Rome: A. Zannetti, 1593) to the fellow Jesuit controversialist Joseph Creswell.

[30] *A true and perfect relation*, F1r.

[31] Ibid., T3v–T4r. The text indicates that Coke repeated at this point his earlier exposition delivered at the trial of the surviving conspirators; see: F1v–F2v. It is interesting that Coke here references a notion of heresy as a hereditary disease. Of course, understanding heresy as a disease was a frequent topos. But the hereditary aspect was of importance to Simancas as it indicated one reason why he was suspicious of the Society of Jesus; namely, their willingness to accept *conversos* (former Jews) into their ranks. For more information on this, see: Robert Maryks, *The Jesuit Order as a Synagogue of Jews* (Leiden: Brill, 2010), esp. pp. 31–40. Admittedly, Coke's exposition is not entirely devoid of reference to texts produced by Jesuits; indeed, he goes on to mention 'Philopater', which was another pseudonym used by Persons.

political thought and, within this discussion, the Jesuits did genuinely espouse political doctrines that, in extreme circumstances, legitimised violence against a tyrannical prince. There was thus a grain of truth to the insinuation that Jesuit doctrine countenanced such violence. A later perennial favourite in elaborating upon this highly qualified assent to violent resistance, though Coke seems to have had no awareness of it in 1606, was *De rege et regis institutione* (1599), a tract penned by the Spanish Jesuit Juan de Mariana. Mariana's work was idiosyncratically extreme and not representative of the general Jesuit position.[32] Yet even the more orthodox Jesuit camp was willing to envisage situations in which the monarch's misdeeds made him as deserving of violent punishment as a common criminal. This attitude was not novel; rather, it found precedent in medieval political theology.[33] Yet this older theology started to clash with the new ideologies then beginning to emerge from the chanceries and cabinets of the early modern state. These ideologies could vary in the way they might either declaim divine right or elaborate upon notions of indivisible sovereignty, but they concurred in their insistence upon the sacrosanct nature of the prince's person.[34]

In his survey of Jesuit political thought, Harro Höpfl writes: 'The charge of teaching and fostering tyrannicide was an inferior surrogate for concrete evidence of active Jesuit complicity'.[35] As inferior as it might have been when it came to demonstrating culpability in a specific case, the evidence pointing to a highly qualified, but nevertheless undeniable, Jesuit approval of tyrannicide provided sufficient material to posit a deeper 'authorial' level of agency from which Jesuits aided and abetted assassins. This, after all, was an age brimming over with plots and assassinations. Stepping back from the particular incident, splicing off an authorial level of agency and, in this manner, trying to make sense of a series of subversions had its advantages. It made it possible to comprehend a series of crimes, which might otherwise have seemed unrelated, by identifying a recurring causal factor in the incitement to such violence issuing forth from Jesuit political thought.

---

[32] For an insightful contextualisation of Mariana's thought, see: Harald E. Braun, *Juan de Mariana and Early Modern Spanish Political Thought* (Aldershot: Ashgate, 2007).
[33] See: Fritz Kern, *Gottesgnadentum und Widerstandsrecht im früheren Mittelalter: Zur Entwicklungsgeschichte der Monarchie* (Leipzig: Koehler, 1914; repr. Darmstadt: Wissenschaftliche Buchgesellschaft, 1980).
[34] For an examination of this conflict in the French context, see: Eric Nelson, *The Jesuits and the Monarchy: Catholic Reform and Political Authority in France (1590–1615)* (Aldershot: Ashgate, 2005).
[35] Harro Höpfl, *Jesuit Political Thought. The Society of Jesus and the State, c.1540–1630* (Cambridge: Cambridge University Press, 2004), p. 324.

This ploy of condemning Jesuits as the 'authors' of conspiracies by pointing to their activities as the 'authors' of texts became the established argumentative strategy adopted in such anti-Jesuit screeds such as Duplessis-Mornay's *Remonstrance* and *L'art d'assassiner les rois*. It resiliently maintained its hold on the minds of diverse anti-Jesuits well into the eighteenth century. Thus, the entry on the Jesuits published in the eighth volume of the *Encyclopédie* in 1762 highlights the argument's staying power. Far from displaying the famed critical spirit otherwise characteristic of this flagship Enlightenment project, this entry represents a catchment basin for several of the anti-Jesuit prejudices that had emerged in the preceding centuries. This is demonstrated by the following passage:

> En 1610, Ravaillac assassine Henry IV. Les Jésuites restent sous le soupçon d'avoir dirigé sa main; & comme s'ils en étoient jaloux, & que leur dessein fût de porter la terreur dans le sein des monarques, la même année Mariana publie avec son institution du prince l'apologie du meurtre des rois.[36]

> [In 1610, Raviallac assassinates Henri IV. The Jesuits remain under the suspicion of having directed his hand; and as though they were jealous of this and their design was to instil terror in the breasts of monarchs, in the same year Mariana published an apology of the murder of kings with his work on the education of the prince].

The authors then draw a parallel to the more recent attempt on the life of Louis XV:

> En 1757, un attentat parricide est commis contre Louis XV. notre monarque, & c'est par un homme qui a vécu dans les foyer de la société de Jésus, que ces peres ont protégé, qu'ils ont placé en plusieurs maisons; & dans le même année ils publient une édition d'un de leurs auteurs classiques, où la doctrine du meurtre des rois est enseignée. C'est comme ils firent en 1610, immédiatement après l'assassinat de Henry IV.[37]

> [In 1757, a parricidal assassination attempt is made on Louis XV, our monarch, by a man who lived in the halls of the Society, whom the fathers had protected, whom they placed in numerous households. And in the same year they publish an edition of a work from one of the classic authors, in which the doctrine of murdering kings is taught. This is the same as what they had done in 1610, immediately after the assassination of Henri IV].

---

[36] *Encyclopédie, ou Dictionnaire raisonné des Sciences, des Arts et des Métiers*, ed. Denis Diderot (Neuchâtel, 1765), 8:514. My translation.

[37] Ibid. My translation.

The entry refers to the re-issue of *Medulla Theologiae Moralis*, a work of casuistry authored by the German Jesuit Hermann Busenbaum in 1645.[38] Because it touches upon the question of tyrannicide, the opponents of the Society seized upon the opportunity to construct a suggestive synchronicity: in the same year that the monarch's life was assaulted, the Jesuits re-issued a publication justifying such attacks. The *Encyclopédists* shared in the anti-Jesuit sentiment and were obviously receptive to such insinuations. The appeal to 1610 to make sense of what happened in 1757 hints at the peculiar feature of the Jesuit as an inveterate king-killer: the image can lay dormant for decades only to be resurrected fully intact when political events call for it. Thus, the entry that the *Encyclopédie* gives for the year 1757 in the Jesuit calendar of infamy ends with the laconic remark: *mêmes circonstances, même conduit* [same circumstances, same conduct].

Damien's attack on Louis XV in 1757 prompted what might be regarded as the culmination of this genre, *Les Jésuites criminels de lèze-majesté*, although circumspection seems to have caused the anonymous author to avoid any reference to the immediate political context and to end the book's enumeration of Jesuit crimes with the murder of Henri IV by Raviallac almost a century and a half earlier. Yet this work still exceeds its predecessors in the amount of material it gathers on historical cases of political violence perpetrated upon heads of state and in the rigour with which it effects a distillation of theological doctrine and real history, or of 'theory' and 'practice'. On the surface, the second part of the tract dealing with history still conforms to the form of a chronicle, but because this part is preceded by a comprehensive exposition of Jesuit doctrine, it is obvious that the sporadic eruptions of political violence proceed from an entrenched body of subversive thought; indeed, the introduction speaks of a 'chain of tradition which has perpetuated itself without interruption'.[39] On the basis of these convictions, numerous assassinations bearing no causal association with the Jesuits are pulled into the orbit of their alleged iniquity.

Given the dramatic nature of its subject matter, any expectations that *Les Jésuites criminels de lèze-majesté* might provide a gripping read are disappointed. In the attempt to emphasise the dastardliness of the Jesuits, the author seems to say little more than: 'not only did they do that, but they also did this'. Nevertheless, this argumentative strategy displays the tell-tale signs of a form of attempted persuasion that, at the time, found application in numerous other contexts beyond the field of anti-Jesuit polemic. Indeed, the Jesuits themselves indulged in the

---

[38] Details about the Busenbaum affair, particularly the condemnation issued by the Parlement of Toulouse on the occasion of its reprinting in 1757, are in Vogel, *Der Untergang der Gesellschaft Jesu*, pp. 162–65.

[39] *Les Jésuites criminels de lèze-majesté* (1758), 'Avis de l'éditeur', i: 'une chaîne de tradition qui s'est perpetuée sans interruption'.

generalised penchant for piling on examples as the rhetorical means of eliciting support for their positions. For example, anti-Machivellian Jesuits attempted to buttress their refutations of the maxims taught by the notorious Florentine humanist and republican by citing countless counter-examples whose collective effect was thought to cast doubt on the lessons contained in *Il Principe* and the *Discorsi*. In his account of this tradition, Robert Bireley points out how the use of these illustrative examples conformed to the means of persuasion favoured by many at the time: 'Their multiplication of examples, a typical form of Baroque argument, was intended to overwhelm the reader and so compel his assent in much the same way that the façade of a Baroque church or palace was meant to impress and evoke the allegiance of the beholder'.[40]

However, it may be that in their exhaustive enumeration of assassinations and conspiracies, the black chronicles reflect more than simply the attempt to persuade and cajole audiences into an abhorrence of the Jesuits. Rather, these black chronicles conform to deep-lying presumptions about the relationship between character and action. In this pre-modern mode of causality, action does not drive a plot forward; rather, actions were recounted to reinforce and affirm character traits.[41] In surveying the bloodshed after the assassination of Henri IV, Duplessis-Mornay asked beseechingly: 'Why all this, I pray you?'[42] Within this framework of action, an answer of sorts was given by pointing to the proclivity for regicide as an incorrigible trait of the Jesuit character and by further insisting that the Jesuit character was constant and unchanging.[43] A German pamphlet published in 1612 maligns the Jesuits by claiming that: 'Königsmord und Fürsten- und Herrenmord steckt einem jeglichen dieser blutgierigen pharisäischen Wesen in der Haut, können nicht anders, ist ihre Natur und Wesen' [Regicide and the murder of princes and lords runs in the blood of every one of these blood-thirsty Pharisees, they cannot do otherwise, it is their nature and their being].[44] A century later, a compilation of anti-Jesuit writings includes the following statement:

[40] Robert Bireley, *The Counter-Reformation Prince: Anti-Machiavellianism or Catholic Statecraft in Early Modern Europe* (Chapel Hill: University of North Carolina Press, 1990), p. 32.
[41] Here, I am transposing ideas from the realm of dramaturgy that Orsolya Kiss has developed in characterising the transition from an 'archaic causation model' to an 'event-oriented, modern causality scheme'. See: 'Reinventing the Plot: J. C. Gottsched's *Sterbender Cato*', *Deutsche Vierteljahrsschrift* 84 (2010): 507–25.
[42] *A Discourse to the lords of the Parliament*, trans. Crashaw, p. 27.
[43] Christine Vogel has described this assertion of an unchanging Jesuit character as an 'axiom of anti-Jesuit conspiracism' ('Kernsatz des antijesuitischen Verschwörungsdenkens'), in *Der Untergang der Gesellschaft Jesu*, p. 187.
[44] Quoted by Johannes Janssen, *Geschichte des deutschen Volkes seit dem Ausgang des Mittelalters, Fünter Band: Die politisch-kirchliche Revolution und ihre Bekämpfung seit der Verkündigung des Concordienformels im Jahre 1580 bis zum Beginne des dreißigjärigen*

'Les Jesuites ont toujours été ce qu'ils sont aujord'hui. L'ambition & le desir de dominer ont toujours fait le Caractere propre de cette Compagnie' [The Jesuits have always been that which they are today. The ambition and desire to dominate have always been the distinctive feature of this company].[45]

Such assertions of invariable wickedness indicate a predilection for conspirator-centred conspiracy theories. By contrast, plan-centred conspiracy theories shift the focus from episodic manifestations of inherent character traits to the unfolding of a narrative. If *Les Jésuites criminels de lèze-majesté* exhibits any narrative at all, then it is provided only by the observed correlation between the rise of the Jesuits and the decline in reverence for the king.[46] The narrative has the rudimentary structure of a comparison between 'before' and 'after': before the Jesuits arrived, the French nation was distinguished by an unsullied reverence for its kings; after their arrival, these kings were exposed to a series of cruel assaults upon their lives. If, in the previous pamphlets, the enumeration of all these assaults, or 'the Blood-thirsty prosecution of Conspiracy upon Conspiracy', as the author of *The Art of Assassinating Kings* describes it, has an enervating effect, this effect in *Les Jésuites criminels de lèze-majesté* is heightened by the fastidiousness with which its anonymous compiler assembles the relevant material.[47]

Yet there are incipient signs of change in the expectations with which readers approached such material. These signs intimate a shift from conspirator-centred to plan-centred conspiracy theories. Vilification of an already identified adversary by tarring them with complicity in conspiracies loses some of its status as the primary purpose of these writings. Instead, their authors make adjustments to the expectations of a reading public, no longer seeking simple corroboration of its prejudices but rather articulating an understanding of history imagined as an unfolding narrative. Thus, readers would soon be privy to glimpses of the motives compelling Jesuits to act in the way they had.

One example is provided by Johann Christoph Harenberg's introduction to his two-volume *Pragmatic History of the Jesuit Order*, published in 1760. There, he appeals to the reader's forebearance, almost apologising for the chronological

---

Krieges im Jahre 1618 (Freiburg im Breisgau: Herder'sche Verlagshandlung, 1886), p. 535. My translation.

[45] *Les Mysteres les plus secret des Jesuites: Contenu en diverses Pieces Originales* (Cologne: Chez les Heritiers de Pierre Marteau, 1727), p. 81. My translation.

[46] *Les Jésuites criminels de lèze-majesté* (1758), p. 188: 'Depuis l'établissement de cette Société les entreprises sur les personnes sacrées des Rois se sont multipliés, & nous avons vu plusieurs fois commettre des attentats inconnus à nos Peres' [Since this Society [i.e. the Society of Jesus] was established its undertakings against the sacred persons of the kings have multiplied and we have seen assassinations committed numerous times against our fathers].

[47] *Art of Assassinating Kings*, p. 78.

approach he has seen himself forced to adopt in ordering the material. The challenge presented by the disparate and seemingly disconnected facts and episodes exceeds his powers of exposition and forces him to revert to the form of a chronicle:

> Ich habe hieselbst die chronologische Methode wählen müssen, weil die Begebenheiten des Ordens so mannigfaltig sind und so oft in einen Zeitpunkt fallen, daß es nicht möglich zu seyn scheinet, dieselben nach dem Zusammenhange der Begebenheiten abzuhandeln.[48]
>
> [I have had to settle for the chronological method as the aspects of this order are so diverse and often so coterminous that it seems not possible to deal with these aspects in terms of their relationship to one another].

Admitting a shortcoming, however, does not necessarily provide cover from criticism. In 1761, the year after Harenberg's work appeared, Anton Ernst Klausing, who later occupied a chair as a professor of antiquities in Leipzig, drew attention to precisely this weakness in Harenberg's exposition. Klausing claimed that Harenberg failed to deliver on the promise of the title he had given to his work. Instead, Harenberg made do with his attempts to group disjointed pieces of information together thematically: 'Es ist allerdings nach dieser Methode dem Hrn. Probst [i.e. Harenberg] sehr leicht gewesen, eine Geschichte der Jesuiten zu schreiben; allein sie ist auch dasjenige noch nicht, was man jetzt in einer solchen Geschichte suchet' [It is admittedly very easy on the basis of this method to write a history of the Jesuits; but it is not that which one now looks for in such a history].[49] Something is missing. Klausing intimates an intention to write a more comprehensive criticism of Harenberg that, presumably, would have more precisely pinpointed the deficit he perceived in Harenberg's work. It seems that he never realised this intention, but some of his comments give a more precise sense of his misgivings. Harenberg's work lacked a system that would tie the heterogeneous pieces of information together. Thus, regarding Harenberg's account of Jesuit missionary work, Klausing writes:

> Wir haben bey den Capiteln von den Missionswerken der Jesuiten gar keine zusammenhängende und vollständige Erzehlung wahrgenommen. Es sind meistentheils nur abgerissene Stücke und einzelne Historien, wodurch man aber noch keinen deutlichen Begriff von dem ganzen Werke einer jedesmaligen Mißion bekommt ...

---

[48] Johann Christoph Harenberg, *Pragmatische Geschichte des Ordens der Jesuiten, seit ihrem Ursprunge bis auf gegenwärtige Zeit*, 2 vols (Halle and Helmstädt: Carl Hermann Hemmerde, 1760), Point 14 in the unpaginated preface (*Vorrede*) of the first volume. My translation.

[49] Anton Ernst Klausing, ed., *Sammlung der Neuesten Schrifften, welche die Jesuiten in Portugal betreffen*, 4 vols (Frankfurt and Leipzig, 1761), 2:XLV.

[We have not been able to perceive in the chapters about the missionary activity of the Jesuits a coherent and complete story. Mostly there are detached pieces and singular stories but one is not given a clear conception of the entire work undertaken by each mission ...].[50]

The criticism of Harenberg's failure to order the historical material satisfactorily corresponds to a presumption on Klausing's part that readers of the time desired some form of over-arching narrative coherence.[51]

An example of a work that at least indicates how to integrate the story of the Jesuit missions, particularly in the case of the South American reductions (i.e. the semi-autonomous settlements for native Indians overseen by Jesuit missionaries), into a grandiose narrative of the order's history was provided by an Italian work titled *Critica di un Romano alle Riflessioni del Portoghese* [*Criticism of a Roman Regarding the Reflections of a Portuguese*] (1759). Klausing translated this text and included it in this same volume of anti-Jesuit writings, the preface of which contained his criticism of Harenberg's efforts.[52] The *Critica di un Romano* belongs to a series of works produced by a Jansenist circle based in Rome, centred around the librarian Giovanni Gaetano Bottari. It evinces a keen awareness for the defensive position in which the Jesuits found themselves in the face of an energetic campaign launched against them by the Portuguese statesman, the Marquis of Pombal.[53] The seventeenth point in this tract introduced a key concept that the authors – in line with an older tradition of anti-Jesuit rhetoric – deemed eligible for consideration as the *telos* of all Jesuit activity. This was the universal monarchy as a vision of order that invoked the distant memory of the Roman empire but that took on increasingly sinister overtones for those who, whether for nationalist or religious reasons, did not identify with the alleged

---

[50] Ibid.

[51] In the eyes of the anonymous reviewer in the *Allgemeine Literatur-Zeitung* 128 (3 May 1791): 217–20, Peter Philipp Wolf was more successful in this regard with the first volume of his *Allgemeine Geschichte der Jesuiten*. Wolf had managed to study the history of the order in its internal coherence ('die Geschichte dieses Ordens im Zusammenhange zu studiren', p. 217) and was capable of discerning a pattern in the history of the order that was more real than the strictly chronological and was connected to the broader political history ('dass er mehr eine gewisse Realordnung, als eine streng chronologische, die den Schauplatz sehr oft verändert, und allenthalben Begebenheiten abgebrochen hinterlässt, beobachtet. Er hat diese vielmehr im Zusammenhange mit der politischen Geschichte vorgetragen', p. 218).

[52] Giovanni Gaetano Bottari et al., *Critica di un Romano alle Riflessioni del Portoghese sopra il memoriale presentato dai PP. Gesuiti al papa Clemente XIII* (Genoa, 1759). For the German translation in the collections compiled by Klausing, see: 'Critik eines Römers über das Sendschreiben eines Portugiesen u.', in Klausing, *Sammlung der Neuesten Schrifften*, 2:108–269.

[53] See: Vogel, *Untergang der Gesellschaft Jesu*, pp. 122–26.

aspirant of such a comprehensive unitary power.[54] After many Europeans attributed such ambitions to the Spanish in the sixteenth and seventeenth century, the focus shifted to the spectre of French hegemony.[55] By the eighteenth century, however, the science of mechanics began to furnish an alternative vision of international order. The talk was of a balance of powers.[56]

The *Critica di un Romano* registers many of these developments in the particularly bold speculation imagining the Society of Jesus – although officially a religious order – as having already achieved the universal monarchy, which eluded the grasp of so many secular powers in the past. According to the author, the series of failed attempts to erect a universal monarchy was sufficient to instruct the Jesuits in the difficulty of their undertaking; indeed, history demonstrated that '... poichè qualora un qualche Monarca potentissimo tirava le sui linee con tutta une monarchia universale, subito gli altri Potentati gli si rivolgevano contro, e glie l'attraversavano efficacemente' [as soon as a powerful monarch had marshalled his strength and cunning to create the universal monarchy the other kings and princes opposed him and thwarted his plans].[57] This was nothing other than the healthy balance of power. Therefore, the Jesuits stood accused of devising a more ingenious plan to achieve their goal; in religion, they recognised an instrument that could transform kings and princes into lifeless marionettes. Politics became a puppet play (*una commedia di burattini*), in which those who move the puppets are hidden from view: 'e così hanno fatto per quasi 200. anni' [in this manner they have ruled for almost 200 years].[58] However, because the Jesuits wearied of this discrete form of universal monarchy, they established their state in Paraguay where they could exercise power without the irksome constraints imposed by a need to work from behind the scenes.

Returning to the specific question of regicide and assassination, the text avoids any attempt to integrate such acts of violence into the larger narrative framework provided by a pursuit of universal monarchy, as easily conceivable as it might seem. However, there were inklings of an attempt to identify the pattern

---

[54] An earlier German example of this assertion, developed in a pamphlet from the period of the Thirty Years War, was printed under the pseudonym Philander Philanax [Johann Seyffert?] in *Außführlicher Tractat Von der Jesuitischen Monarchy* (Frankfurt: Johann Friedrich Weissen, 1633), where, on p. 7, one reads of 'der Jesuiten Intention, die universal Monarchy / directe oder indirecte an sich zu ziehen' [the intention of the Jesuits to seize directly or indirectly the universal monarchy].

[55] For the Protestant German context in the Thirty Years War, see: Peer Schmidt, *Spanische Universalmonarchie oder 'teutsche Libertet': Das spanische Imperium in der Propaganda des Dreissigjährigen Krieges* (Stuttgart: Franz Steiner Verlag, 2001).

[56] For a detailed study of this concept, see: Franz Bosbach, *Monarchia Universalis: Ein Politischer Leitbegriff der Frühen Neuzeit* (Göttingen: Vandenhoeck & Ruprecht, 1988).

[57] *Critica di un Romano*, p. 113.

[58] Ibid., p. 114.

that lent the assassinations a more profound meaning than simply the compulsive expression of a 'villainous practice', as the author of the *Remonstrance* put it. Surveying the series of assassinations in 1610, Duplessis-Mornay could only speak of a 'general murther, an universal slaughter'.[59] Taking a leap of one and a half centuries to arrive at *Les Jésuites criminels de lèze-majesté*, the insinuation conveyed by this work in the wake of the recent attempt on the life of Louis XV is a simple one: the Jesuits are up to their old tricks again.[60] Curiously enough, the German translation hints at a possible line of development. Where the French original uses a verb form in its claim that the Jesuits conspire against the kings, the German translation transforms this into an interesting substantive: the Jesuits are all involved 'in einer Verschwörung wider das Leben der Könige' [in a conspiracy against the kings].[61]

The difference is both slight and significant; while, for the most part, the pamphlets present a series of conspiracies, now these conspiracies have been fused into a singular conspiracy. Obviously, a marginal deviation in a translation is a flimsy basis upon which to rest an argument about a broader narrative unity underpinning disparate events. However, this notion of one large conspiracy that lies behind all the smaller conspiracies and, therefore, provides narrative unity comes to the fore in the remarkable introduction to a pamphlet that formed part of the extensive campaign set in motion by Pombal after the Portuguese monarch, Joseph I, was targeted by an assassination attempt in September 1758.[62] Pombal had old scores to settle with the Jesuits and an attempt on the life of the king represented a perfect opportunity to join the chorus of anti-Jesuit polemic already resonating in France.[63] The *Causes de l'évènement de Portugal* was written in French to reach a wider European audience; in effect, it delivers a brief synopsis of *Les Jésuites criminels de lèze-majesté* by adhering to the same bipartite structure. Yet the opening paragraph is highly innovative in its discussion of the long series of assassinations:

---

[59] *A discourse to the lords of the Parliament*, p. 41.
[60] As noted, *Les Jésuites criminels de lèze-majesté* does not catalogue acts of Jesuit treachery up to the time of its publication but rather ends its historical exposition with the event that inspired the *Remonstrance*, namely the regicide perpetrated upon Henri IV.
[61] *Gefahr der Majestäten*, pp. 21–22.
[62] For details pertaining to the assassination attempt, see: Vogel, *Der Untergang der Gesellschaft Jesu*, pp. 46–49. For Pombal, one can consult Kenneth Maxwell, *Pombal: Paradox of the Enlightenment* (Cambridge: Cambridge University Press, 1995).
[63] For an account of the diplomatic wrangling between Portugal and Rome because of Pombal's campaign, see: Samuel J. Miller, *Portugal and Rome c. 1748–1830: An Aspect of the Catholic Enlightenment* (Rome: Università Gregoriana Editrice, 1978), esp. chapters II and III.

Les attentats affreux qui successivement ont fait gémir deux Royaumes, ne sont point dûs à des causes passageres & accidentelles. Ils ont leur principe dans une conjuration subsistante & persévérante depuis près de deux siècles: conjuration contre la loi de Dieu, contre la vie des Rois & contre les droits de l'humanité. Cette annonce n'emprunte rien de l'emphase ou de l'hyperbole. Ce n'est point par des efforts de raisonnements que l'on prétend en établir la vérité: on ne présentera au lecteur qui doit en juger, d'autres preuves que la traduction exacte des écrits des conjurés, & que les faits constans dans lesquels on retrouve toujours, & en tous lieux, cette même conjuration & les mêmes personnages auteurs de toutes les catastrophes. Puisse la lecture de tant d'horreurs rassemblées & mises en évidence, produire une salutaire indignation, & provoquer le remede qu'exigent également la sureté du trône, l'intérêt de l'humanité & l'honneur de la Religion.

[The horrible assassination attempts that have successively made two kingdoms moan are not due to accidental or passing causes. They have their principle in a conspiracy that has subsisted and persevered for close to two centuries; a conspiracy against the law of God, against the lives of kings and against the rights of humanity. This statement does not rely upon bombast or hyperbole. It is not through the efforts of reasoning that one claims to establish the truth of this: we will present to the discerning reader no other proofs than the exact translation of the writings of these conspirators and the same observed facts in which one encounters at every time and place this same conspiracy and the same authors of all these catastrophes. Reading of so many horrors, compiled and furnished with proofs, induces a salutary indignation and provokes the remedy demanded equally by the security of the thrones, the interests of humanity and the honour of religion].[64]

Although the passage begins by referring to the recent assassination attempts in France and Portugal, it hints at more than the mere enumeration of conspiracies. This is the beginning of a fully-fledged conspiracy theory, evinced by familiar reflexes of this mentality such as the pre-emptive dismissal of chance as an explanation. But the most remarkable aspect is the manner in which the individual conspiracies are now subsumed under the grander conspiracy that has been in motion for over two centuries at the time of writing.[65] Indeed, to

---

[64] *Causes de l'évènement de Portugal: Ouvrage dédié à toute puissance séculière et temporelle* (n.p., 1759). I quote from the re-print included in *Recueil de toutes les pièces et nouvelles qui ont paru sur les affaires des Jésuites, principalement dans l'Amérique Méridionale, & dans le Royaume de Portugal* (n.p., 1760) 2:391–421 at p. 391. My translation. A German translation can be found in Klausing, *Sammlung der Neuesten Schrifften*, 1:41–68.

[65] One can compare this vision with the report sent by Francisco de Almeida, the Portuguese ambassador in Rome, to Pombal on 22 February 1759 as cited by Miller, *Portugal and Rome c. 1748–1830*: 'For two hundred years there has not been a conspiracy into which the Jesuits have not entered universally, as much by the theory and doctrine

prevent the onset of confusion, the author refers to the smaller sub-conspiracies no longer as 'conspiracies'; rather, they have been reduced to the *faits constans*, sub-operations and tactical manoeuvres subordinate to the implementation of a larger plan.

In his investigations into conceptual history, the German historian Reinhart Koselleck offers a schematic possibility for making sense of this development. He does so by drawing attention to the process by which the concept of 'history' as an abstract entity began to ingratiate itself into the consciousness of historical actors and commentators. Whereas in the past 'history' only made sense when it stood in relation to a concrete entity (e.g., a person or a city or a country), during the early modern period it became possible to speak of 'history' as a generalised medium containing within itself all singular histories. Koselleck termed this over-arching abstraction a 'collective singular'.[66] However, the modern concept of 'history' did not stand alone as the only product resulting from a process of collective singularisation; this was a period in which other crucial elements within the semantic field were re-configured in this manner. Thus, Koselleck's observation about 'history' was also valid for the crystallisation of other significant abstractions in this same period. It was, as Koselleck wrote, 'the great period of singularization and simplification which was directed socially and politically against a society of estates. Here, Freedom took the place of freedoms, Justice that of rights and servitudes, Progress that of progressions (*les progrès*, the plural) and from the diversity of revolutions, "The Revolution" emerged.'[67] Koselleck's observation provides the basis for an analogy: the conspiracy that is described in *Causes de l'évènement de Portugal* is the collective singular of the myriad episodic conspiracies that the Jesuits have fomented and instigated. Instead of a conspiracy representing a merely episodic and particularly dramatic departure from politics in its 'business-as-usual' mode, European politics was allegedly

---

which they teach as by their practices' (p. 73). Despite conspicuous similarities between Almeida's statement and the public condemnations of the Jesuits that were being churned out under Pombal's direction, Almeida still adheres to the notion of smaller conspiracies.

[66] For an overview of the various occasions on which Koselleck discussed this concept, see: Kari Palonen, *Die Entzauberung der Begriffe: Das Umschreiben der politischen Begriffe bei Quentin Skinner und Reinhart Koselleck* (Münster: LIT-Verlag, 2004), pp. 208–14.

[67] Reinhart Koselleck, 'Past and Future in Modern History', *Futures Past: On the Semantics of Historical Times*, trans. Keith Tribe (New York: Columbia University Press, 2004), p. 35. Translation of 'Historia Magistra Vitae: Über die Auflösung des Topos im Horizont neuzeitlich bewegter Geschichte', *Vergangene Zukunft. Zur Semantik geschichtlichen Zeiten* (Frankfurt am Main: Suhrkamp, 1989), p. 54. A further example of a collective singular would be 'public opinion', which emerges from aggregating all the individual private opinions.

characterised by a singular conspiracy threading its way through almost the entire early modern period.

The emergence of the concept of 'history' as the result of the collective singularisation of the individual histories obviously was itself a historical process that generated new questions. Even if history now took on the status of a generalised medium in which all other events and sub-histories were embedded, there remained a curiosity about its own form. Of course, progress – another collective singular formed by fusing together the myriad particular progressions – provided one response to this question.[68] But a grand conspiracy theory represented a further option. Repeatedly, Koselleck formulates descriptions of this concept of history that suggest an affinity with aspects of conspiracy. History as a collective singular encouraged the historian 'to elicit secret motives, rather than present chronological series'.[69] It furthermore 'made possible the attribution to history of the latent power of human events and suffering, a power that connected and motivated everything in accordance with a secret or evident plan'.[70] Evidence of history imagined as the unfolding of a 'secret plan' is present, for example, in the drastic conspiratorial vision articulated by Jean Antoine Gazaignes, the canon at the Benedictine monastery of Saint-Benoît, in the introduction to his five-volume, unrestrainedly anti-Jesuit history of the Jesuits: *Annales de la Société des soi-disans Jésuites*. Gazaigne was convinced 'qu'il est dans cette Société un Plan formé, dès sa naissance, d'anéantir la Doctrine & la Morale de Jesus-Christ, de détruire sa Religion & son Culte, de renverser les Thrônes & les Empires, pour, sur ces sacrés débris, élever à ses ambitieux desirs une souveraineté absolue, indépendante, universelle' [that there is within the Society of Jesus a plan, forged at its birth, to annihilate the doctrine and morality of Jesus Christ, to destroy his religion and his worship, to overturn the thrones and the empires in order to raise up, on this sacred debris, an absolute, independent and universal sovereignty in line with their ambitious desires].[71]

---

[68] Koselleck discusses the highly entwined conceptual histories of 'history' and 'progress', particularly in terms of their parallel collective singularisation, in the entry on 'progress' ('Fortschritt') in the *Geschichtliche Grundbegriffe. Historisches Lexikon zur politisch-sozialen Sprache in Deutschland*, ed. Otto Brunner, Werner Conze and Reinhart Koselleck (Stuttgart: Klett-Cotta, 1979), 2:351–53 and pp. 384–90. Consider, in particular, p. 388, where Koselleck summarises the exposition as follows: 'So wird aus den Geschichten der (einzelnen) Fortschritte der Fortschritt der Geschichte' [In this manner, the progress of history emerges out of the histories of the (individual) progressions].

[69] Koselleck, 'Past and Future in Modern History', p. 34.

[70] Ibid., p. 35.

[71] Jean Antoine Gazaignes, 'Dissertation analytique, historique, théologique et critique', *Annales de la Société des soi-disans Jésuites*, ed. Gazaignes (Paris, 1764), 1:ix. My translation.

And yet, curiously, such intimations of a plan-centred conspiracy theory, which occasionally appear in the anti-Jesuit literature of the period, are never fully developed, leaving the impression that the anti-Jesuit tradition had become so sclerotic, and the inherited strategies of defamation so entrenched, as to nip all innovation in the bud. The detailed elaboration of the anti-Jesuit plan-centred conspiracy theory remains, therefore, largely an empty space in the historical record. One reason for this lies in the fact that the need for such innovation was obviated by the dramatic developments to which the vilification of the Jesuits in the mode of conspirator-centred conspiracy theories made their contribution: in 1759, the Jesuits were expelled from Portugal; in 1764, from France; and then, in 1767, from Spain. This all formed the drum roll for the suppression of the Society of Jesus ordered in the papal brief *Dominus ad Redemptor* in 1773. The dubious honour of playing the role of chief protagonist in the grand plan-centred conspiracy theories of the eighteenth century therefore fell to other groups such as the Enlightenment *philosophes* and the Freemasons, whose methodical subversion of the old order came to fruition, according to such theories, in the French Revolution.[72]

Assassination and murder did not, however, provide the means by which opponents of either the *philosophes* or the secret societies linked these groups to subversion. This remained an idiosyncrasy of the anti-Jesuit polemical tradition. And yet, as an idiosyncrasy it evolved. Accusing the Jesuits of complicity in conspiracies on the basis of collusion within the confessional box was a haphazard, hit-and-miss affair; it was not always possible to find evidence, however circumstantial, that the assassin had consulted with Jesuit priests via the confessional. By contrast, the insinuation of a more diffuse influence, achieved through 'seditious writings', was a far more supple and effective way of tying the Jesuits to conspiracies. Indeed, the diffuseness encouraged the sense that Jesuit meddling-in-politics occurred not only as a result of localised conspiracies set in motion by specific acts of 'verbal communication'. When the attempts upon the life of Louis XV in 1757 and Joseph I in the following year inspired the defenders of state sovereignty to reactivate the trope linking the Jesuits with assassination, there were clear signs of a move away from a chronological approach that merely enumerated such instances of conspiratorial action. As some of the material demonstrates, some purveyors of anti-Jesuit sentiment were not averse

---

[72] With the suppression of the society in 1773, the Jesuits do not actually exit the stage on which the drama of conspiracy is played out. Particularly in late eighteenth-century northern (Protestant) Germany, fears were rife that (Ex-)Jesuits had infiltrated the secret societies in whose seclusion they concocted plans to sabotage the Enlightenment. See: Steven Luckert, 'Jesuits, Freemasons, Illuminati, and Jacobins: Conspiracy Theories, Secret Societies and Politics in Late Eighteenth-Century Germany', PhD dissertation (State University of New York, 1993).

to attempting to equate the entire history of the order with one grand conspiracy, perpetrated by means of the nefarious influence exerted by Jesuit doctrine.

Thus, even if the anti-Jesuit polemic does not bear witness to the full shift from conspirator-centred to plan-centred conspiracy theories, it does exhibit clear signs of attempts to amalgamate the smaller conspiracies in a manner similar to the tendency on display in some of the material left behind by the Assassination Information Bureau from the 1970s. In the introduction to *Government by Gunplay*, one of the editors, Sid Blumenthal, felt compelled to 'soft-pedal' the instinctive urge to imagine a broader subversion uniting the repeated jarring acts of political violence: 'History itself, of course, is not a conspiracy. There are, however, conspiracies in history.'[73] In repudiating such an equivalence of history and conspiracy, Blumenthal was most likely referring to the famous essay penned by the historian Richard Hofstadter, whose diagnosis of what he called the 'Paranoid Style in American Politics' was based in part upon a tendency to see 'a "vast" and "gigantic" conspiracy as *the motive force* in historical events'.[74] In other words, those displaying this style were enthralled to the delusion that 'History is a conspiracy'.[75] Such an equivalence, even if fundamentally wrong-headed, is nevertheless startlingly simple and, therefore, immediately comprehensible. Yet its comprehensibility should not be taken for granted. By examining the black chronicles that documented acts of political murder allegedly orchestrated by Jesuits in the early modern period, it is possible to appreciate how the parameters of historical interpretation shifted and evolved, and how such changes gestured in a direction that subsequently allowed for a conflation of history and conspiracy. At certain historical junctures, such a conflation, expressed by the notion that 'History is a conspiracy', often spoke to those afflicted by a particularly pressing need to make sense of an unsettling spate of assassinations.

---

[73] Sid Blumenthal, 'Foreword', *Government by Gunplay*, p. x.
[74] Richard Hofstadter, *The Paranoid Style in American Politics* (Cambridge, MA: Harvard University Press, 1964), p. 29.
[75] Ibid.

PART III

MURDER IN THE COMMUNITY: GENDER, YOUTH AND FAMILY

CHAPTER 13

Negotiating Murder in the *Historiae* of Gregory of Tours

Jeffrey Doolittle

IN HIS *HISTORIAE*, the sixth-century bishop Gregory of Tours (c. 538–94) narrates a brutal killing carried out by Childebert and Chlothar, sons of the famous Merovingian Frankish king Clovis (*Hist.* III.18).[1] Childebert, who was king of Paris (r. 511–558), plotted to seize the kingdom of Orleans from his nephews, heirs of his recently deceased brother Chlodomer. Gregory writes that Childebert was driven by *invidia* [envy] of his nephews, who had become the favourites of Childebert's own mother, Clovis' widow Chlothild (III.18). To carry out his scheme, Childebert turned to another brother, Chlothar, king of Soissons (r. 511–561), and together they devised a ruse to separate the princes from Chlothild. Their nephews, as Gregory repeatedly emphasises, were very

---

[1] Long known as the *History of the Franks*, most scholars now call Gregory's work the *Historiae*. Walter Goffart, 'From *Historiae* to *Historia Francorum* and Back Again: Aspects of the Textual History of Gregory of Tours', in *Rome's Fall and After*, ed. Goffart (London: Hambledon Press, 1989), pp. 255–74. The Latin text is drawn from Gregory of Tours, *Libri historiarum X*, ed. Bruno Krusch and Wilhelm Levison, MGH, SS rer. Merov. 1,1, 2nd edn (Hanover: Hahnsche, 1937–1951), pp. 1–537. Citations in English are from Lewis Thorpe's translations unless otherwise specified, although I have also consulted the more recent (though partial) translation by Alexander Callander Murray. At times, I have also considered the older English translations by Ernest Brehaut and O. M. Dalton. Book/chapter numbers are given in parentheses in the text. See: Thorpe's *Gregory of Tours: The History of the Franks* (New York: Penguin, 1974); Alexander Callander Murray, ed., *Gregory of Tours: The Merovingians* (Toronto: Broadview Press, 2006); Ernest Brehaut, trans., *History of the Franks by Gregory, Bishop of Tours* (New York: Columbia University Press, 1916; reprinted 1969); O. M. Dalton, trans., *The History of the Franks by Gregory of Tours* (Oxford: Clarendon Press, 1927). For an explanation of the manuscript and editorial history of the *Historiae*, see: Martin Heinzelmann, *Gregory of Tours: History and Society in the Sixth Century*, trans. Christopher Carroll (Cambridge: Cambridge University Press, 2001), pp. 192–201; and Pascale Bourgain and Martin Heinzelmann, 'L'oeuvre de Grégoire de Tours: la diffusion des manuscrits', in *Grégoire de Tours et l'espace gaulois: actes du congrès internationale, Tours, 3–5 Novembre 1994*, ed. Nancy Gauthier and Henri Galinié (Tours: Revue archéologique du Centre de la France, 1997), pp. 273–317.

young, only seven and ten years of age.² After succeeding in isolating the boys, Childebert and Chlothar coldly enacted their plan: Chlothar threw the older child to the ground, stabbed him in his armpit and 'crudeliter interfecit' [savagely killed] him (III.18). Upon witnessing the horror of the crime, and with the younger boy's desperate pleas for mercy ringing in his ears, Childebert had a change of heart and begged Chlothar to stop. In response, Chlothar threatened to kill Childebert as well; Chlothar then seized the screaming younger boy and killed him too. To eliminate witnesses, Chlothar and Childebert then slaughtered all the boys' attendants and, Gregory says, left without any compunction for what they had done (III.18).

Violent vignettes such as this one have contributed to the particularly bloody reputation of the *Historiae* and have long captivated historians.³ But while many studies have explored aspects of this violence, a deeper analysis of some of Gregory's bloodiest narratives provides details about his definitions of illegitimate killing and their purpose in his text. The example of Chlothar and Childebert is particularly illustrative: Gregory employs several strategies to demonstrate injustice, including direct statements of impropriety, either in his own voice or that of an interlocutor, the provision of narrative detail highlighting motives and consequences, the use of special terms to emphasise the inhumanity of the act and even the location and context within his books. Gregory affirms that Childebert and Chlothar's killings were committed *crudeliter* [savagely] and poignantly depicts Clothild's grief afterward. From his references to the children's ages and the killers' shameless efforts to kill witnesses, Gregory insinuates that the kings transgressed important norms that align with Salic law injunctions against secretly plotting a killing, hiding evidence of it and, especially, targeting

---

[2] A third nephew, and the only one named by Gregory (Chlodovald), did manage to escape and survive, but spent the rest of his life in a monastery (*Hist.* III.18).

[3] J. M. Wallace Hadrill, 'Blood Feud of the Franks', *Bulletin of the John Rylands Library* 41 (1958–59): 459–87, applied Max Gluckman's anthropological studies of feuding to understand the violence in the *Historiae*. R. F. Newbold provides a quantitative approach to the instances of violence in 'Interpersonal Violence in Gregory of Tours' *Libri Historiarum*', *Nottingham Medieval Studies* 38 (1994): 3–17. For the bishop's role in ameliorating conflicts, see: Edward James, '"*Beati pacifici*": Bishops and the Law in Sixth-Century Gaul', in *Disputes and Settlements: Law and Human Relations in the West*, ed. John Bossy (Cambridge: Cambridge University Press, 1983), pp. 25–45. Guy Halsall, 'Reflections on Early Medieval Violence: The Example of the "Blood Feud"', *Memoria y Civilización* 2 (1999): 7–29 at p. 28. In approaching narratives of violence, Halsall recommends a consideration of the aims, attitudes toward legitimacy and the relationships engendered. For other studies on disputes in Merovingian Gaul, see the essays by Paul Fouracre and Ian Wood in *The Settlement of Disputes in Early Medieval Europe*, ed. Wendy Davies and Paul Fouracre (Cambridge: Cambridge University Press, 1986).

young children.[4] Most significantly, Gregory states that Childebert's sole motive was *invidia* [envy], highlighting its impropriety in prompting acts so contrary to law and custom. In fact, by stating this unworthy motive at the outset of this chapter, Gregory conditions his readers' responses toward moral outrage even before he narrates the evil deeds themselves. These rhetorical techniques invite the audience to ponder the actions that Gregory's historical figures take.

Gregory makes it clear that the murderous deeds of Childebert and Chlothar are wrong. As Walter Goffart and Martin Heinzelmann have argued, such narratives also serve a didactic purpose and help inform Gregory's broader concerns about the responsibilities of royal and episcopal authority.[5] Indeed, Childebert and Chlothar's murders, and countless others like them, constitute evidence for the disordered and sinful nature of the world. For Gregory, each act of illegitimate lethal violence recreates the typologically significant story of Cain and Abel – a narrative that is given a place of prominence in the *Historiae* (*Hist.* I.3) – through the presentation of similar unjust motivations, use of violent force and, in many cases, even similar terminology.[6] Gregory names Cain as a *parecida*, and, in several other striking examples, he uses a similar word, *parricida*, for an unjust killer of a close family member; he also uses the related terms *homicida*, to signify a person with an especially negative reputation for killing, and *homicidium*, to indicate the killing of an innocent person. These labels quickly convey a sense of *mala fama* for certain kinds of killings, which reflects a similar social concern about homicides as witnessed in other sixth-century Merovingian Frankish sources.[7] Gregory provides the figures of the depraved *parricida* driven

---

[4] In Salic Law, certain kinds of killings require a more onerous compensation, and several of these align with the actions of Childebert and Chlothar above. For example, Title XXIV specifies a 24,000 denarii penalty for killing a 'long-haired boy', usually understood as a royal heir under the age of twelve. Title XLI features the same monetary penalty for killings that are concealed or hidden. See: *Pactus Legis Salicae*, MGH Leges nationum Germanicarum 4,1 (Hannover: Hahnsche, 1962), pp. 1–237.

[5] Goffart and Heinzelmann have been two of the most prominent scholars to recast Gregory as a thoughtful and creative historian, and, in different ways, both have argued for a conceptual unity to the *Historiae*. Walter Goffart, *The Narrators of Barbarian History (A.D. 550–800): Jordanes, Gregory of Tours, Bede and Paul the Deacon* (Princeton: Princeton University Press, 1988), pp. 112–234; Martin Heinzelmann's comprehensive rereading of Gregory takes Goffart's discoveries a step farther and argues for a complex Christological vision of society and politics at the centre of the *Historiae*. Heinzelmann finds that Gregory is primarily concerned with demonstrating the joint authority of good kings and bishops over a Christian society. See especially: Heinzelmann, *Gregory of Tours*, pp. 172–92, 202–09.

[6] Goffart, 'From *Historiae* to *Historia Francorum*', p. 74.

[7] For more about the role that murder, specifically of children, plays in classical and medieval literature, see: Margaret E. McKenzie, 'Filicide in Medieval Narrative', PhD

by greed and hatred and the elite *homicida* who delights in the slaughter of innocents as moralising examples for his intended audience of kings and bishops. In the *Historiae* such figures almost always meet violent and bloody ends.

Gregory's monumental historical work, completed shortly before his death, is undoubtedly one of the most important sources for the history of Merovingian Gaul, but also one of the most complicated.[8] Covering all of history from creation until just before Gregory's death in 594, the work comprises ten books and focuses on 'a great many things ... some of them good, some of them bad', in what scholars have long dismissed as a naïve and simplistic anecdotal style. However, as Goffart argues, Gregory had an ambitious plan and envisioned his history as a morally instructive narrative of 'miracles and slaughters'.[9] Heinzelmann suggests that a fundamental break in content may indicate two separate works: Books I–IV, covering 'ancient' history, encompass some 5,774 years since Creation, while Books V through X treat only eighteen years of 'contemporary' history from 575 to 591.[10] Demonstrating the typological links between the 'ancient' and 'contemporary' events in Gregory's work, Heinzelmann emphasises Gregory's selective

---

dissertation (The Catholic University of America, Washington, DC, 2012). McKenzie argues that stories of filicide play a dual role in that they both shock and instruct the audience.

[8] While most scholars have argued for a synchronic composition for the *Historiae*, Murray suggested a composition date around 590 based on strong reflective sentiments throughout the *Historiae*. See: Alexander Callander Murray, 'Chronology and Composition of the Histories of Gregory of Tours', *Journal of Late Antiquity* 1.1 (Spring 2008): 157–96. For more traditional dating, see also: Ian Wood, *The Merovingian Kingdoms, 450–751* (London: Longman, 1994), p. 28; Sam Collins, 'The Written World of Gregory of Tours', in *The Middle Ages in Texts and Texture: Reflections on Medieval Sources*, ed. Jason Glenn (Toronto: University of Toronto Press, 2011), pp. 45–55; Yitzhak Hen, 'Literacy and Orality: The Place of the Written Word in Merovingian Gaul', in *Culture and Religion in Merovingian Gaul, A.D. 481–751* (Leiden: Brill, 1995), pp. 21–42.

[9] Ian Wood, 'The Secret Histories of Gregory of Tours', *Revue Belge de philologie et d'histoire* 71.2 (1993): 253–70; Goffart, *The Narrators of Barbarian History*, pp. 112–234; Murray, 'Chronology and Composition', pp. 157–96.

[10] Heinzelmann sees Book V as starting a very different section of the *Historiae*, as the format becomes more annalistic and the subject more contemporary and local to Tours. Heinzelmann, *Gregory of Tours*, p. 114. Books I–IV were completed around 575/6 and Books V–X were completed near the end of Gregory's life: ibid. Halsall disagrees, arguing that Book V was written first, and then Books I–IV were written afterwards to set it up. See: Guy Halsall, 'The Preface to Book V of Gregory of Tours' Histories: Its Form, Context and Significance', *English Historical Review* 123.496 (2007): 297–317. These latter six books largely coincide with Gregory's episcopate in Tours (573–94 CE). See also: Edward James's analysis of Gregory's chronology in 'Gregory of Tours and the Franks', in *After Rome's Fall: Narrators and Sources of Early Medieval History*, ed. Alexander Callander Murray (Toronto: University of Toronto Press, 1998), pp. 51–66 at p. 57.

retelling of biblical and classical stories and also his deliberate reshaping of contemporary events to make moral points.[11]

While Heinzelmann especially focuses on Gregory's concern about the effects of greed on the world, he notes a related concern with the problem of unjust killings, both in the prominence of the Cain and Abel story from Genesis and Gregory's pervasive and pessimistic frustration with the 'banality of violence' that he so often narrates.[12] After summarising Creation, the first human event in the *Historiae* is the story of Cain, which provides a typology of murder that frames all subsequent killings.[13] Although Gregory mentions the expulsion of Adam and Eve from the Garden of Eden, he implies that the despicable sinfulness of humanity began in earnest only after Cain slew his brother.[14] This 'paradigmatic event' is central to the discussion of Gregory's conception of murder:[15]

> Cognitum autem satellitem, mulier concipit peperitque duos filios. Sed dum Deus unius sacrificium dignanter suscipit, alius invidia inflammante tumiscit, et in fraterni sanguinis effusionem novus parecida consurgens, fratrem opprimit, vincit, interimit.
>
> [Through intercourse with her companion the woman [Eve] conceived and bore two sons. But when God received the sacrifice of the one [Abel] with honor, the other [Cain] was inflamed with envy; he [Cain] rushed on his brother, overcame and killed him, becoming the first parricide by shedding a brother's blood]. (*Hist.* I.2)[16]

Gregory makes several subtle yet significant changes to the Genesis narrative. First, and most notably, although the chapter is entitled 'De Cain et Abel', Eve and her sons are nameless in the text, a shift that underscores the wide applicability of the lessons of the story. Gregory also summarises the story as a brief but powerful statement of *invidia* [jealousy] and resulting murder. He takes the single Bible verse: 'consurrexit Cain adversus Abel fratrem suum et interfecit

---

[11] Heinzelmann advocates considering the material in the early books, especially the refashioned stories from biblical and classical history in Book I, as typologies that prefigure events in the later books. See: Heinzelmann, *Gregory of Tours*, pp. 146–52. This approach has strongly influenced subsequent studies, including those about Merovingian warfare by Laury Sarti, *Perceiving War and the Military in Early Christian Gaul, ca. 400-700 A.D.* (Leiden: Brill, 2013).
[12] Heinzelmann, *Gregory of Tours*, pp. 58–9. Martin Heinzelmann has also argued persuasively that Gregory tends to make his strongest statements through his chapters toward the beginning, middle and end of each of his books.
[13] Ibid., pp. 58–59, 91.
[14] This notion is found elsewhere. See: Horace Jeffery Hodges' re-reading of the interpretation of Cain in *Beowulf* in 'Cain's Fratricide: Original Violence as "Original Sin" in *Beowulf*, *Medieval and Early Modern English Studies* 15.1 (2007): 31–56.
[15] The phrase is Goffart's in *Narrators of Barbarian History*, p. 165.
[16] This translation from Brehaut, *History of the Franks*, I.2.

eum' [And Cain rose up against his brother Abel and killed him] (Gen. 4.8), and adds that Cain became the *novus parecida* [the first parricide] to shed fraternal blood. Gregory's unusual spelling of *parecida* accentuates the novelty of Cain's killing yet still connects the evil deed with the other examples of *parricidae* and *homicidae* encountered subsequently in the *Historiae*.[17] Gregory's retelling of Cain's murder undergirds his concerns regarding illegitimate violence, and the event marks a sad turning point for humanity.[18] At the start of the next chapter, Gregory remarks, 'exhinc cunctum genus in facinus exsecrabile ruit' ['from that moment onwards, the entire human race never ceased to commit one execrable crime after another'] (*Hist.* I.3).[19]

While Heinzelmann interpreted Gregory's Cain and Abel story as foreshadowing an indictment of the greed at the heart of the cycles of internecine civil warfare between the Merovingian royal families, the lessons could also apply to other kinds of killing, including homicide.[20] As evidenced by a quote from Proverbs 26.27 that appears in the *Historiae* in four different contexts, Gregory repeatedly makes it clear that 'qui fodit foveam fratri' [he who digs a hole for his brother], as Cain once did, 'incidet in eam' [will himself fall in].[21] In these contexts, Gregory conflates murderers, conspirators and warring relatives as those who are 'digging holes'. Three of these individuals include Chloderic, a prince of the Ripuarian Franks who acted on his lust for power in coldly killing his father, Sigibert the king (*Hist.* II.40); Leudast, an aristocrat whose life 'had been one

---

[17] This could be a mirage created by the editors of the Latin text. The variation between *parecida*, which Bruno Krusch gives only in this case, and *parricida*, which Gregory uses elsewhere gives pause, and may evoke a discrepancy in classical Latin between the killing of *pares*, *patres* or even the *patria*. Krusch shows that while most manuscript witnesses of the *Historiae* give *parecida* in this passage, in Montecassino, Archivio dell'Abbazia MS cod. 275, the only 'complete' manuscript containing all ten books, as well as the ninth-century manuscript, Heidelberg, Universitats-Bibliothek MS cod. Pal. Lat. 864, the form is *parricida*. See: MGH, SS rer. Merov. 1,1, p. 35. Gregory uses *parricidium* elsewhere to describe Cain's killing, as in *Liber Vitae Patrum*, c. 11, when St Caluppa remarks to the devil 'qui germani dexteram parricidio cruentasti' [you who bloodied the right hand of a brother with parricide]. Jerome does not label Cain as a *parecida*/*parricida* in the Vulgate, but he does in his *Commentaries on Ezekiel*. See: Jerome, *Commentarii in Ezechielem*, 8.27.18, ed. F. Glorie (Turnhout: Brepols, 1964).

[18] See especially: Heinzelmann, *Gregory of Tours*, pp. 146–52.

[19] Goffart, *Narrators of Barbarian History*, p. 210.

[20] Ibid., p. 220. See also: Sarti, *Perceiving War and the Military*, p. 178, who remarks on the problem of distinguishing the scale of violence in Gregory's works. Gregory often uses the same term, *bellum*, to describe large-scale and small-scale violence. While Sarti focuses on Gregory's ideas about warfare, he sees a strong concern in the *Historiae* for preventing other acts of violence, including homicide (p. 90).

[21] The original quote from Prov. 26.27 reads 'Qui fodit foveam incidet in eam et qui volvit lapidem revertetur ad eum', but Gregory tends to add either *patri* or *fratri*. See also: Heinzelmann, *Gregory of Tours*, p. 92.

long tale of perfidious talk' (V.49); and Rauching, an aristocrat who began a conspiracy and rebelled against his king, Childebert II (IX.9). For Gregory, all of these men were later killed justly in recompense for their crimes: Chloderic by a random soldier, Leudast through torture, and Rauching by Childebert's men who slashed him and threw him out of a window.

The close relationship between unjustified warfare and unjustified killing is especially visible at the critical transition from Book IV to V, which is also the context for a fourth quote of Prov. 26.27 (*Hist.* IV.51).[22] As he concludes Book IV, Gregory expresses fatigue at relating so many civil wars culminating with the killing of Sigibert (son of Chlothar above; d. 575 CE), a sentiment he repeats almost verbatim in the prologue of Book V.[23] Gregory sees the warring brothers Sigibert and Chilperic, and Chilperic's son Theudebert, as fulfilling Cain's inheritance. Theudebert, who swore never to attack his uncle Sigibert, is nonetheless ordered to do so by his father. Caught between loyalties, he chooses to betray his uncle instead of his father; still, it is a betrayal nonetheless, and Theudebert dies an especially dishonourable death as his enemies despoil his corpse on the battlefield (IV.50).[24] Similarly, Gregory says that Sigibert, when he hears whispered promises of support from former enemies, could not help but march against Chilperic, despite the warnings of St Germanus. Acting to defend her husband Chilperic, Fredegund then sends assassins to kill Sigibert using poisoned weapons (IV.51). Chilperic, although he survives this engagement, later violently pays with his life as well, and Fredegund too gains a reputation as a murderer, partially because of this incident (VI.46).

In his Prologue to Book V, which Gregory addresses directly to the kings of the Franks, Gregory continues many of the same critiques of violence and killing and looks back to Clovis' reign as a golden age of peace and unity. Having just narrated the devastating cycle of killings between the sons of Chlothar in the previous book, Gregory warns the reader in the Prologue of the next about the deleterious effects of civil wars between the heirs of Clovis. The numbers of killings that Gregory discusses up to this point are connected to the general sense of *discordia* [discord] that he says destroys territories, cities and individual lives

---

[22] Unlike any other book in the *Historiae*, Gregory gives a preface to Book V that specifically addresses all of the violence that came before.

[23] 'It causes me great grief to have to describe these civil wars' (IV.51). Then Gregory echoes himself to begin the next book: 'It gives me no pleasure to write of all the different civil wars which afflicted the Frankish people and their rulers' (V, Prologue).

[24] See also Title LV of the *Pactus Legis Salicae* for concerns about despoiling dead bodies. And see: Katherine Fischer Drew, *The Laws of the Salian Franks* (Philadelphia: University of Pennsylvania Press, 1991), pp. 118–19.

(V, Prologue).[25] As he points out, Gregory has assembled a body of evidence in his *Historiae* that demonstrates that the time spoken of in Matt. 10.21 has drawn near when 'consurgit pater in filium, filius in patrem, frater in fratrem, proximus in propinquum' [The father shall rise up against the son, and the son against the father; brother shall rise up against brother, and kinsman against kinsman] (V, Prologue).[26] Through his linking of biblical examples with parallels in contemporary history, Gregory urges his audience to reflect on their proclivities toward violence, whether on a large scale or a small one and whether between families or within them.

Although many, if not all, of the killings in the *Historiae* have a strong connection to the sin of Cain, those passages featuring individuals that Gregory styles as *parricidae*, like Cain himself, warrant a deeper look. As a legal concept, *parricidium* had a long, if complicated, history in Roman jurisprudence. Ancient Roman jurists distinguished *parricidium* from ordinary homicide as one of the worst crimes imaginable and, correspondingly, gave it one of the worst punishments.[27] While historians continue to debate the Romans' definition of the crime and the forms of punishment it entailed, there are a few points of agreement.[28] The *Digest* of Justinian (c. 530–33 CE), citing the *Institutes* of the third-century jurist Aelius Marcianus, defines a *parricida* as a killer of any one of a long list of specified close family relations.[29] The famous punishment prescribed by the *Lex Pompeia* (55 BCE) involved beating the killer with blood-coloured sticks, then sewing him/her into a sack 'with a dog, a dunghill cock, a viper and a monkey' before finally

---

[25] Heinzelmann, *Gregory of Tours*, pp. 49–50. Heinzelmann sees *discordia*, tied with the atrocities of Chilperic, as one of the *Historiae*'s main themes, but again, subordinated to what he says is Gregory's principal theme of greed.

[26] The verse from Matt. 10.21 which transmits a similar meaning is: 'tradet autem frater fratrem in mortem et pater filium et insurgent filii in parentes et morte eos adficient'.

[27] In addition to the *Theodosian Code* and the *Corpus Iuris Civilis*, the Visigothic Code also contains a section on parricides under Title V. See: S. P. Scott, ed. and trans., *The Visigothic Code* (Boston: Boston Book Company, 1910), pp. 228–30.

[28] For debates about *parricidium* in the Roman legal tradition, see: M. Radin, 'The Lex Pompeia and the Poena Cullei', *Journal of Roman Studies* 10 (1920): 119–30; and J. D. Cloud, 'Parricidium, from the Lex Numiae to the Lex Pompeia de Parricidiis', *Zeitschrift der Savigny-Stiftung für Rechtsgeschichte Romantistiche Abteilung* 88 (1971): 1–66.

[29] The *Lex Pompeia* on parricides states: 'anyone who kills his father, mother, grandfather, grandmother, brother, sister, first cousin on the father's side, first cousin on the mother's side, paternal or maternal uncle, paternal [or maternal] aunt, first cousin (male or female) by mother's sister, wife, husband, father-in-law, son-in-law, mother-in-law, [daughter in law], stepfather, stepson, stepdaughter, patron or patroness, or with malicious intent brings this out, shall be liable to the same penalty as that of the *lex Cornelia* on murderers'. See: *Digest of Justinian*, Book 48, Title 9, in *Vengeance in Medieval Europe: A Reader*, ed. Daniel Lord Smail and Kelly Gibson (Toronto: University of Toronto Press, 2009), p. 47.

throwing the offender into the sea.³⁰ An edict of Constantine dated to 318 and preserved in the *Theodosian Code* (c. 438–9 CE) defines parricide as 'hastening the fate of a parent, or a son, or any person at all of such degree of kinship that killing him is included under the title of parricide', and similarly specifies that the offender should be sewn into a leather sack with snakes and then thrown into the sea or river.³¹

Gregory was likely familiar with these Roman legal ideas about *parricidium* through his source materials including Sallust's *De coniuratione Catilinae* and Orosius' *Historiae adversum Paganos* (c. 416–417 CE), which both contain the term.³² Although Sallust gives *parricidium* a rather different meaning, Orosius, like Gregory, strictly uses *parricidium* to indicate a killing of close family members and draws a very sharp distinction between *parricidae* and other types of murders.³³ Orosius reserves the term for the worst offenders in his history including Oedipus, Romulus, Philip of Macedon, Lysimachus, Publicius Malleolus and Nero; he also mentions the punishment of the sack.³⁴ In his *Liber de miraculis beatae Andreae apostoli*, Gregory mentions a version of the punishment when a Roman procurator orders a Christian boy named Sostratus to be sewn into

---

³⁰ *Digest of Justinian*, Pompeian Law on Parricides, Book 48, Title 9, in Smail and Gibson, *Vengeance*, p. 48. Radin, 'Lex Pompeia', p. 130, notes that this detailed (and frankly, bizarre) punishment involving snakes, dogs, roosters and apes is less about deterrence and more about ritual expiation for the community after a heinous crime that threatens the fabric of society itself.

³¹ *Theodosian Code*, Parricides, Book 9, Title 15, in Smail and Gibson, *Vengeance*, p. 37.

³² Gregory refers to Roman law and the Theodosian Code, in particular. He cites the Theodosian Code once (*Hist*. IV.46), but Wood has argued that this reference does not actually reflect the contents. Ian Wood, 'The Code in Merovingian Gaul', in *The Theodosian Code: Studies in the Imperial Law of Late Antiquity*, ed. Jill Harries and Ian Wood (Bristol: Bristol Classical Press, 2010), pp. 161–77.

³³ Gregory cites Sallust's *De coniuratione Catilinae* twice (*Hist* IV.13; VII.1). Sallust uses *parricida/parricidium* often as a general term for 'a murderer'; he also reserves the term specifically for Catiline or his co-conspirators as traitors to the *patria* [fatherland]. Orosius, another source of Gregory's, uses *parricida/parricidium* frequently to highlight the depravity of the Roman empire under paganism, and draws a sharp distinction between parricide and other types of killing. See: Orosius, *Historiarum adversum Paganos*, ed. Karl Friedrich Wilhelm Zangemeister (New York: Johnson, 1966) and the English translation by A. T. Fear in Orosius, *Seven Books of History against the Pagans* (Liverpool: Liverpool University Press, 2010).

³⁴ See especially the examples of classical parricides including Oedipus at Book I.12.7–10; II.4 (Romulus); III.12 (Philip); III.23 (Lysimachus); V.10 (Ptolemy); and V.16.23 (Publicius Malleolus), as well as the discussion of Nero at VII.7.1–13, in Orosius, *Historiarum adversum Paganos*. The passage on Publicius Malleolus killing his mother also details the punishment of the *culleum parricidii* [sack for a parricide].

the *culleum parricidae* [sack for a parricide] and thrown into a river.³⁵ In the *Historiae*, Gregory identifies two people as *parricidae*: the Burgundian king Sigismund, for killing his son (*Hist.* III.5), and the Gothic princess Amalasuntha, for killing her mother (III.31).³⁶ He also identifies two others as suspected *parricidae*: Gregory's own brother Peter, who was under suspicion for killing his uncle Silvester, a bishop (*Hist.* V.5), and Count Eulalius of Clermont, who was believed to be responsible for killing his mother (X.8). These passages show the destructive power that even the suspicion of *parricidium* can have on one's life and reputation, and with them, Gregory endeavors to present a series of lessons for his audience.

Gregory couches his two royal *parricidae* at the beginning and end of the same book (Book III) amid narratives of conflicts within ruling families; ultimately, both stories emphasise the futility of human endeavour in the face of impending divine punishment. In the first, a veiled statement on the costs of political ambition, Gregory names Sigismund, king of the Burgundians (r. 516–24 CE), a *parricida* for ordering his son to be killed (*Hist.* III.5).³⁷ Gregory devotes the whole of this particular chapter to the explication of Sigismund's crime.³⁸ Sigismund's unnamed second wife, an *uxoris iniquae* [wicked wife] full of *consilium nequam* [evil advice], tells Sigismund that Sigeric, his son from a previous marriage to a daughter of Theodoric the Great, is conspiring to seize the throne and kill him. Gregory says that the king, easily swayed by the *verbis dolosis* [the deceitful words] of his wife, became the *iniquus parricida* [evil parricide] of the young Sigeric.³⁹ Sigismund does not commit the act himself; rather, he supplies

---

³⁵ Gregory uses the same phrase as Orosius. Gregory, *Liber de miraculis beatae Andreae apostoli*, c. 4. Fortunately for Sostratus, a timely earthquake and St Andrew's miraculous intervention save him. MGH SS rer. Merov. 1, 2:829.

³⁶ Both of these royal parricides are quite closely connected to the figure of Theodoric the Great, king of the Ostrogoths. Sigismund was the son-in-law of Theodoric, having married the Gothic king's daughter Ariagna as his first wife. Amalasuntha was Ariagna's sister.

³⁷ Wood sees this episode, which ends with Sigismund's execution at the hands of Chlothild's sons, as lending legitimacy to the Merovingian takeover of Burgundy. Ian Wood, 'Gregory of Tours and Clovis', *Revue Belge de philologie et d'histoire* 63.2 (1985): 249–72 at p. 253.

³⁸ The chapter is entitled 'How Sigismund Killed His Own Son', and is surrounded by similar violent narratives of a conflict between brothers of the Thuringian royal house (*Hist.* III.4), Sigismund's own death at the hands of Clovis' sons (*Hist.* III.6) and the Franks' bloody revenge against the Thuringians (*Hist.* III.7). This is all found in the particularly violent Book III, which follows the story of the Frankish kingdom after the death of Clovis.

³⁹ Gudmund Schuette has pointed out the connection between Gregory's Sigismund story and that of Sigmund and Sinfjötli in Ch. 10 of the *Völsungasaga* in *Sigfrid und Brünhild* (Copenhagen: Jena, 1935). While noting the obvious connections between Sigismund

alcohol to his son and then sends his men to strangle the boy in his sleep. Unlike Gregory's other *parricidae*, Sigismund alone immediately realises his crime and weeps bitter tears.[40] As he often does in especially violent passages, Gregory repeats the essential elements of the story, here through the device of a *senex* [old man] who harshly admonishes Sigismund.[41] The *senex*'s repetition of the details of the murder amplifies the sense of the injustice in the crime: the old man also says the king should save his tears for himself and further describes Sigismund as *parricida saevissimus* [savage parricide], in effect repeating the charge (*Hist.* III.5). The *senex* comments that Sigismund regrets his deeds far too late. The Burgundian king remains a complicated figure; unlike Childebert and Chlothar, Sigismund immediately repents of his deeds and spends his last moments praying at a monastery he had founded. Still, Sigismund's crimes were far too serious and he had to face *ultione divina* [divine punishment]. Sigismund the *parricida* becomes a victim himself in the following chapter as Chlothild's avenging sons kill him, along with his wife and family (*Hist.* III.6).[42] By sacrificing his own son to solidify his hold on power, Gregory says that Sigismund lost his family, his kingdom and his life.

and Sigmund, not least including their shared name, a jealous wife and a poisoned son, George K. Anderson, however, sees a more accurate parallel to the story of King Guntram's wife Marcatrude (*Hist.* IV.25). This story, also involving a stepmother poisoning her stepson, is much briefer than Sigismund's. See: Anderson, trans., *The Saga of the Völsungs: Together with Excerpts from the* Nornagestsháttr *and Three Chapters from the Prose Edda* (Newark: University of Delaware Press, 1982), p. 31; for the passage on Sigmund and Sinfjötli, see pp. 72–73 and Jesse L. Byock, trans., *The Saga of the Volsungs: The Norse Epic of Sigurd the Dragon Slayer* (New York: Penguin, 1990), pp. 50–51. See also: Magnus Rindal, 'Les Burgondes dans la tradition scandinave médiévale', in *Clovis Histoire et Mémoire: Le baptême de Clovis, son echo à travers l'histoire*, ed. Michel Rouche (Paris: Presses de l'Université de Paris-Sorbonne, 1997), 2:453–60.

[40] These details may be related to the fact that Sigismund was also regarded as a rather pious king and martyr.

[41] This trend appears throughout the *Historiae*, especially in narratives of violent deeds. In many episodes, Gregory introduces an interlocutor to either reinforce or contextualise a point he has already made. Archambault argues that this is a classical rhetorical technique and is evidence of a much more meaningful education in the classical tradition for Gregory than has been acknowledged. See: Paul. J. Archambault, 'Gregory of Tours and the Classical Tradition', in *The Classics in the Middle Ages: Papers of the Twentieth Annual Conference of the Center for Medieval and Early Renaissance Studies*, ed. Aldo S. Bernardo and Saul Levin (Binghamton, NY: Center for Medieval and Early Renaissance Studies, 1990), pp. 25–34.

[42] Continuing the lesson in the following chapter, Gregory says that Chlodomer, one of Chlothild's sons, ignored the advice of St Avitus, who warned the young king not to attack Sigismund and his family. When Chlodomer ordered them all killed, divine punishment came for him too, and he ended the chapter dead (*Hist.* III.7).

In the second royal example, Gregory names the Ostrogothic princess Amalasuntha a *parricida* for killing her mother Audofleda (*Hist.* III.31). Amalasuntha's parricide also takes up the entire chapter, but unlike the orthodox Sigismund, Amalsasuntha and Audofleda are both Arians, a fact that at times overshadows the narrative of the killing itself.[43] Gregory's contextual details depict Amalasuntha as disobedient and senseless. He says that Amalasuntha loathes her mother's plans for her to marry a prince and, instead, falls in love with Traguilla, a slave. Audofleda, outraged at this behaviour, sends a band of armed men after her daughter; they kill Traguilla, beat Amalasuntha and bring her back home. Amalasuntha, ostensibly in response to this attack, then poisons her mother during an Arian communion service.[44] Gregory explains the princess's deeds as 'de parte diabuli' [the work of the devil], which implies that her reprisal against her mother was inappropriate and driven more by hatred than a sense of justice (III.32). As with Sigismund, Amalasuntha immediately faced the consequences of her actions, another marker that what she did was unjust. When Amalasuntha's cousin, Theudahad of Tuscany, hears of her evil deeds, he calls her a parricide (*parricidam*) for the sake of a slave and orders that she be locked in a hot bath with a nameless servant and killed (III.31). Theudahad is not declared a *parricida* when he has her killed; instead, Gregory sees Theudahad's killings as divine retribution upon Amalasuntha, an utterly unworthy criminal.[45]

Stark contrasts of purpose distinguish the other two cases of alleged *parricidae*, each found at the beginning and end of the 'contemporary' history section of the *Historiae*; both of these accounts are similar, however, in the important role they assign bishops, whether in formulating an accusation against the *parricida* or establishing the parameters for rehabilitating those accused. In the case of Gregory's brother Peter, a deacon of Langres, Gregory methodically works to disprove the accusation that his slain brother had become a *parricida* in killing his uncle Silvester, the bishop of the city (*Hist.* V.5).[46] When Silvester died a few

---

[43] This chapter is simply titled 'The Daughter of Theodoric, King of Italy'. Amalasuntha is not named, and Theodoric himself seems to loom largest. As with Sigismund's chapter, this passage is also found in the bloody Book III, but here towards the end. The surrounding chapters are also filled with further internecine conflicts between Clovis' sons and a series of chapters focused on stories of the Goths in Spain and Italy, including a long cycle of regicides (*Hist.* III.30) and Theudebert's invasion of Italy (*Hist.* III.32).

[44] Gregory points out that, since both Audofleda and Amalasuntha were Arians, they had separate wine chalices during communion.

[45] Still, Gregory shows that nobody who is associated with the deeds profits. He says that Theudahad had to pay fifty thousand gold pieces as compensation under threat from Amalasuntha's Frankish cousins Childebert, Chlothar and Theudebert. They called the death 'shameful' (*Hist.* III.31).

[46] The chapter is titled 'The Bishops of Langres', but it mostly relates the story of Peter. The chapter is near the beginning of Book V in a series of chapters that tell the story of

days after becoming bishop, Silvester's son *publice* [publicly] called Peter a *parricida*, accusing him of killing Silvester through *maleficiis* [sorcery].[47] Silvester's son then killed Peter in the street with a spear. The suspicion, apparently widely held, was that Peter was *cupidus episcopati* [covetous of the episcopate] and so deserved to be killed, but Gregory uses five strategies to show that Peter did not commit this crime.[48] First, Gregory emphasises a pre-existing rivalry between Peter and another deacon of the city named Lampadius. Gregory says that Lampadius was greedy and stole from the poor, and when Peter revealed this, he earned Lampadius' *odium* [hatred]. Lampadius thus became an implacable foe of Peter and an evil goad in Silvester's son's ear. Second, Gregory provides an alternative explanation for Silvester's mysterious death, identifying him as an *epilenticus* [epileptic], a condition he suffered for a long time, thus deftly removing the possibility of sorcery as a cause of death. Third, Gregory shows Silvester's son as a hotheaded, yet easily manipulated, youth who readily acts on any suggestion of Lampadius and quickly turns to violence against Peter. After killing Peter, Gregory says that Silvester's son fled to Chilperic while, consequently, Guntram confiscated his property, and that, ultimately, this *miser* [wretched soul] turned into a wanderer and was eventually killed himself when he started a needless quarrel with strangers, all further signs of impropriety. Fourth, Gregory repeatedly insists on Peter's innocence, even paraphrasing Gen. 4.10: 'contra eum sanguine insonte ad divinam potentiam proclamante' [his innocent blood cried out against him to divine power]. Fifth, and perhaps most importantly, Gregory details the extraordinary lengths to which Peter went to establish his innocence. Upon being accused, Peter had undertaken a trip to Lyon to swear an oath before Bishop Nicetius and many other witnesses that he had no role in Silvester's death.[49]

In the second example of an allegation, and very much the inverse of the passage about Peter, Gregory strongly implicates Count Eulalius of Clermont as a *parricida* to raise suspicions about his character (*Hist.* X.8). Eulalius is caught

evil men who get their comeuppance. As one of only three passages wherein Gregory directly discusses his family, this chapter is widely cited by historians. See commentary on this passage regarding Gregory's family and ecclesiastical politics in Raymond Van Dam, *Saints and Their Miracles in Late Antique Gaul* (Princeton: Princeton University Press, 1993), p. 56.

[47] Heinzelmann sees Silvester's branch of the family as the Burgundian line of Gregory's relatives through his mother's side. See: *Gregory of Tours*, p. 15.

[48] Gregory introduces this story through reference to a scurrilous letter from his rival, Felix, bishop of Nantes. Felix had alleged that Peter sought to become bishop of Langres (*Hist.* V.5).

[49] This is another relation: Gregory says that Nicetius is his mother's uncle, but his relation to Silvester is not entirely clear. See Heinzelmann's prosopographical table of Gregory's family, in *Gregory of Tours*, p. 10.

in a complicated and seemingly interminable marital dispute with his estranged wife Tetradia before a specially convened council of bishops (*Hist.* X.8).⁵⁰ In the midst of describing Tetradia's theft of Eulalius' property after she went to live with another man, Gregory pauses to give a few background details about Eulalius and none of them are any good. He says that, when he was a reprobate youth, his mother often scolded him, and so Eulalius engendered a deep *odium* [hatred] for her 'quam amare debuerat' [whom he should have loved]. Gregory then says that Eulalius' mother, a holy, orthodox woman, was one day found strangled in her hairshirt, killed while praying in her oratory. Suspicion of the *crimen paricidii* [offence of parricide] fell immediately upon Eulalius, and Gregory makes no attempt to counter it. Indeed, he says the suspicion alone brought about Eulalius' excommunication. As he does with Sigismund's *senex*, Gregory uses an interlocutor to repeat the charge in direct dialogue with the alleged offender; here, Bishop Cautinus says to Eulalius, as the latter begs to receive communion: 'Rumor populi parricidam te proclamant esse' ['Popular rumor has proclaimed you to be a parricide']. Cautinus, no stranger to *mala fama* himself for having once buried an innocent man alive (*Hist.* IV.12), concedes that he has no idea whether Eulalius committed the deed or not, so he places a consecrated host in the alleged parricide's mouth and leaves it to 'beati martiris Iuliani statuo iudicium' [the judgment of the blessed martyr Julian]. Eulalius survives the divine test, is readmitted to communion and, in fact, eventually wins his lawsuit against Tetradia, but surprisingly, Gregory does not portray the count of Clermont as innocent. Rather than turn to a devout life after receiving his second chance, Gregory reports that Eulalius did not change, adding further killings and evil deeds to his already sordid resumé.⁵¹

Considered alongside one another, the four cases of *parricidae* reveal a consistent set of norms against the killing of family members. In all cases where variations of the term *parricida* are employed, Gregory gives a rich narrative of the context and event, allowing opportunities for additional interpretation

---

⁵⁰ The chapter entitled 'Eulalius and His Wife Tetradia' deals entirely with the couple's marital discord. This passage is important for its depiction of canonical and uncanonical marriages, roles of women and the functioning of episcopal courts. See: James, '*Beati pacifici*', p. 30; Lisa M. Bitel, *Women in Early Medieval Europe, 400–1100* (Cambridge: Cambridge University Press, 2002), pp. 86–87.

⁵¹ As the sole survivor of the four individuals named *parricidae*, the case of Eulalius is a significant aberration. The lesson is not so obviously about the parricide itself since Eulalius does not face divine punishment as Sigismund and Amalasuntha do. Instead, this narrative makes a larger point about Tetradia's theft and her eventual restitution of Eulalius' property following the bishops' decision in the case. Context supports this, as the chapter is the last in a short series about the restitution of stolen goods, including Chuppa's raid and forced restitution (*Hist.* X.5); the miraculous release of prisoners at Clermont (X.6); and Childebert II's remission of taxes for the clergy (X.7).

and reflection. Sigismund's deed is declared *iniquus* [evil]. Amalasuntha's is the work of the devil. Even if the accusation is false or rumoured, as with Gregory's brother Peter or Count Eulalius, *parricidium* is an audacious, serious crime that demands justice. Gregory's motives ascribed to the *parricidae* are unjustifiable and destructive: as *invidia* [jealousy] had once motivated Cain, Sigismund's *uxor iniqua* [evil wife] and his own lust for power drives the Burgundian king, and Gregory insinuates that hatred inspires Amalasuntha. Eulalius' *odium* [hatred] of his mother also makes him a principal suspect in her killing.[52] These destructive feelings and influences take the place of the love and loyalty that should have been between family members. Finally, Gregory demonstrates the evil of these deeds most powerfully by detailing what happens to the *parricidae* afterwards. Three take extraordinary steps immediately: Sigismund weeps, repents and goes to a monastery to pray for forgiveness; Peter travels a great distance and swears an oath before a synod of bishops that he did not commit a murder; and Eulalius is excommunicated but submits to the judgment of God by taking a consecrated host into his mouth to reveal his innocence. Still, divine vengeance follows closely for both Sigismund and Amalasuntha, who are both killed soon after the murders attributed to them took place. Gregory holds that Peter, who was also subsequently killed, was killed unjustly, but in highlighting the weight of Silvester's son's charge of *parricida*, Gregory amplifies the difficult situation that his brother faced.

These cases show that Gregory's usage of *parricida* is consistent and reserved for individuals who have committed shame-worthy killings or else used to highlight the severity of an accusation (for Gregory's brother, Peter). Beyond the examples of *parricidae*, fifteen other passages describe killers of siblings, parents, children, nieces/nephews and aunts/uncles, the differences further delineating Gregory's meaning. While four of these cases (*Hist*. II.40; III.4; III.18; V.39) are similar in presentation to the four named *parricidae* – each with rich narrative explanations of the improper contexts of the killing, the unjustified motivations of the killers and their deserved fates – in eleven others, Gregory is either neutral or even supportive in his descriptions of the killers, reflecting the influence of divergent norms of vengeance and family honour that also inform the interpretation of family killings. In four of these cases, although the killings are clearly identified as family affairs, Gregory does not comment much at all, suggesting that he

[52] Barbara Rosenwein, 'Writing Without Fear about Early Medieval Emotions', *Early Medieval Europe* 10.2 (2001): 229–34; Rosenwein, 'Even the Devil (Sometimes) has Feelings: Emotional Communities in the Early Middle Ages', *The Haskins Society Journal* 14 (2003): 1–14; Rosenwein, 'Writing and Emotions in Gregory of Tours', in *Vom Nutzen des Schreibens: Soziales Gedächtnis, Herrschaft und Besitz im Mittelalter*, ed. Walter Pohl and Paul Herold (Vienna: Verlag der Österreichischen Akademie der Wissenschaften, 2002), pp. 23–32.

may see them as justified and, consequently, not deserving of divine punishment (*Hist.* II.28; III.7; III.23; IV.4).⁵³ Two cases are killings of daughters motivated by actual or feared sexual indiscretions (*Hist.* III.26; VI.36).⁵⁴ Finally, in five of the cases, Gregory explains the family killing as vengeance for previous acts of treachery (*Hist.* I.36; II.33; IV.20; IV.50; IV.51). In these five vengeance cases, Gregory is either neutral in tone or openly supportive of the avenging killer. As evidenced by these latter cases that contravene norms proscribing parricides, in instances where an unprincipled family member engages in treachery, adultery or kills someone else in the family, Gregory demonstrates a counter-norm that allows, or even demands, the taking of that life.

Within this small sample size, Gregory's references to *parricida* and *parricidium* in contexts of family killings are fairly consistent; however, his use of the other legal terms, *homicidae* [for killers] and *homicidia* [for their deeds], is both more frequent and more ambiguous. Of the thirteen individuals named *homicidae* and the twenty-two references to *homicidia*, all but one are found in the 'contemporary' history of Books VI–X. This fact, coupled with the contexts of the references themselves, suggests that while Gregory sees *homicidae* and *homicidia* as a sign of humankind's continuing depravity, they also present a special challenge to kings and bishops to render just punishment or to rehabilitate the perpetrators equitably. Gregory's use evokes the language of other sixth-century Merovingian sources, including the canons of Gallic ecclesiastical councils and royal capitularies that similarly reference *homicidium* as a serious social problem.⁵⁵ Like Gregory, the canons do not provide definitions, but they

---

⁵³ Daniel Baraz argues that the level of narrative detail may be a barometer of an author's feelings on violence in *Medieval Cruelty: Changing Perceptions, Late Antiquity to the Early Modern Period* (Ithaca: Cornell University Press, 2003), pp. 49–50. These very terse examples include the killing of King Thorismund by his brothers (*Hist.* II.7); King Gundobad's killing of his brother and his wife (II.28); Theuderic's killing of his relative Sigivald (III.23); and Count Chanao's killings of his brothers (IV.4).

⁵⁴ Under some of the fuller definitions of *parricidia*, such as that in the *Lex Pompeia*, cases of killing spouses and in-laws would also count, which would add two more cases to the total of women killed for sexual indiscretions. There are six cases of killing spouses: Parthenius kills his wife and her lover (III.36); Chilperic kills Galswinth (IV.28); a husband kills his wife and Abbot Dagulf (VIII.19); Magnovald kills his wife (VIII.36); Chilperic and Fredegund kill Audovera (V.39); Alboin's wife kills her husband (IV.41); and a wife has her husband Ambrosius and his brother Lupus killed (VI.13). There are also four cases of killings of in-laws: Chlothar kills the brother of his wife Radegund (III.7); Marcatrude kills her stepson (IV.25); Andarchius kills Ursus (IV.46); and the family of a dishonoured woman fights the family of her husband (X.27). All of these cases could also be considered *parricidia* under Roman and Visigothic law, but Gregory does not use either *parricida* or *parricidia* for any of these.

⁵⁵ Jean Heuclin, 'Le concile d'Orléans de 511, un premier concordat?', *Clovis*, pp. 435–50; Brigitte Basdevant-Gaudemet, 'L'évêque, d'après la législation de quelques conciles mérovingiens', *Clovis*, pp. 471–94.

nevertheless consistently label *homicidium* as one of the capital crimes and speak of excommunication and conditions of penance for those who commit it.[56] The Fourth Council of Orleans (541 CE) identifies a *homicida* as an individual who wilfully 'occidere audeat innocentem' [dares to kill the innocent].[57] This canon and an earlier one from the Council of Epaone (517 CE) also detail a role for bishops to determine penance for *homicidae*, even for those who may have settled with secular authorities or have otherwise avoided secular punishment.[58] Finally, and perhaps most dramatically, the *Decretio* of Childebert II (dated to 595 CE and issued shortly after Gregory's death) establishes the death penalty for cases of *homicidium*, specifically those committed *sine causa* [without a reason], and, in a reversal of the norms evidenced elsewhere in Salic law, eliminates the possibility of compensation from such cases.[59] Gregory goes much further than the prescriptive texts: in addition to demonstrating the disruptions caused by *homicidae* themselves, he also subtly promotes the respective royal and episcopal roles that are necessary to resolve such situations.

Gregory employs language most similar to the canons when he includes *homicidium* as part of a formula of standard offences that are ascribed to evil people or raiding armies. These formulae echo biblical models, such as those

---

[56] In the Conc. Matisconense (581/3 CE): Canon VII specifies 'criminal charges' as those of homicide, theft and sorcery. *Concilia Galliae*, ed. Charles de Clercq (Turnhout: Brepols, 1963), p. 224.

[57] Canon XXVIII, Conc. Aurelianense, (541 CE), *Concilia Galliae*, p. 139. See: Catherine R. Peyroux, 'Canonists Construct the Nun? Church Law and Women's Monastic Practice in Merovingian France', in *Law, Society and Authority in Late Antiquity*, ed. Ralph W. Mathisen (Oxford: Oxford University Press, 2001), pp. 242–55, for discussion of the contexts of these councils. For the close relationship between synods and secular legislating, see: Wood, *Merovingian Kingdoms*, pp. 104–08. For the manuscript transmission of the canons, see: Rosamund McKitterick, 'Knowledge of Canon Law in the Frankish Kingdoms before 789: The Manuscript Evidence', *Journal of Theological Studies* 36.1 (1985): 97–117.

[58] Conc. Aurelianense, *Concilia Galliae*, p. 139. Canon XXXI of the Conc. Epaonense also cites the earlier Canon XXIII from the Council of Ancyra (314 CE), which says that wilful murderers must remain apart from the Church though they may, at the end of life, receive communion. See: Conc. Epaonense, *Concilia Galliae*, p. 32.

[59] *Childeberti secundi decretio*, MGH Leges, Capitularia regum Francorum 1 (Hannover: Hahnsche, 1883), p. 15. 'De homicidiis vero ita iussimus observare, ut quicumque ausu remerario alium sine causa occiderit vitae periculum feriatur: nam non de precio redemptionis se redimat aut componat. Forsitan convenit ut ad solutionem quisque discendat, nullus de parentibus aut amicis ei quicquam adiuvet; nisi qui praesumpserit ei aliquid adiuvare, suum weregildum omnino componat; quia iustum est, ut qui novit occidere, discat morire.' See also: Drew, *The Laws of the Salian Franks*, p. 158. Wood, *The Merovingian Kingdoms*, pp. 103–04, 107–08, 110, 116 discusses both Childebert II and the formulation of Merovingian legislation.

found in Matt. 15.19 and Mark 7.21–23.[60] The scriptural passages name *homicidia* as one example of a long list of capital crimes, which include *furta* [thefts] as well.[61] In the *Historiae* Gregory gives the example of Abbot Dagulf, justly killed (according to Gregory) by the husband of a woman with whom he was having an affair, who previously committed 'furta et homicidia plerumque ... sed et in adulteriis nimium' [a great number of robberies and murders and ... adultery] (*Hist.* VIII.19).[62] *Homicidia* also appear in Gregory's lists of the evil deeds of people and groups, nearly all identified as members of the aristocracy, such as the villainous bishops, Salonius and Sagittarius, who armed themselves like laymen and killed members of their own congregation (V.20, 27); Chlothild (the daughter of King Guntram), whose band of thugs killed clerics and their servants inside churches (IX.40, X.15, X.16); and the unnamed sons of Waddo, a deceased landowner, who lived a dissolute life of killing and theft (X.21). Gregory also uses *homicidia* for the killings of innocent people by various armies on campaign, including the troops of Sigivald (III.16); the men of Desiderius and Bladast around Tours (VI.31); Guntram's army in Poitiers, then in Spain (VII.24, VIII.30); Duke Nicetius' army (VIII.30); Childebert II's troops in Italy (X.3); and the army of Dukes Beppolen and Ebrachar in Brittany (X.9). Even though the term is imprecise in all of these contexts, Gregory's use is clearly negative, and it is a sin especially inherent in the wealthy.[63]

In some situations, Gregory hints at what he means by these formulaic references to *homicidia* because he provides details about that individual's killings

---

[60] Both passages allude to evil that comes from the hearts of men, and Mark 7.21–23 details how such evil thoughts 'defile' men: 'Dicebat autem quoniam quae de homine exeunt illa communicant hominem ab intus enim de corde hominum cogitationes malae procedunt adulteria fornicationes homicidia furta avaritiae nequitiae dolus inpudicitia oculus malus blasphemia superbia stultitia omnia haec mala ab intus procedunt et communicant hominem'.

[61] Heinzelmann has highlighted the role of greed as one of the principal failings of humanity in Gregory's narratives. The close connection between *furta* and *homicidia* in these contexts speaks to the perception that greed leads to a multitude of evil acts. For the relationships between theft and homicide legislation in an Anglo-Saxon context, see: T. B. Lambert, 'Theft, Homicide and Crime in Late Anglo-Saxon Law', *Past and Present* 214 (February 2012): 3–43.

[62] Almost identical listings of 'capital crimes' also occur in the Gallic canons and the work of Salvian of Marseilles. See: *Conc. Aurelianense* (511 CE), 'de homicidis, adulteris et furibus' and again *Conc. Matisconense* (581–583 CE), with 'causa criminale, id est homicidio, furto et maleficio'. Compare this with the fifth-century Gallic writer Salvian's list in *De gubernatione Dei*, IV.9 and VI.3, trans. Eva M. Sanford (New York: Columbia University Press, 1930), pp. 113–16, 162–63.

[63] Gregory's examples reflect the reasoning of Salvian, who advanced the notion that wealthy men, above all others, are susceptible of committing *homicidium*. Salvian, *De gubernatione Dei*, III.10 and IV.5, pp. 94–96, 106–08.

elsewhere. This is the case with Gregory's treatment of the *homicidia* of an aristocrat named Avius. Avius, also known as Vedast, who Gregory calls *miserrimus* [most wretched], committed 'multa furta, adulteria, homicidiaque' [many thefts, adulteries and homicides] (*Hist.* VII.3). In an earlier passage, however, Gregory explains that Avius had become involved with a married woman and schemed with her to kill her husband, a man named Ambrosius (*Hist.* VI.13). At night, with Ambrosius and his brother Lupus asleep after excessive drinking, Avius snuck in and decapitated both men. In the morning, Gregory says the servants expressed horror at the double murder, but no one did anything about it.[64] Afterwards, Avius perpetrated *multa scelera* [many crimes] around Poitiers before encountering a fearsome fellow named *Childericus Saxo* [Childeric the Saxon]. In this instance, Childeric the Saxon and his men serve as the instrument of God's judgment and kill Avius after an exchange of verbal insults.[65] So, while Gregory supplies the formula of wrongful deeds as a way to critique the lifestyle of Avius and others like him, he also provides details of at least two of his 'multa homicidia'.

Gregory also uses *homicidium* as a specific label for acts of killings that have been publicly denounced in some way.[66] The clearest examples come from a story about a Frankish embassy to the Byzantines in the city of Carthage (*Hist.* X.2, 4). In two separate instances in this one episode, a killing is declared to be a *homicidium* by secular authorities. In the first, Gregory says that a *senior urbis* [city leader] of Carthage declared a killing by one of the Frankish envoy's servants of a merchant to be a *homicidium* and gathered a crowd of armed men to find out how it was committed (*Hist.* X.2). When these matters were reported to the Byzantine authorities of the city, Gregory points out that the Frankish servant had been accused of theft, which could possibly give him a motive to kill to redress the insult, but Gregory also states that the man acted impulsively and foolishly. Making matters worse, the Byzantine 'senior urbis' and his crowd then killed two of the Frankish envoys after falsely promising them safety if they emerged from a building without weapons. In the second reference, Gregory

[64] While Gregory clearly thinks that Avius is a dangerous man, his opinion of Ambrosius is not much better, which may be why he emphasises how little people cared about his violent death. Ambrosius seems to be a bad influence; he was greedy, opposed to his brother Lupus joining the church and he encouraged his brother to become intoxicated the night they died (*Hist.* VI.13).
[65] Later, and in similar terms, when Childeric meets his own end after too much drinking, Gregory condemns his 'diversa scelera, homicidia, seditiones multaque alia inproba' [diverse crimes, including homicides, rebellions and much other wickedness] (*Hist.* X.22).
[66] On the public declaration of murder in Iceland, see in this volume: Ilse Schweitzer Van-Donkelaar, 'Bringing Murder to Light: Death, Publishing and Performance in Icelandic Sagas'.

says that Childebert II referred to the people who killed the Frankish envoys also as *homicidas* (*Hist.* X.4). Gregory says that this became an international incident and was, henceforth, negotiated between Childebert and Emperor Maurice through several envoys back and forth (*Hist.* X.4). Other similar examples of this public declaration include: Bishop Praetextatus' false confession before the king and other bishops at a synod in Paris that he committed *homicidium* (*Hist.* V.18); the charges of *homicidium* discussed against the nefarious bishops Salonius and Sagittarius before the council of bishops called by Guntram, king of Burgundy (V.27); the intervention of the hermit Eparchius to save the life of a man who had been accused of *homicidium* and was about to be hanged (VI.8); and a charge of *homicidium* in the context of accusations made against an abbess at another synod at Poitiers (X.16).

Gregory's labelling of certain killers as *homicidae* even more clearly demonstrates a tangible sense of *mala fama* for the murderer combined with subsequent descriptions of his or her irrational or unacceptable motives. Drawing on biblical ideas, the fifth-century Gallic writer Salvian of Marseilles argued in his treatise *De gubernatione Dei* that *homicidae* were defined more by their hatred than by the act of killing itself, but he also claims that those who do kill carry the stain of the label *homicida* for their entire lives as a consequence.[67] Gregory tends to agree, and he uses the term for notorious individuals who have killed for terrible reasons, including hatred, greed, envy and lust for power.[68] Gregory's *homicidae* use poisons, secretly plot against their victims, ignore norms governing sanctuary, kill within holy spaces, threaten their protectors or take vengeance in excessive ways. In some situations, Gregory seems to be comfortable labelling *homicidae* in his own voice. For example, he calls the assassin who snuck into church and killed a reclining Bishop Praetextatus a *homicida* (VIII.31). He also names as *homicidae* both Austregisel and Sichar, two adversaries caught in a serious conflagration in Gregory's city of Tours due to their cycles of inappropriate vengeance that combined excessive thefts and killings. Amongst their many reprisals against one another, Gregory says Austregisel killed four innocent servants while Sichar and his associates killed three men at night (VII.47; IX.19).[69] In most cases, though,

---

[67] Salvian, *De gubernatione Dei*, III.2, pp. 81–82: On several occasions, citing I Jn. 3.15, Salvian prioritises hatred, not commission of *homicidium*, as the defining feature of a *homicida*. At V.2, Salvian states that murderers are not simply murdering at the moment of a killing but that they remain murderers for the rest of their lives since they are 'stained with the blood of the victims'.

[68] There are similar implications of *mala fama* for murderers in other medieval European contexts. In this volume, see: VanDonkelaar, 'Bringing Murder to Light'.

[69] The historiography of this case is expansive, owing to its central place in debates over the nature of feuding culture in the early Middle Ages. See: Gabriel Monod, 'Les aventures de Sichaire: Commentaire des chapitres XLVII du livre VII et XIX du livre IX de

Gregory positions himself rhetorically as a reporter of a charge of *homicida* made by authority figures or those most affected by the crime. In addition to the killers of the Frankish envoys in Carthage (*Hist.* X.4), the other people that Gregory reports as *homicidae* include: (1) the *inimici* [enemies] who killed Bishop Marachar *crudeliter* [cruelly] with a poisoned fish head, condemned as *homicidae* by Marachar's son (V.36); and (2) Eberulf, an unsavoury aristocrat who sought sanctuary at the cathedral in Tours, killed people near St Martin's tomb and threatened Gregory's own life on numerous occasions, who was called a *homicida* by Guntram, king of Burgundy (VII.22). Most of these *homicidae* appear to be aristocrats, but one exceptional royal figure is also described as a *homicida* – the notorious Queen Fredegund, whose many evil deeds fill the latter books of the *Historiae* (VII.7). Against Fredegund, Gregory again does not 'make' the accusation of *homicida* himself – rather it is put in the words of Childebert II.[70] In so doing, Gregory both amplifies the importance of the charge and makes it rhetorically unassailable, as it not only comes from the mouth of a king, but one who was directly affected by Fredegund's evil deeds.

Scholars have long seen an important thematic relationship between Gregory's 'saints and sinners' as Heinzelmann saw – or, as Goffart put it, 'miracles and slaughters' – in the *Historiae*.[71] Gregory interprets the 'miracles and slaughters' of his own day according to biblical archetypes, with the 'slaughters' tied to the emblematic story of the sinner Cain who acted on his feelings of jealousy and killed his brother Abel. Gregory's descriptions of *homicidae* and *parricidae* and their depraved deeds provide some of the most profound evidence for the fall of man; his narratives reveal the depths of moral bankruptcy not only of individuals but of entire kingdoms and peoples. Gregory is concerned about these killings and sees them as a serious social obstacle, but also an unavoidable feature, of a world drenched in sin. Significantly, though, as a prominent and active bishop recording events with an eye towards posterity, Gregory plays the role of a judge himself when he labels certain deeds as *homicidia* or certain individuals as *homicidae* or *parricidae*, specific terms from classical and scriptural sources

---

l'Histoire des Francs de Grégoire de Tours', *Revue historique* 31 (1886): 259–90; N. D. Fustel de Coulange, 'De l'analyse des textes historiques', *Revue des questions historiques* 41 (1887): 5–35; Wallace-Hadrill, 'Blood Feud of the Franks', pp. 459–87; James, 'Beati pacifici', pp. 25–45.

[70] Wood, 'Secret Histories', pp. 258–59. Wood comments on Gregory's ease in describing Fredegund as a 'murderess', which seems to have occurred even during her lifetime and that of her husband Chilperic. Wood says that the label of 'murderess' may have been less concerning to a leader than a charge of adultery since that accusation comes later in his writing.

[71] Heinzelmann, *Gregory of Tours*, pp. 166–72; Goffart, 'From *Historiae* to *Historia Francorum*', p. 74.

that he anticipates will continue to reverberate a special sense of audacity. With his narratives of unjust killings, Gregory both rhetorically demonstrates and actively promulgates the *mala fama* of the individuals whom he associates with these powerful terms.

CHAPTER 14

Poisoning, Killing and Murder in the *Edictus Rothari*

Thomas Gobbitt

*V*ENENUM, OR POISONING, takes a small but interesting role in the early medieval *Edictus Rothari*,[1] the first written version of the Lombard laws, promulgated in the name of King Rothari on 22 November 643.[2] In two adjacent

[1] Throughout this article, I use the standard edition of the laws: for the *Edictus Rothari*, ed. Frederick Bluhme, *Edictus Langobardorum, Legum*, vol. 4 (Hannover: Monumenta Germaniae Historica, 1868), pp. 1–90. Modern English translations of the Lombard laws are taken from Katherine Fischer-Drew, trans., *The Lombard Laws* (Cinnaminson, NJ: University of Pennsylvania Press, 1973), based on Bluhme's edition of the laws.

[2] The prologue and epilogue that frame the *Edictus* (Rothari Prologue and No. 386) explain that the production of a written law-code drew on Lombard customs and the collective memories of the Lombard people. The process, however, was not simply a matter of passively writing down ancient customs but actively emending, adding or omitting details as required. The authority of the laws, then, is presented not as coming directly from the king but from custom. Simultaneously, however, although this was the first instance of a Lombard king legislating, Rothari, with the advice and approval of the principal judges (*primatos iudices*), employed equal authority to update the laws where required. The same customary process of ratification, the Lombard *gairethinx*, was used regardless of whether the laws were derived from the royal court or from customary practice. Rather than drawing on powers inherent to the crown, the framing texts of the *Edictus* themselves legitimate royal power by actively creating this authority and, as with all the early medieval barbarian law-codes, promoting royal ideologies. For a discussion of this and the role of the laws in the ethnogenesis of Lombard identities, see: Walter Pohl, 'Memory, Identity and Power in Lombard Italy', in *The Uses of the Past in the Early Middle Ages*, ed. Yitzhak Hen and Matthew Innes (Cambridge: Cambridge University Press, 2000), pp. 9–28 and, written from the perspective of a highly restricted legal literacy across early medieval western Europe, Patrick Wormald, 'The *Leges Barbarorum*: Law and Ethnicity in the Post-Roman West', in *Regna et Gentes: The Relationship Between Late Antique and Early Medieval Peoples and Kingdoms in the Transformation of the Roman World*, ed. Hans-Werner Goetz et al. (Leiden: Brill, 2003), pp. 21–52. Considerations of the role of literacy in the reduction of Lombard customs to writing are further discussed by Nick Everett, 'Literacy and the Law in Lombard Government', *Early Medieval Europe* 9 (2000): 93–127. In this argument, Everett first appears to equate the lack of surviving manuscripts from the Lombard period (only two are datable to the Lombard period itself: St Gallen, Stiftsbibliothek MS 730 from

clauses in the *Edictus*, the Lombard law-givers outline the extent of composition due in compensation for the act of killing with poison: Rothari No. 141, in which the perpetrator is free, and Rothari No. 142, in which the perpetrator is a *servus aut ancilla* [enslaved man or woman].[3] In both clauses, the composition due is equal to the financial worth of the victim according to their status in Lombard society, to be paid by the poisoner or their owner if the deed was committed by a *servus* or *ancilla*. Poison seems, by its very nature, to be ideally suited for secretive, nefarious killings, and modern scholars have considered poisoning as a means of murder, or attempted murder, within the legal contexts of early medieval law as a whole.[4] Two other clauses in the *Edictus* address cases where a 'homo liber aut mulier libera' [free man or free woman] either plots to poison someone (Rothari No. 139) or else actually administers poison but fails to kill their victim (Rothari No. 140).[5] Rothari No. 142 also discusses plots and non-lethal outcomes of a poisoning attempt when committed by a *servus* or *ancilla*.[6] The Lombard law-givers, then, arranged the clauses on poisoning along two axes, first by descending social class of the perpetrator, free and unfree, then subdividing these in increasing severity of the outcome. The Lombard law-givers never specify the actual types of poison that may have been employed, be it the wrong type of mushrooms ending up in the cooking pot or arsenic left over from silver smelting. Instead, the concern in the *Edictus* is simply that a person, man or woman, free or enslaved, poisoned another. The main focus here is to problematise the relationship of poisoning to killing and murder in the Lombard

the second half of the seventh century and, perhaps, Vercelli, Biblioteca Capitolare Eusebiana MS 188 dating to either the mid eighth or ninth century) with a lack of manuscript production and use, rather than entertaining the possibility of contemporary manuscript loss through overuse of those hypothetical, lost earlier books ('Literacy and the Law', pp. 96–104). However, in his conclusion, he reverses stance and discusses a widespread base of literacy in the Lombard period that continued into the Carolingian era ('Literacy and the Law', pp. 125–27). Everett builds in greater detail on this latter perspective of a prevalent literacy in the Lombard era, legal and otherwise, in Nicholas Everett, *Literacy in Lombard Italy, c. 568–774* (Cambridge: Cambridge University Press, 2003).

[3] Bluhme, ed., *Edictus Langobardorum*, p. 32.

[4] Franck Collard, *The Crime of Poison in the Middle Ages*, trans. Deborah Nelson-Campbell (London: Praeger, 2008); Richard Ireland, 'Medicine, Necromancy and the Law: Aspects of Medieval Poisoning', *Cambrian Law Review* 18 (1987): 52–61. For a discussion of shared features in the legal contexts of early medieval western Europe, see: Maurizio Lupoi, *The Origins of the European Legal Order* (Cambridge: Cambridge University Press, 2007); Maurizio Lupoi, 'A European Common Law Before Bologna', in *Law Before Gratian: Law in Western Europe c. 500–1100*, ed. Per Andersen, Mia Münster-Swendsen and Helle Vogt (Copenhagen: DJØF Publishing, 2007), pp. 1–20.

[5] Bluhme, ed., *Edictus Langobardorum*, p. 32.

[6] Ibid.

legal imagination of the mid seventh century, to break the assumed connection between poisoning and murder, nefariousness and shameful acts, and to demonstrate, instead, that poisoning in the *Edictus*, while still a crime, should be considered in relation to deliberate, open means of killing, but aligned with a broader spectrum of class and gender than killing with more ordinary weapons.

Modern scholarship has paid relatively little attention to poisoning as a crime in the Middle Ages, especially in the legal contexts of the early medieval period. Studies examining violence and the *faida* [feud] tend to overlook the potential role of poisoning as a means of killing.[7] While the law-codes are intended to limit the violence of the *faida*,[8] they do not seek to remove it entirely. Instead, the *faida* is part of the process through which justice was obtained, so that the Lombard laws explicitly state that, in the case of an accidental killing, redress is made through composition only and that, per Rothari No 387, *faida non requiratur* [the feud shall not be required].[9] Although not explicitly stated, the impression given in modern scholarship on early medieval honour violence is that while the *faida* might be brought to redress insult of nefarious murder by poisoning, injury and death inflicted by poison has no place in the honour violence of the *faida*.

Ross Balzaretti's study of female-perpetrated violence in the Lombard laws is comprehensive in its analysis of Lombard socio-legal attitudes surrounding the use of weaponry, but it, similarly, does not address poisoning.[10] Franck Collard prefaces his study on poisoning in the medieval period with the observation that poisoning has been overlooked in modern scholarship as it is assumed to be a

---

[7] See for example: Guy Halsall, 'Reflections on Early Medieval Violence: The Example of the "Blood Feud"', *Memoria y Civilizaión* 2 (1999): 7–29; and the various contributions to Guy Halsall, ed., *Violence and Society in the Early Medieval West* (Woodbridge: Boydell Press, 1998); Belle S. Tuten and Tracey L. Billado, eds., *Feud, Violence and Practice: Essays in Medieval Studies in Honor of Stephen D. White* (Farnham: Ashgate, 2010).

[8] I follow Halsall here and use the early medieval *faida* over the modern translation 'feud' as the latter has gathered multiple meanings from later periods that are anachronistic in the contexts of early medieval justice and society. See: Halsall, 'Reflections on Early Medieval Violence'.

[9] Bluhme, ed., *Edictus Langobardorum*, p. 90; Fischer-Drew, trans., *The Lombard Laws*, p. 129.

[10] Ross Balzaretti, '"These Are Things that Men Do, Not Women": The Social Regulation of Female Violence in Langobard Italy', in *Violence and Society in the Early Medieval West*, ed. Halsall, pp. 175–92. Another notable study on early medieval female-perpetrated violence is that of Nina Gradowicz-Pancer, although her argument focuses specifically on royal Merovingian women, and she argues convincingly that the protagonists' actions should be seen on gender-neutral class lines rather than within a specifically female context. Nira Gradowicz-Pancer, 'De-gendering Female Violence: Honour as an "Exchange of Violence"', *Early Medieval Europe* 11 (2002): 1–18. In this volume, see: Matthew Lubin, 'Poisoning as a Means of State Assassination in Early Modern Venice'.

crime of more 'refined times', in contrast to the modern-day perception of the 'cruelty and bloody violence [considered] typical of the [medieval] period'.[11] He seeks to redress this point and re-contextualises the development of poisoning as a crime in the later medieval period. However, while Collard examines historiographical evidence that spans the entire medieval period, his legal focus is on the laws from around the thirteenth century and onwards. He only briefly outlines the early medieval legal context, noting that the various approaches taken to poisoning in Germanic secular legislation are 'muddled'.[12] Particularly, Collard argues that the early medieval laws on poisoning are a direct inheritance from Roman jurisprudence, in which poisoning is directly attached to homicide as two facets of a single crime. For instance, No. 9.18.1 of the sixth-century *Codex Justinianus*, in a section addressing 'maleficiis et mathematicis et ceteris similibus' [enchanters, magicians and other similar persons], states that 'plus est hominem veneno extinguere quam occidere gladio' [to kill a man with poison is worse than to murder him with the sword].[13] In Roman law, then, poisoning is considered in relation both to magic and to homicide; likewise, poisoning in Roman law is considered a particularly nefarious act, but not as a specific crime in its own right. Collard argues that this Roman inheritance hindered the

---

[11] Collard, *Crime of Poison*, p. 1.

[12] Ibid., p. 12. A similar approach, in which the early medieval period receives even less attention, is taken by Jean de Maleissye, whose focus shifts quickly from classical Antiquity to the 1400s. See: *Histoire du Poison* (Paris: François Bourin, 1991). However, poisoning is addressed in a variety of ways across other early medieval secular law-codes broadly contemporary with the *Edictus Rothari*. Poisoning or witchcraft, alongside adultery and grave-robbing, are given as grounds on which a man may divorce his wife in the *Lex Burgundionum* (c. 500 CE), No. 21.2. Attempting to shoot another with a poisoned arrow is addressed in the *Pactus Legis Salicae* (507–11 CE), No. 17.2, and the *Lex Baiuvariorum* (c. 745 CE), No. 4.21. Giving poison to, or casting a magic spell on, another person, and whether the victim dies or survives, are addressed in the *Pactus Legis Salicae*, Nos 19.1 and 19.2, and the *Lex Ribuaria* (c. 623 CE), Nos 86.1 and 86.2, while preparing poison, a failed attempt to poison or killing by poison are addressed in the *Lex Visigothorum* (642–43 CE), No. 6.2.2, and giving another person poison to drink in the *Lex Baiuvariorum*, No. 4.22. Attacking the king with either weapons or poison is addressed in the *Lex Visigothorum*, No. 2.5.19. Numerous Anglo-Saxon laws address either poisoning or witchcraft, II Æthelstan No. 6, I Edmund no. 6, Pseudo-Edward and Guthrum No. 11, and VI Æthelred No. 7. For further details on the Anglo-Saxon contexts, see: Marianne Elsakkers, 'Anglo-Saxon Laws on Poisoning: An Invitation to Further Investigation', in 'Reading Between the Lines: Old Germanic and Early Christian Views on Abortion', PhD Dissertation (University of Amsterdam, 2010): http://dare.uva.nl/record/1/327030 (accessed 26 August 2016); Felix Liebermann, ed., *Die Gesetze der Angelsachsen*, 3 vols (Halle: Numeyer, 1903–1916).

[13] Paul Krueger, ed., *Codex Iustinianus* (1877): http://droitromain.upmf-grenoble.fr/Corpus/CJ9.htm#18 (accessed 31 August 2016); Fred Blume, trans., *Annotated Justinian Code*, http://www.uwyo.edu/lawlib/blume-justinian/ajc-edition-2/books/book9/book9-18rev.pdf (accessed 31 August 2016).

development of a specific category for poisoning throughout the early medieval period and into the thirteenth century.[14]

The Lombard laws on poisoning, however, do not fit so neatly into Collard's paradigm, which is evident in the overall structure of the *Edictus Rothari*. The *Edictus* comprises a prologue followed by 388 clauses (per the numbering of the modern critical edition), the last three of which form an epilogue to the code. Within the main body of the *Edictus* itself, the laws are organised, approximately, by legal theme, which Nicholas Everett breaks down as:

Laws 1–13, crimes against public authority;
14–145, crimes against private individuals;
146–152, damage to property;
153–177, laws of succession;
178–223, marriage laws;
224–226, manumission;
227–244, property laws;
245–252, obligations;
253–358, minor crimes and damages;
359–366, oaths, pledges, legal procedures;
367–388, miscellaneous affairs and epilogue.[15]

The first (Nos 1–3) and second (Nos 14–145) of Everett's sub-sections are most relevant for poisoning, violence and murder as, in addition to the clauses on poisoning (Rothari Nos 139–142),[16] these contain the main clauses addressing plots, failed and successful attempts at killing a free man by ordinary means (Rothari Nos 10–11),[17] as well as murder (Rothari No. 14)[18] and the killing of

---

[14] Moreover, Collard emphasises that, in contrast to the distinction made in later law between *veneficio* [poisoning] and *maleficium* [witchcraft], both terms are used interchangeably across the early medieval law-codes (see: Collard, *Crime of Poison*, pp. 11–12); Elsakkers makes a similar observation on the dual meanings of both *veneficio* and *maleficium*, as both witchcraft and poisoning, in a discussion that focuses on medicine, abortives and poisoning in the Salic laws. 'Abortion, Poisoning, Magic and Contraception in Eckhardt's *Pactus Legis Salicae*', *Amsterdamer Beiträge zur Älteren Germanistik* 57 (2003): 251–67. Richard Ireland does not discuss the duality in terminology but instead positions poisoning as a nefarious act through its relationship to necromancy, perjury and other immoral activities outlined in Anglo-Saxon and later medieval English laws ('Medicine, Necromancy and the Law', pp. 52–61). In the Lombard laws, the term *venenum* is used consistently throughout (Rothari Nos 139–142) and has been taken in the scholarship to refer exclusively to 'poisoning'; see, for example, the modern English translation of the laws: Fischer-Drew, trans., *The Lombard Laws*, p. 74.
[15] Everett, *Literacy in Lombard Italy*, p.167.
[16] Bluhme, ed., *Edictus Langobardorum*, p. 32.
[17] Ibid., p. 14.
[18] Ibid., p. 15.

aldii [half-free] and various ranks of enslaved people (Rothari Nos 129–138).[19] However, the fine for killing a free woman or girl is listed later in the code, Rothari Nos 200–201,[20] in the section on marriages.[21] The clause on accidental killing is in the trio of clauses that form the epilogue (Rothari No. 387).[22] Everett's 'crimes against public individuals' also include the lists of tariffs for specific injuries inflicted on a victim, with values determined by social rank: first the *homines liberi* [freemen] (Rothari Nos 45–74),[23] then the *aldii* [half-free] and *servi menisteriali* [enslaved people working in the domestic sphere] (Rothari Nos 76–102)[24] and, lastly, at the lowest level of Lombard society, the *servi rusticani* [enslaved people working in the rural sphere] (Rothari Nos 103–126).[25] The laws on poisoning, then, are physically separated in the *Edictus* from the main clauses on the killing of a freeman and murder by some 125 clauses, which suggests a corresponding separation in the legal mentality of the Lombard law-givers; that is, Rothari and his advisors. Rather than seeing poisoning as a sub-set of killing by ordinary means, this separation suggests that poisoning may have been considered in Lombard law as a different category of crime, at least in the instances when the victim was a free person.

The clauses on poisoning in the *Edictus* follow on directly from the monetary assessment of the *praetium* [worth] due for the killing of *aldii* and enslaved people. In the earliest surviving manuscript of the *Edictus*, St Gall, Stiftsbibliothek MS 730, which dates to the second half of the seventh century,[26] each clause is introduced with a capitula number in the margin to the left of the text-block, and the first line of the text is written in red. The initial introducing the clauses is a large majuscule, but it is written by the same scribal hand as that of the main text, and in the same ink as the opening line of the clause. The scribe, therefore, does not demarcate the change of legal theme,[27] but represents all clauses as equal

[19] Ibid., pp. 30–31.
[20] Ibid., pp. 49–50.
[21] Everett, *Literacy in Lombard Italy*, p. 167.
[22] Bluhme, ed., *Edictus Langobardorum*, p. 90.
[23] Ibid., p. 20–24.
[24] Ibid., pp. 24–27.
[25] Ibid., pp. 27–29.
[26] Karl Ubl, ed., 'St Gall, Stiftsbibliothek, 730', *Bibliotheca Legum: A Database on Carolingian Secular Law Texts*: http://www.leges.uni-koeln.de/en/mss/codices/st-gallen-sb-730/ (accessed 26 August 2016).
[27] Where larger decorative initials are present in the St Gall manuscript of the *Edictus Rothari*, they do not mark a larger change of legal theme, but instead are used when the opening initial of the clause varies from the more frequently attested < s >. An example of this can be seen on fol. 28r, lines 7–13, where part of a ten-line < P > is inset into the text block. This initial is line-drawn, with knot-work decorations and green and red fill, and presents a complicated *mise-en-page* in which the scribe inset part of the first three lines of the clause (lines 7–9) inside the bowl of the < P >. This elaborated initial,

sub-divisions within the *Edictus* itself. The movement in the text of the *Edictus*, from the killing of people in the lower strata of Lombard society into the laws of poisoning, does not seem to indicate that the two legal themes were integrally related. However, their proximity may suggest that the lawmakers considered poisoning as a crime to be more closely associated with the lower strata of society. The clauses outlining the *praetium* due for the killing of enslaved people and *aldii* emphasise the rank of the victim, but are not specific with relation to the perpetrator. Moreover, the means of killing is not addressed in any of these clauses apart from the last, Rothari No. 138, which outlines the situation in which the victim is (accidentally) killed by a falling tree felled by one or more other people.[28] The four clauses on poisoning, conversely, emphasise the social rank of the perpetrator and, to the extent that some manner of poison was employed, how the killing (or plot or attempted killing) was committed. Consequently, the laws on the killing of lower ranking people and on poisoning appear as separate, if contiguous, sub-sections within the *Edictus Rothari*. In contrast to Collard's argument that poisoning was treated as an integral part of homicide across the early medieval laws of western Europe,[29] poisoning in the *Edictus* appears to have been positioned as a relatively independent category of crime, as far as permitted by the underlying structure of the *Edictus*. The extent to which the Lombard law-givers considered poisoning as a distinct crime can be further elucidated through an analysis of the specific details of the clauses on poisoning in the *Edictus*, in contrast to those on killing and murder.

The *Edictus Rothari* addresses murder, or *morth* in the Langobardic language, as a very specific type of killing.[30] Cognate words related to the Langobardic *morth* can be found across the Germanic languages; indeed, Old English *morð* and Frankish *murdre* are the etymological ancestors of modern English 'murder'.[31]

however, marks the onset of a sub-section within Rothari No. 136 and outlines a fine for killing the student of a cattleherd, goatherd or oxherd; see: Bluhme, ed., *Edictus Langobardorum*, p. 31. The larger initials in the St Gall manuscript, therefore, do not appear to reflect an attempt by the scribe to introduce a hierarchy into the *mise-en-page*. A similar scribal strategy in selecting initials, which are not an < S > for emphasis, can also be observed in a much later manuscript of the Lombard laws, Milan, Biblioteca Ambrosiana MS O. 53sup, dating to the third quarter of the eleventh century. A detailed codicological and palaeographical comparative study of these two manuscripts would be informative, but that is well beyond the scope of this chapter. See: Thomas Gobbitt, ed., 'Milan, Biblioteca Ambrosiana, MS O 53 sup', in *Manuscripts of the Lombard Laws*: https://thomgobbitt.wordpress.com/lombard-laws/manuscripts-of-the-lombard-laws/ (accessed 21 December 2016).

[28] Bluhme, ed., *Edictus Langobardorum*, p. 31.
[29] Collard, *Crime of Poison*, p. 12.
[30] Rothari No. 14, Bluhme, ed., *Edictus Langobardorum*, p. 15.
[31] Variations of *morð*, *morth*, *murdre* and compound nouns incorporating murder into them can be found or reconstructed across the barbarian laws, including the *Pactus*

Throughout early medieval law, murder is variously defined as a secretive killing in which an attempt was made by the perpetrator to move or hide the body after the act; or else that the killing was a paid-for assassination or undertaken in some other morally nefarious way.[32] Rothari No. 14 begins by stating that 'si quis homicidium in absconse penetraverit in barone libero aut servo vel ancilla, et unus fuerit au taut duo tantum, qui ipsum homicidium fecerint, noningentos solidos conponat' [If anyone secretly kills a freeman or a man or woman slave, if one or two persons commit the homicide, he or they shall pay 900 *solidi* as composition].[33] In the instance of secret killing, then, class distinctions are effectively removed; the composition due for the murder is equal whether the victim was a free man or an enslaved man or woman. The free woman is conspicuously absent from this list, presumably because the composition for killing her, set at 1200 *solidi*, was already higher.[34] When the number of perpetrators behind the murder increases to three or more, the composition due is equal to the *angarathungi* [worth according to rank, sometimes glossed by Anglophone scholars with the Old English 'wergild'] if the victim was a freeman or the *praetium* of an enslaved person. In other clauses of the *Edictus*, including those on poisoning, the term *praetium* is used throughout for both free and enslaved people. Rothari No. 14 concludes by adding a further fine of 80 *solidi* should the murderers also

---

Legis Salicae, the *Lex Ripuaria*, the *Lex Baiuariorum* and the *Leges Alamanorum* as well as the *morth* of the Lombard *Edictus*. Murder as secret killing also appears notably in the opening passage of *Völsunga Saga*: R. G. Finch, ed. and trans., *The Saga of the Volsungs* (London: Nelson, 1965). In this volume, see: Ilse Schweitzer VanDonkelaar, 'Bringing Murder to Light: Death, Publishing and Performance in Icelandic Sagas' and Larissa Tracy, '"Mordre wol out": Murder and Justice in Chaucer'.

[32] Bruce O'Brien discusses the various Germanic varieties and cognates to the English *morð/morðor* in an in-depth analysis of the origins of the English murder fine. Most interestingly, he notes that in Old and Middle English, the sense of secret killing is rarely used (despite the observations made in the *Oxford English Dictionary* entry discussed previously, which includes reference to this early medieval version of the crime within its broader discussion of murder). See: O'Brien, 'From *Morðor* to *Murdrum*: The Preconquest Origin and Norman Revival of the Murder Fine', *Speculum* 71 (1996): 321–57 at pp. 351–52. In this volume, see: Jay Paul Gates, 'Discursive Murders: The St Brice's Day Massacre, *Beowulf*, and *Morðor*'. For 'murder' explicitly being related to poison, see the Old English 'morð-weorc': *Bosworth-Toller Anglo-Saxon Dictionary*: http://bosworth.ff.cuni.cz/023183 (accessed 11 February 2015). Another related, recurrent theme in the early medieval legal definition of murder is the specific disposal of the body in water. For a discussion of the early medieval contexts of murder, see: Graham McBain, 'Modernising the Law of Murder and Manslaughter: Part I', *Journal of Politics and Law* 8 (2015): 9–97 at p. 30.

[33] Fischer-Drew, trans., *The Lombard Laws*, p. 55. 'Composition' being the technical term for the actual moneys paid to the wronged party, or in this case their heirs or owners, in compensation for the offence committed against them.

[34] Bluhme, ed., *Edictus Langobardorum*, pp. 49–50.

commit *plodraub* [plundering the body].³⁵ The law-givers do not define how the victim was murdered, be it by poison or otherwise. The law-givers underline the nefariousness of *morth* through the inclusion of *plodraub* within the same clause, but both of these crimes refer to actions taken by the killer or killers after the victim has died. The killing itself precedes the behaviour which defines whether or not the act was murder. The defining feature of *morth* in Rothari No. 14 is the secrecy of the act; accordingly, the law-givers emphasise the extent of composition due for committing murder.

In most cases in the *Edictus*, the punishment set for a crime is a monetary fine,³⁶ the lowest value being half a *solidus* for relatively minor crimes and injuries,³⁷ and the highest being 1200 *solidi* for the killing of a free woman or girl.³⁸ This situation is complicated somewhat in instances wherein the extent of the fine is calculated in relation to the specific value of the damage that was done: for instance, the value of stolen goods being returned nine-fold,³⁹ or the worth of the victim according to their *praetium* (whether free or enslaved). By comparing the extent of the fines for different crimes, an assessment of the relative severity attributed to each crime by the Lombard law-givers can be postulated. Katherine Fischer-Drew argues that the cut-off line in Lombard law between minor and major crimes was when the fine reached twenty *solidi*. Although she presents this as an integral part of Lombard legal culture,⁴⁰ it should be noted that it was not introduced, or at least made explicit in the laws, until Liutprand No. 152,⁴¹ issued in 735 CE, almost a century after the promulgation of the *Edictus*. Liutprand also made explicit, in a clause promulgated in 724 CE, the various *praetium* for different ranks of freemen: 300 *solidi* if they possessed land, 150 *solidi* if they did not and a further increase if the freeman in question was a royal official (Liutprand

---

[35] Ibid., p. 15; Fischer-Drew, trans., *The Lombard Laws*, p. 55.

[36] Non-monetary punishments, however, include the death penalty for, amongst other reasons, conspiring against the king's life (Rothari No. 1), trying to flee the country (Rothari No. 3), inviting spies into the country (Rothari No. 4) or raising a revolt in the army (Rothari No. 6). Later in the *Edictus*, cutting off a hand is proscribed for minting gold or coin without royal permission or for forging false charters (Rothari Nos 242–243); Bluhme, ed., *Edictus Langobardorum*, pp. 13, 60.

[37] For example, cutting off the fourth toe or little toe of an enslaved field worker (Rothari Nos 123–124, respectively) or cutting the shoot of a vine (Rothari No. 295); see: Bluhme, ed., *Edictus Langobardorum*, pp. 29, 70.

[38] Rothari Nos 200–201; see Bluhme, ed., *Edictus Langobardorum*, pp. 49–50.

[39] Rothari No. 253; see: Bluhme, ed., *Edictus Langobardorum*, p. 62.

[40] Fischer-Drew, trans., *The Lombard Laws*, p. 29. Liutprand No. 152 marks the distinction in severity, by allowing a person who is unable to pay a fine of less than twenty *solidi* to become enslaved until the debt has been worked off, but for unpaid fines of over twenty *solidi*, the debtor becomes enslaved for life; Bluhme, ed., *Edictus Langobardorum*, p. 175.

[41] Bluhme, ed., *Edictus Langobardorum*, p. 175.

No. 62).⁴² Liutprand presented these values as arising from Lombard custom, although whether they actually dated back as far as Rothari's time in the mid seventh century is uncertain.⁴³ Conversely, Rothari clearly outlined the *praetium* of free women, provided they were not killed while acting in a manner deemed unfeminine (i.e. participating in a brawl): 1200 *solidi* (Rothari Nos 200–201).⁴⁴ The *Edictus Rothari* also gives values of composition for the *aldius* [half-free] at sixty *solidi* (Rothari No. 129), and of various ranks of enslaved domestic and agricultural workers, ranging from sixteen to fifty *solidi*, depending on their training and duties (Rothari Nos 130–136).⁴⁵ Even taking the uncertainty surrounding the *praetium* for freemen in the mid seventh century into account, the various values outlined here provide a useful framework for comparing the various compositions assigned in the *Edictus* for the different crimes of plotting, killing and murder by poisoning and other means.

The two clauses on killing by poison in the *Edictus* differ somewhat according to social rank. The first, Rothari No. 141, does not explicitly state the rank of the perpetrator, as it simply begins *si quis* [if anyone]. However, it follows on directly from the two clauses on poisoning with non-lethal outcomes, in which the clause makes clear the rank of the perpetrator as a 'homo liber aut mulier libera' [free man or free woman]: 'Si quis venenum ad bivendum, et qui acceperit, mortuos fuerit, praetium mortui secundum qualitatem personae in integrum componat' [Whoever gives another poison in his drink and that one dies shall pay as composition a sum equal to the full wergild of the dead man in accordance with his rank] (Rothari No. 141).⁴⁶ The specific details of the clause, and those preceding, therefore suggest that the perpetrator discussed here was free born. Moreover, after considering a non-lethal outcome of a poisoning attempt, the final part of the following clause, Rothari No. 142, addresses killing by poison in explicit relation to an enslaved man or woman perpetrator.

> … et si mortuus fuerit, qui accepit tunc dominus servi vel ancillae ipsum hominem in integrum conponat, sic tamen ut servus aut ancilla in ipsa compositione pro quantum adpretiatus fuerit, ad occidendum tradatur et nulla sit redemption aut ecusatio mortis servi vel ancille.
>
> [… and if the one who received the poison dies, then the slave's lord shall pay the full wergild as composition. The value of the slave shall, however, be counted

---

⁴² Ibid., p. 132.
⁴³ Again, Fischer-Drew presents these values as inherent to Lombard legal culture across the Lombard period, and does not draw attention to the specific point in time in which they were introduced in legislation (*The Lombard Laws*, p. 29).
⁴⁴ Bluhme, ed., *Edictus Langobardorum*, pp. 49–50.
⁴⁵ Ibid., pp. 30–31.
⁴⁶ Ibid., p. 32; Fischer-Drew, trans., *The Lombard Laws*, p. 74.

in the amount of the composition, and he or she shall thereafter be killed. And there shall be no redemption or pardon from death for the slave]. (Rothari No. 142)[47]

In both clauses, the composition due for the killing equals the *praetium* of the victim. The most important point of variation is that when the poisoner was an enslaved person, he or she was to be killed as part of the settlement. The composition itself was to be paid by the owner of the enslaved poisoner, but as said owner already had lost the economic value of some property (i.e., they had lost an enslaved worker), the value of the poisoner's *praetium* was subtracted from the fine due. Consequently, in the case of poisonings between enslaved persons with different owners, relatively little financial redress would be due. If we take the values given by Liutprand for a freeman's *praetium* (150–300 *solidi*) as being even loosely comparable to what might have been demanded under Rothari, the significance in difference with the 900 *solidi*, given in the clause on *morth*, is immediately apparent. The composition for killing a freeman by poison or ordinary means is a third or, if he or his family is without land, a sixth of the fine allotted for murder. In the case of the enslaved men and women, for whom the murder fine of 900 *solidi* is also explicitly set, the difference becomes an eighteenth of the value at the highest level, or one fifty-sixth for the very lowest ranking of enslaved peoples.[48] Regardless of the exact figures, the significant degree in difference is apparent between the values awarded for murder in relation to killing by poison. What can be stated here is that poisoning was not explicitly positioned in the Lombard laws as inherently being a form of murder.

The comparable relationship between laws on poisoning and killing by ordinary means, however, is much more apparent as the composition for each is set equal to the victim's worth according to their social rank (Rothari No. 11):

> Si hominis liberi inter se in morte alterius consiliaverint sine regis consilio, et ex ipso tractato mortuus non feuerit, conponat unusquisque, ut supra, solidos viginti; et si ex ipso consilio mortuus fuerit, tunc ille quie homicidia est, conponat ipsum mortuum sicut adpreatiatus fuerit, id est wergild.

> [If freemen without the king's consent plot another man's death, but that one does not die as a result of the agreement, then each of them shall pay twenty *solidi* as composition, as stated above. But if that one [conspired against] dies

---

[47] Ibid., p. 32; Fischer-Drew, trans., *The Lombard Laws*, p. 74.
[48] The murder clause, Rothari No. 14, does not directly address the *aldius* or *aldia* [half-free man or woman], but assuming they were included within its scope, their ordinary *praetium* of sixty *solidi* equals one fifteenth of the 900 *solidi* fine due for murder.

as a result of the plot, then the doer of the deed shall pay the victim's wergild, according as he is valued, as composition]. (Rothari No. 11)[49]

The epilogue to the *Edictus* adds that, in the case when the killing of a freeman was accidental, only the *praetium* needs to be paid, and that there is no further necessity to pursue the *faida*.[50] The law-givers then construct an opposition of deliberate and accidental killing, both atoned for at the same price, but with deliberate killing requiring a lasting enmity. When discussing the deliberate killing by physical means, however, the laws do not mention the requirement for the *faida*; instead, it seems to be silently assumed.

The structure of Rothari No. 10, which first gives the 20 *solidi* fine for conspiring the death of another, and No. 11 is echoed in the later clauses on poisoning; the severity increases in respect to plotting and failed attempts, and concludes with the instance wherein the victim dies. Moreover, a freeman conspiring to kill a person by ordinary means owes the same compensation as the freeman or free woman who conspires to kill with poison (Rothari No. 139); that is, 20 *solidi*.[51] The law-makers even make this point clear in a cross-reference within the later clause: 'Si quis homo liber aut mulier venenum temperaverit et alii ad bivendum dare voluerit, conponat solidos viginti, sicut ille qui de morte alterius consilatus fuerit' [If a freeman or free woman who mixes poison intending to give it to someone to drink shall pay twenty solidi as composition, just as in the case of him who plots the death of someone else].[52] The *Edictus* does not consider plots made by enslaved people who choose to kill by ordinary means or by poison. A comparison of the compositions awarded for plotting, failed attempts, killing and murder by both ordinary means and poisoning is given in Table 14.1. In the Lombard laws, killing can be broadly subdivided into three forms: nefarious 'secretive' killing or *morth* [murder], deliberate but open killing and accidental killing. The descending severity of these types of killing in Lombard legal culture can be inferred from the relative extent of composition awarded for each, and in the case of accidental killing, the removal of the (otherwise silently assumed) need for the pursuit of honour through the *faida*.

The Lombard law-givers only diverge in their approach to poisoning and violence in the case of the failed attempt to kill. There, the composition for a failed attempt to kill is the 20 *solidi* for plotting, outlined in Rothari No. 11, alongside the composition detailed in the tariffs for the specific injuries inflicted on the

---

[49] Bluhme, ed., *Edictus Langobardorum*, p. 14; Fischer-Drew, trans., *The Lombard Laws*, p. 54.
[50] Bluhme, ed., *Edictus Langobardorum*, p. 88.
[51] Ibid., pp. 14, 32.
[52] Ibid., p. 32; Fischer-Drew, trans., *The Lombard Laws*, p. 74.

Table 14.1 Comparison of fines relating to killing, injury and plotting: poisoning versus 'ordinary' means

Crime	Composition due for killing by:	
	Ordinary means	Poisoning
Killing a freewoman or girl	1200 *solidi* (Rothari Nos 200 and 201)	—
Morth (Secretly killing a freeman, or enslaved man or woman)	900 *solidi* (Rothari No. 14)	—
Killing	*Praetium* (Rothari Nos 11, 129-138)	*Praetium* (Rothari No. 141)
Accidental killing	*Praetium*, no requirement for *faida* (Rothari No. 378)	—
Failed attempt to kill	20 *solidi* plus per tariffs for wounds (Rothari No. 11)	½ *Praetium* (Rothari No. 140)
Plotting the death of a freeman	20 *solidi* (Rothari Nos 10 and 11)	20 *solidi* (Rothari No. 139)

victim.[53] Conversely, in the case of poisoning, an undifferentiated composition equal to half the victim's *praetium* is awarded for a failed attempt (Rothari No. 140 when the perpetrator is free, No. 142 when he or she is enslaved). The divergence in approaches taken for calculating the compensation due for failed attempts at killing may be explained by the available extent of medical knowledge. Lisi Oliver presents a detailed analysis of the extent of medical and anatomical knowledge as evidenced by the various Germanic early medieval law-codes.[54] She notes that the injury tariffs almost exclusively address the external body and that, with the exception of the Frisian laws, the internal organs are never mentioned.[55] While specific injuries to the external body could be tallied and counted, the damage inflicted by a failed attempt at poisoning would be to the internal organs. Moreover, any attempt to verify the physical damage inflicted by the poison to the internal organs would have required causing the victim further bodily injury. As such, the specific details of this damage must have been invisible to Lombard legal practitioners assessing the extent of damage the victim had suffered. Here,

---

[53] Rothari Nos 45 to 74, for injuries committed to freemen, Rothari Nos 76 to 102, for the *aldii* and *servi menisteriali* [domestic slaves], and from Rothari Nos 103 to 126, for *servi rusticani* [field slaves]. See: Bluhme, ed., *Edictus Langobardorum*, pp. 20-30; Fischer-Drew, trans., *The Lombard Laws*, pp. 61-71.

[54] Lisi Oliver, *The Body Legal in Barbarian Law* (Toronto: University of Toronto Press, 2011).

[55] Ibid., p. 59.

the effective invisibility of poisoning is most apparent. Setting the composition for a failed poisoning attempt at half the victim's worth simultaneously emphasises the difficulties in assessing the damage inflicted while positioning even a failed poisoning attempt in proportion to the victim's life and worth.[56]

As the Lombard law-givers awarded equal compensation for both plotting and for killing, whether by poison or ordinary means, these two crimes, therefore, must have been viewed in the Lombard socio-legal framework as being of comparable severity. As such, the question arises as to why the Lombard law-givers did not assume that plotting and killing by poisoning were already addressed in the clauses on killing by ordinary means? While no significant variation can be seen in the composition awarded, the Lombard law-givers anticipated a notable variation in the types of perpetrators who might commit these two different means of plotting and killing.

The laws on plotting and killing by ordinary means specifically address a masculine, high-ranking *homo liber* [free man] perpetrator (Rothari Nos 10–11). Female perpetrators of violence by physical means are excluded from consideration here, though they are discussed in some detail by Balzaretti.[57] Elsewhere in the *Edictus*, Rothari addresses female-perpetrated violence, as in Rothari No. 202, which considers women who conspire against their husbands.[58] The possibility that a woman would be the one to act violently is entertained in the following clause (Rothari No. 203), but the methods of killing are not discussed, and the notion that she might orchestrate a killing to be performed by another man is given equal prominence. More explicitly, Rothari No. 378 reduces the composition that would have been awarded to or for a woman killed or injured in a brawl, in which she had actively participated, from 900 *solidi* to the same value of compensation determined 'tamquam si in fratrem ipsius mulieris perpetratum fuisset' [as if it had been perpetrated against a brother of that woman].[59] In addi-

---

[56] Half the victim's worth is also set for numerous other injuries within the *Edictus*, including gouging out eyes or cutting off hands and feet at all social ranks (Rothari Nos 48, 62, 68, 81, 88, 95, 105, 113 and 119), as well as cutting off a freeman's nose (Rothari No. 49). A comparable composition is set for numerous other crimes in the *Edictus*, especially in the cases where an unborn baby is killed inside its mother's womb (Rothari No. 75) or when a freeman is taken by surprise and beaten without the king's consent (Rothari No. 41).

[57] For a detailed analysis of this, see: Balzaretti 'These Are Things that Men Do, Not Women'.

[58] In such a case, the man is permitted to 'do with her what he wishes' (*ea facere quod voluerit*). If she goes as far as to kill him herself, then the proscribed punishment is instant death. See: Rothari, No. 203 (Fischer-Drew, trans., *The Lombard Laws*, p. 92).

[59] Bluhme, ed., *Edictus Langobardorum*, p. 88; Fischer-Drew, trans., *The Lombard Laws*, p. 127. Note that there is a discrepancy in the *Edictus* between the *praetium* of a free woman or girl given, in this clause, as 900 *solidi* (Rothari No. 378) in comparison to the two previous clauses in which the *praetium* was set at 1200 *solidi* for the unwarranted

tion to this reduction in fiscal protection of (free) women, violence by women is also further restricted and appropriate female behaviour circumscribed and reinforced through the imputation of shame for having behaved 'quod inhonestum est mulieribus facere' [in a manner dishonourable for women] (Rothari No. 378).⁶⁰ In all, the Lombard legislators are unwilling to imagine or accept female violence; this is emphasised in Rothari No. 278, which states that neither a free woman (*mulier libera*) nor a female servant (*ancilla*) can be accused of the crime of *hoberos* [breaching another's courtyard] on the grounds that 'absurdum videtur esse, ut mulier libera aut ancilla, quasi vir cum armis vim facere possit' [it seems foolish to think that a woman, free or slave, could commit a forceful act with arms as if she were a man].⁶¹ Balzaretti argues that in the Lombard legislative mentality, then, female violence is a conundrum, something which can only be imagined as an absurdity. He attributes this process of defeminisation to the discomfort of law-makers who, when faced with female violence, resort to 'gendered type-casting' and impute blame to 'that most dangerous of things, women trying to be men'.⁶² Balzaretti concludes his discussion of female violence by emphasising the strict gender polarity in the Lombard laws and the way in which that was used to construct the Lombard social order: 'because men

killing of a freewoman (Rothari Nos 200 and 201). Balzaretti also notes that these constructions of appropriate female behaviour also reflect explicitly on the behaviour expected of men. See: Ross Balzaretti, 'Masculine Authority and State Identity in Liutprandic Italy', in *Die Langobarden: Herrschaft und Identität*, ed. Walter Pohl and Peter Erhart (Vienna: Verlag der Österreichische Akademie der Wissenschaften, 2005), pp. 361–82 at p. 367.

⁶⁰ Bluhme, ed., *Edictus Langobardorum*, p. 88; Fischer-Drew, trans., *The Lombard Laws*, p. 127.

⁶¹ Ibid., p. 67; Fischer-Drew, trans., *The Lombard Laws*, p. 108. It is, perhaps, not surprising that King Liutprand addressed some unintended consequences of this law ninety years later (Liutprand No. 141, from the twenty-second year of his reign, in 734), in which he denounced and legislated against the practice of gathering together a band of free and enslaved women and sending them into another's village or homestead to commit violence. The law also presumes a further limitation of the female potential for perpetrating violence, even in the face of an armed raid, by assuming that these pillaging free and enslaved women were not self-organised women who picked up weapons of their own accord but rather collected groups of women who were given arms by *hominis perfidi et in malitia* [perfidious and evil-minded men]. Moreover, even where female-perpetrated violence undeniably occurred, the law-givers transferred the impetus for it to male agency, assuming that the band of women in question had been gathered and directed by men and that, after the raid, successful or otherwise, those same men would then seek full compensation for any injuries or deaths sustained by the women in the process. Balzaretti also notes that, when female-perpetuated violence is addressed in the Lombard laws, it is only women versus men, never violence between women. See: 'These Are Things that Men Do, Not Women', p. 189; see also: Bluhme, ed., *Edictus Langobardorum*, pp. 112–13, and Fischer-Drew, trans., *The Lombard Laws*, p. 208.

⁶² Balzaretti, 'These Are Things that Men Do, Not Women', pp. 187–88.

were violent', he argues, 'women had, therefore, to be non-violent'.[63] In focusing exclusively on violence by ordinary physical means, the Lombard legal contexts of poisoning have been obscured. It might be assumed, then, that the Lombard law-givers would have constructed poisoning explicitly as a woman's crime and as a socially unacceptable means for male violence.

However, the laws on poisoning in the *Edictus* explicitly address both male and female perpetrators, both free and enslaved. Rothari No. 139 on plotting begins: 'Si quis homo liber aut mulier venenum temperaverit et alii ad bivendum dare voluerit' [If a freeman or free woman mixes poison intending to give it to someone to drink].[64] The following clause on failed attempts to poison begins with an equally explicit statement that the perpetrator might be of either gender: 'Si liber aut libera venenum alii dederit ad bibendum' [If a freeman or free woman gives another poison in his drink].[65] In Rothari No. 142, the same gender equality for the perpetrator is once more stressed, this time at the lower social rank: 'Si servus aut ancilla venenum alicui dederit' [If a man or woman slave gives someone poison].[66] The only exception to this situation is in Rothari No. 141, wherein a poisoning committed by a free person successfully kills the victim; here, the expression of the clause changes to the gender neutral *si quis* [if anyone].[67] While this could reflect the Lombard law-givers restricting the scope of people whom they imagined could kill with poison specifically to exclude freewomen, this conclusion seems doubtful. When it came to the crime of *hoberos*, the law-givers were more than willing to moralise on how a woman could not wield weapons or commit such an act. Instead, this may be a quieter echo of the Lombard law-givers' discomfort with female violence that Balzarreti observed. The *Edictus* appears to acknowledge that a freewoman might well kill by poison, but, in the final instance, the law-givers chose to step delicately around the subject and only to infer it indirectly. Most importantly, however, none of the clauses on poisoning moralise against the woman or man who plots, injures or kills by such means. This contrasts with the treatment of female-perpetrated

---

[63] Ibid., p. 189.
[64] Bluhme, ed., *Edictus Langobardorum*, p. 32; Fischer-Drew, trans., *The Lombard Laws*, p. 74.
[65] Rothari No. 140: Bluhme, ed., *Edictus Langobardorum*, p. 32; Fischer-Drew, trans., *The Lombard Laws*, p. 74.
[66] Bluhme, ed., *Edictus Langobardorum*, p. 32; Fischer-Drew, trans., *The Lombard Laws*, p. 74.
[67] Bluhme, ed., *Edictus Langobardorum*, p. 32; Fischer-Drew, trans., *The Lombard Laws*, p. 74. While 'si quis' clauses are typically taken in modern scholarship to mean 'if any man', Guy Halsall makes a compelling argument for treating this as a gender-neutral phrase in relation to the early sixth-century Frankish *Pactus legis salicae*. See: Halsall, *Settlement and Social Organization: The Merovingian Region of Metz* (Cambridge: Cambridge University Press, 2002), p. 63.

violence by ordinary means discussed previously[68] but aligns exactly with the Lombard law-givers' treatment of physical violence and killing when committed by freemen. In the *Edictus*, then, poisoning is presented as a mode of inflicting violence that could be employed by either gender. Compensation for the crime was extracted from the perpetrator, including their life, if the poisoner was an enslaved man or woman, but, significantly, no shame was imputed to them.

What role then does *venenum* [poisoning] take in the *Edictus* and the mid seventh-century Lombard legal imagination and culture? The modern-day assumption that poisoning is an inherently nefarious act has occluded the way in which poisoning is addressed in the *Edictus*; thus, the assumption must be discounted. In the *Edictus*, poisoning is comparable with killing by ordinary means but set apart in terms of both the physical location in which it is set in the law-code and the scope of perpetrators it envisages. Dishonourable and nefarious crimes in the Lombard laws are either secretive or involve the transgression of gender roles, yet poisoning in the *Edictus* is presented as neither of these. No explicit connection can be drawn between the crimes of *morth* [murder] and poisoning, and the discussion of poisoners in the laws is matter of fact, without imputation of shame or indication that the perpetrator had acted dishonourably. While violence by arms was deemed unfeminine, violence by poison, as constructed in the Lombard laws, appears to present a legitimate means in which a Lombard woman, without being defeminised in the process, could engage equally in causing injury or killing in pursuit of the *faida*. However, poisoning in Lombard law should not be considered as a specifically female crime. In contrast to the construction of binary gender roles, which imputes shame to and masculinises women who commit violence, the laws do not impute shame or dishonour to either men nor women who poison. Poisoning, then, appears to have been a somewhat egalitarian form of killing within the *Edictus*. Moreover, if poisoning is not explicitly deemed nefarious, and it is treated in a comparable fashion to the deliberate open killings by physical means, then the potential for poisoning to be an open, public crime must be considered. The Lombard law-givers' construction of the crime of poisoning allows one to broaden the scope of those who, in Lombard society, could legitimately engage in violence and deliberate killing; likewise, it presents a wider set of contexts in which poison and poisoning might be employed, possibilities that extend far beyond the secretive, heinous and nefarious act of murder.

---

[68] A further example of the imputation of shame to free women for committing specific crimes is theft. The redress from a man is a payment equal to nine times the value stolen. The same amount must also be returned by (the family of) a free woman, but, in addition, the law explicitly states, 'sed vitium suum reputet qui opera indecentem facere temptavit' [let shame be reflected upon her who did this disgraceful deed]. See: Rothari No. 257, Bluhme, ed., *Edictus Langobardorum*, p. 63; Fischer-Drew, trans., *The Lombard Laws*, p. 103.

CHAPTER 15

Murder, Foul and Fair, in Shota Rustaveli's *The Man in the Panther Skin*

G. Koolemans Beynen

SHOTA RUSTAVELI WROTE HIS approximately 6,300-line epic poem *vep'xistqaosani* around 1200 CE in the Caucasus, in Georgia. The title has been translated in various ways, although the literal translation, *In the Leopard Skin*, adequately conveys the theme of the poem: The hero is caught in his animal nature, and the poem tells of his battle to free and control himself. There are five English translations: *The Man in the Panther's Skin* by Marjorie Wardrop, *The Knight in Panther Skin* by Katherine Vivian, *The Knight in the Panther's Skin* by Venera Urushadze, *The Lord of the Panther-skin* by Robert H. Stevenson and *The Knight in the Panther Skin* by Dodona Kiziria and Lyn Coffin.[1] The animal whose skin is so important is called *vep'xi* in Old Georgian, meaning 'leopard'. In Modern Georgian, *vep'xvi*, with an additional *v*, has come to mean 'tiger'; translations use 'panther' or 'tiger', perhaps because of the meaning of Modern Georgian *vep'xvi*.[2] Little is known about the author, whose name means 'Shota from Rustavi'; there are two Georgian towns by that name. He is rumoured to

---

[1] Shot'ha Rust'haveli, *The Man in the Panther's Skin*, trans. Marjorie Wardrop (London: The Royal Asiatic Society of Great Britain and Ireland, 1912; repr. 1966); Shota Rustaveli, *The Knight in Panther Skin*, trans. Katherine Vivian (London: The Folio Society, 1977); Shota Rustaveli, *The Knight in the Panther's Skin*, trans. Venera Urushadze (Tbilisi: Sabchota Sakartvelo, 1968); Shota Rustaveli, *The Lord of the Panther-skin*, trans. R[obert] H[orne] Stevenson (Albany: State University of New York Press, 1977) and Shota Rustaveli, *The Knight in the Panther Skin*, ed. Nodar Natadze, trans. Lyn Coffin, verbatim trans. and ed. Dodona Kiziria (Tbilisi: POEZIA Press, 2015). Georgian does not use capital letters. Georgian words will be transcribed using the Library of Congress Romanization table for Georgian. The Georgian text is from Shota Rustaveli, *vep'xistqaosani* (Tbilisi: Sabchota Sakartvelo, 1975). The English translation is from Wardrop, *The Man in the Panther's Skin*. References to the text of *vep'xistqaosani* will be given by the number of the quatrain in Wardrop's translation, as is usual in Rustaveli studies.

[2] Vaso I. Abaev, 'O fol'klornoi osnove poèmy Shota Rustaveli *Vitiaz' v barsovoi shkure* [On the Folklore Basis of Shota Rustaveli's Poem *The Knight in the Panther Skin*]', *Izvestiia Akademii Nauk SSSR, seriia literatury i iazyka*, 25.4 (July-August 1966): 311; Stevenson, *Lord*, p. xxvi, n. 1.

have been a high court official at the court of Queen Tamar (1184–1213). In 1960, the Russian Academy of Sciences organised an expedition to the Monastery of the Cross in Jerusalem where they found, on a pillar, a fresco of Maxim the Confessor and John of Damascus; between them was the small figure of a kneeling man with a long white beard, accompanied by an epitaph in clumsy Old Georgian asomtavruli letters that reads: 'amis damxat'avsa šotas š[eundve] s ġ[mertma]n [a]min! rust[a]v[e]li' [May God forgive Shota, the painter of this, amen! Rustaveli].[3] *The Man in the Panther Skin* (hereafter *MPS*) has a place in Georgian culture similar to the Bible and Shakespeare's works in English-speaking countries: it is a source of quotations, proverbs and role models.[4] Its importance is illustrated by the fact that it used to be a part of every Georgian woman's trousseau.[5] 'Tinatin', the name of one of the heroines, is a popular name.

The *MPS* starts with idealistic pronouncements about God (1), kings (1), Queen Tamar (3–4), Rustaveli's love for her (5–6) and love in general (8–14), but then the nasty murder of the sleeping Prince of Khvarazmia by Tariel, one of the two heroes of the *MPS*, comes as a shock (542). Tariel's behaviour could be dismissed as the actions of a deranged person: his first appearance in the poem indicates as much when he both asks for help and wants to be left alone (84), while later he calls himself a madman (866, 908). But the real shock is Avtandil's murder of the helpless wine-taster (1093).[6] The two murders show that each murder is not right or wrong in itself, though both are murders of helpless victims; rather, their results determine whether they are right or wrong. Although the murder of a helpless victim is morally bad, the murder of the Prince of Khvarazmia results in the disappearance of Tariel's beloved, and is, therefore, wrong; the murder of the wine-taster results in finding that beloved, and is, therefore, right. Along with the poem's abdications and adoptions, the murders suggest that the same reasoning can be applied to the historical Queen Tamar's ascent to the Georgian throne: if Georgia is flourishing, her ascent must have been right. Rustaveli argues, then, that the end justifies the means, which is a consequentialist ethical philosophy: utilitarianism. The problem with such a reasoning is that it is difficult to predict or anticipate the 'end', that is, the

---

[3] Elguja Khintibidze, *Rustaveli's* The Man in the Panther Skin *and European Literature* (London: Bennett & Bloom, 2011), p. 17; Akaki Gabrielisdze Shanidze, 'Poezdka v Ierusalim [A Visit to Jerusalem]', *Vestnik Akademii nauk SSSR*, 31.8 (August 1961): 91–4. In Old Georgian manuscripts and inscriptions, all but the first and last letter are omitted in frequent words.
[4] Vivian, *Knight*, p. 20.
[5] John Oliver Wardrop, 'Preface', in *The Man in the Panther's Skin*, trans. Marjorie Wardrop, p. iii; David Marshall Lang, *The Georgians* (New York: Praeger, 1966), p. 176.
[6] John Oliver Wardrop, 'Preface', p. vii; Khintibidze, *Rustaveli's*, pp. 90, 91.

results.⁷ Anticipating the results of one's actions is important in consequentialist ethics, and the Arabians are much better in this than the Indians. In the *MPS*, these ethnic terms do not refer to actual ethnic groups but to stages of cognitive development: the term 'Arabians' is used in the *MPS* for people who have the intelligence to foresee the results of their actions while the term 'Indians' stands for people who cannot. For example, when Princess Nestan-Darejan and Tariel, both 'Indians', decide to murder the Prince of Khvarazmia, the results are disastrous, hence their murder is wrong. Avtandil, an 'Arabian', reaches his goal – finding Nestan-Darejan – with his murder of the wine-taster; his murder is, therefore, right.

Rustaveli refers to his poem thus: 'ese ambavi sparsuli, k'art'ulad nat'argmanebi' [This Persian tale, now done into Georgian] (16). Stevenson and Wardrop have assumed that he meant to gain prestige for his poem by presenting it as an originally Persian tale, much like James McPherson ascribed his poems to Ossian.⁸ Persia, after all, enjoyed high prestige in Rustaveli's time.⁹ However, no such Persian tale has been found,¹⁰ and Mariam Karbelashvili has argued that a Persian or Arabic origin is unlikely because of the prominent role of women in the *MPS*.¹¹ But a 'Persian story' need not refer to the geographic origin of the story; in this case, it refers to the ideology of the *MPS*. The *Shahnameh*, too, is 'a Persian tale', and, like the *MPS*, it is a tale with a theory about kingship. Commenting on *Shahnameh's* 'relatively frequent abdications', Dick Davis finds a Middle-Eastern tradition that ascribes to the king 'a quasi-divine position as God's representative on earth'.¹² The *MPS* has a similar theory of kingship: in 1, 39 and 836, Rustaveli defends the divine right of kings: 'misgan ars qovli xelmcip'e saxita mis mierita,' [from Him is every monarch in His likeness](1).

---

[7] Jacques P. Thiroux, *Ethics: Theory and Practice*, 8th edn (Upper Saddle River, NJ: Prentice Hall, 2004), pp. 50–51.
[8] E.g. Stevenson, *Lord*, p. xiii; Donald Rayfield, *Edge of Empires: A History of Georgia* (London: Reaktion, 2012), p. 117; Donald Rayfield, *The Literature of Georgia* (New York: Routledge, 2000), pp. 81–82.
[9] Stevenson, *Lord*, p. xiii; Vivian, *Knight*, p. 25; Rayfield, *Edge*, p. 94; Rayfield, *Literature*, pp. 81–82.
[10] John Oliver Wardrop, 'Preface', *Man*, p. xi; Stevenson, *Lord*, p. xiii.
[11] Mariam Karbelashvili, 'Rustaveli's Poem *The Knight in the Panther's Skin* within the Context of Comparative Studies', *Bulletin of the Georgian Academy of Sciences* 153.3 (1996): 476–77.
[12] Abolqasem Ferdowsi, *Shahnameh: The Persian Book of Kings*, trans. Dick Davis (New York: Penguin, 2006), p. xxiii.

Rustaveli's views are not only Utilitarian[13] for he sees the king 'as a keeper of prosperity in the realm.'[14] His fallacious reasoning here is as follows: monarchs rule by a God-given right, and their rule results in peace; therefore, a successful reign proves that the monarch – Queen Tamar in this case – has the God-given right to rule.[15] Homa Katouzian analyses just such a fallacy, that of affirming the consequent, in *Shahnameh* wherein palace revolutions are justified by their eventual success. Katouzian notes that: 'the *perfect* ruler must have qualities, of which the [Divine] Grace [or *farr*] is only the necessary condition. ... the real test of holding the *farr* was success itself, the fact that the ruler actually held and maintained "supreme power".'[16] Anticipating objections that Queen Tamar's successful reign did not make her claims to the throne legitimate, Rustaveli counters them by referring to a Persian tale, the *Shahnameh* (16), a tale which indicated to Katouzian – and the audience of *Shahnameh* and the *MPS* – that a successful reign *does* legitimise dynastic claims.

Rustaveli's consequentialist ethics aim at justifying the reign of Queen Tamar. Her ascent to the throne was controversial: she was the first female ruler in Georgian history, and her father, Giorgi III, was the younger brother of King Davit V. When the latter died, Davit's son could have succeeded him;[17] instead, he was blinded and castrated and died shortly thereafter.[18] During Tamar's reign, Georgia reached its largest size ever and was the major Christian kingdom of the East, especially after the Fourth Crusade ravaged Constantinople in 1204.[19] Rustaveli gives one example after another showing that the end justifies the means and that, therefore, Tamar's ascent to the throne of Georgia was justified by her successes. He says that he sings Queen Tamar's praises (3–4, 1573), that he is in love with her (15) but also that it is written in praise of Tariel (1576). It may, therefore, not be clear who the poem's hero is, but the consequentialist and utilitarian ethics implied in the two murders in the *MPS* and similar events justify Queen Tamar's right to the throne.

Dianne Farrell, Donald Rayfield, Cecil Bowra, Viktor Zhirmunskii and Eleazar Meletinskii consider the *MPS* a courtly work.[20] Elguja Khintibidze,

---

[13] John Stuart Mill, *Utilitarianism* (London: Parker, Sons and Bourne, 1863), p. 51.
[14] giorgi mč'edlišvili, *šua saukuneebis politikuri azri da vep>xistqaosani* [*Medieval Political Opinion and* The Man in the Panther Skin] (T'bilisi: Mec'niereba, 2000), p. 274.
[15] mč'edlišvili, *šua*, p. 277.
[16] Homa Katouzian, 'Legitimacy and Succession in Iranian History', in *Iran: Politics, History and Literature* (New York: Routledge, 2013), pp. 7, 10.
[17] Rayfield, *Edge*, p. 101; mč'edlišvili, *šua*, p. 273; Ronald Suny, *The Making of the Georgian Nation*, 2nd edn (Bloomington: Indiana University Press, 1994), p. 39.
[18] mč'edlišvili, *šua*, p. 273.
[19] Rayfield, *Edge*, pp. 114, 116.
[20] On the courtly attribution of the text, see: Dianne Ecklund Farrell, *Courtly Love in the Caucasus: Rustaveli's Georgian Epic*, The Knight in the Panther Skin (Pittsburgh:

however, has shown that the love in the *MPS* differs from western courtly love in that its ideal is in 'human happiness, i.e. matrimony'.[21] Moreover, although the poem depicts the typically courtly love between a high-class noble lady and her lower-class lover, the quests in the poem do not prove or test the love of the lover but are more of an affirmation of the logical consequence of that love, what one does for one's beloved. Also, the adultery in the *MPS* differs from most courtly literature in which personal emotions are more important than social conventions like marriage; in the *MPS* adultery is a mere tool to reach a goal, in this case finding Nestan-Darejan's location. Once that has been discovered, the adultery loses its significance and is not mentioned anymore; indeed, it could have been replaced by any other means to find her (e.g. bribery or a magic object). The love in the *MPS* therefore differs significantly from the courtly love described, for example, in the *New Catholic Encyclopedia*.[22] Wardrop mentions the hostility of the Georgian Orthodox Church against Rustaveli.[23] This is most likely because the poem refers to religion in general terms: no mention is made of Christ, Mary or the Trinity, and the heroes and heroines pray to the sun and the planets, the latter addressed by their Arab names.[24] The only known hostile action against the *MPS*, however, was committed by Anton I (1720–1788), the Katholikos or head of the Georgian Orthodox Church, who ordered copies of the *MPS* burned and thrown in the Mtkvari river.[25] The poem's religious vagueness makes it acceptable to adherents of various faiths, but is otherwise hard to explain in a country

University of Pittsburgh Press, 2012), p. 1; Rayfield, *Literature*, p. 80; Cecil Maurice Bowra, *Inspiration and Poetry* (London: Macmillan, 1955), p. 57; Viktor Zhirmunskii, 'Literaturnye otnosheniia vostoka i zapada kak problema sravnitel'nogo literaturovedeniia [Literary Relations between East and West as a Problem of Comparative Literature]', *Trudy iubileinoi sessii LGU: sektsiia fililogicheskikh nauk* (Leningrad: Leningrad State University, 1946), p. 167; and Eleazar Moiseevich Meletinskii, *Srednevekovyi roman* [*The Medieval Novel*] (Moscow: Nauka, 1983), p. 208.

[21] Elguja Khintibidze, *Srednevekovye i renesansnye aspekty poèmy Rustaveli 'vepkhistkaosani'* [*Medieval and Renaissance Trends in Rustaveli's 'Vepkhistkaosani'* (The Man in the Panther's Skin)] (Tbilisi: Tbilisi University Press, 1993), pp. 276–77.

[22] R. H. Green, 'Courtly Love', *New Catholic Encyclopedia*, 2nd edn (Belmont, CA: Thomson Gale, 2003), pp. 318–22.

[23] Rust'haveli, *The Man*, p. iv.

[24] Donald Rayfield, *The Literature of Georgia: A History*, 2nd rev. edn (Richmond, Surrey: Curzon Press, 2000), p. 77; Vivian, *Knight*, p. 22; Howard I. Aronson and Dodona Kiziria, *Georgian Language and Culture: A Continuing Course* (Bloomington: Slavica, 1999), p. 268; Alexander Mikaberidze, *Historical Dictionary of Georgia*, 2nd edn (Lanham, MD: Rowman & Littlefield, 2015), p. 598.

[25] Timothy [Gabashvili], Archbishop of Kartli, *Moxilûa cmindata da sxûata aǧmosavletisa adgilta* [*A Visit to Holy and Other Sites of the East*], ed. Platon Ioseliani (Tpilisi, 1852), p. 154; quoted in Jost Gippert and Manana Tandaschwili, *Schota Rusthaweli, Der Recke im Tigerfell: Ein altgeorgisches Poem. Deutsche Nachdichtung von Hugo Huppert* (Wiesbaden: Reichert Verlag, 2014), p. 7.

that prides itself on being the second state in history to accept Christianity as a state religion (in 334 or 317 CE), a good half century before Byzantium.[26]

The narrative in the poem starts after the Prologue (1–36) with a description of the hunt following the abdication of King Rostevan of Arabia. During the hunt, a mysterious noble appears, clad in a leopard skin: 'mas tansa kaba emosa gare-t'ma vep'xis tqavisa, vep'xis tqavisa k'udive iqo sark'meli t'avisa' [His form was clad in a long coat over which was thrown a panther's skin, his head, too, was covered with a cap of panther's skin] (85). King Rostevan invites the stranger to join in the festivities, which the stranger turns down, a most serious insult among Georgians. When the king's slaves try to enforce the invitation, the stranger fights them off, inflicting bloody casualties. King Rostevan's daughter, Tinatin, then eventually instructs Avtandil, Arabia's commander-in-chief and her lover, to find the stranger. Avtandil finds him – Tariel – who then tells his story.

Tariel is the son of King Saridan, who rules over one of the seven kingdoms of India. King Saridan gives his kingdom away to King Parsadan, ruler over the other six (303), who then makes King Saridan his commander-in-chief. He also adopts Tariel, as his marriage had been childless (308–09), and Tariel eventually succeeds his father as King Parsadan's commander-in-chief. Then, the Queen of India gives birth to a daughter, Nestan-Darejan, and even though Tariel had been adopted unconditionally – for example, without specifying when the adoption could be cancelled – and had started living with his adopted parents, he was sent home and the adoption was cancelled: 'mep'e k'alsa vit' xedvida mep'obisa k'mnisa mct'romsa, mamasave xelt'a mimc'es' [Since the king looked upon the maiden as the heir to the kingship, he gave me back into the hands of my father] (317).[27]

Tariel and Nestan-Darejan grow up and eventually fall in love rather dramatically; indeed, Tariel faints upon first meeting Nestan-Darejan, remaining unconscious for three days: 'samsa dġesa darbazs viqav ar c'oc'xali, arc'a mkvdali' [For three days I was in the palace, neither alive, nor dead] (341). Years later, the king convenes a council and announces his plan to marry his daughter (Nestan-Darejan) to the Prince of Khvarazmia (493) because, as the queen says: 'xvarazmša mep'ea morčmit' mjdomeli, mat'xamc'a švilsa sasiżod č'vent'vis sxva sjobda romeli' [Khvarazmia's shah is a king reigning with power. Who could be better than his son for our son-in-law!] (497). The prospective groom's father is a king, and the marriage would make him an ally of India; his son is, therefore, preferable to Tariel, who is, after all, only one of King Parsadan's employees.

Tariel is part of the council, but he is so shocked by the decision that he meekly agrees. Not so Nestan-Darejan, who is furious when she hears about

---

[26] Rayfield, *Edge*, p. 39.
[27] In Georgian, *mama* means 'father', while *deda* means 'mother'.

the marriage plans (506). The lovers now have several options: they could, for example, try to talk King Parsadan and his queen out of the marriage plans, they could elope or they could overthrow the royal couple and crown themselves king and queen. Instead, Tariel follows Nestan-Darejan's order to kill the prince in his sleep while sparing the prince's soldiers (541).

This murder is the foul murder of the title: its consequences are calamitous since the murder violates not only the laws of hospitality but also the rules of knightly behaviour and fair combat. Killing someone in his sleep is cowardly and completely incomprehensible, especially since Tariel is an almost supernaturally invincible fighter who earlier 'ert'ob srulad amovcqvide cina kerżi razmi ori' [completely destroyed at one onslaught the two front squadrons] (432) of the rebellious Khatavians, who had stopped paying tribute to the Indians. Later, talking about a naval battle, he says: '… ; k'usli vhkar da davuk'c'ie, …' [… I struck [one of the ships] with my heel and upset it] (597). Since Tariel easily destroys 'two front squadrons', he can also easily defeat the Prince of Khvarazmia, about whose prowess in battle nothing is said. There is, therefore, no need to kill him in his sleep. The murder of the prince is about as low as it gets, and the result is utter chaos. But then, later, in Gulansharo, Avtandil commits a similar murder, which results in locating Nestan-Darejan, not chaos. Murder, even in its most reprehensible form, Rustaveli explains, is neither right nor wrong, but one must know when to murder and when not to murder. Tariel and Nestan-Darejan do not, but Avtandil does know when an otherwise cowardly murder is appropriate.

Nestan-Darejan's plan is irrational; that is, she instructs Tariel to pretend that he murdered the prince not because he wanted to marry her but because he objected to the rule of a foreign prince over his 'heritage'. But, first, Tariel's father, King Saridan, voluntarily gave up his kingdom to King Parsadan, which was the right of Georgian kings, though they almost always chose their eldest son as a successor.[28] Hence, Tariel has no right to what his father gave away. Second, his father gave only his own kingdom away and Tariel has no rights to the other six that are part of King Parsadan's kingdom. Nestan-Darejan's plan was that she would then offer to marry him as a face-saving compromise. Tariel would then get what he supposedly wanted, India, while King Parsadan would then supposedly not yield to his demands. But killing a guest, especially the son of a neighbouring ruler (and in his sleep), cannot go unpunished; hence, her plan has no merit, and she and Tariel anticipate the wrong results.

The seriousness of Tariel's violations leaves the king no choice: the murder of the prince must be avenged, and Tariel must be killed. But no army can take on a hero like Tariel, and King Parsadan watches in powerless fury as India collapses in chaos. To make things worse, the king blames his sister Davar for the murder

---

[28] Rayfield, *Edge*, p. 101.

because she was responsible for Nestan-Darejan's upbringing. Davar then arranges Nestan-Darejan's kidnapping and commits suicide (565). After Davar's death, no one knows where Nestan-Darejan is, and Tariel starts a fruitless search that lasts for over three years until Avtandil finally locates her and he and Tariel free her.

The fair murder is a rational murder committed for rational considerations, as Khintibidze and John Oliver Wardrop explain.[29] After hearing Tariel's story, Avtandil takes over the search for Nestan-Darejan because Tariel is too depressed. First, however, he returns to Arabia to get permission from Tinatin to continue his quest as a search for Nestan-Darejan. Avtandil's search is a model of rationality: he goes to where Nestan-Darejan was last seen and then travels around with a group of merchants till they arrive at a large harbour town, Gulansharo.[30] There, pretending to be a merchant, he goes to pay obeisance to the Dean of Merchants, who oversees the trade in Gulansharo. The Dean is absent and his wife, Patman, takes care of his business. Avtandil visits her, and she is attracted to him; he does not discourage her because she seems well informed and may, therefore, help in his search for Nestan-Darejan. She invites him to her house, but on his way to their meeting, a slave of hers meets Avtandil and asks him not to come. Avtandil decides to ignore the message, which is hardly polite, but it turns out to be the right decision. When he arrives, Patman is tense and nervous. The reason soon becomes clear: the King of Gulansharo's wine-taster arrives. His visit had apparently been announced some time before, which is why she tried to cancel Avtandil's visit. The wine-taster, who had been blackmailing Patman into granting him sexual favours, is angered by Avtandil presence. He leaves in a fury, uttering dire threats: 'var šent'a švilt'a šenit'a kbilit'a damajmevelad' [I shall make thee to devour thy children with thy teeth] (1079). Patman tells Avtandil that the wine-taster's revenge will be terrible and asks Avtandil to kill him or flee and abandon her and her family to their fate. Avtandil decides to rescue her and leaves for the wine-taster's house. He enters and kills him as the wine-taster tries to get up from his bed: 'veġar aescra, idumal mok'la, verc'a vc'anit'a' [he gave him no time to rise, privily he slew him, we could not have perceived it] (1093).

This murder is unworthy of a hero like Avtandil, and the act resembles Tariel's murder of the Prince of Khvarazmia. In both cases, a superior fighter kills a weaker opponent while unnecessarily ignoring the rules of fair fight. However, the similarity between the two killings brings out their difference: one is right and one is wrong. Avtandil kills the wine-taster for understandable reasons – not only

---

[29] Elguja Khintibidze, 'Lancelot and Avtandil', *The Kartvelologist: Journal of Georgian Studies* 9 (Autumn 2002): 30–31; John Oliver Wardrop, 'Preface', pp. vii–viii.
[30] Persian *gulan shahr*, 'city of roses'; Stevenson, *Lord*, p. 213 n. 19. Gulansharo could possibly be modelled after Venice.

is the wine-taster blackmailing Patman but he also threatens to kill her, which is problematic because she is Avtandil's only source of information on Nestan-Darejan. Even though that does not make the murder of a defenceless person good, the murder's positive results – finding Nestan-Darejan – make it right. In contrast, Tariel's earlier murder of the prince is impulsive and badly thought out, it ends with disastrous results, and is, therefore, bad and wrong. Avtandil's priority is to keep his source of information, Patman, safe. He could have killed the wine-taster in a fair fight, but any delay in the killing – for instance, giving the wine-taster time to write his last will, get good weapons, say farewell to relatives or pray – could give him an opportunity for revenge and eliminate Avtandil's source of information.

Later in the *MPS* Rustaveli describes how, unbeknownst to Avtandil and Tariel, there were plans to marry Nestan-Darejan to a Kaji prince, which would have made a marriage to Tariel difficult, if not impossible. Therefore, it is imperative – even though in hindsight – to kill the wine-taster because any delay could result in Nestan-Darejan's marriage.

Rustaveli argues that murder is complicated, even in its most despicable forms: one must know when to murder, and one needs a well-developed conceptual apparatus to murder well. A right murder is a murder with right results, and Rustaveli makes a similar argument about other actions like adoptions, adultery, abdications and spending money. The elephant in the room is the historical Queen Tamar, or, rather, her father Giorgi III, who executed his cousin Demna, the son of Giorgi's older brother Davit V, who might have had more rights to the throne than Tamar. This happened when Tamar was probably seventeen years old and seven years before she became queen, which clearly absolves her from any complicity in the crime.[31] But Rustaveli implies that one should know when to commit atrocities, and Queen Tamar's glorious reign justifies Demna's execution, no matter who carried it out.

During his stay in Gulansharo, Avtandil commits adultery in addition to murder. But, like the murder, his adultery is rational and has right results, so Rustaveli does not condemn it. When Avtandil realises that Patman is a useful source of information, he accepts her invitation in the hope that she can lead him to Nestan-Darejan. After Avtandil's murder of the wine-taster, he and Patman spend the night together. Rustaveli explains that Avtandil has mixed feelings about the tryst, saying to himself: 'mnaxet', mijnurno, igi, vin vardia visad, umisod nexvt'a zeda vzi bulbuli msgavsad qvavisad' ['Look at me, lovers, who has a rose of my own! Without her, I, the nightingale, like a carrion-crow, sit on a dung heap'] (1231). Patman has a different perspective, and Rustaveli comments ironically: 'p'atman mas zeda ixarebs mart' vit'a iadonia. t'u qvavi vardsa išovnis,

---

[31] mč>edlišvili, šua, 273; Rayfield, *Edge*, p. 105.

t'avi bulbuli hgonia' [Patman rejoiced in him as if she were a nightingale; if a crow finds a rose, it thinks itself a nightingale] (1232).[32] Rustaveli seems to mock Patman's zeal in the tryst while validating Avtandil's detached moral fortitude. Rayfield calls her Rustaveli's 'Wife of Bath': a 'lowly character ... who lives by [her] wits and appetites' while Avtandil feels free to use her like aristocrats use commoners in a feudal society.[33] But Tariel sets the record straight when he says to her: 'me t'avi šeni midia, dav, guli šeni č'emzeda gardauxdeli didia' ['I adopt thee as my sister. O sister, great is my unpayable debt to thy heart'] (1419). After all, she has been instrumental in finding Nestan-Darejan, and it is not surprising that scholars have looked askance at the 'coldness and wiles' of Avtandil, who treats her rather shabbily.[34]

Avtandil turns out to be right: after spending the night together, Patman provides information that helps him find Nestan-Darejan, and he and Tariel free her. After Nestan-Darejan's liberation, she and Tariel marry, as do Tinatin and Avtandil, and everyone lives happily ever after. This result, Rustaveli tells his readers, justifies the adultery as it does the murder of the wine-taster, reinforcing Rustaveli's argument that Queen Tamar's accomplishments justify her reign, in general, and the fate of her cousin Demna, specifically.

In a similar vein, Rustaveli also describes two abdications: one that is rational, like Avtandil's murder, and another that is irrational and impulsive, like Tariel's. As with the murders, the results of the abdications justify the actions committed by the protagonists, as they do the historical Queen Tamar's reign. King Rostevan's abdication is rational: he realises the country needs a new ruler and wants to be sure that his daughter will be a worthy successor. Therefore, he checks with his advisors and proceeds only after they have approved, assuring him that 'lekvi lomisa scoria, żu iqos, t'unda xvadia' [The lion's whelps are equal (alike lions), be they male or female] (39). On the other hand, King Saridan's abdication (if one could call it that) is irrational and impulsive because he does it out of loneliness: 'xalva moszulda, šeekmna guls kaešant'a jarebi' [He hated solitude; it created hosts of cares in his heart] (302). With his gift, he destroys his family's source of income and forces his son Tariel to become an employee rather than an independent ruler. When Tariel falls in love with Parsadan's daughter (Nestan-Darejan), Parsadan prefers an independent ruler (albeit a future one, the son of the Shah of Khvarazmia) over Tariel as a son-in-law. If Tariel had succeeded his father as king, he would have been considered equal to the Prince of Khvarazmia

---

[32] Rustaveli first uses the Greek word for 'nightingale', iadoni, and then the Turkic, bulbuli, to avoid repetition and to characterise Patman as someone for which there is no Georgian equivalent.

[33] Rayfield, Literature, pp. 79–80.

[34] Khintibidze, Srednevekovye, p. 90.

and would have had better prospects with Nestan-Darejan. King Rostevan's handling of the succession, on the one hand, shows his diligence because he checks with his advisors before his abdication. On the other hand, the impulsiveness of King Parsadan, who does not bother asking anybody's advice about a successor, and who does not ask about his daughter's marital preference, is obvious. He is only interested in the alliance with the groom's father. In not seeking the advice and wisdom of his counsellors, he undermines the stability of his own rule.

King Saridan's abdication is also an impulsive and irrational act of liberality that contrasts with Tinatin's act when she ascends to the throne; indeed, she more or less invites her subjects to empty the state treasury, which they do: 'alap'obdes sačurčlesa missa, vit'a nat'urkalsa' [They pillaged her treasury as 'twere booty from Turks] (55). She does not act on an impulse, like King Saridan, but on the advice of her father who tells her that that is what kings do, that they are supposed to be generous: 'mep'et'a šigan siuxve, vit' edems alva, rgulia ... rasac'a gasc'em, šenia; ... rac' ara, dakargulia' [Munificence in kings is like the aloe planted in Eden ... What thou givest away is thine; what thou keepest is lost] (50). Wardrop notes that Aristotle lists liberality among the virtues, hence both Aristotle and her father consider Tinatin's generosity rational.[35] Medieval Georgia was heavily influenced by Byzantium and its philosophers and theologians, among whom Aristotle was paramount. This liberality, even though recorded around 1200 CE, agrees well with the somewhat exaggerated generosity and hospitality that has long been considered a characteristic of the Georgians and the peoples of the Caucasus.[36] Tinatin, then, more or less bankrupts Arabia but, just as Avtandil knows when to murder, so Tinatin knows when to squander money; likewise, Queen Tamar knows when to murder and, in general, how to rule.

There are two adoptions in the *MPS* and, just like the two murders, there is a right and a wrong adoption. The Indian adoption – King Parsadan's adoption of King Saridan's son – is impulsive and irrational because King Parsadan should have anticipated the possibility of his wife's pregnancy. As it is, the adoption results in a series of disasters. There is also an Arabian counterpart to Parsadan's adoption: King Rostevan, upon being told that Avtandil has left to begin his search for Nestan-Darejan without the king's permission, exclaims: 'va, gazrdilo...', which Marjorie Wardrop translates as 'Alas, my foster-son ...' (802). In 82 and 805, too, Rostevan refers to Avtandil as his 'foster-son', hence Rostevan

---

[35] Marjorie Wardrop, trans., *Man*, p. 9; Aristotle, *Nicomachean Ethics*, 2nd edn., trans. H. Rackham (Cambridge, MA: Harvard University Press, 1975), p. 189; Khintibidze, *Srednevekovye*; Vivian, *Knight*, pp. 3–5.

[36] See: Roger Rosen, *Georgia: A Sovereign Nation of the Caucasus* (Hong Kong: Odyssey, 1999), pp. 13, 41; Neil Wilson et al., *Georgia, Armenia & Azerbaijan* (Hawthorne, Australia: Lonely Planet, 2000), p. 16; Peter Nasmyth, *Georgia: In the Mountains of Poetry* (Richmond, Surrey: Curzon Press, 2001), p. 82.

considers Avtandil his *de facto* adopted son, an adoption with the right results of a rational action. Adoptions may be similar, Rustaveli says, but they may have different consequences. Rational people (and good rulers) know when to adopt, just as they know when to murder. Irrational people do not.

In the *MPS* Rustaveli distinguishes three types of people. First, people like Avtandil and Tinatin, who excel in whatever they do, especially because they can successfully anticipate the results of their actions. They have the ability to think rationally, to anticipate which actions will lead to the desired results. Rustaveli calls these kinds of people 'Arabians', even though neither they nor their cities or regions have Arab names or characteristics. Second, people like King Saridan, King Parsadan, Nestan-Darejan and, especially, Tariel, who, particularly in the first part of the *MPS*, may be good fighters but whose decisions lead to disasters because they lack intelligence and cannot correctly anticipate results. Their actions – a murder, an abdication or an adoption – are disastrous. They are impulsive, and such people Rustaveli labels 'Indians', also without any Indian names or characteristics. Tariel is initially in the second category; that is, he is an outstanding fighter, but he lacks intelligence. For example, he should have spoken up when King Parsadan announced his daughter's marriage and argued that he has a record of victories over the Khatavians; he should have pointed out that his father, like the father of the Prince of Khvarazmia, was a king; and, most importantly, he should have declared that he and Nestan-Darejan were in love. Additionally, he should not have followed Nestan-Darejan's advice to kill the prince but should have tried for a better solution. Third, Tariel, though initially one of the 'Indians', is in a group by himself; that is, he is a third type of person, and a man who has an ability to develop his intelligence and rational thinking, to 'become an Arabian', so to speak, a facility which King Saridan and King Parsadan do not have. Tariel eventually changes, and even surpasses Avtandil, when he comes up with the winning plan for freeing Nestan-Darejan, which shows he has acquired the 'Arabian' intelligence that enables him to anticipate results.

Rustaveli's classification of people into three types ultimately goes back to Alcmaeon of Croton (c. 400 BCE) who distinguished two types of living beings, man and animals, and who taught that man differs from animals in that only man understands, while animals perceive but do not understand.[37] Aristotle agreed with Alcmaeon, as both thought that animals perceive and then act on the basis of the stimuli they receive (e.g. try to eat, avoid or attack what they perceive), while humans use intelligence to decide what to do because they understand

---

[37] Hermann Diels and Walther Kranz, *Fragmente der Vorsokratiker*, 6th edn., 2 vols (Zürich: Weidmann, 1951; repr. 1985), 1: 211–13 (A5), 215 (B1a).

causal relations and can anticipate the consequences of their actions.[38] Rustaveli adds to Alcmaeon's and Aristotle's classification that some humans – the Indians in the *MPS* – can be like animals; that is, they react to stimuli but cannot anticipate the consequences of their actions. Though Indians are like animals, some of them can learn to use their minds, becoming complete humans and foreseeing the results of what they do, like Tariel.

Murder in the *MPS* is the touchstone for cognitive development, and only those who are cognitively well developed and hence rational can handle murder well. And the more repulsive the murder, the better a touchstone it is. Thus, a superior ruler can make reprehensible actions have right results, like Queen Tamar. The rationalisations of the 'correct' murders in the *MPS* justify and rationalise any excesses of Queen Tamar's rule.

The importance of the leopard in the *MPS* is indicated by its occurrence in the poem's title and the cases wherein leopards and people are compared. The leopard and its skin characterise the impulsive stage of cognitive development. Wearing a leopard skin indicates that the wearer is overwhelmed by his impulsive animal nature. Tariel wears the leopard skin throughout the middle part of the *MPS*: he cannot control his animal nature. Avtandil, however, never wears a leopard skin because he controls his animal nature and activates it only when fighting, as he does when fighting the pirates (1020). He is never overwhelmed by his animal leopard nature. When Tariel fights the Khatavians (364–456), he also displays his fighting skills, but he controls his animal nature. Since he has not yet lost Nestan-Darejan, her loss has not yet made him uncontrollable and, therefore, he does not yet appear in a leopard skin. Later, when overwhelmed by grief over her loss, he cannot control himself, and he wears the leopard skin.

Tariel resembles a leopard most of all, although he is never explicitly compared to one because his leopard skin is sufficient. He starts wearing it when Nestan-Darejan's disappearance (565) presents him with an unsolvable problem, and he stops wearing it sometime during Avtandil's stay in Gulansharo (after 672). The most important characters in the *MPS* have a 'leopard episode' in their lives during which they have the leopard's positive (courage) or negative (helpless frustration) characteristic for a short period of time. Tariel, however, has a 'leopard interval'. He spends more than three years after Nestan-Darejan's kidnapping in helpless frustration, indicated by his continually wearing a leopard skin. In short: wearing a leopard skin shows that the person is controlled by his animal nature, while being compared with a leopard signals that the person is either a courageous and good fighter or a person who cannot solve the problem at hand.

---

[38] A[lfred] E[dward] Taylor, *Aristotle*, rev. edn (Mineola, NY: Dover, 1919, repr. 1955), p. 78.

Leopards kill humans, but they do not murder them because, as animals, leopards lack the cognitive ability to murder. And, while in the *MPS* a successful murder is the ultimate test for being a good ruler, Tariel has failed this test; before 672, he still is a 'leopard' without the cognitive capability to murder. He will acquire this capability during Avtandil's stay in Gulansharo. Then, he combines his leopard power to kill with his newly acquired rational powers, murders the soldiers guarding Nestan-Darejan and frees her (1392).

Similar to his distinctions regarding murder, Rustaveli's descriptions of love as actual events, rather than theoretical discourses, begin with the love between Tinatin and Avtandil. Their love is unusual in that there is no beginning of it. When the poem starts, their love is already there – it just is. This is unlike most emotions or events in the *MPS* that have a beginning or a cause. For example, King Parsadan's request that Tariel bring Nestan-Darejan partridges is the beginning of their love (330), but the love between Avtandil and Tinatin is the cause of everything else in the poem. Tinatin says to Avtandil: 'asre git'xra, samsaxuri č'emi gmart'ebs amad orad: pirvel: … merme, č'emi mijnuri xar … cadi, igi moqme žebne …' [This service of mine which I bid thee do befits thee for two reasons: First … Secondly, thou art in love with me … Go, and seek that brother-in-arms …] (129). She tells him she can ask him to search for Tariel because of his love for her, and that is where the poem's actions begin. Khintibidze discusses the philosophical and literary aspects of love in the *MPS* in relation to love's role in other European works,[39] but within the *MPS* love is like the other events in the poem in that it, like murder, has both right and wrong results.

Tinatin and Avtandil's love has right results: happiness for all, including Tariel and Nestan-Darejan (eventually), and, as such, is the opposite of the love between Tariel and Nestan-Darejan. The latter's love has wrong results because it is impulsive and irrational; that is, Tariel faints when first seeing Nestan-Darejan (335), and their love initially results in the murder of the Prince and, then, in long-lasting chaos. But Tinatin, who develops an interest in Tariel, eventually salvages their love, as does Avtandil, who locates Nestan-Darejan. The love of Tinatin and Avtandil thus turns out to be more powerful than the love between Tariel and Nestan-Darejan because rational people, like the former couple, can handle murder, adoptions and love and still obtain right results. Irrational and impulsive people cannot. The love of Tinatin, whose similarity to Queen Tamar has been noted, is all-powerful;[40] eventually, it is more rational and, hence, stronger than the love between Nestan-Darejan and Tariel. After all, until

---

[39] Khintibidze, *Rustaveli's*, pp. 143–64.
[40] Rayfield, *Literature*, p. 79.

recently, Queen Tamar was worshiped as a goddess; thus, one can expect the love of Tinatin, who was modeled after Tamar, to be magically all-powerful.[41]

Friendship is also an important factor in the *MPS*, and scholars have argued whether the poem's primary subject is love or friendship.[42] Among the elements in the *MPS*, friendship is unusual in that it is never rational; indeed, it is always irrational and impulsive, but it always has right results. Tinatin has a sudden, impulsive interest in Tariel; she hears about him in the beginning of the poem after the hunt organised by Avtandil, knows almost nothing about him (like everybody else) and, at the end of the *MPS*, actually sees him for the first time at her wedding to Avtandil. Avtandil's friendship for Tariel is equally irrational and inexplicable as he had been ordered to establish Tariel's identity but, having done so, somehow becomes his friend rather than going home after having fulfilled his quest. When Avtandil and Tariel meet for the first time, they could not be more different: Tariel is depressed, and he ignores or attacks people when he meets them. He also has no idea how to search for Nestan-Darejan. Avtandil sees the solution to Tariel's problems, and he goes about finding Nestan-Darejan in a rational way, but friendship develops between Avtandil and Tariel despite their differences. Statemanship, a grim and Machiavellian affair in the *MPS*, is also counterbalanced by a friendship that can do no wrong: the friendship between Avtandil and Tariel leads to murder (1092) and adultery (1230), but these events are right because of their results. Moreover, their friendship develops after Tinatin has expressed an interest in the mysterious man in the panther skin. Of course, her interest is more motherly than anything else, but it could have made other lovers jealous. Not so Avtandil, whose self-effacing friendship is strong enough to keep him not only from being jealous but also from being envious when Tariel proposes the better plan for freeing Nestan-Darejan. The friendship between Tariel and Asmat (Nestan-Darejan's maid) also leads only to right results. (e.g. 256, 1330–36) The world of the *MPS* is a nasty place, wherein murders of helpless victims (possibly even Queen Tamar's cousin) are justified, but it is brightened by friendship, including a friendship in which a young and inexperienced queen brings two strangers together, randomly but successfully. The magic of friendship is such that it takes hold and eventually allows all to live happily ever after.

Friendship provides a foil for the instances of murder and adultery. On the one hand, Rustaveli claims that human actions, like murder and adultery, are

---

[41] Yves Bonnefoy, 'The Religion and the Myths of the Georgians of the Mountains', in *American, African and Old European Mythologies* (Chicago: University of Chicago Press, 1993), p. 255.

[42] See: Viktor Gol'tsev, *Shota Rustaveli*, 2nd edn (Moscow: GIKhL, 1956), pp. 86–87; Gerhard Deeters, *Georgische Literatur*, Handbuch der Orientalistik, Abt. 1, Bd 7 (Leiden: Brill, 1963), p. 142.

relative: they may be right or wrong depending on their rationality and results, and only rational people handle human actions well. Friendship, on the other hand, is an absolute right. It always results in harmony and peace and, thanks to friendship, even impulsive and irrational love leads to right results. Others have noted this unique quality of friendship. Centuries after Rustaveli, Georg Hegel and, then, Emmanuel Levinas posited that humans receive their identity by being noticed by an 'Other'. Hegel assumes that 'self-consciousness ... *is* only by being acknowledged or "recognized"', without giving a reason why this would be so; it simply happens or it does not.[43] Levinas, on the other hand, sees it as a basic factor in the creation of personalities: 'The Other becomes my neighbor precisely through the way the face summons me ...'. Levinas calls this 'summoning' factor, absent in Hegel, 'guiltless responsibility'.[44] It makes first Tinatin and then Avtandil care for Tariel in a friendship that is irrational and impulsive, yet results in harmony and peace. The love in the *MPS* is more spectacular and more eloquently described than friendship, but it is friendship that gets the job done and brings about happy endings for both couples. Both Levinas and Rustaveli argue that, in humanity, an innate goodness and interest in fellow human beings exists, transforming chaos into goodness. Human actions, Rustaveli explains, are ambivalent, but friendship brings order and goodness in life; indeed, Avtandil's friendship for Tariel compels him to murder the wine-taster, but that eventually brings happiness to the heroes and heroines. Murder, especially the cowardly murder of a sleeping or slumbering opponent, poses the greatest challenge because it is hard to get right results and happiness from such a murder. But Avtandil manages: the murder he commits is right because of the results he gets, and the murder that Tariel commits is right with their friendship. And, as Rustaveli implies, if Georgia was so prosperous under Queen Tamar, then the murder of her cousin must have been rational and right, too.

Murder is a most important and consequential action in the *MPS*; indeed, the murder of the Prince of Khvarazmia explodes society (542) and the murder of the wine-taster (1092) eventually restores it. But murder is nothing more than a tool, although a very powerful one because of the killing it involves. In the *MPS* people use adoption or adultery as tools for social goals, but none of these tools has the impact of murder with its biological and a societal component. Humans are not the only ones who kill other humans, animals do too, but only the leopard has become a part of Georgian culture; its killing only has a biological factor

[43] Georg Friedrich Wilhelm Hegel, 'The Phenomenology of the Spirit', in *The Philosophy of Hegel*, ed. Carl J. Friedrich, trans. James B. Baillie (New York: The Modern Library, 1954), p. 399.
[44] Emmanuel Levinas, 'Ethics as First Philosophy', in *The Continental Philosophy Reader*, ed. Richard Kearny and Mara Rainwater (New York: Routledge, 1996), p. 131.

and no societal implications. It is a 'pure' murderer and, therefore, it is not surprising that the leopard figures in the *MPS* compare human characteristics to those of leopards, especially courage based on hunting and fighting ability. The leopard's importance in Georgian culture is evident from 'the most moving of folk poems', *The Poem of the Youth and the Panther*.[45] The 85-line poem describes a fight between a young hunter and a leopard that does not seem to have had a cause; rather, the leopard suddenly attacks the hunter who happened to be stalking deer. Both die – a draw, so to speak – emphasising the similarities and equality of leopards and people. On the basis of this poem, Ossetian scholar Vaso Abaev proposes that Georgians see the leopard as almost identical with humans and, thus, as a role model: Georgians aim at becoming hunters and fighters as accomplished as leopards.[46] Both leopards and Georgians are good hunters and because they both hunt deer they occupy the same ecological niche. Leopards may kill, but they do not murder because they lack the intelligence to do so. In the *MPS* murder is something leopards cannot do, only people, and, therefore, it is essentially a human act. Claude Lévi-Strauss found a similar situation in the tales of South American Indians who see the jaguar as almost human. These tales are actually stories about what makes people human. The difference between humans and jaguars is that humans have fire, the basis for civilisation, according to the South American Indians; otherwise, a human is basically a jaguar.[47] Abaev argues that the difference between leopards and Georgians is that Georgians have empathy. In *The Poem of the Youth and the Panther*, the mother of the hunter goes to console the leopard's mother, as she, too, has lost a child; the leopard's mother does not commiserate because she cannot empathise. Kevin Tuite refutes this assertion, however, arguing that it is based on only one late nineteenth-century variant of the ballad.[48]

Likewise, material from the *MPS* contradicts Abaev's assertion. Like Abaev and Lévi-Strauss, Rustaveli sees a difference between people and leopards (in his case), but Rustaveli regards people as creatures who think rationally and anticipate the results of their actions. They have intelligence, which leopards lack. Leopards excel at hunting and fighting but not at handling social interactions and causal relations, in which rational thinking is required. Rustaveli compares

---

[45] Rayfield, *Literature*, p. 204; *Anthology of Georgian Poetry*, ed. Mikheil Kvesselava, trans. Venera Urushadze (Tbilisi: Soviet Georgia, 1958), pp. 248–50.

[46] Vasilii Abaev, 'O fol'klornoi osnove poèmy Shota Rustaveli *Vitiaz' v barsovoi shkure*' [On the Folklore Basis of Shota Rustaveli's Poem *The Knight in the Panther Skin*], *Izvestiia AN SSSR, seriia literatury i iazyka*, 25.4 (July–August 1966): 311.

[47] Claude Lévi-Strauss, *The Raw and the Cooked: Introduction to a Science of Mythology* (New York: Harper and Row, 1970), p. 132.

[48] Kevin Tuite, *Violet on the Mountain: An Anthology of Georgian Folk Poetry* (Madison, NJ: Fairleigh Dickinson University Press, 1994), p. 120.

outstanding fighters and courageous people to leopards, but he makes a similar comparison when he wants to show how inept the characters are at activities requiring the ability to anticipate results and solve problems. For example: Avtandil prepares for battle with pirates by donning his armour: 'č'aic'va tansa abjari k'c'evit'a vep'xebr mkrč'xalit'a' [With gesture like a swift panther he clad his form in armour] (1020). The comparison with the panther underlines Avtandil's fighting capability. Similarly, Nestan-Darejan goes to meet the King of Gulansharo: 'adga asre gul-ušišrad, vep'xi iqo anu gmiri' [she rose as fearless as if she were a panther or a hero] (1154); here, the comparison with the leopard indicates her courage, although she is not going to fight.

Additionally, comparisons with the leopard emphasise a character's powerless fury, resentment and frustration caused by his or her inability to find the right solution. First, after her kidnapping by her aunt Davar, Nestan-Darejan arrives in Gulansharo where Patman frees her. Nestan-Darejan stays with Patman and her husband, Usen, the dean of merchants, who try to help her. Nestan-Darejan, alone in a foreign country, does not speak but weeps. If she had used her intelligence, she could have, for example, told her hosts about her relationship to the Indian royal family who would reward her hosts for returning her, or she could have threatened them with the wrath of her lover Tariel or of her Indian relatives. Instead, confused and clueless like a leopard, she sits and mopes: 'vep'xi-avaza pir-k'ušad zis' [The coursing-panther sits sullen-faced] (1137). Second, Tariel explains that he wears the leopard skin because it reminds him of Nestan-Darejan: 'rome vep'xi švenieri saxed misad damisaxavs' [Since a beautiful panther is portrayed to me as her image] (639). He remembers her the way he last saw her, unhappy and unable to control her life and, like a leopard, unable to come up with a logical, rational solution. When she is courageous, she is compared to a leopard (1154), but she is also compared to a leopard when she cannot come up with a plan to reach her goal.

Lastly, when Tariel meets Nestan-Darejan after the announcement of her marriage to the Prince of Khvarazmia, Rustaveli compares her to a panther in her fury: 'k've cva, vit' kldisa napralsa vep'xi pir-gamexebuli' [She crouched, like a leopard on the edge of a rock, her face flashing fury] (506). There is nothing she can do; a leopard can fight and attack, but neither of these actions is appropriate now. She is frustrated because she cannot come up with the right solution. The comparisons with the leopard suggest that the person is at a loss about what to do because (s)he does not find the right solution.

Rustaveli does not portray Nestan-Darejan in a flattering light. True, Tariel is madly in love with her, but the one action for which she is responsible, the murder of the Prince of Khvarazmia, is a disaster. The true heroine of the *MPS* is Tinatin, an all-wise ruling queen who represents Queen Tamar. The structure of the poem dictates that she is portrayed as vastly superior to any other female so as not to confuse the audience into thinking that anyone else is the heroine. The Russian folklorist Skaftymov discusses a similar situation in Russian epic songs (the *byliny*) in which various heroes are portrayed against the background of Russian history, including Prince Vladimir, the eventual king and saint. The audience of the *byliny* could, of course, mistake Vladimir for the hero of the poem, but he was portrayed as lazy and slow-witted to prevent this from happening. Marxist folklorists explain Vladimir's portrayal as evidence for the democratic and anti-monarchist nature of Russian folk-art, but Skaftymov argues that Vladimir's image aimed at keeping him apart from the real hero of the *byliny*.[49] In the *MPS*, too, Nestan-Darejan's image is clearly distinguished from that of Tinatin.

While the leopard provides a role model for men in both the *MPS* and in Georgian folklore, no one animal serves as a role model for women, although women, especially Arabian women, have intelligence and can foresee the results of their actions. Also, they use men to carry out their plans, tell men what to do and bring them in contact with each other. Men are inclined to hunt and fight, like 'leopards', but women tell them what to hunt and fight for, and with whom to fight. For example, the *MPS* begins when Tinatin sends Avtandil on a quest. True, King Rostevan made an earlier independent decision to abdicate in favour of his daughter Tinatin, but this is a decision to turn all future decisions over to a woman, as she will be the Queen of Arabia. Later, Avtandil decides, after having found Tariel and so fulfilled his quest, to broaden his search to include Nestan-Darejan as well, seemingly another independent male decision. But first, he returns home to Arabia for Tinatin's approval. Clearly, Tinatin is in charge. Hence, even decisions by men turn out to be decisions by women, perhaps justifying Queen Tamar's independent rule.

Likewise, the two murders are just special cases of women telling men what to do. Since successful murders in the *MPS* are the test for successful leadership, it follows that only women, like Queen Tamar, are successful leaders. The first murder takes place when Nestan-Darejan, upon hearing she has been betrothed to the Prince of Khvarazmia, orders Tariel to kill the prince. The second murder begins when Patman gives Avtandil the choice to kill the wine-taster or leave her to her fate, which really is not a choice. There is a clear similarity between the two female-instigated murders in the *MPS* and the death of Queen Tamar's cousin Demna, whose death facilitated Tamar's ascent to the throne (although even 900 years later, there are no indications she ordered it).[50] Women also facilitate contacts between people. Tinatin brings Tariel to Avtandil's attention

---

[49] Aleksandr Pavlovič Skaftymov, *Poètika i genezis bylin: Očerki* [*The Poetics and Genesis of the Byliny: Essays*] (The Hague: Mouton, 1970), pp. 127–28.

[50] mč'edlišvili, *šua*, p. 273.

(114, 152). Also, Asmat (Nestan-Darejan's maid) is the liaison between Tariel and Nestan-Darejan, and later, she introduces Avtandil to Tariel when Avtandil, having noticed Tariel's generally aggressive behaviour, is reluctant to approach him. Lastly, Patman helps Avtandil find Nestan-Darejan, who has disappeared into Kajistan. Like Tinatin and Asmat, Nestan-Darejan brings people together; for example, from her prison, she writes a letter to Tariel, asking him to take care of her father, and so she brings those two men together (1283). In her concern for her father and Tariel, she is like Tinatin, whose interest in Tariel brings him and Avtandil together. Abaev may have been partially right when he proposed that Georgians see empathy as the defining characteristic of humans in opposition to leopards for, in the *MPS*, women have empathy.[51]

Women create society – they do the networking and even (or especially) murder. They are the only ones who instigate the murders, even though men do the actual killing. The cruel and suspicious death of her cousin Demna throws a shadow over Queen Tamar's reign. Rustaveli tackles this problem head-on by arguing that murders, even the most despicable ones, can be right if handled by a rational person, whereas irrational and impulsive people bungle murders. On the one hand, this can be read as an effort to support Queen Tamar, who did tell men what to do; on the other hand, it can simply reflect the cultural reality in the Caucasus, even nowadays, where women are influential and enjoy high social prestige.[52]

This does not apply only to murders; indeed, Rustaveli gives several examples showing that rational people do no wrong. Rustaveli bases the *MPS* on utilitarianism, a philosophy which has been described as 'cold and unsympathizing'[53] since it reduces emotions and judgements to a mere 'utility calculus'.[54] The Prince of Khvarazmia would have agreed, as would the wine-taster and Patman, although Patman receives at least some token of appreciation. But Rustaveli provides a counterbalance to the coldness of his ethics, not only in his love for Queen Tamar (5, 15, 17), but also in Avtandil's friendship for Tariel. Avtandil has been described as cold and perfidious,[55] but his warm and self-effacing friendship

---

[51] Abaev, 'O fol'klornoi', p. 131.
[52] George Tarkhan-Mouravi, 'Georgia', in *Countries and Their Cultures*, ed. Melvin Ember and Carol R. Ember, (New York: Macmillan Reference USA, 2001), 2:842; Irina Babich, 'Turkey and the Caucasus', *Encyclopedia of Women and Islamic Cultures: Family, Law and Politics*, ed. Suad Joseph and Afsāna Nağmābādī (Leiden: Brill, 2003), 2:235–36; John Colarusso, 'Peoples of the Caucasus', in *Worldmark Encyclopedia of Cultures and Daily Life*, ed. Paul Hocking (Farmington Hills, MI: Gale, 2009), 5:381.
[53] Mill, *Utilitarianism*, p. 28.
[54] Robert Solomon, *The Big Questions: A Short Introduction to Philosophy*, 6th edn (New York: Harcourt, 2002), p. 280.
[55] Khintibidze, 'Lancelot and Avtandil', pp. 30–31.

lifts Tariel out of his years-long depression. Rustaveli seems to be arguing that though everyone messes up eventually, the danger lies in the potential for sliding into a long depression like Tariel did. Rustaveli does not discuss mistakes in the abstract; rather, he gives concrete examples like abdications, murders and adoptions. He points out that mistakes happen when people act impulsively, but there is hope for them, and they can become like the rational Arabians. Just as Tariel loses his impulsive character, so impulsive people can become rational. Murders cannot be undone, but people can become rational and improve like Tariel (and Queen Tamar), and they can live on and do good.

More importantly, murder is a most powerful tool to manage society. Tools are ethically neutral: they are neither good nor bad though they can be more or less effective for a certain purpose. But tools can be dangerous: the carpenter can hit his thumb and the Golem can run amuck.[56] It takes a rational mind to handle tools well, even more so with murder. Queen Tamar had such a mind, but even for those without such a mind, there is hope. The secret to shedding an impulsive personality, becoming rational and managing tools and actions well (including murder), Rustaveli explains, is the friendship of someone, even a stranger who, to quote Levinas, is summoned to responsibility.[57]

---

[56] *No Star Too Beautiful: Yiddish Stories from 1382 to the Present*, ed. and trans. Joachim Neugroschel (New York: Norton, 2002), p. 491.

[57] Levinas, 'Ethics', p. 131.

CHAPTER 16

A Multiple Poisoning in the City of Valencia: Sanxo Calbó's Crime (1442)*

Carmel Ferragud

SOME CRIMES, PARTICULARLY MURDER, leave their mark on a community. Their cruelty and their impact on society are so shocking that they appear in the chronicles and are sometimes spoken about from generation to generation.[1] On 19 February 1442, in the presence of Joan Sifre, the knight who acted as the *justícia criminal* [judge] in the city of Valencia,[2] Pere Roquer (profession unknown) accused his father-in-law Sanxo Calbó (a former craftsman working in textiles as a shearer and *apuntador*)[3] of having poisoned several members of his family. This poisoning killed Isabel (Calbó's daughter and Roquer's

---

* This work has been carried out as part of research projects FFI2011-29117-C02-01 (2012–2015) and FFI2014-53050-C5-3-P (2015–2018) of the Ministry of Economy and Competitiveness (MINECO) the Spanish Government, co-financed with FEDER funds of the European Union. This paper was translated by Andrew Stacey.
[1] See, for example, the case of the crime of Paiporta, in which one family murdered the family next door in a hamlet in the *huerta* of Valencia. Numerous chronicles and literary and notarial sources mentioned the case. See: Antonia Carré, 'Jaume Roig, autor de l'Espill (segle XV): dels protocols notarials a la literatura', *Estudis Històrics i Documents dels Arxius de Protocols* 30 (2012): 87–105.
[2] The *justícia criminal*'s court was established by a privilege of James II in 1321, according to which civil and criminal jurisdiction, united since the conquest of Valencia in 1238, would come under the control of two judges. The criminal judge was responsible for guarding the city; capturing wrong-doers and those carrying prohibited weapons; considering punishments imposed for those unsheathing a sword, gambling or going around at night without a light; judging slander cases, crimes with wounds or mutilations and homicides; and any other criminal acts, including crimes committed up to 100 miles out to sea. This judge imposed fines and corporal punishments on those condemned. See: Rafael Narbona, 'El Justicia Criminal: Una corte medieval valenciana, un procedimiento judicial', *Estudis Castellonencs* 3 (1986): 287–310 and Pablo Pérez García, 'Origen y configuración de una magistratura urbana de la Valencia foral: el justicia criminal', *Estudis* 13 (1988): 21–73.
[3] A *shearer* finished the surface and trimmed the edges of woollen fabrics with large scissors; an *apuntador* folded pieces of cloth, creased them and passed a thread through the hem of each to affix a seal.

wife) and his grandmother (also called Isabel), but left behind the accuser and Roquer's mother, Estévena (who was also poisoned), with serious after-effects, along with a little baby (Calbó's grandson and the son of Roquer and Isabel who was indirectly poisoned thorough breastfeeding from Isabel) and, finally, a housemaid called Joana.

In one of the quires in a volume of the city of Valencia's *justícia criminal* the whole trial is preserved in all its procedural form, from the accusation, the taking of statements by witnesses for the prosecution, the defence and the final sentence.[4] This is unusual; normally, trials were put down in writing in fragments distributed in different quires and even in different volumes. This fragmented process of recording events makes consulting the sources difficult, and, occasionally, it means that only part of the process survives. The case presented here is, therefore, quite exceptional because the whole judicial process is preserved from the complaint to the execution of the judgment in the same quire.

Immediately after the accusation, Sanxo Calbó must have been apprehended due to the seriousness of the crimes, although there is no news about it. On 20 February, he was taken from the city jail to answer his son-in-law's accusations. The next morning, the trial lawyers were appointed by both parties and the judge established a period of time for witnesses to be found. Between 22 February and 24 March, a total of forty witnesses paraded through the courthouse, of whom only six were women. This last point is strange, considering that many aspects reported by the witnesses were related to domestic life. In many of the known judicial proceedings referring to crimes committed inside the house, whether civil or criminal, numerous women appear among the witnesses interrogated. The home was where they spent most of their time because their everyday activities and their social lives were based there. However, this preference for women as witnesses was not the case in the crime here. The witnesses, especially former professional colleagues and customers, were chosen to testify to their version of Calbó's good or bad reputation. These people represented different social and labour categories: craftsmen (eight *apuntadors*, a cloth dealer or *draper*, a glover, a dyer, a hosier, a tanner and a broker); medicine practitioners (two doctors, two apothecaries and a barber); a priest; two notaries and two shopkeepers. There were higher status witnesses involved as well, including four citizens (*ciutadans honrats*) and two knights, who were members of the nobility.

Their contributions were very unequal; while some witnesses gave numerous details for one or more of the points into which the judge divided the accusation,

---

[4] Valencia, Arxiu del Regne de València (ARV), Justícia Criminal (JCr), p. 87. I have normalised the original sources, cited in Catalan, in respect to punctuation and spelling. The date of the testimony is given in parentheses as the folios of the trial are not numbered. I have been unable to find evidence for the execution of this sentence.

others hardly said anything relevant to the case or to the establishment of a verdict. Some witnesses were summoned to corroborate the bad or good reputation of the accused and to clarify aspects of Calbó's past that might be related to the crime or to the personality of the poisoner.[5] Therefore, most of them were Calbó's former colleagues. Other witnesses were friends or relatives who could supply information. On the whole, this is the story of how a craftsman's life degenerated into criminality, how he was moved by dark desires to obtain wealth, even at the cost of sacrificing the lives of his blood relatives. After listening to numerous witnesses, the *justícia criminal*, with doubts but with clear evidence of guilt, decided to subject the accused to torture to elicit a confession. Calbó confessed in detail about how he poisoned all the victims and what the motives were for his commission of such a horrific crime.

Crimes of poisoning had always been a great public concern. The first examples of criminal procedures in Valencia regarding poisoning date from 1280, when some individuals were accused of using *realgar* [red arsenic] to commit murder.[6] Unfortunately, the volumes in the series of the *justícia criminal*, the most important source for finding these cases, have been conserved in a scant and irregular way for the fourteenth and fifteenth centuries in Valencia. It is impossible to say whether it was a habitual crime, but the *justícia criminal* does provide some very interesting qualitative information about criminal poisoning. The conclusions of the material in the *justícia criminal* are similar to those in different parts of Mediterranean Europe.[7] Crimes with poison are rare in this area of the Mediterranean in relation to the total number of murders committed, and the most recurring cases are those of the wife who, in collusion with her lover, poisons her husband, who is ignorant of their clandestine relationship.[8]

---

[5] Public reputation (*fama pública*) is at heart a testimony of quality by members of a community that provides the judge with public knowledge about certain facts related to a case. For discussions of *fama* in murder cases elsewhere in medieval Europe, see in this volume: Jeffrey Doolittle, 'Negotiating Murder in the *Historiae* of Gregory of Tours' and Ilse Schweitzer VanDonkelaar, 'Bringing Murder to Light: Death, Publishing and Performance in Icelandic Sagas'.

[6] See the documents in *Llibre de la Cort del Justícia de València (1280–1282)*, ed. Enric Guinot Rodríguez, M. Àngels Diéguez and Carmel Ferragud (Valencia: Universitat de València, 2008), pp. 153, 167–68.

[7] For similar accounts of poisoning as a method of murder in various medieval communities, see in this volume: Thomas Gobbitt, 'Poisoning, Killing and Murder in the *Edictus Rothari*' and Matthew Lubin, 'Poisoning as a Means of State Assassination in Early Modern Venice'.

[8] There are various published trials of crimes of poisoning from the area of the Crown of Aragon against the backdrop that I comment on here. For the case of Barcelona, see three poisonings in 1373–1374, in Carlos López Rodríguez, *Sexe i violència en la Corona d'Aragó. Processos criminals dels segles XIII al XV* (Valencia: Universitat de València, 2014), pp. 179–241. A similar case, in fourteenth-century Valencia, on which I am

Matrimony is a habitual context in poisoning crimes. Proximity and intimacy encouraged the use of poisons to do away with the hated partner. This is repeated in several places during the medieval and early modern periods, reinforcing many stereotypes about women as poisoners.[9] But, in addition, people's imaginations played a decisive role in this respect, causing many communities to believe that the crime of poisoning was particularly the work of women. It was a long-standing cultural legacy, originating in classical Antiquity but highly developed in the Middle Ages, which survived into the twentieth century. The biblical story of original sin and the role of Eve is closely associated with the origins of the criminal use of poison by women. Literature is full of these kinds of accounts, written by clergymen especially. Étienne de Fougères, Jean Raulin, Álvaro Pelayo, Bernardino de Siena and Antonino Pierozzi are some of the medieval authors who fuelled this image of women as poisoners.[10] However, neither the documents conserved, nor the case of Calbó, confirm this point in any way. In Valencia, as in the rest of Europe, there is a trend (largely misogynist) of associating women with the handling of toxic products in order to concoct potions for illicit and criminal purposes.[11] Nevertheless, stubborn reality reveals a different situation, since, in the majority of cases, crimes of poisoning were committed by men.

Among his laws of 1261, the king of the Crown of Aragon, James I, introduced one that punished poisoning severely, especially if women were involved. If a man was guilty of murder by poison, he would be hanged, whereas a woman would

---

currently working, is a particularly long and complex court case in which Joan Berbegal and his aunt Francesca were accused of having sexual intercourse and of having poisoned Bartomeu Sanxo, the uncle and husband. See: ARV, JCr, manus 1, fol. 1ff, 45 (11 January 1380).

[9] Franck Collard, *Le crime de poison au Moyen Âge* (Paris: Presses Universitaires de France, 2003), p. 125 (*The Crime of Poison in the Middle Ages*, trans. Deborah Nelson-Campbell [Westport, CT: Praeger, 2008]); Alessandro Pastore, *Veleno: Credenze, crimini, sapere nell'Italia moderna* (Bologna: Il Mulino, 2010), pp. 100–1. For the case of Valencia, see: Rafael Narbona, 'Tras los rastros de la cultura popular. Hechicería, supersticiones y curanderismo en la Valencia medieval', in *Memorias de la ciudad: Ceremonias, creencias y costumbres en la historia de Valencia* (Valencia: Ajuntament de València, 2003), pp. 241–59 at pp. 254–55. Examples from Barcelona can be found in Joaquim Miret i Sans, *Sempre han tingut béch les oques: Apuntacions per la historia de les costumes privades* (Barcelona: F. Badia, 1905–1906), 1:65–75, 2: 28–48.

[10] Collard, *Le crime*, pp. 111-13.

[11] The misogynist text par excellence of Valencian literature of the period – although in a clearly humorous vein – is the famous *Espill*, by the royal and city doctor Jaume Roig. In it, criticisms of women poisoners are also reflected. See an edition with comments in this respect in Jaume Roig, *Espill*, ed. Antònia Carré (Barcelona: Barcino, 2006), pp. 123–27, 624–25.

be burnt at the stake.¹² Poisoning – a horrifying, abominable crime perpetrated insidiously and secretly, which gave the unwary victim no chance to defend him- or herself – was considered the greatest of all crimes, the greatest of all betrayals, and it had to be punished in the most terrifying way.¹³ For this reason, the judge was implacable in his verdict, and Calbó was sentenced to death.

Arsenic was omnipresent and was, therefore, the most feared poison during the Middle Ages. Since Antiquity, it was known in its two natural forms as sulphurs: *orpiment* [yellow arsenic] and *realgar* [red arsenic]. It was used in a variety of ways and in different prescriptions for its healing properties, especially as a corrosive for treating the wounds of people and animals.¹⁴ However, its high toxicity also made it ideal for killing and exterminating pests, like rodents. The ease with which it was obtained by apothecaries and alchemists, and with which it could be supplied to deadly effect because it is odourless and tasteless, made arsenic an ideal (and frequent) poison to commit crimes.¹⁵ And yet, Joana the maid is the only person in this trial who testified that she had been suspicious of the powders that Calbó used. When she saw the powder that he wished to pour in Isabel's syrup, and witnessed an argument that he had had with Estévena (Isabel's mother-in-law), she realised that it was not sugar candy that Calbó had used but something altogether different. She confronted the poisoner about the deaths as soon as the household came back from Isabel's funeral. Nobody else ever seemed to notice the powder being used, despite the fact that Calbó poured it in several meals and drinks over time. This lack of evidence highlights the great difficulty in discovering arsenic as a cause of death, and it illustrates the viability of using it in the commission of a crime without arousing too much suspicion.

The rise in the number of apothecaries, where the sale of poisons was habitual, facilitated access to, and the spread of, toxins.¹⁶ In order to control the abuse

---

¹² *Furs de València*, vol. 7, ed. Germà Colón and Arcadi Garcia (Barcelona: Barcino, 1999), p. 104.

¹³ Collard, *Le crime*, pp. 137–48, 217. Pastore, *Veleno*, p. 101. In several Italian cities, poisoners were liable to the death penalty, sometimes even for attempted poisoning. Poisoning was often linked to witchcraft and black magic, and there was greater insistence on the mechanisms used than on the damage caused. Trevor Dean, *Crime and Justice in Late Medieval Italy* (Cambridge: Cambridge University Press, 2010), pp. 156–58.

¹⁴ For its uses in surgery, see: Michael McVaugh, *The Rational Surgery of the Middle Ages* (Florence: Sismel-Edizioni del Galluzzo, 2006), pp. 212–13, 259. The blacksmith and horse doctor from Barcelona, Jaume de Montserrat, was used to having *realgar*, arsenic and other poisons in his house 'per les cures que ha a fer de les bèsties' [for healing the beasts]. López Rodríguez, *Sexe i violència*, p. 115.

¹⁵ John Parascandola, *King of Poisons: A History of Arsenic* (Washington, DC: Potomac Books, 2012).

¹⁶ This opinion has been expressed by Collard, *Le crime*, pp. 53–54. Arsenic is found in some of the few known inventories of apothecaries. The apothecary Arnau Bertran had, in his workshop, an ounce of ground orpiment and another half-pound in a jar (nearly

of these substances, municipal governments (and even kings) regulated their control and sale, and these measures were gradually adopted in many cities. At the beginning of the fourteenth century, the municipal government of Barcelona refused to let apothecaries and their assistants sell *realgar*. Only doctors of renowned prestige (*bons e coneguts*) could act as vendors of the substance, and they could only possess it if they swore that they would use it for medical purposes. Moreover, Jews were not allowed to either buy or sell it. If they did, the fine rose to the remarkable sum of 1,000 *sous*, and if a convicted Jew could not pay it, he lost a hand.[17] The Valencian authorities' concern about the presence of toxic products became obvious at the beginning of the fifteenth century when King Alfonso the Magnanimous enacted a new law in 1417.[18] From that moment onwards, deadly poisons, like arsenic, *argent viu soblimat*[19] and any other toxins could only be sold and dispensed to the people who needed them by certain Christian apothecaries and spice dealers who had to be chosen by the *jurats* [councillors] of the city, the town or other location in the kingdom, and who were considered suitable by the inspectors (*veedors*). Any person who broke this law would be fined 50 *morabatins*. The law also made it compulsory for owners of the material to guard poisons and for the purveyors of the toxic goods to sell and dispense them in person. If the transaction was not done this way, traffickers in the poisons would have to pay the same fine, half of which would be for the king and the rest for the prosecution.

The sheer number of apothecaries (and spice dealers and shopkeepers) meant that it was easy for purveyors of toxic goods to escape control. Barcelona had experienced the same situation in the fourteenth century as Valencia did in

178 gr) including other delicate products like henbane seeds, brimstone and laudanum. See: ARV, Protocols of Vicent Saera, 2728 (12 January 1423). The apothecary Ramon Amalric had an *arroba* and 4 pounds of powdered orpiment (12,070 gr), and mention is made of a little wooden box for this product (*argent sublimat* 23 pounds). See also: Valencia, Arxiu del Reial Col·legi Seminari de Corpus Christi de València (ACCV), notary Gerard de Ponte, 25027 (14 January 1404).

[17] Barcelona, Arxiu Històric de la Ciutat de Barcelona, Llibre de Consell, I-2, fol. 35r (3 July 1313). In 1351 an ordinance of Peter the Ceremonious made it obligatory to supervise the sale of toxic products in Barcelona. However, from 1372 onwards, the storage and sale of poisons would be regulated on a local level and both apothecaries and spice dealers could sell them. Jean-Pierre Bénézet, *Pharmacie et médicament en Méditerranée occidentale (XIIIe-XVIe siècles)* (Paris: Champion, 1999), pp. 171–72. On the prohibitions dealing with Jews and women in Valencia, see: David Nirenberg, *Comunidades de violencia: La persecución de las minorías en la Edad Media* (Barcelona: Península, 2001) [first published as *Communities of Violence: Persecution of Minorities in the Middle Ages* (Princeton: Princeton University Press, 1996)], pp. 173–75.

[18] *Furs de València*, vol. 8, ed. Germà Colón and Arcadi Garcia (Barcelona: Barcino, 1999), pp. 139–40.

[19] Mercury – used in medicine, as a colourant and to make metals.

the fifteenth century. The control and monopoly of the apothecaries was gradually imposed because their expertise, in contrast to that of the simple retailers, was a profound concern for the authorities. However, no special emphasis was given to the matter of dangerous products in the articles of the apothecaries' guild of Valencia, created on 20 March 1431. This was almost certainly because the idea was to consolidate the group and thereby avoid disputes. The articles concerning sociability and religion were mixed up with more technical, professional ones, such as the regulation of access to the practice of the medical arts, the apprenticeship process and the examination, licensing and opening of individual workshops.[20] The articles refer also to the advisability of observing the laws regarding the title of doctors, including those who regulated the art of the apothecaries. And yet, as usually happened with many other laws, practitioners and suppliers did not always comply with the law.[21] It seems that any resident of Valencia could easily acquire poisonous products such as arsenic, as in Calbó's case.

Calbó purchased the arsenic in two places: the workshops of Joan Agostí, to whom he referred as a shopkeeper and spice dealer (*botiguer, especier*), and that of the apothecary Martí Martínez.[22] In both cases, the same reasons were given: Calbó needed the product to exterminate the rats in the house of the Jaume and Mateu Pujades, who were knights. The rats in the garden next to the Pujades' home were very large, and they got inside the house, damaging the study where they devoured the owners' papers.

The owners of the house testified that one Miquel Raimer, the housekeeper, must have purchased the arsenic, but it seems that he had asked Calbó to do it because Calbó went to both apothecaries on two occasions, barely a few days apart, and, in both cases, he repeated to the owners that the ground arsenic they had sold him was ineffective and that he wanted something more potent. The

---

[20] Faustino Barberá, *Nuestra farmacia retrospectiva: Manuscrito histórico, Códice del antiguo colegio de boticarios de Valencia* (Valencia, 1906), pp. 4–9.

[21] However, some apothecaries were scrupulous about the sale of arsenic due to the risks it entailed, and they considered its indiscriminate sale to be irresponsible. See the opinion of the Barcelona apothecary Miquel Tosell, a member of the royal household, in López Rodríguez, *Sexe i violència*, pp. 238–39.

[22] Joan Agostí was an apothecary with a workshop in the city of Valencia, although, in the trial, he was always referred to as a shopkeeper (*botiguer*). His information is recorded from the year 1386. The only information I have about Agostí are the annual payments made to him every year by the authorities of Valencia and Castelló de la Plana for annuities. See: Valencia, Arxiu Municipal de València (AMV), Protocol of Jaume Desplà, 2 (24 November 1386) and 4 (13 November 1387) and ARV, Protocols of Andreu Julià, 1264, s.f. (2 July 1415). If the shopkeeper, Joan Agostí in this case, was the same person and not a son, he was already an old man. For Martí Martínez, I have been unable to find a single reference.

price he paid in each of the four purchases was two deniers. It was a very low price, which shows how easy it was to get hold of the product. Moreover, the amount of poison purchased was very large – half a quarter – and the apothecaries were surprised that he did not have enough to kill all the rodents. Calbó replied that he used to throw the surplus arsenic down the drain to prevent harming anyone. The shopkeeper Agostí justified his sale of arsenic saying that Calbó was someone known to him who did not seem suspicious.

The documentary evidence shows that the laws were quite ineffective and that any apothecary or shopkeeper could have arsenic and other poisons in his workshop. There was a certain degree of precaution about how the customers could use the toxic substances, but no strict controls were put in place, and the mere fact that the purchaser was known to the apothecary was sufficient. Nevertheless, the crime committed by Calbó compelled the municipal government to consider a new regulation. A councillor named Guillem Saera took the initiative, claiming that 'en la dita ciutat generalment se venia arcènich e abeuratges verinosos, que no s'i servava orde algú, la qual cosa era molt perillosa a moltes gents' [in the said city arsenic and other poisonous concoctions were generally sold without any order being observed, which was very dangerous for the people].[23] He refers to a recent event just a few days earlier that raised the alarm about the danger of selling these substances without control, and he said that regulating them would benefit the public greatly. Although it is not made explicit, they were talking about the Calbó case. Therefore, on 9 May, the municipal government passed a law for the purpose of implementing more exhaustive controls: 'Provehí, stablí e ordenà que en tota la ciutat e terme de aquella, d'ací avant no s'i puxa tenir per a vendre arcènich ni abeuratges verinosos, sinó dues bones persones deputadores e elegidores per los honorables jurats cascun any ... persones expertes, ço que·ls parria, a beneffici e utilitat de la cosa pública de la dita ciutat' [It was ordered that throughout the city and its territory, from thereon only two people chosen by the *jurats* every year may sell arsenic or poisonous potions ... Expert people, those that seem the best, for the benefit and usefulness of the city].[24]

However, the new law passed in the wake of Calbó's trial did not prevent another such crime a decade later: that of Riudaura in the city of Valencia in 1453. Riudaura poisoned his wife and his parents, all of whom died, and he also tried to poison his parents-in-law and his sister-in-law. Riudaura was punished the same way as Calbó, but unlike Calbó, Riudaura's crime was collected in a famous chronicle by Melcior Miralles, the priest of King Alfonso the Magnanimous.[25]

---

[23] AMV, Manual de Consells, A-32, fol. 56v (9 May 1442).
[24] Ibid.
[25] 'En l'any de .M.CCCC.LIII., dimarts a .XIII. de march, estant justícia en Rianbau de Crueles, pengaren Riuda[u]ra, lancer, lo qual confessà que avia morta sa muler primera

It is not clear why Miralles chose to record the crime committed by Riudaura but not that committed by Calbó. It must surely have been due to the public resonance of the Riudaura case and to the fact that the attention paid to him had also been drawn to them personally. Because of the position he held in the cathedral, Miralles must have been aware of everything going on in the city. If he wrote about this crime, it was because of the personal and social impact of the case, but as it is the only poisoning recorded in his diary, it suggests exactly how exceptional this kind of crime was in the city of Valencia.

Calbó's crime was both exceptional and particularly insidious. One day, Calbó laced some sweets (*confits*) with arsenic. Taking the poisoned candy to his house, Calbó invited everyone there to try them, urging his daughter Isabel and her grandmother to have more. Immediately after swallowing them, they began to feel ill: 'aquelles hagueren mal de ventrell e gran turbació en llur persona e cap e començaren a pervocar en vòmit' [they had terrible stomach ache, great dizziness and general discomfort and they began to vomit] (19 February). A neighbour named Joana gave a detailed description of the suffering of the people poisoned in Roquer's house, testifying that she heard terrifying screaming and vomiting. Many neighbours entered the house to see what was happening. The distress and the vomiting were horrifying. Isabel 'anava lo ventre rocegant per terra de la gran dolor e del gran mal e basqua que tenia' [was dragging herself around the floor because of the pain and the feeling that she was about to vomit] (22 February). During that time, as the witness said, 'axí segueren malavegant, adés gitant-se adés levant-se, e axí malavegaren fins que moriren' [[Isabel] and the others who had been poisoned would get up and lie down, always restless] (22 February). The poison gave them no respite.

But Calbó did not stop at poisoning the sweets; indeed, he poured it into the wine and into the water in the well that supplied the house: 'hagué arçenich e pólvores verinoses e de aquelles meté e y hi meté en la ampola del vi e en lo pou e en tot ço que podia per què matàs totes les dites persones e altres que fossen en la casa del dit en Pere Roquer' [he obtained arsenic and poisonous powders and placed them in a bottle of wine, in the well and in everything he could in order to kill all the people who were in Pere Roquer's house] (19 February). Isabel and

ab metzines, e matà som pare e sa mare ab metzines, e donà metzines ha son sogre e sogra e cunyada. Lo qual Ridaura meteren viu davall son pare e deval sa mare en la fosa, e, tret de la fosa, pengaren-lo en lo Mercat' [On Tuesday 13 March 1453, being *justícia* en Rianbau de Crueles, was hanged Riudaura, lancer, who confessed to killing his wife and his parents with poison and to giving poison to his parents-in-law and his sister-in-law. As punishment, Ridaura was buried, while still alive, under his parents inside their grave, and, once he was removed from that grave, he was hanged in the market square]. Melcior Miralles, *Crònica i dietari del capellà d'Alfons el Magnànim*, ed. Mateu Rodrigo (Valencia: Universitat de València, 2011), p. 230.

her grandmother were the first ones affected, followed soon after by Roquer and his mother, Estévena, the suckling baby and Joana the maid. Isabel's death throes lasted twenty-five days from the moment she began eating the sweets. Roquer, his son and his mother managed to survive, but not without terrible consequences. Months after the poisoning, both still exhibited symptoms of paralysis of their limbs and experienced terrible pains. Roquer also said that other people outside the household who had drunk that water were afflicted.

The poisoning began around All Saints Day, 1 November 1442. At several points during the trial, Roquer said that he was still suffering the after-effects of the poison five months later, which supports his claim for the start date of the poisoning. Isabel's grandmother died first, although she had managed to care for her granddaughter during her illness. Isabel finally succumbed to the poison on Saint Catherine's Day, 25 November.

Although the poisoning was apparently indiscriminate, Calbó made sure his daughter ingested more than the others. Everyone in the house was ill, so nobody could attend to Isabel's needs, leaving Calbó to look after her and enabling him to do everything in his power to finish her off: 'li metia en tot quant prenia metzines e pólvores verinoses' [he put poisonous powders in everything she was taking] (19 February). The doctor who visited Isabel during the first illness, which was diagnosed as indigestion, was the physician, master in arts and medicine, Joan d'Exulbe (or de Xulbi).[26] During his interrogation, he said that Calbó came to him asking to visit her. D'Exulbe observed her urine and her stomach problems, diagnosing it as 'fleuma, viscós, mulcilaginós, aderent a les parets del ventrell' [viscous and mucilaginous phlegm stuck to the walls of the stomach].[27] He prescribed a purgative to induce vomiting. Once the medicine had been administered, Isabel expelled all that viscous material with great difficulty. Finally, he prescribed a syrup (*exarob*): 'e tallar aquella matèria viscosa mulcilaginosa, per ço que la natura la pogués pus fàcilment expel·lir' [and stop

---

[26] He was appointed the city's examiner of doctors for the years 1420, 1422, 1424, 1430, 1435, 1438 and 1442. He held the post of *obrer de la ciutat* in 1433 and was the bishop of Valencia's personal doctor. See: ACCV, notary Pere Ferrandis, 971, s.f. (26 February 1436). He died before 1448. See: ACCV, notary Joan d'Aragó, 16.704, s.f. (20 April 1448). The doctors interrogated in the trial did not issue an expert report, contrary to the usual practice at the time in the courts of Valencia, at least in the known cases, as can be seen in Carmel Ferragud, 'Los peritajes médicos en la Valencia bajomedieval: los casos de envenenamiento', *Dynamis* 36.1 (2016): 119–41. It seems that they refrained from answering the question of whether they thought that poisoning had occurred. Furthermore, too much time had passed for the corpses to be disinterred and analysed.

[27] Analysis of urine was one of the methods of obtaining information about a possible poisoning. See: Laurence Moulinier-Brogi, *L'Uroscopie au Moyen Âge: 'Lire dans un verre la natura de l'homme'* (Paris: Champion, 2012), p. 16. However, in this case, uroscopy did not give the doctor any clues.

that viscous and mulcinaginous matter, so that nature might expel it easily] (22 February). On a later visit, Roquer's mother, Estévena, told him about the confrontation she had had with Calbó because she knew that he had poured a white powder into the syrup. She asked the doctor if he had ordered this to be done, and he said he had not. Then d'Exulbe asked Calbó for an explanation, and he answered that his daughter 'era fastigosa de rebre exarob e medecines e que per ço li metia çucre candi' [found it very difficult to take syrup and other medicines and so he added sugar to it] (22 February). The doctor's reply was clear: 'mal fahia, car lo exarob era ja de si dolç, e que ell, dit Sanxo Calbó, no y devia metre de si res sens consell del metge' [he had acted wrongly, as the syrup was already sweet, and Sanxo Calbó should not have put anything in without consulting the doctor] (22 February). After those visits, Isabel and her grandmother got better and could leave the house. He could not give an opinion about what happened with the next illness, which caused their deaths, because he did not treat them.

Calbó's motives for committing this murder are rooted in his life story. Apparently, Calbó was brought up by his uncle, Sanxo Calbó the elder. He may have been an orphan and had been taken in, but the younger Calbó claimed during the trial that he had lived for over thirty years with his uncle and aunt, the elder Calbó and the elder Isabel (the widow of a tipstaff of King John I, named Tibaud de Barrenes).[28] The elder Calbó married his nephew Calbó to his stepdaughter Margarida in 1418.[29]

The younger Calbó and Margarida had two daughters, Úrsula and Isabel. The former died aged fifteen during the plague of 1439, called in the chronicles the *huytena mortaldad*, an especially virulent epidemic.[30] The latter was one of the victims of the poisoning along with her grandmother Isabel. This old woman played a very important part in arranging the marriage between Isabel the younger and Pere Roquer. On 4 February, the elder Isabel donated a house located in the port district of Valencia (Grau de la mar) to her granddaughter, but it was not the only donation the couple received. Guillem Bernís, a parish priest from Xirivella, granted them a house in the parish of Sant Pere and, moreover, a tax-exempt house with an adjoining field in Massanassa, a small village in the *horta* [the rural hinterland] of Valencia.[31] The priest's relationship to this

---

[28] About Barrenes, see: Josep M. Roca, *Johan I d'Aragó* (Barcelona: Institució Patxot, 1929), pp. 146, 338.

[29] This genealogy has been reconstructed with data from the ACCV, notary Jaume Vinader, 9533, s.f. All the following information about the family and their relationships comes from that source.

[30] Agustín Rubio Vela, 'Las epidemias de peste en la ciudad de Valencia durante el siglo XV. Nuevas aportaciones', *Estudis Castellonencs* 6 (1994–95): 1179-1221 at pp. 1200–02.

[31] ACCV, notary Jaume Vinader, 9533, s.f. (both documents on 4 February 1440).

family is unknown, but he is mentioned on several occasions during the trial as a person with whom they had some sort of ties.

That same day in February, before the same notary, Isabel the younger (still a maiden) married Pere Roquer with her grandmother's and her father's consent. For this, she provided a very generous dowry of 14,500 *sous* (the royal money of Valencia), comprising a house and an annual pension.[32] Then, Roquer added the sum of 7,500 *sous* as *creix* to increase the dowry. The provost Francesc Daries and the nobleman Pere Boïl Lladró de Vilanova acted as witnesses in the document, which suggests that the family was quite well connected. The next day, the younger Isabel (now Roquer's wife) signed another document in the presence of a notary granting her father, Sanxo Calbó, *inter vivos*, all the rights to half of the annuity of 500 *sous* in the dowry. The notary passed this information on to the syndic of Llíria, the town that paid the pension, and from that moment onwards, Calbó was the beneficiary of 250 *sous*.[33]

Very little is known about the Roquer family. Pere was a citizen of Valencia; however, his father Feliu was from Sant Feliu de Guíxols, a town in Catalonia, and Estévena's origins are unknown, though she was living with the newlyweds at the time of the poisoning. Nothing can be said either about the Roquer family's occupations, although they probably worked as traders.

Shortly after his marriage to Margarida, the younger Calbó began working with his uncle until he inherited the workshop with all the tools in 1428. The uncle also made his namesake's two daughters his heirs as a mark of his affection for his nephew, who benefitted greatly from this generosity.

The elder Calbó had held an important position in the *apuntadors'* corporation, and everyone referred to him as *lo prohom* [the distinguished citizen].[34] The young Calbó worked in this workshop until 1437, but Calbó the younger was always referred to in the trial as a former (*olim*) *apuntador* and shearer because although he had worked for at least twenty years in these trades, at the time of the trial, it had been five years since he had done anything with them. For many years, the business prospered. In the beginning, the younger Calbó had his own apprentices and assistants, and his good work as a craftsman was acknowledged,

---

[32] It was a dowry that exceeded the usual amount for the merchant class, which was around 12,000 *sous*, though the average was actually 4,000. See: José Mª Cruselles, 'Ideas sociales y estrategias familiares en el mundo urbano (la ciudad de Valencia, 1485–1500)', ed. Luis Miguel Enciso Recio, *La burguesía española en la Edad Moderna* (Valladolid: Universidad de Valladolid, 1994), 2:1369–83 at p. 1372.

[33] ACCV, notary Jaume Vinader, 9533, s.f. (5 March 1440).

[34] This may very well be the Sanxo Calbó who took part in a commission in February 1407 to talk to the king about some matters relative to the city. See: *Documents de la pintura valenciana medieval y moderna*, ed. Lluïsa Tolosa, Ximo Company and Joan Aliaga (Valencia: Universitat de València, 2011), p. 151.

among others, by the *apuntador* Bernat Bonjoc. Nevertheless, the younger Calbó was expelled from the profession after having been repeatedly accused of committing fraud in the performance of his work. It seems that the officials of the profession insisted he stand down before being publicly accused, threatening him with public shame if there was a trial. The testimony of an *apuntador*, Joan Figueres, supports this: 'per no fer-li vergonya públicament que li fos dit, no sab per qui, que·s jaquís de dit offici e que no·n usàs, per ço que no li'n haguessen affer affronte públicament' [in order not to publicly shame him, someone in the profession told him not to carry on if he did not want to be shown up in public] (9 March). Pere d'Aloça said that Calbó used to steal pieces of cloth when he cut them, and that, in respect to the younger Calbó, 'bé sab que fa pocha faena e és larch en despesa' [[he] knew that he worked little and spent a lot] (23 January). One of his former employees who worked in his shop for two years, Joan Llarguet, was of the same opinion, saying 'que lo hom que despén e no guanya, per força se a ampobrir' [that the man who spends and does not earn will eventually be poor] (23 February). D'Aloça also said that he suspected Calbó whenever cloths disappeared from his workshop, although he later discovered the real thief and apologised to Calbó. A cloth maker named Joan Garcia spoke of several thefts of pieces of cloth that he had discovered when he had given Calbó a job. He also claimed that Calbó had accused his own assistants, and that he already had this habit of stealing when he worked with his uncle. Calbó was accused not only of professional fraud but also personal theft and murder. He was accused of having stolen a silver cup from a doctor named Civera, which he melted down to obtain its value in money,[35] and then he was suspected of having one Pere Sastre murdered. So, by reputation, Calbó was known as a swindler, a thief and a murderer before he was put on trial for poisoning his daughter and other members of his family.

The prosecutor strove to show that Calbó had been wandering around like a vagabond, unemployed since he lost his workshop.[36] An *apuntador* named Lluís Romero claimed that the workshop had been ceded to Calbó by his uncle for ten years, a period that expired just when Calbó abandoned the profession. Other witnesses said that the workshop had been rented, which suggests that it must have passed into his ownership. However, after losing his job, Calbó had substantial financial problems. Questioned by the judge about whether he had been tried previously for other crimes, Calbó admitted that he had been in prison for

---

[35] It was without doubt Gil Civera, *in artibus et medicina magister*, recorded in Valencia in those years. See: ACCV, notary Pere Ferrandis, 971, s.f. (14 February 1436).

[36] The forcefulness with which the influential Franciscan Francesc Eiximenis expressed himself in this respect is remarkable. He thought that those who wandered idly about the city ought to be expelled. See: Francesc Eiximenis, *Regiment de la cosa pública*, ed. Daniel de Molins de Rei (Barcelona: Barcino, 1927), p. 177.

debt and that the loss of his workshop forced him to find money to live. Indeed, in 1437, after he stopped working, he decided to rent his house out for 340 *sous* a year. Calbó was then appointed *justícia* of the port district of Valencia.[37] At this point, he said that his real reason for leaving his profession was the demands of the duties that he had to perform as a judge. He also added a pension of 800 *sous* for food that he received from the *legítima* (the part of the inheritance that must be set aside for one's heirs) that he earned from the property of his daughter who had died during an epidemic. From that moment onwards, his income was derived from three sources: the rent, the salary from the position of *justícia* and the food pension. Everything seems to indicate that Sanxo Calbó had developed a strategy – fraudulently in some cases, it would seem – to accumulate enough money, thanks mainly to a variety of incomes, without working in any profession. There was no other alternative – after being discredited as a prestigious artisan – if he wanted to maintain his way of life. Some witnesses testified that Calbó liked spending money, which Roquer corroborated, confirming that Calbó was desperate for more property and an increase in his fortune.

At some point before the murders and the trial, Calbó married a second time to a woman named Joana. There is no information about the death of his first wife. During the trial, the prosecution emphasised Joana's bad reputation and the poor relationship between the couple, eventually casting doubt on the validity of their marriage. Although no mass was ever said to celebrate the marriage, it was formalised with the relevant licence. Roquer claimed that Joana was merely Calbó's mistress and, therefore, that they did not live according to Christian precepts. Joana seems to have contributed to this shady image herself. According to the testimony of Bernat Palau, Joana lived on *Carrer de l'Aiguardent* (a kind of liquor), she got drunk, she was mad and she was a procuress. Indeed, Roquer accused Calbó of prostituting his own daughter, Isabel, and his wife. Apparently, Joana threw Calbó out of the house after a quarrel, as Calbó himself admitted. He went to live with a sister for a while, but then his daughter Isabel asked him to move into her house, to which Roquer agreed. For a few months, Calbó lived with them and shared their table, occasionally contributing a sum of money. According to Roquer: 'és fort mal home de mala vida, mal cristià que no ha rahell en Déu ni amor a son prohisme' [he is a man who leads a bad life, a bad Christian who has neither roots in God nor loves his neighbour] (19 February). Calbó did

---

[37] Municipalities usually had their own officers of justice, who were elected every year. After his election by municipal authorities, Calbó was sworn as a new *justícia de loch de Vilanova del grau de la mar de València* on 25 December. See: AMV, Manuals de Consells, A-31, fols 158v and 162r. Calbó held this same post the following year, this time by purchasing it from a man in the household of *Mossèn* Antoni Sanç, provost of Valencia cathedral, for a price of 30 florins [1 *florí* (gold coin) = 12 *sous*] (testimony, 10 March, of Joan Amalric).

not observe the Lenten fasts imposed by the Church; he ate meat, he was not seen at Mass and, Roquer added, 'és molt astuciós en mal, mal crestià, e home de mala vida e conversació molt pobre, lo qual desigava e havia molt gran desig de haver béns e patrimoni' [he very cunningly causes bad things to happen, he is a bad Christian, a man who leads a bad life and whose conversation is poor, and who very much wanted to have a lot of money] (19 February).[38] Roquer's intent was to highlight Calbó's immorality and the fact that he was a bad Christian who could not be trusted, but this evidence also explains how Calbó came to be living with his daughter and her family.

Not long after Roquer and Isabel were married, she became pregnant and the young couple decided to ask for a loan from an unknown party to purchase furniture and to do some work on the house. Indebtedness was very common in Valencia for young couples starting a new life, but Roquer said that this expenditure infuriated his father-in-law, who began to threaten them. Isabel was surprised by the loan request and remembered how, after her sister Úrsula had died when she was still a maiden, and also ill, her father had forced her (Isabel) to make out a will in which she made him her heir. Isabel suspected that this was why he was angry: Roquer and Isabel were spending money that Calbó wanted to inherit eventually. It was around that time when she decided to change her will. She called the notary Cremades and made her son her heir, leaving her father an annual pension of 500 *sous*. This is how Calbó managed to get his hands on at least part of his daughter's money. In the event that her father and son died, her husband (Roquer) would be the beneficiary. However, there was yet another change. Roquer maintained that his father-in-law convinced Isabel to make out a will in his favour even though Calbó protested that it had actually been his daughter's wish to make this later change in July. In an attempt to deflect suspicion from himself, Calbó accused Roquer of beating Isabel. Calbó said that, on one occasion, he found his daughter at her house with a dislocated foot. Calbó claimed that Isabel had told him that her husband had injured her, which is why she wanted to change her will:

> 'pare mon marit me tracta mal e me ha ferida e yo vull mudar lo testament que fiu en poder d'en Cremades, car en aquell yo lexava tot ço del meu a mon marit e ara vull-ho mudar, puys que tinch fill. E axí, si us plau, anem a casa d'en Roqua, lo blanquer, e allí faré mon testament'

> ['father, my husband mistreats me and has injured me, and that is why I wish to change the will I made with Cremades, as in it I left everything to my husband, and therefore I now wish to leave it to my son. That is why I ask you to go with

[38] The municipal council of Valencia was sensitive to these questions, since, on 22 July 1447, it agreed that the *justícia civil* would fine those who did not observe the holiday in church festivals the amount of 60 *sous*.

me to the house of Roca, the tanner, and there I shall make out a new will']. (20 February)

To support Calbó's claim that he had done nothing wrong to his daughter, and that she had acted free from his coercion when she granted him the pension of 500 *sous*, Roca was called to give evidence (Calbó was the nephew of Roca's wife). In Roca's opinion, Calbó had no reason to kill his daughter, and Roca had never heard a bad word from Isabel about her father for many years.

Roquer admitted that, while it was true that he had hit his wife on a few occasions, he had not caused her any lasting damage,[39] further arguing that he did not influence her decision to change her will. Calbó, however, boasted about how much he loved his daughter and his grandson, so much so that he was only happy when he took them to the market or for a walk around a square. He was also very fond of the woman who had looked after him almost all his life. He cunningly asked how, given his obvious affection for his family, he could do them any harm. But at the same time, Roquer also accused his father-in-law of repeatedly wanting to kill his grandson: 'que lo dit en Sancho Calbó portant a veguades al braç lo fillet [...], nét seu, lo strenyia fahent-lo croxir les costelles perquè pogués fer morir' [that when Sanxo Calbó held Pere Roquer's son, his own grandson, in his arms he squeezed him, crushing his ribs to kill him] (19 February). For this reason, Calbó was forbidden from picking up his grandson.

Once Calbó managed to get his daughter to change her will in his favour, he decided to act and devised the crime. All of these manoeuvres orchestrated by Calbó were designed to get money from his daughter and, ultimately, they led to his conviction and his punishment, though he used various arguments to defend himself against these accusations.

An important argument in Calbó's defence was based on the accepted medical treatments for poisoning. Some people developed their own remedies in their homes. The maid Joana, who was living in Roquer's house at the time, testified that she also fell victim to the poison, but as soon as she realised that her pain and discomfort were almost certainly the result of a toxin, she went

---

[39] It was not at all infrequent for men to beat their wives. Civil and canon law accepted that husbands could discipline their wives, but, at the same time, it delimited the excesses that led to unlawful violence that was disruptive of domestic order and, by extension, social order. See: Hannah Skoda, 'Violent Discipline or Disciplining Violence? Experience and Reception of Domestic Violence in Late Thirteenth- and Early Fourteenth-Century Paris and Picardy', *Cultural and Social History* 6.1 (2009): 9–27. On gender violence in the Hispanic Middle Ages, see the studies published in María Jesús Fuente Pérez and Remedios Morán Martín, eds., *Raíces Profundas: La violencia contra las mujeres (Antigüedad y Edad Media)* (Madrid: Polifemo Ediciones, 2011).

to her house, took *triaga* (an antidote) with strawberry tree water[40] and then drank ash with oil and vomited. She survived, but as a result of the poisoning and the cure, she lost most of her teeth (26 February). The attitude of the maid was strange because it seems she did not notice that the rest of the household was affected. Whether she did or not, it does not appear in her testimony during the trial. Joana's actions illustrate the fact that when people thought they had been poisoned, they turned to many different kinds of cures. This was the usual medical network based on healthcare diversity in which neighbours, friends, relatives and others took part. People were used to choosing the best option from all of the healing possibilities.[41] The attitude shown by different people in this trial towards the possibility of having been poisoned clearly suggests widespread panic about being poisoned in all areas of society, which was not surprising because of the suffering, the after-effects and the danger of death.[42]

But in this case, as the women were dying slowly of this poison, a merchant named Françoi Tria (a neighbour of Roquer's) searched for Roquer because of the terrible state the women were in. As soon as the priest *Mossèn* Ferrer Abellà saw them, he was sure that they had been poisoned, and that if swift action was not taken, they were going to die. He went back home and prepared some powders mixed with cordial waters that were touched by an amulet, the unicorn's horn (*oricorn*).[43] It took effect immediately, and the women survived; however, the symptoms immediately turned into pain in the legs and arms and then paral-

---

[40] Both could be obtained easily from apothecaries. Bénézet, *Pharmacie et médicament*, pp. 675-78. *Triaga* was a universal antidote composed of dozens of simples. It was considered by Arnau de Vilanova to be the greatest of medicines due to the different applications it had, although there were important controversies over its use and production. See: *De amore heroico: De dosi tyriacalium medicinarum*, ed. Michael R. McVaugh, AVOMO, vol. 3 (Barcelona: Barcino, 1985), pp. 58-71. Michael R. McVaugh, 'Theriac at Montpellier 1285–1325', *Suchoffs Archiv* 56 (1972): 113–24. With respect to the strawberry tree, there is a powerful mythological tradition that links it to strong curative powers. The ease with which this tree sprouts anew tallies with this. Its vitality is enormous, its leaves always green, which is a symbol of immortality. In Barcelona, we also know of the case of an alleged poisoning in which a *triaga* that was kept at home was promptly resorted to. See: López Rodríguez, *Sexe i violència*, p. 180.

[41] María Luz López Terrada, 'Las prácticas médicas extraacadémicas en la ciudad de Valencia durante los siglos XVI y XVII', *Dynamis* 22 (2002): 85–120. This has been highlighted recently for the case of England in Sara Butler, *Forensic Medicine and Death Investigation in Medieval England* (New York: Routledge, 2015), pp. 218–19.

[42] Pastore, *Veleno*, p. 30.

[43] The use of various amulets and talismans and particularly unicorn horn was habitual among the nobility, civilians, ecclesiastics and monarchs of the period. See: Roca, *Johan I*, pp. 399-403 and Michael R. McVaugh, *Medicine Before the Plague: Practitioners and their Patients in the Crown of Aragon, 1285–1345* (Cambridge: Cambridge University Press, 1991), pp. 157-58. For the case of Castile, see: Flora Ramires, 'Le poison chez les Trastamare: De l'empoisonnement réel à l'imaginaire de l'empoisonnement', *Cahiers de*

ysis. Abellà understood that this was preferable to dying and, for these new ailments, there were other remedies. These amulets and talismans were habitually used by the elites, but their use as an antidote by a minor clergyman in this case suggests that people in Valencia from all walks of life, priests included, trusted them.[44] The priest tried to save the victims with his knowledge of poison, but, ultimately, he did not succeed.

Others went to healers and diviners, recognised for their special knowledge, for antidotes. Joan Freixa (a relative of the younger Isabel's) and his wife Úrsula stayed in the house to help. After the four members of the family had been affected by the poison, Freixa went to the Moorish quarter to look for a Moor who knew how to recognise poisonings. There he found a man who made *espardenyes* (a kind of shoes), who had helped them previously. He was called Mahomat *l'Espardenyer*, and everyone referred to him by his beard (*barbudet*). They also asked Freixa to take the Moor to the house of *Mossèn* Bernís, where he had been before. The latter was a priest from Xirivella, a benefactor of the family.

Freixa had a hard time finding Mahomat *l'Espardenyer*, but after asking various people, and making a couple of trips to the Moorish quarter, he succeeded. When the Moor introduced himself to Roquer, the latter asked him if he knew how to divine things about poisons (20 March). The Moor said that he did not but he knew someone who did. Three days later, he came back to Roquer saying that another Moor had told him about the poisonings in the house and that, if they wanted, he could give them a syrup as a cure. Roquer's family agreed, and Mahomat returned with three small bottles for the afflicted, staying to have lunch in the house. When they drank from the bottles, according to Roquer, the afflicted members of the family got better immediately. Nevertheless, Freixa said that when he went back to the house, Isabel told him that she had felt worse after drinking the syrup.

A neighbour named Margarida arrived to shroud Isabel's grandmother when she died, and stayed for a few days to help the younger Isabel in her convalescence, so she was present when the Moor gave the bottles of syrup to Roquer for his wife and mother. She was surprised by the high price Roquer had paid, nine silver *reals* of Valencia, because she doubted its efficacy and thought it did more harm than good. She was not the only one. One day, another woman named Moratona shouted at the Moor in the street, reproaching him for what she thought was the result of the medicine: it had killed one woman and left

recherches médiévales et humanistes 17 (2009): 53–69. In general, see: Collard, *Le crime*, pp. 83–85.

[44] The use of poison could enable priests not to stain their hands with blood, which they so abhorred. They could also use their knowledge of the properties of elements of nature for criminal purposes. See: Collard, *Le crime*, pp. 109–11. About the use of amulets and talismans in Valencia see: Narbona, 'Tras los rastros', pp. 244, 246, 256.

the other two debilitated. It may be that Moratona simply disapproved of what she considered negligence on the part of the healer, but it is also possible that she was voicing the type of opinion common at that time in Valencia about the Moors and the ambivalent relations they maintained with the Christian community: at times complicit and friendly, and, at others, adversarial, accusatorial and marked by suspicion and hate.[45] Accusations of malpractice against Moorish or Jewish healers were far more frequent than those against Christian doctors. The laws also prohibited from practising medicine men who had not studied at the university and thus had not been properly examined or licensed.

A witness named Miquel Martí shed a different light on this matter. He said that one day he was talking to Mahomat, who used to sell him linen. The Moor told him that he felt rather uneasy because, in his efforts to help, the Calbó family had been hostile to him. He said that *Mossèn* Bernís (his good friend) had asked him for help on behalf of the poisoned family. The first victim of the poisoning had already died, and they feared the worst. Mahomat told them that he knew someone who could help them (not giving the name), who supplied him with the syrup. After being paid for it, the procurer had handed over the syrup to Mahomat, who administered it, and now the family were demanding their money back. From the Moor's point of view, nothing had been done incorrectly. Mahomat responded promptly to the family's requests and supplied them with the medicine, so he did not understand the reasons for the family's annoyance and the demand for the money to be returned.[46]

However, Calbó tried to capitalise on this state of affairs, implying that the Moor might be responsible for the two women's ills instead of him:

> se'n congoxà ab ell que de què era lo dit exarop, ne de hon lo havia haüd, e aquell dit moro, no sabent dar desexida en lo dit feyt, dix que no l'havia fet lo dit exarop e que altri lo fahia, e que ell no y sabia res. Et de ffet, lo dit Sanxo Calbò lo meneçà que·l faria prendre, e de fet ho haguera fet sinó que li fon donat a entendre e preguar que no u fes, que·l dit moro no era home maliciós e no crehia que mentalment volgués matar a negú.

> [he got annoyed with him and asked him what that syrup was and where he had got it from, and the Moor, at a loss, said that someone else had given it to him.

---

[45] Carmen Barceló, *Minorías islámicas en el País Valenciano: Historia y dialecto* (Valencia: Universitat de València, 1984), pp. 92–100.

[46] Realistically, a patient only had any chance of getting their money back in the case of a failed treatment when a notarial contract existed. This only occurred in a few cases between a private individual and a healer. Reports of malpractice were few and far between. Complaints prompted by patient dissatisfaction most often tended to be directed essentially against those practising without a licence, Jewish and Muslim medical practitioners, and those of low status. See: McVaugh, *Medicine Before the Plague*, pp. 184–87.

And, in fact, Sanxo threatened to report him and would have done so had it not been for the fact that the others dissuaded him, saying that he was not an evil man who wished to do anyone any harm]. (2 March)[47]

The remedies themselves, and the neighbours' help, were the first resort in a case of poisoning. The complicity, the trust and the close ties with the city's Muslims were still very strong in the mid fifteenth century, making it possible to seek widespread remedies normally prohibited by the Church. The gradual deterioration in relations between Christians and Muslims in the city and kingdom of Valencia reached its high point about the same time. In 1455, the Moorish quarter was attacked and destroyed and, consequently, there was a movement of conversions and baptisms.

Accusing a Moor of trickery was not a bad option for Calbó's defence. On many occasions, important preachers in the city, such as Vincent Ferrer or Francesc Eiximenis, were hostile towards people who devoted themselves to the divinatory arts, but[48] they had a very different attitude toward prestigious physicians and surgeons. In one of his sermons, Ferrer compared the world to a large hospital. Jesus Christ, the greatest of doctors, had descended from paradise (which the preacher called *Studium*), to heal the waiting men in the rooms, the same as physicians. Thus, he established a metaphor that ennobled the doctor trained at the university as one compared to the son of God. Not all medical practitioners were valued equally, however. Physicians and surgeons trained in Galenism – the medical doctrine upon which rested all matters relating to knowledge about health, disease and the development of therapies to preserve health or to heal the sick – particularly in the universities, enjoyed a high reputation and social status above any other healers.[49] In defending his innocence, Calbó claimed that he quickly sought good doctors to attend to his daughter: 'ab tota diligència que podia trebalava en haver bons metges e solicitar aquells que venguessen' [as diligently as he could he worked to find good physicians and asked them to come] (2 March). This was Calbó's strategy for avoiding the

---

[47] Mª Carmen Barceló, 'La morería de Valencia en el reinado de Juan II', *Saitabi* 30 (1980): 49–71.

[48] For the Franciscan Eiximenis, all those who practised divination should be considered necromancers and, therefore, expelled from the city. See: Eiximenis, *Regiment*, p. 135. The Valencian Dominican Vincent Ferrer also warned continually in his sermons against turning to diviners. See: Miguel Llop, *San Vicente Ferrer y los aspectos socioeconómicos del mundo medieval* (Valencia: Universitat de València, 1995), p. 111.

[49] See: Luis García Ballester, 'The Construction of a New Form of Learning and Practicing Medicine in Medieval Latin Europe', *Science in Context* 8 (1995): 75–102; Nancy Siraisi, *Medieval and Early Renaissance Medicine: An Introduction to Knowledge and Practice* (Chicago: University of Chicago Press, 1990), pp. 20–23 and Carmel Ferragud, *Medicina i promoció a la baixa Edat Mitjana (Corona d'Aragó, 1350–1410)* (Madrid: Consejo Superior de Investigaciones Científicas, 2005).

accusation of poison: if he was the most diligent and attentive when caring for his relatives, and looking for the best medical care, he could not possibly have wanted to kill them.

In Calbó's defence, the apothecary Joan Amalric spoke positively of Calbó's diligence and Roquer's negligence in looking for healers: 'hun dia veu que en Sanxo Calbò portava hun orinal ab orina, e dix-li que era de sa filla e que la anava a mostrar a mestre Loís Gil, car mestre Exulbi la havia jaquida per ço com son gendre no·l volia pagar' [one day he saw that Sanxo Calbó was carrying a chamber pot with urine, and he told him it was his daughter's; he was taking it to the master Lluís Gil because the master Exulbe had refused it as his son-in-law was not paying him] (10 March). The court records refer to an alleged doctor, Ferragut, as *lo prohom* (the distinguished citizen), which emphasises his status.[50] Although there were several medical practitioners with this surname in Valencia at that time, the most important one was the bachelor of medicine and surgeon, Joan Ferragut. Calbó may have mentioned him, using the opinion of this prestigious surgeon and physician to avoid the accusation of poisoning: 'a hoÿt dir a·n Ferragut, lo prohom, qui l'era anat a veure, que si·s tenia a regiment ell guarria, e que no havia mal de metzines' [he had heard Ferragut, *lo prohom*, say that he had gone to see him, and that if he followed a strict regime he would get better, and that he had not been poisoned] (20 February).[51]

Ultimately, Calbó wanted the symptoms of the poisoning to look like those of indigestion and drinking too much alcohol, so one of his strategies was to accuse the people living in the house of gluttony and drunkenness. He said that one day in September they had had pork for dinner, and his daughter felt so ill that she asked him to call a confessor and the physician Joan d'Exulbe so that he could treat her.[52] He said that Roquer's mother was very fond of wine, which is why her face was bloated, adding that the doctor Miquel Climent (who treated her) had advised her to stop drinking, which she refused to do, saying that no doctor had ever prohibited her from doing it. But he also claimed that, after the first attack,

[50] On Joan Ferragut, see: Carmel Ferragud, 'El coneixement expert dels cirurgians en la cort del justícia criminal de la ciutat de València durant els segles XIV i XV: la pràctica de la dessospitació', in *Expertise et valeur des choses au Moyen Âge*, II: *Savoirs, écritures, pratiques*, ed. Laurent Feller and Ana Rodriguez (Madrid: Casa de Velásquez, 2016), pp. 315–29.

[51] Josep Sanchis Sivera, *Quaresma de Sant Vicent Ferrer predicada a València l'any 1413* (Barcelona: Barcino, 1927), pp. 27–31.

[52] The first law introduced in the laws (*furs*) of Valencia relative to the practice of medicine was the obligation for doctors to convince their patients to receive confession before beginning the cure, echoing what had been ordered in the Fourth Lateran Council (1215). See: Luis García Ballester, Michael R. McVaugh and Agustín Rubio Vela, *Medical Licensing and Learning in Fourteenth-Century Valencia* (Philadelphia: University of Pennsylvania Press, 1989) 6:42–43.

both granddaughter and grandmother had recovered and left the house healthy and cheerful enough to watch the Saint Dionysius procession, which was very popular in Valencia, an observation that was corroborated by several witnesses. However, this feast day is celebrated on 9 October, to commemorate the establishment of the Christian kingdom of Valencia after King James I's conquest,[53] so Calbó was referring to an episode before the poisoning to confuse people's understanding of the sequence of events.

Calbó also tried to use his love and care for his grandson as part of his defence. Roquer argued that the baby's indisposition was linked to his mother's milk, which must also have been poisoned. But Calbó refuted the accusations:

> E del fillet de la dita na Ysabel és ver que aquell una nit li vench vòmit e gità [...] ell [...] dix a la dita na Ysabel: 'filla tu est malalta e cries aquest minyó. Més valdria que li hagueses dida, si no tu perdràs a ell e a tu matexa'. E ell, dit confessant, pres lo dit minyó en sos braços e porta'l a casa d'en Pastor, la muller del qual criava, e dona-li hun reyal perquè li tingués aquella nit. E allí lo tingueren, e lo cendemà lo tornaren a casa

> [And it is true that one night Isabel's baby son vomited and Calbó said to Isabel, 'My daughter you are ill and you are breast-feeding a baby. You had better take him to a wet nurse, otherwise both you and he will die.' And he, a witness, took the baby in his arms and took him to Pastor's house, whose wife was breastfeeding, and he gave her a *real* for that night. And the next day they brought him back home]. (20 February)

Suckling babies were constantly taken to wet nurses, and there were several institutions that provided milk to foundlings.[54] The mother's illness, or her inability to breastfeed, meant that she resorted to wet nurses temporarily. Calbó insisted that he had acted swiftly to prevent Isabel from passing on the sickness to the baby because he loved his grandson and wanted him to be well, and so could not possibly have poisoned him.

Calbó's arguments failed, however, because once he was subjected to torture he confessed to putting arsenic in the syrup, in the salt cellar, in the broth, in a pot and in the sweets. He also confessed to lying to get the property of his daughter Úrsula, who died in the plague. He confessed that he was motivated by hatred for Roquer and that he wanted to get his hands on his daughter Isabel's goods. The *justícia criminal* was clear in its judgment: Isabel and her namesake grandmother had died because of the arsenic that they had ingested, which was

---

[53] Rafael Narbona, *El nou d'octubre: ressenya històrica d'una festa valenciana (segles XIV–XV)* (Valencia: Universitat de València, 1997).

[54] Agustín Rubio Vela, 'La asistencia hospitalaria infantil en la Valencia del siglo XIV: pobres, huérfanos y expósitos', *Dynamis* 2 (1982): 159–91 at pp. 163–65.

administered by Calbó, and that Roquer and his mother Estévena were very weak, and partially paralysed, for the same reason.

According to the Valencian laws (*furs*), when someone killed a close relative, he or she was sentenced to death, by being buried alive under the body of the person who was murdered until they themselves died.[55] However, it seems that the punishment was not carried out exactly in this way since Calbó was sentenced to be buried beneath his daughter and then, after being disinterred while still alive, to be hanged until he was dead:

> declaram lo dit Sanxo Calbó deure ésser soterrat viu en la fossa en la qual fon sepellida la dita na Ysabel, filla sua, e lo cos de aquella ésser mès sobre aquell dit Sanxo. En aprés, lo dit Sanxo Calbó deure ésser portat a penjar e deure ésser penjat en les forques del mercat de la dita ciutat, en manera que muyra naturalment e la ànima sia separada del cos.
>
> [We declare that Sanxo Calbó must be buried alive in the grave where his daughter Isabel was buried, and that her body be placed on top of Sanxo's. Then Sanxo Calbó must be taken to be hanged on the gibbet in the city's market, so that he may die a natural death and his soul may leave his body].

The excessiveness of the punishment may have made the act of burial with the victim symbolic in that the exhibition of the corpse was probably meant to act as a warning to the public.

The case of Sanxo Calbó is an anomalous episode involving people from the middle class in the city of Valencia in the mid fifteenth century. We observe them going about their daily lives, the different places they moved in and the ways they socialised, in the privacy of the home or in the street. We also see them contacting all sorts of people – regarding their profession, their religion and their social status – in the most diverse ways, but forced to do so by a crime. Calbó had all the qualities needed in this urban context to succeed and to progress in his life: firm patronage provided by his uncle, a profession in which he had established himself and a notable marriage. In short, in his case, all the conditions necessary for social promotion were in place. Nevertheless, he became an anomaly. His personality, his ambitions, his dishonesty as a craftsman in violating the principles established by his corporation and other diverse circumstances led him to break the law necessary for the functioning of the *res publica*. He became a criminal and committed the most horrendous and abominable of crimes, poisoning members of his family because of his hatred for his son-in-law and his greed. This case shows the social fascination with a macabre crime (*parricide*)

---

[55] *Furs de València*, pp. 7, 104. We have no information of any women being sentenced to die this way.

and the horror of its indiscriminate nature; that is, the attempt to kill all those living under the same roof, blood relatives or not.

The case illuminates the variety of meanings that poison, particularly arsenic, had for medieval society – its handling, its virtues and its risks. The people of Valencia were genuinely appalled by the damage arsenic could do, and yet its sale and use were habitual, despite the controls established in the laws. Indeed, people were used to handling it. The case is also an example of the mobilisation of numerous healthcare and medical resources that medieval urban society was equipped with to attend to people who had been poisoned.

Calbó's crime also illustrates the means that the authorities had at their disposal for investigating a complex case and for administering justice in accordance with the principles of Roman law. The laws of Valencia were created in 1261 within the strictest tradition and influence of the university of Bologna. The innovations put into practice by this new law code enabled the authorities to play a significant role as judges (with varying degrees of academic training) who carried out a judicial investigation either on their own initiative (*inquisitio*) or by way of denunciation, that was based on evidence set down in writing. It was the authorities' duty to restore order and to avoid the repetition of similar acts; to offer a deterrent, laws could be toughened as a result of the most shocking crimes. In the final analysis, the citizens had to be reassured that cases as heinous as this one were exceptional, that those who violated the law would face the full force of it and wind up a corpse, dangling in the market square as a potent sign for the rest of society.

CHAPTER 17

A Case of Mariticide in Late Medieval France

Patricia Turning

TUCKED INSIDE THE ARCHIVES of the southern French city of Toulouse is the story of Clare de Portet.[1] The events surrounding this woman provide a unique opportunity to consider a nuanced connection between gender, murder and the spectacle of public executions in the fifteenth century. Preserved in a jurisdictional dispute from 1428, it is impossible to know with certainty if the case survives because of sheer happenstance, or if contemporaries recognised it as something exceptional and important. On 28 May that year, the royal seneschal of Toulouse found Clare, from the nearby town of Portet, guilty of adultery with Bertrandus Savari, a soldier working as a sailor on the local Garonne river during a lull in war. The two were also deemed culpable of killing her husband, whose dead body they hid under the staircase of her house. For these crimes, the seneschal condemned her to run the city streets of Toulouse as a 'walk of shame', to forfeit all of her goods to the court, and to be decapitated *au talhador* [at the chopping block] before the city's Royal Treasury. Afterwards, the seneschal ordered her body to be suspended from the city's gallows while her head was to be taken to Portet and displayed on a pike: 'Qui ainsi fera ainsi périra' [And thus she shall perish].[2] On the determined day, however, the execution did not go off smoothly. Clare ran the town and authorities presumably confiscated her possessions, but after the seneschal's officers loaded her into the executioner's cart and started to wheel her to the site of her beheading, a group of municipal administrators (known as *capitols*) and their sergeants burst through the crowd of spectators and physically stopped the vehicle. This was not an act of chivalry or benevolence; instead, the civic officials insisted that they (and not the seneschal) should have the right to execute her for the murder. After hours of intense public confrontation between the royal and local officials, the result was

---

[1] Toulouse, Archives municipales de Toulouse [AMT], AA60, AA61, AA62. It is also the subject of a brief chapter in Roger Merle, *Les grandes affaires criminelles de Toulouse* (Toulouse: Privat, 1978), pp. 29–32.

[2] AMT, AA6, AA60.

a four-year jurisdictional battle over who had the right to decapitate this woman for the betrayal and death of her husband.

The archival records of this case raise a number of fundamental questions about the particularity of this specific crime and execution. At the time, France was engaged in the Hundred Years' War, with English forces steadily occupying the northern territory after Henry V's victory at Agincourt in 1415. The Dauphin Charles granted a teenage girl the opportunity to rally French resistance from the south, but in 1431 the English captured the same Joan of Arc, condemned her and burned her at the stake for heresy and witchcraft in the northern city of Rouen. In light of these political concerns, the contentious efforts of these secular administrations to decapitate Clare de Portet in the southern realm are really striking because of the time and resources involved. In addition, the documents do not indicate what happened to Clare's lover, the sailor who presumably participated in the murder, and who certainly lived with her while the corpse of her husband rotted nearby. In terms of violent acts (and especially in criminal investigations of murder), the male offender typically carried the brunt of the legal blame because judges perceived the female as an easily manipulated, and physically limited, participant in the crime.[3] It is unusual that Clare was the lone focus of this jurisdictional dispute. Perhaps even more remarkable is the execution itself, because examples of authorities beheading a female criminal for murder throughout the Middle Ages are few and far between. Trevor Dean mentions a case from Bologna in 1344 when the city's *podestà* convicted and beheaded a woman for crushing her newborn baby's throat with her bare hands, but that is the extent of the details.[4] In most of the scholarly literature and in the archival cases from late medieval France, authorities subjected women to specific public punishments, and decapitation simply was not one of them. In fact, French officials preferred hanging over beheading for even the most hardened of male criminals. Even if the story of Clare de Portet endures in the archives today because it is, indeed, exceptional to all that is known about gender and medieval crime and punishment, the case establishes that by the fifteenth century, in some circumstances, authorities saw just an offender – not a woman, but a criminal – who needed to die in a spectacular fashion. In this respect, the gravity of the crime and the status of the participants trumped any sensitivity to the fact that Clare was a woman. The murder of her husband became a pressing opportunity for competing jurisdictions to demonstrate their power and control over the inhabitants of Languedoc.

---

[3] Barbara Hanawalt, 'The Female Felon in Fourteenth-Century England', *Viator* 5 (1974): 253–68 at p. 256.

[4] Trevor Dean, *Crime in Medieval Europe 1200–1550* (Harlow: Pearson Education, 2001), p. 79.

Because of the nature of Toulouse's archival sources, there are limits to which definitive conclusions may be drawn from this case about the multifaceted meanings surrounding the execution of murderous women at the end of the Middle Ages. Most glaringly, many of the criminal cases do not even include indications of guilt or innocence, let alone official sentences. But this narrative of Clare de Portet allows historians to contemplate the fifteenth century as an era of transition in the French judicial process. This is not to say that gender was abandoned universally, but perhaps the tumultuous opening of the century forced secular authorities to ignore presumptions of the 'typical' female criminal, and to demonstrate their power and relevance by controlling the punitive performance that unfolded in the civic space. The lack of a public outcry at the beheading of Clare de Portet may suggest that the culture of death and dying was becoming less sensitive about protecting or minimising the participatory criminal role of a woman convicted of adultery and murder and that killing one's husband warranted the full weight of the law.

The central issue at stake in the case of Clare de Portet (which developed into a judicial dispute of such magnitude) was the rank of this young French woman's slain spouse. According to the archival records, her husband was a royal sergeant who, while stationed in Portet, married Clare, a local girl. Again, from a broader political perspective, this case took place during the Hundred Years' War when the prestige of the monarchy and its royal authority was drastically undermined by the looming threat of English forces. Throughout France, even during periods of truce, displaced marauders and soldiers caused chaos in the countryside, which heightened a sense of obligation and action from judicial authorities. Although both Esther Cohen's work on Paris and Jacques Rossiaud's study of Dijon confirm that the war did not dramatically alter the nature of crime in the cities, still, the increase in thefts and robberies in the rural areas influenced perceptions of justice for urban administrations.[5] Cohen explains that, during the Hundred Years' War, Parisian officials considered 'the power of law ... geared to keep order so as to uphold authority', and that crime was perceived as 'not a violation of law or justice, but merely as a transgression against the power of authority'.[6] In this era of social displacement and persistent instability, royal administrators grasped at opportunities to maintain their legitimate

---

[5] Jacques Rossiaud, 'Prostitution, Youth and Society in the Towns of Southeastern France in the Fifteenth Century', in *Deviants and the Abandoned in French Society*, ed. Robert Forster and Orest Ranum (Baltimore: Johns Hopkins University Press, 1978), pp. 1–46 at p. 7.

[6] Esther Cohen, 'The Hundred Years' War and Crime in Paris, 1332–1488', in *The Civilization of Crime: Violence in Town and Country since the Middle Ages*, ed. Eric A. Johnson and Eric H. Monkkonen (Chicago: University of Illinois Press, 1996), pp. 109–24 at p. 121.

relevance, and this required a firm control over the semblance of order and a certain amount of credible privilege for their officers, so there would have been legal and political concern about a royal officer stationed in the south.

Hence, the disappearance of a royal sergeant in Portet did not pass unnoticed for long; authorities were at Clare's door months after the murder and placed her case in the jurisdiction of the royal seneschal. In this circumstance, the fact that the seneschal sentenced Clare to such an extensive punishment implies that gender was not always a determining factor in rendering executions. Here was a case where a woman's crime was an attack not only on the head of her household but also a representative of the head of state, and so the only fitting final punishment for murder was decapitation, regardless of her sex. Her sentence included the loss of all her goods to the crown, and running the streets of the city, as was customary for a wife found guilty of adultery in Languedoc.[7] It is possible that her husband's rank conferred a more privileged status that afforded her transportation in a chariot to the site of her demise. This position, however, did not protect Clare de Portet from a public execution, and may have demanded a very deliberate display of her head and body after death. Sending her severed head to Portet visibly signified the extension of royal justice beyond the provincial capital of Toulouse. In the context of the larger concerns of the war, it may have been imperative that the seneschal make an example of Clare, proving his effectiveness in the local legal realm by establishing that not even a woman was exempt from the ramifications of this type of treason and treachery against a royal official.[8] In this era of military volatility, perceptions of order may have transcended perceptions of gender.

It is also important to remember that the only reason the scenario is preserved in the archives of Toulouse is because of the jurisdictional dispute that followed after the *capitols* stopped her execution. There are other instances in medieval corporal punishment in which the public reaction or an official reprieve saved the condemned from imminent death. In 1443, a crowd in Amiens saved four clerks from execution out of reverence for their office by grabbing the cart from the executioners and escorting the prisoners to asylum and safety.[9] A woman could step forward and propose marriage to a criminal. Officials perceived this arrangement as an option to reintegrate the criminal back into society as he

---

[7] Jean-Maris Carbasse, "'Currant nudi": Le répression de l'adultère dans le Midi médiéval, XIIe-VXe siècles', in *Droit, histoire et sexualité*, ed. Jacques Poumarede and Jean-Pierre Royer (Lille: Publications de l'Espace juridique, 1987), pp. 83–102.

[8] For more on murder as treason in medieval French law, see in this volume: Emily J. Hutchison, 'Defamation, a Murder *More* Foul?: The "Second Murder" of Louis, Duke of Orleans (d. 1407) Reconsidered' and Jolanta N. Komornicka, 'Treacherous Murder: Language and Meaning in French Murder Trials'.

[9] Dean, *Crime in Medieval Europe*, p. 136.

would be saved by domesticity and afforded the opportunity to serve the community by marrying an unwed spinster or a reformed prostitute.[10] To some men, having to spend the rest of his life with an unwanted woman was a fate worse than death.[11] But on the day of the execution back in 1428, the municipal *capitols* and their officers did not stop Clare de Portet's chariot outside the town hall on its way to her decapitation out of compassion for her sex or conviction of her innocence. No one from the audience came to her defence because they viewed her as an abused wife trying to escape a violent husband. Instead, this protest in Toulouse signalled the municipal *capitols'* refusal to surrender their power and role in the judicial process to the royal seneschal.

The records indicate that the commotion surrounding Clare de Portet's chariot lasted two hours as the crowd of Toulousains grew, inflaming tensions. The municipal *capitols* complained that the royal judge did not have the authority to hear cases of crimes committed in the city and vicariate of Toulouse. That right, they claimed, had been granted to the *capitols* by King Philip III in 1283. Philip mandated that the *capitols* had the right to preside over all trials concerning crimes committed in the city and surrounding territory of Toulouse in the name of the king, thus establishing the local officials as the first source of justice for the citizens. A royal official sat in on the trials, purely as an observer. The *capitols* interrogated defendants and witnesses, handled lawyers and rendered their verdicts, but the final step in the criminal process, punishing the convicted criminal, had to be approved by the royal vicar or his representative.[12] With the proclamation in 1283, King Philip theoretically shifted the power to punish out of the hands of the *capitols* and into the vicar's, and even though the *capitols* still retained the power to preside, the king thus placed his royal representative at the top of the local judicial hierarchy.

In medieval France, the right to punish criminals gave legitimacy to political administrations, both royal and municipal. Toulouse's *capitols* held on to this privilege well into the fourteenth century (and seemingly into the fifteenth century) for several reasons, in direct defiance of the king's proclamations. The public nature of criminal punishments allowed Toulouse's population to be involved in the civic rituals of law and order. The spectacle not only assured the constituents that their local officials fulfilled the obligations of their office but it also provided the people with the ritual elements of punishments they

---

[10] Esther Cohen, "'To Die a Criminal for Public Good': The Execution Ritual in Late Medieval Paris', in *Law, Customs, and the Social Fabric in Medieval Europe: Essays in Honor of Bryce Lyon*, ed. Bernard Bacharach (Kalamazoo, MI: Western Michigan Press, 1990), pp. 280–304 at p. 295.

[11] Esther Cohen, *The Crossroads of Justice: Law and Culture in Late Medieval France* (Leiden: Brill, 1993), p. 194.

[12] AMT, AA3:4, and duplicated in registers AA4:1, AA5:30, AA53:27.

demanded for justice. In addition, the *capitols* aspired to subvert royal authority and dominance in the city and to maintain autonomy and resistance to the royal vicar and his guards who had intruded upon their jurisdictional territory. In Toulouse in particular, this competition was a lingering tension stemming from the royal conquest of Languedoc after the Albigensian Crusade in 1229 and the Capetian efforts to integrate the region into their realm through a structured legal hierarchy. Municipal and royal leaders fought to secure the power to punish criminals because the process demonstrated authority to the city's inhabitants through horrific spectacles performed in their living and working spaces. Public punishments bound the citizens (as spectators) with their officials (as enforcers) in the restoration of law and order within the community, and so certain crimes necessitated public events in order to provide restitution to the victims and their families.

In the case of Clare de Portet, the *capitols* claimed that the royal seneschal's death sentence was completely void because his court did not alert them about the trial and verdict until after the fact. But, as the murdered husband was a royal sergeant, the seneschal's officials insisted that this trumped the *capitols'* claims over the case. It is hard to believe that either side debated these issues very eloquently in the heat of the moment, surrounded by a mob of spectators and officers holding arms. After several hours, the *capitols* refused to release their hold on the cart (in the meantime, Clare de Portet was no doubt confused and perhaps a bit optimistic of escaping death), and the highest officials retired to the nearby church of Saint Barthélémy to continue the discussion.[13] Eventually, they decided that the only solution was to refer the matter to the royal Parlement (which was meeting in Poitiers) and to the count of Foix, who served as lieutenant general.[14] The municipal officers escorted Clare to the prison in the town hall where she waited for four years – until 16 May 1432 – when the crown exercised its justice and a royal executioner finally decapitated her. For delaying the proceedings and for questioning the authority of the crown, Parlement ordered the city of Toulouse to pay 10,000 gold coins and to forfeit a portion of its criminal jurisdiction. In the proceedings, no one questioned Clare's guilt in the murder of her husband. The authorities debated only who had the lawful jurisdiction to cut off her head, which indicates that larger forces were at play beyond criminal justice. Her case became an opportunity for the public posturing of sovereignty between regional and royal officials.

---

[13] AMT, AA6/61.
[14] AMT, AA6/62.

From a historiographic perspective, the relationship between women, gender and deviance at the end of the Middle Ages is a complex one.[15] For some scholars, the answers to questions about felonious women rest in the quantitative data, which establishes that women were statistically less involved in crime than men. For example, James Given has found that, in England during the mid thirteenth century, less than 10 per cent of accused killers were women, and in the first half of the fourteenth century, women committed only 10 per cent of reported felonies.[16] In France, at the end of the fourteenth century, of the 127 people who appeared in the *Registre criminal du Châtelet* (1389–1392), nineteen were women, all accused of theft.[17] Guy Geltner's study of Italian cities reveals that women were represented in the records of offences punishable by imprisonment, but again, fewer were involved in the judicial or punitive process than their male counterparts. In Venice, women committed 17 per cent of thefts prosecuted during the years 1270 to 1347, and 14 per cent between 1348 and 1403.[18] Barbara Hanawalt speculates that the low number of females represented in criminal records could come from the bias of male judges and juries who hesitated to arrest or punish the 'weaker sex'.[19] Beyond numeric consideration of women's participation (or lack thereof) in punishable crime, another matter of scholarly focus is distinguishing female deviance from male.[20] As a result, some works conceive of female crime primarily in terms of sexual offences such as prostitution, concubinage or adultery. But women did participate in theft, burglary or the reception of stolen goods as well as brutal crimes such as murder, which complicates any neat binary constructs of either masculine or feminine criminal behaviour. Despite gendered notions of women as passive and non-violent players in the illicit world, individual cases from these same studies also reveal that women were just as likely to commit serious crimes as men, just not as frequently.

For offences like theft, regional variations abound, although, typically, female offenders came from the lower ranks of society and committed petty acts out of

---

[15] For the complex attitude towards women in early modern English society, especially those who killed their own children, see in this volume: Dianne Berg, 'Monstrous Un-Making: Maternal Infanticide and Female Agency in Early Modern England'.

[16] James B. Given, *Society and Homicide in Thirteenth-Century England* (Stanford, CA: Stanford University Press, 1977), pp. 134–49.

[17] M. Henri Duplès-Agier, ed., *Registre criminel du Châtelet de Paris du 6 Septembre 1389 au 18 Mai 1392*, 2 vols (Paris: Charles Lahure, 1861–1864).

[18] Guy Geltner, 'A Cell of their Own: The Incarceration of Women in Late Medieval Italy', *Signs* 39.1 (2013): 27–51 at p. 30.

[19] Hanawalt, 'Female Felon', p. 256.

[20] For a discussion of gender constructs of criminal violence in the early Middle Ages, see: Ross Balzaretti, '"These Are Things that Men Do, Not Women": The Social Regulation of Female Violence in Langobard Italy', in *Violence and Society in the Early Medieval West*, ed. Guy Halsall (Woodbridge: Boydell Press, 1998), pp. 175–92.

desperation or opportunity. In England, for example, women were more likely to steal food and clothing than their male counterparts.[21] In Paris, the *Registre criminal du Châtelet* contains cases of prostitutes such as Marion du Pont and Marion de la Court who stole money and goods from customers. Under torture, Marion du Pont confessed to robbing from a series of different clients' households and hotel establishments, and for these crimes she was sentenced to death.[22] Similarly, in 1375, the court of Bologna found a prostitute named Lisia guilty of stealing both money and clothes from taverns and clients over the span of two years.[23] Besides overt petty theft, women are also found in the criminal records engaging in the transmission of stolen goods and, in at least one case, a wife named Ameline de Warlus made a pretty good career of it while running a second-hand clothes shop in Paris. According to witness testimony (and after two sessions of torture), officials at the Châtelet determined that Ameline had an elaborate network of thieves who would discreetly notify her when they had clothes for her to purchase, which she could then sell for a profit.[24] For Bronislaw Geremek, this case in particular illuminates a connection between the marginalised world of theft and the world of trade, in which women very frequently served as the conduit.[25] For her role in the crime, Ameline de Warlus was sentenced to the pillory and banishment from the city, but for another woman, named Perrette Mauger, her facilitation of the resale of stolen goods for a band of thieves resulted in the death penalty in 1460.[26]

In terms of violent crimes such as assault or murder, it is more difficult to reconcile generalisations with the specifics found in extant court documents, especially from Toulouse. Some scholars like Dean have argued that while women did participate in physical attacks, the resulting wounds were not, inherently, as severe.[27] Whereas men had access to weapons and brute strength, women were physically less strong and limited to using their fists. The argument could be made that men kill, women wound. As a result, some studies suggest that judges tended to be more lenient in their consideration of female perpetrators. For instance, in England, when husband and wife acted together in committing a crime, jurors would convict the husband and acquit the wife on the grounds that

---

[21] Hanawalt, 'Female Felon', p. 262.
[22] *Registre criminel*, 2:386.
[23] Dean, *Crime in Medieval Europe*, p. 76.
[24] *Registre criminel*, 1:157–64.
[25] Bronislav Geremek, *The Margins of Society in Late Medieval Paris*, trans. Jean Birrell (Cambridge: Cambridge University Press, 1987), pp. 263–9.
[26] Ibid., p. 269.
[27] Dean, *Crime in Medieval Europe*, p. 77.

she 'could not contradict her husband's wishes'.[28] Medieval notions of gender presumably made it difficult for judicial authorities to accept that the 'fairer' or 'weaker' sex was capable of posing a dangerous physical threat to its community in any substantial, thus, punishable, capacity.

Specific cases reveal exceptions to these notions, however. The archives of Toulouse hold a criminal register (dated from April to October 1332) containing fifty-two cases that offer remarkable insight into the daily lives, tensions and concerns of the people who interacted with each other in the streets of the city as well as a sense of how a municipal court treated women accused of physical violence. The manuscript contains accounts of three married women listed as primary defendants, all in aggressive confrontations. Ricarda was married to Arnaldus de Bolbenas, a merchant of Carreria Nova in Saint Cyprian.[29] Bernarda was the wife of Arnaldus Durandi, a tavern keeper of barrio Alte Rippe.[30] Gualharda, wife of Arnaldis Aynerii de Petra Lada, was identified and charged as a conspirator with a male neighbour for orchestrating an assault and publicly humiliating a woman with a bad reputation.[31] All three women stood accused of vicious crimes against individuals who were not in their immediate families. Wives were not relegated to the sphere of the home, tucked away from the social and economic activity of the city. Instead, they actively engaged in the public realm as they feuded with neighbours and stood trial for their misdeeds in the *capitols'* courtroom. Although the women stood trial for brutal attacks, their actions could also constitute attempted murder, which provides further evidence that there is not a singular type of female criminality. Women could be confrontational, ruthless and scheming, not just stereotypical sexual or indirect offenders.

In the case of Ricarda, she assaulted a woman named Vitalia in the course of an ongoing feud. She publicly threatened this next-door neighbour, eventually gaining entrance to her house and striking her with a *magnum lapidem* [large rock] tucked into her clothing. According to the deposition, with one blow, Vitalia collapsed to the ground and had to be confined to bed for a long time; her husband feared that she was in mortal danger.[32] There is a certain amount of premeditation to this case as Ricarda did not frantically grab a rock in a scuffle outside but instead hid it until the moment of attack. The notary recorded that Vitalia was in physical peril and could have died, indicating the severity of her wounds. Ricarda's attorney postponed the case and, alas, the register contains no

---

[28] Henry Summerson, 'Maitland and the Criminal Law in the Age of *Bracton*', in *The History of English Law: Centenary Essays on 'Pollock and Maitland'*, ed. John Hudson (Oxford: Oxford University Press, 1996), pp. 115–43 at p. 117.

[29] AMT, FF57, p. 129. This manuscript has a modern pagination that is followed here.

[30] Ibid., p. 151.

[31] Ibid., p. 245.

[32] Ibid., p. 129.

testimony or verdict, but when feuds like this dissolved into violence, the *capitols* and their court became a broader venue for these interpersonal disputes, beyond the immediate vicinity of the city streets. The litigants brought cases to trial to seek some public retribution and acknowledgement of the tensions that could sprout during the daily frustrations of urban living, which also demonstrates the physical aggression that women could unleash to harm, or possibly kill, a rival.

The next female defendant was Bernarda Durandi, who entered the tavern of Guillelmus Amusse one day as he sold wine and other goods to his many clients. Bernarda, the wife of a fellow tavern owner from the same neighbourhood, wanted to return a *scutella* [dish] she purchased from Guillelmus' wife, but the proprietor refused to issue a refund. Because the transaction occurred in front of several witnesses, Bernarda apparently perceived this as an insult and she started screaming furiously at the wife that *pro malium infortunium eveniret eis* [bad things would come to her].[33] Bernarda stormed out of the tavern, only to return a short while later with a dagger concealed beneath her clothes. Confronting Guillelmus, she drew the dagger and stabbed him repeatedly in the chest until he fell back to the floor, injured. But this did not satisfy Bernarda, who seems to have wanted him dead. According to the court records, the next day she recruited several corrupt men to assist her plan of eliminating her foe. She instructed the men to go to Guillelmus' house in the middle of the night and bang on the door, shouting that they wanted to buy some wine. When Guillelmus opened the door to greet his customers, the armed men attacked him, wounding him in the head. Bernarda was an angry woman, but not irrational. She took the time to secure male accomplices to complete her vengeance, not because of physical weakness, but because she needed the element of surprise. This case also demonstrates the lengths to which a woman would go to seek personal restitution for a perceived insult: if she could not avenge herself with an assault with a deadly weapon, she simply employed malefactors to complete the task.

In the third case, a merchant named Guillelmus Calveti and a woman named Gualharda conspired against their neighbour Alamanda, wife of Petrus Bergonhonis.[34] What is known of the case comes from Alamanda's complaint to the *capitols* in court that the two defendants publicly defamed her character and threatened her safety on numerous occasions. She said that they told their neighbours that they would not break bread with her and would in fact 'panem suum comedent in lecto' [break bread in her bed] and 'taliter esset signata in eius facie pro semper cognosceretur et esset defformata dicte eius facie' [leave a mark on her face so she would always be recognised and deformed].[35] These disparaging

[33] Ibid., p. 151.
[34] Ibid., p. 245.
[35] Ibid.

remarks, taken as a whole, seemingly accuse Alamanda of illicit sexual conduct and allude to prostitution. Prostitutes were not allowed to socialise or to be welcomed into respectable homes and the threat of 'breaking bread' in her bed could be a symbolic accusation that she had hosted many men in that location. Aspiring to scar her face would not only socially isolate her but also impugn her reputation. Some cultures believed that a woman with a permanent mark on her face did not have sexual integrity.[36] But the accused defendants Guillelmus Calveti and Gualharda were not content to slander Alamanda's reputation and social standing in their neighbourhood; indeed, they also coordinated a ritual humiliation to drive her from it. The couple forced Alamanda to cross over a bridge from the suburb into the city of Toulouse, and denounced her way of life as they made her walk *cum pauperina mulier* [like a poor woman].[37] The procession ended in a vineyard outside the city where the two conspirators then directed some malefactors to Alamanda's location. The men beat her so badly that she was discovered half-dead. When the *capitols* summoned Guillelmus Calveti and Gualharda to stand trial for these accusations, both proclaimed their innocence of any misdeed.[38] Although the sources are silent on the outcome of this case, there is no indication from the proceedings that the female of the duo was anything less than an equal participant in the allegations. Like Clare de Portet, Toulouse's officials did not exhibit sympathy or excuse Gualharda for her role in this harassment.

What is important about these three examples is that, within the span of seven months in 1332, the *capitols* of Toulouse heard the charges against these women for dramatic and public affronts against the community. Comparing them with the cases that involved male defendants from the same register, there is little to no difference in the formulaic layout of the notary's work or in the way the *capitols* treated the offenders. In these circumstances, the perceived constructs of medieval gender did not affect the way officials viewed women. These proceedings did not portray the women as weak or feeble or as passive accomplices

---

[36] From a literary perspective, the best example of this phenomenon is perhaps Marie de France's *Bisclavret*, in which a werewolf bites off the nose of his disloyal wife and her children are born with the same infliction. *The Lais of Marie de France*, trans. Glyn S. Burgess and Keith Busby (New York: Penguin Classics, 1999), pp. 68–72. I thank Albrecht Classen for pointing this out to me, as well as other significant literary analogies below. Valentin Groebner argues more specifically that the severing of a nose signified an assault against the sexual honour of an individual, both in criminal punishments sanctioned by the municipal governments and through duels fought between rivals. A husband in late medieval Germany, for example, could punish his wife for infidelity by cutting off her nose. Groebner, *Defaced: The Visual Culture of Violence in the Late Middle Ages*, trans. Pamela Selwyn (New York: Zone Books, 2004), pp. 67–86.

[37] AMT, FF57, p. 245.

[38] Ibid., p. 246.

or marginal instigators. In 1332, there was no sense that the female constitution deserved anything less than serious repercussions in Toulouse. When considered individually, these cases, to some degree, undermine the quantitative data that seemingly minimises the female criminal's role in the medieval judicial system.

However, assaulting and conspiring against their neighbours is one thing; wives who killed their husbands is quite another. Claude Gauvard insists that medieval mariticide was a very rare phenomenon that was generally the product of many long years of spousal abuse. She offers as example a case from 1415 in which Marie la Mugière from Sens testified in court that she had endured eighteen years of suffering at the hands of her blind husband. The final straw came one evening after a long day of harvesting grapes when she found that her husband had ruined a separate stash of grapes. When she confronted him, a fight ensued during which he physically threw her out of the house. She returned indoors with force and, in the process of the subsequent struggle with her spouse, administered a lethal blow. The court exonerated her for killing him because it concluded that she had endured years with this abusive and burdensome man and 'in other cases, she was always a woman of a good life'.[39] William Chester Jordan found similar sympathy for an Exeter wife, named Alice, who plotted with a female friend to murder her husband, Richard le Blunt.[40] Whereas the authorities caught and convicted both women of the crime, they only executed the accomplice, Margaret, for her role as conspirator. The wife escaped being burned at the stake when a group of respectable men and women (and two chaplains) from the community interrupted the execution and escorted her to a church where she received asylum and, eventually, the ability to abjure the realm for exile in France. Jordan reads this as evidence that people were willing to afford Alice this judicial privilege because there was known excessive spousal abuse, although it may also be the case that Alice had strong personal or familial connections at play as well.[41] Hanawalt provides another self-defence case that is less transparent: an English woman claimed that, one night, her husband was struck by a fit of violent insanity and, out of desperation, she slit his throat and smashed his skull with a bill hook. Rather than put her fate in the hands of the court, she fled to a church to secure asylum.[42] This situation indicates

---

[39] Claude Gauvard, 'De grace especial': Crime, état et société en France à la fin du Moyen Âge (Paris: Publications de la Sorbonne, 1991), 1:314.

[40] William Chester Jordan, From England to France: Felony and Exile in the High Middle Ages (Princeton: Princeton University Press, 2015), p. 49.

[41] This notion of community intervening in cases of domestic violence has also been addressed by Sara M. Butler in 'The Law as a Weapon in Marital Disputes: Evidence from the Late Medieval Courts of Chancery, 1424–1529', Journal of British Studies 43.1 (2004): 291–316 at pp. 313–15.

[42] Hanawalt, 'Female Felon', p. 260.

that women understood how to employ the necessary rhetoric after murdering a spouse while also acknowledging the limits of communal or legal credulity.

There are cases of wives plotting with lovers to murder their husbands but, unlike many tales of courtly love, it is not so clear that the woman was impotent in the crime – that she schemed while the man carried it out.[43] In a well-documented case from the Île de France in 1369, these circumstances unfold in the high ranks of society.[44] The victim of the design was a wealthy nobleman named Even Dol, a counsellor to the king who received the privileges and protection of that title. Apparently, he also loaned money to those who needed it, but he was ruthless and heartless in calling in those debts. He was married to Ameline, the daughter of the war treasurer of King Charles V. The well-connected couple came to know Roland de Santeuil, a clerk and sellsword (mercenary), who needed a loan from Even to pay a ransom in Spain. Heavily in debt, Roland began to visit the Dol house under the pretence that he was courting their daughter, Michelete. In the process, Roland learned the rhythms of the household, started an amorous relationship with Ameline and plotted with her to get rid of the patriarch, Even Dol. With one blow, Roland would be rid of his financial obligation, and Ameline would be out of an unhappy marriage. The murder was an ambush: an assailant struck and killed Even Dol with a sword as he was travelling to Paris. Shortly thereafter, royal authorities arrested the wife and the lover and pursued the case aggressively because of the *sauvegard* afforded to Even Dol due to his rank and title. Although the records indicate that the murderous pair confessed to the crime under torture, there is no clear indication of how the two were punished. In this scenario, however, the wife was obviously in no position to kill her husband with a weapon or to organise an attack in the forest where her husband was most vulnerable; the court most likely saw her as an accomplice who hatched the plan and knew the risk involved, even though she did not deliver the fatal blow. But still, she saw an opportunity for happiness and perhaps passion, while protecting her status and wealth, and this came at the cost of her husband's life.

Even at the lowest of demographic levels, women could manipulate a lover to do away with a husband who stood in the way of their relationship. The register from the Châtelet de Paris includes a case from 1391 involving Belon, the wife of Drion Anceau. The document contains notification from a lesser French court which informed Parisian officials that, before it executed a criminal named

---

[43] Again, Marie de France provides an example of this in the story of *Equitan*, wherein a seneschal's wife plots (unsuccessfully) with her lover, the king, to get rid of her husband by making him jump, unaware of the true heat, into boiling water. *The Lais*, pp. 56–60.

[44] Annik Porteau-Bitker, 'Un crime passionnel au milieu du XIVe siècle', *Revue historique de droit français et étranger* 59 (1981): 635–51.

Thevenin Tout Seul for other crimes, he had confessed that, earlier that year (with the consent of Belon), he had murdered her husband by strangling him with his bare hands, after which they collectively disposed of the body by tossing it in a nearby river. The lower court wanted the Parisian officials to find and punish her. When confronted and interrogated, Belon (not surprisingly) protested her innocence, testifying that Thevenin Tout Seul acted alone in this crime. In her initial deposition, she recounted that, during the time she and her husband lived in a hotel, Thevenin Tout Seul was another guest who propositioned her for sex on multiple occasions. Although she resisted, one night before the feast of All Saints (1 November) he approached her and tried to seduce her one last time. Belon recalled that he had professed his love, intimating that if her husband was dead, they could get married. All she had to do, he had continued, was to leave the door to their room unlocked.[45] Not thinking much of it, one night before she had joined her husband in bed, she left the hinge unfastened. She claimed she woke up around three o'clock in the morning to find Thevenin kneeling by her bed; he whispered, 'tay-toi; ce sui-je. J'ay fait' ['be quiet; it's me. I did it'].[46] Then, she rolled over to find that he had strangled her husband to death. Desperate and afraid, she helped him to dispose of the body; they kept their distance for a few days so as not to arouse suspicion among the other residents of the hotel.

Eventually, they fled to join a band of travelling minstrels and *guiterne* players. The couple had separated when Thevenin left for Paris to find employment. In her testimony, she insisted that she never had sex with Thevenin until after the murder, further claiming to have been a victim of this persistent man's manipulations to get rid of her husband. This defence did not impress the court, which found her guilty and sentenced her to be burned at the stake. In her final moments of life, she finally confessed that her husband had been a bad provider and, out of desperation, she had sex with Thevenin in return for money and goods. As this adulterous relationship ran its course, the couple turned to murder and the anonymity of a transient life to try to find happiness together. In the end, it cost them their lives. The records indicate that Belon was so poor she had no possessions for the courts to confiscate after her death, which, in many ways, supports her second version of the story. Her spouse did not necessarily abuse her, but he neglected her, and so she looked for a chance to have a better life. And while she, like Ameline, did not physically murder her husband, she still was an active participant in disposing of the evidence and, in this case, she met her fate at the stake.

Without a male accomplice, the other way in which a woman could be implicated in harming her husband was through diabolical assistance, which

---

[45] *Registre criminel*, 2:55–61.
[46] Ibid., 2:57.

generally resulted in a trial for witchcraft. Although the *Registre criminel* contains a couple of trials of lower-class women convicted and burned at the stake for love magic,[47] the first witchcraft trial in Europe, in which a woman was accused of gaining sinister power after having had sexual intercourse with a demon, was held in fourteenth-century Ireland. Alice Kyteler of Kilkenny outlived several of her husbands and, in the process, inherited a good amount of money. Once her stepchildren started to resent her prosperity, rumours swirled that she manipulated her spouses through the diabolical, first luring them in with love magic and then killing them with the aid of the devil.[48] Officials built a case claiming that Alice had a demon lover and that she participated in Sabbaths wherein she sacrificed to the devil. This was confirmed with the confession of a former servant under torture. When her fourth husband became ill in 1324, pressure mounted in the community that forced Alice to flee to England for refuge. Although Alice does not perfectly fit the profile of the defendants targeted during the peak of the witch craze in the early modern period, her story still suggests a certain social incredulity that a woman could engage in these deadly misdeeds on her own, without the help of some other force or collaborator.[49] So among the highest and lowest echelons of society, women conspired with their lovers – or supposedly sought the help of the devil – to get rid of husbands. But Clare de Portet stood alone as the culpable and punishable party.

Unfortunately, Toulouse's archival records do not reveal exactly how Clare killed her husband, but they do indicate that the murder took place at the end of 1427 or early 1428; the seneschal condemned her at the end of May 1428. Given the speed of the medieval justice system, it is possible that for a good four or five months Clare hid her husband's rotting corpse under the stairs of her house while she and her boyfriend lived as a couple, systematically selling her late husband's possessions. Although a violent demise at the hand of her lover is always a possibility, Clare might have had the opportunity to stab her husband herself or to poison him either with herbs or a more creative toxin.[50] For example, in 1280, in

---

[47] For example, Ibid., 1:327–61 and 2:280–343.
[48] L. S. Davidson and John O. Ward, eds., *The Sorcery Trial of Alice Kyteler: A Contemporary Account (1324) Together with Related Documents in English Translation, with Introduction and Notes* (Binghamton, NY: Pegasus Press, 2004).
[49] Michael D. Bailey, *Magic and Superstition in Europe: A Concise History from Antiquity to the Present* (New York: Rowland and Littlefield, 2007), p. 123. See in this volume: Bridgette Slavin, 'Secret Killing and Murder by Magic in the Law of Adomnán'.
[50] For more on poisoning as a method of murder, particularly by women, see in this volume: Thomas Gobbitt, 'Poisoning, Killing and Murder in the *Edictus Rothari*', and Ben Parsons, 'Imps of Hell: Young People, Murder and the Early English Press'. There are also multiple examples of men dosing the food of their victims with poison. See in this volume: Carmel Ferragud, 'A Multiple Poisoning in the City of Valencia: Sanxo Calbó's Crime (1442)'.

northern France, authorities banished the wife of Gillot de Dors for attempting to kill her husband by feeding him what she believed to be a lethally toxic toad.[51] Whatever the cause of death, the murderer(s) could have conceived of a method that would have left the corpse in a condition tolerable enough that they could live with it for several months without a bloody mess or overwhelming odour. Anything too gruesome, perhaps, would have resulted in a more concerted effort to dispose of the carcass or severed limbs as a priority, especially considering the sanitary conditions of the Middle Ages. But then again, the audacity of the couple in keeping the dead husband under the stairs might explain why the seneschal issued such an extensive and public punishment to be played out in the streets of Toulouse. Clare and her lover eschewed religious rituals and societal norms, murdering a husband and royal officer and not even bothering to dispose of the evidence. It was an insult on all fronts (spiritual and secular) that could only be rectified with the most extreme punishment.

By the end of the Middle Ages, judicial administrations in France had standardised the rituals of public executions to the extent that everything – from the use of city space to the dress – reflected the status of the offender and the severity of the crime. Before execution, a common criminal was stripped to the waist, while a nobleman wore his livery of rank and office; a common criminal was hanged, while a person of rank was beheaded with a sword. Even transportation to the site of execution carried meaning: common criminals were strapped to a hurdle (or a wooden board) and dragged by horses to the location of execution, while a noble was transported in a cart.[52] In this way, the authorities signified their control over the orchestrated execution – they moved the culprit, he did not move himself. In the hands of secular officials, the dying and death of a criminal created a deliberate showcase for their power and of the way in which they could restore order to the community.[53]

It is difficult to assess how often judicial authorities publicly punished criminals because of the limitations of the archival sources. Most of the statistical evidence from medieval France indicates that the number of people executed was relatively low compared with the number of people charged with crimes. Between 1387 and 1400, for example, the Parisian Parlement heard more than

---

[51] Eugène Janin, 'Documents relatifs à la peine du banniessment (treizième et quatorzième siècles)', *Bibliothèque de l'École des chartes* 3 (1846): 419–26 at p. 420. Another example of a married woman and poison is found in Steven Bednarski, *A Poisoned Past: The Life and Times of Margarida de Portu, a Fourteenth-Century Accused Poisoner* (Toronto: University of Toronto Press, 2014).

[52] Cohen, *The Crossroads of Justice*, p. 187.

[53] I make this case for Toulouse in Patricia Turning, *Municipal Officials, Their Public and the Negotiation of Justice in Medieval Languedoc* (Leiden: Brill, 2012).

two hundred cases, of which only four ended in capital punishment.[54] In Arras, the municipal government ordered corporal punishment, mutilation and capital executions infrequently, averaging only one death sentence a year in the fifteenth century.[55] Jacques Chiffoleau found that the administration of fifteenth-century Avignon preferred to punish criminals with a prescribed set of financial fines, although papal justice had an arsenal of spectacular chastisements like drawing and quartering at its disposal.[56] On the continent, outside of France, this may have been the case as well. David Nicholas has shown that execution for crime did not occur very often in fourteenth-century Ghent. He argues that the bailiff of the city imposed the death sentence in less than 10 per cent of cases each year and, in fact, preferred banishment to the death sentence.[57] Geltner has effectively documented the rise of prisons as punitive institutions in the Italian communes of Venice and Florence by the end of the Middle Ages.[58] Public punishment was not an arbitrary or senseless weapon of cruelty for secular jurisdictions.

However, the importance of executions and punishments in the urban milieu resides not in the frequency but in the public, ritual meaning behind the events. Cohen asserts that medieval authorities and chroniclers created a 'visual trick' through these spectacular executions.[59] Even though the death sentences may not have occurred regularly, she argues, the painstaking processions to the gallows and bloodshed of the prisoner left a lasting impression upon spectators, leading them to recall the particularity and individuality of each execution. With a single decapitation or mutilation, a municipal government could make a statement both about its power and its intolerance for certain crimes that could endure for decades. However, historians have debated exactly how to unpack the notion of public punishment as ritual drama. Spierenburg argues that executions were a combination of religious and secular elements, which were intended to provide the criminal with numerous opportunities to confess, to repent and to be reconciled with God before death.[60] A passive crowd stood by as witness to the solemn procession as priests and clergy accompanied the convict to the scaf-

[54] Gauvard, 'De grace especial', p. 897.
[55] Robert Muchembled, *Le temps des supplices: De l'obéissance sous les rois absolus, XVe-XVIIIe siècle* (Paris: A Colin, 1992), p. 57.
[56] Jacques Chiffoleau, *Les justices du pape: délinquance et criminalité dans la région d'Avignon au XIVe siècle* (Paris: Publication de la Sorbonne, 1984), pp. 211–42.
[57] David Nicholas, 'Crime and Punishment in Fourteenth-Century Ghent (first part)', *Revue Belge de philologie et d'histoire* 48 (1970): 289–334 at pp. 328–29.
[58] G. Geltner, *The Medieval Prison: A Social History* (Princeton: Princeton University Press, 2008).
[59] Cohen, '"To Die a Criminal for Public Good"', p. 300.
[60] Peter Spierenburg, *The Spectacle of Suffering: Executions and the Evolution of Repression, from a Preindustrial Metropolis to the European Experience* (Cambridge: Cambridge University Press, 1984), pp. 46–52, 61–63.

fold. But Gauvard insists that medieval spectators were actively engaged in the whole process (which she believes was lacking in any spiritual tone) and that viewers were prepared to intervene in certain circumstances. If an executioner failed to offer a clean blow with his axe, or a rope broke before a criminal was successfully hanged, the audience could take it as a sign of God's mercy. In both interpretations, administrations gave careful consideration to the preparation of any execution or punishment in order to appease the public and to advance their judicial or social agenda.

What this means is that given the ramifications of and intentions behind these events, many authorities chose their criminals with discretion. For example, in Paris outsiders and transients suffered the majority of the executions involving amputations, mutilations or bodily remains left displayed on pikes or gibbets.[61] The most common profile of the executed criminal was a young lower-class male, unsettled and unmarried.[62] The Parisian authorities assigned lesser monetary sentences to local inhabitants who had financial and social ties to the community, unless the crime was treason against the king or especially heinous in its nature.[63] These studies imply that if royal or municipal governments chose to demonstrate their authority through the spectacles of punishment, someone who resided on the fringes of the general public became the most viable candidate, perhaps because there would be no popular protest against the execution. But it appears that in Toulouse, the *capitols* chose to publicly punish prisoners who had committed crimes that resonated with the community in some way. The men and women executed or ritually chastised had disturbed the balance of order within Toulouse, and only through their punishment could it be restored. One of the best examples is the famed Aimery Berenger Affair of 1332, which dramatically altered the judicial composition of the city for decades.[64] The public execution of a university student's squire became the fodder of a massive jurisdictional dispute between royal and municipal officials, which resembled that of Clare de Portet: namely, who has the right to kill particular offenders.

---

[61] Rodrigue Lavoie, 'Les statistiques criminelles et le visage du justicier: justice royale et justice seigneuriale en Provence au Moyen Âge', *Provence historique* 115 (1979): 3–20 at pp. 15 and 18.

[62] The administration of early modern Amsterdam also favoured this demographic of convicted criminals. Spierenberg, *The Spectacle of Suffering*, pp. 153–65.

[63] Rodrigue Lavoie, 'Justice, criminalité et peine de mort en France au Moyen Âge': Essai de typologie et de régionalisation', in *Le Sentiment de la mort au moyen âge: Études présentées au Cinquième colloque de l'institut d'études médiévales de l'Université de Montréal*, ed. Claude Sutto (Montreal: Université de Montréal, 1979), pp. 31–55 at p. 54.

[64] Patricia Turning, 'The Right to Punish: Jurisdictional Disputes between Royal and Municipal Officials in Medieval Toulouse', *French History* 24 (2010): 1–19.

Toulouse and the surrounding region of Languedoc utilised customary punishments to display this sovereignty, such as sentencing criminals and moral offenders to run the town. The *capitols* of Toulouse created a mobile performance of chastisement, in which a large amount of space and a variety of people witnessed the municipal authorities' ability to reestablish justice in the city. Officers dragged the culpable parties to a designated site, whereupon the civic trumpeter announced the crimes and sounded his horn before leading the procession of humiliation throughout the most populous and frequented streets during broad daylight. Variations abounded regarding the treatment of the defendants and the crimes that warranted this punishment. At times, the criminals had to wear objects that revealed their offences. On other occasions, executioners whipped the prisoner as he ran the town, inviting the public to join in the taunts and throw objects as well. Customary law dictated that adulterers run nude. In one illustration from a thirteenth-century Toulouse manuscript, the female defendant leads her lover by a rope tied around his penis.[65] Leah Lydia Otis found several examples of prostitutes and procurers in Languedoc sentenced to this punishment in the fifteenth and sixteenth centuries.[66] For particularly heinous crimes, running was replaced with dragging, and the procession ended in death. In 1290, the consuls of nearby Albi sentenced B. Salomonis of Noailles *qui, ut dicebatur, carnaliter cum quadam vacca se immiscebat* [who carnally knew a certain cow] to be tied to the tail of a horse, dragged throughout the streets of the city, decapitated and then burned.[67] In running the town, the sound of the trumpeter's horn signalled to the people of Toulouse that a public offender was passing through their streets. Standing in their doorways, armed with garbage to be thrown or just passing judgement, spectators knew that the *capitols* had caught and reprimanded a danger to their society, like the adulterous murderer Clare de Portet.

Other urban authorities, including the *capitols*, could also establish their role in high justice through the physical presence of gallows and pillories. Throughout the thirteenth century, the municipal authority erected both temporary and permanent structures in various sectors of Toulouse. Gallows, the wooden frames used for hangings, held a tremendous amount of symbolic authority to the people of the Middle Ages.[68] In fact, in France, Capetian kings regulated how many executed criminals each of the gallows could hold in order to maintain royal dominance over lesser jurisdictions. Dukes' gallows could hang eight criminals at a time and counts' were limited to six. The king's gallows in Paris,

[65] Paris, Bibliothèque nationale, MS lat. 9187, fol. 30v.
[66] Leah Lydia Otis, *Prostitution in Medieval Society: The History of an Urban Institution in Languedoc* (Chicago: The University of Chicago Press, 1985), pp. 91, 95.
[67] Archives municipales d'Albi, FF 7, fol. 1v.
[68] Henri Ramet, *Histoire de Toulouse* (Marseille: Toulouse Tarride, 1977), p. 202. Dean, *Crime in Medieval Europe*, pp. 124–25.

however, could suspend the bodies of as many as sixty prisoners at the same time. Criminals condemned to death at the gallows were not simply hanged until their neck broke. Instead, they suffered the slow process of strangulation, their bodies left on display after death until decay and decomposition freed the various parts of their corpse dangling from the ropes and chains.[69] Even a woman convicted of murder like Clare de Portet would not have faced this sentence in the south of France as most authorities reserved 'suspension' for men convicted of murder, treason, arson or violent attacks.[70]

Although historians have long believed that authorities never hanged female convicts because medieval attitudes toward women found it indecent to leave their bodies exposed, Cohen argued that fears of the supernatural were a more likely explanation.[71] No female convict was hanged in Paris before 1449.[72] Instead, officials sentenced any woman convicted of a capital offence either to be buried alive with her victim or burned at the stake to destroy her body completely. Nineteenth-century historians insisted this was an attempt to preserve female modesty by preventing the prolonged display of her body, but considering that authorities frequently whipped naked prostitutes and adulteresses in public, Cohen finds this explanation less than satisfying. Instead, she believes that there was a fear within medieval popular culture that all women possessed supernatural powers of some sort. Because of their perceived physical and intellectual weakness, women were supposedly more likely to consort with the devil, and this satanic relationship made them strong and threatening to men.[73] But this generalisation leans more towards anthropological understandings of gender and punishment rather than what the archival sources reveal.

Cohen continues, arguing that felonious females were considered especially dangerous because of the combination of demonology and their actual crimes and so, to prevent her from returning as an evil spirit, the female convict's body was either secured in the ground or completely wiped off the face of the earth.[74] Folke Ström found cases of women who had murdered a child, where the authorities first impaled her with an oak stake while she either lay in a grave or

---

[69] Roger Grand, 'Justice criminelle, procédures et peines dans les villes aux XIIIe et XIVe siècles', *Bibliothèque de l'École des chartes* 102 (1941): 51–108 at p. 99.
[70] Cohen, *The Crossroads of Justice*, p. 191.
[71] Jean Gessler, 'Mulier suspensa: à délit égal peine différente?' *Revue Belge de philologie et d'histoire* 18 (1939): 974–88. Cohen refutes Gessler's argument in Ester Cohen, 'Symbols of Culpability and the Universal Language of Justice: The Ritual of Public Executions in Late Medieval Europe', *History of European Ideas* 11 (1989): 407–16 at pp. 412–13.
[72] Gessler, 'Mulier suspensa', p. 981.
[73] Cohen, *The Crossroads of Justice*, p. 95.
[74] Cohen, 'Symbols of Culpability', p. 413.

on the ground, and then buried her on the spot.⁷⁵ In Aurrillac, after two women strangled all of their children, they were transported to the *fourches* where executioners burned them to ashes. In 1495 a young girl from Metz, who had 'taken her child by the feet, struck it against the wall and killed it', then 'threw it in the well of the house', suffered a similar fate.⁷⁶ Germany stands as a regional variation, in that in some cases female criminals were drowned so that the purifying force of the water carried the corpse away.⁷⁷ According to this line of argument, the authorities, therefore, punished female criminals in ways that explicitly removed the malefactor from the public eye and eliminated the (perceived/real) threat of her body from the community as a whole. Again, this position does not take into consideration that some crimes could transcend these constructs of women and the supernatural and assume far greater political or jurisdictional weight in their community.

Decapitation as corporal punishment carried a whole litany of meanings in the Middle Ages. From a literary perspective, severed heads play a role in the hagiography of cephalophoric saints and in vernacular epics, like *Beowulf*, or in the Middle High German *Nibelungenlied*.⁷⁸ From a practical point of view, judicial authorities chose decapitation because it provided the clearest proof of death. Even after the head was detached, it could be appropriately displayed while preserving the temporary facial identity of the criminal. Historically, though, this was a punishment primarily reserved for men of noble status and for extreme crimes like treason. In Germanic penal law, it was one of the earliest prescribed punishment for rape.⁷⁹ But it evolved, particularly in England, as reserved for heads of state or heads of household who had committed acts of treason. Apparently, William the Conqueror brought this tradition to England, employing it to keep the nobles in line by displaying severed heads as a sign of his power.⁸⁰ Here, status protected them from more gruesome executions because decapitation was a quicker, less painful death. However, it also signified the gravity of the crime, in which the nobleman had undermined his position of prominence and authority; it was only fitting that his death involved him losing his head. English sovereigns chose to perform their restoration of order and jus-

---

[75] Folke Ström, *On the Sacral Origin of the Germanic Death Penalties* (Stockholm: Hakan Ohlssons Baktrycheri, 1942), p. 210.
[76] Gonthier, *Le châtiment du crime*, p. 164.
[77] Ströme, *On the Sacred Origin*, pp. 171–78.
[78] See, for example, the many articles in *Heads Will Roll: Decapitation in the Medieval and Early Modern Imagination*, ed. Larissa Tracy and Jeff Massey (Leiden: Brill, 2012). Ström, *On the Sacral Origins*, pp. 166–67.
[79] Ström, *On the Sacral Origins*, p. 162.
[80] Howard Engel, *Lord High Executioner: An Unashamed Look at Hangmen, Headsmen, and their Kind* (Willowdale, Ontario: Key Porter Books, 1996), p. 106.

tice and to symbolise their power over the living through decapitation, while French authorities preferred hanging as the primary mode of punishment.[81]

In the end, what is truly striking about the case of Clare de Portet is that there is no indication anywhere in the archival records that this exceptional punishment for a woman – who took a lover, murdered her husband, hid his body in her house and lived alongside it with her accomplice – was anything but appropriate. Of course, there is always the possibility that municipal and royal officials had this real conversation and a notary failed to record it in the jurisdictional proceedings. But its absence could suggest that, by the fifteenth century, the gender or sex of the offender played less of a role in the execution of justice than historians searching for a neat binary construct of masculine/feminine criminality and official chastisement might assume, and that maybe this public and extreme punishment of a woman was more commonplace than the extant archival sources seem to reveal. Ultimately, this case may speak more about the male authorities' desire to perform their power through control of public punishments, rather than any hesitation or reservation on the behalf of officials toward decapitating a female murderer. To the judicial system of fifteenth-century Toulouse, Clare's beheading fit the crime that upset the status quo of both the household and the kingdom. Thus, her death for the murder of her husband filled a purpose of establishing a semblance of royal order in an environment that was perpetually threatened by a myriad of disorders.

---

[81] Tracy and Massey, 'Introduction', *Heads Will Roll*, pp. 1–14 at p. 8.

CHAPTER 18

Monstrous Un-Making:
Maternal Infanticide and Female Agency
in Early Modern England

Dianne Berg

IN THE SPRING OF 1616, Margaret Vincent, a gentlewoman 'of good parentage ... good education ... and being careful, as it seemed, of her soul's happiness' was converted '(by the subtle sophistry of some close Papists) ... to a blind belief of bewitching heresy' and became convinced that her family's Protestantism imperiled their eternal salvation.[1] Her husband, Jarvis, rebuffed her pleas for Roman Catholic conversion, accounting such 'persuasions ... vain and frivolous, and she undutiful to make so fond an attempt, many times snubbing her with some few unkind speeches'. This spousal resistance 'bred in her heart a purpose of more extremity' until at last she 'resolved the ruin of her own children ... to save their souls (as she vainly thought)' from being 'brought up in blindness and darksome errors, hoodwinked (by her husband's instructions) from the true light'. Accordingly, she waited until Jarvis was away and on 9 May – Ascension Day or Holy Thursday – she dismissed her maidservant and 'like a fierce and bloody Medea' strangled her two young sons, aged two and five, laying their corpses 'upon the bed, sleeping in death together'. (The Vincents' youngest child was 'abroad at nurse' and thus survived.)

The anonymous author of the contemporary prose pamphlet, *A Pittilesse Mother who most unnaturally at one time murthered two of her own children at Acton within six miles of London*, writes that the crime scene 'might have burst an iron heart asunder and made the very Tiger to relent' but Vincent – 'still animated forward by instigation of the Devil' – instead tried to take her own life, 'being of this strange opinion, that she herself by this deed had made Saints of her two children in heaven'. The murderous mother's attempt to join the saints she had

---

[1] Anonymous, *A Pittilesse Mother That at One Time Murdered Two of Her Own Children at Acton, etc.* (London, 1616); Tufts University Libraries, Early English Books Online, http://eebo.chadwyck.com.ezproxy.library.tufts.edu/home (accessed 12 December 2016). All quotations are from this source.

'made' was interrupted by her servant's return 'at the very instant of this deed of desperation', and the tract goes on to detail Vincent's 'violent rage', ensuing fit of madness and shocking lack of remorse:

> But blindness so prevailed that she continued still in her former stubbornness, affirming (contrary to all persuasive reasons) that she had done a deed of charity in making them Saints in Heaven that otherwise might have lived to destruction in Hell, and likewise refused to look upon any Protestant book as Bible, meditation, prayer book, and such like, affirming them to be erroneous and dangerous for any Romish Catholic to look in. Such were the violent opinions she had been instructed in, and with such fervencies therein she continued that no dissuasions could withdraw her from them, no, not death itself, being here possessed with such bewitching willfulness.

A Pittilesse Mother portrays a once exemplary woman 'possessed with such bewitching willfulness' that she can no longer distinguish good from evil, or 'right faith' from 'the Devil's temptation'. In the grip of this grievous error, Margaret Vincent collapses her own confused subjectivity with that of her children until the association is so 'deranged, consuming, and dangerous' that no choice remains but to eliminate herself and them for their collective good.[2] But despite the pamphlet's censure of 'this creature not deserving mother's name', for Vincent, the earthly 'undoing' of her family was wholly commensurate with the role of loving Christian parent. By sacrificing the children 'bred in her own body, and cherished in her own womb with much dearness full forty weeks', she secured their most essential safety by preserving their souls. It was only after three days of counselling by 'certain godly preachers ... that her heart by degrees became a little mollified and in nature somewhat repentant for these her most heinous offences', and Vincent was (according to the pamphlet's narrative) convinced she had acted 'only by the Devil's temptation' and 'eternally deserved hellfire for the murder of her children'.

The popular analogical framing of the domestic realm as a microcosm of the community, the state and a well-ordered universe made the early modern household a place where wives and mothers held positions of simultaneous authority and subjugation, with female power exercised privately in the interests of maintaining a masculine public order. Protestant rhetoric extolled an ideal of companionate matrimony akin to a partnership: a 'marriage of true minds' that did not translate to an equal balance of power but instead espoused the male/female, work/home division of authority that would inform the western family model for centuries to come, allocating women power in a domestic context distinct from the public, political realm of men. This arrangement gave women

---

[2] Frances E. Dolan, *Dangerous Familiars: Representations of Domestic Crime in England, 1550–1700* (Ithaca: Cornell University Press, 1994), p. 142.

responsibility for establishing and maintaining household order while remaining answerable to their husbands' superior authority: a place for everyone, and everyone in his or her appointed (and appropriately gendered) place. But in practice, the personal was deeply political: Margaret Vincent's desire to control her family's spiritual destiny challenged and undermined her husband's duty to his private household and to his nation's official, public – and legally enforced – religion, making the children's murder a profoundly seditious act. A woman who killed her offspring rejected, abandoned and ultimately reversed her political and 'natural' roles in the production of a stable and godly family, household and community: a monstrous unmaking in which her material female energy disrupted power structures conceptualised as male. Through her destruction of what she had created and nurtured, the infanticidal mother became a peculiarly subversive amalgam of traitor and apostate.

The fact that Margaret Vincent's misguided attempt to 'save' her children occurred via the 'charming persuasions' of papists highlights a worrisome flaw in the analogical scheme: the weakness of the feminine vessel. As *A Pittilesse Mother* cautions, 'hardly the female kind can escape their enticements, of which weak sex they continually make prize ... and by them lay plots to ensnare others, as they did by this deceived gentlewoman'. A virtuous matron so readily 'deceived' by proponents of a heretical religion exemplified contemporary concerns about women as vulnerable points in the body politic: portals through which pernicious forces might creep to undermine an only superficially stable whole. The pamphlet's author describes the newly converted Vincent's efforts to lead Jarvis down the same wicked path:

> For she, good soul, being made a bird of their own feather, desired to beget more of the same kind, and from time to time made persuasive arguments to win her husband to the same opinion, and deemed it a meritorious deed to charge his conscience with that infectious burden of Romish opinions, affirming by many false reasons that his former life had been led in blindness, and that she was appointed by the Holy Church to shew him the light of true understanding. These and such like were the instructions she had given her to entangle her husband in and win him if she might to their blind heresies.

Wise husbands – recalling Adam's uxorious folly – were on guard against such 'persuasions' and careful to assert sovereignty in religious as well as practical matters. Women were considered especially vulnerable to malign influence, and their inherently inferior intellectual capacity and emotional nature made them worryingly receptive to cunning papist sophistry. Given this axiomatic frailty, a woman's most positive impulses (including Christian zeal and maternal tenderness) could be twisted to diabolical purpose, and such fears were expressed in representations of hitherto 'good' mothers whose love became so perverted that they killed their children in what they believed were their best interests.

Infanticide is a crime historically associated with unruly female passion. Peter Hoffer and N. E. H. Hull write that in the early modern period it 'was a crime for which women were indicted far more frequently than men ... almost exactly the opposite of the distribution of the sexes in murders and manslaughters of adult victims'.[3] This disparity is partially due to the fact that women were less likely to engage in the types of civilian violence – street combat, private duels or crimes of sexual jealousy – in which men were killed. Childcare, however, was almost exclusively women's work, meaning that when women became angry or frustrated, the closest victim of their anger might well be a child, and often their own child. But this association is not to suggest that maternal infanticide was commonplace, or viewed as anything but a tragic aberration; while most murdered children died at their mothers' hands, these cases were rare, and the spectre of the loving nurturer who violently subverts her natural role wielded a conceptual power far beyond any danger she realistically posed. Indeed, such anxieties indicate more global concerns about the state of the family, the family as microcosmic state and the need to reinforce the *status quo* at home and abroad. The sensational tone and lurid imagery employed by popular representations of murderous mothers express not only the horror these crimes evoked but also the urge to neutralise the domestic and social threat they embodied. The 'true relations' of such crimes in pamphlets and ballads reveal an abiding fascination with women who kill and a desire to cast them, in J. A. Sharpe's terms, as 'willing central participants in a theatre of punishment'.[4] In this way, texts like *A Pittilesse Mother* appropriate and manipulate infanticide narratives, providing a titillating glimpse of maternal violence in the interest of preserving patriarchal order.

Early modern ideas about women's moral, ethical and intellectual frailty belonged to a well-established western tradition.[5] From Genesis' portrait of Eve (the prototypical havoc-wreaking, insufficiently monitored female) to the writings of St Jerome; from medieval antifeminism to Renaissance humanism (Erasmus describes women as 'talkative, fickle and superstitious'); from misogynist Protestant reformers like John Knox to the 'woman-hating' pamphleteer John Swetnam, masculine suspicion and criticism were in plentiful supply.[6] The inconsistent, frivolous nature of the weaker sex was fodder for sermons, homilies, polemical tracts and conduct literature, and both sides of the Reformation

---

[3] Peter C. Hoffer and N. E. H. Hull, *Murdering Mothers: Infanticide in England and New England 1558–1803* (New York: New York University Press, 1984), p. 98.

[4] J. A. Sharpe, '"Last dying speeches": Religion, Ideology, and Public Execution in Seventeenth Century England', *Past and Present* 107 (1985): 144–67 at p. 148.

[5] See, in this volume: Patricia Turning, 'A Case of Mariticide in Late Medieval France'.

[6] Desiderus Erasmus, *De duplici copia verborum ac rerum comentarii duo*, ed. Craig Thompson, trans. Betty Knott, *The Collected Works of Erasmus* (Toronto: University of Toronto Press, 1975), p. 583.

divide employed the trope of the spiritually and psychologically infirm woman to serve their respective agendas. Lucy Underwood writes of a contemporary Catholic account in the Archives of the Archdiocese of Westminster, which presents the Vincent murders as the work of a female mind unhinged not by demonic possession and/or heresy but by religious persecution: 'Madness, not Catholicism, caused Margaret Vincent's unnatural actions, and madness was the result of Protestant oppression ... Where *A Pittilesse Mother* insists on a premeditated murder, the Catholic report makes it a panicked reaction' to the threat of her children being removed as punishment for her 'violent' recusancy.[7]

In this alternate reading, *A Pittilesse Mother*'s cautionary 'tale of papist child-slaughter' becomes the story of a well-intentioned, but emotionally unstable, mother made desperate by institutionalised religious intolerance: 'for the Protestant writer, the moral is that Catholicism turns loving parents into monsters; for the Catholic writer, that Protestant tyranny drives burdened souls to lunacy'.[8] But whether Vincent's crime resulted from diabolic influence or the pressure of an abusive state religion on a fragile psyche, she responded by destroying her children, her husband's patrimony and the domestic commonwealth she was entrusted to maintain. These actions may have sprung from misguided conversion to a 'false' faith or from the intolerable tension between her private spiritual beliefs and her public duties as a wife, mother and citizen in a Protestant nation; however, viewed from either perspective, the murderous mother enacts a moral, emotional and/or mental weakness explicitly gendered as female, a designation made even more disruptive given her putatively 'natural' role as caregiver.

Given the space *A Pittilesse Mother* devotes to Vincent's 'stubbornness' and 'undutiful' efforts to convert her family, it is striking that her final words remain a mystery, an omission that complicates the restoration of 'right' faith the pamphlet implies. Underwood points out that although *A Pittilesse Mother* claims she 'repented her actions', the author 'does not quite say Vincent reconverted to Protestantism, stopping at "Thus she was truly repentant, to which (no doubt) but by the good meanes of these Preachers she was wrought unto"'.[9] In a period and print medium that privileged such details for their sensation value as much as for their didactic function, the particulars of Vincent's trial, execution and scaffold speech are conspicuous by their absence. Moreover, *A Pittilesse Mother*'s bathetic tone clearly seeks an emotional response from readers. It seems unlikely

---

[7] Archives of the Archdiocese of Westminster, Series A, vol. 15, no. 98, in Lucy Underwood, *Childhood, Youth, and Religious Dissent in Post-Reformation England* (New York: Palgrave Macmillan, 2014), p. 176.
[8] Underwood, *Childhood*, p. 176.
[9] Ibid., p. 238.

that a writer who relates how one victim retained 'a countenance so sweet [it] might have begged mercy at a tyrant's hand' as his 'fierce and bloody mother … parted the soul and body' would miss an opportunity to describe that mother's eventual remorse and public reckoning in equally melodramatic terms.

It may be that the Protestant pamphlet's reference to the 'free confession' and 'patient mind' with which Vincent received her judgment were generic formalities, but it is intriguing that 'good gentlewomen' are urged to simply 'Forgive and forget her' since 'she is not the first that hath been blemished with blood nor the last that will make a husband wifeless'. The absence of any confession or gallows speech raises questions about why the narrator – simultaneously condemning her transgressions and urging 'forgiveness' – silences Vincent rather than allowing her to speak, or even ventriloquising a conventional expression of remorse. In its erasure or elision of her final words, *A Pittilesse Mother* strips Vincent of both her voice and any lingering subjectivity beyond the object lesson of her crime and punishment, while its closing admonition that 'Countrymen of England' beware 'that dangerous sect' conflates standard anti-papist cant with deep-seated anxieties about wilful, unruly women. Despite her constrained authority and limited personal agency, the murderous mother's ability to 'make a husband wifeless' (and a father childless) posed a threat to patriarchal order made only marginally less discomfiting when couched in anti-Catholic rhetoric. The tract's dismissal of the individual woman behind the murders attempts to reduce Vincent to a 'type', consigning her to the long list of morally weak, headstrong women who people contemporary misogynist polemic.

Despite her subsidiary position in the analogical scheme, the early modern housewife wielded substantial power, even when contained within her designated sphere of influence. As homemakers, wives and mothers create and shape the household through their practical management of everyday domestic affairs; they also 'make' the family via the somatic materiality of pregnancy, childbirth, the production of breast milk, the selection of midwives and wet-nurses and early childhood education and discipline. In these ways, mothers simultaneously engender the nation and ensure its future; as David Cressy observes, 'Without childbearing there could be no patriarchy, without human procreation no social reproduction. The woman's work of childbearing made mouths to feed and hands to work, new subjects, citizens, and Christians'.[10] But a negative symbiosis inheres in this social and biological interdependence. The childbearing woman manufactures 'new subjects, citizens, and Christians', but only if she performs certain actions; all a pregnant woman or recently delivered mother has to do is nothing for a growing foetus or an infant to die.

---

[10] David Cressy, *Birth, Marriage, and Death: Ritual, Religion, and the Life Cycle in Tudor and Stuart England* (Oxford: Oxford University Press, 1997), p. 15.

During pregnancy and the post-natal period, maternal bodies nourish their offspring to promote the developing infant's growth and early survival; after weaning comes the work of ensuring the child continues to thrive until it can feed, protect and eventually fend for itself. But failure or refusal to perform these functions, or even simple neglect or incompetence, threatens the whole system; moreover, the fragility of babies and young children meant they met with frequent accidents and could be deliberately done away with under the guise of mischance. There were many ways in which the childbearing woman's protean, generative capabilities could be used for *un*making, and this capacity to destroy what she had 'cherished in her own womb' – possibly without detection or consequences – imbued the mother with tremendous psychological force. Naomi J. Miller addresses the early modern period's multivalent 'codes of maternity' in her essay on the speaker's self-infantilisation in Shakespeare's sonnet 143 ('Lo, as a careful housewife'), noting that '[i]n a variety of early modern texts, mothers offer the potential for both nurture and rejection, sustenance and destruction'.[11] Miller writes that the one-two punch of maternal authority and sexuality was a particularly 'powerful combination in a society that had marked anxieties over the positions of women', where mothers were 'sometimes represented as Madonna and monster at once' in texts that veered between eulogising those who sacrificed themselves for their children's sake (e.g. *The Honour of Virtue*, a 1620 pamphlet that praises Elizabeth Crashaw, the poet's stepmother, for her admirably selfless death in childbirth) and denouncing others like Margaret Vincent as 'without all motherly pity'.[12]

This perceived duality is, at least, partly attributable to the female body's changeable nature, a physical incoherence directly related to that body's sexual and reproductive functions. Anxieties about women's weirdly unstable corporeality stretch back to Antiquity, when Hippocratic medicine held that women's skin was more porous than men's, leaving them 'susceptible to passions, [and] less protected against corrupting ingestions'.[13] The female body's shape-shifting penetrability renders it inferior to its less plastic masculine opposite, yet its ability to incubate, procreate and cultivate life grants women power to 'bridge the gap between two bodies, becoming both one and two at once through the gifts of gestation and milk', thereby making its very instability a disquieting strength.[14] Medieval and early modern anxieties about women's moral

[11] Naomi J. Miller, 'Playing "the mother's part": Shakespeare's Sonnets and Early Modern Codes of Maternity', in *Shakespeare's Sonnets: Critical Essays*, ed. James Schiffer (New York: Routledge, 2000), p. 347.
[12] Ibid., p. 348.
[13] Rebecca Kukla, *Mass Hysteria: Medicine, Culture, and Mothers' Bodies* (Lanham, MD: Rowman and Littlefield, 2005), p. 5.
[14] Ibid., p. 1.

inconstancy are rendered more legible when contextualised by this disturbing mutability. In addition to her volatile flesh – expanding and contracting, generating, expelling and sometimes losing life through miscarriage, stillbirth or childbed mortality – the sexualised woman's association with bodily fluids had prodigious cultural import, especially with regard to blood. Ariane Belizet writes that while 'blood itself is not necessarily gendered, the act of bleeding *is*, and the bleeding associated with domestic rites and relationships is almost always considered feminine'.[15] From the onset of menses to the hymeneal bleeding of nuptial consummation, which 'initiated the domestic unit and established domestic hierarchy by embodying patriarchal control over the new wife's body', women's blood and the act of bleeding separated them not only from men but also from their unsexualised pre-pubescent selves.[16] Belizet presents the loss of virginity as a contract written in the bride's own blood, affirming her 'physical, spiritual, and mental submission to her husband's will, not just at the moment of consummation but as the most important factor of her new identity as wife … bloody wedding sheets serve as evidence of a marriage's consummation and represent the bride's first task of housewifery'.[17] This foundational association links bloodshed to the performance of marital obedience and to the conceptual identity of 'wife' itself. In a culture in which sexual consummation rendered a marriage both valid and (in most cases) indissoluble, the fact that this bond was partially forged via the woman's bleeding lays the groundwork for a relationship wherein willing submission becomes rhetorically indistinguishable from enforced subjugation: a condition that never exists without the danger of rebellion.

Menstrual and marital blood marked important changes in women's cultural status and identity, and the blood of childbirth was equally fraught with signification. The potential for wifely insubordination caused a great deal of masculine unease in this period, and a woman's transition from bleeding bride to bleeding mother gave an additional valence to her mysterious propagative power. Beyond the deeply gendered nature of the event itself, the bleeding that followed childbirth meant that new fathers were forbidden sexual access to their wives during the post-partum period. In this way, the blood accompanying the transformation from wife to mother interrupted and temporarily suspended a husband's patriarchal control over his wife's body. This period of relative autonomy was brief – generally four to six weeks – but important, and observance of the customary 'gander month' ensured that the mother was excused from most regular obligations. In his compendious conduct book, *Of Domesticall Duties*, the clergyman

---

[15] Ariane M. Balizet, *Blood and Home in Early Modern Drama: Domestic Identity on the Renaissance Stage* (New York: Routledge, 2014), p. 89.
[16] Ibid., p. 36.
[17] Ibid., pp. 36–37.

and polemicist William Gouge cautioned that newly delivered women required rest to make a proper recovery: 'The mother at that time by reason of her travail and delivery is weak, and not to have her head troubled with many cares'.[18] As Gouge notes, this hiatus was intended to allow the post-partum woman some much-needed peace and quiet, but it was also meant to insulate her from ordinary activities (and from most other people) while she was still 'green', a term used to indicate female sickness in general but 'primarily related to the condition of "greensickness", amenorrhea, the stoppage of menses or terms'.[19]

Women's blood had a variety of negative implications in this period, from menstruation's association with the purging of excess humors (and possible poisonous properties) to the 'after-purging' that followed delivery, symptomatic of a new mother's 'weakness and uncleanness'. According to custom, 'green women' were expected to remain at home, avoid sexual relations and eschew church attendance in the time between confinement and 'churching', a controversial ceremony presented variously as a service of thanksgiving, a public celebration of safe deliverance or a retrograde by-product of heathen superstition. With roots in Hellenic, Hebrew and Catholic traditions, churching seemed designed to provoke Protestant anxieties, and Puritans inveighed against it vigorously. In addition to the custom's troubling antecedents and slippery function, its focus on the maternal body risked valorising women's lived, messy corporeality within the sacred and patriarchal space of the church. It is pleasing to think of the ways in which early modern mothers contrived to turn their post-natal sequestration into a quasi-holiday, and their reintroduction to the community into a celebration of female bodies in the face of institutional suspicion. Excused from household and marital duties, a woman who survived the trial of childbirth could deploy her perceived weakness to advantage: resting, eating, drinking and visiting with female relatives and gossips. In this way, misogynist ideas about post-partum bodies and their 'unclean' leakages reprieved new mothers from wifely obligations, while the churching ritual carved out a space where their procreative bodies were honoured, even as their parturient pain and blood heralded the new servitude of motherhood.

The ordinary wife and mother was no stranger to life's gory corporeality beyond the birthing chamber, and the daily routine of kitchen and pantry included its share of carnage. Wendy Wall's vivid portrayal of the early modern housewife '[e]mptying and dismembering bodies when they are almost cold, trafficking in warm blood, and ripping guts from live chickens' as she 'isolated and

---

[18] William Gouge, *Of domesticall duties eight treatises* (London, 1622); Tufts University Libraries, Early English Books Online: http://eebo.chadwyck.com.ezproxy.library.tufts.edu/home (accessed 11 November 2016).

[19] Cressy, *Birth, Marriage, and Death*, p. 203.

manipulated the boundary between animation and death' graphically illustrates this intimate familiarity with flesh and blood.[20] The act of changing animals into carcasses and thence into sustaining, wholesome food is a profoundly transformative one, comprising both making and unmaking: livestock are bred, sheltered, reared and cared for until ready for slaughter, at which point the unmade animal becomes the finished meal. This quotidian violence was wholly unremarkable yet incongruent with the image of maternal tenderness as women performed, on a private scale, actions judged necessary, but socially marginalised, in the wider community.[21] Moreover, contemporary domestic treatises stress the figurative concept of an embodied home wherein the husband functions as the head, and the well-ordered household is a healthy body. Should the woman of the house – ancillary to the head but superior to lesser members – employ her homely skills beyond the kitchen, she materially and notionally dismembers the family, the community to which it belongs and the patriarchal framework underpinning analogical thought.[22]

Dolan observes that 'infanticide statutes articulated fears about women's capacity for violence rather than accurately describing their behavior', but although the rarity of such crimes exposes them as largely unjustified, these fears have deep cultural roots.[23] Anxieties about doting mothers becoming infanticidal monsters reach back to Medea, to whom early modern child-killers are sometimes compared in ballads and broadsheets. Taken in this context, it is significant that Margaret Vincent's delusion first manifests as wilful obstinacy: the formerly 'discreet' and 'modest' woman seeks to dictate her family's religion, and when denied that power, she seizes it by killing them. Comparing her to 'a bloody Medea', *A Pittilesse Mother* describes Vincent's bloodlust as insatiable once aroused: 'These two pretty children being thus murdered ... she began to grow desperate and still to desire more and more blood, which had been a third murder of her own babes, had it not been abroad at nurse and by that means could not be accomplished. Whereupon she fell into a violent rage'. The

---

[20] Wendy Wall, *Staging Domesticity: Household Work and English Identity in Early Modern Drama* (Cambridge: Cambridge University Press, 2002), p. 13.

[21] Raphael Hythloday, the narrator of More's *Utopia*, notes that livestock in that idealised society are slaughtered by slaves in 'special places without the town ... for the Utopians ... think that pity and good-nature ... are much impaired by the butchering of animals' and view 'the desire for bloodshed, even of beasts, as a mark of a mind that is already corrupted with cruelty, or that at least by the frequent returns of so brutal a pleasure must degenerate into it'. Thomas More, *Utopia* (New York: Dover Publications, 1997), pp. 38–39, 51.

[22] See Karl Steel on the notional connection between butchers and social disruption, and butchery's potential to confuse human and animal bodies in *How To Make A Human: Animals and Violence in the Middle Ages* (Athens: Ohio State University Press, 2011).

[23] Dolan, *Dangerous Familiars*, p. 131.

pamphlet explicitly casts her crime as one of vengeful disobedience – 'she made her husband fatherless of two as pretty children as ever came from woman's womb' – adding the destruction of his heirs and patrilineal 'house' to her litany of misdeeds.

In another literary echo of a murderous woman addressing a man bereft of heirs, Vincent's insistence that 'what's done is past … and I nothing at all repent it' illustrates her 'bewitching willfulness', evoking Lady Macbeth's '[t]hings without all remedy/ Should be without regard; what's done, is done' (*Macbeth*, 3.2.12–13).[24] Although her infanticide may be only metaphorical, the 'fiend-like' queen's abrupt and shocking shift from the wistful nostalgia of 'how tender 'tis to love the babe that milks me' to dashing its brains out suggests the terrifying coexistence of nurturing and murderous impulses. *A Pittilesse Mother*'s author expounds at some length on Vincent's monstrous subversion of her motherly feelings and functions:

> Oh, that the blood of her own body should have no more power to pierce remorse into her iron-natured heart, when pagan women that know not God nor have any feeling of his deity will shun to commit bloodshed, much more of their own seed. The cannibals that eat one another will spare the fruits of their own bodies; the savages will do the like; yea, every beast and fowl hath a feeling of nature, and according to kind will cherish their young ones. And shall woman, nay, a Christian woman, God's own image, be more unnatural than pagan, cannibal, savage, beast, or fowl?

Murderous mothers are often linked to the monstrous, the uncivilised, the 'savage' and the non- or semi-human. Whereas Elizabeth Crashaw was a 'phoenix' for giving her life in childbirth, Margaret Vincent is 'tygerous' and 'wolfish' in her violation of maternal love and duty, and *A Pittilesse Mother* contrasts her unfavourably with one of the animal kingdom's more admirable mothers:

> This Mistress Vincent, now deserving no name of gentlewoman, being in her own house fast locked up only with her two small children, the one of the age of five years, the other hardly two years old, unhappily brought to that age to be made away by their own mother, who by nature should have cherished them with her own body, as the pelican that pecks her own breast to feed her young ones with her blood. But she, more cruel than the viper, the envenomed serpent, the snake, or any beast whatsoever … takes away those lives to whom she first gave life.

Unlike the selfless mother bird, Vincent does not 'cherish' her young, but is aligned with proverbially vicious species like vipers, serpents and snakes. These

---

[24] William Shakespeare, *The Tragedy of Macbeth*, in *The Norton Shakespeare*, ed. Stephen Greenblatt et al. (New York: W. W. Norton, 1997).

'envenomed' animals are traditionally connected to insincerity, guile and falsehood, as in the juxtaposition of snake imagery with Vincent's betrayal of her children's faith and trust:

> This creature not deserving mother's name, as I said before, not yet glutted nor sufficed with these few drops of innocent blood ... She came unto the elder child of that small age that it could hardly discern a mother's cruelty nor understand the fatal destiny fallen upon the other before, which as it were seemed to smile upon her as though it begged for pity, but all in vain, for so tyrannous was her heart that without all motherly pity she made it drink of the same bitter cup as she had done the other.

In place of the mother pelican's life-giving blood, Vincent offers her 'innocent', uncomprehending child the 'bitter cup' of murder (and, in another echo of Lady Macbeth, while it was smiling in her face). Being herself deceived by the Devil's 'cunning instruments', the spiritual sustenance and eternal salvation she thinks to offer her children is actually poison: 'a witchcraft begot by Hell and nursed by the Romish sect, from which enchantment God in Heaven defend us'.

The pamphlet's comparison of Margaret Vincent to axiomatically toxic non-humans is congruent with Reformation depictions of sin, falsehood and heresy, especially with regard to Roman Catholicism. Edmund Spenser offers a captivating analogue to *A Pittilesse Mother*'s portrait of malformed maternity in the figure of Errour, the hideously fecund serpent/monster in Book One of *The Faerie Queene*. When the well-meaning but feckless Redcrosse Knight enters the creature's den, deep within the wandering wood, he encounters this nightmarish family scene:

> ... he saw the vgly monster plaine,
> Halfe like a serpent horribly displaide,
> But th'other halfe did womans shape retaine,
> Most lothsom, filthie, foule, and full of vile disdaine ...
> And as she lay vpon the durtie ground,
> Her huge long taile her den all ouerspred,
> Yet was in knots and many boughtes vpwound,
> Pointed with mortall sting. Of her there bred
> A thousand yong ones, which she dayly fed,
> Sucking vpon her poisonous dugs, each one
> Of sundry shapes, yet all ill fauored:
> Soone as that vncouth light vpon them shone,
> Into her mouth they crept, and suddain all were gone.
> (*The Faerie Queene*, 1.1.14.6–9; 1.1.15.1–9)[25]

---

[25] Edmund Spenser, *The Faerie Queene* (New York: W. W. Norton & Co., 1992), p. 10. Book, canto and line numbers are given in parentheses.

This monstrous mother 'horribly' combines the properties of a poisonous serpent – 'whom God and man does hate' – with those of a human female, and Spenser's description of its 'womans shape' as 'lothsom', 'filthie' and 'foule' makes it unclear whether the speaker refers to the total package or, specifically, to the way the Errour's hybrid animality perverts her feminine characteristics. The 'durtie ground' and disarray of her tail 'in knots and many boughtes' adds a sense of slatternly disorder to the scene, suggesting a correlation between the creature's domestic chaos and her unbridled fertility. Errour is also an actively nursing mother, and the passage evokes contemporary ideas about the effect of diet, environment and humoral theory on lactating women, and the shaping influence of breast milk on developing infants.[26] The wandering knight is aghast at the creature's reproductive capabilities: the flood of matter emerging from her 'beastly body' includes Catholic rhetoric allegorised as 'Deformed monsters fowle, and blacke as inke' and 'poyson horrible and blacke' spewing from 'her filthy maw' (1.1.18.3; 1.1.22.7; 1.1.20.1–3).[27] Spenser's graphic portrayal of papist superstition transmitted from mother to child as the monster's 'fruitfull cursed spawne of serpents small' feed from her 'poysonous dugs' and upon her blood until 'Their bellies swolne ... with fulnesse burst' aligns with prevailing apprehensions about women as weak vessels, easily filled with false doctrine (1.1.22.6; 26.5).

A Pittilesse Mother echoes these concerns as it relates how Margaret Vincent, misled by 'Popish persuasions', becomes 'a creature ... whose life's overthrow may well serve for a clear looking-glass to see a woman's weakness in, how soon and apt she is won unto wickedness, not only to the body's overthrow but the soul's danger'.[28] The putative ease with which women were 'won unto wickedness' accounts for anxieties about wives and mothers changing from virtuous helpmeets to homicidal monsters, a transformation that Sandra Clark notes 'follows the homiletic concept of the "chain of vice", whereby the soul once

---

[26] See Spenser's own well-documented disapproval, in *A View of the Present State of Ireland*, of English mothers who hired Irish wet-nurses, for fear that impressionable children might absorb the moral qualities, social values, religious beliefs and other characteristics of the Irish along with their first food. Edmund Spenser, *A View of the Present State of Ireland* (Oxford: Oxford University Press, 1970).

[27] Shannon Garner-Balandrin notes how Errour's 'womb-like mouth, her abiogenetic bile, and the porousness of her body provide a humeral horror of generative excess'. See: 'Into Something Rich and Strange: Early Modern English Romance and Ecotheory', PhD dissertation (Northeastern University, 2016), p. 49.

[28] Spenser provides a contrast to Errour in Charissa, who emerges from her 'fruitfull nest' accompanied by 'a multitude of babes.../ Whom she still fed, whiles they were weake & young' (1.30.1–2; 29.8; 31.1.3). This paragon of Protestant domestic virtue happily nourishes her children, but, unlike the slovenly Errour, she is careful to wean and 'thrust them forth still, as they wexed old' (1.31.3).

infected by sin becomes increasingly prone to graver and graver moral lapses.'[29] By demonstrating how swiftly a Christian gentlewoman, 'well beloved and much esteemed of all that knew her for her modesty and seemly carriage' could 'fall into the hands of Roman wolves ... to have the sweet lamb, her soul, thus entangled by their persuasions', *A Pittilesse Mother* presents a potent reminder of how today's wilfulness might become tomorrow's anarchy.

The overdetermined relation between larger power structures and a married woman's capacity to create and nurture a 'little commonwealth' stands in stark contrast to the situation faced by mothers of illegitimate children. Most murdered infants were killed by unmarried women trying to escape the social and financial consequences of bearing a bastard child; so closely were infanticide and illegitimacy connected in the public imagination that, in 1624, the crime became a specific offence. The Act to Prevent the Destroying and Murthering of Bastard Children penalised single women not only for killing their children but also for concealing the fact, and (implicitly) for becoming pregnant in the first place, thereby making a murdered infant the evidence of its mother's crime as well as the victim:

> If any woman shall endeavor privately, by drowning or secret burying, or in any other way, either by herself or the procurement of others, to conceal the death of any such issue of her body, male or female, which being born alive, should by the laws of this realm be a bastard, and that she endeavour privately either by drowning or secret burying thereof, or any other way, either by herself or the procuring of others, so to conceal the death thereof, as that it may not come to light, whether it be born alive or not, but be concealed, in every such case the mother so offending shall suffer death as in the case of murder except such mother can make proof by one witness at the least, that the child (whose death was by her intended to be concealed) was born dead.[30]

An unmarried woman who became pregnant was not only a walking embodiment of sin and incontinence but also a practical nuisance. Such women tended to be poor and were often employed in domestic service, from which they would likely be dismissed should their condition come to light, making them a financial burden on the community. An illegitimate child was a personal, material and moral catastrophe that could easily drive a woman with few options to desperation, and the fallen, unwed mother, rooted in the harsh economic realities of female employment, was a recurring cautionary figure in broadsheets and pamphlets.

---

[29] Sandra Clark, *Women and Crime in the Street Literature of Early Modern England* (Basingstoke and New York: Palgrave Macmillan, 2003), p. 126.

[30] R. W. Malcolmson, 'Infanticide in the Eighteenth Century', in *Crime in England 1550–1800*, ed. J. S. Cockburn (Princeton: Princeton University Press, 1977), pp. 196–97.

Unlike their unwed sisters, 'honest' matrons who killed their children were more likely to be judged insane or as victims of diabolic influence. When able or inclined, married women were also permitted to plead their case and to portray themselves as loving parents who had fallen victim to madness, evil influences or a mistaken impulse to protect their children, as in the Vincent case or that of the Anabaptist Mary Champion. Champion was adamant that her infant son should not be baptised until he was an adult, and when she met resistance from her Presbyterian husband, John (whom the 1647 pamphlet, *Bloody Newes from Dover*, laconically describes as 'much perplexed'), 'she took a great knife and cut off the Child's head'.[31] The tract's title page features a shocking woodcut of Champion brandishing the child's severed head as its body lies bleeding on the floor, while the accompanying text relates how 'when her husband came in, she called him into a little Parlour, where the poore Infant lay bleeding, uttering these words: Behold husband, thy sweet Babe without a head, now go and baptize it; if you will, you must christen the head without a body: for here they lye separated'.[32]

It is worth noting the disparate ways in which the English criminal justice system treated petty treason and infanticide, the two violent crimes most associated with women, and the ways in which marital status played an important role in how these criminals were judged and punished. A married woman who killed her spouse committed not simple murder but a crime against the state. This offence was punishable by burning (as opposed to the more typical hanging), and decried as especially terrible given the conjugal bond between the killer and her victim. By contrast, an unmarried infanticidal woman was shown little mercy in comparison with matrons guilty of the same crime; whereas marriage made husband-killing worse, it ameliorated the censure directed at women who killed their children. The tone of contemporary infanticide accounts toggles between censorious didacticism, voyeuristic prurience and Christian pity, and if the guilty woman is married, most texts also express hope for her soul's salvation, even as her body is consigned to the gallows. This tacit concern, even sympathy, for mothers who brutally subvert their primary social and biological role sits incongruously alongside salacious details like Mary Champion's decapitated infant, or the elaborate picnic packed by Elizabeth Barnes 'to intice [her] child unto its slaughter', producing a heady brew of horror and melodrama with a reclamation chaser.[33] Witness how *A Pittilesse Mother*'s characterisation of Margaret

---

[31] *Bloody newes from Dover. Being a true relation of the great and bloudy murder, committed by Mary Champion (an Anabaptist) who cut off her childs head, being 7. weekes old, and held it to her husband to baptize* (London, 1647); Tufts University Libraries, Early English Books Online: http://eebo.chadwyck.com.ezproxy.library.tufts.edu/home (accessed 11 November 2016).

[32] Ibid.

[33] Dolan, *Dangerous Familiars*, p. 162.

Vincent ascribes her 'undutiful' behaviour to spiritual error: 'Oh, blinded ignorance! Oh, inhumane devotion! Purposing by this to merit Heaven, she hath deserved (without true repentance) the reward of damnation'. Yet once removed from malign influences and counselled by 'certain Godly preachers', Vincent comprehends and regrets the wickedness of her actions, and the pamphlet closes on a relatively charitable note: 'Her offence was begot by a strange occasion but buried, I hope, with true repentance'.

The explicit woodcuts and sensational rhetoric of these texts ensured their success as popular page-turners, but the possible redemption they extend for wives who have otherwise 'deserved … the reward of damnation' contrasts sharply with the treatment doled out to their unwed counterparts. After Margaret Vincent accepts the 'celestial consolations' of Protestant clerics, she is restored to her former faith's promise of redemption: 'Her judgment and execution she received with a patient mind, her soul no doubt hath got a true penitent desire to be in Heaven, and the blood of her two innocent children so wilfully shed (according to all charitable judgements) is washed away by the mercies of God'. A married woman who confessed her sin and begged pardon from God and her husband reassumed her proper, subordinate position in her own marriage and, in the broader analogical scheme, her 'true repentance' brought some hope of grace. But unmarried child-killers received no such 'charitable judgements': following execution, their corpses were surrendered for dissection, a fate reserved for particularly wicked criminals, and one which carried weightier consequences than public shame and physical suffering. Since penetrating a corpse imperiled the soul, this post-mortem dismemberment irrevocably denied such women any hope of salvation. Although guilty of the same crime, and condemned to the same ignominious earthly end, infanticidal women who were neither contained nor constrained by the bonds of marriage were denied privileges accorded their 'honest' contemporaries in this world and the next one.

Patriarchal authority is an abstract albeit powerful concept, but challenges to that authority can take frighteningly physical form. Infanticide exposes occluded aspects of mothering by demonstrating how women might not only desire but actively cause their children's deaths, and the murderous mother retains special potency across historical periods. Witness the rhetorical frenzy that surrounds infanticidal women compared with their male counterparts in the modern press, where the condemnatory, gendered preoccupations of early modern pamphlets are echoed by sensationalist reporters who employ a similar queasy mix of mawkish sentimentality, righteous indignation and slavering bloodlust.[34] Parents who

---

[34] A recent example is the case of Bella 'Baby Doe' Bond, a Boston toddler killed by her mother's boyfriend because he believed she was a demon. Although the child's mother was charged as an accessory after the fact, the degree of vilification heaped upon her

kill are always bad, but mothers who do so inhabit a separate category of moral, spiritual or psychological weakness, even if they act for what they imagine to be good reasons; compare early modern responses to murderous mothers claiming madness or diabolic influence with current attitudes towards post-partum depression and psychosis.[35] Mothers unwilling or unable to perform their 'natural' duties often express feelings of inadequacy, fear and guilt that resonate across centuries, whether as symptoms of illness or evidence of 'true repentance'.

Perhaps these troubling urges indicate a defect in the maternal organism, a symptom of women's fundamentally mutable, unstable nature. Or they may be the necessary inverse of the exhausting commitment, the passionate emotions and the surrender of personal desire and physical autonomy that mothering requires. The (presumably male) authors who chronicle these crimes in the early modern period seek to contain disruptive female agency run amok, reifying order via the 'unnatural' woman's contrition and punishment while providing a warning to others. But, in the end, such efforts fail to exorcise the spectre they raise. Whether a by-product, a waste product or a fatal flaw in the ideology of motherhood itself, maternal infanticide lies outside the realm of masculine control, a perversion of the feminine art and craft of childrearing with the potential to undermine, dismember and destroy the very systems mothers are charged with perpetuating.

---

far outweighed that directed at the actual killer by virtue of her relationship to the victim: http://www.wcvb.com/article/bella-was-demon-and-it-was-time-for-her-to-die-mom-s-boyfriend-allegedly-says/8226801 (accessed 15 December 2016).

[35] An especially compelling analogue to the Vincent murders is the 2002 case of Andrea Yates, the evangelical Texas Christian who drowned her five children, believing she was sending them to heaven and ridding the world of sin through her own execution. See: Deborah W. Denno, 'Who is Andrea Yates? A Short Story About Insanity', *Duke Journal of Gender and Law Policy* 10.1 (2003): 1–60.

CHAPTER 19

Imps of Hell: Young People, Murder and the Early English Press*

Ben Parsons

ON 5 AUGUST 1664, Samuel Pepys paid a visit to William Joyce, husband to a cousin on his mother's side, and rode with him to Highgate. As the two men travelled together, their conversation turned to the subject of murder, in particular the death of Walter Clun, an actor who had been robbed, bound and left to die by a group of assailants earlier that week.[1] Joyce proved especially fascinated by the crime, excitedly recounting 'the manner of it … and manner of having it found out', taking Pepys through the various scraps of information he had gleaned about Clun's final moments.[2] Since the case had already made its way into the press by this point, appearing in the hastily written broadside *An Egley on Mr Clun*, much of his knowledge seems to have been culled from the printed news discourse that Pepys himself enthusiastically consumed.[3] Ultimately, however, merely reading about the crime was not enough: Joyce also insisted on hunting out the exact spot where Clun had died, taking a detour to Kentish Town to find where he had 'laid in a ditch, and … bled to death through his struggling'.[4]

In many respects, the scene described by Pepys seems remarkably contemporary. Joyce's treatment of murder as entertainment, his delight in specific circumstantial detail and even his attraction to the site where Clun was killed is reminiscent of the ways in which murder has been marketed and consumed by news media and its audiences throughout the twentieth and twenty-first

---

* The author would like to thank the AHRC for funding the research on which this chapter is based.
[1] On Clun's career and death, see: John Astington, *Actors and Acting in Shakespeare's Time: The Art of Stage Playing* (Cambridge: Cambridge University Press, 2010), p. 195.
[2] Samuel Pepys, *Diary*, ed. Robert Latham, 10 vols (London: HarperCollins, 2000), 5:233–34.
[3] *An Egley upon the most execrable murther of Mr. Clun* (London: Edward Crowch, 1664): Wing E481. See: Kate Loveman, *Samuel Pepys and His Books. Reading, Newsgathering, and Sociability 1660–1703* (Oxford: Oxford University Press, 2015), pp. 42–44, 80–107.
[4] Pepys, *Diary*, 5:234.

centuries.⁵ With his eager absorption of printed reports of violent crime, Joyce seems to differ little from the 'readers of Sunday papers' discussed by Orwell in his sardonic analysis of 'the murders which have given the greatest amount of pleasure to the British public'.⁶ But the question is how seriously these similarities should be taken. It is true that the resemblance between early modern reading habits and later practices has often dominated scholarly discussion of early print culture. The growing body of criticism on Tudor and Stuart murder narratives has tended to stress the parallels between crime pamphlets and the popular journalism of more recent periods, at times using one to interpret the other.⁷ Sandra Clark, for instance, regards chapbooks on female killers as products of the same 'fascination' with 'women's acts of extreme disorder' currently visible in the tabloid press, while Daniel Cohen uses seventeenth-century murder accounts to understand 'the pattern of writing and reporting' in the United States during the nineteenth and twentieth centuries.⁸ In both of these cases, the early modern and later presses are seen as fundamentally equivalent, to the extent that one can serve as a paradigm for reading the other.

While these analogies are undeniably suggestive, they bring with them a danger of overlooking discrepancies between the two forms of reportage. Although pamphlets and newspapers might arise out of similar interests and imperatives, there are numerous junctures at which they pursue radically different paths. A case in point is murder committed by children and young adolescents.⁹ Murder by young people is, in some respects, an archetypal 'newsworthy

---

⁵ See, for instance: A. V. Seaton and J. J. Lennon, 'Thanatourism in the Early 21st Century: Moral Panics, Ulterior Motives and Alterior Desires', in *New Horizons in Tourism: Strange Experiences and Stranger Practices*, ed. T. V. Singh (Cambridge, MA: CABI, 2004), pp. 63–82.

⁶ George Orwell, 'Decline of the English Murder', in *Complete Works*, ed. Peter Davison, 20 vols (London: Secker and Warburg, 1996–98), 18:108–10 at p. 108.

⁷ For the general history of early modern news discourse, see: Michael Harris, 'The Structure, Ownership and Control of the Press, 1620–1780', in *Newspaper History from the Seventeenth Century to the Present Day*, ed. George Boyce, James Curran and Pauline Wingate (London: Constable, 1978), pp. 82–97.

⁸ Sandra Clark, *Women and Crime in the Street Literature of Early Modern England* (Basingstoke and New York: Palgrave Macmillan, 2003), pp. ix–x; Daniel A. Cohen, 'Blood Will Out: Sensationalism, Horror, and the Roots of American Crime Literature', in *Mortal Remains: Death in Early America*, ed. Nancy Isenberg and Andrew Burstein (Philadelphia: University of Pennsylvania Press, 2003), pp. 31–55 at p. 32.

⁹ It is notoriously difficult to pinpoint the frontier between minority and majority in early modern culture. While the period inherited a well-defined scheme of distinct *aetates* from the Middle Ages, which set the upper limit of *pueritia* (childhood) at fourteen or fifteen, in practice, the threshold of maturity proved much more fluid. Across the seventeenth century, religious and legal discourse increasingly tended to drive the age of responsibility up to eighteen, twenty or later; marriage typically occurred in the late twenties for both sexes. For the sake of cogency, this essay will discuss murderers below

murder' as it often attracts a degree of attention out of proportion with its actual frequency. Whereas juvenile offenders were only responsible for around 1.2 per cent of the murders in the United Kingdom in the last three decades of the twentieth century, their crimes invariably provoked 'intense media frenzy'; likewise, the nine cases that made their way into print between 1641 and 1675 probably represent around 1.4 per cent of the total number of homicides in London for the same period.[10] But this type of crime is also notable for generating markedly different responses across the two periods. Each type of news discourse negotiates murderous youngsters in specific ways, drawing on a distinct nexus of attitudes in order to understand the offender and the offence. As a result, their differences in approach expose larger ruptures in conceptions of youth and crime, as each form of reportage looks to a different set of ideas to make sense of its object. In the process, they do not merely highlight the fluid relationship between culpability and maturity across the two periods but challenge several engrained ideas about the nature of the pre-adult period in early modern culture.

As a number of prominent cases over the last few decades highlights, and as analysis of those cases has shown, modern journalism encounters profound difficulties when confronted with killings carried out by children and other young people.[11] In the words of Bob Franklin and Julian Petley, while these homicides might 'trigger an exceptional and overwhelming flood of newspaper coverage',

the age of eighteen, specifically those belonging to the periods of *pueritia* and early *adolescentia* in the traditional schema. See: Deborah Youngs, *The Life-Cycle in Western Europe* (Manchester: Manchester University Press, 2006), pp. 96–125, Lawrence Stone, *The Family, Sex and Marriage in England* (New York: Harper and Row, 1977), pp. 40–46; Michael Mascuch, 'The Godly Child's "Power and Evidence" in the Word', in *Children and Their Books*, ed. G. Avery and J. Briggs (Oxford: Clarendon Press, 1989), pp. 103–26 at p. 109; Keith Thomas, 'Age and Authority in Early Modern England', *Proceedings of the British Academy* 62 (1976): 205–48 at p. 225.

[10] Emilia Mugnai, 'Serves you right!: Playing Populist Politics with Children Who Kill', *Childright* 176 (2001): 10–11 at p. 10; Paul Cavadino, 'The Case for Change', in *Children who Kill*, ed. Paul Cavadino (Winchester, UK: Waterside Press, 2002), pp. 9–19. On murder rates in the late seventeenth century, see: J. A. Sharpe, *Crime in Early Modern England, 1550–1750*, 2nd edn (London: Pearsons, 1999), pp. 263–68; Julius R. Ruff, *Violence in Early Modern Europe 1500–1800* (Cambridge: Cambridge University Press, 2001), p. 130; Manuel Eisner, 'Long-Term Historical Trends in Violent Crime', *Crime and Justice* 30 (2003): 83–142 at p. 96. The figures quoted here are based on the Bills of Mortality for 1658–1700; see: William Farr, *Appendix to the Third Annual Report of the Registrar General of Births, Marriages and Deaths* (London: George Eyre and William Spottiswood, 1841), p. 12.

[11] In addition to the studies cited below, see: Maggie O'Neill and Lizzie Seal, *Transgressive Imaginations: Crime, Deviance and Culture* (Basingstoke: Palgrave, 2012), pp. 20–41; Sana Nakata, *Childhood Citizenship, Governance and Policy: The Politics of Becoming Adult* (London: Routledge, 2015), pp. 72–99; John Springhall, '"The Monsters Next Door: What Made Them Do It?" Moral Panics Over the Causes of High School

this is marked by a slippage away from the '"normal" requirements of reporting' often 'in favour of undiluted, vitriolic editorialising'.[12] Patricia Holland adds that responses to underage killers tend to be informed by 'hysterical condemnation' above all, causing reportage to 'break free of social explanations' and instead 'to express the horror felt ... excluding any attempt to explore the history or context of the event'.[13] Overall, the depiction of killer youngsters in contemporary news discourse is characterised by disturbance and 'panic', as the circumstances of their crimes are repeated more out of a sense of traumatised disbelief than for any entertainment value they might possess.[14]

What seems to grant juvenile murderers this power is the resistance they offer to the mechanisms that make crimes comprehensible. As the field of media studies has made clear, newspaper journalism (especially in its commercial forms) often tends towards the process that Raymond Williams describes as 'dramatization' or 'fictionalization': although it delivers information that is factual at root, it tends to present it as quasi-fictive 'stories', strategically collapsing the 'boundaries between news and entertainment'.[15] The purpose of this approach, as Stewart Hall notes, is to interpret events on behalf of a particular readership, rendering them intelligible by accommodating them into familiar narratives. Hall sees the press as foremost amongst 'the institutions ... responsible for describing and explaining the events of the world' and claims that it achieves this end by 'maintaining a preferred or delimited range of meanings' when relaying information.[16] Similar observations also underpin Stanley Cohen's influential work on the media as a 'way of coping' with perceived crises, as this also sees the press as a machinery by which potentially disturbing occurrences can be channelled into conventional narratives.[17] Murders committed by the young, how-

---

Multiple Shootings', in *Moral Panics over Contemporary Children and Youth*, ed. C. Krinsky (Farnham: Ashgate, 2008), pp. 47–69.

[12] Bob Franklin and Julian Petley, 'Killing the Age of Innocence: Newspaper Reporting and the Death of James Bulger', in *Thatcher's Children?: Politics, Childhood and Society in the 1980s and 1990s*, ed. Jane Pilcher and Stephen Wagg (London: Falmer Press, 1996), pp. 136–57.

[13] Patricia Holland, *Picturing Childhood: The Myth of the Child in Popular Imagery* (London: I. B. Tauris, 2004), p. 119.

[14] Joel P. Best, 'Locating Moral Panics within the Sociology of Social Problems', in *Moral Panic and the Politics of Anxiety*, ed. Sean Hier (London: Routledge, 2011), pp. 37–52.

[15] Raymond Williams, *Writing in Society* (London: Verso, 1983), p. 19; Dick Rooney, 'Thirty Years of Competition in the British Tabloid Press', in *Tabloid Tales: Global Debates over Media Standards*, ed. Colin Sparks and John Tullock (Lanham, MD: Rowman and Littlefield, 2000), pp. 91–109 at p. 91.

[16] Stuart Hall, 'The Rediscovery of "Ideology": Return of the Repressed in Media Studies', in *Culture, Society and the Media*, ed. Michael Gurevitch, Tony Bennett, James Curran and Janet Woollacott (London: Methuen, 1982), pp. 56–90 at pp. 67–68.

[17] Stanley Cohen, *Folk Devils and Moral Panics*, 3rd edn (London: Routledge, 2002), p. 1.

ever, seem to defy these processes on a range of fronts. On the one hand, the very scarcity of these events makes it difficult for narratives to cohere around them. Their anomalous status prevents them from being treated in archetypal terms: put simply, the very fact that such murders are rare makes it 'hard to understand what motivates them' and so 'forces us to think beyond our normative categories'.[18] But at the same time, they short-circuit many of the narratives used to make murder intelligible, not merely falling outside them, but dissolving their fundamental logic. In the first place, the murderous child or youth confuses the simple binarism on which most popular reportage is predicated, upsetting the balance between 'clearly defined (innocent) victim and (blameworthy) perpetrator'.[19] As Colin Hay writes, the young are emphatically blameless in orthodox journalistic rhetoric, usually functioning 'as idealized innocent victims in relation to which the deviancy of the other is defined': when the murderer is also young, this seesaw effect cannot establish itself and, as a result, 'conventional conceptions of innocence and guilt become deeply problematised'.[20] Similarly, the undeveloped nature of the youngster presents a further obstacle, prohibiting the usual speculation into psychological motivation by which 'adult killers and abusers' are customarily 'pathologized'.[21] Since youths effectively lack a formative history, they defy explanation in such terms, often triggering a desperate hunt for other external 'causes' in society at large.[22] In short, murders committed by children and adolescents seem to put modern-day journalistic narratives under particular strain, often imploding the systems by which homicide is usually understood.

The newsbooks of the early modern period, on the other hand, follow a different course when faced with murders carried out by young people. The divergence is not complete, however. The pamphlets call on many of the same mechanisms for making sense of crimes, showing much the same reliance on established narratives evident in the contemporary press. The interpretive element Hall describes, in fact, seems embedded in murder discourse from its inception: as Randall Martin writes, the murder chapbook seems to have evolved out of the

---

[18] Sarah Kember, *Virtual Anxiety: Photography, New Technologies, and Subjectivity* (Manchester: University of Manchester Press, 1998), pp. 69–70.

[19] Shani D'Cruze, Sandra L. Walklate and Samantha Pegg, *Murder* (London: Routledge, 2013), pp. 79–80.

[20] Colin Hay, 'Mobilization Through Interpellation: James Bulger, Juvenile Crime and the Construction of Moral Panic', *Social and Legal Studies* 4 (1995): 197–223 at pp. 200–01.

[21] Howard Davis and Marc Bourhill, 'Crisis: The Demonization of Children and Young People', in *'Childhood' in 'Crisis'?*, ed. Phil Scraton (London: Routledge, 1997), pp. 28–57 at pp. 45–47.

[22] See: Marjorie Heins, *Not in Front of the Children: 'Indecency', Censorship, and the Innocence of Youth* (New York: Hill and Wang, 2001), pp. 201–27; David James Smith, *The Sleep of Reason* (London: Faber and Faber, 2011).

wider discourse of the 'newsworthy wonder' or 'the marvellous', a genre which by its very nature demands inquiry into the phenomena recounted.[23] Hence the earliest pamphlets on murder – such as those published by 'D. S.' and Arthur Golding in 1573, or the similar work produced by Anthony Munday, 'Ævesham' and Thomas Johnson in the 1580s and 90s – tend to cast murder in explicitly 'wondrous' terms: each killing and its detection is presented as a 'maruellous apparance', a mysterious violation of 'naturall reasons' that requires deciphering, like the 'prodigies' collected by Wolffhart or Boaistuau.[24] This drive to interpret murder usually leads early modern authors to 'fictionalize' events along the lines that Williams outlines. The murder pamphlets quickly developed a set of distinctive conventions by which they could transform 'the raw material of domestic mishap, criminal enormity and local tragedy' into 'stylised narratives suitable for sale'.[25] A relatively stable group of formulaic components thus came to govern the pamphlets; they contain such recurrent features as the miraculous or providential discovery of the killer, an emphasis on their general movement towards 'spiritual redemption', a climactic 'scaffold speech', and close reference to a general typology of sinners or criminals.[26] This explains why they proved such a key resource for early modern dramatists, who could find in newsbooks current events organised into readymade quasi-dramatic form.[27] Like the modern

---

[23] Randall Martin, *Women, Murder, and Equity in Early Modern England* (London: Routledge, 2008), pp. 85–86. See: Lorraine Daston, 'Marvelous Facts and Miraculous Evidence in Early Modern Europe', in *Wonders, Marvels, and Monsters in Early Modern Culture*, ed. Peter G. Platt (London: Associated University Presses, 1999), pp. 76–105.

[24] D. S., *A true reporte or description of an horrible, wofull, and moste lamentable murther* (London: Henry Kirkham, 1573): STC 21485; Arthur Golding, *A briefe discourse of the late murther of master George Saunders* (London: Henry Bynneman, 1573), sig. C3–C3v (STC 11985); Anthony Munday, *A view of sundry examples, reporting many straunge murthers* (London: John Charlewood, 1580): STC 18281; 'Ævesham', *A most straunge, rare, and horrible murther* (London: Thomas Purfoote, 1586): STC 11377; [T]homas [J]ohnson, *A world of wonders. A masse of murthers. A couie of cosonages* (London: Abel Jeffes, 1595): STC 14068.5; Conrad Wolffhart, *The doome warning all men*, trans. Stephen Batman (London: Henry Bynneman, 1581), fol. 3v (STC 1582).

[25] Peter Lake with Michael Questier, *The Anti-Christ's Lewd Hat: Protestants, Papists and Players in Post-Reformation England* (New Haven: Yale University Press, 1993), pp. 7–8.

[26] Peter Kirwan, *Shakespeare and the Idea of Apocrypha: Negotiating the Boundaries of the Dramatic Canon* (Cambridge: Cambridge University Press, 2015), p. 86; Nadia Bishai, 'Blacke Bookes: Ephemeral Production and Early Modern Playwrights', in *Encountering Ephemera: 1500–1800; Scholarship, Performance, Classroom*, ed. Joshua B. Fisher (Newcastle upon Tyne: Cambridge Scholars Press, 2013), pp. 95–134; David Stymeist, 'Criminal Biography in Early Modern News Pamphlets', in *Taking Exception to the Law: Materializing Injustice in Early Modern English Literature*, ed. Donald Beecher et al. (Toronto: University of Toronto Press, 2015), pp. 137–61.

[27] See: Frances E. Dolan, *Dangerous Familiars: Representations of Domestic Crime in England, 1550–1700* (Ithaca: Cornell University Press, 1994), pp. 150–61; Betty S. Travitsky,

articles discussed by Williams and Hall, 'fictionalization' is a central function of early modern news discourse.

Nevertheless, when the pamphlets deal with the young, further complexities emerge. Again, there are a few admitted parallels, as later conventions are, at points, already beginning to crystallise. As work on early modern child-murder has repeatedly shown, newsbooks often describe crimes against the young in idealised terms that look forward to later media: the murdered child is usually depicted as a figure of absolute innocence, 'harmless ... helplesse and hopelesse' or a 'poore harmelesse soule'.[28] However, when juveniles are killers rather than victims, the story is very different. At this point, the newsbooks and newspapers decisively part company. Although this order of crime was no more common in the sixteenth and seventeenth centuries than in the twentieth and twenty-first, when it does occur, it elicits profoundly dissimilar reactions. On the whole, the early modern reports experience less difficulty, let alone 'moral panic', in interpreting murders performed by young people. Beneath the emotive language customarily used by pamphleteers, there is a much greater willingness to treat immature criminals as extensions, rather than breaches, of existing values and systems. A case in point is the anonymous *News from Tybourn* (1675). When this text records the crime of 'a little boy about 14 years of age' – identified by a handwritten note in one copy as Joseph Dyson – who was arrested 'for murthering a Citizen and Silk man', it does not seem to regard him with particular anxiety.[29] Dyson is awarded no special distinction as a criminal on account of his age, being merely treated as an item in a general catalogue of delinquency. His story is sandwiched between 'W. N.', who 'Confessed that he had been a great oppres-

'Husband-Murder and Petty Treason in English Renaissance Tragedy', in *Disorder and the Drama*, ed. Mary Beth Rose (Evanston, IL: Northwestern University Press, 1990), pp. 171–98; John G. Bellamy, *Strange, Inhuman Deaths: Murder in Tudor England* (Stroud: Sutton, 2005), pp. 171–87; Tiemen de Vries, *Holland's Influence on English Language and Literature* (Chicago: C. Grentzebach, 1916), pp. 282–87; Sandra Clark, *The Plays of Beaumont and Fletcher* (Hemel Hempstead, UK: Harvester Wheatsheaf, 1994), pp. 17–18.

[28] *The horrible murther of a young boy of three yeres of age* (London: A. P., 1606), pp. 4, 7 (STC 6552); John Taylor, *The vnnaturall father* (London: I. T., 1621), sig. Bv (STC 23808a). See: Peter C. Hoffer and N. E. H. Hull, *Murdering Mothers: Infanticide in England and New England, 1558–1803* (New York: New York University Press, 1981); Anne-Marie Kilday, *A History of Infanticide in Britain, c. 1600 to the Present* (Aldershot: Palgrave, 2013), pp. 23–50; Ken MacMillan, *Stories of True Crime in Tudor and Stuart England* (London: Routledge, 2015), pp. 47–52, 132–38, 173–76. In this volume, see: Dianne Berg, 'Monstrous Un-Making: Maternal Infanticide and Female Agency in Early Modern England'.

[29] *News from Tybourn* (London: D. M., 1675), p. 6 (Wing N1026). The annotation naming Dyson appears in the copy held at the London Metropolitan Archives. Subsequent references to this text are in parentheses.

sor of the poor in his Office', and 'G. F.', arrested for 'robbing upon the High way, and firing a Pistol at a Watch man' (*News from Tybourn*, 6–7). Although the author acknowledges Dyson's immaturity as a point of interest, noting that 'he had so soon imbru'd his hands in blood', it presents him as the moral and mental equal of any other prisoner: 'had he been older he could not have been more sensible of his act, nor more apprehensive of his approaching death' (*News from Tybourn*, 7). The text, in short, shows no sense that Dyson's minority renders him problematic as a criminal. It places him at the same level as the other entries on its list rather than singling him out for particular attention.

Such unconcern is the general rule when early modern news discourse approaches youngsters guilty of murder. Even when authors seem to attach particular gravity to these cases, their claims usually stem from sensationalist rhetoric rather than a real sense of confusion or horror. This pattern can be seen in the example of an apprentice shoemaker 'aged thirteen years and a Month' and named only as 'Daniel', who stabbed to death another apprentice in 1675. The immediate cause of the attack was a minor dispute over clothing: 'the Prisoner cut the others Apronstrings, and the other attempting to cut his, the Prisoner took a Three-penny Knife, and stab'd him in the Belly'.[30] The crime itself features in two of the early proceedings of the Old Bailey.[31] One of these reports treats the murder in extraordinarily charged terms that might be taken to indicate shock, at least at first glance. It prefaces its account with a scandalised meditation on social decline, treating the offence as a radical departure from normality: the author laments that 'every Age, nay, every Sessions brings forth new Crimes, and many times more Prodigious then the former' before launching into its 'Cursery' of this 'Murther committed by a Boy' (*Narrative of the proceedings*, sig. A2). Nevertheless, such declarations cannot be taken at face value. On the one hand, the claim that this is an unprecedented offence seems to be a product of traditional language rather than a failure of it. The newsbook is, in fact, attempting to cast the murder in 'marvellous' terms, like Golding and Munday before it: its use of the term 'Prodigious' and its insistence that Daniel represents an 'aberration in the natural order' both emulate the vocabulary of wonder literature, looking back to the roots of early modern murder reportage.[32] On the other hand, its horrified tone is entirely absent from alternative reports of the murder.

---

[30] *A narrative of the proceedings at the Sessions* (London: John Millet, 1676), sig. A2 (Wing N210). Subsequent references to this text are in parentheses.

[31] See: Andrea McKenzie, 'Making Crime Pay: Motives, Marketing Strategies, and the Printed Literature of Crime in England 1670–1770', in *Criminal Justice in the Old World and the New: Essays in Honour of J.M. Beattie*, ed. Greg T. Smith, Allyson N. May and Simon Devereaux (Toronto: University of Toronto Press, 1998), pp. 235–69.

[32] Alexandra Walsham, *Providence in Early Modern England* (Oxford: Oxford University Press, 1999), p. 169.

The second account of the proceedings simply lists the crime after the murder of a bailiff, applying to it the offhand description 'another unhappy Murther ... by the discord of two young Lads'.[33] This additional author does not see the crime as a new species of wrongdoing at all but treats it as an entirely unremarkable occurrence.

A corollary of this indifference is a general willingness to accommodate juveniles into existing murder narratives and to read them as established types of murderer. In most reports, youngsters who kill do not register as anomalous offenders who need to be interpreted along new lines but are readily drawn into given categories of killer. Such a process can be seen in contemporary responses to two similar crimes, one that occurred at Plymouth in 1677, the other in the London parish of St Martin in the Field in 1675. In each case, a young maid-servant was implicated in multiple poisonings within a single household. At London, a girl of 15 was found to have served food laced with 'Ratsbane' to the 'two Gentlewomen' acting as her guardians; although both women recovered, under questioning, the maid confessed to having murdered her 'sickly and troublesome' mother a year earlier, along with a 'Maid that was sick of the Small-pox'.[34] At Plymouth, four members of the family of William Weeks were poisoned with 'Crude Arsenick', two fatally. After a brief investigation, the poison was found to have been administered by two maids in the household, one of whom was Anne Evans, 'a Poor Child' and ward of parish 'being then about Twelve or Thirteen years old'.[35] Although Anne was more an accomplice than an instigator, having been directed by the other, older maid, she was burned at the stake for her involvement, while her partner-in-crime was hanged.

In both of these cases, there is, again, a marked lack of interest in the ages of the girls, as other details are privileged instead. Whereas the pamphlets do call attention to their youth, even describing them as 'barbarously unnatural' on account of it, they are still able to draw them into recognisable networks of meanings (Quick, *Hell open'd*, 3). This process is perhaps at its most conspicuous when the girls are defined as members of a household. The authors place heavy emphasis on the domestic setting of their crimes: for instance, Anne finds the poison when 'going out into the Garden to gather Herbs, amongst the Marygolds' and stores it 'in a Salt-Seller' (Quick, *Hell open'd*, 8), while the poisoning at St Martins came to light after 'a Cat, happening to lick up part of what one of the Ladies had cast, fell into a strange fit of trembling' (*Horrid News*, 5).

---

[33] *A true narrative of the proceedings at the Sessions-house in the Old-Bayly* (London: D. M., 1676), pp. 4–5 (Wing T2815A).

[34] *Horrid news from St. Martins* (London: D. M., 1677), p. 6 (Wing H2864). Subsequent references to this text are in parentheses.

[35] John Quick, *Hell open'd, or, The infernal sin of murther punished* (London: Francis Eglesfield, 1676), p. 9 (Wing Q207). Subsequent references to this text are in parentheses.

The home is, then, at the core of the texts, informing the details they assemble; the murders take place against a backdrop of pets, crockery and kitchen gardens. This strand of meaning is emphasised even further by repeated allusion to food, with the reports showing a particular interest in meals and eating. The material dealing with Anne Evans dedicates a great deal of space to the preparation of food by Anne and her fellow conspirator, whether or not it contributed to the poisoning of the Weeks family. It describes at various points the serving of 'a Pot of Beer' flavoured with 'Nutmeg and Sugar' and 'a piece of Beef, and part of a Neck of Veal and Cabbidge, and Carrots', before finally reaching the 'Dish of Pottage ... and very little Bread' with which Evans and her associate poisoned their employers (Quick, *Hell open'd*, 9–12). Accounts of the London poisoning follow a similar course, basing the girl's guilt on the fact that 'Provision' in the house 'pass'd through nobodies hands but hers' (*Horrid News*, 4–5).

Numerous factors can be seen at work beneath these references. In the first place, they again show indifference towards the ages of the girls, characterising the two killers as household servants rather than youngsters. While their immaturity is flagged up in passing, their identities are quickly subsumed into the domestic context that preoccupies the pamphlets; they are regarded as servants first and foremost. In fact, of the three pamphlets published on Anne Evans, only one makes any mention of her age at all, with another omitting even her name; all three instead describe her principally by her professional designation, as 'Maid Servant in the House' or 'Apprentice Maid'.[36] But at the same time, these allusions also serve to attach other valuations to the murderers, identifying both girls with a common figure in the criminal typology of the period – the 'discontented' woman, exemplified by such characters as Dominica and Denisa in Reynold's murder 'histories'.[37] As Vanessa McMahon writes, this type is a widespread and potent one in the early modern imagination: such a figure uses poison, itself seen as 'a woman's weapon', to attack her husband or master 'without his knowledge' from the relatively closed space of the kitchen; in so doing, she enacts a parodic inversion of female responsibilities, using her role within the household to 'usurp the husband's legitimate marital power ... via her secret rebellion'.[38] So pervasive is this figure that she often merges with another murderous stereotype, that of the

---

[36] *The poysoners rewarded* (London: J. M., 1687): Wing P2744; *A Barbarous Murder Committed at Plimouth* (London: John Millet, 1676): Wing H2865. Subsequent references to these texts are in parentheses.

[37] John Reynolds, *The Triumphs of Gods Revenge Against the Crying and Execrable Sin of Murther* (London: Sarah Griffine, 1656), pp. 433–44 (Wing R1308A).

[38] Vanessa McMahon, *Murder in Shakespeare's England* (Basingstoke: Palgrave Macmillan, 2004), pp. 108–09. See also: Margaret Hallissy, *Venomous Woman: Fear of the Female in Literature* (New York: Greenwood Press, 1987), and, in this volume, Thomas Gobbitt, 'Poisoning, Killing and Murder in the *Edictus Rothari*'. However, there are also examples

witch, as Emese Bálint has shown.³⁹ The heavy emphasis on their function in the household conflates both girls with this conventional figure, turning them into a perennial threat from the kitchen made concrete. By accentuating their duties, the chapbooks generalise each into murderous women, not girls, who behave along lines familiar to the reading public. But the larger point here is that the immaturity of the girls does not create the same friction apparent in twentieth-century media. It does not prevent the absorption of juvenile killers into standard patterns for understanding murder. While their age is recognised, it is treated more as a novelty than an obstacle, receiving passing comment but not preventing their identification as a recognised 'type' of offender. It certainly does not provoke any larger questions about guilt or responsibility, or prompt any misgivings that these categories might not be fully applicable to such figures or their actions.

Similar processes appear in accounts of murders carried out by apprentices. Here, temporal identity carries such little weight that it is often difficult to establish whether an apprentice is in fact a boy or an adult. The label 'apprentice' could, of course, encompass a wide variety of ages: sources indicate that apprenticeships could begin at ten or fourteen and last until the boy was eighteen, twenty-four or even 'thirty yeres of age'.⁴⁰ However, specific detail seems to interest the pamphlets very rarely. More usually, the age of an apprentice can only be inferred from references to his recent 'ripenesse of yeares' or from claims that his story should inspire 'vertuous undertakings in Children'; otherwise, like housemaids, boy killers are defined by their social position alone.⁴¹ This pattern can be witnessed in the case of George Bridges, who was hanged at Monmouth in 1672 for assisting his master in killing his mother, cutting the woman's throat as she 'lay gasping' after her son shot her in the head.⁴² Bridges is invariably described as 'Servant' or 'his Boy': he is only identified by his age in

---

of men dosing the food of their victims with poison. See, in this volume: Carmel Ferragud, 'A Multiple Poisoning in the City of Valencia: Sanxo Calbó's Crime (1442)'.

³⁹ Emese Bálint, 'Imagining Pain in a Sixteenth-Century Hungarian Poisoning Trial', in *The Sense of Suffering: Constructions of Physical Pain in Early Modern Culture*, ed. Jan Frans van Dijkhuizen and K. A. E. Enenkel (Leiden: Brill, 2009), pp. 423–42 at p. 426.

⁴⁰ Thomas Lupton, *Siuqila, Too Good To Be True* (London: Henry Bynneman, 1580), p. 39 (STC 16951.5); *Anno quinto reginae Elizabethe .xii. of Ianuary* (London: Richard Jugge and John Cawood, 1564), fol. 22 (STC 9464.5); Thomas Emerson, *A Concise Treatise on the Courts of Law of the City of London* (London: J. Nichols, 1794), pp. 66–67. See: Ilana Krausman Ben-Amos, 'Service and the Coming of Age of Young Men in Seventeenth-Century England', *Continuity and Change* 3 (1988): 41–64; Patrick Wallis, Cliff Webb and Chris Minns, 'Leaving Home and Entering Service: The Age of Apprenticeship in Early Modern London', *Continuity and Change* 25 (2010): 377–404.

⁴¹ *The Apprentices Warning Piece* (London: Henry Walker, 1641), sig. A2 (Wing M2582); *Heavens Cry Against Murder* (London: Henry Brome, 1657), p. 2 (Wing H1346). Subsequent references to these texts are in parentheses.

⁴² *A most barbarous murther* (London: Edward Horton, 1672), pp. 5, 8 (Wing M2868B).

one of the two newsbooks based on the case, wherein he is called 'a Boy of about fifteen years of Age' or, more obliquely, an 'Imp of Hell'. Nonetheless, even here, the author goes on to treat him as an 'unhappy servant' above all, even asking that the reader overlook his age and see him as 'young indeed in years, but old in wickedness'.[43] As these examples make clear, offenders of this type tend to be submerged into their social standing as forcibly as serving maids. They are defined almost exclusively as apprentices rather than in terms of physical maturity; their status as children, youths or adults is not only of little obvious interest to the texts but it is actively overlooked in favour of vocational status.

This indifference to age enables pamphleteers to treat apprentices much like serving-maids and to identify them with stock types of criminal. The chapbooks tend to present boy killers as variations on one of the period's most pervasive cultural and literary types, the riotous apprentice. This was a favourite scapegoat for urban disorder throughout the sixteenth and seventeenth centuries, from the early Tudor morality plays onwards.[44] Apprentice murderers are thus shown to be immersed in a wider urban youth culture, as their crimes are presented as offshoots of habitual 'Gaming and Drinking, and such-other base and dishonest courses' (*Heavens Cry Against Murder*, 4), or 'Drunkenness, Gaming, Purloining, and Fornication'.[45] More importantly, their crimes are also forced into a penitential structure derived from morality drama, as the chapbooks stress the killer's movement from corruption to redemption in the face of punishment, bringing 'strong statements of morality, repentance and deterrence' to the fore.[46] This approach is typified by the treatment of Nathaniel Butler, whose case attained a degree of notoriety in the late 1650s.[47] Butler was a cloth-drawer's apprentice who stabbed and smothered John Knight, a fellow apprentice with whom he was lodging, in the course of robbing Knight's master. An incidental remark in one newsbook suggests that Butler was about fourteen or fifteen at the time of the assault.[48] The case attracted a high degree of interest from booksell-

---

[43] *The Bloody murtherer* (London: Henry Lloyd, 1672), pp. 7, 10 (Wing B3259).
[44] Roger B. Manning, *Village Revolts: Social Protest and Popular Disturbances in England, 1509–1640* (Oxford: Clarendon Press, 1988), pp. 159–70; Paul S. Seaver, 'Apprentice Riots in Early Modern London', in *Violence, Politics, and Gender in Early Modern England*, ed. Joseph P. Ward (New York: Palgrave, 2008), pp. 19–21.
[45] George Meriton, *Immorality, Debauchery, and Profaneness, Exposed to the Reproof of Scripture* (London: John Harris and Andrew Bell, 1698), p. 40 (Wing M1800).
[46] MacMillan, *Stories of True Crime*, p. 189.
[47] On Butler, see: Lincoln B. Faller, *Turned to Account: The Forms and Functions of Criminal Biography in Late Seventeenth- and Early Eighteenth-Century England* (Cambridge: Cambridge University Press, 1987), pp. 103–09; Lake with Questier, *Anti-Christ's Lewd Hat*, pp. 159–75.
[48] See: *Blood Washed Away by Tears of Repentance* (London: W. G., 1657), sig. A5v (Wing B6285).

ers, inspiring no fewer than four competing pamphlets, many denouncing the 'Lying and false Relations' of the others.[49] It also inspired a particularly forceful level of dramatisation. One of the booklets, *Heavens Cry Against Murder*, goes to great lengths to align murderer and victim with vice and virtue, fixing them at opposing ends of the moral and socioeconomic spectrum. For this text, Butler is a 'Harpy' and 'bloody Assassinate', the child of 'Parents now ... fallen to decay, and suspected in their Credit'; he is not merely corrupt but corruptive, bribing his master to employ another in his place so that he can be free to drink, gamble and even 'perswade other young Men to cozen and to deceive their Masters'. His victim, on the other hand, is his 'too too honest friend' who is 'well descended from a worthy and worshipful Family of the *Knights* in *Berkshire*'. Even Knight's association with Butler is born out of an underlying piety, as he was said to have encountered Butler during 'their ingrafting into the visible Church in the same Font' (*Heavens Cry Against Murder*, 4–6).

Despite these excesses, all four accounts fix the events to the same basic plot. Butler starts off as a naïve boy born 'in *Hamshire* seven miles beyond Farneham' who is led into 'drinking, abusing himself with women, and other vices' after coming to London.[50] He kills Knight to sustain this 'licentious course of life' and is almost immediately overcome with remorse; he is then apprehended and dies repenting his sins (*Full and Truest Narrative*, 9). As might be expected, this last part of the sequence receives the greatest attention, even at times eclipsing the crime itself. One pamphlet dedicates twelve of its thirty pages to quoting what it claims is Butler's 'Unfained Repentance ... written with his owne Hand' and offers a portrait of him in gaol as 'one whose penitence, and I hope reall contrition spake much of a Saint ... instead of a bloody and unhuman wretch' (*Blood Washed Away*, sig. C); another licensed by Robert Tichborn, Lord Mayor of London, consists almost entirely of 'conferences' and 'Discourses' between 'this doubting staggering poor Wretch' and various ministers and officials who visited him at Newgate.[51] Indeed, owing to these portrayals, Butler's story crosses into homiletic discourse at the end of the seventeenth century: the career of this 'great Company-keeper' is listed by Samuel Ward and George Meriton among their 'several exemplary Judgments ... of God's severe Justice'.[52] Butler's life is

---

[49] 'A Lover of Truth', in *A Full and the Truest Narrative of the most Horrid, Barbarous and Unparalled Murder* (London, 1657), p. 2, fol. 1 (Wing F2292). Subsequent references to this text are in parentheses.

[50] Compare *Blood Washed Away*, sig. A5v, which places his birth 'near unto *Basingstoke*'.

[51] Randolph Yearwood, *The Penitent Murderer* (London: Thomas Newcombe, 1657), p. 30 (Wing Y23).

[52] Samuel Ward, *A Warning-Piece to all Drunkards and Health-Drinkers* (London: Langley Curtis, 1682), pp. 33–34 (Wing W931); Meriton, *Immorality, Debauchery, and Profaneness*, p. 40. Butler's story also appears as an implicit sign of moral chaos during the

then turned into an illustrative morality narrative akin to a sermon exemplum: he undergoes the same cycle of temptation, sin and repentance as the wayward urban youths of *Hick Scorner* (c. 1512), *Mundus et Infans* (1522), *Like Will to Like* (1568), *Eastward Hoe* (1605), Hogarth's *Industry and Idleness* (1747) or the popular ballad 'An Apprentice of London' (c. 1624).[53] His age makes no obvious difference to his identification with this type, causing no interpretive problems and sparking no doubts about his responsibility. While he may be little more than a child, he is treated like any other apprentice-criminal, to the extent that he even symbolises the excesses of this group as a whole, embodying 'the lust of unbridled youth' (*Blood Washed Away*, sig. C1v).

The framework pressed on to Butler's life proves just as robust in similar pieces. A near-identical course is also followed by responses to Thomas Savage, who bludgeoned a maidservant in 1668 during a robbery, and Peter Moore, who poisoned his master in 1641 in order to escape his service. Both seem to have been of similar age to Butler. While they are again placed in the opaque category of 'apprentice', Moore was probably younger than eighteen, since he appealed to his parents 'that they out of hand might buy out my time' before his training was complete and shortly before killing his master; likewise, a pamphlet published three years after Savage's execution makes him 'under sixteen years of age'.[54] Again, the crimes are presented as products of the urban milieu and 'bad company': Moore allegedly killed so that he might 'imbrace iniquity' even more freely (*Apprentices Warning Piece*, sig. A3), while Savage sought to please

---

Commonwealth in *Royall and loyall blood shed by Cromwell* (London: H.B., 1662), fols 45–46v (Wing R2101).

[53] Martha Tuck Rozett, *The Doctrine of Election and the Emergence of Elizabethan Tragedy* (Princeton: Princeton University Press, 1984), p. 85; G. K. Hunter, *English Drama, 1586–1642: The Age of Shakespeare* (Oxford: Oxford University Press, 1997), pp. 323–26; Ronald Paulson, *Hogarth: Art and Politics* (Cambridge: Cambridge University Press, 1992), pp. 95–97. The 'Apprentice of London' offers a particularly vivid illustration of the hazy distinction between fictional structures and factual reportage in the murder pamphlets: on the one hand, the name of its main character was repeatedly evoked as an archetype for discussing and defining actual instances of juvenile crime; on the other, the story was eventually absorbed into news discourse itself, being presented as an actual, recent occurrence in two late chapbooks. See: *The Prentice's Tragedy* (London: W. O.,[c.1699]), Wing A3587B; *Memoirs of George Barnwell* (London: Sherwood, Neely and Jones, 1817); Civicus, 'To Henry Stonecastle, Esq.', *Universal Spectator* 172 (22 January 1732): 1; 'George Barnwel parallel'd', *Gentleman's Magazine* 653 (January 1732): 568; William Jackson, *Newgate Calendar*, 6 vols (London: A. Hogg, 1795), 4:109. On the history of the text, see: Ralph Cohen, 'Literary History and the Ballad of George Barnwel', in *Augustan Studies: Essays in Honour of Irvin Ehrenpreis*, ed. Douglas Lane Patey and Timothy Keegan (London: Associated University Presses, 1985), pp. 13–31.

[54] Richard Alleine, *A Murderer Punished and Pardoned* (London, 1671): Wing A997.

'the Whore that enticed him ... with her Spiders Web of wickedness'.[55] Much like the accounts of Butler, the chapbooks show the boys being undone by 'fear, horror, and guilt of Conscience' (*Apprentices Warning Piece*, sig. A2v), coming to sincere repentance once arrested and heading to their executions 'desiring all people, especially young persons to take warning ... what company they addicted themselves unto' (*Gods Justice Against Murther*, 9). The same basic sequence of corruption by the city environment, inevitable sin and eventual penance is, therefore, imposed on all three crimes. Although the murders have clear disparities – motive, circumstance, method and victim are different in each case – these are quietly glossed over in order to fit them into a uniform narrative. Even when apprentices play a peripheral role in murders, they tend to be packaged into the same trajectories. In 1669, a group consisting of 'six men and one bloody woman' was arrested for cutting the throat of John Taylor, a former chaplain and minister, in a garden at Shoreditch.[56] The youngest member of the group was George Rhodes, an apprentice pawnbroker, convicted largely on the basis that he was 'able to give no account of where he was that night'.[57] While Rhodes' part in the crime was at best marginal, the newsbooks still force him into the established penitential narrative: although one author admits that Rhodes 'said little' before his execution, he still feels compelled to add that he 'seemed to be very penitent, weeping bitterly' and blames his death on 'keeping ill company'.[58] Once again, the newsbooks show no compunction in drawing boys into a morality-style plot, applying such a template without hesitation. Unlike twentieth-century newspaper reports of murderous youngsters, the age of the offenders does not disturb the process of fictionalisation to the least degree; these figures can be smoothly integrated into readymade definitions of murderer with little sense of unsuitability or eccentricity.

Overall, it is clear that early modern news discourse sees no reason to exempt the young from its ruling methods of understanding murder. In the first place, the minority of the offenders does not carry much weight for the newsbooks, let alone generate any obvious signs of disquiet. The general lack of emphasis on age suggests that the authors and their presumed audience were untroubled by the basic idea of a child or youth committing murder. Since pamphlets would often exaggerate alarming features of particular crimes to attract potential buyers, much like later commercial media, their silence on this front is extremely telling;

---

[55] *Gods Justice Against Murther* (London: John Clarke, 1668), p. 8 (Wing G959A). Subsequent references to the text are in parentheses.
[56] *A Perfect Narrative of the Robbery and Murder Committed near Dame Annis so Cleer* (London: William Godbid, 1669), p. 31 (Wing P1503).
[57] *An Exact Narrative of the Bloody Murder and Robbery* (London: R. Taylor, 1669), p. 5 (Wing E3665).
[58] *Exact Narrative*, p. 8.

their failure to advertise the age of offenders suggests that readers were unlikely to be moved by this detail as it was insufficiently 'sensational' to merit exploitation.[59] Indeed, their interest in the crimes probably owes more to the special horror with which early modern culture regarded petty treason, given that many of the crimes were committed by an inferior against a social superior.[60] But at a more structural level, when maidservants and apprentices are found to have killed, they are drawn into the ruling narratives of the early modern reports with little obvious resistance, prompting no questions about culpability. Time and again, pamphleteers can be seen to identify them with particular criminal archetypes and to lock them into conventional cycles of sin and penance, without any indication of indecision or sense of impropriety. In other words, there is not the same degree of shock or doubt found in later cases; the implicit systems of the early modern press prove more than capable of processing these crimes without impediment, drawing them unreservedly into their established taxonomies. In short, children and youths provoke no debates about criminal responsibility, but can be judged in much the same terms as adult transgressors.

This raises some obvious questions: why, exactly, killer youngsters should lack the disruptive effect that features so markedly in more recent reportage, and why the newsbooks should be so at ease conceiving of them as criminals. The findings assembled so far suggest that there is some tacit element in early modern attitudes towards the young that allow the pamphlets to encode them in this way; the lack of explicit discussion certainly indicates that news discourse is following a deeper cultural assumption. Yet identifying what guides this behaviour is highly complex. It is rendered especially difficult by the fact that juvenile criminals do, at times, present interpretive problems to sixteenth- and seventeenth-century culture. In particular, they challenge the field of law, in which there is much less willingness to condemn them out of hand. One witness to this position is the barrister Sir Matthew Hale, whose *Historia placitorum coronae* (c. 1670) wavers considerably when trying to fix the frontiers of culpability and 'the privilege of infancy'. Attempting to synthesise existing practice, Hale locates a discrepancy between the *aetas pubertati*, 'determined antiently ... to be twelve years for both sexes', and the age at which offenders are able to 'discern between good and evil', which traditionally commences 'after fourteen years'.[61] Procedure is clear above and below these levels: 'an infant above fourteen and under twenty-one' should be punished to the full extent of the law, for 'if the law should not

[59] On these commercial strategies, see: Lake with Questier, *Anti-Christ's Lewd Hat*, pp. 19–23.
[60] Matthew Lockwood, 'From Treason to Homicide: Changing Conceptions of the Law of Petty Treason in Early Modern England', *The Journal of Legal History* 34 (2013): 31–49.
[61] Sir Matthew Hale, *Historia placitorum coronæ: The History of the Pleas of the Crown*, ed. Sollom Emlyn and George Wilson, 2 vols (London: E. and R. Nutt, 1778), 1:25–26.

animadvert upon such offenders by reason of their nonage, the kingdom would come to confusion'; on the other hand, 'if an infant be above seven years old and under twelve years ... and commit a felony, in this case *prima facie* he is to be judged not guilty' (*Historia placitorum*, 1:25–6). In other words, definitions of puberty and legal responsibility do not fully match up; the age at which physical maturity is attained and the age at which full moral awareness is reached do not completely coincide. There is a gap of two years between the two states; between the ages of twelve and fourteen, there exists a shadowy period in which defendants 'might or might not be guilty according to the circumstances of the fact' – they are considered adults but lack judgement and liability (*Historia placitorum*, 1:22). The assured valuations in the chapbooks, therefore, dodge wider uncertainties about whether young people can, in fact, be deemed responsible for their offences. Many of these cases, such as Anne Evans and 'Daniel', fall into precisely the indeterminate period that Hale puzzles over. Nonetheless, these murderers are fastened to firm valuations by the pamphleteers, their culpability beyond doubt: Evans is straightforwardly guilty, 'a Slave and Vassal of the Devil' (Quick, *Hell Opend*, 22, 48), despite being only thirteen years old at most, while Daniel is simply a 'mallefactor' (*Narrative of the proceedings*, sig. Ai). The newsbooks are largely content to overlook the ambiguities presented by their subjects' age; they deflect the problems that youngsters carry with them in legal theory and practice, despite their reliance on trials for their material.

One possible explanation for the pamphleteers' unconcern, and their evasion of the problems Hale articulates, is their ability to consult a wider range of discourses than jurisprudence alone. Although largely dependent on the law courts, their authors nevertheless can look to a number of cultural centres, and so have a wide range of conceptions at their disposal. This approach can be seen in their preference for social classifications over temporal or physical categories. Such definitions seem to be taken from contemporary middle-class culture, wherein the transition from childhood to adulthood is often understood in similar terms. As several commentators have observed, early modern authors within the urban professional classes tended to use social and economic factors to calculate the 'ripeness' of an individual, looking to changes in status rather than the body to determine maturity. Hence Ilana Krausman Ben-Amos and Elizabeth Foyster argue that marriage represented the chief point of entry into adulthood in the period, being 'an important signpost in this process of maturation, if not the most important', while other critics have noted that further rituals carried comparable weight, such as the attainment of 'capacity' in a given trade or the general acquisition of other 'binding social commitments'.[62] The movement

---

[62] Ilana Krausman Ben-Amos, *Adolescence and Youth in Early Modern England* (New Haven: Yale University Press, 1994), p. 32; Elizabeth A. Foyster, *Manhood in Early Modern*

from minority to majority is thus seen in bourgeois circles as an accumulation of roles and responsibility above all, rather than a collection of anatomical signs: in the words of the Puritan Francis Rous, gaining 'ripeness and manhood' involves being 'lanched forth like a full built ship into the world on a sea of cares', or being propelled into a network of social obligations.[63] The fact the newsbooks use these definitions is, no doubt, at least partly reflexive; after all, the pamphlets circulated within the same middle-class urban culture from which these ideas originated. However, this deployment can also be seen as a deliberate rhetorical choice as these definitions go a long way towards defusing the problems that Hales runs into. By describing the murderer in professional terms, rather than specifying a numeric age, the pamphlets muddy the distinction between child and adult. When described as 'apprentice' or 'maidservant', the killer appears both youthful and fully grown at once since these terms cut across the boundary between the two ages. Indeed, there are points when this confusion does seem to be part of a deliberate policy: for instance, one of the booklets on Thomas Savage links him with boyhood and manhood at the same time, depicting him with a full beard on its frontispiece while branding his crimes 'youthful extravagancies' (*Gods justice against murther*, 2). These manoeuvres, in turn, allow the newsbooks to draw their subjects into criminal typologies; by blurring the lines between youth and adult with these wilfully indistinct terms, the pamphleteers imply that their subjects are fully accountable for their actions, brushing aside their immaturity and questionable level of responsibility. In short, the pamphleteers deliberately choose the vision of the young person most conducive to their projects, one which allows them to insist on the criminality of their subject, manipulating them to fit the demands of their discourse.

Nevertheless, this is only one of the conceptions of youth the newsbooks select. Despite their overriding interest in social identities, the chapbooks also draw repeated attention to the bodies of offenders, both male and female. Typical in this regard is the account of the St Martin's poisoning, where the anatomy of the perpetrator is repeatedly evoked. Her physiology is made particularly visible during the girl's interview by the authorities, as the writer gives a detailed sketch of her posture and demeanour: it is reported that 'she is strictly questioned, and at first denied it, though the changeable Colours in her face, and trembling disorder gave her tongue the lye' (*Horrid News*, 5). The sense that child criminals are betrayed by their own physicality becomes something

---

England: Honour, Sex and Marriage (London: Routledge, 1999), p. 65; Mary Abbott, *Life Cycles in England, 1560–1720: Cradle to Grave* (London: Routledge, 1969), p. 69; Claire Sponsler, *Drama and Resistance: Bodies, Goods, and Theatricality in Late Medieval England* (Minneapolis: University of Minnesota Press, 1997), p. 90.

[63] Francis Rous, *Meditations of Instruction, of Exhortation, of Reprofe* (London: John Legat, 1616), p. 441 (STC 21342).

of a commonplace in the literature, as similar allusions appear in the accounts of Nathaniel Butler's murder. According to this set of texts, Butler is detected not merely by the presence of 'some scattering hairs' he left in his victim's hands but by the outward traces of his troubled conscience, which left his face looking 'so sadly and ghastly' (*Full and Truest Narrative*, 3–4) and 'dejected ... being as it seems smitten' (*Heavens Cry Against Murder*, 7). Alongside these details, the body makes a further appearance when chapbook authors try to classify these crimes. Blood is often evoked as a symbol for the murders, even in cases without any obvious injury or violence. Thus, Peter Moore's poisoning of his master is 'a deed which now doth make each Artery to quake' (*Apprentices Warning Piece*, sig. A3), while the St Martin's case is said to possess a 'Sanguine Complexion' (*Horrid News*, 7). In either case, blood seems to be less a synonym for aggression, given the clandestine methods employed, and more a general, descriptive heading for the killings.

In singling out these two details, the newsbooks seem to connect their remarks to contemporary medical understanding of the immature body. Throughout the early modern period, conventional thinking still tended to regard puberty in humoral terms inherited from medieval medicine, especially from the work of Avicenna.[64] According to this view, pubescents' bodies were dominated by blood, which supposedly provided the warmth and moisture necessary for growth; at the same time, however, blood was also thought to render their temperaments volatile and unstable, figuratively 'heating' appetite, behaviour and intellect.[65] The persistence of this idea can be seen in Stephen Batman's 1582 encyclopedia, *Batman upon Bartholome*. Batman's work is itself a meeting point between the medieval and modern: it is based on Trevisa's fourteenth-century translation of Bartholomaeus Anglicus' *De proprietatibus rerum* (c. 1245), but freely incorporates material 'as hath bene brought to light ... to time present', particularly by the likes of Paracelsus and Conrad Gessner.[66] Yet despite this modernisation, when Batman considers juvenile physiology, his remarks fall back entirely on medieval thinking. He describes youngsters as 'hot and moyst of complection ... through stirring and mouing of the heate of the flesh and of humours', adding that these conditions make them changeable and irritable in disposition, being 'lightly and soone wroth, and soone pleased

---

[64] Avicenna, *The Canon of Medicine of Avicenna*, trans. O. Cameron Gruner (New York: AMS Press, 1929), p. 69.

[65] See: Hannah Newton, *The Sick Child in Early Modern England, 1580–1720* (Oxford: Oxford University Press, 2012), pp. 65–90.

[66] See: Elizabeth Joy Keen, *Journey of a Book: Bartholomew the Englishman and the Properties of Things* (Canberra: ANU Press, 2007), pp. 127–60.

... lyghtly they forgiue'.⁶⁷ Substantially the same position is sketched out by Henry Cuffe a few decades later. Although Cuffe presents his work as starting from first principles and empirical observation, his description of the immature constitution also stresses its traditional bloodiness: 'so see wee the same body in our youth and child-hood, diuersly tempered, our infancy ful of moisture, as the fluid soft substance of our flesh manifestly declareth'.⁶⁸ Cuffe also assigns a number of behavioural effects to blood, arguing that its liquidity generates a general lack of intellectual discipline, represented by loose 'sportfulnesse, talke, and learning'.⁶⁹ Similar comments on the 'the moisture of Childrens bodies' or adolescence as the time of 'bloods Predominancy in the Body' continue to occur throughout early modern medicine.⁷⁰

The newsbooks' emphasis on young murderers as 'Sanguine' or 'bloudy' is no doubt aligned with these longstanding medical conceptions, using them to shore up their judgements. At points, the link appears expressly. Hence, one late piece on a murderous apprentice begins with a treatise on the anatomy of the young and its attendant social problems, opining that 'the juvenile mind is constitutionally sanguine' and, as a result, is 'wild and fanciful' before its 'dangerous heat is tempered by experience'.⁷¹ The same reasoning can also be glimpsed in references to the minds of offenders, as the psychological processes attributed to the children often recall properties assigned to blood. For instance, the reports on the apprentice named Daniel take care to point out that 'his Memory was as much Corrupted as his mind' while killing his colleague (*Narrative of the Proceedings at the Sessions*, 3). This detail again makes veiled reference to blood, which was thought to compromise recollection owing to its fluidity: according to Cuffe, 'children haue so slippery and short memories' because of the influence of the humour, as 'their braines too great humidity ... is disabled to keepe the impressions of the outward senses obiects' in the same way that water is 'least fit to retaine any figure imprinted' (*Differences of the Ages*, 125–6). The descriptions of children being undone by their physical appearance also seems to pick up on an assumption running through the medical texts; namely, that the minds of children are basically indistinguishable from their material bodies, with one directly determining the other. In their references to blood, therefore, the

---

[67] Stephen Batman, *Batman vppon Bartholome* (London: Thomas East, 1582), fols 3v, 73 (STC 1538).
[68] Henry Cuffe, *The Differences of the Ages of Mans Life* (London: Arnold Hatfield, 1607), pp. 113–14 (STC 6103).
[69] Cuffe, *Differences of the Ages*, pp. 113–14.
[70] John Pechey, *A General Treatise of the Diseases of Infants and Children* (London: R. Wellington, 1697), p. 83 (Wing P1023); Alius Medicus, *Animadversions on the Medicinal Observations of Frederick Loss* (London: William Willis, 1674), p. 108 (Wing B178).
[71] *Memoirs of George Barnwell*, sig. A2v.

chapbooks draw on another idea of youth, as they look to the medical understanding of puberty to help construct their narratives.

In terms of their functions within the texts, these allusions seem to have two distinct roles. On the one hand, they have a metaphoric purpose, providing a symbolic hinge on which ideas of immaturity and homicide can be brought together since both are equally 'bloody'. As a result, they further rationalise the crimes for their readership, levering them into an established conceptual vocabulary. But at the same time, the humoral references also imply a causal relation between blood and murder, suggesting that the humour's volatility is ultimately responsible for violence. That the heat of blood can prompt aggression is again a truism in early modern culture. For instance, in a series of sermons on the dangers of youth, the Welsh minister Daniel Williams argues that the 'overheated Spirit' of 'Young Men' does not merely mean that they are 'apt to be peevish and cross' but leads directly to 'Lasting Enmities, Quarrels, Murthers'.[72] Likewise, the influential pedagogue Richard Mulcaster turns to the language of criminality when describing the 'unwholesome and superfluous humors' of youthfulness, calling them 'common murtherers of a multitude of scholars'.[73] The same logic seems to hover in the background of the newsbooks as their repeated allusions to blood, with its dual connotations of youth and instability, implicates the humour as a trigger for crime. Again, the murder pamphlets deliberately seek out conceptions of minority most closely suited to their own designs. They carefully choose ideas that allow them to depict youngsters as unambiguously guilty, incorporating definitions that support their larger presentation of their subject.

Collectively, therefore, these remarks reveal precisely why young people are not encountered as alien objects by early modern news discourse, despite the problems they raise in relation to criminal responsibility and the difficulties they present to later media. The wider culture of the seventeenth century provided numerous methods for interpreting minors that might evade these issues; the writers of pamphlets could call on a range of semantic resources to render youngsters acceptable as criminals, from the social categorisation of middle-class culture to the standard medical understanding of immature physiology. Each of these conceptions allows the pamphlets to crowbar the young into their criminal typologies in various ways. In fact, these ideas do not represent the limit of meanings from which news discourse could draw. After all, as scholarship has widely recognised, the newsbooks could also present juveniles as antitheses of crime, depicting them as absolute victims whose deaths testify to the 'monstrous

---

[72] Daniel Williams, *The Vanity of Childhood and Youth* (London: John Dunton, 1691), p. 34 (Wing W2657).

[73] Richard Mulcaster, *Positions Concerning the Training up of Children*, ed. William Barker (Toronto: University of Toronto Press, 1994), p. 35.

and inhuman' cruelty of their killers.[74] Even apprentices could be made to serve this function despite their traditional venality: hence, John Wattle, who beat his apprentice to death at Maidstone in 1680, is made all the more 'perfidious' and 'unmerciful' by his choice of victim, as his 'barbarous usuage' is the worse for being directed at a 'Youth of about eighteen years of Age'.[75] The point is that young people prove intensely malleable in the pamphlets. They can be made to serve whatever purpose their authors require of them, being equally amenable to charges of guilt and guiltlessness. They do not have to resist narratives of crime because they can be shaped to fit any role, simply by reading them through the appropriate lens.

This might in fact be where the murder pamphlets have greatest value: they show the profound instability of early modern youth at a conceptual level. Their treatment of young people highlights how many overlapping ideas were circulating in sixteenth- and seventeenth-century English culture, and how no one view carried absolute authority. As these texts illustrate, it is less the case that children 'did not exist' as a distinct group in the period, or that young people were seen merely as 'miniature adults', and more that they were overdetermined and overlaid with multiple, competing valuations.[76] As a result, children and adolescents can be made into murderers or victims as the occasion demands, and the problems their immaturity raises can be dismissed merely by concentrating on one of the many potential meanings they contain. A central distinction between early and later news discourse is, then, a greater appreciation of the complexity of the young in the earlier texts. The newsbooks clearly have horizons beyond the monolithic, sentimental view of youth that predominates in modern journalism, with its single-minded emphasis on 'innocence, dependency and powerlessness': they bear witness, it might be said, to the gradual simplification of youngsters over time within the discourse they initiated.[77] Ultimately, they lay bare deep-running fractures within the supposedly stable, biological category of immaturity, not only exposing the variety of contemporary opinion, but revealing progressive discontinuities over time.

---

[74] Kilday, *A History of Infanticide*, p. 19.
[75] *Proceedings at the Assizes Holden at Maidstone* (London, 1680), pp. 1–2 (Wing F2316A).
[76] Philippe Ariès, *Centuries of Childhood: A Social History of Family Life*, trans. Robert Baldick (New York: Alfred A. Knopf, 1962), p. 125; John Demos, *Family Life in a Plymouth Colony* (Oxford: Oxford University Press, 1970), p. 57. See: Linda A. Pollock, *Forgotten Children: Parent-Child Relations from 1500 to 1900* (Cambridge: Cambridge University Press, 1983), pp. 43–54.
[77] D'Cruze, Walklate and Pegg, *Murder*, p. 80.

Conclusion

Hannah Skoda

Taken together, these articles serve as a powerful corrective to lazy stereotypes of the Middle Ages as horrifically and unthinkingly brutal. It is perhaps ironic that a volume devoted to the subject of murder should have this effect, and certainly we do not emerge with any rose-tinted illusions about the level of violence in medieval life. But we do gain a sense of the complexity and sophistication of responses to fatal violence. Whether or not medieval reasoning resonates with our own, contemporaries wrote, spoke about and listened to accounts of violence with an almost obsessive interest which went beyond the prurient. As these essays reveal, it was a subject whose dubious moral framework provoked anxiety and ambivalence.

Of course, if murder was a common medieval literary theme, this was partly because of its theatrical potential: it has drama, often mystery and a good deal of human interest. A medieval crowd-pleasing example which usefully embodies many of the observations which follow about this volume is the play *La Femme du Roy de Portugal* (1876): it contains multiple murders.[1] This is a reworked narrative from the *Vie des Pères*, a popular collection of miracle stories from the mid thirteenth century, surviving in over thirty manuscripts.[2] The play version was produced for the annual festivities of the Parisian guild of goldsmiths. Over the course of the play, the soon-to-be-Queen is raped by the King's Seneschal, whom she subsequently murders. Realising that this jeopardises her role as a virgin on her wedding night, she persuades another woman to replace her for the one night, only to find the other woman unsurprisingly reluctant to relinquish her place. The Queen, in despair, murders the woman who is attempting to usurp her place. Condemned by law to death, she is rescued at the last minute by the efforts of the Blessed Virgin Mary. The story makes splendid theatre, keeping the audience breathless with the melodrama and tension of it all. It is also a highly

---

[1] *Les miracles de Nostre Dame par personnages*, ed. Gaston Paris and Ulysse Robert, 7 vols (Paris: Librairie de Firmin Didot, 1876–93), I:151–202.

[2] *La Vie des Peres*, ed. Félix Lecoy, 3 vols (Paris: Société des anciens textes français, 1987–1999), II:84–109.

problematic tale, not least because of the extreme levels of violence, and it is surely this problematic nature which was designed to keep the audience rapt by a series of moral and legal knots which cannot easily be disentangled. In the first place, as a spectator, it was and is hard to work out where one's sympathies lie. The Queen clearly suffers appallingly, and yet her reaction is a terrifying one. She kills by setting her victims alight, and, given the propensity of late medieval dramatists to indulge in lavish pyrotechnics, this must have shocked and awed the audience.[3] Literature works so often by engaging our compassion, and as we oscillate, as an audience, between sympathy and horror, we are left in disarray as to the identity of the real victim. In the second place, the play toys with attempts to categorise an act like this on a scale of justifiability. In trying to assess the heinousness of a crime, medieval audiences would have looked for clues like a sense of justice being done, the absence or presence of 'hot anger', the degree of premeditation or the openness or secrecy of a particular crime. The Queen's murderous actions trouble all these distinctions: she is raging with fury, but her actions are at least strategic; her crimes are spectacular and highly public, and yet she tries to keep her true motivation secret. The legal reaction to her crimes (and that of the Church, since she confesses to a chaplain who then betrays her) is predictably harsh, and yet this categorisation is challenged by the miraculous intervention of the Virgin Mary. Every attempt by the audience to make sense of what is going on is frustrated and challenged by the layering of different and competing normative discourses about murderous violence and what might justify it.

But what is most striking about this tale is its almost total lack of interest in the victims of the violence. In the case of the Seneschal, this is unsurprising. The tale implies that he got what was coming to him and that is that. In the case of the woman who agreed to sleep with the King in his new bride's place, this is more shocking to a modern audience. And yet, this lack of interest in the personhood of the victim on an emotional or even on an ethical level seems to characterise many of the cases treated in this volume. Whilst all the articles analyse medieval discourses about particular types and cases of murder, rarely do these medieval accounts show the slightest interest in the personhood of the victim; that is, unless it be in the most generic sense, for instance regarding the victim's status. The *Historia* of Gregory of Tours, discussed by Jeffrey Doolittle, is an exception wherein the murder by Childebert and Clovis is dramatised through a powerful evocation of Clothild's grief afterwards. Even here, though, where there is a much clearer sense of the personal implications of killing, Gregory's main point is not about individuals but about the disordered and sinful nature of the world. In the most extreme sense, this denial of attention to the personhood of the

---

[3] See, for example: Laura Weigert, *French Visual Culture and the Making of Medieval Theater* (Cambridge: Cambridge University Press, 2012), p. 221.

victim is illustrated by Anne Latowsky's comments on the comedic potential of murder in several of the Old French fabliaux. These tales sometimes rely on 'corpse comedy', and, as Latowsky shows, such humour depends on the complete evacuation of any sympathy for the victim himself. In the case of the Old French fabliaux, this was largely achieved through rendering the victim as the stock figure of the lecherous priest, who was a disappointment to his vocation, to his community and to God.

As these articles show, then, medieval responses to murder tended to evince interest in the victim only in so far as this shed light on the implications for the community as a whole. To modern audiences, this may seem callous, but it is an instance of how a theme like murder can reveal a far more community-oriented way of thinking, communities both horizontal and vertical or hierarchical. The identity of the victim mattered mainly in so far as the relative status of victim and perpetrator affected the judgement of the crime as it carried implications for the social hierarchy and cohesion of the whole community. So, for instance, Thomas Gobbitt shows how Lombard laws rendered the price of composition for poisoning someone equal to the financial worth of the victim. Such an injunction arose not from any personal interest in the victim but from a recognition of the importance of restoring social hierarchies which could, in this case, be rendered in precisely quantifiable terms. Doolittle discusses the importance of the distinction between *parricidium* and *homicidium* in Gregory's work, the former referring to the killing of close family members. Once again, the classification, but not the identity, as such, of the victim really matters. The seriousness of these murderous acts lay in their rending of families and of the ties of normal social life, not in the personal loss experienced by the victim. If classifications of victims and perpetrators really mattered because of the implications for social cohesion, it is again very telling that these classifications were so different from modern ones. What mattered most was social status and kinship relations. As Ben Parsons points out, the age of the perpetrator attracted rather little attention, surprisingly enough, with young killers condemned because they were killers, not because they were adolescents.

Community, of course, was also knit together by notions of honour. Who the victim was emphatically mattered in the context of vengeance, honour and resulting feuds, although again this was about collective identities and motivations rather than individual personhood. It is a quite different way of thinking about murder from modern interest in victim impact, which may attempt to quantify but remains resolutely personal. The feuds of the Icelandic sagas, as analysed here by Ilse Schweitzer Van Donkelaar, are a case in point. Killing and its consequences were bound up in the very public performance of feuds, whose role in maintaining a precarious social balance depended precisely upon this sense of publicising honourable motivation and family reputation.

In the later medieval period, as the definition of political communities evolved, so too did the implications of murder. Rather than concern for the personhood of the victim, the implications for horizontal communities and social cohesion lay at the heart of legal, moralising and narrative reactions. By the fourteenth century, political communities could be more clearly articulated as body politics dependent upon the role of the king at the head, and the communal implications of murder were therefore more explicitly read as treasonous. In killing someone, a perpetrator disrupted the body politic and, by implication, injured most seriously the interests of its head, the monarch. As Jolanta Komornicka shows in the context of French murder trials coming before the Parlement of Paris between 1254 and 1320, the legal semantics of murder increasingly associated it with treason. As she observes, this was not an equation made regarding every crime; for instance, crimes against property were not characterised in such terms. Murder was increasingly seen as a crime which disrupted the entire political community, and, in many ways, the actual victim mattered less and less.

On the other hand, what mattered more and more were the jurisdictional implications of murder. The murder itself was just the beginning of the story. What really mattered for many of these political communities was the statement to be made by stamping promptly and judicially on the matter. If the killing itself affected the cohesion and harmony of the whole community, the way in which it was jurisdictionally dealt with was perhaps the most powerful statement of relative political power in the medieval western world. Patricia Turning's discussion of the surviving documents about an adulterous woman who murdered her husband in sixteenth-century Toulouse makes this case particularly strongly. As a woman who overturned that most fundamental hierarchy of patriarchy by killing her husband, one might expect the social and familial implications of this to have dominated the subsequent documentation of the case. What actually happened was a four-year wrangle between the royal jurisdictional officers and the municipal 'capitols' over who had the right to prosecute and execute her. Jurisdiction and its far-reaching implications for definitions of relative power and political community trumped even fundamental gender hierarchies. The dead victim barely warranted comment.

Likewise, accepting the jurisdictional conclusions of a particular governmental body was often the most communally significant dimension of a murder case. As Pinchas Roth powerfully explains in the context of medieval Jewish responses to executions of Jewish murderers by Christian authorities, the choice of whether or not to grieve for the condemned man was one that carried enormous implications for the entire Jewish community and went far beyond any concern for the life of that individual. Mourning Jews who were executed by Christian authorities was a way of rejecting that jurisdictional authority. This method was used sparingly, however, and a sophisticated distinction was made between justice and power; indeed, the significance of mourning was enlisted to emphasise the inherent difference between those Jews who were legitimately and judicially condemned by regular courts and those who were executed by a state whose interests could not be so easily aligned with the prerogatives of justice, but rather reflected raw power. Once again, the implications of murder stretched far beyond the personal impact on the victim and his or her family, beyond the identity of the perpetrator, to produce dramatisations of the relationship between different religious and political communities.

If the implications of murder were read as threats to communities rather than the individuals involved, what really seemed to matter to the nature of that threat was the idea of secrecy or openness. In case after case, across the period, what distinguished murder from homicide was the secrecy of the crime. As Larissa Tracy puts it, all murder was homicide, but not all homicide was murder; what distinguished murder and made it especially heinous was its lack of openness. Truly, it was a crime of dishonesty, of deception and of secrecy. The Lombard laws of the seventh century, as Gobbitt shows, are explicit in condemning secrecy as particularly appalling. So too do the laws of early medieval Ireland. The Lombard laws devote particular attention to what happened to the body after the violent act: plundering or hiding the body was an element of added disrespect which made the crime all the more nefarious. The Old Irish laws, as Bridgette Slavin demonstrates, condemn supernaturally-induced killings most particularly because of their invisibility. Fast-forwarding to late medieval France, Komornicka also shows that there was even more concern about secrecy and dissimulation than there was about the question of premeditation.

Why was secrecy so abominable? Once again, this must be read in the context of the notion of community. Any community is bound together by a key quality: trust (though many would argue that its corollary, fear, can also be a powerful binder). Horizontal communal ties are founded on trust; that is, we need to know what to expect from our neighbours, and we need to be able to trust each other to respect our possessions and persons. Vertical political communities were also based upon trust. Monarchs and governments could command respect and obedience because people trusted that they would behave in specific ways and even provide a level of protection. Trust can be threatened in all kinds of ways, of course, but openness is surely fundamental to it. As a case like that of the Icelandic sagas shows, even high levels of feuding need not erode a sense of social cohesion if the feuding is visible and publicised. If, however, crimes take place in secret and one never knows who perpetuates the betrayal, that fundamental social glue of trust begins to come apart. Schweitzer Van Donkelaar explains that medieval Icelandic society relied on the fundamental prerogative of any killer to reveal his or her deed. She goes on to show how this clear distinction between secrecy and publicity was troubled by the sagas' often riddle-like, character-driven narratives of violent deeds, in which the perpetrator both publicises and obscures his deed. Komornicka points out that the *Livre de Jostice*, an early fourteenth-century French compilation of customary law, defines murder as treachery precisely because it betrays trust. This is why poisoning was also deemed such a heinous crime: its invisibility renders it particularly terrifying. Carmel Ferragud discusses the case of Sanxo Calbó who was accused of poisoning multiple members of his family in Valencia in 1442. His actions are horrific, not just because of the sheer scale of his violence, but because he violated the fundamental bond of trust which holds a family together and, by extension, a whole society. His deeds were committed through trickery and deception as his relatives believed that they were merely accepting his hospitably offered drinks and sweets. Trickery and deception are what marked this man out as a devil.

Where does the issue of secrecy and openness leave premeditation? As Komornicka comments in the late medieval French case, dissimulation seems to trump even premeditation in defining the heinousness of a crime, though the two are not unconnected. Premeditation implies a degree of cunning and planning which is, and seems always to have been, deeply distasteful. It implies concealment, dissimulation and trickery. But unlike the dominant condemnation of secrecy, the question of premeditation provoked a good deal more ambivalence. The case of the Queen of Portugal in *La Femme du Roy de Portugal* toys explicitly with the ethical ambivalence in assessing rational motives versus irrational anger, and careful planning versus spontaneous rage. On the one hand, if a murder was premeditated, its logic was more likely to be considered rational, perhaps even understandable. On the other hand, premeditation implies concealment, and cunning and was even more threatening to the community, whether that community was local or political. This latter sense is potently illustrated by medieval attitudes towards crimes committed because of insanity. If judged insane, a murderer could not have planned or intended the crime, and its implications were deemed to be less far-reaching. If not of sound mind, the perpetrator cannot have had such clear intention, there can have been no premeditation and, therefore, the case did not amount to a criminal act of murder. Effectively, this was also the position of continental Roman law, which privileges the notion of intention in judging crimes.[4] But there were other ways of thinking about these implications, as these articles highlight. Or rather, if intention mattered, the nature of that intention was the key. If legal responses were about justice, so too could killing be justified as an act of justice if the intention behind it could be demonstrated to be bona fide. Of course, this is the problematic logic underpinning *La Femme du Roy de Portugal*. It is the unimpeachable logic of

---

[4] See, for example: Jean-Marie, Carbasse, *Histoire du droit pénal et de la justice criminelle* (Paris: Presses Universitaires de France, 2000), pp. 319–20.

the Queen's crime, her desire to redress two injustices – rape and usurpation – which render the audience reaction so complex and ambivalent towards her extreme outburst of violence. In general, of course, it was far easier to claim the justice of a killing if it was done on behalf of the state. This much is clear in the work of Matthew Lubin on early modern Venice. Poisoning seems to have been worryingly common in Venice in the period, and it is described as being particularly appalling in legal handbooks because of its secretive aspect. However, there were also many state-sponsored poisonings as acts of political assassination; indeed, it was an important tool against the Ottomans. As such, it was justifiable despite its premeditation because it was state-sponsored and because the underlying intention was one which supported the well-being of the body politic. The eleventh-century St Brice's Day massacre, described by Jay Paul Gates, may be a similar case in point. Aethelred II ordered the assassination of all Danes living in England in 1002, in what appears to have been an appallingly premeditated and cruelly executed act of genocide. Later chroniclers like William of Newburgh certainly gloss it this way. However, there was an alternative perspective, one put eloquently by the more contemporary Anglo-Saxon chronicle. In this reading, the mass killing was an act of justice provoked by a Danish plot to assassinate the king which followed the precepts of the recent law of *morð* (or *morðor*), which made it possible to hold an ethnic group responsible for political subversion.

In other words, whilst premeditation implies concealment and secrecy, and renders a crime particularly distasteful, it can also be used to explore the rational intentions behind a killing, which allows killers to present themselves as guardians of justice. Fascinatingly, in the case of medieval Georgia, as G. Koolemans Beynen asserts, Shota Rustaveli's *Man in the Panther Skin* (c. 1200) posits a thoroughly utilitarian view of killing which judges its justifiability according to its outcome and relies heavily on a sense of the intention, premeditation and rationality of the perpetrator. A killing which achieves the resolution of a knotty problem might thereby be justified. As the title of the text hints, a panther (or, in fact, a leopard) can kill, but not murder, because it lacks the cognitive ability to plan and rationalise a killing. The protagonists of this tale must demonstrate their humanity and must rise above the animals, and they are able do this by demonstrating their rationality, even if this involves carefully premeditated and instrumental killing.

All this bears witness, once again, to the complexity of medieval thinking on the subject. There are no easy answers, and straightforward dichotomies allowing one to judge the implications of killing are rapidly broken down. Part of the complexity in thinking about murder lies in the multiple intertwined discourses surrounding it. Obviously, legal frameworks – Roman, customary, English common law and canon law – have much to say on the subject, but moral discourses occasionally provide alternative interpretations. Literary texts also tend to explore and exploit the gaps and disjunctions between these frameworks.

As these articles demonstrate, it is clear that the role of law was not to forbid so much as to categorise. Indeed, the dilemmas described in these essays are largely framed by the categories of crime produced by law in an effort to try and distinguish between different kinds of killing and to work out which ones carried the greatest threat to the community. Such a process echoes that of anthropologists who often see law as a fundamental way of categorising, labelling and making sense of the world, as much as an instrument of control; indeed, in some contexts, geographical or historical, the coercive power of law is minimal, but its role in framing reality remains very important.[5] Moral, ethical and religious discourses in the Middle Ages tended, though, to challenge the straightforward categorisations produced by law, whether one is referring to the complex pettifogging of professional lawyers or the organically evolving logic of customary law. The plot and dramatic tension of *La Femme du Roy de Portugal* hinges precisely on the sense that legal categorisations of the actions of the Queen fail to take a holistic view of what has happened. The situation is clearly more complex than black and white legal regulations can ever accommodate. The intervention of the Blessed Virgin Mary is the ultimate plot twist, as well as a powerful admission that law is simply an inadequate discursive framework to comprehend the complexity of human action.

In some cases, the logic underlying the categorisations imposed through law is challenged. In the context of Malory's *Morte Darthur*, Dwayne C. Coleman demonstrates law's foundation in categories of innocence and guilt, and contrasts the way in which, in terms of chivalric culture, shame and honour, rather than innocence and guilt, were the operative concepts. The clash of these benchmarks produced gaps and problems in the application of law to crime and its assessment. In Arthuriana, the motif of the judicial combat tackles, head-on, the question of the relationship between divinely-inspired ethical judgements and legal judgements. Most interestingly, in the chivalric Arthurian context, the clash between cultures of shame and cultures of guilt create (in a literary sense) a rich tapestry of interwoven and complex judgements. Coleman shows how the text's admiration for the heroic is rooted, not in the application of law, but in an ethos of chivalry, reputation and honour, and that whilst this is clearly lauded, it is embedded with a sense of the tragic.

Related to the question of honour and shame is one of reputation. Although medieval law famously gives great weight to the question of reputation in assessing

---

[5] See, for example: Paul Dresch, 'Legalism, Anthropology, and History', in *Legalism: Anthropology and History*, ed. Paul Dresch and Hannah Skoda (Oxford: Oxford University Press, 2012), pp. 1–38; John Bossy, 'Postscript', in *Disputes and Settlements: Law and Human Relations in the West*, ed. Bossy (Cambridge: Cambridge University Press, 1983), pp. 287–94.

likely culpability, this was not a means of assessing the heinousness of the crime but rather a way of determining the likely culpability of the perpetrator.[6] In other words, reputation counted against the accused as far as the fact-finding part of a trial went, but not as much in interpreting and assessing the crime itself. As Schweitzer Van Donkelaar shows, radical disjunctions could emerge between legal and other social and ethical assessments of murder, depending on different emphases on reputation. She examines the tensions between the assessment of murder in Icelandic law-codes and in the thirteenth- and fourteenth-century sagas, arguing that sagas judged the implications and seriousness of murder according to the reputation and subsequent behaviour of the killer, trumping the kinds of categorisations framed by the legal codes themselves.

There is, of course, another powerful way of responding to killing, which corresponds neither to medieval legal frameworks nor to the alternative categorisations of religious-ethical frameworks. This is to reject violence altogether; to argue that, whatever the circumstances, the second commandment enjoins people not to kill, and that is the end of the story. It is to suggest that attempts to channel violence in particular directions, to justify its use against certain foes or in the defence of honour, is to miss the point. Such a view was extremely rare in the Middle Ages, but there are traces of it here and there as contemporaries bemoaned high levels of violence and began to wonder about its ultimate justifiability. As Lucas Wood argues, the early thirteenth-century *Queste del Saint Graal* may critique earthly chivalric values altogether. If earthly chivalry was about honour, glory and violence in the service of one's peers and of God, then there was another kind of chivalry which one might pursue, according to this text – the moral code of 'chevalerie celestielle', which was driven by a higher goal of spiritual service to God. Whereas other romances often focus on distinguishing between good and bad violence, the *Queste* rejects such distinctions wholesale. Since all violence causes bloodshed, such distinctions theoretically amount to a kind of disingenuous pedantry. Radically, the text proposes an alternative 'quest' which promises a more enduring kind of meaning. And it is very striking, as Wood shows, that at a structural level, in the more violent portions of the text, there is very little resembling meaningful plot: the relentless drive of killing after killing effectively evacuates narrative and purpose. It is a potent critique of every kind of killing. Wood suggests that this view may be understood in the context of the early twelfth-century Peace of God movement and the sermons of Bernard of Clairvaux. The powerful rhetoric of these campaigns railed against the ubiquitous violence of European knights yet the message was that this violence might

---

[6] See, for example: *Fama, The Politics of Talk and Reputation in Medieval Europe*, ed. Thelma Fenster and Daniel Lord Smail (Ithaca: Cornell University Press, 2003).

be re-channelled against the Infidel. The *Queste* seems to go farther than this, and, in doing so, is a truly radical text.

The *Queste*'s critique is made most powerfully at a structural level, whereby meaningful plot progression is broken down by a cycle of pointless violence. And indeed, as a whole, this volume demonstrates the profound importance of how violence was narrativised. A murder is never the end of the story; attention to the shaping of narratives is, of course, part and parcel of the work of the historian or literary critic. We access events, listening to the voices of the past through the remaining sources, and we need to be always alert to the processes of construction which have enabled, constrained and shaped those sources. This is particularly apparent in the case of legal sources, where, as Natalie Zemon Davis most famously points out, narratives of events are carefully constructed to fit legal norms, to correspond to existing structures and formulae and, most importantly, to attempt to bring about the desired legal outcome.[7] Literary scholars are naturally highly attuned to these processes, and historians have been able to learn from their approaches in order to appreciate the palimpsests of meaning which constitute the surviving documents. Reading sources, most particularly for crime and deviance, requires close attention to the conventions, formulae and structures which produced them. The essays in this volume, however, demonstrate that something more is at stake. Put simply, the documents on which we rely for accounts of murder were produced, not for the sake of future historians, but in order to *do* things. These documents are historical agents in their own right; in other words, a letter of remission, for example, is part and parcel of the historical events and process surrounding the murder that scholars may be investigating. Thinking about sources as historical agents is useful more generally, but it is a process that sharpens when addressing events like murders. Fraught social disruptions like these produced documents which mediate, negotiate, challenge and shape the social and legal outcomes of killings.

Emily Hutchison's article on the assassination of the duke of Orleans reveals this point with particular clarity. Not only did the assassination produce a veritable spate of aggressive documents and accounts on both sides of the factional divide, but the combined effect of the documents attempting to justify the murder was described by opponents as itself 'a murder'. The sources upon which scholars rely were a part of the process of factional conflict, as the enemies of Orleans attempted to destroy the dead duke's reputation; in essence, the legal and the political were tightly intertwined. As Hutchison points out, reputation was as politically valuable as life itself, so to describe this process as a form of assassination is not far-fetched. The murder itself stretched, then, far beyond the

---

[7] Natalie Zemon Davis, *Fiction in the Archives: Pardon Tales and their Tellers in Fifteenth-Century France* (Stanford, CA: Stanford University Press, 1990).

initial act of violence, and it was one both perpetrated and perpetuated through the very documents upon which scholars rely to reconstruct events. The duke of Burgundy could claim to have been carrying out justice, whilst his Orleanist enemies vehemently asserted the heinous illegality of his action.

Many of these cases revolve around competing narratives as Gates points out regarding the St Brice's Day Massacre. He contrasts initial reactions to the massacre, which presented it as a legal reaction to a political violation perpetrated against the king for which an entire ethnic group was deemed accountable according to the recently promulgated law of *morð*, with later discourses which were keen to portray events as genocide in an attempt to shore up ideas of Englishness. The earlier discourse was one which permitted the strengthening of ideas about religion and lordship, as well as ethnicity. In this case, the narrativisation of collective murders forms part of a wider historical process of political identity construction around such poles as religion, lordship and ethnicity.

Naturally, narratives of violence could be very effective ways to demonise particular groups. As Andrew McKenzie-McHarg shows in the case of the Jesuits, or as Dianne Berg argues with respect to Catholic and Protestant antagonism in the early modern period, repeatedly associating certain groups with acts of heinous violence was a very effective way of disempowering and discrediting them. McKenzie-McHarg's study of the growth of a widespread set of conspiracy theories about the Jesuits reveals insights into the insidiously destructive work that the sources can affect. In the case of early modern England, associating Catholics with cases of infanticide was an effective and surprisingly subtle way to shore up Protestant narratives about the importance and centrality of family values.

Many of these documents were generated by legal responses to violence, but again, it emerges over the course of these essays that the law was not a simple check on physical brutality but, rather, part of the historical process of social dislocation and violent behaviour. As Tracy points out in her study of murder, torture and punishment in Chaucer, medieval contemporaries were well aware of the inherent and problematic violence of law itself. She demonstrates how the methods of justice in many of Chaucer's *Canterbury Tales* undermine their own ambition of containing violence by sanctioning practices such as torture. The dichotomy between law and violence is broken down: indeed, it is shown never to have been tenable. And for the medievalist, the important lesson is that the dichotomy between violent event and documentary witness is equally untenable. The documents and narratives so vividly analysed and explored here were powerfully engaged, destructive and violent themselves. To return to *La Femme du Roy de Portugal*, the point is made with typical brutality. The Queen's confessor, who revealed her terrible secret, is thrown onto the executioner's pyre instead of the Queen herself. In the final analysis, his public narrative of her crimes is deemed an even more heinous crime than the Queen's own murderous violence.

Again and again, we are reminded that medieval societies really worried about murder and homicide. Levels of violence may have been higher than in our own cultures, but the sense of anxiety and hesitation about how to deal with it continue to resonate. If violence often feels ubiquitous in the texts studied here, it is perhaps precisely because it was deemed so problematic and because even those texts themselves were recognised as potential agents of cruelty.

Select Bibliography

Akehurst, F. R. P. 'Good Name, Reputation, and Notoriety in French Customary Law'. In *'Fama': The Politics of Talk and Reputation in Medieval Europe*, ed. Thelma Fenster and Daniel Lord Smail. 75–94. Ithaca: Cornell University Press, 2003.

Ankarloo, Bengt and Stuart Clark, eds. *Witchcraft and Magic in Europe: The Middle Ages*. Philadelphia: University of Pennsylvania, 2001.

Aptowitzer, Victor. 'Observations on the Criminal Law of the Jews', *Jewish Quarterly Review* 15 (1924): 55–118.

Armstrong, Dorsey. *Gender and the Chivalric Community in Malory's* Morte Darthur. Gainesville: University Press of Florida, 2003.

Assaf, Simhah. *Bate ha-din ve-sidrehem ahar hatimat ha-Talmud* [*The Courts and Their Procedures after the Close of the Talmud*]. Jerusalem: Ha-Po'alim, 1924.

———. *Ha-Onashin ahare hatimat ha-Talmud* [*Punishments after the Close of the Talmud*]. Tel Aviv: Ha-Poel ha-Zair, 1922.

Assis, Yom Tov. 'Crime and Violence among the Jews of Spain (13th–14th Centuries)'. *Zion* 50 (1985): 221–40.

Balzaretti, Ross. 'Masculine Authority and State Identity in Liutprandic Italy'. In *Die Langobarden: Herrschaft und Identität*, ed. Walter Pohl and Peter Erhart. 361–82. Vienna: Verlag der Österreichische Akademie der Wissenschaften, 2005.

Baraz, Daniel. *Medieval Cruelty: Changing Perceptions, Late Antiquity to the Early Modern Period*. Ithaca: Cornell University Press, 2003.

Barceló, Mª Carmen. 'La morería de Valencia en el reinado de Juan II', *Saitabi* 30 (1980): 49–71.

———. *Minorías islámicas en el País Valenciano. Historia y dialecto*. Valencia: Universitat de València, 1984.

Barker, Sheila. 'The Art of Poison'. *The Medici Archives* 85 (2008). http://www.theflorentine.net/articles/article-view.asp?issuetocId=3464

Bar-Levav, Avriel. 'Leon Modena and the Invention of the Jewish Death Tradition'. *The Lion Shall Roar: Leon Modena and His World*, ed. David Malkiel. 85–101. Jerusalem: Magnes Press, 2003.

———. 'Ritualisation of Jewish Life and Death in the Early Modern Period'. *Leo Baeck Institute Year Book* 47 (2002): 69–82.

Barmash, Pamela. *Homicide in the Biblical World*. Cambridge: Cambridge University Press, 2005.

Barron, W. R. J. 'The Penalties for Treason in Medieval Life and Literature'. *Journal of Medieval History* 7 (1981): 187–202.

Bayless, Martha. *Sin and Filth in Medieval Culture: The Devil in the Latrine.* New York: Routledge, 2012.
Bednarski, Steven. *A Poisoned Past: The Life and Times of Margraida de Portu, a Fourteenth-Century Accused Poisoner.* Toronto: University of Toronto Press, 2014.
Bedwell, Laura K. 'The Failure of Justice, The Failure of Arthur'. *Arthuriana* 21.3 (2011): 3–22.
Bellamy, John G. *Strange, Inhuman Deaths: Murder in Tudor England.* Stroud: Sutton, 2005.
———. *The Tudor Law of Treason: An Introduction.* London: Routledge and Kegan Paul, 1979.
———. *Crime and Public Order in England in the Later Middle Ages.* London and Toronto: Routledge and Kegan Paul, 1973.
———. *The Law of Treason in England in the Later Middle Ages.* Cambridge: Cambridge University Press, 1970.
Bénézet, Jean-Pierre. *Pharmacie et médicament en Méditerranée occidentale (XIIIe-XVIe siècles).* Paris: Champion, 1999.
Berkowitz, Beth. *Execution and Invention: Death Penalty Discourse in Early Rabbinic and Christian Cultures.* Oxford: Oxford University Press, 2006.
Beynen, G. Koolemans. 'The Evolution of Courtliness in Shota Rustaveli's "The Man in the Panther Skin": From Neoplatonism to Modernity'. In *Cultures courtoises en mouvement*, ed. Isabelle Arseneau and Francis Gingras. 149–54. Montréal: Presses de l'Université de Montréal, 2011.
Billoré, Maïté and Myriam Soria, eds. *La trahison au Moyen Âge: De la monstruosité au crime politique (Ve–XVe siècle).* Rennes: Presses Universitaires de Rennes, 2009.
Bireley, Robert. *The Counter-Reformation Prince. Anti-Machiavellianism or Catholic Statecraft in Early Modern Europe.* Chapel Hill: University of North Carolina Press, 1990.
Blumenthal, Sid and Harvey Yazijian, eds. *Government by Gunplay: Assassination Conspiracy Theories from Dallas to Today.* New York: Signet, 1976.
Bondurand, Édouard. 'Les coutumes de Lunel: Texte de 1367'. *Mémoires de l'Académie de Nîmes* 8 (1885): 35–78.
Brand, Itzhak. 'Religious Recognition of Autonomous Secular Law: The Sitz im Leben of R. Nissim of Girona's Homily (no. 11)'. *Harvard Theological Review* 105 (2012): 163–88.
Breatnach, Liam. *A Companion to the Corpus Iuris Hibernici.* Dublin: Dublin Institute for Advanced Studies, 2005.
Broedel, Hans Peter. 'Gratuitous Examples and the Grateful Dead: Appropriation and Negotiation of Traditional Narratives in Medieval Exemplary Ghost Stories'. In *Translatio or the Transmission of Culture in the Middle Ages and the Renaissance: Modes and Messages*, ed. L. H. Hollengreen. 97–112. Turnout: Brepols, 2009.
———. *The Malleus Maleficarum and the Construction of Witchcraft: Theology and Popular Belief.* Manchester: Manchester University Press, 2003.
Brown, Warren C. *Violence in Medieval Europe.* Harlow: Longman, 2011.
Bruce, Scott G., ed. *The Penguin Book of the Undead: Fifteen Hundred Years of Supernatural Encounters.* New York: Penguin Books, 2016.
Burrows, Daron. *The Stereotype of the Priest in the Old French Fabliaux: Anticlerical Satire and Lay Identity.* Bern: Peter Lang, 2005.

Busato, Davide. *Venezia Criminale*. Venice: Helvetia, 2013. http://www.venezia.net/22/12/2013/veleni-e-magia-gli-veneziani-facevano-fuori-i-parenti-con-che-veleni.html

Butler, Sara M. *Forensic Medicine and Death Investigation in Medieval England*. New York: Routledge, 2015.

———. *The Language of Abuse: Marital Violence in Later Medieval England*. Leiden: Brill, 2007.

———. 'Women, Suicide, and the Jury in Later Medieval England'. *Signs: Journal of Women in Culture and Society* 32.1 (2006): 141–66.

Cavadino, Paul, ed. *Children Who Kill*. Winchester, UK: Waterside Press, 2002.

Charles-Edwards, Thomas. *The Medieval Gaelic Lawyer*. Quiggin Pamphlets on the Sources of Mediaeval Gaelic History 3. Cambridge: University of Cambridge, Department of Anglo-Saxon, Norse and Celtic, 1999.

Chiffoleau, Jacques. 'Sur le crime de majesté médiéval'. In *Genèse de l'état moderne en Méditerranée: Approches historique et anthropologique des pratiques et des representations. Actes des tables rondes internationales tenues à Paris les 24, 25 et 26 septembre 1987 et les 18 et 19 mars 1988*. 183–213. Collection de l'École française de Rome 168. Rome: École française de Rome, 1993.

Clark, Sandra. *Women and Crime in the Street Literature of Early Modern England*. Basingstoke and New York: Palgrave Macmillan, 2003.

Cloud, J. D. 'Parricidium, from the Lex Numiae to the Lex Pompeia de Parricidiis'. *Zeitschrift der Savigny-Stiftung fur Rechtsgeschichte* 88 (1971): 1–66.

Cohen, Daniel A. 'Blood Will Out: Sensationalism, Horror, and the Roots of American Crime Literature'. In *Mortal Remains: Death in Early America*, ed. Nancy Isenberg and Andrew Burstein. 31–55. Philadelphia: University of Pennsylvania Press, 2003.

Cohen, Esther. *The Crossroads of Justice: Law and Culture in Late Medieval France*. Leiden: Brill, 1993.

———. 'Patterns of Crime in Fourteenth-Century Paris'. *French Historical Studies* 11 (1980): 307–27.

———. 'Violence Control in Late Medieval France: The Social Transformation of the Asseurement'. *Tijdschrift voor Rechtsgeschiedenis* 51 (1983): 111–22.

Cohen, Stanley. *Folk Devils and Moral Panics*, 3rd edn. London: Routledge, 2002.

Collard, Franck. *The Crime of Poison in the Middle Ages*, trans. Deborah Nelson-Campbell. Westport, CT: Praeger, 2008

———. '*Secundum artem et peritiam medicine*: Les expertises dans les affaires d'empoisonnement à la fin du Moyen Âge'. In *Experts et expertise au Moyen Âge. Consilium quaeritur a perito*. 161–73. Paris: Publications de la Sorbonne, 2012.

———. 'Poison et empoisonnement dans quelques œuvres médicales latines antérieures à l'essor des *Tractatus de venenis*'. In *Terapie e guarigioni*, ed. Agostino Paravicini Bagliani. 363–393. Convegno internazionale. Impruneta: SISMEL, 2010.

Cuttler, Simon Hirsch. *The Law of Treason and Treason Trials in Later Medieval France*, ed. Walter Ullmann. Cambridge Studies in Medieval Life and Thought. Cambridge: Cambridge University Press, 1981.

D'Cruze, Shani, Sandra L. Walklate and Samantha Pegg. *Murder*. London: Routledge, 2013.

Dahood, Roger. 'English Historical Narratives of Jewish Child-Murder, Chaucer's *Prioress's Tale*, and the Date of Chaucer's Unknown Source'. *Studies in the Age of Chaucer* 31 (2009): 125–40.

Daston, Lorraine. 'Marvelous Facts and Miraculous Evidence in Early Modern Europe'. In *Wonders, Marvels, and Monsters in Early Modern Culture*, ed. Peter G. Platt. 76–105. London: Associated University Presses, 1999.

Davies, Wendy and Paul Fouracre. *The Settlement of Disputes in Early Medieval Europe*. Cambridge: Cambridge University Press, 1986.

Davis, Howard and Marc Bourhill. 'Crisis: The Demonization of Children and Young People'. In *'Childhood' in 'Crisis'?*, ed. Phil Scraton. 28–57. London: Routledge, 1997.

Dean, Trevor. *Crime in Medieval Europe 1200–1550*. Harlow: Pearson Education, 2001.

de Maleissye, Jean. *Histoire du Poison*. Paris: François Bourin, 1991.

Dolan, Frances E. *Dangerous Familiars: Representations of Domestic Crime in England, 1550–1700*. Ithaca, NY: Cornell University Press, 1994.

Dumolyn, Jan and Jelle Haemers. 'Patterns of Urban Rebellion in Medieval Flanders'. *Journal of Medieval History* 31 (2005): 369–93.

Eisner, Manuel. 'Long-Term Historical Trends in Violent Crime'. *Crime and Justice* 30 (2003): 83–142.

Emerson, Thomas. *A Concise Treatise on the Courts of Law of the City of London*. London: J. Nichols, 1794.

Espinosa, Aurelio M. 'Hispanic Versions of the Tale of the Corpse Many Times Killed'. *The Journal of American Folklore* 49 (1936): 181–93.

Faller, Lincoln B. *Turned to Account: The Forms and Functions of Criminal Biography in Late Seventeenth- and Early Eighteenth-Century England*. Cambridge: Cambridge University Press, 1987.

Ferragud, Carmel. *Medicina i promoció a la baixa Edat Mitjana (Corona d'Aragó, 1350–1410)*. Madrid: Consejo Superior de Investigaciones Científicas (CSIC), DL, 2005.

———. 'El coneixement expert dels cirurgians en la cort del justícia criminal de la ciutat de València durant els segles XIV i XV: la pràctica de la dessospitació'. In *Expertise et valeur des choses au Moyen Âge*, II. *Savoirs, écritures, pratiques*, ed. Laurent Feller and Ana Rodriguez. 315–29. Madrid: Casa de Velasquez, 2016.

———. 'Los peritajes médicos en la Valencia bajomedieval: los casos de envenenamiento'. *Dynamis*, 36.1 (2016): 119–41.

Finke, Laurie A. and Martin B. Shichtman. 'No Pain, No Gain: Violence as Symbolic Capital in Malory's *Morte d'Arthur*'. *Arthuriana* 8.2 (1998): 115–34.

Finucane, R. C. *Appearances of the Dead: A Cultural History of Ghosts*. Buffalo: Prometheus Books, 1984.

Flint, Valerie. 'The Demonization of Magic and Sorcery in Late Antiquity: Christian Redefinitions of Pagan Religions'. In *Witchcraft and Magic in Europe: Ancient Greece and Rome*, ed. Bengt Ankarloo and Stuart Clark. 277–348. Philadelphia: University of Pennsylvania Press, 2002.

———. *The Rise of Magic in Early Medieval Europe*. Princeton: Princeton University Press, 1991.

Ford, Franklin. *Political Murder: From Tyrannicide to Terrorism.* Cambridge, MA: Harvard University Press, 1985.

Fornaciari, Gino, et al. 'A Medieval Case of Digitalis Poisoning: The Sudden Death of Cangrande Della Scala, Lord of Verona (1291–1329)'. *Journal of Archaeological Science* 54 (February 2015): 162–67.

Foucault, Michel. *Discipline and Punish: The Birth of the Prison*, trans. Alan Sheridan. New York: Vintage Books, 1995.

Fouracre, Paul. '"Placita" and the Settlement of Disputes in Later Merovingian Francia.' In *The Settlement of Disputes in Early Medieval Europe*, ed. Wendy Davies and Paul Fouracre, pp. 23–44. Cambridge: Cambridge University Press, 1986.

Fraher, Richard M. 'Preventing Crime in the High Middle Ages: The Medieval Lawyers' Search for Deterrence'. In *Popes, Teachers, and Canon Law in the Middle Ages*, ed. James Ross Sweeney and Stanley Chodorow. 212–33. Ithaca: Cornell University Press, 1989.

Frank, Moses. *Kehilot Ashkenaz u-bate dinehen (The Communities of Ashkenaz and their Courts)*. Tel Aviv: Devir, 1938.

Fraser, Antonia. *The Gunpowder Plot: Terror and Faith in 1605.* London: Phoenix, 2002.

Fuente Pérez, María Jesús, and Morán Martín, Remedios, eds., *Raíces Profundas: La violencia contra las mujeres (Antigüedad y Edad Media)*. Madrid: Polifemo Ediciones, 2011.

Garofolo, Andrew. 'Guilty but Mentally Ill'. *History of Forensic Psychology.* Online: http://historyforensicpsych.umwblogs.org/the-insanity-defense-outline-by-andrew-garofolo/guilty-but-mentally-ill/

Garrett, Jane. *The Triumphs of Providence: The Assassination Plot, 1696.* Cambridge: Cambridge University Press, 1980.

Gates, Jay Paul and Nicole Marafioti, eds., *Capital and Corporal Punishment in Anglo-Saxon England.* Woodbridge: Boydell Press, 2014.

Gaughan, Judy E. *Murder Was Not a Crime: Homicide and Power in the Roman Republic.* Austin, TX: University of Texas Press, 2010.

Gauvard, Claude. *'De grace especial': Crime, état et société en France à la fin du Moyen Âge.* Paris: Publications de la Sorbonne, 1991.

———. 'Fear of Crime in Late Medieval France'. In *Medieval Crime and Social Control*, ed. Barbara A. Hanawalt and David Wallace. 1–48. Minneapolis: University of Minnesota Press, 1999.

Geltner, Guy. *The Medieval Prison: A Social History.* Princeton: Princeton University Press, 2008.

———. 'Medieval Prisons: Between Myth and Reality, Hell and Purgatory'. *History Compass* 4 (2006): 10.1111/j.1478-0542.2006.00319.x.

Given, James B. *Society and Homicide in Thirteenth-Century England.* Stanford, CA: Stanford University Press, 1977.

Goldberg, Sylvie Ann. 'Common Law and Jewish Law: The Diasporic Principle of dina de-malkhuta dina'. *Behemoth: A Journal on Civilisation* 2 (2008): 39–53

Goodich, Michael. *Other Middle Ages: Witnesses at the Margins of Medieval Society.* Philadelphia: University of Pennsylvania Press, 1998.

Gonthier, Nicole. *Le châtiment du crime au Moyen Âge: XIIe-XVIe siècles.* Rennes: Presses Universitaires de Rennes, 1998.

Gordon, Stephen. 'Disease, Sin and the Walking Dead in Medieval England, c.1100–1350: A Note on the Documentary and Archaeological Evidence'. In *Medicine, Healing and Performance*, ed. Effie Gemi-Iordanou et al. 55–70. Oxford: Oxbow Books, 2014.

Gouron, André. *La science du droit dans le Midi de la France au Moyen Âge*. Aldershot: Ashgate, 1984.

Grand, Roger. 'Justice criminelle, procédures et peines dans les villes aux XIIIe et XIVe siècles'. *Bibliothèque de l'École des chartes* 102 (1941): 51–108.

Green, David A. *When Children Kill Children: Penal Populism and Political Culture*. Oxford: Oxford University Press, 2008.

Halberstam, Chaya. *Law and Truth in Biblical and Rabbinic Literature*. Bloomington: Indiana University Press, 2010.

Hall, Dianne. 'Women and Violence in Late Medieval Ireland'. In *Studies on Medieval and Early Modern Women: Pawns or Players?*, ed. Christine Meek and Catherine Lawless. 131–40. Dublin: Four Courts Press, 2003.

Halsall, Guy. *Settlement and Social Organization: The Merovingian Region of Metz*. Cambridge: Cambridge University Press, 2002.

———. 'Reflections on Early Medieval Violence: The Example of the "Blood Feud"'. *Memoria y Civilización* 2 (1999): 7–29.

———, ed. *Violence and Society in the Early Medieval West*. Woodbridge: Boydell Press, 1998.

Halttunen, Karen. *Murder Most Foul: The Killer and the American Gothic Imagination*. Cambridge, MA: Harvard University Press, 1998.

Hamel, Sébastien. 'L'application de la peine de mort par les justices municipales: L'affaire Berthe du Jardin au parlement de Paris (1369–1398)'. *Violences souveraines au Moyen Âge: Travaux d'une école historique*, ed. François Foronda, Christine Barralis and Bénédicte Sère. 29–37. Paris: Presses universitaires de France, 2010.

Hammer, Carl. 'Patterns of Homicide in a Medieval University Town: Fourteenth-Century Oxford'. *Past and Present* 78 (1978): 3–23.

Hanawalt, Barbara. 'Violent Death in Fourteenth- and Early Fifteenth-Century England'. *Comparative Studies in Society and History* 18 (1976): 297–320.

Harries, Jill. 'Courts and the Judicial System'. In *Oxford Handbook of Jewish Daily Life in Roman Palestine*, ed. Catherine Hezser. 85–101. Oxford: Oxford University Press, 2010.

Hodges, Horace Jeffery. 'Cain's Fratricide: Original Violence as "Original Sin" in *Beowulf*'. *Medieval and Early Modern English Studies* 15:1 (2007): 31–56.

Hoffer, Peter C. and N. E. H. Hull. *Murdering Mothers: Infanticide in England and New England, 1558–1803*. New York: New York University Press, 1981.

Holdsworth, William. *A History of English Law*. 16 vols. London: Methuen & Co., 1871–1944.

Horowitz, Elliott. 'The Jews of Europe and the Moment of Death in Medieval and Modern Times'. *Judaism: A Journal of Jewish Life and Thought* 44 (1995): 271–81.

———. *Reckless Rites: Purim and the Legacy of Jewish Violence*. Princeton: Princeton University Press, 2006.

Hurnard, Naomi D. *The King's Pardon for Homicide before A.D. 1307*. Oxford: Oxford University Press, 1969.

James, Edward. '"*Beati pacifici*": Bishops and the Law in Sixth-Century Gaul'. In *Disputes and Settlements: Law and Human Relations in the West*, ed. John Bossy. 25–45. Cambridge: Cambridge University Press, 1983.

Jardine, Lisa. *The Awful End of Prince William the Silent: The First Assassination of a Head of State with a Handgun*. New York: HarperCollins, 2007.

Jones, Karen. *Gender and Petty Crime in Late Medieval England: The Local Courts in Kent, 1460–1560*. Woodbridge: Boydell Press, 2006.

Jones, Michael. 'Trahison et l'idée de lèse-majesté dans la Bretagne du XVe siècle'. In *La faute, la répression et le pardon: Actes du 107e Congrès national des sociétés savantes, Brest, 1982, section de philologie et d'histoire jusqu'à 1610*. 91–106. Paris: C.T.H.S., 1984.

Jordan, William Chester. *From England to France: Felony and Exile in the High Middle Ages*. Princeton: Princeton University Press, 2015.

Kaeuper, Richard W. *Chivalry and Violence in Medieval Europe*. Oxford: Oxford University Press, 1999.

———. 'The King and the Fox: Reaction to the Role of Kingship in Tales of Reynard the Fox'. In *Expectations of the Law in the Middle Ages*, ed. Anthony Musson. 9–21. Woodbridge: Boydell Press, 2001.

Kaye, J. M. 'The Early History of Murder and Manslaughter'. *The Law Review Quarterly* 83 (1967): 365–95.

Kelly, Fergus. *A Guide to Early Irish Law*. Dublin: Dublin Institute for Advanced Studies, 2005.

Kelly, Henry Ansgar. 'Inquisition, Public Fame and Confession: General Rules and English Practice'. In *The Culture of Inquisition in Medieval England*, ed. Mary C. Flannery and Katie L. Walter. 8–29. Cambridge: D. S. Brewer, 2013.

Khintibidze, Elguja. *Srednevekovye i renesansnye aspekty poèmy Rustaveli 'Vepkhist'q'aosani'* [*Medieval and Renaissance Trends in Rustaveli's* The Man in the Panther's Skin]. Tbilisi: Tbilisi University Press, 1993.

———. *Rustaveli's 'The Man in the Panther's Skin' and European Literature*. London: Bennett & Bloom, 2011.

Kilday, Anne-Marie. *A History of Infanticide in Britain, c. 1600 to the Present*. Aldershot: Palgrave, 2013.

Kirschenbaum, Aaron. *Jewish Penology: The Theory and Development of Criminal Punishment among the Jews Throughout the Ages*. Hebrew; Jerusalem: Magnes Press, 2013.

———. *Self-Incrimination in Jewish Law*. New York: Burning Bush Press, 1970.

Kisch, Guido. *The Jews in Medieval Germany: A Study of Their Legal and Social Status*, 2nd edn. New York: Ktav Publishing House, 1970.

———. 'The "Jewish Execution" in Mediaeval Germany'. *Historia Judaica* 5 (1943): 103–32.

Klein, Birgit. 'Jewish Legal Autonomy in the Middle Ages: An Unchallenged Institution?'. *Zutot* 3 (2003): 121–34.

Kleinman, Ron S. 'Civil Law as Custom: Jewish Law and Secular Law – Do They Diverge or Converge?'. *Review of Rabbinic Judaism* 14 (2011): 11–36.

Komornicka, Jolanta N. 'Man as Rabid Beast: Criminals into Animals in Late Medieval France'. *French History* 28 (2014): 157–71.

Kors, Alan Charles and Edward Peters, eds., *Magic and Witchcraft in Europe 400–1700: A Documentary History*. Philadelphia: University of Pennsylvania Press, 2000.

Koven, Mikel. 'Traditional Narrative, Popular Aesthetics, *Weekend at Bernie's*, and Vernacular Cinema'. In *Of Corpse: Death and Humor in Folklore and Popular Culture*, ed. Peter Narváez. 294–310. Logan: Utah State University Press, 2003.

Kutys, J. 'GBMI vs. NGRI: An Annotated Bibliography'. *The Jury Expert: The Art and Science of Litigation Advocacy* (November 2009). Online: http://www.thejuryexpert.com/2009/11/guilty-but-mentally-ill-gbmi-vs-not-guilty-by-reason-of-insanity-ngri-an-annotated-bibliography/.

Lacy, Norris J. *Reading Fabliaux*. 2nd edn. Vestavia Hills, AL: Summa Publications, 1999.

———. 'Subject to Object: Performance and Observation in the Fabliaux'. *Symposium* 56 (2002): 17–23.

Lamansky, Vladimir. *Secrets d'État de Venise*. St Petersburg, Russia: Imperial Press, 1884.

Lambert, T. B. 'Theft, Homicide and Crime in Late Anglo-Saxon Law'. *Past and Present* 214 (February 2012): 3–43.

Lamm, Maurice. *The Jewish Way in Death and Mourning*. New York: David, 1969.

Lanhers, Yvonne. 'Crimes et criminels au XIVe siècle'. *Revue historique* 240 (1968): 325–38.

Landman, Leo. *Jewish Law in the Diaspora: Confrontation and Accommodation*. Philadelphia: Dropsie College, 1968.

Lecouteux, Claude. *The Return of the Dead: Ghosts, Ancestors, and the Transparent Veil of the Pagan Mind*, trans. Jon E. Graham. Rochester, VT: Inner Traditions, 1996.

Lemesle, Bruno. 'Trahisons et idées de trahison sous les princes angevins et normands (1050–1150)'. In *La trahison au Moyen Âge: De la monstruosité au crime politique (Ve–XVe siècle)*, ed. Maïté Billoré and Myriam Soria. 229–38. Rennes: Presses Universitaires de Rennes, 2009.

Levy, Brian J. *The Comic Text: Patterns and Images in the Old French Fabliaux*. Amsterdam: Rodopi, 2000.

———. 'Le fabliau et l'exemple: Étude sur les recueils moralisants Anglo-Normands'. In *Épopée animale, fable, fabliau: Actes du IVe Colloque de la Société Internationale Renardienne, Évreux, 7-11 septembre 1981*. 311–20. Paris: Presses Universitaires de France, 1984.

———. 'Performing Fabliaux'. In *Performing Medieval Narrative*, ed. Evelyn Birge Vitz, Nancy Freeman Regalado and Marilyn Lawrence. 123–40. Cambridge: D. S. Brewer, 2005.

L'Engle, Susan. 'Justice in the Margins: Punishment in Medieval Toulouse'. *Viator* 33 (2002): 133–65.

Lockwood, Matthew. 'From Treason to Homicide: Changing Conceptions of the Law of Petty Treason in Early Modern England'. *Journal of Legal History* 34 (2013): 31–49.

López Rodríguez, Carlos. *Sexe i violència en la Corona d'Aragó. Processos criminals dels segles XIII al XV*. Valencia: Universitat de València, 2014.

Lorberbaum, Yair. *In God's Image: Myth, Theology, and Law in Classical Judaism*. Cambridge: Cambridge University Press, 2015.

Lorcin, Marie-Thérèse. 'Les Revenants dans les fabliaux'. *Reinardus* 2 (1989): 91–101.

Lourie, Ilana. 'Mafiosi and Malsines: Violence, Fear and Faction in the Jewish Aljamas of Valencias in the Fourteenth Century'. In *Actas del III congreso internacional encuentro de las tres culturas*, ed. Carlos Carrete Parrondo. 69–102. Toledo: Ayuntamiento de Toledo, 1988. Republished in Elena Lourie, *Crusade and Colonisation: Muslims, Christians and Jews in Medieval Aragon*. Aldershot: Variorum, 1990.

Lynch, Andrew. *Malory's Book of Arms: The Narrative of Combat in* Le Morte Darthur. Cambridge: D. S. Brewer, 1997.

Lyon, Bryce. *A Constitutional and Legal History of Medieval England*, 2nd edn. New York: Norton, 1980.

Macé, Laurent. 'La trahison soluble dans le pardon? Les comtes de Toulouse et la félonie (XIIe–XIIIe siècles)'. In *La trahison au Moyen Âge: De la monstruosité au crime politique (Ve–XVe siècle)*, ed. Maïté Billoré and Myriam Soria. 369–83. Rennes: Presses Universitaires de Rennes, 2009.

MacMillan, Ken. *Stories of True Crime in Tudor and Stuart England*. London: Routledge, 2015.

Malkiel, David. *A Separate Republic: The Mechanics and Dynamics of Venetian Jewish Self-Government, 1607–1624*. Jerusalem: Magnes Press, 1991.

Manning, Roger B. *Village Revolts: Social Protest and Popular Disturbances in England, 1509–1640*. Oxford: Clarendon Press, 1988.

Martin, Randall. *Women, Murder, and Equity in Early Modern England*. London: Routledge, 2008.

McBain, Graham. 'Modernising the Law of Murder and Manslaughter: Part I'. *Journal of Politics and Law* 8 (2015): 9–97.

McGrath, Kate. 'The Politics of Chivalry: The Function of Anger and Shame in Eleventh- and Twelfth-Century Anglo-Norman Historical Narratives'. In *Feud, Violence and Practice: Essays in Medieval Studies in Honor of Stephen D. White*, ed. Belle S. Tuten and Tracey L. Billado. 55–70. Farnham: Ashgate, 2010.

McKenzie, Andrea. 'Making Crime Pay: Motives, Marketing Strategies, and the Printed Literature of Crime in England 1670–1770'. In *Criminal Justice in the Old World and the New: Essays in Honour of J. M. Beattie*, ed. Greg T. Smith, Allyson N. May and Simon Devereaux. 235–69. Toronto: University of Toronto Press, 1998.

McLaughlin, Terence. *The Coward's Weapon*. London: Robert Hale, 1980.

McMahon, Vanessa. *Murder in Shakespeare's England*. Basingstoke: Palgrave Macmillan, 2004.

McSheffrey, Shannon and Julia Pope. 'Ravishment, Legal Narratives, and Chivalric Culture in Fifteenth-Century England'. *Journal of British Studies* 48 (2009): 818–36.

McVaugh, Michael R. *Medicine Before the Plague: Practitioners and their Patients in the Crown of Aragon, 1285–1345*. Cambridge: Cambridge University Press, 1991.

McWalter, J. C. 'On Some Historical Poisons'. *Pacific Review* 6.1 (1891): 4–7.

Merback, Mitchell B. *Beyond the Jewish Badge: Anti-Judaism and Antisemitism in Medieval and Early Modern Visual Culture*. Leiden: Brill, 2007.

——— . *The Thief, the Cross and the Wheel: Pain and the Spectacle of Punishment in Medieval and Renaissance Europe*. Chicago: University of Chicago Press, 1999.

Meyerson, Mark D. 'The Murder of Pau de Sant Martí: Jews, *Conversos*, and the Feud in Fifteenth-Century Valencia'. In *'A Great Effusion of Blood'? Interpreting Medieval Violence*, ed. Mark. D. Meyerson, Daniel Thiery and Oren Falk. 57–78. Toronto: University of Toronto Press, 2004.

Miller, William Ian. *Bloodtaking and Peacemaking: Feud, Law, and Society in Saga Iceland.* Chicago: University of Chicago Press, 1990.

Monkkonen, Eric H. *Crime, Justice, History.* Columbus: Ohio State University Press, 2002.

Moore, R. I. *The Formation of a Persecuting Society: Power and Deviance in Western Europe, 950–1250.* Oxford: Blackwell, 1987.

———. 'Heresy as Disease'. In *The Concept of Heresy in the Middle Ages (11th–13th c.)*, ed. Willem Lourdaux and Daniel Verhelst. 1–11. Leuven: University Press, 1976.

Mousnier, Roland. *The Assassination of Henry IV: The Tyrannicide Problem and the Consolidation of the French Absolute Monarchy in the Early Seventeenth Century*, trans. Joan Spencer. London: Faber and Faber, 1973.

Müller, Miriam. 'Social Control and the Hue and Cry in Two Fourteenth-Century Villages'. *Journal of Medieval History* 31 (2005): 29–53.

Musson, Anthony. *Medieval Law in Context: The Growth of Legal Consciousness from Magna Carta to the Peasants' Revolt.* Manchester: Manchester University Press, 2001.

Narbona, Rafael. 'El Justicia Criminal: Una corte medieval valenciana, un procedimiento judicial'. *Estudis Castellonencs* 3 (1986): 287–310.

———. *El nou d'octubre: ressenya històrica d'una festa valenciana (segles XIV-XV).* Valencia: Universitat de València, 1997.

———. 'Tras los rastros de la cultura popular: Hechicería, supersticiones y curanderismo en la Valencia medieval'. In *Memorias de la ciudad: Ceremonias, creencias y costumbres en la historia de Valencia.* 241–59. Valencia: Ajuntament de València, 2003.

Newbold, R. F. 'Interpersonal Violence in Gregory of Tours' *Libri Historiarum*'. *Nottingham Medieval Studies* 38 (1994): 3–17.

Nicholas, D. M. 'Crime and Punishment in Fourteenth-Century Ghent (first part)'. *Revue Belge de philologie et d'histoire* 48 (1970): 289–334.

Nirenberg, David. *Communities of Violence: Persecution of Minorities in the Middle Ages.* Princeton: Princeton University Press, 1996.

Nolan, Maura. '"Acquiteth yow now": Textual Contradiction and Legal Discourse in the Man of Law's Introduction'. In *The Letter of the Law: Legal Practice and Literary Production in Medieval England*, ed. Emily Steiner and Candace Barrington. 136–53. Ithaca: Cornell University Press, 2002.

Nykrog, Per. *Les fabliaux: Nouvelle édition.* Geneva: Droz, 1973.

O'Brien, Bruce. 'From *Morðor* to *Murdrum*: the Preconquest Origin and Norman Revival of the Murder Fine'. *Speculum* 71 (1996): 321–57.

Obringer, Frédéric. *L'aconit et l'orpiment: Drogues et poisons en Chine.* Paris: Fayard, 1997.

O'Neill, Maggie and Lizzie Seal. *Transgressive Imaginations: Crime, Deviance and Culture.* Basingstoke: Palgrave, 2012.

Orwell, George. 'Decline of the English Murder'. In *Complete Works*, ed. Peter Davison, 20 vols. London: Secker and Warburg, 1996–1998.

Palmer, Richard. 'Physicians and the Inquisition in Sixteenth-Century Venice: The Case of Girolamo Donzellini'. In *Medicine and the Reformation*, ed. Ole Peter Grell and Andrew Cunningham. 118–33. London: Routledge, 1993.

Parascandola, John. *King of Poisons: A History of Arsenic*. Washington, DC: Potomac Books, 2012.

Passamaneck, Stephen M. *Modalities in Medieval Jewish Law for Public Order and Safety*. Cincinnati: Hebrew Union College Press, 2009.

Pastore, Alessandro. *Veleno: Credenze, crimini, sapere nell'Italia moderna*. Bologna: Il Mulino, 2010.

Pennington, Kenneth. *The Prince and the Law, 1200–1600: Sovereignty and Rights in the Western Legal Tradition*. Berkeley: University of California Press, 1993.

Peyroux, Catherine R. 'Canonists Construct the Nun? Church Law and Women's Monastic Practice in Merovingian France'. In *Law, Society and Authority in Late Antiquity*, ed. Ralph W. Mathisen. 242–55. Oxford: Oxford University Press, 2001.

Pinto-Mathieu, Elisabeth. *La 'Vie des Pères': Genèse de contes religieux du XIIIe siècle*. Paris: Champion, 2009.

Po-Chia Hsia, Ronnie. *Trent 1475: Stories of a Ritual Murder Trial*. New Haven: Yale University Press, 1992.

Radulescu, Raluca L. '"Oute of mesure": Violence and Knighthood in Malory's *Morte Darthur*'. In *Re-Viewing Le Morte Darthur*, ed. K. S. Whetter and Raluca L. Radulescu. 119–31. Cambridge: D. S. Brewer, 2005.

Ramires, Flora. 'Le poison chez les Trastamare. De l'emposionnement réel à l'imaginaire de l'empoisonnement'. *Cahiers de recherches médiévales et humanistes* 17 (2009): 53–69.

Reynolds, Andrew. *Anglo-Saxon Deviant Burial Customs*. Oxford: Oxford University Press, 2009.

Ribémont, Bernard. 'Le "crime épique" et sa punition: Quelques exemples (XIIe-XIIIe siècles)'. In *Crime and Punishment in the Middle Ages and Early Modern Age: Mental-Historical Investigations of Basic Human Problems and Social Responses*, ed. Albrecht Classen and Connie Scarborough. 29–42. Berlin: De Gruyter, 2012.

Riisøy, Anne Iren. 'Deviant Burials: Societal Exclusion of Dead Outlaws in Medieval Norway'. In *Cultures of Death and Dying in Medieval and Early Modern Europe*. Helsinki: University of Helsinki, 2015.

Rosenwein, Barbara. 'Even the Devil (Sometimes) has Feelings: Emotional Communities in the Early Middle Ages'. *Haskins Society Journal: Studies in Medieval History* 14 (2003): 1–14.

———. 'Writing and Emotions in Gregory of Tours'. In *Vom Nutzen des Schreibens. Soziales Gedächtnis, Herrschaft und Besitz im Mittelalter*, ed. Walter Pohl and Paul Herold. 23–32. Vienna: Verlag der Österreichischen Akademie der Wissenschaften, 2002.

———. 'Writing Without Fear about Early Medieval Emotions'. *Early Medieval Europe* 10:2 (2001): 229–34.

Roth, Pinchas. 'Later Provençal Sages – Jewish Law (Halakhah) and Rabbis in Southern France, 1215–1348'. PhD dissertation, Hebrew University of Jerusalem, 2012.

———. 'Legal Strategy and Legal Culture in Medieval Jewish Courts of Southern France'. *AJS Review* 38.2 (2014): 375–93.

Rousseaux, Xavier. 'La répression de l'homicide en Europe occidentale (Moyen Age et Temps modernes)'. *Genèses* 19 (1995): 122–47.

Rubin, Miri. *Gentile Tales: The Narrative Assault on Late Medieval Jews*. Philadelphia: University of Pennsylvania Press, 2004.

———. *Charity and Community in Medieval Cambridge*. Cambridge: Cambridge University Press, 2002.

Ruff, Julius R. *Violence in Early Modern Europe 1500–1800*. Cambridge: Cambridge University Press, 2001.

Russell, Jeffrey Burton. *Satan: The Early Christian Tradition*. Ithaca: Cornell University Press, 1981.

———. *The Devil: Perceptions of Evil from Antiquity to Primitive Christianity*. Ithaca: Cornell University Press, 1977.

Saperstein, Marc. *Leadership and Conflict: Tensions in Medieval and Early Modern Jewish History and Culture*. Oxford: Littman Library, 2014.

Scattergood, John. 'Social and Political Issues in Chaucer: An Approach to *Lak of Stedfastnesse*'. In his *Reading the Past: Essays on Medieval and Renaissance Literature*. 192–98. Dublin: Four Courts Press, 1996.

Schenck, Mary Jane. 'Orality, Literacy and the Law: Judicial Scenes in the Fabliau'. *Reinardus* 8 (1995): 63–75.

———. *The Fabliaux: Tales of Wit and Deception*. Amsterdam: Benjamins, 1987.

Sharpe, J. A. *Crime in Early Modern England, 1550–1750*, 2nd edn. London: Pearsons, 1999.

Shemesh, Aharon. *Punishments and Sins: From Scripture to the Rabbis*. Hebrew; Jerusalem: Magnes Press, 2003.

Shilo, Shmuel. *Dina de-Malkhuta Dina: The Law of the State is Law*. Jerusalem: Jerusalem Academic Press, 1974.

Shoemaker, Karl. *Sanctuary and Crime in the Middle Ages, 400–1500*. New York: Fordham University Press, 2011.

Shoham-Steiner, Ephraim. 'The Medieval Jewish Underworld: Jewish Involvement in Crime in Medieval Europe'. Tikvah Working Paper 08/11: http://www.nyutikvah.org/pubs/1011/0811Steiner.html.

Shoval, Ilan. *Jews and Muslims as Servi Regis in the Kingdom of Aragon, 1076–1176: A Comparative Study of Minorities in a Medieval Frontier Society*. Jerusalem: Ben-Zvi Institute, 2010.

Siraisi, Nancy. *Medieval and Early Renaissance Medicine: An Introduction to Knowledge and Practice*. Chicago: University of Chicago Press, 1990.

Skoda, Hannah. *Medieval Violence: Physical Brutality in Northern France 1270–1330*. Oxford: Oxford University Press, 2013.

———. 'Violent Discipline or Disciplining Violence? Experience and Reception of Domestic Violence in Late Thirteenth- and Early Fourteenth-Century Paris and Picardy'. *Cultural and Social History* 6.1 (2009): 9–27.

Smail, Daniel Lord. *The Consumption of Justice: Emotions, Publicity, and Legal Culture in Marseille, 1264–1423*. Ithaca: Cornell University Press, 2003.

——— and Kelly Gibson, eds. *Vengeance in Medieval Europe: A Reader*. Toronto: University of Toronto Press, 2009.

———. 'Hatred as a Social Institution in Late-Medieval Society'. *Speculum* 76.1 (2001): 90–126.

Soloveitchik, Haym. 'A Note on the Penetration of Roman Law in Provence'. *Tijdschrift voor Rechtsgeschiednis* 40 (1972): 227–29.

———. 'Religious Law and Change: The Medieval Ashkenazic Example', *AJS Review* 12 (1987): 205–21.

Soyer, François. 'Living in Fear of Revenge: Religious Minorities and the Right to Bear Arms in Fifteenth-Century Portugal'. In *Vengeance in the Middle Ages: Emotion, Religion and Feud*, ed. Susanna A. Throop and Paul R. Hyams. 85–103. Farnham: Ashgate, 2010.

Spierenburg, Pieter. *A History of Murder: Personal Violence in Europe from the Middle Ages to the Present*. Cambridge: Polity Press, 2008.

———. *The Spectacle of Suffering: Executions and the Evolution of Repression from a Preindustrial Metropolis to the European Experience*. Cambridge: Cambridge University Press, 1984.

Stanislawski, Michael. *A Murder in Lemberg: Politics, Religion and Violence in Modern Jewish History*. Princeton: Princeton University Press, 2007.

Steinmetz, Devora. *Punishment and Freedom: The Rabbinic Construction of Criminal Law*. Philadelphia: University of Pennsylvania Press, 2008.

Stuhmiller, Jacqueline. 'Iudicium Dei, iudicium fortunae: Trial by Combat in Malory's le Morte Darthur'. *Speculum* 81.2 (2006): 427–62.

Stymeist, David. 'Criminal Biography in Early Modern News Pamphlets'. In *Taking Exception to the Law: Materializing Injustice in Early Modern English Literature*, ed. Donald Beecher et al. 137–61. Toronto: University of Toronto Press, 2015.

Terpstra, Nicholas, ed. *The Art of Executing Well: Rituals of Execution in Renaissance Italy*. Kirksville, MO: Truman State University Press, 2008.

Thompson, C. J. S. *Poisons and Poisoners, with Historical Accounts of Some Famous Mysteries in Ancient and Modern Times*. London: H. Shaylor, 1931.

Toureille, Valérie. *Vol et brigandage au Moyen Âge*. Paris: Presses Universitaires de France, 2006.

Tracy, Kisha G. 'Representations of Disability: The Medieval Literary Tradition of the Fisher King'. In *Disability in the Middle Ages: Reconsiderations and Reverberations*, ed. Joshua R. Eyler. 105–18. Farnham: Ashgate, 2010.

Tracy, Larissa. *Torture and Brutality in Medieval Literature: Negotiations of National Identity*. Cambridge: D. S. Brewer, 2012.

———. '"So He Smote of Hir Hede by Myssefortune": The Real Price of the Beheading Game in *Sir Gawain and the Green Knight* and Malory'. In *Heads Will Roll: Decapitation in the Medieval and Early Modern Imagination*, ed. Larissa Tracy and Jeff Massey. 207–31. Leiden: Brill, 2012.

———. 'Wounded Bodies: Kingship, National Identity, and Illegitimate Torture in the English Arthurian Tradition'. *Arthurian Literature* 32 (2015): 1–29.

———. 'The Uses of Torture and Violence in the Fabliaux: When Comedy Crosses the Line'. *Florilegium* 23 (2006): 143–68.

Trenchard-Smith, Margaret. 'Insanity, Exculpation and Disempowerment in Byzantine Law'. In *Madness in Medieval Law and Custom*, ed. W. J. Turner. Leiden: Brill, 2010.

Turning, Patricia. *Municipal Officials, Their Public and the Negotiation of Justice in Medieval Languedoc*. Leiden: Brill, 2012.

Tuten, Belle S. and Tracey L. Billado, eds. *Feud, Violence and Practice: Essays in Medieval Studies in Honour of Stephen D. White*. Farnham: Ashgate, 2010.

Vallerani, Massimo. *Medieval Public Justice*, trans. Sarah Rubin Blanshei. Washington, DC: The Catholic University of America Press, 2012.

Watson, Gilbert. *Theriac and Mithridatium: A Study in Therapeutics*. London: Wellcome History Medical Library, 1966.

Westerhof, Danielle. *Death and the Noble Body in Medieval England*. Woodbridge: Boydell Press, 2008.

White, Stephen D. 'Alternative Constructions of Treason in the Angevin Political World: Traïson in the *History of William Marshal*'. *e-spania* (2007): 1–47. http://e-spania.revues.org/document2233.html

Wood, Ian. 'The Code in Merovingian Gaul'. In *The Theodosian Code: Studies in the Imperial Law of Late Antiquity*, ed. Jill Harries and Ian Wood. 161–77. Bristol: Bristol Classical Press, 2010.

———. *The Merovingian Kingdoms, 450–751*. London and New York: Longman, 1994.

———. 'The Secret Histories of Gregory of Tours'. *Revue belge de philologie et d'histoire* 71:2 (1993): 253–70.

———. 'Disputes in Late Fifth- and Sixth-Century Gaul: Some Problems'. In *The Settlement of Disputes in Early Medieval Europe*, ed. Wendy Davies and Paul Fouracre. 7–22. Cambridge: Cambridge University Press, 1986.

Wormald, Patrick. 'The *Leges Barbarorum*: Law and Ethnicity in the Post-Roman West'. In *Regna and Gentes: The Relationship Between Late Antique and Early Medieval Peoples and Kingdoms in the Transformation of the Roman World*, ed. Hans-Werner Goetz et al. 21–52. Leiden: Brill, 2003.

Index

Æthelstan 31, 32, 46, 52, 336 n. 12,
abortion 34–45, 336 n. 12, 337 n. 14,
adultery 326, 328, 331 n. 70, 336 n. 12, 354, 358–9, 364–5, 395, 397–8, 401
adventure 159, 160, 163–4, 179–80, 183–6, 189–90, 195–9, 204, 210
Albania 231, 251–3
allegory 182, 205
Amalasuntha, Queen of the Ostrogoths 320, 322, 324 n. 51, 325
analogical thought 418–9, 422, 426, 432
apothecary 375 n. 16, 376 n. 16, 377–8, 391
aristocracy 182, 184, 191–3, 328
Arthur, King 9, 13, 179–205, 206–26
Augustine of Hippo 26–7
Avicenna 235 n. 30, 452

Bede 49 n. 6, 126, 313 n. 5
Beowulf 10–11, 47–76, 140 n. 3, 315 n. 14, 415
Bernard of Clairvaux 190, 192–3, 193 n. 30, 194 n. 33, 201, 464
   De laude novae militiae (*In Praise of the New Knighthood*) 192–4, 201
betrayal 53, 64, 70, 76, 99–100, 103, 105–6, 110, 116, 118, 123, 207, 214, 239, 264–6, 317, 375, 396, 428, 460,
blood 63, 82, 86, 116, 121, 132–4, 144, 166, 176, 182, 184, 188, 189, 190–1, 200–2, 207, 217, 247, 254, 255, 258, 261, 263, 265–8, 279, 298, 312, 314–8, 320 n. 38, 322 n. 43, 323, 330 n. 67, 336, 355, 373, 388 n. 44, 394, 410, 417, 422, 424–9, 431–2, 441, 446–8, 452–4, 464,

blood feud 146, 211, 215, 312 n. 3, 331 n. 69, 335 n.7,
bloodguilt 196
bloodshed 148, 156, 208, 286, 297, 411
Boort, Sir 183, 200–4
Bosnia 244, 249
Bracton, Henry
   On the Laws and Customs of England [*Bracton*] 7, 11, 118–25, 128, 133, 135–6, 403 n. 28,
breach of courtyard (*hoberos*) 347–8
breastfeeding 372, 392

Cáin Adamnáin 9, 19–46
Cain (and Abel) 59 n. 52, 60, 204, 313, 315–6, 331,
Chapelain, Le 159–78
Charlemagne 31–2, 46
charter 69–72, 75–6, 341 n. 36,
Chaucer, Geoffrey 3–4, 9, 11, 12, 115–136, 466
childbirth 236 n. 33, 422–7
Childebert II,
   Decretio 327
Chrétien de Troyes 181, 185, 188, 224
Christie, Agatha 1
churching 425
Clovis, King of the Franks 311, 317, 320–2, 326 n. 55, 457
Cohen, Esther 85 n. 39, 96 n. 5, 104, 111 n. 57, 169, 397, 399 n. 10
Collard, Franck 98 n. 10, 105, 234, 334 n. 4, 335, 374 n. 9
comedy 11, 12, 131 n. 43, 159–78, 458
composition, fines 54, 334–5, 340–6

concealment 4, 20, 22, 123 n. 23, 140 n. 3, 141, 145, 148, 150, 155, 157, 461–2
corpse(s) 12, 19 n.12, 20, 83 n. 32, 117, 134, 141, 145, 149, 150, 159–78, 236, 238, 247, 317, 380 n. 26, 393–4, 396, 409, 410, 414, 415, 417, 432, 458
Council of Epaone (517 CE) 327
crusade 182, 192, 194, 281 n. 2, 353, 400

Dalmatia 231, 245, 250, 252–3
Dean, Trevor 5, 8, 11, 89 n. 52, 104 n. 31, 375 n. 13, 396, 398 n. 9, 402, 413 n. 68
defamation 13, 254–80, 281, 307
demonic powers 20, 24, 26–7, 33
  possession 171, 176, 421
duinetháide 9, 19–25, 32, 34, 42 n. 103, 46, 141

Egil's Saga 141, 154 n. 42,
epaid 27, 28, 29–31, 33, 36, 42
Eyrbyggja Saga 155–7, 147, 149, 150 n. 36
embodied home 426
emotion 155, 158, 204, 219, 223, 276 n. 87, 325 n. 52, 354, 363, 369, 419, 421, 433, 457
enslaved man (servus) 334, 342, 348
enslaved woman (ancilla) 232, 334, 340, 342, 347, 348
ethnicity 48, 69–71, 466
execution 11, 15, 69 n. 75, 73 n. 87, 77–95, 116, 120, 124, 128, 130, 132–3, 175, 199, 205, 218, 223, 255, 257 n. 14, 258, 261, 266, 275, 288, 292, 320 n. 37, 358, 372, 395–400, 406, 410–5, 421, 432–3, 447–8, 459
  beheading (decapitation) 77, 84, 135, 169, 215, 395–9, 411, 415–6
  burning 259 n. 18, 466
  death penalty 31, 89, 203, 327, 341 n. 36, 375, 402
  executioner 7, 203, 466

fabliaux 9, 12, 159–78, 458
fama 13, 142 n. 10, 216, 224 n. 60,

publica fama (fama pública) 216, 373 n. 5
female violence 335 n. 10, 347–8, 401 n. 20
feud 10, 20, 59, 60, 63–7, 89, 90, 111–2, 141, 144, 146–9, 153, 176, 187–8, 206–26, 330 n. 69, 335, 403, 404, 458, 460
  faida 335, 344–5, 349
folkloric motifs 162, 165
Fourth Council of Orleans (541 CE) 327
freeman (homo liber) 334, 342, 344–6, 348,
free woman (mulier libera) 334, 342, 347
Il Friuli medico 250

Gauvard, Claude 89 n. 53, 98 n. 8, 100 n. 16, 107 n. 45, 258–9 n. 17, 260, 261 n. 29, 262 n. 32, 33, 272 n. 65, 273, 279, 406, 411 n. 54, 412
Gawain, Sir (Gauvain) 12, 13, 179–205, 206–26,
grave-robbing (plodraub) 341
Gregory of Tours,
  Historiae 14, 311–32
  Liber de miraculis beatae Andreae apostoli 319–20
Guinevere, Queen 206, 209, 213, 215–22, 225

'half-free' (aldius, aldia) 342, 343 n. 48
Hanawalt, Barbara 96 n. 5, 97 n. 6, 98 n. 8, 100 n. 16, 104, 107 n. 43, 261 n. 28, 267 n. 48, 396 n. 3, 401, 402 n. 21, 406,
honour 272, 274, 315, 378
humour 115, 159–78, 452–4, 458

Iceland 6, 9–10, 12, 21, 52 n. 22, 111 n. 56, 139–58, 329 n. 66, 340 n. 31, 458, 460, 464
illegitimacy 189, 430
internal organs 345
irony 161, 167, 176, 186, 190, 229 n. 7
Isidore of Seville 27
Islam 130, 389 n. 46, 390

judicial combat 208, 210, 222, 463
jurisdiction 81, 97, 121, 371 n. 2, 395–8, 400, 411–3, 415–6, 459
Justinian
   Digest 227, 229, 232, 318, 319 n. 30

killing, accidental 223, 335, 338, 344–5
killing, attempted 222–3, 334, 339, 403,
Kyteler, Alice 409

Lancelot 179, 187–8
Lancelot, Sir 181, 183, 185–8, 196 n. 38, 207, 208, 210, 213, 215, 217, 219–26
laws
   VI Æthelred 336 n. 12
   II Æthelstan 31 n. 53, 336 n. 12
   Bretha Étgid 21, 34, 41–2, 45
   Britton 119
   Codex Justinianus 336
   Coutumes de Beauvaisis 7, 102, 160, 261 n. 29, 262 n. 32, 268 n. 49
   Edictus Rothari 6, 232 n. 15, 333–49, 373 n. 7, 409 n. 50
   I Edmund 336 n. 12
   Fleta 119
   Glanvill 118, 123 n. 23, 267 n. 48
   Grágás 6, 12, 140–51, 158
   Halakhah 11, 77, 82
   Jónsbók 6, 140, 143, 146, 148, 151, 158
   Leges barbarorum 333 n. 2
   Lex Baiuvariorum 336 n. 12
   Lex Frisionum 6
   Lex Pompeia 318–9, 326 n. 54,
   Lex Ribuaria 336 n. 12
   Lex Visigothorum 38, 336 n. 12
   Mirror of Justices 119
   Pactus Legis Salicae 313 n. 4, 317 n. 24, 336 n. 12, 337 n. 14, 348 n. 67
   Pseudo-Edward and Guthrum 336 n. 12
   Roman 7–8, 38, 78, 80, 99, 119, 124, 232, 244, 319 n. 32, 336, 394, 461
   Salic 312–3, 327, 337 n. 14
Laxdæla Saga 149–50, 151 n. 37, 153

'little commonwealth' 430
loyalty 52, 54, 70, 99, 104, 133 n. 52, 203–4, 219, 220, 226, 264–6, 325
lýsa víg (*lýsing*) 143, 149, 151–2, 156–8

magic, 9, 19–46, 172, 232–3, 238, 248, 336, 354, 364, 375 n. 13, 409
   maleficium 35–40, 101, 103, 232, 337 n. 14
   witchcraft 31, 149, 238 n. 35, 336 n. 12, 337, 375, 396, 409, 428
Malory, Sir Thomas 13, 181 n. 5, 182 n. 7, 206–26, 463
   Le Morte Darthur 13, 206–26, 463
materia medica 233, 243 n. 61
maternity, motherhood 417–33
Medea 417, 426
medicine 234, 247, 337 n. 14, 372, 376 n. 19, 380–1, 387 n. 40, 388–9, 391, 423, 452–3
miles Christi 12, 180, 193, 202
misadventure, death by 120–121, 195
misogyny 374, 420, 422, 425
monstrosity 10, 33 n. 65, 54, 56–9, 60, 65–6, 184, 421–3, 426, 428–9
murder (killing, secret) 5 n. 18, 9, 19–46, 119, 216, 340
   massacre 11, 47–76, 116, 126, 201, 462, 466
   definition of 3–4, 11, 125, 248 n. 83, 261, 330, 340, 438
   genocide 48–9, 65, 69, 73, 76, 462, 466
   homicide 1–14, 19–25, 27, 30–7, 40–2, 45–6, 52, 64, 89, 90, 97–8, 101, 107, 112, 117–25, 135, 139–42, 145, 147–8, 152, 160, 181–5, 188, 191 n. 26, 193–4, 197–200, 202, 206, 212, 216, 222, 230, 236, 239–40, 255, 261–4, 266, 270–2, 275, 277, 286, 313, 316, 318, 327 n. 56, 328 n. 61, 329, 336, 339–40, 371 n. 2, 436–8, 454, 460, 467
   infanticide 4, 8–9, 15, 417–33, 466
   killing (open/public) 344, 349
   morð 4, 11, 21, 141, 339, 340 n. 32, 462, 466

morðbeala 10, 59
morðor 47–76, 119, 340 n. 32, 462
morðvíg 141–2
morth 4, 339, 339–40 n. 31, 341, 343–5, 349
motives for 5, 14, 55 n. 36, 96, 100, 150, 153, 215, 298, 305, 312, 325, 330, 373, 381, 461
    aggravating circumstances 108–9, 110
mourir 4
murtrir 4
ocir 4, 174, 179, 205
parricide 263, 285, 295, 315–6, 319–22, 324, 393
premeditation 4, 102, 103, 104, 107, 112, 218, 222, 403, 457, 460–2
regicide 3, 8, 13, 261, 291, 297, 301, 302 n. 60, 322
supernaturally induced 9, 20, 23, 25, 27, 32–5, 40, 45–6, 460
tuer 4, 102, 257, 263
tyrannicide 8, 13, 255, 262, 294, 296
víg 4, 21, 141–3, 147, 151–2, 154, 156–7

Nibelungenlied 415
níðingsverk 141–2, 154–5
Njal's Saga 151–3

Orosius 319, 320 n. 35
Ottoman 229, 231, 244–5, 250, 252–3, 462
outlawry 52, 70, 140 n. 3, 141, 145–7, 155

Parlement of Paris 11, 96–7, 105, 258, 259 n. 19, 269–71, 459
peace 3, 10, 47–8, 54, 57–61, 63–4, 66–7, 69–70, 73–5, 88, 109, 112–3, 120–1, 123 n. 23, 145–6, 158, 192, 201–3, 215, 219, 255 n. 6, 256, 261–2, 269, 272, 276, 317, 353, 365, 425, 464
Pentecost oath 206–7, 209, 211–13, 218–23
physician(s) 228, 235, 238, 240, 242, 247, 380, 390–1

plotting 101, 103–4, 109 n. 52, 204, 312, 342, 344–8, 407
pogrom 48, 55, 68, 70, 73, 75
poison 13–4, 28, 32 n. 59, 33, 38, 44 n. 113, 101, 103, 105–8, 110, 197, 209, 213, 218–21, 227–53, 281 n. 2, 317, 321 n. 39, 322, 330–1, 333–49, 371–94, 409, 410 n. 51, 425, 428–9, 442–4, 447, 451–2, 458, 461–2
    arsenic 227–8, 238, 240, 243, 334, 373, 375–9, 392, 394, 442
    theriac (*theriaca Veneta*) 234, 242–3, 387
    veneficium 32 n. 59, 229, 232, 239, 248–9
    venenum 228–9, 232, 337 n. 14, 342, 344, 348–9
priest(s) 12, 39–41, 88, 106, 117, 133–6, 159–78, 201, 287–9, 292, 306, 372, 378, 381, 387–8, 411, 458
prowess 12, 152, 155, 180–3, 191, 193–7, 209–10, 222–6, 356

Queste del Saint Graal 12, 179–205, 464

rebels 231, 258
Registre criminal du Châtelet 259 n. 18, 401–2
reputation 13, 15, 124, 126–7, 139–55, 157–8, 181 n. 5, 186, 190, 206–26, 230 n. 9, 233, 241, 243, 248 n. 83, 249, 257–62, 268–9, 272–9, 281, 312–3, 317, 320, 372–3, 383–4, 390, 403, 405, 458, 463–5
revenant(s) 12, 161, 168–70, 177

Sacristain II 159–78
Sallust 319
Salvian of Marseilles 328 n. 62, 330
sagas 9–10, 12, 139–58, 458, 460, 464
satire 12, 115, 119, 133, 159, 170
Satan 130, 134, 198, 414
secrecy 19–46, 104, 112, 140, 151, 239, 249, 262–3, 341, 457, 460–2

shame 14, 125, 128, 131, 140 n. 3, 141–2, 147–8, 151, 153–8, 173, 175, 192, 204, 211, 215, 217–8, 221–4, 254, 261–6, 269, 276, 279, 312, 322 n. 45, 325, 335, 347, 349, 383, 395, 432, 463
Sigismund, King of Burgundy 245, 320–5
skaldic verse 157
Spenser, Edmund 428–9
  Faerie Queen 428–9
St Brice's Day (massacre) 11, 47–76, 462, 466
state-sponsored assassination 13, 227–53, 281 n. 2, 462

Theodosian Code 32, 318 n. 27, 319
tournament 4, 187, 190–1, 198 n. 43, 218
treason 4, 11, 14, 53, 64 n. 63, 68, 70, 96–114, 116, 128 n. 32, 132, 160, 188, 204, 208, 215–6, 218–23, 229 n. 8, 239, 244, 255, 258 n. 14, 259 n. 20, 261, 267, 276, 278, 291–3, 398, 412, 414–5, 431, 449, 459
  petty 107 n. 43, 431, 440 n. 27, 449

trial 96–114, 122, 125–6, 128, 130, 135, 207–8, 213, 219–25, 238 n. 35, 244, 256, 262–4, 271 n. 61, 273, 275, 292–3, 372, 373 n. 8, 375, 377 n. 22, 378, 380–4, 387, 399–400, 403–5, 409, 421, 425, 450, 459, 464

Valencia, Kingdom of 9, 14, 371–94, 461,
Venice 13, 32 n. 59, 94, 227–53, 401, 411, 462
  Venetian-Ottoman conflict 245, 253
Vie des Pères 177, 456
violence
  legitimate 111, 113, 114, 316
  illegitimate 114, 316
Völsungasaga 9, 10 n. 39, 320–1 n. 39, 340

Wife's Lament 9
worth (forms of compensation)
  angarathungi 340
  lóg n-enech 21
  praetium 338–46
  wergild 53, 147, 340, 342–6

www.ingramcontent.com/pod-product-compliance
Lightning Source LLC
Chambersburg PA
CBHW061340300426
44116CB00011B/1928